Multidimensional Perspectives and Global Analysis of Universal Health Coverage

Yeter Demir Uslu
Istanbul Medipol University, Turkey

Hasan Dinçer
Istanbul Medipol University, Turkey

Serhat Yüksel
İstanbul Medipol University, Turkey

A volume in the Advances in Medical Diagnosis, Treatment, and Care (AMDTC) Book Series

IGI Global
DISSEMINATOR OF KNOWLEDGE

Published in the United States of America by
IGI Global
Medical Information Science Reference (an imprint of IGI Global)
701 E. Chocolate Avenue
Hershey PA, USA 17033
Tel: 717-533-8845
Fax: 717-533-8661
E-mail: cust@igi-global.com
Web site: http://www.igi-global.com

Library of Congress Cataloging-in-Publication Data

Names: Demir Uslu, Yeter, 1977- editor. | Dinçer, Hasan, 1982- editor. | Yuksel, Serhat, 1983- editor.
Title: Multidimensional perspectives and global analysis of universal health coverage / Yeter Demir Uslu, Hasan Dinçer, Serhat Yüksel, editors.
Description: Hershey, PA : Medical Information Science Reference, [2020] | Includes bibliographical references and index. | Summary: "This book examines multidimensional perspectives of universal health coverage"-- Provided by publisher.
Identifiers: LCCN 2019039496 (print) | LCCN 2019039497 (ebook) | ISBN 9781799823292 (hardcover) | ISBN 9781799823308 (ebook)
Subjects: MESH: Universal Health Insurance | Delivery of Health Care--economics | Health Services Accessibility--economics | Health Policy
Classification: LCC RA412.3 (print) | LCC RA412.3 (ebook) | NLM W 100 | DDC 368.38/2--dc23
LC record available at https://lccn.loc.gov/2019039496
LC ebook record available at https://lccn.loc.gov/2019039497

This book is published in the IGI Global book series Advances in Medical Diagnosis, Treatment, and Care (AMDTC) (ISSN: 2475-6628; eISSN: 2475-6636)

British Cataloguing in Publication Data
A Cataloguing in Publication record for this book is available from the British Library.

Advances in Medical Diagnosis, Treatment, and Care (AMDTC) Book Series

ISSN:2475-6628
EISSN:2475-6636

MISSION

Advancements in medicine have prolonged the life expectancy of individuals all over the world. Once life-threatening conditions have become significantly easier to treat and even cure in many cases. Continued research in the medical field will further improve the quality of life, longevity, and wellbeing of individuals.

The **Advances in Medical Diagnosis, Treatment, and Care (AMDTC)** book series seeks to highlight publications on innovative treatment methodologies, diagnosis tools and techniques, and best practices for patient care. Comprised of comprehensive resources aimed to assist professionals in the medical field apply the latest innovations in the identification and management of medical conditions as well as patient care and interaction, the books within the AMDTC series are relevant to the research and practical needs of medical practitioners, researchers, students, and hospital administrators.

COVERAGE

- Critical Care
- Internal Medicine
- Patient-Centered Care
- Diagnostic Medicine
- Medical Procedures
- Cancer Treatment
- Emergency Medicine
- Alternative Medicine
- Disease Management
- Disease Prevention

IGI Global is currently accepting manuscripts for publication within this series. To submit a proposal for a volume in this series, please contact our Acquisition Editors at Acquisitions@igi-global.com or visit: http://www.igi-global.com/publish/.

The Advances in Medical Diagnosis, Treatment, and Care (AMDTC) Book Series (ISSN 2475-6628) is published by IGI Global, 701 E. Chocolate Avenue, Hershey, PA 17033-1240, USA, www.igi-global.com. This series is composed of titles available for purchase individually; each title is edited to be contextually exclusive from any other title within the series. For pricing and ordering information please visit http://www.igi-global.com/book-series/advances-medical-diagnosis-treatment-care/129618. Postmaster: Send all address changes to above address.

Titles in this Series

For a list of additional titles in this series, please visit:
https://www.igi-global.com/book-series/advances-medical-diagnosis-treatment-care/129618

Handbook of Research on Medical Interpreting
Izabel E.T. de V. Souza (Osaka University, Japan) and Effrossyni (Effie) Fragkou (National and Kapodistrian University of Athens Greece)
Medical Information Science Reference • © 2020 • 400pp • H/C (ISBN: 9781522593089) • US $345.00

Quality Assurance in the Era of Individualized Medicine
Anastasius S. Moumtzoglou (P. & A. Kyriakou Children's Hospital Greece)
Medical Information Science Reference • © 2020 • 346pp • H/C (ISBN: 9781799823902) • US $285.00

Diagnosing and Managing Hashimoto's Disease Emerging Research and Opportunities
Mahmoud Sakr (Alexandria University, Egypt)
Medical Information Science Reference • © 2020 • 263pp • H/C (ISBN: 9781522596554) • US $245.00

Using Narrative Writing to Enhance Healing
Jennifer Lynne Bird (Oxbridge Academy, USA)
Medical Information Science Reference • © 2020 • 355pp • H/C (ISBN: 9781799819318) • US $275.00

Strategies to Overcome Superbug Invasions Emerging Research and Opportunities
Dimple Sethi Chopra (Punjabi University, India)
Medical Information Science Reference • © 2020 • 284pp • H/C (ISBN: 9781799803072) • US $225.00

Advanced Applications of Nanotechnology in Cancer Detection and Therapy
Alireza Heidari (Faculty of Chemistry, California South University, USA)
Medical Information Science Reference • © 2020 • 280pp • H/C (ISBN: 9781799801399) • US $275.00

For an entire list of titles in this series, please visit:
https://www.igi-global.com/book-series/advances-medical-diagnosis-treatment-care/129618

IGI Global
DISSEMINATOR OF KNOWLEDGE

701 East Chocolate Avenue, Hershey, PA 17033, USA
Tel: 717-533-8845 x100 • Fax: 717-533-8661
E-Mail: cust@igi-global.com • www.igi-global.com

Editorial Advisory Board

Table of Contents

Detailed Table of Contents

The purpose of this study is to reveal the relationship between the economic development of countries and the importance they attach to health. In this context, macroeconomic data on the economic development levels and health of 127 countries were included in the study. In the application part of the study, clustering and cross-table analysis were used. As a result of the k-means clustering analysis, a 76.4% similarity was found between the three countries groups and the economic development levels. Therefore, it is possible to talk about significant relationships between health expenditures/investments and economic development. In addition, it is seen that 90% of the country group that attaches importance to health expenditures consists of developed countries.

This article describes how due to the globalization activities, where competition is very intense and economic, technological and international environmental elements are also very active and uncertain. In the 21st century, the concept "management" stands out so that all institutions, including health institutions, can see their present and future locations, anticipate opportunities and threats, adapt to all the changes that have taken place, make their services more effective and sustain their success. Organizations need leaders who are open to teamwork, encouraging, creative, sociable, energetic, attaching importance to their subordinates' feelings, thoughts, needs and expectations, taking care to develop high quality relations with their subordinates and respecting their subordinates. Within the scope of the study, the understanding of leadership in health institutions and the importance of leadership are emphasized; the effects of leadership on the motivation, satisfaction and performance of the employees

Recently, one of the inventive developments penetrating many industries is blockchain technology. In the era of globalization and digitalization, blockchain has garnered interest in various application fields from health data management to clinical trials. In this study, we aimed to explore blockchain applications in healthcare with an explorative perspective with a scientometrics analysis. With this analysis, the trends and evolutionary relations between health and blockchain technology were examined via the queries in the Web of Science database. In the analysis, the author keyword co-occurrences were used for demonstrating concept relationships. To understand the new emerging study field, VosViewer was used for network visualizations and CiteSpace free java-based software was used for scientometrics analysis. As a result, it can be implied that the main focus areas of the studies on blockchain are solving payment systems, digital identity, and privacy and security issues in healthcare field.

Health exports have increased to 100 billion dollars per year and it has become an important item in service exports all over the world. Demographic structures are changing with the old population in developed countries, and health tourism among countries has increased. This chapter aims to study health tourism in European Union, aiming to create a single market with member countries and with free movement of people among member countries. EU policy permits member countries' citizens to get health service from any other member country. A literature review shows that the differences between member countries' national health systems is one of the main issues to be resolved and that the countries with old populations who need health care affect health tourism from developed countries with old population countries to countries with young population like Spain. Along with the legislation, ethical, social issues, and standard international rules accepted by all countries covering all aspects of health tourism must be set by international organisations like the WHO to avoid potential risks for the patients.

Section 2

This study investigates the relationship between health care expenditure and income inequality empirically. Using data from a large panel of countries covering a sizeable period of time, how level and composition of health care expenditures correlate with income inequality is studied via the panel data fixed effects estimation methodology. These estimations yield several robust findings. First, there is a significant positive correlation between income inequality and reliance on private resources for health care financing. Second, there exists a significant negative correlation between health care expenditure per capita and income inequality. Third, there is a significant negative correlation between income inequality and health care expenditure as a share of GDP. Next, this study analyzes a select group of well-established democracies with developed economies to detect if health expenditure and income inequality variables correlate with public beliefs and preferences. Empirical analyses reveal that indeed belief and preferences accord well with policy choices.

With the development of new communication technologies and the change and transformation of mobile applications, communication styles also acquire a different dimension. Currently, individuals can access information about many health-related issues easily and quickly. Mobile applications also provide support to individuals in this area anywhere at any time. However, awareness about mobile applications and their availability is important at this point. While the transformation in the technological field makes life easier for users, not everyone (young, old, disabled,

In this study, 16 countries in the MENA region (United Arab Emirates, Bahrain, Djibouti, Algeria, Egypt, Iran, Jordan, Kuwait, Lebanon, Morocco, Malta, Oman, Qatar, Saudi Arabia, Tunisia, and Yemen) were included to the sample and was analyzed, by using a panel data method Pedroni Cointegration test, that relationship between "health expenditures" and "life expectancy at birth" in 2000-2016 period these countries. As a result of the analysis, there was no relationship between health expenditures and life expectancy at birth. Although health expenditures do not have a direct impact on life expectancy at birth, If the MENA region countries take needed measures (such as; to attach importance to institutionalization and functionality in health, focusing on disadvantaged groups, and to encourage investments of hospital and personnel), the inequalities in health outcomes would be reduced.

The emergence of social networking systems as mainstream applications and an inherent element of daily life is a phenomenon observed throughout the world as the worldwide social media users exceeds 2.7 billion. Similar to other sectors, healthcare organizations have also started benefiting from social media in distinct ways such as collecting feedback, educating, communicating and supporting patients and citizens. Social networks can act as remarkable channels for healthcare providers, governmental institutions, pharmaceutical companies, hospitals and others to educate, communicate to, listen, connect to and engage existing and potential customers, patients, physicians and healthcare professionals. Despite the various benefits offered, health institutions, health professionals and stakeholders are reluctant to utilize social media due to several barriers and lack of expertise. This chapter aims to provide a better understanding on the ways healthcare companies can utilize social networks in detail to overcome use barriers and obtain related benefits.

The purpose of this study is to define the concept of public-private cooperation, to talk about its advantages and disadvantages and to examine its reflections on the health sector. In this context, the main features of the Public Private Partnership and the financing models applied throughout the world have been mentioned by making extensive literature review. In addition to this, the effects of public-private cooperation on health sector practices are discussed and the benefit of the synergy created as a result of cooperation is emphasized. In the literature review, the creation of Public Private Partnerships for various purposes together with various financing models, the services public and private sector provide for a common purpose, the risk sharing resulting from all these factors have been discussed. It is stated that the provision of compulsory public services by the government in cooperation with the private sector adds value to projects both in terms of innovation and time cost.

There is a positive relationship between the health level of the society and its economic development. The main reason is that improving quality of the lives and increasing lifetime has lead to higher economic performance. This evaluates the relationship between health expenditure and infant mortality rate in OECD countries. In the analysis process, 20 different countries in the OECD are selected and annual data of these countries for the years between 1980 and 2017 is evaluated with the help of Kao panel cointegration and Dumitrescu-Hurlin causality analysis. The findings show that there is long term relationship between health expenditure and infant mortality rates in OECD countries. Another important conclusion is that there is a causality analysis from health expenditure to the infant mortality rate. While considering these results, it is recommended that OECD countries should take some actions in order to increase health expenditure so that it can be possible to decrease infant mortality rate.

The main objective of the chapter was to examine the effect on the motivations of Pygmalion perception of health workers working in public-private hospitals operating in TRB1 region (Elazığ, Malatya, Tunceli, and Bingöl) and to analyze the mediator role of self-efficacy and leadership in this effect. For this purpose, employees of all

Foreword

I have been working in the fields of finance, economy and health for many years. Therefore, I have had the opportunity to study many studies in these three important areas. What stands out here is the limited number of studies dealing with these areas together. In the majority of studies, finance, economics and health issues were analyzed separately. One of the important results I have reached in these examinations is that there is a need for new studies on health finance.

This book focuses on a very important issue, such as universal health coverage. This issue is important not only for developing countries but also for developed countries. Every country aims to provide easy access to health services to its citizens. The most important point here is that this situation is quite costly. Therefore, health expenditure issues need to be well managed. Therefore, it is thought that the studies on health finance will be very guiding.

I would like to firstly congratulate the editors Prof. Yeter Demir Uslu, Prof. Hasan Dinçer and Prof. Serhat Yüksel for generating this book. I believe that this book makes an important contribution to the literature.

Selman Duran
İstanbul Medipol University, Turkey

Preface

Universal health coverage refers to the healthcare services that are provided to all citizens. In other words, it means that all people in the country can reach different types of the healthcare services which are necessary for their lives. In this definition, it can be understood that universal health coverage includes the citizens who do not have financial power to pay for healthcare services. Thus, almost all countries in the world try to take actions to reach an effective universal health coverage system. With the help of this issue, it can be possible to increase the quality of the life of the citizens.

The main purpose of this book is to define the significance of universal health coverage by considering different issues. While making analysis for different concepts related to the universal health coverage, it can be possible to make qualified recommendations for the governments to improve this situation. Therefore, it can be said that this project makes a significant contribution to the literature by focusing on an important topic.

Target audience and potential users of this book are defined below.

- Researchers
- Academicians
- Policy Makers
- Government Officials
- Upright Students in the concerned fields
- Members of Chambers of Commerce and Industry
- Top managers of the companies

This book consists of four different sections. In section 1, there are four different chapters. In chapter 1, the relationship between health investment and economic development is identified. Chapter 2 tries to evaluate the relationship between leadership characteristics and motivation and satisfaction in health institutions. In chapter 3, a scientometric analysis is performed for blockchain technologies in healthcare. Chapter 4 focuses on the relationship between health export and health tourism role in European Union countries.

Four chapters are also included in section 2. Chapter 5 makes an analysis to understand the relationship between health expenditure and income inequality. Moreover, chapter 6 tries to identify the accessibility for everyone in health communication mobile application usage. Chapter 7 focuses on the depression rate, GDP growth rate, health expenditure and voice and accountability. Additionally, chapter 8 describes he health ecosystem in NIS with the case of university hospitals in Turkey.

In addition, section 3 has also four different chapters. Chapter 9 evaluates the impact of strategic management and strategic thinking on performance in the public health sector. Furthermore, chapter 10 makes an analysis about the Broken Windows Theory in terms of patient safety. In chapter 11, the relationship between health expenditures and life expectancy at birth is identified for MENA countries with the help of cointegration methods. Chapter 12 aims to understand the ways of improving health and efficiency with strategic social media use in health organizations.

In section 4, there are also four different chapters. Chapter 13 is related to the public-private partnerships and its reflections to the health sector. The effects of health expenditure to decrease infant mortality rate in OECD countries are identified in chapter 14. On the other hand, chapter 15 focuses on the mediating role of self-efficacy and leadership in Pygmalion perception of the workers. Finally, the factors which affects the convergence of per-capita health expenditures in the EU member countries are determined in chapter 16.

Acknowledgment

The editors would like to acknowledge the help of all the people involved in this project and, more specifically, to the authors and reviewers that took part in the review process. Without their support, this book would not have become a reality.

First, the editors would like to thank each one of the authors for their contributions. Our sincere gratitude goes to the chapter's authors who contributed their time and expertise to this book.

Second, the editors wish to acknowledge the valuable contributions of the reviewers regarding the improvement of quality, coherence, and content presentation of chapters. Most of the authors also served as referees; we highly appreciate their double task.

Yeter Demir Uslu
İstanbul Medipol University, Turkey

Hasan Dinçer
İstanbul Medipol University, Turkey

Serhat Yüksel
İstanbul Medipol University, Turkey

Section 1

Chapter 1
Identifying the Relationship Between Health Investment and Economic Development:
A Cluster Analysis for Developing, Developed, and Least Developed Countries

Serkan Eti
https://orcid.org/0000-0002-4791-4091
Istanbul Medipol University, Turkey

Yaşar Gökalp
Istanbul Medipol University, Turkey

Nurcan Okçuoğlu Tosun
Istanbul Medipol University, Turkey

ABSTRACT

The purpose of this study is to reveal the relationship between the economic development of countries and the importance they attach to health. In this context, macroeconomic data on the economic development levels and health of 127 countries were included in the study. In the application part of the study, clustering and cross-table analysis were used. As a result of the k-means clustering analysis, a 76.4% similarity was found between the three countries groups and the economic development levels. Therefore, it is possible to talk about significant relationships between health expenditures/investments and economic development. In addition, it is seen that 90% of the country group that attaches importance to health expenditures consists of developed countries.

DOI: 10.4018/978-1-7998-2329-2.ch001

INTRODUCTION

Economic growth is an extremely important variable for the success of a country's economy. It is an indispensable element of the economic policies of many countries, especially developed countries. The phenomenon of economic growth is one of the most debated issues of economists in all periods. Today, it is one of the most important social and economic issues that least developed, developing and even developed countries have emphasized. It is expressed as economic growth that a country widening its production limit by increasing the amount of scarce resources or improving their quality or reaching higher production levels by changing production technology and institutional framework (Üstünel, 1988). The increase in the national income of the countries is an important indicator in terms of economic growth. When the literature is analyzed, GDP (Gross Domestic Product) has been used in the national income calculations since the beginning of 1990s instead of GNP (Gross National Product) in order to measure economic growth (Ertek, 2017; Murat & Yılmaz-Eser, 2013; Ersin and Eti, 2017). While developed countries attach importance to economic growth, in other words, the change in real GDP over the years, developing countries give more importance to the concept of economic development than to the concept of economic growth. Economic development encompasses economic as well as social and political spheres such as economic growth, reduction of income imbalances and unemployment, and the modernization of economic and social institutions (Dinçer et al., 2018a, 2018b, 2018c; Özel, 2012). The differences in the growth rates of the countries have made it inevitable to investigate the factors that determine economic growth and to take these factors into consideration while determining policies.

Economists have therefore developed different theories of economic growth. Endogenous growth theory, which was developed as a reaction to growth theory, is of great importance. Internal growth theory has examined capital in two parts as physical and human capital. Because of physical and human capital on economic growth, it is emphasized that the factors affecting human capital will indirectly contribute to economic growth (Başar et al., 2016). There are many factors affecting human capital. Education and health, which is one of the main factors of human capital, will increase the efficiency of investments made in these areas in the long term. Therefore, it can be said that individuals can directly affect the human capital level (OECD, 2001). Education enables individuals to increase their knowledge and specialize in specific subjects. Health, on the other hand, affects the return on investment in human capital positively along with other indicators, especially the life span of individuals (Akça, 2015). Therefore, any kind of investment in people will contribute to economic growth. When the countries with high economic development are examined, it is seen that the education and health levels of these countries are generally high (Çetin & Ecevit, 2010).

All systems and organizations in the world aim to realize a society consisting of healthy individuals and healthy individuals. Because the basis of security, power, knowledge and happiness are healthy individuals. Today, the most accepted definition of universal health is the definition made by WHO (Larson, 1991). According to this definition, health; it is a state of complete physical, mental and social well-being as well as the absence of any illness and weakness. As it can be understood from the definition, health services to be provided to states by individuals; disease elimination, elimination of the factors that cause the disease or prevention measures (Koçak et al., 2017). All expenses incurred to provide these services are collected under health expenditures (Dinçer and Yüksel, 2019).

The increase in the importance of human capital especially after the second world war has increased the importance given to health and health expenditures. During this period, national health services brought public health to a large extent (Yılmaz & Yentürk, 2015). In some countries, the provision and financing of health care is fully provided by the public, while in others it can be covered by both the public and private sectors. The method of providing the financing of the countries, economic, political, historical, technological, etc. It is shaped depending on variables such as. In addition, the continued economic development of countries, the increase in demand for health services due to technological developments in medicine and changes in health policies may lead to an increase in health expenditures and spending dynamics (Daştan & Çetinkaya, 2015). When we look at the recent years, the increase in health expenditures is quite remarkable. Especially in developed countries, the share of health expenditures is relatively higher than in developing countries. Due to the increasing economic and educational levels in developed countries, individuals have become more sensitive to health issues with the increase in living standards, changing health perceptions and increasing health expectations (Shi et al., 2019).

In many studies, the increase in education levels of countries shows that there is a parallel between economic growth and health expenditures (Taban & Kar, 2003). Mushkin (1962) showed that simultaneous investments in education and health have positive effects on the economic development process. In this context, he found that healthy and educated people behave more effectively as consumers and producers in society (Kamacı & Yazıcı, 2017). Since healthy people will be better educated, it is observed that the workforce that grows from these people is increasing production and productivity. In addition, educated people will question the existing situation and seek different and more qualified health services in case of insufficiency (Koçak et al., 2018). In hospitals equipped with more luxurious and technological equipment, they will be in expectation of receiving health services by specialist professionals.

In recent years, the most important factor that increases health expenditures is considered as technological progress. Particularly, high costs in the purchase and use of diagnostic technological tools and equipment are one of the main factors that increase expenditures. For example, according to OECD 2010 Health statistics, the use of MRI (Magnetic Resonance Imaging) and CT (Computed Tomography Devices) has increased rapidly in recent years. Between 2000 and 2008, the increase in per capita MRI equipment in OECD countries was more than doubled. MRI and CT devices are very costly to purchase and use. These costs vary from country to country (Yereli et al., 2016). On the other hand, the unnecessary use of these devices or the inconsistency of the tests at the diagnostic stage is another factor that increases the expenditures. Long-term examination appointments, failure to get results on time, or more comfortable service seekers of the system may cause the patients to shift to the private sector. In this case, it causes cost increase in health services.

An indicator of the level of development of countries is also measured by the size of the resources they devote to R&D expenditures. While the competition among developed countries is at a high level, developing countries are in research and development studies since they do not yet understand the importance and severity of the lack of resources or problems (Dinçer et al., 2019a,b,c). Therefore, they fall behind in the competition. Developed countries need to produce health services both in order to make their people healthy and protect against infectious diseases, and to take precautions against an epidemic that may emerge in other countries and spread all over the world. They need to invest more in R&D. In particular, the R&D studies carried out by the developed welfare states for infectious diseases increase health expenditures considerably and create a burden on their budgets. The technological infrastructure required for health care services and the training of trained personnel, tools and equipment require high costs (Akın, 2007). Although the share allocated for R & D studies and new technological developments in the short-term seems to be a burden, these expenditures, which are considered in the long-term, turn into investments and contribute greatly to the national economy. The fact that the US has a voice in the world medical device market by 41%, the EU by 23% and Japan by 10% is proof of this situation (Arık et al., 2016). While developed countries are at the forefront of R & D and innovation studies, developing countries concentrate more on production activities (Yaylalı et al., 2010). For every reason, every country in the world makes several health expenditures within the framework of its own health understanding and opportunities. Today, these health expenditures are increasing rapidly and constitute a large market share worldwide.

This study aims to group health expenditures and investments in countries. In this respect, it is aimed to identify the countries that make similar health expenditures and health investments in the countries examined. Subsequently, the groups formed will be taken into consideration and compared with economic growth levels. On the other hand, it will be investigated whether there is a similarity between the economic growth levels of countries and the importance they attach to health. In this context, 127 countries will be grouped with k-means clustering method, taking into account health items. The variables to be used in the analysis will be provided in the world bank.

In line with the issues mentioned in the introduction, this study analyzes the similarities between the health expenditures and health investments of the countries and their economic growth levels. For this purpose, 27 variables belonging to 127 countries belonging to the mentioned concepts were examined by the clustering method. According to the results obtained, health expenditures and health investments can be compared with the economic levels of the countries. In the studies in the literature, it is seen that the relationship between these variables is mostly examined by country or country groups. Therefore, in this study, 127 countries are examined, and a large data set is taken into consideration and it is thought to contribute to the literature. Also, when the literature is examined, it is determined that the expenditures and investments made by the countries in the field of health are generally handled by restricting them to public expenditures. Therefore, considering the health expenditures with 27 variables, it is thought that the grouping of countries will contribute to the literature.

The study consists of four different parts. In this introduction, which constitutes the first part of the study, economic growth, health expenditures, and health investments are emphasized. In this section, definitions of concepts used in the study are given. In addition, the relationship between them has been put forward conceptually. In the second part of the study, the literature on economic growth, health expenditures, and health investments will be included. As a result of the literature analysis, the deficiency will be determined. Thus, the originality of the study will be emphasized. In the third section, brief information about the clustering method will be given. Besides, theoretical knowledge and clustering literature will be emphasized. Afterward, the results and findings of the application will be shared. Also, in the last part of the study, the importance of health expenditures and investments on the contribution of the national economy will be highlighted.

LITERATURE REVIEW

The World Health Organization (WHO, 2005) associated the vast majority of the difference in economic growth between developed and developing countries with Health Care. This is an indication of a positive correlation between health investments and economic growth. For this reason, studies investigating the relationship between health investments and economic development of countries are examined.

Hartwig (2009) conducted a study to measure the impact of health capital formation on long-term economic growth. This article was conducted using panel Granger-causality analysis. Using empirical methodology, it reviews the question of whether health capital formation in wealthy countries promotes GDP growth. The results do not support the view that health capital formation promotes long-term economic growth in the OECD region. With the Abuja Declaration in 2001, African leaders agreed to devote 15% of government spending to health spending, but by 2013 only five African countries had achieved this goal. Piabuo and Tieguhong (2017) aimed to present a comparative analysis of the impact of health expenditures between countries in the CEMAC sub-region and the other five African countries that reached the Abuja declaration. The data of this study were taken from the World Economy Indicator (2016) database and the panel of ordinary least square (OLS), fully modified ordinary least square (FMOLS) and dynamic ordinary least square (DOLS) were used as econometric technic of analysis. As a result of this study, it was concluded that health expenditures had a positive and significant effect on economic growth in both cases. In addition, there was a long-term relationship between health expenditure and economic growth for both country groups. Bedir (2016) conducted a study to examine the relationship between health expenditures and economic growth in developing countries. From 1995 to 2013, a modified version of the Granger (1969) causality test proposed by Toda and Yamamoto (1995) and Dolado and Lütkepohl (1996) was used in European, Middle Eastern African and Asian countries. The results show that incomes are an important factor in explaining the difference in health expenditures between countries. Therefore, it is seen that the increase in income level increases health expenditures for some developing market economies. Aluko and Marvelous (2018) conducted a study to examine the impact of public health spending on economic growth in Nigeria between 1995 and 2016. Ordinary Least Squares (OLS) and Error Correction Model (ECM) were used to estimate the long-term and short-term effects of public health expenditure, while time-series data and econometrics tools were used to test stagnation, causality, and cohesion. According to the results of Ordinary Least Squares (OLS) analysis, there is a positive relationship between public health expenditure and economic growth in Nigeria in the long term. Similarly, according to the results of the Error Correction Model (ECM) analysis, public health spending in Nigeria has a short-term impact on economic growth. Sarpong et al. (2018) conducted a study to examine the impact of health on long-term economic growth in 35 selected Sub-Saharan African countries using panel data covering the period 1997-2016. Data analyzed using panel cointegration tests, panel Granger causality tests, and the dynamic OLS estimator indicate that health human capital is an important determinant of long-term economic growth in Sub-Saharan Africa. It was concluded that the increase in health human capital provided by health expenditures per capita increased growth by 0.207 percent. In addition, the causal link between economic growth and health is two-sided.

Chakroun (2010) conducted a study to investigate the potential impact of national expenditures on the relationship between health care and national income. Using a panel threshold regression model, data specific to 17 OECD countries over the period 1975–2003 was analyzed. Unlike previous analyzes, empirical results of the study show that health care is a necessity rather than a luxury. Moreover, the relationship between health expenditure and income varies by time and between countries. Cebeci and Ay (2016), on the BRIC countries and Turkey, conducted a study to examine the effects of economic growth and health movement with a panel regression analysis. This study aims to explain the relationship between health and economic growth with panel data analysis. BRICS countries and Turkey made on this study covers the period 2000-2014. According to the results obtained from the econometric study, it was concluded that health expenditures had a significant impact on economic growth. Lawrence Babatunde (2014) conducted a study to assess the impact of health spending on economic growth in Nigeria. Multiple regression analysis was applied in this study. According to the analysis results, gross capital formation, total health expenditures and labor productivity are important determinants of economic growth in Nigeria while it shows that life expectancy rate has a negative effect on growth in the period covered by the study. As a result, it is suggested that the government should encourage savings and investments in the economy, increase spending on healthcare provisions, increase labor productivity levels, and prioritize security and life issues in Nigeria. Cetin and Ecevit (2010) conducted a study to measure the impact of health expenditures in OECD countries on economic growth by using panel regression analysis. Data were collected from 15 OECD countries between 1990-2006. The relationship between health expenditures and economic growth was estimated by panel OLS method within the Pooled Regression Model. According to the empirical results, no statistically significant relationship was found between health expenditures and economic growth. Tang and Huang (2016) created a regression model and conducted a study on the impact of human capital investments in health on economic growth in Hunan Province, China. The study was carried out by regression analysis of Hunan's time series data from 1978 to 2008. As a result of the study, it was concluded that health human capital investment did not only affect the health level of individuals but also played a decisive role on the impact of economic growth. Health investments are made in at least two directions; one is medical investment, the second is health investments. Both complement each other and improve people's health. Therefore, ensuring that individuals have health awareness is an important part of health investments that cannot be neglected. Mehrara et al. (2010) conducted a study to estimate the relationship between health expenditure and income for 16 OECD countries in the period 1993-2007. In this study, panel flat transition regression model with individual effects was used. Income elasticity for all OECD members is estimated at approximately 2.59. According to these results, health expenditure can be considered as a luxury. In addition, the estimated income elasticity of health expenditures over time and in countries was found to be highly variable.

Sunkanmi and Oke (2012) were conducted to examine the relationship between health spending and economic growth in Nigeria, covering the period 1970-2009. This study was conducted using the multivariate cointegration technique proposed by Johansen. The cointegration equation shows some deviations that the allocation to health services is very inadequate. Therefore, it is recommended that a significant proportion of the national budget be allocated to health services in order to have more robust health care programs that can promote economic growth in Nigeria. Eryigit et al. (2012), for the period 1950-2005 using annual time series data, education-health expenditures in Turkey, a long-term relationship between defense spending and economic growth has carried out a study in order to investigate experimentally. In order to estimate these relationships, the cointegration method, which allows the existence of structural breaks, was used. The results show that there are two common integrative vectors with statistically significant structural breaks in the system. According to the long-term equations defined, education and health expenditures positively affect economic growth, while defense expenditures are negatively affected. In addition, the results show that there is a budget balance between education-health and defense expenditures. Elmi and Sadeghi (2012) conducted a study to investigate the causal and cointegration relationships between economic growth and health expenditures in developing countries between 1990 and 2009. This study focuses on panel cointegration and causality within the framework of VECM. As a result of the study, it was concluded that there is a short-term causality from GDP to health expenditures, while there is no short-term causality from health expenditures to economic growth. Similarly, it is concluded that there is a dual causality and long-term relationship between economic growth and health expenditure. It also confirms the health-induced growth hypothesis in developing countries.

Li and Huang (2009) conducted a study to examine the relationship between health, education and economic growth in China. In this empirical analysis, the relationship between real GDP growth per capita and health investment in physical capital, human capital and production function is evaluated. Panel data models were used in the estimation based on the data obtained from the period 1978-2005. Empirical evidence suggests that both health and education have a significant positive impact on economic growth. Eggoh (2015) and colleagues conducted an empirical study examining the relationship between education and health and economic growth through a large sample of 49 African countries. As a result of the study conducted using traditional cross-sectional and dynamic panel techniques, it has been concluded that education and health expenditures negatively affect economic growth for an African country due to inefficiency, corruption, bureaucracy and lack of investment. In addition, it was concluded that health expenditures contribute more to economic growth than education variables. Halıcı-Tuluce, Dogan and Dumrul (2016) conducted a study to examine the relationship between health expenditures and economic development. This study examines the relationship between health spending and economic growth using panel data covering low- and high-income countries. Using the dynamic panel data methodology, twenty-five high-income and nineteen low-income economies were analyzed for the period 1995-2012 and 1997–2009. The relationship between health expenditures and economic growth in the short term and the one-way causality relationship between public health expenditures and economic growth in the long term were determined. In high-income countries, while there is a two-way causality for both private and public health expenditures in the short term, there is a one-way causality between economic growth and private health expenditures in the long run. In addition, private health expenditures have negative effects on economic growth and public health expenditures have both negative and statistically significant effects. Gong, Li, and Wang (2012) conducted a study to analyze the impact of health investment and therefore health capital on physical capital accumulation and long-term economic growth in an extended Ramsey model with the Arrow-Romer production function and Grossman (1972) utility function. Using a panel of data from China's individual provinces, it was concluded that economic growth is associated with both health growth rate and health level. The growth in health capital always facilitates economic growth. However, since health investments can affect physical capital investment, it can be said that excessive investment in health may adversely affect economic growth. Gyimah-Brempong and Wilson (2004) conducted a study to investigate the effects of health human capital on per capita income growth in Sub-Saharan Africa and OECD countries. In this study using the Solow growth model, panel data and a dynamic panel estimator, it was found that per capita income growth rate was strongly and positively influenced by health human capital stock and investment after controlling other variables. In sub-Saharan African countries, the relationship between health human capital and income growth is similar to the structure of the relationship in OECD countries.

Reeves et al. (2013) conducted a study to determine whether investment in the health sector affects economic growth. The working method was determined by Using cross-national fixed effects models covering 25 EU countries from 1995 to 2010, determining the financial multipliers before and during the recession that started in 2008. The multiplier for total government expenditure was found to be 1.61. In addition, there is a significant heterogeneity among expenditure types. Titus Ayobami and Adebayo (2017) conducted a study to examine the level of government spending, economic growth and poverty in Nigeria. In this study, government expenditures are divided into health and education components. Annual secondary data covering the period between 1980 and 2014 were analyzed using the Vector autoregressive

(VAR) technique. According to the results of the analyzes, the government's health and education expenditures increase economic growth. Similarly, the increase in economic growth has led to poverty reduction in the country. In addition, evidence from the variance decomposition analysis showed that economic growth and health spending in Nigeria has the potential to affect the level of poverty. Moreover, the findings show that health expenditures and education expenditures made to the state have greater potential in increasing economic growth and per capita consumption expenditures. Sahnoun (2018) conducted a study to examine the relationship between health expenditures and economic growth in Tunisia. In Tunisia, non-stationary time series have been used to measure the relationship between health expenditure and economic growth over a period of forty-four years. According to the results, it is understood that there is a positive relationship between health expenditures and economic growth. Wang and Granados (2019) conducted a study to examine the relationship between mental health and economic development in China in the 21st century. Individual data and city-level variables were used to investigate the relationship between macroeconomic variables and health outcomes. Individual data were obtained from the Longitudinal Study of China Health and Retirement (CHARLS). The relationship between economic conditions and mental health in China was investigated using three consecutive questionnaires in 17,000 adult cohorts aged 45 and over, covering a total of 42,000 observations interviewed in 2011, 2012, 2013 and 2015. The relationship between economic conditions and mental health in China was investigated. It was concluded that economic growth was associated with increased symptoms of depression and cognitive impairment. Heshmati (2001) conducted a study using the augmented Solow growth model to investigate the relationship between OECD countries' gross domestic product (GDP) and per capita health expenditure (HCE). The empirical analysis is based on data from OECD countries for the period 1970-1992. The results show that OECD countries approach the fixed income per capita at 3.7% per year. It shows that health expenditures positively affect economic growth and convergence rate.

Spiteri and von Brockdorff (2019) conducted a study to investigate the relationship between economic development and health outcomes in Europe in the context of cardiovascular diseases. In the first place, an empirical model was constructed using data on cardiovascular disease deaths in 27 European countries, with GDP per capita in each country from 2003 to 2014. According to the results, there is a statistically significant inverted U-shaped relationship; whereby as income increases mortality rates first rise, before declining at subsequent levels of development. It is emphasized that improvements in public health systems, especially in developing countries, continue with the efforts to increase economic growth. Narayan, Narayan and Mishra (2010) conducted an empirical study to investigate the relationship between health and economic growth with data from 5 Asian countries covering the period

1974-2007. This relationship is modeled within the framework of the production function and two important conclusions are reached. Firstly, it is concluded that the variables share a long-term relationship in all four variables of the growth model, and secondly, health, investment, export, EDRD (the interaction term between education and R & D) and R & D contribute positively to economic growth. Aslan et al. (2015) conducted a study using time series data for seven industrialized countries (France, Germany, England, Italy, Japan, Canada, and the United States) between 1980 and 2009 to investigate the causality between health spending and economic growth. A classic Cobb-Douglas production function, including health spending, labor, capital, the number of patent applications, and the total number of higher education students, suggests a long-term relationship between growth and health expenditure, according to the results of the study. Atılgan et al. (2016) hypothesis-driven growth for the health of Turkey's economy with health expenditure in order to examine empirically conducted a study examining the relationship between economic growth dynamics. The growth hypothesis is that there is a positive relationship between health expenditure and economic growth. The limited test approach, the autoregressive distributed lag approach (ARDL) and Kalman filter modeling were used to examine the cointegration relationship between economic growth and health expenditure in the period 1975-2013. According to the results of the study, a 1% increase in health expenditures per capita would lead to a 0.434% increase in the gross domestic product per capita. Furthermore, the results of the ARDL model show that health expenditures have a positive effect on GDP and economic growth in both long and short term. Kurt (2015) conducted a study examining the direct and indirect effects of public health expenditures on economic growth using the Feder-Ram model. The data used in the study of Turkey's economy in the years 2006-2013, total production, total government health expenditure, health expenditure was obtained from treatment and medication. According to the results obtained from the study of general government expenditure on health as a direct impact on economic growth in Turkey and the indirect positive effects were found to be significant as it has been found that negative and significant. Accordingly, the improvement of the health sector in Turkey and that there is a need for improvement is evident.

AN ANALYSIS ON 127 DIFFERENT COUNTRIES

In this study, 127 countries were analyzed through macro data. In this section, first of all, information is given about data collection. Then, descriptive statistics of the data were shared. Then, cluster analysis was applied to the variables. Cross-table analysis was applied between these clusters and economic development.

Data Set and Method

In this study, it is aimed to cluster the countries on the health base. For this purpose, the values of health expenditures and investment items of countries were obtained from the World Bank site. The developed, developing and underdeveloped countries that were taken under the study were given in the Appendix A.

Clustering analysis was analyzed on 127 countries in the table. The variables which are considered in the analysis are given in Table 1.

The descriptive statistics for 27 variables are summarized in the Table 2. These variables were used to measure health expenditures and health investments.

Cluster Analysis and Methodology

A set is defined as a community of mathematical objects. The clustering analysis is the method that groups the n observations within the framework of their characteristics. Thus, as a result of the analysis, homogenous clusters are formed within themselves and a heterogeneous structure is formed among themselves (Hair et al., 2014). Cluster analysis is a statistical method. Therefore, the assumptions of the analysis are available (Eti, 2019). In this context, it is required that there are no extreme extremes in the observation values and no multiple correlations. It is a very preferred method because of its low assumptions.

Cluster analysis basically consists of four stages.

- Creating Data Matrix
- Obtaining the Similarity or Distance Matrix
- Determination of Clustering Method
- Interpretation of Results

There are two types of methods in determining the clusters. These are called hierarchical and nonhierarchical methods. Hierarchical methods are divided into two as agglomerative and divisive methods. The most widely used nonhierarchical method is the k-means clustering method. Apart from this method, method clustering, fuzzy clustering methods are also available. In these methods, the number of sets is predetermined (Alpar, 2017). The analysis is used in many areas such as marketing, psychology, economics, and health.

Ulder et al. (2018) conducted a study on Type 2 diabetic patients. This study aimed to find the pathways causing the disease. Bayesian non-negative matrix factorization (bNMF) was applied for this purpose. As a result of the analysis, 5 clusters were determined. These clusters have been determined to have strong properties specific to each tissue. Barreto et al. (2007) used clustering analysis to

Table 1. Variables for clustering analysis

Variables
Maternal Mortality Ratio
Lifetime Risk of Maternal Death
Immunization, Measles
Mortality Rate, Infant
Domestic Private Health Expenditure Per Capita
Domestic Private Health Expenditure
Out-Of-Pocket Expenditure Per Capita, PPP (Current International $)
Out-Of-Pocket Expenditure Per Capita (Current US$)
Out-Of-Pocket Expenditure (% Of Current Health Expenditure)
Domestic General Government Health Expenditure Per Capita, PPP (Current International $)
Domestic General Government Health Expenditure Per Capita (Current US$)
Domestic General Government Health Expenditure (% Of GDP)
Domestic General Government Health Expenditure (% Of Current Health Expenditure)
Current Health Expenditure Per Capita, PPP (Current International $)
Current Health Expenditure Per Capita (Current US$)
Current Health Expenditure (% Of GDP)
Incidence of Tuberculosis
Tuberculosis Case Detection Rate
Immunization, DPT
Immunization, Hepb3
Mortality Rate, Neonatal
Mortality From CVD, Cancer, Diabetes or CRD Between Exact Ages 30 And 70
Mortality Rate, Under-5
Cause of Death, By Non-Communicable Diseases
Cause of Death, By Injury
Cause of Death, By Communicable Diseases And Maternal, Prenatal And Nutrition Conditions
Prevalence of Anemia Among Children

solve the location routing problem. They have integrated clustering techniques into the traditional location routing problem. Kılınçarslan et al. (2018) benefited from clustering analysis in concrete. In this study, clustering analysis was used in the mechanical strength of aggregate types. As a result of the analysis, three different groups were identified. Differences in clusters were investigated.

Table 2. Descriptive statistics

	N	Minimum	Maximum	Mean	Std. Deviation
Maternal Mortality Ratio	127	3,00	1360,00	200,6299	255,79384
Lifetime Risk of Maternal Death	127	0,00	5,94	0,9227	1,37350
Immunization, Measles	127	20,00	99,00	86,2835	14,86708
Mortality Rate, Infant	127	2,20	91,60	26,1787	22,21120
Domestic Private Health Expenditure Per Capita	127	1,94	4734,01	228,7465	479,79678
Domestic Private Health Expenditure	127	3,29	83,00	41,6590	17,70121
Out-Of-Pocket Expenditure Per Capita, PPP (Current International $)	127	4,36	1056,95	271,6168	256,12654
Out-Of-Pocket Expenditure Per Capita (Current US$)	127	1,94	1056,95	157,0846	205,64746
Out-Of-Pocket Expenditure (% Of Current Health Expenditure)	127	3,29	81,63	35,4042	18,42674
Domestic General Government Health Expenditure Per Capita, PPP (Current International $)	127	4,07	5275,89	702,6693	1118,27801
Domestic General Government Health Expenditure Per Capita (Current US$)	127	2,12	5155,60	493,4578	1034,76677
Domestic General Government Health Expenditure (% Of GDP)	127	0,39	9,42	3,2283	2,09232
Domestic General Government Health Expenditure (% Of Current Health Expenditure)	127	5,17	88,25	48,0873	21,63520
Current Health Expenditure Per Capita, PPP (Current International $)	127	31,86	9535,95	1086,9807	1510,33709
Current Health Expenditure Per Capita	127	16,64	9535,95	730,6334	1429,23002
Current Health Expenditure	127	2,53	18,32	6,5832	2,61726
Incidence of Tuberculosis	127	0,79	788,00	127,5716	149,61483
Tuberculosis Case Detection Rate	127	22,00	100,00	72,5354	16,43641
Immunization, DPT	127	23,00	99,00	87,0630	15,06586
Immunization, Hepb3	127	22,00	99,00	86,5669	15,09157
Mortality Rate, Neonatal	127	1,40	46,30	15,2047	11,71464
Mortality From CVD, Cancer, Diabetes or CRD Between Exact Ages 30 And 70	127	9,30	30,80	19,5417	5,40242

continued on following page

Table 2. Continued

	N	Minimum	Maximum	Mean	Std. Deviation
Mortality Rate, Under-5 (Per 1,000 Live Births)	127	2,70	130,80	35,5992	33,51373
Cause of Death, By Non-Communicable Diseases	127	25,40	95,30	66,1331	23,61491
Cause of Death, By Injury	127	2,60	29,60	8,9638	3,97809
Cause of Death, By Communicable Diseases and Maternal, Prenatal And Nutrition Conditions	127	1,50	67,10	24,9071	22,21219
Prevalence of Anemia Among Children	127	7,80	86,50	37,9496	19,15598

Abualigah et al. (2018) studied the problem of optimization. They used the Krill-herd algorithm together with clustering analysis. In the application part of the study, the clustering of text documents is emphasized. Clustering performance was evaluated by Krill herd algorithm. The success of the proposed method has been tested with thirteen algorithms in the literature. As a result, the best results were obtained. Zhao et al. (2018) conducted a study in the field of urban planning. The study also carried out a study on the public transportation system. In the method part of the study, a station focused clustering analysis was applied. The 89 metro stations in Nanjing in China are considered as a sample. K-medoids clustering method results were considered. It was included in the study in the surrounding offices, factories, and hospitals. Choreography analysis was applied to the relationship of the related centers to land use.

Palomo-Duarte et al. (2019) benefited from clustering analysis in the field of education. In this study, a 3D based video was designed and tested to teach foreign languages. In the application part of the study, 102 students who want to learn German are included. The students were evaluated before, during and after the training. The skills such as grammar, vocabulary and writing knowledge were compared and classified. As a result of the analysis, some students did not benefit from the game. It was determined that such students could develop a language with conventional and guided learning. Zhang et al. (2018) used clustering analysis and simulated Monte -Carlo simulation. The k-means algorithm is considered as the clustering analysis method. In this study, the multi-room room equalization was emphasized. As a result of the analysis, it was determined that the spatial distribution of the early reflections in the same cluster is regular and predictable.

Blackhurst et al. (2018) discussed the supply chain. Petri net and triangulation clustering were utilized to evaluate the large and complex structure of the supply chain. In the related study, strategies to reduce distortion in the supply chain have been evaluated. Aljarah et al. (2019) worked on the optimization of the gray worm healing algorithm. The problem in question is weakness tendency in early convergence. It has hybridized with Tabu research in order to eliminate the discretion. The performance of the method was compared with various clusters for measurement. As a result, it has been determined that the proposed method can be used for clustering applications.

Umer et al. (2018) They conducted a study on public health in Pakistan. Malaria is a serious health problem for Pakistani people. In this study, health data between the years 2011-2016 are taken into consideration. The study aimed to identify clusters of high-risk disease areas in the country. For this purpose, 1593409 cases were evaluated. Clustering analysis was fully utilized in identifying high risk areas. Zhang (2018) proposed a fuzzy clustering analysis. In this study, hierarchical clustering analysis was developed with Pythagorean fuzzy numbers. In the application part, 10 different smartphone brands are discussed. The price, performance and appearance criteria of the smartphones in question were taken into consideration. Ghahari et al. (2018) used clustering analysis in neuroscience. In this study, the purpose of separating the clustering analysis was highlighted. Thus, we focused on the separation of sorting spikes of RGCs in visual warning systems to retinas of wild field mice without human intervention.

Jiménez-Murcia et al. (2019) conducted a study on gambling disorder. In the method part of the study, the two-step clustering technique was used. As a result of the analysis, three clusters were obtained. The demographic information of the individuals such as entering origin, sex, education level, civil status, employment status, age, age of GD onset, duration of the gambling problem, GD severity and gambling related variables in the related clusters, which are named as high, medium and light, were examined. Li et al. (2018) conducted a study on urban design. This study also benefited from satellite images. In urban planning, the region is grouped by the k-means clustering method according to the structure of the buildings. As a result of the study, small differences in estimated energy consumption were determined. Gallo et al. (2018) aimed to investigate the effects of the Kyoto protocol on agriculture and forestry. A method is proposed for the analysis of the objective. According to the result of the analysis, four clusters were formed. In the analysis of the study, 189 nations and 64 properties were used.

Analysis Results

The study was conducted on the 2015 data of 127 countries in the World Bank. Three clusters were formed by the K-means algorithm. Then, chi-square analysis was used for the similarity between these clusters and economic growth. Distribution of 127 countries according to their economic growth is given in the Table 3.

As a result of the clustering analysis, 127 countries were divided into 3 groups. The 27 variables were considered for this analysis. These groups and the cross-table of economic development levels are given in Table 4. According to the table, it can be seen that 62,50% of the first group consists of the least developed countries. Similarly, the majority of the second group consists of developing countries. Almost all of the last group is developed countries. Based on this table, when the economic growth of the country is envisaged by looking at the health expenditures and investments, 76.4% (97/127) of the country has the accuracy ratio.

When the table is examined, it is seen that there is a similarity between the groups formed and economic growth (chi-square statistic = 107,853, $p < 0,001$). As a result of the analysis, it is seen that there is a similarity between the three clusters formed with the similarities of health expenditures and investments and economic growth.

Considering Turkey, Turkey is a developing country. As a result of clustering analysis, it has been determined that developing countries have similarities to health expenditures and investments. However, the Czech Republic, despite being a developed country, follows a health policy similar to a developing country.

Table 3. Frequency of countries

	Frequency	Percent
Least Developed	35	27,6
Developing	75	59,1
Developed	17	13,4
Total	127	100

Table 4. Crosstabulation of economic growth and clusters

		Cluster Number			
		1	2	3	Total
Economic Growth	Least Developed	30	4	1	35
	% within Cluster Number of Case	62,50%	5,90%	9,10%	
	Developing	18	57	0	75
	% within Cluster Number of Case	37,50%	83,80%	0,00%	
	Developed	7	0	10	17
	% within Cluster Number of Case	10,30%	0,00%	90,90%	
	Total	68	48	11	127

The summary statistics of the 27 variables included in the study were analyzed. ANOVA was used to show the significance of the difference between the groups statistically. Group statistics and difference test results are given in Table 5.

As a result of the post hoc test, it was examined which variables differed in groups. For example, "Maternal mortality ratio" was found to differ in all groups. The first group had the highest average, while the third group had the lowest average. In another variable, "Cause of death, by injury", while the difference between the first two groups was not statistically different, the third group was different from the other groups. This variable is both low and distinctive in the third group.

SOLUTIONS AND RECOMMENDATIONS

Countries continue to work to maintain their economic development. Health is the most important element of economic development. If health is taken in general, health expenditures should be directed to sustain economic growth.

FUTURE RESEARCH DIRECTIONS

In this study, 127 countries whose data can be accessed are studied. We recommend working with a wider country data. Furthermore, the use of other clustering methods will provide originality for future studies.

CONCLUSION

Economic growth is an important factor for countries. Therefore, countries focus on the factors that affect economic growth. The most important of these elements are the physical and human capital of the countries. Some of the arguments that make up the relevant capital are education and health issues. It is seen that developed countries have invested in health and education fields in order to increase efficiency. Therefore, investments and expenditures on healthcare have an important role in the development and economic growth of countries.

The concept of health, by definition, includes not only disease but also health protection and rehabilitation. In this context, all kinds of activities to be carried out both at the time of illness and before and after the illness are important. All kinds of expenditures and investments made for this purpose are called as health expenditures and investments. These expenditures and investments are a sub-subject of economic activity and they affect the growth.

Table 5. Descriptive statistics of groups (Mean ± Standard Deviation)

	Member of Groups			F	p
	1	2	3		
Maternal Mortality Ratio	454,85±253,39[a]	52,5±57,28[b]	7±3,03[c]	95,882	<0,001
Lifetime Risk of Maternal Death	2,24±1,47[a]	0,14±0,19[b]	0,01±0,01[c]	79,824	<0,001
Immunization, Measles	74,81±16,83[a]	93,09±7,93[b]	94,27±3,88[b]	35,647	<0,001
Mortality Rate, Infant	50,01±16,52[a]	13,07±8,27[b]	3,24±0,94[c]	159,333	<0,001
Domestic Private Health Expenditure Per Capita	35,13±32,86[a]	198,8±155,91[b]	1258,71±1174,61[c]	54,2	<0,001
Domestic Private Health Expenditure	46,86±19,61[a]	40,82±15,31[a]	24,12±9,83[b]	8,442	<0,001
Out-Of-Pocket Expenditure Per Capita, PPP (Current International $)	72,28±64,86[a]	334,53±211,34[b]	752,57±188,26[c]	82,569	<0,001
Out-Of-Pocket Expenditure Per Capita (Current US$)	26,99±23,48[a]	164,53±127,93[b]	678,73±199,17[c]	155,464	<0,001
Out-Of-Pocket Expenditure (% Of Current Health Expenditure)	40,5±20,21[a]	35,09±16,18[a]	15,11±5,26[b]	9,691	<0,001
Domestic General Government Health Expenditure Per Capita, PPP (Current International $)	77,53±124,91[a]	621,78±469,09[b]	3930,6±909,64[c]	349,328	<0,001
Domestic General Government Health Expenditure Per Capita (Current US$)	31,02±52,52[a]	319,33±285,45[b]	3587,8±1080,46[c]	422,546	<0,001
Domestic General Government Health Expenditure (% Of GDP)	1,66±1,15[a]	3,61±1,33[b]	7,69±1,53[c]	105,358	<0,001
Domestic General Government Health Expenditure (% Of Current Health Expenditure)	30,18±16,57[a]	56,23±15,79[b]	75,88±9,83[c]	57,6	<0,001
Current Health Expenditure Per Capita, PPP (Current International $)	202,26±199,81[a]	1031,19±610,19[b]	5292,46±1681,34[c]	261,464	<0,001
Current Health Expenditure Per Capita	79,03±83,14[a]	524,78±403,41[b]	4846,54±1911,61[c]	272,042	<0,001
Current Health Expenditure	5,83±2,96[a]	6,51±1,72[a]	10,32±2,69[b]	16,474	<0,001
Incidence of Tuberculosis	262,02±158,21[a]	52,1±58,62[b]	7,43±1,93[c]	62,312	<0,001

continued on following page

Table 5. Continued

	Member of Groups			F	p
	1	2	3		
Tuberculosis Case Detection Rate	56,38±13,25[a]	81,66±8,97[b]	86,64±1,21[c]	92,578	<0,001
Immunization, DPT	77,02±16,94 [a]	92,72±10,36 [b]	95,91±2,07 [b]	23,571	<0,001
Immunization, Hepb3	76,9±17[a]	92,59±10,59[b]	91,55±6,12[b]	20,872	<0,001
Mortality Rate, Neonatal	27,85±7,8[a]	8,36±5,09[b]	2,3±0,57[c]	171,048	<0,001
Mortality From CVD, Cancer, Diabetes or CRD Between Exact Ages 30 And 70	21,97±3,96[a]	19,2±5,22[b]	11,03±1,46[c]	26,083	<0,001
Mortality Rate, Under-5 (Per 1,000 Live Births)	71,56±26,84[a]	15,35±9,95[b]	3,87±1,08[c]	154,618	<0,001
Cause of Death, By Non-Communicable Diseases	39,56±12,93[a]	81,1±10,38[b]	89,57±1,95[c]	226,203	<0,001
Cause of Death, By Injury	10,26±3,3[a]	8,66±4,27[a]	5,17±1,18[b]	8,698	<0,001
Cause of Death, By Communicable Diseases and Maternal, Prenatal and Nutrition Conditions	50,18±13,78[a]	10,24±7,43[b]	5,27±1,28[c]	242,91	<0,001
Prevalence of Anemia Among Children	58,06±14,64[a]	28,01±5,96[b]	11,61±1,3[c]	167,942	<0,001

When the literature is examined, the studies between economic growth and health are remarkable. In this concept, the relationship between the economic growth and health expenditures of the countries is examined by econometric analysis. In this study, more than one country was analyzed. This is the most important factor that constitutes the originality of the study. In addition, the studies in the literature have analyzed public expenditures as health expenditures. This excludes other areas of health from analysis. In the study, the use of other macro data has allowed us to look at a wider perspective.

In this study, it has been tried to group the countries in terms of their importance to health expenditures and investments. In addition, the relationship between these groups and economic growth was examined. For this purpose, 127 countries were included in the research. The k-means cluster analysis was applied based on the health expenditure and investment items of the countries. As a result of the analysis, 3 different groups were determined. Chi-square analysis was used for the relationship between these groups and development levels.

As a result of the study, the similarities of the countries in terms of health expenditures and investments were determined. With the help of this similarity, 3 different country groups were obtained. When the characteristics of these groups are examined, it is seen that the first group is behind the other two groups in terms of health. It was observed that the first group was less important than the other groups in terms of both the concept of health and their expenditure / investments. Similarly, it was found that the third group attaches importance to health expenditures and investments compared to other countries.

In addition, in the analysis part of the study, the economic development levels of the countries in these three groups were examined. For this purpose, chi-square analysis was applied. According to the analysis, 76.4% similarity was found between health groups and economic development levels. This similarity was statistically significant ($p < 0.001$). As a result of the cross-table analysis, it was found that 90.9% of the countries in the third group were developed countries. As a result, it can be interpreted that developed countries attach importance to health expenditures and investments. Similarly, it is seen that 62.5% of the countries constituting the first group are underdeveloped countries. In general, while it is seen that the group of countries that attach importance to health expenditure and investment is composed of developed countries, it is concluded that those who do not put the sector in the foreground are less developed countries.

As a result, if countries want to achieve sustainable economic growth, they should attach importance to health spending and investments. For this purpose, sensitivity should be given to any argument that constitutes the subject of health. In both public and private sectors, expenditures and investments in health should be supported. In this context, their tendency towards R & D studies, technological developments and education issues should be ensured. In these activities, all kinds of arguments that are particularly complex and expensive should be produced within the country and exported to other countries. Thousands of new technical devices to be produced means dozens of factories to be opened and tens of factories to employ hundreds of thousands of people should be remembered. This situation will not only have to spend high costs for the health sector and bring equipment from abroad, and thanks to the investments made, it will provide job opportunities to people and contribute directly to the economy. In addition, healthy individuals increase human capital. The healthy individual is more open to learning. The person who learns and develops himself / herself specializes in the field; i.e. healthy workers are more efficient. In the meantime, the education of healthy people means that the investment will be made longer. Because healthy people live longer and work actively. Therefore, it would be correct to say that there is a two-way relationship in the field of health and education. This makes a positive long-term contribution to economic prosperity and growth. As the number of specialist health personnel per person increases, the accuracy rate of the diagnoses made will increase and the number of examinations and the number of extra procedures performed will decrease. It is a known fact that every extra transaction affects the national economy negatively. When this situation is prevented, it will lead to a decrease in the cost of health services provided by the public sector and increase the productivity. This will make a positive contribution to economic growth.

REFERENCES

Abualigah, L. M., Khader, A. T., & Hanandeh, E. S. (2018). A combination of objective functions and hybrid Krill herd algorithm for text document clustering analysis. *Engineering Applications of Artificial Intelligence*, *73*, 111–125. doi:10.1016/j.engappai.2018.05.003

Akça, H. (2015). Beşeri Sermaye Harcamaları: Türkiye'de Yaşanan Gelişmeler Ve Sonuçlar Üzerine Bir İnceleme. *Ekonomi Bilimleri Dergisi*, *7*(2), 33–57.

Akın, C. S. (2007). *Sağlık ve sağlık harcamalarının ekonomik büyüme üzerine etkisi: Türkiye'de sağlık sektörü harcamaları*. Çukurova Üniversitesi Sosyal Bilimler Enstitüsü, İktisat Anabilim Dalı, Yayınlanmamış Yüksek Lisans Tezi.

Aljarah, I., Mafarja, M., Heidari, A. A., Faris, H., & Mirjalili, S. (2019). Clustering analysis using a novel locality-informed grey wolf-inspired clustering approach. *Knowledge and Information Systems*, 1–33.

Alpar, R. (2017). *Uygulamalı çok değişkenli istatistiksel yöntemler*. Detay Yayıncılık.

Aluko, O. O., & Marvelous, A. I. (2018). Public health expenditure and economic growth in Nigeria: An error correction model. *Journal of Economics, Management and Trade*, 1-11.

Aslan, A., Menegaki, A. N., & Tugcu, C. T. (2016). Health and economic growth in high-income countries revisited: Evidence from an augmented production function for the period 1980–2009. *Quality & Quantity*, *50*(2), 937–953. doi:10.100711135-015-0184-2

Atilgan, E., Kilic, D., & Ertugrul, H. M. (2017). The dynamic relationship between health expenditure and economic growth: Is the health-led growth hypothesis valid for Turkey? *The European Journal of Health Economics*, *18*(5), 567–574. doi:10.100710198-016-0810-5 PMID:27260182

Ayobami, O. T., & Ayinla, A. A. (n.d.). Government expenditure, Economic Growth and Poverty Level in Nigeria: A Disaggregated Approach.

Barreto, S., Ferreira, C., Paixao, J., & Santos, B. S. (2007). Using clustering analysis in a capacitated location-routing problem. *European Journal of Operational Research*, *179*(3), 968–977. doi:10.1016/j.ejor.2005.06.074

Başar, S., Künü, S., & Bozma, G. (2016). Eğitim ve Sağlık Harcamalarının Ekonomik Büyüme Üzerine Etkisi: Türkiye Üzerine Bir Uygulama. *Igdir University Journal of Social Sciences*, (10).

Bedir, S. (2016). Healthcare expenditure and economic growth in developing countries. *Advances in Economics and Business*, *4*(2), 76–86. doi:10.13189/aeb.2016.040202

Blackhurst, J., Rungtusanatham, M. J., Scheibe, K., & Ambulkar, S. (2018). Supply chain vulnerability assessment: A network based visualization and clustering analysis approach. *Journal of Purchasing and Supply Management*, *24*(1), 21–30. doi:10.1016/j.pursup.2017.10.004

Cebeci, E., & AY, A. (2016). The Effects Of Health Expendıtures On Economıc Growth: A Panel Regressıon Analysıs On Brıcs Countrıes And Turkey. *Dumlupinar University Journal of Social Science/Dumlupinar Üniversitesi Soysyal Bilimler Dergisi*.

Çetin, M., & Ecevit, E. (2010). Sağlık harcamalarının ekonomik büyüme üzerindeki etkisi: OECD ülkeleri üzerine bir panel regresyon analizi.

Chakroun, M. (2010). Health care expenditure and GDP: An international panel smooth transition approach. *International Journal of Economics*, *4*(1), 189–200.

Daştan, İ., & Çetinkaya, V. (2015). OECD Ülkeleri ve Türkiye'nin Sağlık Sistemleri, Sağlık Harcamaları ve Sağlık Göstergeleri Karşılaştırması. *SGD-Sosyal Güvenlik Dergisi*, *5*(1), 104–134.

Dinçer, H., Hacıoğlu, Ü., & Yüksel, S. (2018c). Conflict Risk and Defense Expenses and Their Impact on the Economic Growth. In Handbook of Research on Military Expenditure on Economic and Political Resources (pp. 1–23). Hershey, PA: IGI Global. doi:10.4018/978-1-5225-4778-5.ch001

Dinçer, H., & Yüksel, S. (2019). Identifying the causality relationship between health expenditure and economic growth: An application on E7 countries. *Journal of Health Systems and Policies*, *1*, 5.

Dinçer, H., Yuksel, S., & Adalı, Z. (2018a). Relationship Between Non-Performing Loans, Industry, and Economic Growth of the African Economies and Policy Recommendations for Global Growth. In Globalization and Trade Integration in Developing Countries (pp. 203–228). Hershey, PA: IGI Global. doi:10.4018/978-1-5225-4032-8.ch009

Dinçer, H., Yüksel, S., Adalı, Z., & Aydın, R. (2019a). Evaluating the Role of Research and Development and Technology Investments on Economic Development of E7 Countries. In Organizational Transformation and Managing Innovation in the Fourth Industrial Revolution (pp. 245-263). Hershey, PA: IGI Global.

Dinçer, H., Yüksel, S., Korsakienė, R., Raišienė, A. G., & Bilan, Y. (2019b). IT2 hybrid decision-making approach to performance measurement of internationalized firms in the baltic states. *Sustainability, 11*(1), 296. doi:10.3390u11010296

Dincer, H., Yüksel, S., & Martinez, L. (2019c). Balanced scorecard-based Analysis about European Energy Investment Policies: A hybrid hesitant fuzzy decision-making approach with Quality Function Deployment. *Expert Systems with Applications, 115*, 152–171. doi:10.1016/j.eswa.2018.07.072

Dinçer, H., Yüksel, S., & Şenel, S. (2018b). Analyzing the global risks for the financial crisis after the great depression using comparative hybrid hesitant fuzzy decision-making models: Policy recommendations for sustainable economic growth. *Sustainability, 10*(9), 3126. doi:10.3390u10093126

Eggoh, J., Houeninvo, H., & Sossou, G. A. (2015). Education, health and economic growth in African countries. *Journal of Economic Development, 40*(1), 93–111. doi:10.35866/caujed.2015.40.1.004

Elmi, Z. M., & Sadeghi, S. (2012). Health care expenditures and economic growth in developing countries: Panel co-integration and causality. *Middle East Journal of Scientific Research, 12*(1), 88–91.

Ersin, İ., & Eti, S. (2017). Measuring the Waste-Conscious and Saving Habits of the Youth in Turkey: The Sample of Istanbul Medipol University. *Uluslararası İslam Ekonomisi ve Finansı Araştırmaları Dergisi, 3*(3), 41–49.

Ertek, T. A. (2007). Temel ekonomi: (Basından örneklerle). *BETA Bulletin of Experimental Treatments for AIDS.*

Eryigit, S. B., Eryigit, K. Y., & Selen, U. (2012). The long-run linkages between education, health and defence expenditures and economic growth: Evidence from Turkey. *Defence and Peace Economics, 23*(6), 559–574. doi:10.1080/10242694.2012.663577

Eti, S. (2019). The Use of Quantitative Methods in Investment Decisions: A Literature Review. In Handbook of Research on Global Issues in Financial Communication and Investment Decision Making (pp. 256–275). Hershey, PA: IGI Global. doi:10.4018/978-1-5225-9265-5.ch013

Gallo, C., Faccilongo, N., & La Sala, P. (2018). Clustering analysis of environmental emissions: A study on Kyoto Protocol's impact on member countries. *Journal of Cleaner Production*, *172*, 3685–3703. doi:10.1016/j.jclepro.2017.07.194

Ghahari, A., Kumar, S. R., & Badea, T. C. (2018). Identification of Retinal Ganglion Cell Firing Patterns Using Clustering Analysis Supplied with Failure Diagnosis. *International Journal of Neural Systems*, *28*(8), 1850008. doi:10.1142/S0129065718500089 PMID:29631502

Gong, L., Li, H., & Wang, D. (2012). Health investment, physical capital accumulation, and economic growth. *China Economic Review*, *23*(4), 1104–1119. doi:10.1016/j.chieco.2012.07.002

Gyimah-Brempong, K., & Wilson, M. (2004). Health human capital and economic growth in Sub-Saharan African and OECD countries. *The Quarterly Review of Economics and Finance*, *44*(2), 296–320. doi:10.1016/j.qref.2003.07.002

Hair, J. F., Black, W. C., Babin, B. J., & Anderson, R. E. (2014). *Multivariate data analysis: Pearson new international edition*. Essex: Pearson Education Limited.

Halıcı-Tülüce, N. S., Doğan, İ., & Dumrul, C. (2016). Is income relevant for health expenditure and economic growth nexus? *International Journal of Health Economics and Management*, *16*(1), 23–49. doi:10.100710754-015-9179-8 PMID:27878709

Hartwig, J. (2010). Is health capital formation good for long-term economic growth? –Panel Granger-causality evidence for OECD countries. *Journal of Macroeconomics*, *32*(1), 314–325. doi:10.1016/j.jmacro.2009.06.003

Heshmati, A. (2001). On the causality between GDP and health care expenditure in augmented Solow growth model. SSE/EFI.

Jiménez-Murcia, S., Granero, R., Fernandez-Aranda, F., Stinchfield, R., Tremblay, J., Steward, T., ... Perales, J. C. (2019). Phenotypes in Gambling Disorder Using Sociodemographic and Clinical Clustering Analysis: An Unidentified New Subtype? *Frontiers in Psychiatry*, 10.

Kamacı, A., & Yazıcı, H. U. (2017). OECD Ülkelerinde Sağlik Harcamalarinin Ekonomik Büyüme Üzerindeki Etkisinin Ekonometrik Analizi. *Sakarya İktisat Dergisi*, *6*(2), 52–69.

Kılınçarslan, Ş., İnce, E. Y., Tuncay, E. B., & Yağmurlu, F. (2018). Clustering Analysis of Normal Strength Concretes Produced with Different Aggregate Types. *Open Chemistry*, *16*(1), 918–922. doi:10.1515/chem-2018-0100

Koçak, O., Arslan, H., & Eti, S. (2017). Belediyelerde sosyal politika uygulamaları ve Pendik belediyesi örneği. *Uluslararası Toplum Araştırmaları Dergisi*, *7*(12), 119–144. doi:10.26466/opus.311278

Koçak, O., Beki, A., & Eti, S. (2018). The Effects of the Different Activities on the Depression Level of Older People. *OPUS Uluslararası Toplum Araştırmaları Dergisi*, *8*(15), 1241–1266.

Kurt, S. (2015). Government health expenditures and economic growth: A Feder-Ram approach for the case of Turkey. *International Journal of Economics and Financial Issues*, *5*(2), 441–447.

Larson, J. S. (1991). *The measurement of health: Concepts and indicators* (Vol. 31). Greenwood Publishing Group.

Li, H., & Huang, L. (2009). Health, education, and economic growth in China: Empirical findings and implications. *China Economic Review*, *20*(3), 374–387. doi:10.1016/j.chieco.2008.05.001

Li, X., Yao, R., Liu, M., Costanzo, V., Yu, W., Wang, W., ... Li, B. (2018). Developing urban residential reference buildings using clustering analysis of satellite images. *Energy and Building*, *169*, 417–429. doi:10.1016/j.enbuild.2018.03.064

Mehrara, M., Musai, M., & Amiri, H. (2010). The relationship between health expenditure and GDP in OECD countries using PSTR. European Journal of Economics. *Finance and Administrative Sciences*, *24*, 1450–2275.

Muhsin, K. (2003). Kamu harcama çeşitlerinin ekonomik büyüme üzerine etkisi. *Ankara Üniversitesi SBF Dergisi, 58*(3).

Murat, S., & Eser, B. (2013). Türkiye'de Ekonomik Büyüme ve İstihdam İlişkisi: İstihdam Yaratmayan Büyüme Olgusunun Geçerliliği. *Emek ve toplum, 2*(3), 92-123.

Narayan, S., Narayan, P. K., & Mishra, S. (2010). Investigating the relationship between health and economic growth: Empirical evidence from a panel of 5 Asian countries. *Journal of Asian Economics*, *21*(4), 404–411. doi:10.1016/j.asieco.2010.03.006

Odubunmi, A. S., Saka, J. O., & Oke, D. M. (2012). Testing the cointegrating relationship between health care expenditure and economic growth in Nigeria. *International Journal of Economics and Finance*, *4*(11), 99–107. doi:10.5539/ijef.v4n11p99

OECD. (2001). *Strategies for Sustainable Development*. France.

Oni, L. B. (2014). Analysis of the growth impact of health expenditure in Nigeria. *IOSR Journal of Economics and Finance*, *3*(1), 77–84. doi:10.9790/5933-03117784

Özel, H. A. (2012). Ekonomik Büyümenin Teorik Temelleri. *Çankırı Karatekin Üniversitesi İİBF Dergisi*, *2*(1), 63-72.

Özer, A. R. I. K., İleri, Y. Y., & Buğra, K. A. Y. A. (2016). Sağlık Hizmetlerinde Tıbbi Cihaz Sektörü. *Hacettepe Sağlık İdaresi Dergisi*, *19*(2).

Palomo-Duarte, M., Berns, A., Yañez Escolano, A., & Dodero, J. M. (2019). Clustering analysis of game-based learning: Worth it for all students? *Journal of Gaming & Virtual Worlds*, *11*(1), 45–66. doi:10.1386/jgvw.11.1.45_1

Piabuo, S. M., & Tieguhong, J. C. (2017). Health expenditure and economic growth-a review of the literature and an analysis between the economic community for central African states (CEMAC) and selected African countries. *Health Economics Review*, *7*(1), 23. doi:10.118613561-017-0159-1 PMID:28593509

Reeves, A., Basu, S., McKee, M., Meissner, C., & Stuckler, D. (2013). Does investment in the health sector promote or inhibit economic growth? *Globalization and Health*, *9*(1), 43. doi:10.1186/1744-8603-9-43 PMID:24059873

Sahnoun, M. (2018). Does Health Expenditure Increase Economic Growth: Evidence from Tunisia? *Romanian Economic Journal*, *20*(67).

Sarpong, B., Nketiah-Amponsah, E., & Owoo, N. S. (2018). Health and Economic Growth Nexus: Evidence from Selected Sub-Saharan African (SSA) Countries. *Global Business Review*.

Shi, X., Li, J., Wang, F., Dinçer, H., & Yüksel, S. (2019). A Hybrid Decision-Making Approach for the Service and Financial-Based Measurement of Universal Health Coverage for the E7 Economies. *International Journal of Environmental Research and Public Health*, *16*(18), 3295. doi:10.3390/ijerph16183295 PMID:31500288

Spiteri, J., & von Brockdorff, P. (2019). Economic development and health outcomes: Evidence from cardiovascular disease mortality in Europe. *Social Science & Medicine*, *224*, 37–44. doi:10.1016/j.socscimed.2019.01.050 PMID:30738235

Tang, L., & Huang, H. (2016). A Study on the Influences of human capital investment in health on economics growth in Hunan Province. *International Journal of Simulation--Systems, Science & Technology*, *17*(49).

Udler, M. S., Kim, J., von Grotthuss, M., Bonàs-Guarch, S., Cole, J. B., Chiou, J., ... Mercader, J. M. (2018). Type 2 diabetes genetic loci informed by multi-trait associations point to disease mechanisms and subtypes: A soft clustering analysis. *PLoS Medicine*, *15*(9). doi:10.1371/journal.pmed.1002654 PMID:30240442

Umer, M., Zofeen, S., Majeed, A., Hu, W., Qi, X., & Zhuang, G. (2018). Spatiotemporal Clustering Analysis of Malaria Infection in Pakistan. *International Journal of Environmental Research and Public Health*, *15*(6), 1202. doi:10.3390/ijerph15061202 PMID:29880778

Üstünel, B. (1988). *Ekonominin Temelleri, 5.* Baskı.

World Health Organization. (2005). *World health development indicators.* Washington, D. C.

Yaylalı, M., Yusuf, A. K. A. N., & Cem, I. Ş. I. K. (2010). Türkiye de Ar&Ge Yatırım Harcamaları Ve Ekonomik Büyüme Arasındaki Eş-Bütünleşme Ve Nedensellik İlişkisi: 1990–2009. *Bilgi Ekonomisi ve Yönetimi Dergisi*, *5*(2).

Yereli, A. B., Kobal, İ., & Köktaş, A. M. (2016). *Türkiye'de Sağlık Harcamalarını Arttıran Faktörler.* İstanbul: Uluslararası Bilgi, Ekonomi ve Yönetim Kongresi, İstanbul Üniversitesi İktisat Fakültesi.

Yılmaz, V., & Yentürk, N. (2015). Türkiye'de sağlık harcamalarına tarihsel bir bakış. *İstanbul Bilgi Üniversitesi Sivil Toplum Çalışmaları Merkezi*, 1-17.

Zhang, X. (2018). Pythagorean fuzzy clustering analysis: A hierarchical clustering algorithm with the ratio index-based ranking methods. *International Journal of Intelligent Systems*, *33*(9), 1798–1822. doi:10.1002/int.21915

Zhang, Z., Zhu, G., & Shen, Y. (2018). Data clustering analysis of early reflections in small room. *The Journal of the Acoustical Society of America*, *144*(4), EL328–EL332. doi:10.1121/1.5065073 PMID:30404478

Zhao, X., Wu, Y. P., Ren, G., Ji, K., & Qian, W. W. (2019). Clustering Analysis of Ridership Patterns at Subway Stations: A Case in Nanjing, China. *Journal of Urban Planning and Development*, *145*(2), 04019005. doi:10.1061/(ASCE)UP.1943-5444.0000501

KEY TERMS AND DEFINITIONS

GDP: Gross Domestic Product
GNP: Gross National Product
VAR: Vector AutoRegressive
MRI: Magnetic Resonance Imaging
CT: Computed Tomography Devices

APPENDIX 1

Countries Considered for Analysis

Afghanistan, Angola, Albania, United Arab Emirates, Argentina, Armenia, Austria, Azerbaijan, Burundi, Belgium, Benin, Burkina Faso, Bangladesh, Bulgaria, Bosnia and Herzegovina, Belarus, Belize, Bolivia, Brazil, Botswana, Central African Republic, Chile, China, Cote d'Ivoire, Cameroon, Congo, Dem. Rep., Congo, Rep., Colombia, Costa Rica, Cyprus, Czech Republic, Germany, Djibouti, Dominican Republic, Algeria, Ecuador, Egypt, Arab Rep., Spain, Estonia, Ethiopia, Fiji, France, Gabon, Georgia, Ghana, Guinea, Gambia, The, Guinea-Bissau, Greece, Guatemala, Guyana, Honduras, Croatia, Haiti, Indonesia, India, Ireland, Iran, Islamic Rep., Iraq, Italy, Jamaica, Jordan, Kazakhstan, Kenya, Kyrgyz Republic, Cambodia, Liberia, St. Lucia, Sri Lanka, Lesotho, Lithuania, Luxembourg, Latvia, Morocco, Moldova, Madagascar, Mexico, Macedonia, FYR, Mali, Montenegro, Mongolia, Mozambique, Mauritania, Malawi, Malaysia, Namibia, Niger, Nigeria, Nicaragua, Netherlands, Nepal, Oman, Pakistan, Panama, Peru, Philippines, Papua New Guinea, Poland, Portugal, Paraguay, Romania, Russian Federation, Rwanda, Sudan, Senegal, Solomon Islands, Sierra Leone, El Salvador, Serbia, South Sudan, Suriname, Slovak Republic, Sweden, Eswatini, Chad, Togo, Thailand, Tajikistan, Turkmenistan, Tunisia, Turkey, Tanzania, Uganda, Ukraine, Uruguay, United States, Venezuela, RB

Chapter 2
Evaluation of the Relationship Between Leadership Characteristics and Motivation and Satisfaction in Health Institutions

Zafer Adiguzel
https://orcid.org/0000-0001-8743-356X
Medipol Business School, Istanbul Medipol University, Turkey

ABSTRACT

This article describes how due to the globalization activities, where competition is very intense and economic, technological and international environmental elements are also very active and uncertain. In the 21st century, the concept "management" stands out so that all institutions, including health institutions, can see their present and future locations, anticipate opportunities and threats, adapt to all the changes that have taken place, make their services more effective and sustain their success. Organizations need leaders who are open to teamwork, encouraging, creative, sociable, energetic, attaching importance to their subordinates' feelings, thoughts, needs and expectations, taking care to develop high quality relations with their subordinates and respecting their subordinates. Within the scope of the study, the understanding of leadership in health institutions and the importance of leadership are emphasized; the effects of leadership on the motivation, satisfaction and performance of the employees

DOI: 10.4018/978-1-7998-2329-2.ch002

INTRODUCTION

Due to the nature of their activities in the environment in which they live, health institutions interacting with many different individuals and organizations must provide effective and high quality services, manage technology and human resources successfully, and manage the problems experienced within the to produce permanent solutions and to ensure the continuous development of the institution. In order to achieve this, the presence of leaders with strong characteristics in health institutions is very important. The level of interactions they have with their subordinates as well as the characteristics required by healthcare leaders are another issue that needs to be carefully examined. This unique interaction relationship between leader and subordinate, which develops over time, is called "leader-member interaction" in the literature (Yukl, 2010).

In health institutions where different and more sensitive service delivery is realized compared to institutions in other sectors; the inconsistency and uncertainty of the demands, the existence of complex service delivery processes, the necessity of providing services in coordination in large and complex teams, and the rapid development and change of technology and medicine increase the importance of both leadership and the level of interaction between the leader and subordinates. Because any relationship or communication disorders or conflicts between the leader and the subordinate will affect the quality of the health service and the health status of the patient will be reflected. Therefore, it is essential that healthcare leaders develop high quality relationships with their subordinates based on mutual support, trust, respect and understanding. The interaction relationship between the leaders and subordinates affects the atmosphere in the organization and affects many individual and organizational output variables such as performance, organizational commitment, job satisfaction, burnout and intention to quit (Dulebohn et al., 2012).

Due to the nature and sensitivity of the services provided in health institutions, there is a greater need for exhibiting and promoting extra behaviors. Because the insufficiencies in the organizational citizenship behaviors of the employees may lead to a decrease in individual and total performance and as a result, inadequacy in the provision of health services may occur (Kolade et al., 2014). For this reason, it is thought that health professionals who have stronger communication with their leaders, who receive more supportive behavior from their leaders and who receive more consultancy, who love their leaders and who are satisfied with their relationship with their leaders, will voluntarily go beyond their expectations by spending more effort and time (Van Yperen et al., 1999). Leadership is an entire process that involves influencing and directing the activities of one person to achieve the goals of individuals or groups (Rost, 1993). As life quality and duration increases, the importance of healthy living and health institutions has increased. When the competitive environment is considered, health institutions like other businesses need strong leaders with vision, who are aware of their mission to keep themselves superior to their competitors and to carry them to the future without shaking. People who can respond to changing competition conditions in a timely manner and with new methods and continuously improve their management knowledge and at the same time lead these services are of great importance (Uno and Zakariasen, 2010). Leadership in health services is of great importance in terms of following innovations and adapting to current situations. In this case, in order for health workers to produce quality health services and work efficiently, innovative, knowledge-based collaborative, collective employees, leaders who can communicate well, distribute authority to their subordinates and who can trust them are needed. Health care workers determine the quality of health service with the level of performance they perform in their duties and patient satisfaction or dissatisfaction occurs in proportion to the quality of the service. The aim of this study is to investigate the relationship between the concepts of leadership, job satisfaction and motivation towards the organizational commitment of the employees.

LEADERSHIP

Managers, which is one of the main functions of the manager, also means leading the organization (Stogdill, 1974). The concept of management has been the subject of continuous discussion as thought and practice throughout the historical process (Bass and Stogdill, 1990). Managers are ambassadors trying to realize the harmonious goals of organizational elements (Hunt, 1991). Leadership is the process of having one's wishes by making employees want them in line with their wishes (Mahsud et al., 2010). It develops by changing over time. It is seen that the concepts of manager and leadership are unchangeable in practice (Vroom and Jago, 1988). A manager is a person who works for and on behalf of others, strives to achieve predetermined organizational objectives, plans the work within the organization, ensures its implementation and controls the final results (Yammarino, 2013). The leader is the person who determines the goals of the group and influences the other members of the group in the direction of these goals and directs them to behave in this direction (Newstrom et al., 1993).

Leadership is a concept that has been researched and conducted since ancient times (Northouse, 2018). In this context, the emergence of rational organizations did not diminish the need for leadership, but rather increased it. In particular, it is known that written procedures, rules, etc. do not determine the functioning of the process alone, and that the most important dynamics in the management of the human element are the manager and leader behaviors. Leadership can be defined as the process of bringing together a group of people around a common goal and vision, with their own voluntary will, blending their knowledge and skills with the leader's personal, behavioral and organizational characteristics and thus achieving the determined vision by successfully accomplishing the goals (Hughes, 1993; Yukl, 2011). Since leadership is a status created by the fact of living in a group, people living in communities; they need people who take initiative, produce solutions to problems and integrate society around a common goal (Daft, 2014; Yukl et al., 2013). This is the reason for the existence of leadership. Mankind is witnessing the fastest change experienced throughout history. In this period of rapid changes and developments, which are called the post-industrial society, the information age or the information society, perhaps more leadership and leaders are needed in the social and organizational sphere (Kâhya, 2013).

Within the framework of the studies and investigations on leadership, researchers have made many definitions based on the impressions they have obtained according to their individual conclusions. Some of these definitions are as follows:

- Leadership is a process that cannot be precisely formulated (Güney, 2000).
- It can be said that leadership is the behavioral pattern of the mobilization and maintenance of the structure with expectations and relations (Duygulu, 2007).
- Leadership as a process is defined as the influence of one person on the activities of other people and directing the activities under certain conditions in order to realize certain individual and group objectives (Ertürk, 2000).
- Leadership is more about gathering people around a common goal rather than dominating (Gezici, 2007).
- Ability to influence, motivate and direct organizational members towards leadership, targeted goals (Serinkan, 2008).

Leader; is a person who can read and see the future well in all definitions, influences its followers, guides and follows the group that gives confidence with their knowledge and experience (Hargreaves and Fink, 2012; Schein, 2010). "Leadership is a part of life. Through their vision, great leaders have taken great responsibilities and cost to the societies throughout the history in order to reach and develop more than the current situation (Duygulu, 2007). In this context, the power sources of leadership and leadership concepts in health institutions are discussed.

Leadership Power Supplies

Power is the ability to achieve goals. Physically, this achievement is achieved by spending energy and psychologically with the power and motivation of perseverance (Hodgkinson and Partington, 2008). French and Raven (1968) divided the power supplies that leaders would use to influence their followers into five groups. These; Reward Power: The leader can use it as a power tool if he can reward or punish his audience. Expressed rewards can be realized by means of wage increase, additional payment, promotion, more responsibility, more important work, status change, praise, appreciation, and group honoring (Meydan and Polat, 2010).

Coercive Power: It is opposed to reward power and based on punishment. The coercive force reflects the power of the leader to control and punish if subordinates oppose his directives. This power is based on fear. Anything that scares group members can be a source of power (Hersey et al., 1979; Bakan and Büyükbeşe, 2010).

Legal Power: In the organizational hierarchy, the power of influencing the behavior of subordinates because of their positions is the legal force. Here, subordinates, they feel compelled to obey orders and orders from the upper echelons (Coleman, 1997; Deniz and Çolak, 2008).

Expertise Power: This power, which is related to the knowledge, experience and expertise of the leaders or managers, is one of the most effective tools in business performance. It is the most useful way to influence other people in the organization (Chan, 2010; Titrek and Zafer, 2009).

Charismatic Power: Charismatic power is directly related to the personality traits of the leader (House et al., 2004). The fact that the personality of the leader can inspire the audience, and express their desires and hopes is the basis of this resource. The leader for subordinates is the epitome of ideal (Kouzes and Posner 2006). Therefore, subordinates who try to identify with the leader develop personal relationships such as loyalty and sympathy, and fulfill his wishes because he loves his leader and thinks he/she is a good person (Conger and Kanungo, 1998; Çetin, 2009).

Leadership in Health Institutions

Good leadership is important for every organization as well as for health organizations. The success of the organization is realized with the leader (Mahoney, 2001). There is a need in healthcare institutions for effective leaders who are intellectually oriented, targeted for team success and who use authority in a participatory way (Goodwin, 2000). Effective health services leadership includes strategic, vision setting, achieving goals, communicating with subordinates, motivating them, creating opportunities from innovation, finding new and effective solutions to problems (Dennis et al., 2010). The key person in health institutions that can strengthen the quality of health care is the leader (Hartley and Fletcher 2008). According to Breemhaar and Van Den Borne (1991), a successful leader empowers staff, creates a climate of mutual trust, improves job satisfaction, improves patient care quality, and builds organizational commitment to achieve organizational goals such as facilitating health care (Murphy, 2005). Leaders are of great importance in establishing a hospital culture that can provide high performance (Leatt and Porter, 2003). To this end, leaders create a culture based on quality patient care using safe and effective tools (Burns, 2001). Opportunities and training should be provided to increase the participation of individuals in the organization in the process of service quality and safety. Leaders should create a list of codes that identify acceptable, appropriate and useful behavior, identify inappropriate and disruptive behavior, and manage the process well to avoid any harm (Trastek et al., 2014).

According to health professionals, the top leader in health should be able to compete well, analyze hospital service processes well and increase the value of health services (Plsek and Wilson, 2001). Considering the factors that health organization leaders should consider in order to achieve organizational goals, health organizations display a system characteristic. The characteristics of a successful organization are (Gordon, 2010):

- Shared vision and goals,
- A shared plan to achieve the objectives,
- Clearly specify the role of each member,
- Individual authority of each individual,
- Understand the strengths and weaknesses of the roles of other members,
- Effective communication,
- Monitoring members' services,
- Supporting other members when needed and
- Mutual trust.

Importance and Place Of Leadership in Health Institutions

Leaders in health institutions are also expected to be more specific and more successful than other institutions (Lantz, 2008). A person who is a leader in health institutions is expected to be more intellectual, expert in different fields, innovative, giving importance to personnel motivation, strategic, creative, visionary, using authority effectively (Wikström and Dellve, 2009). According to health professionals, the top leader in health should be able to compete well, analyze hospital service processes well and increase the value of health services (Uysal et al., 2012). In addition to providing a higher quality service for healthcare workers, it is one of the main objectives of the health sector to stand out in the competitive environment in order to survive and maintain its success by starting out with the logic that health institutions are also a business in today's conditions. Therefore, the leader who is able to do all these is the most important condition for hospital success (Uysal et al., 2012). The specialization brought by the high technology in the health sector and the fact that a large number of people from different fields are in operation also raises various management difficulties and the difficulty of channeling human resources to the same target. Therefore, the existence of a single leadership style that facilitates the management of all these elements becomes difficult (Hanson and Ford, 2010). In this context, there are various elements different from other commercial services in hospitals that use the most intensive technology and manpower resources in the health sector evaluated in the service sector category. In this direction, while the management of financial resources, tools and equipment are at stake, the human resources in the organization are led. A leader in a hospital should determine a leadership vision based on the current conditions of the hospital and the expectations of the employees, and convince the human resources with which they work together in line with this vision (Robbins et al., 2001; Kumar, 2013). However, a leader should prepare mission statements for people from different specialties who have come together under the same institution, and should create a structure that will facilitate the operation of the system with its internal audit even in the absence of audit (Karahan, 2008).

Health institutions are very problematic and their employees experience burnout syndrome and stress. In addition, budget is one of the important issues in hospitals. Therefore, a person who can lead a health institution is expected to be able to cope with all of these (Koçak and Özüdoğru, 2012). Leadership behaviors in health sector can create commitment and inefficiency (Hartley and Benington, 2010). The inefficiency in the health sector can be a risk for the development of human health, which can lead to serious problems. However, in principle, a healthcare business must have a leadership style that is codified within the organizational culture.

According to Tengilimoğlu and Yiğit (2005), the main results of leadership in the hospitals that use the most intensive technology and manpower in the health sector are as follows:

- "Maintain the long-term competitiveness of the organization in order to preserve its existence and integrity, not only up-to-date.
- To be able to gain the competitive advantage by creating the creativity of a wide variety of manpower and working intensively.
- Define a vision for the employees and direct the employees from the lowest to the highest level in line with this vision.
- Bring the organization forward by bringing it to a level that can compete with today's conditions.
- To ensure the satisfaction of the staff by taking all these precautions and exhibiting these behaviors. (Tengilimoğlu and Yiğit, 2005).
- Health sector managers need to have multiple leadership qualities to manage a complex labor-intensive process.

Expectations of Healthcare Professionals From The Leader

Managers need to know their employees very well in order to increase efficiency and quality in all institutions (Jasper and Jumaa, 2008). Motivation of employees should be well analyzed by managers. The work environment also affects the motivation of the person in the social environment (Borowski and Daya, 2014). It is effective for the managers to have information about the employee outside the business environment. In order to increase the motivation of employees, rewarding, recognition by managers and positive communication established in the business environment should be provided. There is no motivation problem in the employees who are cared for by the manager, who value their ideas about the work area, communicate and provide sincere solutions to their problems. The leader should always be planned, controlled and able to make decisions on the spot. It is due to the fact that the jobs have a continuous productivity and that the employees can reach a high level of satisfaction (Gezici, 2007; Stankūnas et al., 2012). Organizations that cannot satisfy their employees cannot survive, and even if they do, they cannot achieve sufficient performance from the employee and accordingly, they cannot ensure the optimum efficiency of the organization. Health sector is a sector that is open to continuous development and change due to its service area. For this reason, in this continuously developing system, where the conditions of the day are essential, the employee should also be open to this development in the leaders as well as to develop himself, and should take initiatives to support and develop the employees in order to adapt to the working environment and the system of the organization (Uysal et al., 2012). This issue is even more important especially in the health sector. Because the health sector serves human health and mistakes often cannot be compensated. Effective and successful leaders who provide services for human health, such as health care, are expected to motivate their employees in this process, add excitement to the event, and manage the process by supporting their staff in every aspect (Gün and Aslan, 2018).

At the heart of the health sector are health workers. The success of an organization is primarily due to the satisfaction of the employees. In an organization where the patient is not satisfied, the negative reactions of the patient will also be reflected to the employee to whom he/she is a one-to-one contact. Therefore, the manager should know how to please the patient as well as the employee. It is known that a job that becomes monotonous and routine, poor working conditions and unfair management style creates dissatisfaction in personnel (Şencan, 2013). Employees provide better quality service as long as they provide satisfaction from the work they do. Therefore, managers should try to meet not only the material economic and social needs of the employees, but also their emotional and psychological needs in order to ensure complete integrity (Weberg, 2012). The performance of the employee who feels that he is with the manager is also high. Leaders should support, appreciate, encourage and encourage the employee to be more successful. The staff expects their managers to appreciate themselves. At the same time, employees should always have access to the manager.

Intercultural Leadership and Cultural Intelligence

The fact that organizations operate across national boundaries and the growing complexity of manpower culturally, ethnically and internationally requires leaders to understand and manage interactions within different cultures (Van Dyne et al., 2010). Since leadership in an intercultural environment requires influencing one of the different cultures, it is imperative that leaders have knowledge of different cultures. What characteristics people attribute to leaders and which behaviors are necessary for leadership are perceived differently in different cultures (Hofstede, 1993). Because of these differences in perception, there are great differences in the interpretation of leader behaviors and characteristics from culture to culture (Yukl, 2008). For example, many researchers (Peterson and Hunt, 1997) stated that culture has an effect on leadership behaviors and that different leadership behaviors are effective in different cultures. Therefore, one of the important situational elements in determining the effectiveness of leadership in an intercultural environment is culture.

With the studies, there is an increasing accumulation of knowledge for the relationships between culture, dimensions that form culture and leadership (Dickson et al., 2003). However, the inclusion of cultural dimensions in leadership research has further complicated efforts to understand and determine leader effectiveness in an intercultural setting (Chen and An, 2009). Instead, researchers have tried to explain the individual differences and intercultural activity by turning to the question "Why are some individuals more effective than others in different cultures?". Accordingly, research focusing on individual differences such as social intelligence (Aditya and House, 2002), cultural intuition (Javidan and House, 2001) and relational skill (Clark and Matze, 1999) have shown that these skills and skills contribute positively to leadership in the intercultural environment. Recently, research on individual differences in intercultural activity has been concentrated on the concept of cultural intelligence (Ng, 2013).

Cultural intelligence is a set of abilities that enable the individual to function effectively and be successful in a different cultural environment or in a multicultural environment (Earley and Ang, 2003). Sternberg and Detterman's (1986) cultural intelligence based on the multidimensional intelligence model; It consists of metacognitive, cognitive, motivational and behavioral components (Ang and Van Dyne, 2008). Metacognitive cultural intelligence refers to the mental processes used by the individual in acquiring and understanding cultural information and the control of these processes. This dimension of intelligence includes the ability to plan, construct, monitor and review mental models of other cultures. While metacognitive cultural intelligence is more concerned with mental processes, cognitive cultural intelligence includes information acquired by individuals through education and experience about norms, practices and customs of different cultures. Cognitive cultural intelligence, as well as knowledge of universal thinking about cultures, includes information about cultural differences. Motivational cultural intelligence expresses the capacity of the individual to direct his/her energy and attention in this direction in order to work in and learn about intercultural environments. This dimension of intelligence is related to the individual's interest and desire to interact with people from different cultures. Finally, behavioral cultural intelligence is defined as the capacity to properly demonstrate verbal or non-verbal behavior when interacting with people from different cultures (Ang and Van Dyne, 2008; Ng et al., 2012).

Research has shown that cultural intelligence contributes to the intercultural performance of individuals (Earley and Ang, 2003), is effective in intercultural adaptation (Templer et al., 2006) and reduces burnout (Maslach and Leiter, 2016). Cultural intelligence also has positive contributions to leadership effectiveness in an intercultural environment. For example, a qualitative study found that the leader's cultural intelligence is important in managing subordinates with different cultural backgrounds (Deng and Gibson, 2008). In a study conducted in teams composed of people from different cultures, it was seen that the leader's cultural intelligence contributed positively to leadership performance and teamwork (Groves and Fcycrherm, 2011). In addition, it has been shown that cultural intelligence is the determinant of international leadership potential (Ang and Van Dyne, 2015). These results reveal the importance of cultural intelligence in explaining leadership potential and effectiveness in an intercultural environment.

Intercultural Leadership Activity

Overall, measuring leadership performance is a difficult and controversial issue. It is stated that there is no best and only way to measure leader effectiveness (Hogan et al., 1994). In most of the definitions made about the concept of leadership, it is stated that leaders are effective on the attitudes and behaviors of subordinates (Yukl, 2008). Although the information obtained from different sources is important, some researchers suggest that attitudes and behaviors of subordinates should be examined in measuring leader performance (Bass and Stogdill, 1990; Sheridan, 2005). Similarly, it has been suggested that the actual performance of leaders can only be measured by variables such as job satisfaction, commitment and organizational citizenship of subordinates (Yukl, 2008). Riggio and Cole (1992) showed that there is a positive relationship between leader performance and job satisfaction of subordinates. In another study, it was found that there is a positive relationship between subordinates' job satisfaction caused by leader and leader behaviors (Bartolo and Furlonger, 2000). Organizational citizenship behaviors of subordinates positively correlated with leadership has been demonstrated by research (Purvanova et al., 2006).

Leadership in an intercultural environment refers to the process of influencing and motivating people belonging to different cultures in order to achieve the specified goals and objectives (Dubrin, 2010; Allard et al., 2017). It has been shown that a leader working in an intercultural environment can overcome the difficulties faced by cultural intelligence (Earley and Mosakowski, 2004). For example, individuals with high cultural intelligence can consciously question their cultural assumptions and, if necessary, create new methods and rules for social communication and interaction. Through cultural knowledge, it can better evaluate the culture of a society and its elements and systems. At the same time, these individuals are willing, they can easily direct their energy and attention towards the intercultural environment and show flexibility in exhibiting behavior specific to intercultural interaction (Seiler, 2007). For this reason, it is expected that leaders with high cultural intelligence have an impact on their attitudes and behaviors when working with people from different cultures in an intercultural setting (Normore and Collard, 2009).

As an indicator of leadership effectiveness in an intercultural setting, subordinates may have job satisfaction from the leader. In general, job satisfaction can be defined as a reaction of employees' feelings about their jobs (Spector, 1997). According to Luthans (1995), job satisfaction is a concept that predominates in the emotional aspect and can often be expressed by the extent to which the work meets the expectations of the employees. Because the nature of the work involves different elements, job satisfaction consists of many related components (Spector et al., 2000). These are mostly components such as work, wages, promotion opportunities, leadership/management style and colleagues. Job satisfaction, which is a component of job satisfaction, is directly influenced by the characteristics and behaviors of the leader (Spector, 1997). For example, Frawley and Fasoli (2012) showed that how perceptions of subordinates perceive their leaders positively or negatively affects job satisfaction. Verbal or non-verbal communication between the leader and subordinates determines the quality of the relationship between them (Yrle et al., 2002) and this affects the job satisfaction of subordinates from the leader (Collard and Wang, 2005). However, studies have shown that there is a positive relationship between leadership and job satisfaction of subordinates caused by the leader (Yukl, 2008). Leaders with high cultural intelligence can easily direct energy and attention to intercultural interaction through their cognitive strategies (Triandis, 2006) and be flexible in displaying appropriate verbal or non-verbal behavior (Ng 2013). Therefore, subordinates working with a leader with high cultural intelligence are expected to have high job satisfaction from the leader.

IMPORTANCE OF WORK PRODUCTIVITY IN HEALTH SECTOR

As the demands of the societies for health services increase day by day, the analysis of the elements that affect the efficient and effective use of hospitals gains more importance (Candoğan and Erigüç, 2006). While the conditions experienced in institutions can be a source of motivation, it can sometimes become a source of stress (Tunceli et al., 2005). For this reason, the managers of the organization have to take into account the business conditions (material and moral). Among the employees working in health institutions, especially nurses and doctors are directly involved with the patient; The unpleasant behaviors of the patients due to their negativities, in short, the attitude of the patients can easily turn into a cause of stress. It is also difficult for individuals under stress to be successful and happy (Boles et al., 2004).

These situations, where the health of the individual is threatened, and intense stress due to uncertainty and obscurity, affect the health personnel as well as the sick individual (Letvak and Buck 2008). In the studies conducted with health workers, it was found that stress factors in the work environment adversely affect the physical and mental health and job satisfaction of health workers (Lerner and Henke, 2008). Although no negative attitudes are encountered in an environment where patients are present, the harmony of the environment can easily make the patient and the patient sick if there are problems with other variables in his/her life (Pelletier et al., 2004). In the reflection of these symptoms on job performance, decrease in attention and concentration level and related errors, increased interpersonal relations, depersonalization, decrease in work efficiency, decrease in working speed, frequent illness and increase in the frequency of reporting because it is easier, the loss of labor resulting from this is remarkable (Lerner et al., 2003). In addition, insufficiencies in health care and unbalanced distribution of services and staff create frustration and tension in employees. In addition, job-related tension has institutional implications, such as lowering productivity and productivity, reducing job satisfaction, delaying work, never making up an apology or leaving the job completely, and ultimately the retention of experienced staff due to wages (Sünter et al., 2006).

JOB SATISFACTION

Many literature studies have been conducted in order to explain the satisfaction or dissatisfaction of employees in business life and from the results obtained from these studies, approaches and theories related to movement have been put forward (Faragher et al., 2005). The theories related to job satisfaction are called as motivation theories in the literature. Motivation is the force that pushes individuals towards their goals. This power is of two kinds, internal and external. As mentioned in this study, attitudes towards work interact with internal and external factors. One of the most important of these factors is motivation. There is a significant relationship between motivation and job satisfaction. As the motivation increases, job satisfaction increases. From this assumption, theories about motivation and job satisfaction will be explained. The theories related to job satisfaction consist of content and process theories. Scope theories are composed of theories that motivate the employee and include the motivating factors and explain the internal factors. Process theories, on the other hand, consist of theories aiming at explaining external factors which are the cause of human behavior (Weiss, 2002; Lund, 2003). It is not possible to think separately about motivation and job satisfaction. Job satisfaction arises with motivation and new satisfaction leads to new motivation (Saari and Judge, 2004). Motivation and behavior of individuals with high job satisfaction in a positive course is simpler to progress (Judge et al., 2000). If the employee does not reach satisfactorily, the process returns to the beginning, causing anxiety and this is negatively reflected in performance (Karlıdağ et al., 2000).

The high level of job satisfaction of the employees is also an indication that the organization is well managed (Lum et al., 1998). Reduction in job satisfaction leads to many results. Some of them are absenteeism, low morale, restlessness, disciplinary problems and dismissal. As a result, decreases in job satisfaction cause both individuals and organizations to reach their goals (Örücü et al., 2006). It is known that the high level of job satisfaction is effective on the productivity of the employees, their commitment to work and organization, and the increase of the quality of the work done (Lu et al., 2005). If the employee thinks that his/her expectations from his/her job and work environment are not met at a sufficient level, job dissatisfaction occurs (Aziri, 2011). Job dissatisfaction may negatively affect employee health and may lead to mental and behavioral disorders in individuals (Erdoğan, 1996). Emotional (stress, anxiety, helplessness) and physical (insomnia, muscle pain, headache) breakdowns were found in employees with low job satisfaction and a significant relationship was found between job dissatisfaction (Akıncı, 2002).

Basaran (1991) explains the effects of job dissatisfaction on working individuals as follows:

- Job dissatisfaction causes excessive anxiety and fear feelings by disrupting mental health in employees.
- It causes many discomforts on the employee such as heart, stomach disorders, adjustment disorders and muscle pain.
- Due to the fact that the rest time given in the work is very low and the work requires some repetitions and monotony, it creates boredom.
- Dissatisfaction causes employees to follow a belligerent and aggressive attitude.

- Insatiable employees do not adopt organizational goals and alienate their organizations and disrupt the functioning of the organization.

Organizational Results of Job Satisfaction

Executives play an important role in improving the working environment, communicating with employees, ensuring employee participation and feedback, and giving autonomy to employees. For this reason, the behavior and attitude of the managers and the support they give to the employees are a very effective factor in ensuring the satisfaction of the employees (Griffin et al., 2001).

Businesses that cannot provide job satisfaction face many problems. Some of these are:

- High absenteeism
- Low inefficiency
- Increased alienation, stress and resentment
- Strikes coming to the agenda
- Disciplinary problems
- Increase in employee turnover
- Damage or sabotage of machinery or facilities

As a result of this, high work tension, increased insurance costs and subsequent judicial costs. All these results of job dissatisfaction create increases in direct or indirect cost items of enterprises (Türk et al., 2003). Moreover, the importance of providing job satisfaction is better understood when separation of employees who experience job dissatisfaction is taken into consideration, such as orientation training about the system and policies of the organization, loss of time in this process, increase in operating costs and decrease in customer satisfaction, even if they are experienced (Özdemir, 2006).

MOTIVATION CONCEPT

Motivation is the sum of efforts to constantly and willingly mobilize people for a specific purpose. It is defined as the power that drives people for a specific purpose and to dream of a situation in which one can be satisfied enough for himself in the future (Leonard et al., 1999). Motivation can be defined as motive and motivator. Motive is the force that drives a person for a specific purpose (Argon and Eren, 2004). "Motivation, on the other hand, is the creation of a work environment that satisfies the needs of the organization and the individuals, and is influenced and motivated by the individual to act" (McClelland, 1987). Motivation; ability of employees to take action in order to achieve their goals means that they have the enthusiasm and self-sacrifice necessary to achieve the impulse and result for a specific purpose and can be considered as a set of actions or actions that mobilize (Peters, 2015). Motivation is a fine balance and must be well maintained (Hofstede, 1980). A manager's greeting to his/her employee and asking his/her memory will have a motivating effect, and vice versa. Today's managers have to deal closely with motivation. The success of managers depends on their subordinates working in channeling their business goals and spending their knowledge, skills and skills in this direction (Herzberg, 2017). In other words, motivation is closely related to employee performance. It is not expected that the employee who is not motivated or not encouraged to perform high is expected. Scientists have addressed motivation in three different ways. These are psychology, business life and motivation within the organization (Karakuzu, 2013).

In psychology, motivation and motivation are explained by the initiation and continuation of behavior towards a goal (Osterloh and Frey, 2000). Motivation is the process of exhibiting behaviors that enable people to meet their various needs. In this process, behavioral differences may also occur due to the continuous change of human needs in line with the requirements of the age. This constant change is the dynamic of motivation. Psychology states that motivation is effective in initiating behaviors by examining human behaviors. The diversity of human behavior is closely related to the psychology of people in achieving the goals of the employees and the objectives of the enterprise (Karakuzu, 2013).

Work motivation is the process of influencing or motivating the individual to take action by creating a work environment that satisfies the needs of the individual and the organization (Deci and Ryan, 2008). In other words, work motivation is the shaping and regulation of the behaviors of the employee and the management within the organization in realizing the wishes and aims of the person, that is the employee himself/herself and the organization (Dörnyei and Ushioda, 2013). Here, motivation has been the most important area of interest of institutions (Karakuzu, 2013). In this respect, the concept of motivation has come to the forefront as a requirement of maximizing the benefits of employees in achieving the desired corporate performance outputs.

"Organizational motivation can also be defined as a set of effects that initiates and maintains an employee. It is natural that one is motivated for his own purposes. But motivation for organizational purposes is artificial. From this point of view, it is very important to motivate the employees of the organization for their work, unless the individual is motivated for organizational purposes, organizational actions will not be at the desired level. People have been brought to organizations to realize a purpose. This purpose can be production or service. They are given some things in return for their services so that they are constantly encouraged in a certain direction." Organizational motivation is the formation of one-to-one relationships with the organization and the behavior of the employees in line with the objectives of the organization. Employees whose behavior is shaped within the organization for organizational purposes will be motivated and organizational actions will reach the desired level (Karakuzu, 2013).

MOTIVATION TOOLS

Economic Tools

Money (Income): It is difficult for a person to concentrate on his/her work and be productive if the salary he/she receives as a result of his/her work is not sufficient to keep the standard of living at the desired level. Money is important for employees due to the fact that it serves as a tool that satisfies the needs of people, is an incentive tool, and satisfies people. The increase in wages will cause the employee to increase his/her morale level with enthusiasm and to act with a sense of ownership (Vaitkuviene et al., 2010). An employee who does not get his financial return in time or who does not get enough money will be reluctant against his job in a work environment in which he is working and spending time.

Awards: Rewarding in human resources management is very important. Success in management starts with rewarding successful staff. Rewarding successful employees encourages them to work harder and increases their commitment to management. Therefore, the rewarded success leads to continuous success, while the non-rewarded success leads to failure (Margarita, 2013). The award is a gift to the employee despite its effective and productive work. Factors that motivate employees should be known and appropriate personalized methods should be used when determining the rewarding methods in institutions.

Participation in Profit: the portion of the income earned at the end of each working period is given to the employees. It is a very effective method to ensure that employees work more enthusiastically and with performance (Mangi et al., 2015). Performance based supplementary payment system has been implemented in all institutions by the Ministry of Health in recent years. In this way, it is expected that patient satisfaction will be ensured as a result of providing better quality health care services, and employees' satisfaction will increase with the additional payments they will receive in direct proportion to their performance.

Social Helps: Social services may include service, periodic food aid, marital assistance, nursery, local, guest house, etc. Service availability is an important issue especially in metropolitan cities in order to prevent the loss of time in reaching work and to ensure compliance with working hours. Opening nurseries in institutions will increase the motivation of employees as they create the idea that they do not move away from their children. In addition, the aid given on holidays and special occasions will contribute to the budget of the families and make them feel that they are considered by the management level. Employees who find accommodation in the guesthouses of their institutions in different cities will feel part of a large organization (Borowski and Daya, 2014). Organizational commitment and motivation of the employees will be increased.

Psycho-Social Tools

Being Recognized: Appreciating employees is an important element of motivation. As a result of the successful work of the employees, it is the most powerful and simplest element of motivation to be praised, congratulated and appreciated by the superiors in written or verbal form (Fugate et al., 2004). Appreciating employees in order to support the working atmosphere positively and to ensure the continued continuation of positive behaviors is an element that should not be missed.

Status and Value: Status; the position of a person in the administrative hierarchy in the institution in which he works, the status of the staff, the degree of authority and responsibility. Giving authority and responsibility to the personnel who come to the fore with their work will increase their desire to do their own work and will also create dynamism among other employees and will reveal the desire to come to the forefront and gain status with their work (Gimson et al., 2009). Providing employees with a business environment in which they can access all kinds of promotions will cause them to realize their potential and enable them to develop themselves.

Respect for Private Life: People have a life outside of business. Family relations, social activities, etc. constitute the individual's private life. For an employee to work efficiently, it is very important that his life outside of work is organized. Tolerance of his/her child to participate in important school activities and understanding of his/her family in case of getting permission in case of health problems will increase his/her integration with his/her institution and his sense of gratitude. It should not be forgotten that busy working hours will cause problems in the private life of the person.

Giving a Worthy Job: Doing a job worth doing is also one of the motivation tools. In addition to working to maintain a person's life, seeing that it is beneficial to society will increase the sense of satisfaction. Health professionals will strive to provide better service when they see the value and satisfaction of their contribution to human health (Elstad, 1998). The intensity of emotion created by a smiling and compassionate hand reaching out to them at the point where health care recipients and their relatives are most helpless will be created by both the service recipient and the donor.

Security: Pension, accident, illness, life, unemployment insurance, such as the economic protection of the employee during his life forms of economic protection makes the employee energetic and zealous (Bonnes and Secchiaroli, 1995). At the same time, if the employee can look to the future with confidence and is not constantly rotated, he will adapt himself better to the work environment. Creating a work environment in which employees feel secure is essential for their motivation and their stability in the organization.

Independence in the Study: In organizations, most people want to work independently, to move freely, to take initiative, to take responsibility and to do business on their own (Peker and Aytürk, 2002). People don't like working under pressure, getting involved and giving orders. People who think that they do not have the right to speak in the institution they work for cannot think about the transition to different institutions because they cannot provide sufficient satisfaction. Managers who analyze the differences of their employees and determine the management style appropriate to their personality structures can be successful.

Suggestion Systems: Providing a work environment in which employees can express their ideas clearly, and evaluating and applying the suggestions received form a democratic work environment. A leader who attaches importance to the different thoughts of the employees; to feel themselves as part of the team, to distinguish the more talented and creative ones, to make them feel that they are important will provide the emergence of creative powers and ideas (Fries 2009).

Social Activities: Activities such as picnics, entertainment and food organizations, organizing trips, etc. that will bring together the employees and their families outside the work will increase communication and increase organizational commitment and motivation. With the time spent together outside the business environment, employees will have time to get to know each other with their different characteristics and this will lead to the development of communication channels by creating sincerity (Trist, 1990).

Organizational and Managerial Tools

Opportunities for Promotion: As people gain experience in their work, they will find their powers and responsibilities insufficient. Promotion is a reward for successful staff and a good incentive tool. However, criteria regarding promotion opportunities should be clearly defined and merit should be considered by management. In order to be promoted, the motivation of the employees will decrease in a work environment where it is thought that reference should be taken from somewhere rather than merit.

Purpose Union: Employees in organizations do not need to work effectively and efficiently without a certain goal to be achieved (Peker and Aytürk, 2002). Setting the right and right target is one of the best sources of motivation. The fulfillment of these objectives facilitates the satisfaction of high-level needs such as self-fulfillment. In order to achieve this, those who are in the management level in the first place need to set certain goals for themselves so that they can motivate employees towards this goal. It is essential for the success of the organization that the management level and the employees act synchronously for the same purposes.

A Just and Continuous Discipline System: Opportunities should be provided in which employees can express their dissatisfaction. The motivation of employees who think that the complaints are examined and finalized in a fair manner will increase. Employees who feel that the complaints are not justified and that the procedure consists of the procedure will stop using this mechanism after some point. In addition, encountering a situation such as mobbing as a result of the complaint transmission about their superiors will cause unrest in the working environment. Care should be taken to ensure that the grievance mechanism is fair and protects the rights of employees.

Physical Working Conditions: It is important for the motivation that the workplace is in proper physical conditions. Working in a spacious, ventilated, heated and clean environment will have a positive effect on the motivation of the employees. Improving the working environment and conditions is an issue that should not be omitted because it creates an environment in which employees can work comfortably.

Motivation Process

The process of motivation is the process of acting with the effect of a motive to take a certain action (Kanfer, 1990). Motivation is important to the extent that it affects individual behaviors. Motivation and performance are directly proportional, the individual will perform to the extent that he is motivated (Latham and Pinder, 2005). The overlap of the objectives of the employees with the objectives of the organizations and the provision of a work environment that can meet the needs of the employees will increase the performance (Katzell and Thompson, 1990). In organizations with advanced management skills, managers manage the motivation process successfully thanks to effective human resources management, who can interpret what motivates employees well (Miner, 1978). Providing employees with a business environment in which to improve themselves, encouraging them to participate in decisions and giving responsibility will contribute to their identification with the workplaces. Therefore, the motivation and commitment of the employees who see the success of the organization as their success will also increase (Williams et al., 2001).

Some of the benefits of working with motivated people include:

- The work is performed within the specified time period and in accordance with the correct standard.
- People enjoy doing business and think they are valued.
- Employees do more work because they do what they want to do.
- Success is monitored by the people concerned and there is no need for oversight.
- Their morale is high, which provides a good work environment (Keenan, 1996).

In today's conditions where competition conditions are becoming more severe, the institutions need to make the motivation process functional by prioritizing the desires and desires of the manpower they manage in order to gain competitive advantage.

There are four basic steps in the motivation process:

- Need; motivation begins with the need for certain things.
- Stimulation is the formation of any power in order to satisfy the need in the individual.
- When an individual's need arises and is stimulated to fulfill that need, a certain behavior is reached.
- Satisfaction, the individual's behavior, to the extent that the individual achieves the satisfaction of the individual reaches.

Motivation is a concept that should be dealt with in two aspects. The impulse that motivates an individual and drives him to behavior can sometimes be internal and sometimes external. The first aspect is the spontaneous emergence of the motive and the motivation of the individual, corresponding to a need. This power comes from within and motivates oneself. An intrinsically motivated individual makes effort because he wants to and gives the prize to himself. There is a direct relationship between the work done and the award and the employee receives this award while doing the work (Steers et al., 2004). Pleasure is obtained from the work done and satisfaction is obtained in the process of doing the work (Eren, 1993). The needs of the individual such as self-satisfaction needs, values, goals, competence and sense of development are the sources of intrinsic motivation (Petri and Govern, 2012). The self-motivated individual is open to development and leads to change in development.

External motivation, on the other hand, is the process of direct motivation of individuals for the achievement of a job, especially at the organizational level. Extrinsic motivation originates from the outside of the person, enabling the person to act with reinforcement or reward from the environment. The various awards and performance-enhancing practices described in detail in the motivation tools section come to the forefront. It is necessary to internalize external sources of motivation.

Motivation tools appropriate to the personalities of the employees should be used in order to achieve the expected activity and provide a peaceful working environment (O'Neil et al., 2012). Those in the management level can provide efficiency in their organizations by analyzing the structure of the organization and the profile of the employees, using the right techniques and managing the motivation process in the best way.

Performance

The effects of the business environment on individual well-being and performance are relatively central in the new perspective of organizational health. Researchers have focused on the relationships between various variables that provide personal characteristics, environmental conditions and job comfort. In the literature, performance is discussed under two headings, usually individual and organizational. There are two important types of individual performance behaviors. These; task performance and situational performance. Task performance behaviors include basic technical skills and activities related to a person's profession and job. Situational performance behaviors include assisting colleagues and colleagues, making extra efforts and developing their organization (Miller et al., 1999). Situational performance is especially important for organizational health in two aspects. First, situational behavior is beneficial for the whole organization. For example; When an employee spends time and effort to help a colleague in his group, he may reduce the level and performance of his own output, but increase the overall output level and organizational performance of the workgroup. Secondly, situational behaviors contribute to increasing the motivation of individuals (Miller et al., 1999).

A number of statistical studies have shown that the costs caused by an unhealthy organization are far beyond those predicted. For example, a study by Evanoff (1994) in the United States suggests that direct and indirect medical costs caused by work stress have risen from $ 80 billion to $ 150 billion, which are not added to the costs caused by low productivity (Shoaf et al., 2004). Therefore, there is an increase in the number of studies aimed at examining the effects of a healthy organization on individual and organizational output and performance. Jaffe (1995) suggests that the concept of organizational health encompasses two factors. These are (Browne, 2000): the performance of the organization (such as profitability, productivity and competition) and employee health/job satisfaction (such as physical and mental health of employees and job satisfaction). Studies on organizational health reveal that work stress, job performance and organizational climate affect organizational health in different ways (Code and Langan-Fox, 2001; Miller et al., 1999). Individual welfare, goodness and happiness result in psychological comfort and job satisfaction.

As a result, individual satisfaction provides organizational performance and success (Miller et al., 1999).

SOLUTIONS AND RECOMMENDATIONS

Organizational commitment of health workers may be weakened due to practices restricting professional development. However, in terms of their commitment to work, health workers see their work as a whole and act more in line with the expectations of the organization in order to perform their jobs better. Emotional commitment levels of healthcare workers are higher than other commitment components. It can be stated that organizational commitment levels of health personnel are lower than normative commitment and continuity commitment. As the education levels of healthcare workers increase, general organizational commitment levels may decrease. In some studies, it is seen that educational status negatively affects the commitment to the organization. However, in some studies, as the level of education increases, commitment to the organization decreases. The reason for this is that because of the increase in the level of education and training of health professionals, their commitment to the health institution may decrease because of their self-confidence. As the working time of health workers increases, their commitment to the organization increases. Health professionals spend a long time in their workplaces. In the light of these data, it can be concluded that working time has a positive effect on the level of commitment to the organization. As wage income of health workers increases, their loyalty and motivation to health institution increases. In the light of these data, it would be correct to apply wage policies that structure the health sector. Because, health workers who have to stay overtime act positively both in terms of motivation and commitment in case they receive their labor. However, as health care workers' emotional commitment to the organization increases, their performance may decrease. Employees with a high level of loyalty continue to remain in the organization due to the high cost of leaving the organization, and because of their obligation to work, they do not show high performance. The reason for this may be the decrease in their performance due to the feeling that they are obliged to perform their obligatory duties rather than willingly because they continue to work in the health institution in the face of the difficulties of changing the location in the family. As job satisfaction levels of health workers increase, organizational commitment levels increase. High job satisfaction of healthcare workers increases their commitment to work and reduces their tendency to leave the organization where they live. Health workers who are satisfied with their work are less affected by the negative situations caused by various reasons. Organizational commitment of health workers decreases as job stress increases. The health sector itself is one of the most difficult and responsible occupations. Given this situation, health workers work in a stressful environment. It is inevitable that healthcare workers who spend more working time in the workplace may experience stress in a stressful environment. However, health workers, who continue to stay in the organization with their own consent, experience less work stress. So he is pleased with his work. Leadership style is the basis of the positive and negative conditions experienced by the employees within the organization. Leadership style has a significant impact on the management of health institutions. Therefore, it is necessary to examine the direction of leadership style in the face of situations that may be experienced in health institutions.

FUTURE RESEARCH DIRECTIONS

The most important element for success in today's conditions is that managers have leadership qualities, that is, they are defined as leading managers and that they use motivation resources effectively considering the employee profile. In employee - manager relations, the leader of the manager; being polite and sincere, taking care of employees' problems and valuing them, taking into consideration their emotions, thoughts and discourses, honoring them, appreciating what they are doing, explaining the events, giving confidence and making them feel important, increase the motivation of employees. The aim of management is to win people first, then to work effectively and efficiently, to use resources economically and rationally and to implement management functions successfully. Therefore, the presence of leaders who can manage them without giving orders will increase the job satisfaction in the institutions.

It will have the necessary infrastructure to carry a leadership institution with leadership characteristics to success. Providing leadership training to those in the management level is an issue that needs to be emphasized. In this way, managers who participate in training programs to develop their leadership capacity will adapt to the renewed conditions and make progress in this direction day by day. Successful leader; is a person who uses his / her power to influence individuals in an appropriate and appropriate manner by giving new perspectives to employees, demonstrating management skills in resolving conflicts and having high empathic thinking ability. Observes the personalities and capacities of the employees well and uses motivation techniques appropriate to the employee profile for the success of the organization. It should not be expected that institutions should be managed with the same management approach under all circumstances. According to the approach called contingency theory, different conditions require different leadership styles. The most appropriate leadership behavior; organizational culture is determined by employee profile and experiences.

The leader will be the source of motivation for the employees by adopting the transformational leadership style that reconciles the present and the future, giving the group momentum, creating a vision and determination. Leading managers are those who frequently give feedback to employees to show how important their performance is at work, contribute to their personal development, and encourage people to do what is best for them, but not the best for them. Health institutions employees are kind and compassionate to the people they serve, but they expect to be treated in the same way. Health is a subject that is vulnerable to abuse, since people have the weakest points, and those working in this field and those in the management level need to pay maximum attention to ethical values. Due to the matrix structure of health services, postponement, non-error, and special conditions, ethical values and teamwork should be given importance. In order to increase organizational commitment, leading managers need to use motivation methods in line with the employee profile effectively.

CONCLUSION

Today, organizations should be able to keep up with the rapid technological changes, ensure their continuity in the sector where continuous innovations are experienced and use their resources in the most effective way. Organizations with sufficient economic power should have the technological devices required by the sectors. Thus, they must have the ability to cope with other organizations in an intense competitive environment. That is, they must move to an advantageous position. Those who work in organizations are ahead of all other inputs. Because those who work are in a position to control and implement the policies of the organization. In this context, the importance that organizations attach to employee employment is becoming more and more important. Organizations that want to be successful must integrate with their employees and mutually embrace each other's values. One of the service sectors where employees work under intense stress is the health services sector. Health sector; It is a sector where the level of specialization is high and unpredictable demands and uncertainties are intense and it is also an important sector because it covers urgent and non-delayable services. When the results of the evaluated studies are compared, it is seen that the commitment levels of different occupational groups in the health sector are different from each other. These occupational groups are midwives and nurses. This difference between health workers is due to the fact that working conditions under more intensive work load and stress affect their commitment to the organization. The fact that the employees in the occupational group stated that their working conditions are more difficult and that they remain in the organization even though they find it inadequate to pay and reward shows that their commitment to continuity is high.

According to the occupational information and the results of the study, it was found out that health workers work under a heavy workload and that the excessive workload affects their family and social lives as well as their lives negatively. Excessive workload was seen as the most important factor that weakened the organizational commitment of health workers and caused them to experience intense stress. Among health workers, nurses and ancillary health personnel experience serious role uncertainty and this uncertainty negatively affects their motivation and job satisfaction levels, leading to weakening of organizational commitment levels. Another stress factor for health workers can be listed as working conditions and workload, salary level, performance pressure, occupational risks and inadequate rewards. The stress levels of the departments, colleagues and working system health workers differ significantly. Health institutions have different structures due to the gradual provision of health services. As these structural differences affect service delivery and working conditions, it is another result obtained from the studies that the organizational commitment levels of health workers working in different health institutions are different from each other. The perception of injustice regarding the insufficiency and distribution of wage level is one of the most important factors determining the organizational commitment levels of health workers. It is thought that the introduction of a performance-based supplementary payment system for health workers may positively affect their performance. The high level of job satisfaction of the employees is directly effective in the high level of organizational commitment. It has been an important result obtained from the study, in which the employees with high loyalty to the work have high loyalty to the organization. Health workers' job satisfaction levels are higher than their overall organizational commitment.

REFERENCES

Aditya, R., & Hause, R. J. (2002). Interpersonal acumen and leadership across cultures: Pointers from the GLOBE study. In *Proceedings of the 9th Kravis-de Roulet Leadership Conference*. Lawrence Erlbaum Associates Publishers.

Akıncı, Z. (2002). Turizm sektöründe işgören iş tatminini etkileyen faktörler: Beş yıldızlı konaklama işletmelerinde bir uygulama. *Akdeniz Üniversitesi İktisadi ve İdari Bilimler Fakültesi Dergisi*, *4*, 1–25.

Allard, S., Qayyum, M. A., & Mehra, B. (2017). Intercultural leadership toolkit for librarians: Building awareness to effectively serve diverse multicultural populations. *Education Libraries*, *30*(1), 5–12. doi:10.26443/el.v30i1.231

Ang, S., & Van Dyne, L. (2008). *Handbook of Cultural Intelligence: Theory. Measurement and Application*. Routledge.

Ang, S., & Van Dyne, L. (2015). *Handbook of cultural intelligence*. Routledge. doi:10.4324/9781315703855

Argon, T., & Eren, A. (2004). İnsan Kaynakları Yönetimi. Nobel Yayın Dağıtım.

Aziri, B. (2011). Job Satisfaction: A Literature Review. *Management Research & Practice, 3*(4).

Bakan, İ., & Büyükbeşe, T. (2010). Liderlik "türleri" ve "güç kaynakları" na ilişkin mevcut-gelecek durum karşılaştırması. *Karamanoğlu Mehmetbey Üniversitesi Sosyal ve Ekonomik Araştırmalar Dergisi,* (2), 73-84.

Bartolo, K., & Furlonger, B. (2000). Leadership and job satisfaction among aviation fire fighters in Australia. *Journal of Managerial Psychology, 15*(1), 87–93. doi:10.1108/02683940010305324

Başaran, İ. E. (1991). *Örgütsel Davranış İnsanın Üretim Gücü*. Ankara: Gül Yayınevi.

Bass, B. M., & Stogdill, R. M. (1990). *Bass & Stogdill's handbook of leadership: Theory, research, and managerial applications*. Simon and Schuster.

Boles, M., Pelletier, B., & Lynch, W. (2004). The relationship between health risks and work productivity. *Journal of Occupational and Environmental Medicine, 46*(7), 737–745. doi:10.1097/01.jom.0000131830.45744.97 PMID:15247814

Bonnes, M., & Secchiaroli, G. (1995). Environmental psychology: A psycho-social introduction. *Sage (Atlanta, Ga.).*

Borowski, A., & Daya, U. (2014). Employee motivation tools. In *Human capital without borders: Knowledge and learning for quality of life. Proceedings of the management, knowledge and learning international conference*. Academic Press.

Breemhaar, B., & Van den Borne, H. W. (1991). Effects of education and support for surgical patients: The role of perceived control. *Patient Education and Counseling, 18*(3), 199–210. doi:10.1016/0738-3991(91)90129-S

Browne, J. H. (2000). Benchmarking HRM practices in healthy work organizations. *American Business Review, 18*(2), 54.

Burns, J. P. (2001). Complexity science and leadership in healthcare. *JONA: The Journal of Nursing Administration, 31*(10), 474–482. doi:10.1097/00005110-200110000-00011 PMID:11676217

Candoğan, A. K. C. A., & Erigüç, G. (2006). Hastane çalışanlarının yöneticileri ve çalışma arkadaşları ile yaşadıkları çatışma nedenlerine yönelik bir araştırma. *Hacettepe Sağlık İdaresi Dergisi, 9*(2), 126–153.

Çetin, S. (2009). Vizyon yönetimi. *Selçuk Üniversitesi Sosyal Bilimler Enstitüsü Dergisi*, (22), 95-103.

Chan, S. H. (2010). The influence of leadership expertise and experience on organizational performance: A study of Amanah Ikhtiar Malaysia. *Asia Pacific Business Review, 16*(1-2), 59–77. doi:10.1080/13602380802503566

Chen, G. M., & An, R. (2009). A Chinese model of intercultural leadership competence. In The SAGE handbook of intercultural competence (pp. 196-208). Sage.

Clark, B. D., & Matze, M. G. (1999). A core of global leadership: Relational competence. *Advances in global leadership, 1*, 127-161.

Code, S., & Langan-Fox, J. (2001). Motivation, cognitions and traits: Predicting occupational health, well-being and performance. *Stress and Health: Journal of the International Society for the Investigation of Stress, 17*(3), 159–174. doi:10.1002mi.897

Coleman, J. A. (1997). Authority, power, leadership: Sociological understandings. *New Theology Review, 10*(3).

Collard, J., & Wang, T. (2005). Leadership and intercultural dynamics. *Journal of School Leadership, 15*(2), 178–195. doi:10.1177/105268460501500205

Conger, J. A., & Kanungo, R. N. (1998). *Charismatic leadership in organizations*. Sage Publications.

Daft, R. L. (2014). *The leadership experience*. Cengage Learning.

Deci, E. L., & Ryan, R. M. (2008). Self-determination theory: A macrotheory of human motivation, development, and health. *Canadian Psychology, 49*(3), 182–185. doi:10.1037/a0012801

Deng, L., & Gibson, P. (2008). A qualitative evaluation on the role of cultural intelligence in cross-cultural leadership effectiveness. *International journal of leadership studies, 3*(2), 181-197.

Deniz, M., & Çolak, M. (2008). Örgütlerde çatışmanın yönetiminde gücün kullanımı ve bir araştırma. *Elektronik Sosyal Bilimler Dergisi, 7*(23), 304–332.

Dennis, R. S., Kinzler-Norheim, L., & Bocarnea, M. (2010). Servant leadership theory. In *Servant leadership* (pp. 169–179). London: Palgrave Macmillan. doi:10.1057/9780230299184_14

Dickson, M. W., Den Hartog, D. N., & Mitchelson, J. K. (2003). Research on leadership in a cross-cultural context: Making progress, and raising new questions. *The Leadership Quarterly*, *14*(6), 729–768. doi:10.1016/j.leaqua.2003.09.002

Dörnyei, Z., & Ushioda, E. (2013). *Teaching and researching: Motivation*. Routledge.

Dubrin, A. J. (2010). *Impression management in the workplace: Research, theory and practice*. Routledge. doi:10.4324/9780203865712

Dulebohn, J. H., Bommer, W. H., Liden, R. C., Brouer, R. L., & Ferris, G. R. (2012). A meta-analysis of antecedents and consequences of leader-member exchange: Integrating the past with an eye toward the future. *Journal of Management*, *38*(6), 1715–1759. doi:10.1177/0149206311415280

Duygulu, S. (2007). *Servis sorumlu hemşirelerine yönelik hazırlanan transformasyonel liderlik eğitim programının liderlik uygulamaları üzerine etkisi* [Doctoral dissertation]. Hacettepe Üniversitesi Sağlık Bilimleri Enstitüsü.

Earley, P. C., & Ang, S. (2003). *Cultural intelligence: Individual interactions across cultures*. Stanford University Press.

Earley, P. C., & Mosakowski, E. (2004). Cultural intelligence. *Harvard Business Review*, *82*(10), 139–146. PMID:15559582

Elstad, J. I. (1998). The psycho-social perspective on social inequalities in health. *Sociology of Health & Illness*, *20*(5), 598–618. doi:10.1111/1467-9566.00121

Erdoğan, İ. (1996). *İşletme Yönetiminde Örgütsel Davranış*. İstanbul: Beta Yayınları.

Eren, E. (1993). *Yönetim psikolojisi. 4. Baskı* (pp. 193–255). İstanbul: Beta Basım Yayım Dağıtım.

Ertürk, M. (2000). *İşletmelerde Yönetim ve Organizasyon (3. Baskı)*. İstanbul: Beta Yayınevi.

Evanoff, B. (1994). Psychophysiologic stressors and work organization. In L. Rosenstock & M.R. Cullen (Eds.), *Textbook of clinical occupational and environmental medicine*. Academic Press.

Faragher, E. B., Cass, M., & Cooper, C. L. (2005). The relationship between job satisfaction and health: A meta-analysis. *Occupational and Environmental Medicine*, *62*(2), 105–112. doi:10.1136/oem.2002.006734 PMID:15657192

Frawley, J., & Fasoli, L. (2012). Working together: Intercultural leadership capabilities for both-ways education. *School Leadership & Management, 32*(4), 309–320. doi: 10.1080/13632434.2012.708328

French, J., & Raven, B. (1968). The bases of social power. *Studies in Social Power*, 150-167.

Fries, A. (2009). *Daydreams at work: Wake up your creative powers*. Capital Books.

Fugate, M., Kinicki, A. J., & Ashforth, B. E. (2004). Employability: A psycho-social construct, its dimensions, and applications. *Journal of Vocational Behavior, 65*(1), 14–38. doi:10.1016/j.jvb.2003.10.005

Gezici, A. (2007). *Yöneticilerin liderlik stillerinin çalışanların iş tatmini üzerindeki etkileri: özel eğitim kurumlarında öğretimsel liderlik ve bir uygulama. Yayınlanmamış Yüksek Lisans Tezi*. Kütahya: Dumlupınar Üniversitesi SBE.

Gimson, A., Moskaliuk, J., & Kimmerle, J. (2009). Using wikis for organizational learning: functional and psycho-social principles. *Development and Learning in Organizations: An International Journal.*

Goodwin, N. (2000). Leadership and the UK health service. *Health Policy (Amsterdam), 51*(1), 49–60. doi:10.1016/S0168-8510(99)00072-X PMID:11010225

Gordon, R. D. (2010). Dispersed leadership: Exploring the impact of antecedent forms of power using a communicative framework. *Management Communication Quarterly, 24*(2), 260–287. doi:10.1177/0893318909360213

Griffin, M. A., Patterson, M. G., & West, M. A. (2001). Job satisfaction and teamwork: The role of supervisor support. *Journal of Organizational Behavior: The International Journal of Industrial. Occupational and Organizational Psychology and Behavior, 22*(5), 537–550. doi:10.1002/job.101

Groves, K. S., & Feyerherm, A. E. (2011). Leader cultural intelligence in context: Testing the moderating effects of team cultural diversity on leader and team performance. *Group & Organization Management, 36*(5), 535–566. doi:10.1177/1059601111415664

Gün, İ., & Aslan, Ö. (2018). Liderlik Kuramları ve Sağlık İşletmelerinde Liderlik. *Journal of Health and Nursing Management, 5*(3), 217–226.

Güney, S. (2000). *Davranış Bilimleri (2. Baskı)*. Ankara: Nobel Yayın Dağıtım.

Hanson, W. R., & Ford, R. (2010). Complexity leadership in healthcare: Leader network awareness. *Procedia: Social and Behavioral Sciences, 2*(4), 6587–6596. doi:10.1016/j.sbspro.2010.04.069

Hargreaves, A., & Fink, D. (2012). *Sustainable leadership* (Vol. 6). John Wiley & Sons.

Hartley, J., & Benington, J. (2010). *Leadership for healthcare*. Policy Press.

Hartley, J., & Fletcher, C. (2008). Leading with political awareness: Leadership across diverse interests inside and outside the organisation. In *Leadership perspectives* (pp. 163–176). London: Palgrave Macmillan. doi:10.1057/9780230584068_12

Hersey, P., Blanchard, K. H., & Natemeyer, W. E. (1979). Situational leadership, perception, and the impact of power. *Group & Organization Studies, 4*(4), 418–428. doi:10.1177/105960117900400404

Herzberg, F. (2017). *Motivation to work*. Routledge. doi:10.4324/9781315124827

Hodgkinson, L., & Partington, G. H. (2008). The Motivation for Takeovers in the UK. *Journal of Business Finance & Accounting, 35*(1-2), 102–126. doi:10.1111/j.1468-5957.2007.02063.x

Hofstede, G. (1980). Motivation, leadership, and organization: Do American theories apply abroad? *Organizational Dynamics, 9*(1), 42–63. doi:10.1016/0090-2616(80)90013-3

Hofstede, G. (1993). Cultural constraints in management theories. *The Academy of Management Perspectives, 7*(1), 81–94. doi:10.5465/ame.1993.9409142061

Hogan, R., Curphy, G. J., & Hogan, J. (1994). What we know about leadership: Effectiveness and personality. *The American Psychologist, 49*(6), 493–504. doi:10.1037/0003-066X.49.6.493 PMID:8042818

House, R. J., Hanges, P. J., Javidan, M., Dorfman, P. W., & Gupta, V. (Eds.). (2004). *Culture, leadership, and organizations: The GLOBE study of 62 societies*. Sage publications.

Hughes, R. L. (1993). *Leadership: Enhancing the lessons of experience. Burridge, IL* : Richard D. Irwin, Inc.

Hunt, J. G. (1991). *Leadership: A new synthesis*. Sage Publications, Inc.

Jaffe, D. T. (1995). The healthy company: Research paradigms for personal and organizational health.

Jasper, M., & Jumaa, M. (Eds.). (2008). *Effective healthcare leadership*. John Wiley & Sons.

Javidan, M., & House, R. J. (2001). Cultural acumen for the global manager: Lessons from project GLOBE. *Organizational Dynamics, 29*(4), 289–305. doi:10.1016/S0090-2616(01)00034-1

Judge, T. A., Bono, J. E., & Locke, E. A. (2000). Personality and job satisfaction: The mediating role of job characteristics. *The Journal of Applied Psychology, 85*(2), 237–249. doi:10.1037/0021-9010.85.2.237 PMID:10783540

Kâhya, C. (2013). *Dönüştürücü ve etkileşimci liderlik anlayışları ile örgütsel sessizlik arasındaki ilişkide örgütsel güvenin rolü*. Erzurum: Atatürk Üniversitesi Sosyal Bilimler Enstitüsü Yayımlanmamış Doktora Tezi.

Kanfer, R. (1990). Motivation theory and industrial and organizational psychology. In Handbook of industrial and organizational psychology (pp. 75-130). Academic Press.

Karahan, A. (2008). Hastanelerde liderlik ve örgütsel bağlılık arasındaki ilişkinin incelenmesi. *Sosyal Bilimler Dergisi, 10*(1).

Karakuzu, A. (2013). *Sağlık Çalışanlarında Motivasyon ve Motivasyonu Etkileyen Faktörler (Kırklareli Örneği)*. İstanbul: Beykent Üniversitesi Sosyal Bilimler Enstitüsü Yüksek Lisans Tezi.

Karlıdağ, R., Ünal, S., & Yoloğlu, S. (2000). Hekimlerde iş doyumu ve tükenmişlik düzeyi. *Türk Psikiyatri Dergisi, 11*(1), 49–57.

Katzell, R. A., & Thompson, D. E. (1990). Work motivation: Theory and practice. *The American Psychologist, 45*(2), 144–153. doi:10.1037/0003-066X.45.2.144

Keenan, K. (1996). *Yöneticinin kılavuzu, zamanı doğru kullanma. Translation: E. Koparan*. İstanbul: Remzi Kitabevi.

Koçak, R. D., & Özüdoğru, H. (2012). Yöneticilerin liderlik özelliklerinin çalışanların motivasyonu ve performansı üzerindeki etkileri: Kamu ve özel hastanelerinde bir uygulama. *Ticaret ve Turizm Eğitim Fakültesi Dergisi, 1*, 76–88.

Kolade, O., & Ogunnaike, O. (2014). Organizational citizenship behaviour, hospital corporate image and performance. *Journal of competitiveness, 6*(1), 36-49.

Kouzes, J. M., & Posner, B. Z. (2006). *The leadership challenge* (Vol. 3). John Wiley & Sons.

Kumar, R. D. (2013). Leadership in healthcare. *Anaesthesia and Intensive Care Medicine, 14*(1), 39–41. doi:10.1016/j.mpaic.2012.11.006

Lantz, P. M. (2008). Gender and leadership in healthcare administration: 21st century progress and challenges. *Journal of Healthcare Management, 53*(5), 291–301. doi:10.1097/00115514-200809000-00004 PMID:18856135

Latham, G. P., & Pinder, C. C. (2005). Work motivation theory and research at the dawn of the twenty-first century. *Annual Review of Psychology, 56*(1), 485–516. doi:10.1146/annurev.psych.55.090902.142105 PMID:15709944

Leatt, P., & Porter, J. (2003). Where are the healthcare leaders" the need for investment in leadership development. *Healthcare Papers, 4*(1), 14–31. doi:10.12927/hcpap.2003.16891 PMID:14660891

Leonard, N. H., Beauvais, L. L., & Scholl, R. W. (1999). Work motivation: The incorporation of self-concept-based processes. *Human Relations, 52*(8), 969–998. doi:10.1177/001872679905200801

Lerner, D., Amick, B. C. III, Lee, J. C., Rooney, T., Rogers, W. H., Chang, H., & Berndt, E. R. (2003). Relationship of employee-reported work limitations to work productivity. *Medical Care, 41*(5), 649–659. doi:10.1097/01.MLR.0000062551.76504.A9 PMID:12719689

Lerner, D., & Henke, R. M. (2008). What does research tell us about depression, job performance, and work productivity? *Journal of Occupational and Environmental Medicine, 50*(4), 401–410. doi:10.1097/JOM.0b013e31816bae50 PMID:18404013

Letvak, S., & Buck, R. (2008). Factors influencing work productivity and intent to stay in nursing. *Nursing Economics, 26*(3), 159. PMID:18616053

Lu, H., While, A. E., & Barriball, K. L. (2005). Job satisfaction among nurses: A literature review. *International Journal of Nursing Studies, 42*(2), 211–227. doi:10.1016/j.ijnurstu.2004.09.003 PMID:15680619

Lum, L., Kervin, J., Clark, K., Reid, F., & Sirola, W. (1998). Explaining nursing turnover intent: job satisfaction, pay satisfaction, or organizational commitment? *Journal of Organizational Behavior: The International Journal of Industrial. Occupational and Organizational Psychology and Behavior, 19*(3), 305–320. doi:10.1002/(SICI)1099-1379(199805)19:3<305::AID-JOB843>3.0.CO;2-N

Lund, D. B. (2003). Organizational culture and job satisfaction. *Journal of Business and Industrial Marketing, 18*(3), 219–236. doi:10.1108/0885862031047313

Luthans, F. (1995). *Organizational Behavior, international edition.* İstanbul: Literatür Yayıncılık.

Mahoney, J. (2001). Leadership skills for the 21st century. *Journal of Nursing Management, 9*(5), 269–271. doi:10.1046/j.1365-2834.2001.00230.x PMID:11879469

Mahsud, R., Yukl, G., & Prussia, G. (2010). Leader empathy, ethical leadership, and relations-oriented behaviors as antecedents of leader-member exchange quality. *Journal of Managerial Psychology, 25*(6), 561–577. doi:10.1108/02683941011056932

Mangi, A. A., Kanasro, H. A., & Burdi, M. B. (2015). Motivation tools and organizational success: A criticle analysis of motivational theories. *The Government-Annual Research Journal of Political Science, 4*(4).

Margarita, I. Å. (2013). Motivation tools though lenses of prospective employees. *Entrepreneurship and Sustainability Issues, 1*(2), 116–123. doi:10.9770/jesi.2013.1.2(6)

Maslach, C., & Leiter, M. P. (2016). Burnout. In Stress: Concepts, Cognition, Emotion, and Behavior (pp. 351-357). Academic Press.

McClelland, D. C. (1987). *Human motivation*. CUP Archive.

Meydan, C. H., & Polat, M. (2010). Liderin Güç Kaynaklari Üzerine Kültürel Bağlamda Bir Araştirma. *Ankara Üniversitesi SBF Dergisi, 65*(4), 123–140.

Miner, J. B. (1978). Twenty years of research on role-motivation theory of managerial effectiveness. *Personnel Psychology, 31*(4), 739–760. doi:10.1111/j.1744-6570.1978.tb02122.x

Murphy, L. (2005). Transformational leadership: A cascading chain reaction. *Journal of Nursing Management, 13*(2), 128–136. doi:10.1111/j.1365-2934.2005.00458.x PMID:15720482

Newstrom, J. W., Davis, K., & Pierce, J. L. (1993). Organizational behavior: Human behavior at work.

Ng, K. Y., Van Dyne, L., Ang, S., & Ryan, A. M. (2012). Cultural intelligence: A review, reflections, and recommendations for future research. In *Conducting multinational research: Applying organizational psychology in the workplace* (pp. 29-58). APA.

Ng, R. (2013). Cultural intelligence. In The Encyclopedia of Cross-Cultural Psychology (pp. 310-313). Academic Press.

Normore, A. H., & Collard, J. (Eds.). (2009). *Leadership and intercultural dynamics*. IAP.

Northouse, P. G. (2018). *Leadership: Theory and practice*. Sage publications.

O'Neil, H. F. Jr, Drillings, M., & O'Neil, H. F. (2012). *Motivation: Theory and research*. Routledge.

Örücü, E., Yumuşak, S., & Bozkır, Y. (2006). Kalite Yönetimi Çerçevesinde Bankalarda Çalışan Personelin İş Tatmini ve İs Tatminini Etkileyen Faktörlerin İncelenmesine Yönelik Bir Araştırma. *Celal Bayar Üniversitesi İİBF Yönetim ve Ekonomi Dergisi*, *13*(1), 39–51.

Osterloh, M., & Frey, B. S. (2000). Motivation, knowledge transfer, and organizational forms. *Organization Science*, *11*(5), 538–550. doi:10.1287/orsc.11.5.538.15204

Özdemir, F. (2006). *Örgütsel iklimin iş tatmin düzeyine etkisi: tekstil sektöründe bir araştırma. Yayımlanmamış doktora tezi*. Adana: Çukurova Üniversitesi, Sosyal Bilimler Enstitüsü.

Peker, Ö., & Aytürk, N. (2002). *Yönetim Becerileri (2. Baskı)*. Ankara: Yargı Yayınevi.

Pelletier, B., Boles, M., & Lynch, W. (2004). Change in health risks and work productivity over time. *Journal of Occupational and Environmental Medicine*, *46*(7), 746–754. doi:10.1097/01.jom.0000131920.74668.e1 PMID:15247815

Peters, R. S. (2015). *The concept of motivation*. Routledge. doi:10.4324/9781315712833

Peterson, M. F., & Hunt, J. G. J. (1997). International perspectives on international leadership. *The Leadership Quarterly*, *8*(3), 203–231. doi:10.1016/S1048-9843(97)90002-3

Petri, H. L., & Govern, J. M. (2012). *Motivation: Theory, research, and application*. Cengage Learning.

Plsek, P. E., & Wilson, T. (2001). Complexity, leadership, and management in healthcare organisations. *BMJ (Clinical Research Ed.)*, *323*(7315), 746–749. doi:10.1136/bmj.323.7315.746 PMID:11576986

Purvanova, R. K., Bono, J. E., & Dzieweczynski, J. (2006). Transformational leadership, job characteristics, and organizational citizenship performance. *Human Performance*, *19*(1), 1–22. doi:10.120715327043hup1901_1

Riggio, R. E., & Cole, E. J. (1992). Agreement between subordinate and superior ratings of supervisory performance and effects on self and subordinate job satisfaction. *Journal of Occupational and Organizational Psychology*, *65*(2), 151–158. doi:10.1111/j.2044-8325.1992.tb00491.x

Robbins, C. J., Bradley, E. H., Spicer, M., & Mecklenburg, G. A. (2001). Developing leadership in healthcare administration: A competency assessment tool/Practitioner application. *Journal of Healthcare Management*, *46*(3), 188–202. doi:10.1097/00115514-200105000-00010 PMID:11372221

Rost, J. C. (1993). *Leadership for the twenty-first century*. Greenwood Publishing Group.

Saari, L. M., & Judge, T. A. (2004). Employee attitudes and job satisfaction. *Human Resource Management: Published in Cooperation with the School of Business Administration, The University of Michigan and in alliance with the Society of Human Resources Management, 43*(4), 395-407.

Schein, E. H. (2010). *Organizational culture and leadership* (Vol. 2). John Wiley & Sons.

Seiler, S. (2007). *Determining factors of intercultural leadership: A theoretical framework. In Cultural challenges in military operations* (pp. 213–228). Rome: NDC.

Şencan, N. (2013). Sağlık çalışanları ve eczacılar üzerinde yapılan iş doyumu ve örgütsel bağlılık araştırmaları. MÜ. *Eczacılık Dergisi.*, *17*, 106.

Serinkan, C. (2008). *Liderlik ve Motivasyon Geleneksel ve Güncel Yaklaşımlar*. Ankara: Baskı, Nobel Yayın Dağıtım.

Sheridan, E. (2005). *Intercultural leadership competencies for United States business leaders in the new millennium* [Doctoral dissertation]. University of Phoenix.

Shoaf, C., Genaidy, A., Karwowski, W., & Huang, S. H. (2004). Improving performance and quality of working life: A model for organizational health assessment in emerging enterprises. *Human Factors and Ergonomics in Manufacturing & Service Industries*, *14*(1), 81–95. doi:10.1002/hfm.10053

Spector, P. E. (1997). *Job satisfaction: Application, assessment, causes, and consequences* (Vol. 3). Sage publications.

Spector, P. E., Chen, P. Y., & O'Connell, B. J. (2000). A longitudinal study of relations between job stressors and job strains while controlling for prior negative affectivity and strains. *The Journal of Applied Psychology*, *85*(2), 211–218. doi:10.1037/0021-9010.85.2.211 PMID:10783537

Stankūnas, M., Sauliūnė, S., Smith, T., Avery, M., Šumskas, L., & Czabanowska, K. (2012). Evaluation of leadership competencies of executives in Lithuanian public health institutions. *Medicina*, *48*(11), 85. doi:10.3390/medicina48110085 PMID:23455893

Steers, R. M., Mowday, R. T., & Shapiro, D. L. (2004). The future of work motivation theory. *Academy of Management Review*, *29*(3), 379–387.

Sternberg, R. J., & Detterman, D. K. (1986). *What is intelligence? Norwood*. New York: Ablex.

Stogdill, R. M. (1974). *Handbook of leadership: A survey of theory and research*. Free Press.

Sünter, A. T., Canbaz, S., Dabak, Ş., Öz, H., & Pekşen, Y. (2006). Pratisyen hekimlerde tükenmişlik, işe bağlı gerginlik ve iş doyumu düzeyleri. *Genel Tıp Dergisi*, *16*(1), 9–14.

Templer, K. J., Tay, C., & Chandrasekar, N. A. (2006). Motivational cultural intelligence, realistic job preview, realistic living conditions preview, and cross-cultural adjustment. *Group & Organization Management*, *31*(1), 154–173. doi:10.1177/1059601105275293

Tengilimoğlu, D., & Yiğit, A. (2005). Hastanelerde liderlik davranışlarının personel iş doyumuna etkisini belirlemeye yönelik bir alan çalışması. *Hacettepe Sağlık İdaresi Dergisi*, *8*(3), 374–400.

Titrek, O., & Zafer, D. (2009). İlkögretim Okulu Yöneticilerinin Kullandıkları Örgütsel Güç Kaynaklarına İlişkin Öğretmen Görüşleri. *Kuram ve Uygulamada Eğitim Yönetimi*, *60*(60), 657–674.

Trastek, V. F., Hamilton, N. W., & Niles, E. E. (2014). Leadership models in health care—A case for servant leadership. *Mayo Clinic Proceedings*, *89*(3), 374–381. doi:10.1016/j.mayocp.2013.10.012 PMID:24486078

Triandis, H. C. (2006). Cultural intelligence in organizations. *Group & Organization Management*, *31*(1), 20–26. doi:10.1177/1059601105275253

Trist, E. (1990). *Culture as a psycho-social process. The Social Engagement of Social Science*. London: Free Association.

Tunceli, K., Bradley, C. J., Nerenz, D., Williams, L. K., Pladevall, M., & Lafata, J. E. (2005). The impact of diabetes on employment and work productivity. *Diabetes Care*, *28*(11), 2662–2667. doi:10.2337/diacare.28.11.2662 PMID:16249536

Türk, S., Aydoğan, E., & Kansu, N. (2003). İçsel Motivasyonun İş Tatmini Üzerindeki Etkisi, Türk Tarih Kurumu Matbaası ve Nurol Matbaası'nda Yapılan Bir Araştırma, 1. Matbaa Teknolojileri Sempozyumu, Eylül, Ankara. Matbaa Teknolojileri Sempozyumu, Eylül, Ankara. Retrieved from http://w3.gazi.edu.tr/web/msturk/yayinlar/pdf/motive.pdf

Uno, H., & Zakariasen, K. (2010). Public health leadership education in North America. *Journal of Healthcare Leadership*, *2*, 11–15. doi:10.2147/JHL.S9727

Uysal, Ş. A., Keklik, B., Erdem, R., & Çelik, R. (2012). Hastane yöneticilerinin liderlik özellikleri ile çalışanların iş üretkenlik düzeyleri arasındaki ilişkilerin incelenmesi. *Hacettepe Sağlık İdaresi Dergisi*, *15*(1), 25–57.

Vaitkuviene, L., Balvociute, R., & Stoskus, S. (2010). The comparative analysis of employee motivation tools: The case of Lithuanian and Swedish manufacturing companies. *Oranizciju Vadyba*, *3*, 97–113.

Van Dyne, L., Ang, S., & Livermore, D. (2010). Cultural intelligence: A pathway for leading in a rapidly globalizing world. In *Leading across differences* (pp. 131-138). Academic Press.

VanYperen, N. W., Van Den Berg, A. E., & Willering, M. C. (1999). Towards a better understanding of the link between participation in decision-making and organizational citizenship behaviour: A multilevel analysis. *Journal of Occupational and Organizational Psychology*, *72*(3), 377–392. doi:10.1348/096317999166734

Vroom, V. H., & Jago, A. G. (1988). *The new leadership: Managing participation in organizations*. Prentice-Hall, Inc.

Weberg, D. (2012). Complexity leadership: A healthcare imperative. *Nursing Forum*, *47*(4), 268–277. doi:10.1111/j.1744-6198.2012.00276.x PMID:23127241

Weiss, H. M. (2002). Deconstructing job satisfaction: Separating evaluations, beliefs and affective experiences. *Human Resource Management Review*, *12*(2), 173–194. doi:10.1016/S1053-4822(02)00045-1

Wikström, E., & Dellve, L. (2009). Contemporary leadership in healthcare organizations: Fragmented or concurrent leadership. *Journal of Health Organization and Management*, *23*(4), 411–428. doi:10.1108/14777260910979308 PMID:19862865

Williams, M., Burden, R. L., & Al-Baharna, S. (2001). The role of the individual in motivation theory. In *Motivation and second language acquisition*. Second Language Teaching & Curriculum Center.

Yammarino, F. (2013). Leadership: Past, present, and future. *Journal of Leadership & Organizational Studies*, *20*(2), 149–155. doi:10.1177/1548051812471559

Yrle, A. C., Hartman, S., & Galle, W. P. (2002). An investigation of relationships between communication style and leader-member exchange. *Journal of Communication Management*, *6*(3), 257–268. doi:10.1108/13632540210807099

Yukl, G. (2008). How leaders influence organizational effectiveness. *The Leadership Quarterly*, *19*(6), 708–722. doi:10.1016/j.leaqua.2008.09.008

Yukl, G. (2011). Contingency theories of effective leadership. In The SAGE handbook of leadership (pp. 286-298). Academic Press.

Yukl, G., & Mahsud, R. (2010). Why flexible and adaptive leadership is essential. *Consulting Psychology Journal: Practice and Research*, *62*(2), 81–93. doi:10.1037/a0019835

Yukl, G., Mahsud, R., Hassan, S., & Prussia, G. E. (2013). An improved measure of ethical leadership. *Journal of Leadership & Organizational Studies*, *20*(1), 38–48. doi:10.1177/1548051811429352

Chapter 3
Applying Blockchain Technologies in Healthcare:
A Scientometric Analysis

Zehra Ozge Candereli
Izmir Katip Celebi University, Turkey

Serhat Burmaoglu
https://orcid.org/0000-0002-5537-6887
Izmir Katip Celebi University, Turkey

Levent B. Kidak
Izmir Katip Celebi University, Turkey

Dilek Ozdemir Gungor
Izmir Katip Celebi University, Turkey

ABSTRACT

Recently, one of the inventive developments penetrating many industries is blockchain technology. In the era of globalization and digitalization, blockchain has garnered interest in various application fields from health data management to clinical trials. In this study, we aimed to explore blockchain applications in healthcare with an explorative perspective with a scientometrics analysis. With this analysis, the trends and evolutionary relations between health and blockchain technology were examined via the queries in the Web of Science database. In the analysis, the author keyword co-occurrences were used for demonstrating concept relationships. To understand the new emerging study field, VosViewer was used for network visualizations and CiteSpace free java-based software was used for scientometrics analysis. As a result, it can be implied that the main focus areas of the studies on blockchain are solving payment systems, digital identity, and privacy and security issues in healthcare field.

DOI: 10.4018/978-1-7998-2329-2.ch003

INTRODUCTION

When innovation in healthcare is considered, economic wealth and better public health appear as two of the most prominent topics. As the access to care improves and technological innovation brings new perspectives in the medical field, new driving forces such as public expectations, more strict food and drug security measures, improved traceability and précised medicine increase come to the stage. The demand-side drivers force the health system to transform classical approaches into innovative ways to confront these demands in a cost-effective, appropriate and compatible manner (Petre, 2017a).

From a holistic perspective, healthcare is a complex ecosystem which brings together different services such as promotion, diagnosis, treatment, and rehabilitation. All these services are provided by different parties e.g. hospital, clinics, public sector, private sector, pharmaceutical and medical equipment manufacturers, private/public insurance facilities. As a result, patient healthcare data are scattered and fragmented among different parties of the healthcare system which makes data exchange and collaboration between institutions hard in current healthcare systems. However, patients need to secure and share their data whenever and wherever it is necessary. Due to the importance and sensitive nature of health data, their management is cumbersome in this context (Pilkington, 2017; Dubovitskaya et al., 2017; Szewczyk, 2017).

In many countries, paternalistic government policies prevent individuals from having access to their own health data. Individuals do not have full control of their health record. Current centralized structures of Electronic Health Records (EHR) are subject to hacking, strict security regulations, and excessive overhead costs (Simic et al., 2017; Swan, 2015: 56; McFarlane et al, 2017).

On the other hand, there are advancements in ICT enable cost-effective, technology-based, personalized solutions in the healthcare industry. Wearable devices, e-health, m-health, telehealth are all launched as the use of ICT and ICT based-products such as sensors, internet of things (IoT), cloud systems, remote monitoring system have become financially feasible. Therefore, these developments help patients track their vitals and health parameters while accumulating data in enormous amounts. Patient data acquired by many different devices, providers, and systems cause privacy, security concerns as well as issues related to big data. Therefore, healthcare services (paradigm) are shifting from a centralized, hospital-oriented model toward a distributed patient-centric model.

Rising expectations from healthcare-service providers necessitate improvements in operational efficiency in the healthcare industry and the use of data from various structured and unstructured resources is the key to success. Although a "killer app" does not seem possible in the near future, blockchain technology has the potential to overcome the aforementioned issues (COCIR, 2017).

Satoshi Nakamoto introduced blockchain technology, without mentioning its name explicitly (Mattila, 2016), in 2008 with a white paper in which Bitcoin is proposed as an electronic payment system based on a decentralized peer-to-peer network, without any need for intermediation. Shortly, blockchain is a protocol and widely acknowledged as a major breakthrough in fault-tolerant distributed computing, following decades of research in this field. As it was proposed, the first field of application was the finance sector. Yet blockchain is considered as a promising technology which has the potential to make significant improvements in different industries such including healthcare.

Because of these considerations, in this study, blockchain and healthcare relationship is analyzed with scientometrics. The study is outlined as follows. In the second section blockchain literature is reviewed and the technology is explained. Then, in the third section the literature related to blockchain and healthcare studies are reviewed. The fourth section describes the research methodology and in fifth section is presented findings. The final section discusses the possible effects of blockchain technology on healthcare.

REVIEW OF BLOCKCHAIN LITERATURE

Globalization has found its true meaning with the developments in network technologies and the Internet. In this age, digital platforms changing the business models and whole society by enabling connected structure via cloud-based systems (Kushida et al., 2011; Pon et al., 2014; van Alstyne et al. 2016). Big data approach has been applied to these digital platforms and unprecedented solutions revealed from the data mountains. This perspective can enable a light-weight financial system, inter-organizational record-keeping, and multiparty data aggregation (Greenspan, 2016).

One of these technologies is blockchain, which is accepted today as a general purpose technology (GPT) like steam engine, electricity, and the Internet (Catalini and Gans, 2016). GPTs typically lead to subsequent innovation and productivity gains across multiple industry verticals, sustaining new technological paradigms and economic growth for multiple years (Bresnahan and Trajtenberg, 1995; Helpman and Trajtenberg, 1998; Rosenberg and Trajtenberg, 2001; Moser and Nicholas, 2004; Basu and Fernald, 2007). According to Naughton (2016), blockchain technology will be the most important information technology invention of our age.

Briefly, blockchain can be defined as a distributed ledger that contains all transaction executed in the Bitcoin network. This technology is described with three words as (i) disintermediated, (ii) censorship-resistant, and (iii) tamper-proof

(Seppala et al., 2016). The ledger network is open and participants do not need to trust each other to interact. All transactions are verified and recorded by the nodes of the network through cryptographic algorithms, without supervisors, central authority, human intervention, and any other third-party organizations.

The reliability of the network is provided by the majority of nodes, even if some of them may be dishonest or malicious. For making human intervention or controlling authority unnecessary, a verification process is performed through a mathematical mechanism, called 'proof-of-work'. Proof-of-work systems run by "mining[1]", which does not serve for the purpose of verifying transactions, but for building a credible commitment against an attack. Consensus about the true state of a distributed ledger therefore emerges and becomes stronger as time (and blocks) go by. If a bad actor wanted to reverse a past transaction it would have to spend a disproportionate amount of resources to do so. This is the result of the bad actor not only having to outpace the growth rate of the legitimate chain, but also of having to re-compute all blocks after the one that is being manipulated.

Since the network always takes the longest valid chain as the true state of the ledger (i.e. as the "consensus"), the task of altering a past block of transactions and imposing it on the rest of the network becomes increasingly difficult as the chain is extended. As a result, in proof-of-work systems, a blockchain is only as secure as the amount of computing power dedicated to mining it. This generates economies of scale and a positive feedback loop between network effects and security: as more participants use a crypto-currency, the value of the underlying token increases (because the currency becomes more useful), which in turn attracts more miners (due to higher rewards), ultimately increasing the security of the ledger.

The main idea of the blockchain protocol is decentralization and permisionless attendance. However, there are different blockchains as permissioned like private, public etc. The steps of the Blockchain protocol is demonstrated in Figure 1.

It is clear with the explanation of blockgeeks.com that blockchain process is paperless, disintermediated, unaltered, reliable and free. These characteristics make this system more popular especially for reducing transaction costs at first. These costs include the cost of verification and the cost of networking (Catalini and Gans, 2016). By using the blockchain protocol, for the first time in history, value could be reliably transferred between two distant, untrusting parties without the need of a costly intermediary.

However, the Blockchain technology has also some technical challenges and limitations that have been identified. Swan (2015) presents seven technical challenges and limitations for the adaptation of Blockchain technology in the future:

Figure 1. Blockchain process
(Source: https://blockgeeks.com/wp-content/uploads/2016/09/infographics0517-01-1.png)

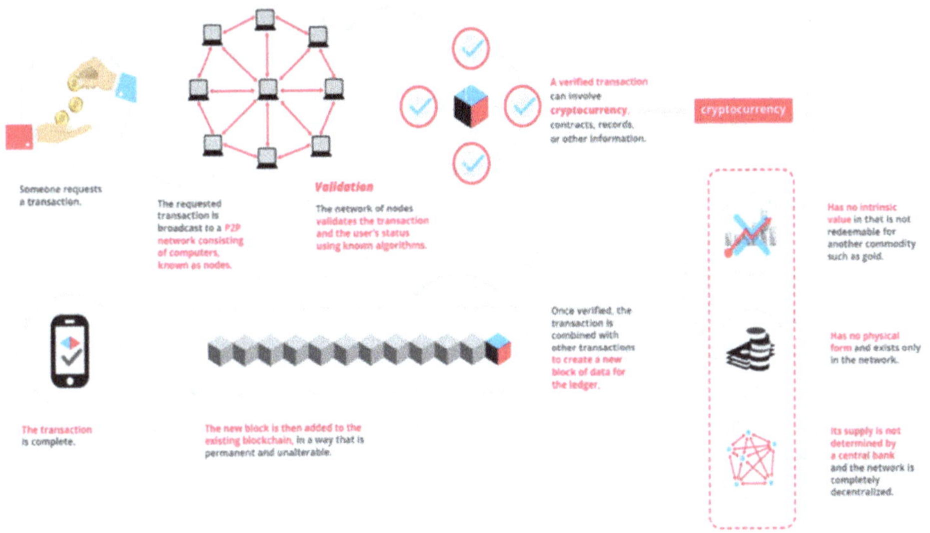

- **Throughput:** The potential throughput of issues in the Bitcoin network is currently between 4 to 7 transactions per second (tps), Ethereum 20 tps and these are limited when compared to VISA (56.000 tps) and PayPal (193 tps).
- **Latency:** To create sufficient security for a Bitcoin transaction block, it takes currently roughly 10 minutes to complete one transaction. To achieve efficiency in security, more time has to be spent on a block, because it has to outweigh the cost of double spending[2] attacks. Bitcoin protects against double spending by verifying each transaction added to the block chain, to ensure that the inputs for the transaction have not been spent previously. This makes latency a big issue in blockchain currently. Making a block and confirming the transaction should happen in seconds, while maintaining its security. To complete a transaction e.g. in VISA takes only a few seconds, which is a huge advantage compared to Blockchain.
- **Size and Bandwidth:** At the moment, the size of a blockchain in the Bitcoin network is over 100GB (http://www.coinfox.info/news/6700-bitcoin-blockchain-size-reaches-100-gb). When the throughput increases to the levels of VISA, blockchain could grow 214PB in each year. The Bitcoin community assumes that the size of one block is 1MB, and a new block is created every ten minutes. Therefore, there is a limitation in the number of transactions that can be handled (on an average of 500 transactions in one block). If the

Blockchain needs to control more transactions, the size and bandwidth issues have to be solved.

- **Security:** The current Blockchain has a possibility of a 51% attack. In a 51% attack, a single entity would have full control of the majority of the network's mining hash-rate and would be able to manipulate Blockchain. To overcome this issue, more research on security is necessary.
- **Wasted Resources:** Mining Bitcoin wastes huge amounts of energy ($15million/day). The waste in Bitcoin is caused by the Proof-of-Work effort. There are some alternatives in industry fields, such as Proof-of-Stake. With Proof-of-Work, the probability of mining a block depends on the work done by the miner. However, in Proof-of-Stake, the resource that is compared is the amount of Bitcoin a miner holds. For example, someone holding 1% of the Bitcoin can mine 1% of the "Proof-of-Stake blocks". The issue with wasted resources needs to be solved to enable more efficient mining in Blockchain.
- **Usability:** The Bitcoin API for developing services is difficult to use. There is a need to develop a more developer-friendly API for Blockchain. This could resemble REST APIs.
- **Versioning, Hard Forks, Multiple Chains:** A small chain that consists of a small number of nodes has a higher possibility of a 51% attack. An issue also emerges when chains are split for administrative or versioning purposes.

Beyond these limitations, according to Yli-Huumo et al. (2016), scalability is also an issue that needs to be solved for future needs. Therefore, to identify and understand the current status of research conducted on blockchain, it is important to gather all relevant research. It is then possible to evaluate what challenges and questions have been tackled and answered, and what the most problematic issues in blockchain are at the moment.

Due to the fact that the maturity of blockchain technology is still relatively low, the technological know-how is mainly concentrated to a small group of blockchain users in the World. However, in a decade the Blockchain platform has been approved with its bespoken characteristics. Hence, the idea behind it is to make the technology more widespread. It can be envisioned that the perspective will have potential to be improved with these common applications. For today there are many application areas of Blockchain, and here one of them is mentioned.

As an irreversible and tamper-proof public records repository for documents, contracts, properties, and assets, the Blockchain can be used to embed information and instructions, with a wide range of applications from private to public (Atzori, 2015). The most popular application is *smart contracts* which can be described as tamper- proof, self-executing and automatically enforceable. Based on Mattilla et al. (2017) American cryptographer Nick Szabo published an article in which he outlined the concept of smart contracts first in 1994. However, because of the immature technology and ICT infrastructure at that time, the idea could not find a way for application. Beyond Szabo's smart contract definition, today smart contracts are accepted as a set of promises in a digital form including protocols within which the parties perform on these promises. The Blockchain technology enables smart contracts to be programmed and embedded to the system easily. Moreover, it can be envisioned that these smart contract systems may be improved with self-execution and self-enforcement to be fully automatized in autonomous organizations. With these improvements in smart contracts it is envisioned to reach Decentralized Autonomous Organization/Corporations/ Societies (DAOs/DACs/DASs). In this concept, self-sufficient agents derived from artificial intelligence are capable of executing tasks without human involvement, for which the Blockchain can provide additional functionality. DAOs operate independently of their developers. In their structure, humans are moved from the center of the organization to its outskirts, as the system is used to organize human activity algorithmically. An open organization based on smart contracts may solve the problem of bad leadership or issues with the transparency of the organization. However, if left unregulated and ungoverned, errors in the programming code may prove to be very harmful or even dangerous. The DAO is still in the development stage and so it reveals new types of risks. The organizational character of the DAO in itself raises the question of, for instance, the distribution of liability for damages within such new types of applications. In addition, it involves ties to the question of determining the correct legal entity in economic activity based on new models of co-operation. Hence, developing technology is not only adequate for making the application common, but also social side should be handled with a holistic perspective.

Because of these evolutionary improvements in Blockchain, Swan (2015) described the technology as "fundamental for forward progress in society as Magna Carta or the Rosetta Stone" (Swan, 2015, p. 16). Again, based on Mattila (2016), the Blockchain technology is shifting society in two aspects. Firstly, it enables directly and reliable transactions of any assets over the Internet between any parties by providing censorship-resistant, disintermediated, tamper-proof digital platforms (Mattila & Seppälä, 2015; Mattila, 2016). Secondly, for enterprise- and industry- level systems, blockchain technology is providing efficiency gains on top of existing structures by removing the constant need for actively intermediated data-synchronization and concurrency control by a trusted third party (Mattila, 2016; Mattila et al., 2016). Therefore, the blockchain platform can be described as more democratic and equal for all nodes in the network. The main idea is accepting all parties sharing the same platform without having privileges and no third-party will provide other ones these privileges. Hence, the blockchain technology can enable all the participants to produce a platform together in a distributed manner, without having to trust each other in almost any capacity (Seppälä & Mattila, 2016; Mattila, 2016).

The deployment of blockchain technology in the healthcare industry will be undoubtedly disruptive. However, due to characteristics of the healthcare ecosystem, it is not expected to serve as a magic bullet to solve every emerging problem. Instead, it will be an evolutionary journey for blockchain-based healthcare systems or applications (Das, 2017). As it has the potential to transform healthcare delivery by enforcing patient-centric systems and improving security, privacy and interoperability; in time it may turn into a technical standard that enables individuals, healthcare providers, healthcare entities and medical researchers to securely share electronic health data (Rabah, 2017; Linn and Koo, 2016).

BOUNDARIES BETWEEN HEALTHCARE AND BLOCKCHAIN LITERATURE

COCIR (2017) revealed an illustrative Healthcare Blockchain Ecosystem and projected potential applications based on blockchain as supply chain management, drug verification, secure exchange of data for reimbursement, control over personal EHR, and management of clinical trials. Capgemini (2017) examined the issue from a holistic perspective and asserted that blockchain applications could benefit the healthcare ecosystem as a whole conceptually. In addition, the elimination of third-party entities and middlemen would reduce administrative costs and increase efficiencies in processing of claims. Distributed ledger and built-in authentication controls would lower the risk of data theft and fraud. Capgemini (2017) concluded that this would foster higher levels of trust in electronic transactions, which would spur electronic payments and thereby reduce payment (accounts receivable) timelines. Furthermore, these studies accepted the use of blockchain technology in the healthcare field promising and disruptive.

According to Frost and Sullivan Report (2017) cited by Das (2017), the potential uses of blockchain in healthcare from the data management perspective were classified. The report demonstrated the use of five general blockchain-based healthcare which are as follows: clinic health data exchange and interoperability, claims adjudication and billing management, drug supply chain and provenance, pharma clinical trials and population health research, cybersecurity, and healthcare IoT. They are believed to indicate more outsanding opportunities, but their uses are employed at various levels by different health systems and countries. Moreover, in order to create globally integrated applications and build collaboration among different industry/parties; standards, and frameworks have to be established.

While use cases e.g. blockchain-based EMR and healthcare data management have the potential to eliminate the burden and cost of health data reconciliation and facilitate interoperability, other use cases e.g., claim adjudication, billing management, drug supply chain, clinical trails have the potential to reveal new economic benefits, effective solutions and quality healthcare services by disintermediating high-cost gatekeepers and automating transactional services across healthcare workflows (Frost and Sullivan, 2017).

However, Hölbl et al. (2018) indicated that blockchain technology in healthcare is mainly applied for healthcare data management including data sharing, health records and access control and rarely used for supply chain management, audit trail management and other scenarios, like drug prescription management and auditing (Hölbl et al., 2018).

After reviewing the literature, the potential use cases of blockchain in healthcare are decided to group in five fields of application. Following sub-headings are the group names and groups explained below.

Healthcare Data Management

One of the most prominent topics in blockchain and healthcare relation is healthcare data management including data storage, exchange and sharing e.g. blockchain-based EMR. According to McFarlane et al. (2017), current electronic medical record (EMR) systems can not meet effective patient-provider relationship and deliver a limited capability of exchange of information among parties. The new healthcare paradigm requires effective and optimal care delivery to produce better care outcomes for patients. These needs force healthcare providers to be able to effectively coordinate and collaborate with other health care organizations and subsidiary health organizations such as laboratories and pharmacies in care delivery. They proposed a "Patientory Blockchain Network" which empowers patients, clinicians, and healthcare organizations to access, store and transfer information safely, thus improving care coordination while ensuring data security since it adheres to HIPAA compliance requirement (McFarlane et al., 2017; www.patientory.com).

Azaria et al. (2016) also proposed that "MedRec" prototype was decentralized health record management system facilitate data sharing, authentication and auditability. They suggested that it was integrated with existing data storage infrastructure and thus provided patients a detailed, immutable history and access control healthcare data via smart contracts. Dubovitskaya et al. (2017) also proposed blockchain based EMR prototype relating oncology patients. They designed a permission blockchain to manage and share clinical data with consent and authorization.

Another one of the blockchain-based and EMR-related implementation was collaboration between Guardtime which was data security firm and the Estonian eHealth Foundation. All citizens were provided a national eID card which links their EMR data with their blockchain-based identity. Every update and access to healthcare records via immutable, time-stamped data logs were registered in the blockchain and a "keyless signature" was returned and stored next to the record. These signatures have served as an electronic timestamp which could prove when changes were made, while the blockchain independently has verified who made them. In doing so, government has secured and managed the health records of over a million Estonians because the system facilitates improved access to vital information for health professionals, while simultaneously guaranteeing patient confidentiality and the integrity of their files (Angraal, 2017).

For medical data exchange among cloud service providers which was trustless parties, Xia et al. (2017) proposed MeDShare which was blockchain-based data sharing system. The system relies on smart contracts and access control mechanisms to effectively monitor data and also detect and cancel unauthorized access and tampering. In this way, cloud service providers could provide secure data sharing, data provenance and auditing on medical data with each other. Brennan (2017) asserted that Healthcoin encourage people for healthy life and diabetes prevention. Based on Brennan's proposal, Healthcoin allowed to individuals, suppliers, insurers and goverments across the globe to manage people's lifestyle change by offering exercising, eating right, better mental health as well as biomakers like weight, heart rate, sugar level etc. to a database run on the blockhain. Healthcoin's algorithm then could calculate the changes or improvement in the patient's health, accordingly, they earned a certain amount of Healthcoins could be used to decrease insurance cost, recognize achievement. In addition, patients could choose to share the information with friends, doctors, goverment or public health organization using it for research (Brennan, 2017).

Healthcare Data Gateway (HDG) which is a smart App proposed by Yue et al. (2016) has ensured that people manage personal healthcare data via blockchain storage system. Thus, patients could share their health data in secure way because private blockchain cloud-based application has notable features such as "purpose-centric access control" which provides patients to control their own data and "secure multi-party computation" without violating privacy with third party for patient data processing.

Several researchers also suggested that diverse blockchain-based healthcare data management scenarios such as e-health solutions (Liu, 2017; Dias et al., 2018), electronic prescriptions (Seitz et al., 2017), mobile health applications (Liang et al., 2017), healthcare data in cloud (Al Omar et al., 2019).

As a result, blockchain technology with immutable, cryptographically secured, time-stamped log features enable precise, real-time and longitudinal health data for all healthcare stakeholders.

Claims Adjudication and Billing Management

For maintaining of healthcare delivery, claims data apart from health data has been substantial input especially in revenue cycle. Governments have the right to speak about how services are billed and money is collected but in current patient billing management systems are complex and related to the transparency and trust because claims data flows through different organizations and incline to manipulation by parties and so this result in fraudulent, excessive billing or billing for non-performed services (Rabah, 2017; Yip, 2017).

It can be assertedt that, blockchain based systems, which have the features like smart contract and verifiable ledger of all service and payment activities, can create more effective solutions via notary function for reducing healthcare billing-related issues. Thus, blockchain can help reduce fraud, extra payment, the need for intermediaries, administrative costs and waiting time for providers and payers (Randall et al., 2017; Das, 2017).

Yip (2017) stated that decentralizing system based blockchain can be alternative payment model. Based on Yip (2017)'s findings, it can be said that, blockchain will provide to add and update claim data much faster than current system and even payers and Bitcoin may be connected to private blockchains and thus patients can pay from a single point for the healthcare services they receive from multiple parties.

Culver (2016) proposed that smart contract, an agreement between provider and patient or government, can enable near real-time automating the majority of claim adjudication and payment processing activities. Thus, complex and ambiguous agreements will be turned into clear and transparent smart contracts and this will trigger to cut down administrative cost, transaction time and middleman.

Partnered with Capital One, Gem Health developed *GemOS* which is a blockchain-based ecosystem for exchanging claim data between and within organizations. It formed global identifiers to trace data and these identifiers connect to each other and record the location of data of a person and organization on a blockchain, along with the necessary consents and sharing policies (Allison, 2017).

Drug Supply Chain Integrity and Provenance

Clauson et al. (2018) stated that supply chain manangement in healthcare is quite important because of its directly affects on patient life and outcomes. Healthcare delivery consists of many different inputs and drug supply chain is big part in terms of both quantity and cost and thus vulnerable to fraudulent attacks. It is well known that drug supply chains contain multiple countries, organizations, and products which have various legal, trade and regulatory enforcement. This nature of the chain makes it difficult to guarantee the chemical components of drugs. With the globalization of the pharmaceutical supply chain, drug counterfeiting is a major problem in this industry and public health. Many companies and blockchain start-ups try to find out blockchain based solutions such as simulation models, and prototyping for drug supply chain (Mackey and Nayyar, 2017; Clauson et al., 2018).

Blockchain based system has potential to create formal registry to track products and components by adding to immutable and timestamped log at every step of process (from manufacture to end user). Furthermore, adding the functionalities such as private keys and smart contract, system could provide transparency, trustworthy, authenticity, proof of ownership of the drug source (Das, 2017; Angraal, 2017; Engelhardt, 2017).

However, according to Mackey et al. (2019), the blockchain-based drug supply chain develops slowly when compared to other industries (e.g., food supply). Since there are no common global policies and regulatory standards, blockchain-based solutions need a consortium on which the concerned parties compromise. Thus, governance can be ensured on who will participate in the chain and how the data will be verified.

The MediLedger Project is a collaborative approach among cross-industry partnerships which have same standards. By forming a consortium, it aims to tackle serialization and other business problems (www.mediledger.com). Similarly, Hyperledger which is blockchain network cross-industry is backed by Linux Foundation and commenced a project for fighting counterfeit medicine. By using tracking and timestamp features of blockchain technology, it could make easy to determine when and where a drug was produced (Taylor, 2016).

Pharma Clinical Trails, Biomedical Research and Population Health Research

Clinical trials are composed of multiple stakeholders, an essential part of which is patient, similar to the drug supply chain and so they have the same challenges like regulatory standards (Mackey et al., 2019). Furthermore, in clinical trials, reproducibility, data sharing, personal data privacy concerns, patient enrollment as well as missing data, endpoint switching, data dredging, and selective publication are a big problem and crucial safety issues for patients. Besides, these challenges result in knowledge gaps for healthcare stakeholders and health policymakers (Benchoufi and Ravaud, 2017; Nugent et al., 2016). Therefore, these issues affect research outcomes and quality because trials could take a long time and outcomes are important for the future of drugs and human health. The use of distributed ledger and time-stamped immutable records will provide traceability and guarantee patients' privacy (Dubovitskaya et al., 2017).

Moreover, using smart contracts can act as trusted administrators which are able to improve the transparency and accountability of data reporting during clinical trials, by immutably capturing all aspects of data including trial registration, protocol, subject registration, consent, clinical measurements, survey, tests, and statistic, etc. This can reduce waste, reporting errors and accusations of data manipulation or selective reporting. (Nugent et al., 2016; Petre, 2017b; Cocir, 2017).

In terms of biomedical research, healthcare data are obtained from different resources such as hospital, patient-related data including consent data, health plan data, genomic, laboratory, etc., clinical trial data, drug supply chain data, and internet of medical things like wearable devices, sensors, etc. In this manner, all data need to authenticity, integrity, provenance, and privacy. Thanks to the features of blockchain, they could be securely stored, time-stamped, current, and transparent (Kuo et al., 2017).

Blockchain-based solutions can improve trust among researchers, suppliers, patients, and other communities and this could help trigger collaboration among them. Therefore, researches can increase in medical field like precision medicine and population health because blockchain technology enable secure way to an ample set of standardized non-patient identifiable information in real-time from different ethnic and socio-economic backgrounds and various geographical environments. Particularly, real-time access to data could allow providers/ researchers to enhance care coordination in emergency case and quickly determine and interfere with environmental conditions in public health like epidemics (Linn and Koo, 2016).

Irving and Holden (2016) presented proof of concept study, they used a copy of the clinicaltrials.gov study protocol based on previously reported prespecified endpoints and planned analyses. By using public and private key produced from the protocol, they incorporated a transaction into the blockchain and so they provided a time-stamped record. As a result, the transaction was completed in a short time and it was low cost. Besides, they confirmed the authenticity of the original protocol and independently verifiable method to audit.

Many researchers also proposed blockchain-based solutions including MedRec (Ekblaw et al., 2016), Healthbank (Mettler, 2016) for clinical and biomedical research.

Cyber Security and Healthcare IoT

Recently, not only current systems have ineligible health IT security infrastructure but also cyber attacks on health data and medical devices are increasing. Thus, they might be exposed to numerous breaches and cyber attacks by external hackers and internal attackers at organizational and individual level. Moreover, as health information technologies improve, current health IT security infrastructure has difficulty in supporting these technologies such as connected health, internet of medical things (IoMT) including wearable devices, sensors, etc., remote patient monitoring, and cloud-based device (Rabah, 2017). This gap increases privacy and security concerns about the transfer and logging of data transactions.

According to Berg Insight Report (2018), the number of remotely monitored patients around world was 16.5 million in 2017 and the market acceptance continues to grow. The number estimated to reach 83.4 million by 2023.

However, due to the characteristics of health data, both their security and privacy need to be ensured in the best way and their accessibility need to be ensured to provide quality healthcare. As mentioned above, blockchain-enable solutions have the potential to cope with the challenges e.g. interoperability, security, privacy and reliability (Brodersen et al., 2016; Rabah, 2017; Deloitte, 2018; Hölbl et al., 2018; Griggs et al., 2018).

Concerning this, Dwivedi et al. (2019) indicated that "the inability to delete and change information from blocks makes blockchain technology the best technology for the healthcare system." They suggested a combination of the private key, public key, blockchain, and other lightweight cryptographic primitives like Ring signature in order to reduce security and privacy concerns about IoT which has resource constraints.

Griggs et al. (2018) proposed a private blockchain based on the Ethereum protocol for enabling secure analysis and management of medical sensor like remote patient monitoring. They used smart contracts integrated with Wireless Body Area Networks (WBAN) systems like smart devices to provide real-time patiens monitoring and medical interventions by sending notifications to patients and healthcare providers in a HIPAA compliant manner.

Angeletti et al. (2017) stated that in the era of Internet of Things (IoT) when internet-based services uncontrollably grow, a huge amount of data, also called big data flow, consistently from different devices and so we need privacy-preserving applications where people maintain control of their own data. They presented a digital health application for using IoT data in clinical trials. In recruiting phase, in order to select desired patient profile meeting criteria, a clinical research institute need accurate data and trusted devices, but in terms of participants, they need privacy of their health data. Thus, they proposed IoT such as wearable devices are equipped with a tamper-proof memory space where the manufacturer places a private key. On the other hand, personal health data are not shared publicly until an individual is enrolled.

The Challenges to Blockchain-Based Solutions

On the other hand, blockchain technology has technical, organizational and behavioral economic challenges and limitations before it has been used in healthcare industry.

The maturity of blockchain technology is still relatively low. During the deployment of blockchain technology, the healthcare industry will face both technical challenges such as interoperability, scalability, throughput, latency, size and bandwidth, security, wasted resources, etc., and some organizational and behavioral economic challenges, for instance, adoption and incentives for participation, costs of operating blockchain technology and regulatory consideration etc. (Swan, 2015; Krawiec et al., 2016; Siyal et al., 2018; Gordon and Catalini, 2018; Katuwal et al., 2018). The challenges and their explanations are summarized in Table 1.

Current implementations of blockchain technology in healthcare are either prototyping stage or development phase, and they have the immature infrastructure. Therefore, it needs more research, experimental implementations, and investments for evaluating its effect on services and outcomes.

Table 1. Challenges of blockchain in healthcare

	Blockchain challenges
Technical	• The number of transactions in healthcare sector is enormous and it needs high-volume and high-frequency transactions of clinical data but blockchain e.g. permissionless blockchain faces volume and storage constraints. • At the same time, a blockchain consumes significant computing power to process transactions. The cost of computing power is derived from the volume and size of transactions submitted through the network. • For blockchain-based solutions to operate effectively, stakeholders e.g. healthcare providers, patient, and insurance must be willing to cooperate and set standards about what data is stored on or off the blockchain, what size and format is offered etc., especially cross-border sharing of data. • Likewise, it needs technically access control policies and synchronization mechanisms to operate in complex and diverse communication systems e.g. IoT devices. • Although blockchain implementations are pseudonymous, namely, identity is typically obscured behind a public key, it can not ensure transactional privacy for each public key and so the value of transactions are publicly visible
Organizational	• Because it is a novel technology, blockchain has an uncertain cost of operations for healthcare sector, • A network of co-operation of multiple stakeholders (nodes) must be found to provide the computing power necessary to generate blocks after a transaction is produced. Thus it needs incentives e.g. financial, operational for participation, • For integration with multiple parties, healthcare policy makers should be executively collaboration and make regulatory framework as to patient's privacy like HIPAA.
Behavioral	• Patient-controlled data can be risky e.g. losting key, • Blokchain is still in progress stage and so it confronts social challenges e.g. cultural shift, social acceptance and so it need to be users education, incentive etc.

METHODOLOGY AND DATA

In this study, we aimed to explore blockchain applications in healthcare with explorative perspective by using scientific publications indexed in WoS. Author keyword co-occurrences was used for demonstrating concept relationships. We believe that demonstrating big picture by using science visualization techniques will give opportunity to understand the new emerging study field and contribute existing literature. CiteSpace, free java-based software, was used for scientometrics analysis and VosViewer was used for network visualizations.

It is clear that WoS is not a health-focused index like PUBMED and MEDLINE but its coverage and metadata are accepted as powerful than others. Mongeon and Paul-Hus (2016) compared databases based upon journal coverage and found that for comparative research evaluation, databases should be carefully used due to their biases. Moreover, they did not conclude that one database was superior to the other in terms of journal coverage.

A number of free and commercial software tools are available to carry out the mapping study. Each has its strengths and weaknesses based on different characteristics to carry out science mapping analysis. Cobo et al. (2011)'s study can be reviewed for further comparative information about these tools. Among those, the present study used Citespace II (Chen 2006) software, which takes a set of bibliographic records as its input and models the intellectual structure of the underlying domain in terms of a synthesized network based upon a time series of networks derived from each year's publications. As CiteSpace is easy to use and has some favorable features, it was chosen for the purpose of the present study. Some of the visuals were generated by using VosViewer (van Eck and Waltman, 2007) free Java-based software.

ANALYSIS AND FINDINGS

Blockchain publications were retrieved by using lexical search query as "TS=(("blockchain" OR "distributed ledger" OR "cryptocurrenc*") AND ("health" OR "healthcare")) OR TI=(("blockchain" OR "distributed ledger" OR "cryptocurrenc*") AND ("health" OR "healthcare"))" in WoS. TS refers to topic sentence and TI refers to Title. 198 publications were reached with this query and after preprocessing data were analyzed.

First analysis was performed by using author keywords. Co-occurrence analysis was applied. Keyword co-occurrence analysis has been applied in several domains for understanding the dynamics of a scientific field. Keywords were clustered based on co-occurrences. As proposed by Chen and Song (2017), clusters were considered the embodiment of an underlying specialty. Therefore, all clusters represented various aspects of the analyzed domain. Cluster members were scrutinized in each cluster by identifying structural and temporal metrics of research impact and evolutionary significance. Timeline view of these clusters demonstrated in Figure 2.

In Figure 2, every vertical line represents different cluster and other arcs represent links between different keywords in clusters. Top to down order of clusters only refer to the higher number of members in the cluster. Plus signs represent frequency of usage of keywords. When the order of clusters considered from top to down, first cluster was labeled as "thing security" and its focus was mostly on privacy and security issues. It is clear that these issues were the critical challenges for medical informatics. Second cluster was labeled as "current research topics" based on titles of the clustered articles. In these cluster, payment systems mostly discussed in healthcare by using cryptocurrencies like Ethereum or Bitcoin. In third cluster, internet-based applications of healthcare were discussed and their distributed aspects were scrutinized. Electronic medical records were discussed in fourth cluster and trust aspect of blockchain platforms were examined. Fifth cluster was including blockchain applications and its some extensions like smart contracts. Last cluster was connection of health system and smart city concept.

It can be asserted that there were not many articles and focused terms to be called as emergent in analyzed dataset. However, mean publication year was seen as 2017 and focus of articles were about overcoming health challenges. Therefore, it can be implied that studies on blockchain will make contribution especially for solving payment system, digital identity, privacy, and security issues.

Figure 2. Timeline view of keyword co-occurrence network

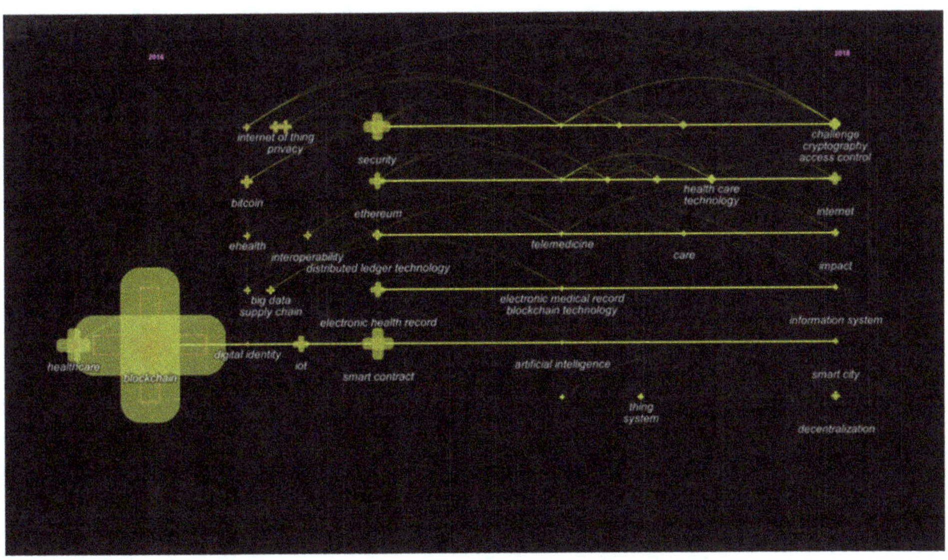

After analyzing keyword co-occurrences, it can be beneficial to see the country collaborations on the same subject. Country collaboration network map was prepared by using Vos Viewer (van Eck and Waltman, 2007) as demonstrated in Figure 3.

As can be seen in Figure 3, there were 9 clusters which were colored differently. USA, China, England, and South Korea published more articles than others when the size of circles considered. As in keyword co-occurrences network analysis, because of the low number of publications it is not easy to demonstrate some hot points in Figure 2. However, German-Chinese collaboration, USA-Japan collaboration, European network, and England-Pakistan-UAE collaboration may seem interesting.

CONCLUSION

In this study, blockchain technology has been reviewed to understand whether it can be a cure for these challenges in healthcare. Even, blockchain technology is not mature, there were many studies in many fields which were promising. In this chapter, we tried to review real cases and visualize cognitive space of intersection of health and blockchain concepts. Finally, it can be asserted that healthcare system has important challenges regarding privacy, security and interoperability.

We identified six clusters in author keyword co-ocurrences network map. However, we couldn't identify emerging concepts with high frequency because of low number of publications in the field. We envisioned that privacy and security issues might

Figure 3. Country collaboration network map

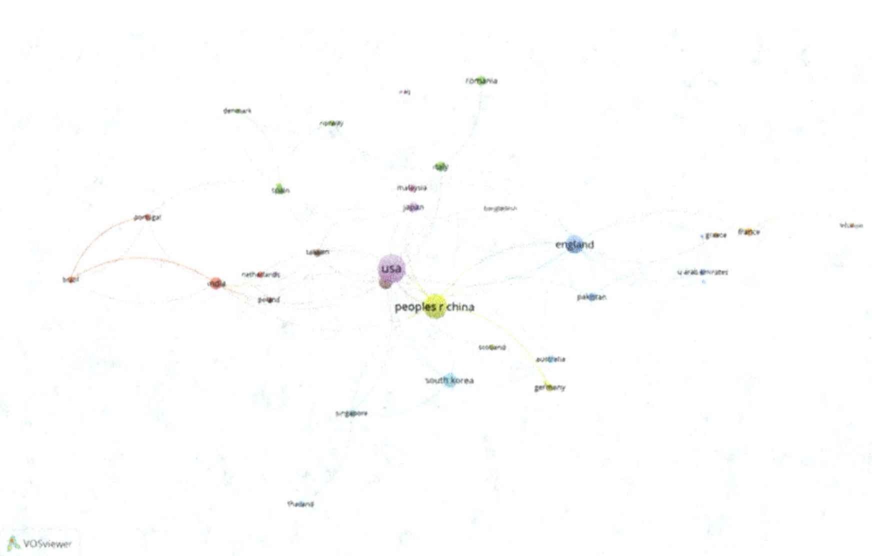

be the first focus of blockchain studies in healthcare. Then, interoperability and payment systems will be integrated by establishing operating standards of blockchain technology in health field.

For further studies, focus issues that we emphasized with this study should be examined in detail and *Scopus, PUBMED and MEDLINE data should be combined with WoS data by eliminating duplicate problem.*

REFERENCES

Al Omar, A., Bhuiyan, M. Z. A., Basu, A., Kiyomoto, S., & Rahman, M. S. (2019). Privacy-friendly platform for healthcare data in cloud based on blockchain environment. *Future Generation Computer Systems*, *95*, 511–521. doi:10.1016/j.future.2018.12.044

Allison, I. (2017). Gem shows off first blockchain application for health claims. International Business Times. Retrieved from https://www.ibtimes.co.uk/gem-shows-off-first-blockchain-application-health-claims-1622574

Angeletti, F., Chatzigiannakis, I., & Vitaletti, A. (2017, September). The role of blockchain and IoT in recruiting participants for digital clinical trials. In *Proceedings of the 2017 25th International Conference on Software, Telecommunications and Computer Networks (SoftCOM)* (pp. 1-5). IEEE. 10.23919/SOFTCOM.2017.8115590

Angraal, S., Krumholz, H. M., & Schulz, W. L. (2017). Blockchain technology: Applications in health care. *Circulation: Cardiovascular Quality and Outcomes*, *10*(9), e003800. doi:10.1161/CIRCOUTCOMES.117.003800 PMID:28912202

Azaria, A., Ekblaw, T. V., & Lippman, A. (2016). MedRec: Using Blockchain for Medical Data Access and Permission Management. In *Proceedings of the 2016 2nd International Conference on Open and Big Data (OBD)* (pp. 25-30). Academic Press. 10.1109/OBD.2016.11

Benchoufi, M., & Ravaud, P. (2017). Blockchain technology for improving clinical research quality. *Trials*, *18*(1), 335. doi:10.118613063-017-2035-z PMID:28724395

Brennan, B. (2017). Healthcoin – blockchain-enabled platform for diabetes prevention. *Blockchain Healthcare Review*. Retrieved from https://blockchainhealthcarereview.com/healthcoin-blockchain-enabled-platform-for-diabetes-prevention/

Brodersen, C., Kalis, B., Leong, C., Mitchell, E., Pupo, E., Truscott, A., & Accenture, L. (2016). *Blockchain: Securing a New Health Interoperability Experience*. Accenture LLP.

Capgemini. (2017). Blockchain: A healthcare endustry review. Retrieved from https://www.capgemini.com/wp-content/uploads/2017/07/blockchain-a_healthcare_industry_view_2017_web.pdf)

Chen, C. M. (2006). Citespace II: Detecting and visualizing emerging trends and transient patterns in scientific literature. *Journal of the American Society for Information Science and Technology*, *57*(3), 359–377. doi:10.1002/asi.20317

Clauson, K. A., Breeden, E. A., Davidson, C., & Mackey, T. K. (2018). *Leveraging blockchain technology to enhance supply chain management in healthcare. Blockchain in Healthcare Today*. doi:10.30953/bhty.v1.20

Cobo, M. J., Lopez-Herrera, A. G., Herrera-Viedma, E., & Herrera, F. (2011). Science mapping software tools: Review, analysis, and cooperative study among tools. *Journal of the American Society for Information Science and Technology*, *62*(7), 1382–1402. doi:10.1002/asi.21525

Cocir. (2017) Beyond the hype of blockchain in healthcare. Retrieved from http://www.cocir.org/uploads/media/17069_COC_Blockchain_paper_web.pdf

Culver, K. (2016). Blockchain Technologies: A whitepaper discussing how the claims process can be improved. In *Proceedings of the ONC/NIST Use of Blockchain for Healthcare and Research Workshop*. ONC/NIST.

Das, R. (2017). Does Blockchain Have A Place In Healthcare? *Pharma&Healthcare*. Retrieved from https://www.forbes.com/sites/reenitadas/2017/05/08/does-blockchain-have-a-place-in-healthcare/#552cb0c91c31

Deloitte. (2018). Blockchain to blockchains in life sciences and health care-What broader integration is making possible today. Retrieved from https://www2.deloitte.com/content/dam/Deloitte/us/Documents/life-sciences-health-care/us-lshc-tech-trends2-blockchain.pdf

Dias, J. P., Reis, L., Ferreira, H. S., & Martins, Â. (2018). Blockchain for access control in e-health scenarios.

Dubovitskaya, A., Xu, Z., Ryu, S., Schumacher, M., & Wang, F. (2017). Secure and Trustable Electronic Medical Records Sharing using Blockchain. In *Proceedings of the AMIA 2017 Annual Symposium Proceedings*. Academic Press.

Dwivedi, A. D., Srivastava, G., Dhar, S., & Singh, R. (2019). A decentralized privacy-preserving healthcare blockchain for iot. *Sensors (Basel)*, *19*(2), 326. doi:10.339019020326 PMID:30650612

Engelhardt, M. A. (2017). Hitching Healthcare to the Chain: An Introduction to Blockchain Technology in the Healthcare Sector. *Technology Innovation Management Review.*, *7*(10), 22–34. doi:10.22215/timreview/1111

Frost and Sullivan. (2017). Blockchain Technology in Global Healthcare, 2017–2025. Retrieved from http://www.frost.com/sublib/display-report.do?searchQuery= blockchain&id=K1DB-01-00-00-00&bdata=aHR0cHM6Ly93d3cuZnJvc3QuY 29tL3NyY2gvY2F0YWxvZy1zZWFyY2guZG8%2FcGFnZVN pemU9MTImcXVlcnlUZXh0PWJsb2NrY2hhaW4mbWFya2V0Q29kZXM9SEMmZmlsdGVyU3dpdG NoPWZhbHNlQH5AU2VhcmNoIFJlc3VsdHNAfkAxNTE1MjU0MDg1NDk3

Gordon, W. J., & Catalini, C. (2018). Blockchain technology for healthcare: Facilitating the transition to patient-driven interoperability. *Computational and Structural Biotechnology Journal*, *16*, 224–230. doi:10.1016/j.csbj.2018.06.003 PMID:30069284

Griggs, K. N., Ossipova, O., Kohlios, C. P., Baccarini, A. N., Howson, E. A., & Hayajneh, T. (2018). Healthcare Blockchain System Using Smart Contracts for Secure Automated Remote Patient Monitoring. *Journal of Medical Systems*, *42*(7), 130. doi:10.100710916-018-0982-x PMID:29876661

Hölbl, M., Kompara, M., Kamišalić, A., & Nemec Zlatolas, L. (2018). A systematic review of the use of blockchain in healthcare. *Symmetry*, *10*(10), 470. doi:10.3390ym10100470

IBM. (2016). Blockchain: The Chain of Trust and its Potential to Transform Healthcare – Our Point of View. Retrieved from https://www.healthit.gov/sites/default/files/8-31-blockchain-ibm_ideation-challenge_aug8.pdf

Irving, G., & Holden, J. (2016). How blockchain-timestamped protocols could improve the trustworthiness of medical science. *F1000 Research*, 5. PMID:27239273

Katuwal, G. J., Pandey, S., Hennessey, M., & Lamichhane, B. (2018). Applications of Blockchain in Healthcare: Current Landscape & Challenges.

Krawiec, R. J., Housman, D., White, M., Filipova, M., Quarre, F., Barr, D., . . . Tsai, L. (2016, August). Blockchain: Opportunities for health care. In *Proc. NIST Workshop Blockchain Healthcare* (pp. 1-16). Academic Press.

Kuo, T. T., Kim, H. E., & Ohno-Machado, L. (2017). Blockchain distributed ledger technologies for biomedical and health care applications. *Journal of the American Medical Informatics Association*, *24*(6), 1211–1220. doi:10.1093/jamia/ocx068 PMID:29016974

Liang, X., Zhao, J., Shetty, S., Liu, J., & Li, D. (2017, October). Integrating blockchain for data sharing and collaboration in mobile healthcare applications. In *Proceedings of the 2017 IEEE 28th Annual International Symposium on Personal, Indoor, and Mobile Radio Communications (PIMRC)* (pp. 1-5). IEEE. 10.1109/PIMRC.2017.8292361

Linn, L., & Koo, M. (2016). Blockchain for health data and its potential use in health it and health care related research. In *Proceedings of the ONC/NIST Use of Blockchain for Healthcare and Research Workshop*. ONC/NIST.

Liu, W., Zhu, S. S., Mundie, T., & Krieger, U. (2017, October). Advanced block-chain architecture for e-health systems. In *Proceedings of the 2017 IEEE 19th International Conference on e-Health Networking, Applications and Services (Healthcom)* (pp. 1-6). IEEE. Retrieved from https://www.iim.ftn.uns.ac.rs/is17/papers/28.pdf

Mackey, T. K., Kuo, T. T., Gummadi, B., Clauson, K. A., Church, G., Grishin, D., ... Palombini, M. (2019). 'Fit-for-purpose?'–challenges and opportunities for applications of blockchain technology in the future of healthcare. *BMC Medicine, 17*(1), 68. doi:10.118612916-019-1296-7 PMID:30914045

Mackey, T. K., & Nayyar, G. A. (2017). A review of existing and emerging digital technologiesto combat the global trade in fake medicines. *Expert Opinion on Drug Safety, 16*(5), 587–602. doi:10.1080/14740338.2017.1313227 PMID:28349715

McFarlane, C., Beer, M., Brown, J., & Prendergast, N. (2017). Patientory: A Healthcare Peer-to-Peer EMR Storage Network v1. 0. Retrieved from https://patientory.com/patientory_whitepaper.pdf

Mediledger. (n.d.). Retrieved from https://www.mediledger.com/

Mettler, M. (2016). Blockchain technology in healthcare: The revolution starts here. In *Proceedings of the 2016 IEEE 18th International Conference on e-Health Networking, Applications and Services (Healthcom)*. IEEE.

Mongeon, P., & Paul-Hus, A. (2016). The journal coverage of web of science and scopus: A comparative analysis. *Scientometrics, 106*(1), 213–228. doi:2-015-1765-5. doi:10.10071119

Nugent, T., Upton, D., & Cimpoesu, M. (2016). Improving data transparency in clinical trials using blockchain smart contracts. *F1000 Research, 5*, 2541. doi:10.12688/f1000research.9756.1 PMID:28357041

Petre, A. (2017a). Leveraging Sustainable Innovation in Healthcare. Retrieved from http://www.ancapetre.com/leveraging-sustainable-innovation-healthcare

Petre, A. (2017b). Blockchain use cases in healthcare. Retrieved from https://www.linkedin.com/pulse/blockchain-use-cases-healthcare-anca-petre

Pilkington, M. (2017). Can Blockchain Improve Healthcare Management? Consumer Medical Electronics and the IoMT. doi:10.2139srn.3025393

Rabah, K. (2017). Challenges & Opportunities for Blockchain Powered Healthcare Systems: A Review. *Mara Research Journal of Medicine & Health Sciences*, *1*(1), 45–52.

Randall, D., Goel, P., & Abujamra, R. (2017). Blockchain Applications and Use Cases in Health Information Technology. *J Health Med Informat*, *8*(276), 2.

Report, B. I. (2018) mHealth and Home Monitoring. Retrieved from http://www.berginsight.com

Seitz, J., & Wickramasinghe, N. (2017). Blockchain technology in e-health: The case of electronic prescriptions in Germany. In *Proceedings of the XVII International Scientific Conference on Industrial Systems*. Academic Press.

Simic, M., Sladic, G., & Milosaljevic, B. (2017). A Case Study IoT and Blockchain powered Healthcare. In *Proceedings of the 8th PSU-UNS International Conference on Engineering and Technology (ICET-2017)*. Academic Press.

Siyal, A., Junejo, A., Zawish, M., Ahmed, K., Khalil, A., & Soursou, G. (2019). Applications of Blockchain Technology in Medicine and Healthcare: Challenges and Future Perspectives. *Cryptography*, *3*(1), 3. doi:10.3390/cryptography3010003

Swan, M. (2015). *Blockchain Blueprint for a New Economy*. USA: O'Reilly Media.

Szewczyk, P. (2017). *Potential applications of the blockchain technology in helthcare*. Zeszyty Naukowe. Organizacja i Zarządzanie/Politechnika Śląska.

Taylor, P. (2016). Applying blockchain technology to medicine traceability. Retrieved from https://www.securingindustry.com/pharmaceuticals/applying-blockchain-technology-to-medicine-traceability/s40/a2766/#.XLt6tOgzY2y

Van Eck, N. J., & Waltman, L. (2007). Bibliometric mapping of the computational intelligence field. *International Journal of Uncertainty Fuzziness and Knowledge-Based Systems*, *15*(5), 625–645. Available: 488507004911 doi:10.1142/S0218

Xia, Q. I., Sifah, E. B., Asamoah, K. O., Gao, J., Du, X., & Guizani, M. (2017). MeDShare: Trust-less medical data sharing among cloud service providers via blockchain. *IEEE Access*, *5*, 14757–14767. doi:10.1109/ACCESS.2017.2730843

Yip, K. (2017). Blockchain & alternate payment models. In *Proceedings of the ONC/NIST Use of Blockchain for Healthcare and Research Workshop*. ONC/NIST.

Yue, X., Wang, H., Jin, D., Li, M., & Jiang, W. (2016). Healthcare data gateways: Found healthcare intelligence on blockchain with novel privacy risk control. *Journal of Medical Systems*, *40*(10), 218. doi:10.100710916-016-0574-6 PMID:27565509

ENDNOTE

1 Mining: Nodes in the network compete to solve a mathematical puzzle that requires the consumption of computing power. Once the puzzle solved the new block of transactions is accepted by the network and committed to the Blockchain. The network nodes which is called miners rewarded with newly generated coins.

2 Double-spending is the result of successful spending of money more than once.

Chapter 4
Health Export and Health Tourism Roles in European Union Countries

Yurdagül Meral
https://orcid.org/0000-0001-9244-1994
Istanbul Medipol University, Turkey

ABSTRACT

Health exports have increased to 100 billion dollars per year and it has become an important item in service exports all over the world. Demographic structures are changing with the old population in developed countries, and health tourism among countries has increased. This chapter aims to study health tourism in European Union, aiming to create a single market with member countries and with free movement of people among member countries. EU policy permits member countries' citizens to get health service from any other member country. A literature review shows that the differences between member countries' national health systems is one of the main issues to be resolved and that the countries with old populations who need health care affect health tourism from developed countries with old population countries to countries with young population like Spain. Along with the legislation, ethical, social issues, and standard international rules accepted by all countries covering all aspects of health tourism must be set by international organisations like the WHO to avoid potential risks for the patients.

DOI: 10.4018/978-1-7998-2329-2.ch004

INTRODUCTION

The Constitution of the World Health Organization (1946) and the World Health Organization and the United Nations Children's Fund (UNICEF) have prepared in their common declaration of Almatı (1978) have defined health as "Not only the absence of illness or disability, but also physical, mental and social well-being and a fundamental right" (World Health Organisation, 2006). As health is seen as a type of service that should be given priority because of its importance for individual and society (Aktan, Işık, 2010), health is an integral part of basic human rights, and can be defined as "an individual's to request from the society, from the government, his health to be able to be protected, and if necessary to be treated and to benefit from the opportunities provided by the society " (Bilgili, 2008).

HEALTH TOURISM

Tourism is regarded as a leisure activity and includes, in a sense, the consumption of goods and services that are not required (Urry, 2002). Health tourism is also defined as externalization of health and health services (Kher, 2006). At the same time, it is defined as "export of patients" and importation of medical services (Herrick, 2007). Another definition of health tourism is organized trips from one's own place to another in order to protect or improve one's mental and physical health (Carrera, 2006). Health tourism covers people's travels from their permanent living and workplaces and temporary accommodation necessities (Olalı, 1988),

According to (UNWTO, 2017), the difference between definitions of tourism, health tourism and wellness tourism are: Tourism (travel) activity helps wellbeing. Health tourism covers both subtypes tourisms i.e. wellness and medical tourism. In other words, health tourism covers both mental, spiritual health via medical and wellness-based tourism. The first subtype of tourism is wellness tourism which covers items like healty eating, fitness, relaxation etc. The second subtype of tourism is the medical tourism, which covers diagnosis, cure, treatments, preventation etc.

As the data of health tourism covers many aspects therefore the statistical data showing the size and growth estimates vary, according to Medical Tourism Association, the market size is 100 billion US Dollars and according to Patients Beyond Borders the market is between 45,5 to 72 million dollars (World Tourism Organization and European Travel Commission, 2018). With the increase in the health care costs, middle- and low-income countries increased medical tourism (Hopkins and et al, 2010). In other words, Medical tourism high-income countries' patients travelled to low- and middle-income countries to have cheaper medical care (Mazzaschi, 2011).

Connell claims that although medical tourism has increased in the past years, reliable estimates are not available because it is difficult to identify medical tourists (Connell, 2013). Medical tourism income has been estimated about 60 billion United States dollars (US$) per year and is expected to grow about 20% annually (Heung, Küçükusta, Song, 2011). In 2007, an estimated 50 000–120 000 residents of the United States of America travelled abroad to obtain medical services (Johnson, and Garman, 2010). UK's estimate for the year 2010 is that 63 thousand went abroad for medical care (Hanefeld, Horsfall, Lunt, Smith, 2013). According to some of the estimates, Thailand received 104830 medical tourists in 2010 (Noree, Hanefeld, Smith, 2010).

The first dimension of health tourism is planning and realization of travels (Glinos, Baeten, 2006); the second dimension includes the provision of accommodation, health care and other complementary services to those coming for the purpose of health care (Turner, 2008); the third dimension includes the patient's return to his / her country after receiving health care and controlling the recovery process when necessary (Kültür ve Turizm Bakanlığı, 2009).

The most preferred countries in the field of health tourism are; US, India, Cuba, Costa Rica, Thailand, Singapore, Colombia, Malaysia, Turkey, Mexico, Germany and South Korea. South and Central American countries generally provide services to American citizens seeking treatment options outside the United States due to very high treatment costs. Malaysia, on the other hand, receives approximately 75% of its patients for better medical care from the immediate surroundings, such as Indonesia and the Philippines. The most common transboundary patient movement in the European countries is the movements within the Union. For example, 60% of patients coming to Belgium from outside the country come from the Netherlands and 92% come from neighboring EU countries (Sağlık Bakanlığı, 2019).

REASONS OF HEALTH TOURISM

It is generally accepted that the patient prefers to receive health care from the nearest location to his / her home and is not willing to travel abroad for treatment purposes (Brouwer, et al, 2007). In addition to geographical proximity, cultural and linguistic proximity is also effective in choosing patients where they want to be treated. The idea of receiving services in another country has increased with the development of mass tourism and the increase in people's experience of living in foreign countries with the increase income (Connell, 2006).

Economic

Generally, small populations or small countries prefer patients to receive health care in a foreign country instead of making expensive and uneconomical investments (Glinos, Baeten, 2006). The direction of patient mobility is generally from countries where treatment costs are high, providing low-cost, high-tech services (Bookman, 2007). While mobility within the EU is from countries where treatment costs such as the UK, Ireland, Denmark, Germany and Switzerland to countries where treatment costs are relatively low, such as Poland, Hungary and Slovenia. The direction of patient mobility in the world is in developing countries that offer "first class service at third-rate prices (South Africa, Singapore, Argentina) (De Arrellano, 2007).

Quality

Patients who are not satisfied with the health service provided in their home country may think that the health service provided in a foreign country is of a higher quality and go to this country for treatment (Hermans, 2000). In the United States, the Joint Commission controls the standards of health care, in UK and in Hong Kong, Trent International Accreditation bodies controls the affiliated hospitals and health care organizations standards of healthcare (Bertinato and Canapero, 2010).

The driving force is mainly the difference and comparison between the option to stay in a home country and the option to move to a foreign country (Glinos, Baeten, 2006).

Unavailable Health Service

The national health institution may not be able to provide this health service within the country on the grounds that it is unethical (such as the prohibition of abortion in Ireland for ethical reasons) or that it is highly experimental and devoid of scientific evidence (Cortez, 2008).

Ambiguity Between Doctor and Patient

The information asymmetry between the patient and the doctor forces the healthcare consumer to choose under uncertainty (Erdem, Yıldırım, 2003).

Competition

In health tourism, where the competition is quite high, it is seen that the hospitality dimension of the service provided has become increasingly prominent. "Five-star hospitals", which do not smell like hospitals and hotels where nurses work is are an extreme indicator of this trend (Flower, 2006).

Lastly, cross-border mobility of health personnel may affect the mobility of patients as well (Carrera, 2006).

FACTORS AFFECTING HEALTH TOURISM

Accreditation

Accreditation systems such as JCI, TEMOS or ACHSI has enabled insurance reimbursement institutions to facilitate travel for therapeutic purposes. The accreditation or encouragement of health institutions by the countries that aspire to health care provision has accelerated the development of this sector. For example, in the United States "JCI - Joint Commission International" has accredited more than 300 foreign health facilities where the majority of them are located in US, Turkey, Thailand, India, Dubai and the United Arab Emirates.

Intermediary Institutions

As a matter of fact, the US Travel industry has seen this important opportunity in the market and the intermediary institutions have arranged health tourism packages including air ticket, accommodation and surgical expenses claiming to save up to 80% compared to the costs in the USA. It is claimed that for example a 123,000 USD cardiovascular surgery in the US, including all-inclusive mediation is provided for $ 15,000 in Thailand (http://www.thaiwebsites.com/cost-medical-treatment.asp).

Excluded Treatment

In most western countries, the exclusion of cosmetic, dental and aesthetic operations from health insurance coverage and the presence of people in need of such health care have led to the pursuit of cheap treatment in foreign countries.

International Agreements

Medical tourism has become an important outsourcing sector globally. As in the case of Japan, it is preferable to send people to countries where retirement nursing homes and gerontology services are provided at a lower price, instead of providing them in the country. In this way, both a cost-effective solution is produced and its own work power can be used in more strategic areas. In the UK, the NHS has a sub-contract with India on the provision of medical services. The best example of outsourcing services in tourism is from Japan. In addition, agreements with private insurance companies in the US with JCI accredited international hospitals are increasing day by day.

The success of health tourism in Asia increases global interest and competition. For example, Southeast Asia countries want to attract 1 million patients with a revenue target of $ 2.5 billion in 2015, even though there are relatively high destinations in thermal health tourism travel. If this goal is achieved, at least 20,000 new jobs will be opened. Dubai has implemented the Dubai Healthcare City project to prevent Middle Eastern tourists from going to Asia. Health tourism targets the middle-income group and all groups in the developed countries, while it targets the upper income group in the developing countries. For example, high-income citizens of countries such as Kenya or Ukraine spend billions of dollars each year on health expenses abroad. In Japan, it is seen as prestige that middle- and upper-income groups have gone abroad, for example Thailand or Singapore, even for simple health services. In addition, Japan's encouraging elderly population to go to elderly health care centers in foreign countries shows the different contribution levels of countries to the health tourism sector. It is estimated that by 2019, only 1,9 million American patients from the United States will travel outside their country for receiving health services to overseas countries (Patients Beyond Borders, 2019).

EUROPEAN UNION AND HEALTH TOURISM

Tourism has entered into acquis with the Maastricht Treaty, symbolizes the conflict between liberal ideology and interventionist ideology and is part of the European integration process from the beginning. This difference of opinion manifests itself as "neoliberalism" and "regulated capitalism (Egan, 2010). These two different approaches also determine the countries' attitudes towards cross-border mobility and European integration in the field of health. In the case of health services, there is a production process carried out by the public or private sector and the consumption of health services in order to protect or improve health (Mazgit, 1988).

Regulated capitalism includes market regulatory measures (state intervention), social market economy-social solidarity, welfare state and distribution policy in order to integrate social dimension into integration; social dialogue and social partnership. It supports the strengthening of the European Parliament and the participation of social groups in decision-making via increasing the powers of supranational institutions; facilitating decision-making processes; (Egan, 2010). The social rules of the member states, which have a long history and become a long-established tradition, form the basis of the social dimension of European integration (Dinan, 2005).

In terms of production, medical technology and pharmaceutical companies play an important role in Western economies (Freeman, 2000). Health systems are shaped by the economic, social, cultural and political structure of the society in which they live. Social and political values affect the preferences of the health system and play a decisive role on the health policies implemented, the institutions established and the types of services developed (Thomas, 2003). In the twentieth century, this power was generally the state that intervened in the field of health. The right to access to health has started to be seen as a defining element of democracy and citizenship rights. As a natural consequence of this, the vast majority of health expenditures are generally covered by public sources and health issues are generally handled within the public bureaucracy (Freeman, 2000).

European Community activities include contributing to the high level of health protection. In fact, domestic market practices also include social objectives for the protection of consumers and health (European Union, Directive 93/42 / EEC). Some directives even have the purpose of regulating or limiting market forces, like the 89/105 / EEC directive on price control and regulation in the pharmaceutical industry (Busse, Wissar, Berman, 2002). The change created by these pressures in the welfare state is multifaceted and continuous (Hay, Watson, Wincott, 1999).

Cross-border patient mobility has led to the interconnection between the economic and social systems of the member states and the European internal market, which is the basis of European economic integration (Busse, Wissar, Berman, 2002).

Mobility is one of the defining characteristics of European integration; because the European internal market, which is at the focal point of European integration, is based on four fundamental freedoms; free movement of goods, services, capital and persons. Cross-border mobility if the free movement of persons is based on moving from one Member State to another; If it is manifested by going to another region within the same country, that is interregional mobility. People seeking health care in this country, for example, tourists or long-term residents in that foreign country, do not fall within the scope of cross-border patient mobility because they are ill during their stay abroad (Gilnos, Baeten, 2006).

While the proportion of EU citizens traveling across borders is high (80%), the proportion of those traveling for health services (2-5%) among this group and the per capita expenditure on health tourism in the EU (EUR 2.75) are relatively low, cross-border patient mobility within the EU is expected to increase over time. Within the EU, the share of expenditures on cross-border patient mobility in public health expenditures is 1%. This corresponds to € 9.7 billion (European Union, 2008).

EU Welfare State Models and Health

The welfare state is one of the main features of all member states and the European social model, the patient is offered a certain level of safety net. In general, social security systems consider access to health care as a right within the borders of the country and reimburses the treatment they receive in their country (Jorens, 2002).

Member countries' health systems are financed by taxes or contributions from employees and employers. The fact that health services are financed in different ways brings together the coexistence of different political and economic actors, each of whom wishes to protect and develop their own interests (Freeman, 2000). An important part of health services other than individual interventions are social services (Kornai, Eggleston, 2001). In institutional terms, health systems are carried out as part of the overall social security system (Hervey, McHale, 2004).

Welfare states are nation states and national welfare states are among the main institutions of European social policy (Leibfried, 2000). With the regulations following the industrialization, concrete steps were taken in the social security system. The main feature of this period is the implementation of risk-specific and limited scope of insurance (Meryem & Alper, 2000).

Before giving examples of national health systems of European Union member countries and single insurance market in EU the the two main models of European Union i.e. The Conservative Welfare State Model and The Scandinavian or Social Democrat model will be defined and the differences will be given in this part of the study.

The protection of health and the provision of social security are among the duties of the welfare state. The welfare state has evolved in Europe with the development of the nation state in the historical process, and three basic models have emerged that differ in terms of financing and distribution of services. The welfare state is a structure that emerges in societies where the belief that the welfare of the individual is too important to be left to informal regulations and private initiatives (Briggs, 1961). According to Briggs's definition, the welfare state has three main functions: first, providing individuals and their families with minimum income security regardless of their employment or labor market situation; second, to a certain degree of confidence in the face of social risks, such as illness, unemployment, old age, which may lead to individual or familial problems; the third is to provide the best standards without discrimination to all citizens in the agreed social work areas.

The Scandinavian or Social Democrat Model

This model is basically financed by taxes as part of a "public service state", the principle of universality applies. In the liberal model, while cash aids are more dominant, in the social democratic model, the provision of social services by the state is important (Katrougalos, & Lazaridis, 2003). There are strong trade unions, participatory working relationships with a high degree of collective bargaining (Andersen, Gallie). The social democratic welfare states aim full employment, where the goal is to ensure that people rely on their own income and that they are less dependent on the welfare services and programs provided by the state (Gökbunar, Özdemir, & Uğur, 2008). For example, the US's model, which promotes personal flexibility, initiative and accountability and where the state intervention approach is accepted as negative is quite different from the European social model, there is no American social model (Dinan, 2005).

In the post-1970 period, the development boundaries of the European welfare state became questionable and debates on the necessity of restructuring in the welfare state came up (Koray, 2005). Opinions on the reduction of health costs and the limitation of state funding have led to requests for the withdrawal of the state from the health field (Moran, 1999).

The welfare concept in Europe is dynamic (Şenkal, 2007). Because welfare state practices in Europe are composed of compositions that emerge at different points on the axis of liberalism on one end and social democracy on the other. Different syntheses express the mix of different values such as liberal-social synthesis, market and welfare state, individual morality and social responsibility, competition and social solidarity, productivity and social security, depending on time and country. The liberal approach recognizes that citizenship consists mainly of fundamental rights and freedoms and political rights and sees the fulfillment of other needs as individual responsibility. The social-democratic approach places great responsibility on the state and political democracy in improving economic-social conditions (Koray, 2005).

The most frequently used classification of welfare states is Esping-Andersen's "Three Worlds of Welfare Capitalism" classification. Esping-Andersen analyzes the welfare state according to the total expenditure on social programs or the level of redistribution of the system; it also regulates the classification system according to whether the program is universal and that people can make a living without trusting the labor market (Esping-Andersen, Gallie, Hemerijck, & Myles, 2002).

The Conservative Welfare State (The Continental European Model)

This model is also referred to as the 'Continental European' model. It has a statist, corporatist (provided by social institutions) and a family-centered structure (Esping-Andersen, Gallie, Hemerijck, & Myles, 2002).

At the heart of this welfare model is social insurance, which is largely funded from employee and employer premiums and supported by the state in some countries by transferring funds from taxes. Non-state actors are effective in the organization and distribution of services (management, distribution of insurance funds and provision of services). In time, the union of actions and management between the aid funds established by trade unions and employers has been largely ensured and these funds have been allowed to maintain their existence together (Şenkal, & Sarıipek, 2007). In a conservative approach, the state intervenes to a minimum. In this respect, it differs from the individualist liberal model and the social democratic model that provides protection to the whole society (Gökbunar, Özdemir, & Uğur, 2008). The Conservative-Corporatist model depends on social class and status. A narrow space is left for private insurance coverage (Pestieau, 2006).

European Union and Single Insurance Market

With the Single Insurance Market of the European Union, it is aimed that both insurance companies and consumers to be free to use and purchase insurance products under the same conditions as local companies and consumers anywhere in the member countries by removing restrictions on the provision of insurance services at national borders. In Europe, before the European Single Insurance Market integration process, there are two different regulatory and supervisory philosophies called "Continental Model" and "Anglo Saxon Model (Ennsfellner, Dorfman, 1998). Insurance covering all European Countries also help EU countries citizens to be mobile withing the EU countries as well.

The insurance models are can be grouped as Continental Insurance Model and the Anglo Saxon Insurance Model. The definition, advantages and disadvantages of these two models can be summarized as follows;

Continental Insurance Model

The advantage of this model is to ensure the stability and transparency of the markets, but its disadvantage is that this stability is achieved through tight regulation and limited product diversity and low competition levels (Ennsfellner and Dorfman, 1998). The continental model has historically been applied in Germany, Austria, Italy, to some extent in France and in some other countries where controls for compulsory traffic insurance third party liability insurance premiums are made (Pickering and Matthews, 1997).

Anglo Saxon Insurance Model

It is a liberal approach that emphasizes the freedom of companies to work. According to this model, insurance regulation is more flexible and insurance companies can determine premiums and identify their own products without regulatory control. Drabbe (1994) states that the inspection of insurance products is done only once, once the product is marketed, but additional arrangements may be introduced to protect the policyholder, such as the execution of business rules. He suggested that each member state could find its own balance between regulation and consumer protection on the one hand, competition and the wider product range on the other, while improving the surveillance systems. As a result, establishing the European Union Single Insurance Market has required the unification of national insurance markets that differ not only in regulatory traditions but also in the philosophy of how to provide insurance (Ennsfellner and Dorfman, 1998). During the creation of the European Union Single Insurance Market throughout the European Commission, the European Commission adopted the Anglo-Saxon model by asserting that in the integration of the insurance It has supported.

Brittan (1990) mentions that establishing a single insurance market in the EU through the operation of insurance and reinsurance companies in any of the Member States and through the freedom of establishment (FOE-freedom of establishment) in the EU, or through freedom of service (FOS-freedom of service) should be completely free. On the other hand, Labilloy (2003), claims that the main purpose of the establishment of the Insurance Association in Europe is that the European insurance companies, independent from their own main member states to benefit from equal competition conditions in this large market and to be in a more competitive environment, which enables to provide consumers cheaper, diversified insurance products with quality. Drabbe (1994), stated that the primary objective of the member states in the single insurance market is to ensure that insurance companies fulfill their obligations to policyholders and the second objective is to strengthen the position of policyholders against the insurance sector. He argues that consumer protection is the primary objective, due to differences in insurance legislation between Member States. De Haan et al. (2009) states that all business lines are audited in France, Italy and Luxembourg, while in Belgium life insurance and compulsory motor third party liability insurance were audited wherelse in Netherlands only life insurance was audited.

Paleari (2018) in his study, where a comparative analysis of the complexity and variability of insurance systems against losses caused by natural disasters for residences in EU-28 countries; the results show that firstly, very high rates of insurance use are often associated with the direct inclusion of government into the program, at the same time, interim solutions were developed by many EU countries, and that it was not related whether volunteer or compulsory. Second finding is that as the link between insurance and risk reduction is not automatic, creative support measures are tested by EU-wide insurance programs and their success is often controversial and should be further investigated. Last, he found that the form of government compensation does not directly affect insurance penetration rates, but the certain degree of coordination degree between insurance companies and only after state compensation has an advantage of improving effective allocation of financial resources in risk management.

Cummins (2016), as a result of his study investigating the effects of competition in the EU life insurance market on the soundness of the insurance industry, found that competition increased the robustness of the European Union life insurance markets in the period 1999-2011. The strengthening effect of competition is greater for financially weak insurance companies. Competition, measured by the Boone indicator, provides evidence across countries about the relationship between robustness and competition in the life insurance market. As a result of the analysis of 10 European Union (EU) life insurance markets with Boone in the post-regulation period of 1999-2011, the results measure the competition based on the reallocation of profit from inefficient insurers to efficient ones, the results show that efficiency is the mechanism by which competition contributes to insurance solvency. The strengthening effect of competition is greater for healthy insurers than for healthy insurers.

Malafronte (2015) provides new empirical evidence on the nature and determinants of disclosure practices in the European insurance market in the period 2005-2010 in his survey of disclosure practices by insurance companies. The main results show that insurers tend to invest in the amount of risk information rather than the disclosure quality of the annual report, that the risk information is directed at highly financially trained people and that investment in quality requires less resources than needed. Furthermore, the analysis also shows that insurer level characteristics significantly affect the amount of risk information disclosed in terms of size and technical provisions and country level variables. In years affected by the financial crisis, the level of risk disclosure increases as insurance companies use disclosures as a means to ensure their independence from the global financial crisis.

In another study, (Eling & Schaper, 2017) found that liberalization and widespread economic changes had a major impact on the business environment of European life insurance companies over the last decade, and the multi-stage study by Fried, Schmidt, and Yaisawarng (1999) to determine the impact of the changing environment on the productivity and efficiency of European life insurance companies. The results of the data analysis show that, when 970 life insurance companies from 14 European countries are considered, the main factors of productivity are economic, capital market and insurance market conditions. Although there was no technical change in the European life insurance sector, an increase in productivity was observed in the 2002-2013 period, which can be explained by more challenging business conditions in the 2000s. The results emphasize the need to control the business environment in efficiency studies across countries. Otherwise, the efficiency of companies operating under less favorable business conditions is underestimated. Moreover, it suggests that a complex work environment can probably take into account technical downtime and reflect significant technical efficiency.

NATIONAL HEALTH SYSTEMS OF EUROPEAN UNION MEMBER COUNTRIES

European countries in 1950's, the first example of welfare states is the Christian centrist group of Germany, Austria, the Netherlands and Belgium. In this group, the welfare state offers generous social achievements, but its scope is average or above average, but it is not universal. In the social democratic group led by Sweden and Norway, the welfare state has developed almost universally, but the social achievements offered are limited at low or moderate levels (Cousins, 2007). During the period from 1950 to the mid-1970s, with the effect of favorable external economic conditions, economic growth and welfare state practices were carried out together with Keynesian economic policies within the market economy and social expenditures increased the share of GDP (Koray, 2005)

Southern European countries differ from others with low social spending levels (average 21.7%). Expenditure focuses on pensions and health expenditures (40% and 25% respectively), with little share in welfare services (Cousins, 2007).

The way in which health funds operate is either determined by national legislation (Austria, France, Germany, Luxembourg and the Netherlands) or strictly controlled by the statutory regulations of the state. In order to collectively fund contracts with service providers, health funds use incomes from members' premium payments (Saltman, 2004).

The national health systems of countries may have different characteristics, which are given below.

Belgium

Belgium has adopted the Gent system. These funds are unique non-profit organizations and the board of directors is partly selected by fund members (except France) (Saltman, 2004).

Netherlands

Private health insurance has three main functions: creating an alternative for statutory health insurance (Netherlands); providing services for risks not covered by social insurance by completing services not provided by statutory insurance (for example, some dental treatments) provides assurance in addition to people's existing health

Table 1. EUROPEAN UNION - List of exporters for the selected service

Exporters	Exported value in 2013	Exported value in 2014	Exported value in 2015	Exported value in 2016	Exported value in 2017
European Union (EU 28) Aggregation	74,204,915	75,492,541	60,751,916	64,817,979	61,056,750
United Kingdom	30,805,463	31,395,497	22,632,547	23,803,868	19,307,612
Ireland	11,209,864	11,573,094	11,441,133	10,224,160	10,891,032
Germany	8,617,036	10,612,543	9,519,120	9,738,560	9,760,799
France	9,627,449	6,305,965	3,913,897	7,477,586	6,622,057
Luxembourg	3,571,623	3,819,665	3,231,820	3,247,661	3,598,653
Spain	2,039,410	2,165,229	2,098,354	2,102,794	2,304,838
Italy	2,404,672	2,474,092	2,017,392	1,995,276	1,892,533
Belgium	1,909,291	1,899,882	1,593,729	1,587,328	1,879,773
Netherlands		1,388,958	1,030,878	1,396,848	1,281,028
Sweden	539,758	612,156	627,423	574,527	716,656
Austria	1,153,807	934,020	530,134	517,679	487,663
Greece	553,270	573,016	342,591	334,832	484,174
Poland	333,638	257,164	418,099	460,960	467,709
Denmark	273,813	324,095	268,619	300,497	322,049
Czech Republic	269,085	275,924	229,111	247,001	259,269
Portugal	131,446	120,733	139,742	132,738	147,202
Cyprus	25,227	23,881	26,618	74,112	128,163
Malta	82,320	88,466	80,962	95,129	117,743
Slovenia	92,411	105,873	104,918	102,983	113,832
Finland	129,617	98,851	102,034	101,766	103,836
Slovakia	41,558	56,386	57,228	39,932	59,469
Romania	128,005	78,547	84,898	69,250	45,902
Hungary	38,885	30,260	27,079	26,108	29,024
Croatia	32,813	32,141	20,871	20,256	22,226
Estonia	4,116	3,980	3,105	3,982	5,027
Latvia	29,210	2,653	2,218	3,318	4,326
Bulgaria	161,128	229,918	206,731	137,943	3,347
Lithuania		9,552	665	885	808

Source: ITC, UNCTAD, WTO trade in services Unit: US Dollar thousand

insurance (Wasem, etal, 2004). Supplementary health insurance is a form of insurance that is often adopted in tax-financed health systems to increase "consumer choice seçim and access to different health services in health care (Mossialos, Thomson, 2004).

United Kingdom

The British national health system was established on the principle of free provision of health care (Hervey and McHale, 2004). Contracted service providers may be from public or private sector (Freeman, 2000). In the UK, the state intervened to protect workers against social risks for a long time. Apart from the Poverty Act of 1601, a law was adopted in 1897, which envisages the responsibility of the employer in the event of an occupational accident. The National Insurance Law, which entered into force in 1911, introduced regulations in the fields of sickness, disability and unemployment insurance. In subsequent laws, widows and orphans were attached monthly. In terms of the management of social insurance, the British system has given the public authorities broad powers. The Beveridge report, published in 1942, was the source of radical change (Güzel ve Okur, 2002). The liberal welfare state model was developed by William Beveridge in 1942 by the Commission under the Beveridge Report. It is based on efforts to put it into practice after World War II. The model focuses on groups that have no or very low income; it provides minimum social security. The state is taking measures for individuals who cannot reach the "state of well-being ıyla through their efforts; depending on the need to prove that social assistance offers. Social services are not developed outside health and education. The aim of social programs is to strengthen the market and market entry, by providing low minimum income for everyone or by actively contributing to private welfare programs. As a result of this model, which opposes the direct intervention of the state for social welfare, a society structure divided into two classes emerges. England after 1980 is considered to be the representative of this model within the EU (Koray, 2005). Social policy in the UK focuses on reconciling the universal social rights offered to citizens and the effectiveness of the market (Johnson, 1987) Trade unions are not strong, labor relations are not coordinated as in the Scandinavian model, wage bargaining is not centralized (Esping-Andersen, 2002).

France

In France, the law of 1928, which is the basis of social insurance legislation, formed the roof of the French social insurance system until the general regulation in 1945. Prior to this, although there are special regulations for some occupational groups, the practices are seen as scattered and unsuccessful (Güzel, Okur & Caniklioğlu, 2002).

Germany

The first social insurance system, the German Social Insurance System, was established by laws enacted between 1880-1890. The unique conditions of this period, Germany's higher level of industrialization compared to other European countries, the increase in the number of workers living in poverty in cities, the economic conditions of 1877, and the living conditions that became difficult with the social crisis, led Otto von Bismarck's traditional repression policy and at the same time, by providing the state with a social quality of workers to integrate with the system and to neutralize the socialist thought currents. Social services in Germany depend on the business relationship rather than on the right to citizenship (Johnson, 1987).

Spain

Spain is a country receiving retired migration, and the number of long-term residents (more than three months a year) in Spain is increasing. The coordination of social security systems and Schengen Agreement have been effective in increasing mobility within the scope of Regulation 1408/71. The retirees who settle in Spain generally come from the richer Nordic countries (Scandinavian countries, France, Germany). There is a group of retirees called 'fake tourists' or 'floating population', who have been in Spain for more than three months and have not registered and formalized their status. In this group, they enter and exit between Spain and their own countries and use their homes in Spain as their second homes. Pensioners who do not officially document their long-term residence in Spain can receive emergency health care with the European Health Insurance Card when they need health care (Rosenmöller & Lluch, 2006).

FUTURE RESEARCH DIRECTIONS

It is recommended to set the international rules and ethical norms which will be accepted by all parties involved including the patients receiving and sending country of health tourism.

Furthermore, the reasons why patients seek care outside countries must be investigated as well. Patients receiving health care in other countries and returning bank to their home countries must be researched as well whether they are followed up afterwards in their home countries and if they were satisfied with the health service given abroad.

CONCLUSION

World health export or tourism export is important for all countries, of which globally the amount of health export exceeds nearly hundred billion dollars. The health tourism is different from other tourism sectors as the well being of the medical tourist is very important not only during the medical treatment, also after returning home country the necessary precautions must be arranged to take care of the medical tourist. Furthermore, the governments, while motivating health tourism in their countries for foreigners well being, local residents well being must not be neglected. Health is a basic human right and every human being health is the responsibility of states.

European Union countries, with free movement of the citizens among countries have increased mobility of patients as well, as the EU policy permits citizens to get health service from any member country. The tourism import countries must provide the medical tourists, safe and secure environment, the legislation, quality of health service, accreditation and certification of health tourism premises. Health tourism can contribute to the country's welfare, unlike other tourism areas, it may not be seasonal.

The different national health systems adaptation to the one single insurance and health system is not easy as they all have different aspects, therefore health directory was not accepted easily by all countries. As the cost of health care is more expensive in old member countries however it is cheaper in new member countries, the movement of patients are from high cost old member countries to low cost new member countries.

As in Hudson et al (2011) their literature review suggests that policies covering thee ethical, legal, social aspects of the medical tourism is very important. The data available is not reliable yet however especially the countries giving medical service must be very cautious.

Ethical issues have to be covered before it is too late, as it has been mentioned already by Norea et al's publication in the Bulletion of the World Health Organisation, that not sufficient information was given to the (Crooks, 2010) and that low-middle income local citizens organs or surrogacy services were sold to foreign patients (Crush and Maswikwa, 2012) and (Whittaker, 2010). Lastly, an Australian boy was abondened by his Australian parents, born with down syndrome from a surrogate mother in Thailand (Guardian, 2014). As the mobility increases, to avoid such cases, the policies covering all aspects of medical tourism must be prepared and be accepted by all parties involved.

Furthermore, the estimates are not reliable, therefore a standard reporting system, which will distinguish medical tourist from others must be set to get reliable data for health tourism.

REFERENCES

Aktan, C. C., & Işık, A. K. (2010). *Sağlık Hizmetlerinin Sunumu ve Alternatif Yöntemler*. Retrieved from http://www.canaktan.org/ekonomi/saglik-degisim-caginda/pdf-aktan/sunum-alternatif.pdf

Bertinato, L., & Canapero, M. (n.d.). *Health Tourism-the Growth Phenomenon.* Asian HHM. Retrieved at https://www.asianhhm.com/healthcare-management/health-tourism

Bilgili, Ö. (2008). *Özel Sağlık Kurum ve Kuruluşları Personeli: İstihdamı ve Sosyal Güvenlikleri.* Unpublished doctoral dissertation, Dokuz Eylül Üniversitesi, İzmir, Turkey.

Bookman, M. (2007). *Medical tourism in developing countries.* Springer. doi:10.1057/9780230605657

Briggs, A. (1961). The welfare state in historical perspective. *European Journal of Sociology. Archives Européennes de Sociologie*, *2*(2), 221–258. doi:10.1017/S0003975600000412

Brittan, L. (1990). European insurance in a single market. *Tijdschrift voor Economie en Management*, *35*(4), 411–423.

Brouwer, W., Van Exel, J., Hermans, B., & Stoop, A. (2003). Should I stay or should I go? Waiting lists and cross-border care in the Netherlands. *Health Policy (Amsterdam)*, *63*(3), 289–298. doi:10.1016/S0168-8510(02)00120-3 PMID:12595128

Busse, R., Wismar, M., & Berman, P. C. (Eds.). (2002). *The European Union and health services: the impact of the single European market on member states* (Vol. 50). IOS Press.

Carrera, P. M., & Bridges, J. F. (2006). Globalization and healthcare: Understanding health and medical tourism. *Expert Review of Pharmacoeconomics & Outcomes Research*, *6*(4), 447–454. doi:10.1586/14737167.6.4.447 PMID:20528514

Connell, J. (2006). Medical tourism: Sea, sun, sand and… surgery. *Tourism Management*, *27*(6), 1093–1100. doi:10.1016/j.tourman.2005.11.005

Connell, J. (2013). Contemporary medical tourism: Conceptualisation, culture and commodification. *Tourism Management*, *34*, 1–13. doi:10.1016/j.tourman.2012.05.009

Cortez, N. (2008). Patient without borders: The emerging global market for patients and the evolution of modern health care. *Industrial Law Journal*, *83*, 71.

Cousins, M. (Ed.). (2007). *Welfare Policy and Poverty*. Combat Poverty Agency.

Crush, J., Chikanda, A., & Maswikwa, B. (2012). Patients without borders: Medical tourism and medical migration in Southern Africa.

De Arellano, A. B. R. (2007). Patients without borders: The emergence of medical tourism. *International Journal of Health Services*, *37*(1), 193–198. doi:10.2190/4857-468G-2325-47UU PMID:17436992

De Haan, J., Oosterloo, S., & Schoenmaker, D. (2009). *European financial markets and institutions*. Cambridge University Press. doi:10.1017/CBO9780511806230

Dinan, D. (2005). *Ever closer union: an introduction to European integration*. Palgrave Macmillan.

Drabbe, H. (1994). The Internal Market for Insurance: A Reality? *The Geneva Papers on Risk and Insurance. Issues and Practice*, *19*(2), 135–143. doi:10.1057/gpp.1994.11

Egan, M. (2010). The single market. *European Union Politics*, *3*, 258–274.

Eling, M., & Schaper, P. (2017). Under pressure: How the business environment affects productivity and efficiency of European life insurance companies. *European Journal of Operational Research*, *258*(3), 1082–1094. doi:10.1016/j.ejor.2016.08.070

Ennsfellner, K. C., & Dorfman, M. S. (1998). The Transition to a Single Insurance Market in the European Union. *Risk Management & Insurance Review*, *1*(2), 35–53. doi:10.1111/j.1540-6296.1998.tb00071.x

Erdem, R., & Yıldırım, H. H. (2003). Sağlık hizmetlerinde vekalet ilişkisi ve arzın talep yaratması problemi. *Hacettepe Sağlık İdaresi Dergisi*, *6*(2), 3–26.

Esping-Andersen, G., Gallie, D., Hemerijck, A., & Myles, J. (2002). *Why we need a new welfare state*. USA: Oxford University Press. doi:10.1093/0199256438.001.0001

European Council. (2008). Commission staff working document - Accompanying document to the proposal for a Directive of the European Parliament and of the Council on the application of patients' rights in cross-border healthcare - Impact assessment. Retrieved from https://eur-lex.europa.eu/legal-content/EN/ALL/?uri=CELEX:52008SC2163

Flower, J. (2006). Five-star hospitals. *Strategy and Business*, *42*, 66.

Freeman, R. (2000). *The politics of health in Europe*. Manchester University Press.

Fried, H. O., Schmidt, S. S., & Yaisawarng, S. (1999). Incorporating the operating environment into a nonparametric measure of technical efficiency. *Journal of Productivity Analysis*, *12*(3), 249–267. doi:10.1023/A:1007800306752

Glinos, I. A., & Baeten, R. (2006). A literature review of cross-border patient mobility in the European Union. *Observatoire social européen, Europe for patients*.

Gökbunar, R., Özdemir, H., & Uğur, A. (2008). Küreselleşme kıskacındaki refah devletinde sosyal refah harcamaları.

Güzel, A., Okur, A. R., & Caniklioğlu, N. (2002). Sosyal güvenlik hukuku.

Hanefeld, J., Horsfall, D., Lunt, N., & Smith, R. (2013). Medical tourism: A cost or benefit to the NHS? *PLoS One*, *8*(10), e70406. doi:10.1371/journal.pone.0070406 PMID:24204556

Hay, C., Watson, M., & Wincott, D. (1999). *Globalisation, European integration and the persistence of European social models*. Sussex European Institute, University of Sussex.

Hermans, H. E. (2000). Cross-border health care in the European Union: Recent legal implications of 'Decker and Kohll'. *Journal of Evaluation in Clinical Practice*, *6*(4), 431–439. doi:10.1046/j.1365-2753.2000.00250.x PMID:11133126

Herrick, D. M. (2007). *Medical tourism: Global competition in health care*. Heal Wheel India. Retrieved from http://www.heal-wheel-india.com/white-pappers/Medical-Tourism-Global-Competition-in-Health-Care-NCPA-Report.pdf

Hervey, T. K., & McHale, J. V. (2004). *Health law and the European Union*. Cambridge University Press. doi:10.1017/CBO9780511617553

Heung, V. C., Kucukusta, D., & Song, H. (2011). Medical tourism development in Hong Kong: An assessment of the barriers. *Tourism Management*, *32*(5), 995–1005. doi:10.1016/j.tourman.2010.08.012

Hopkins, L., Labonté, R., Runnels, V., & Packer, C. (2010). Medical tourism today: What is the state of existing knowledge? *Journal of Public Health Policy*, *31*(2), 185–198. doi:10.1057/jphp.2010.10 PMID:20535101

Hudson, N., Culley, L., Blyth, E., Norton, W., Rapport, F., & Pacey, A. (2011). Cross-border reproductive care: A review of the literature. *Reproductive Biomedicine Online*, *22*(7), 673–685. doi:10.1016/j.rbmo.2011.03.010 PMID:21498121

Johnson, N. (1987). *The welfare state in transition: The theory and practice of welfare pluralism*. Univ of Massachusetts Press.

Johnson, T. J., & Garman, A. N. (2010). Impact of medical travel on imports and exports of medical services. *Health Policy (Amsterdam)*, *98*(2-3), 171–177. doi:10.1016/j.healthpol.2010.06.006 PMID:20619919

Jorens, Y. (2002). The right to health care across borders. In *The impact of EU law on health care systems* (Vol. 39, pp. 83–122). Peter Lang.

Katrougalos, G., & Lazaridis, G. (2003). *Southern European welfare states*. New York: Problems, Challenges and Prospects. doi:10.1057/9780230523722

Kher, U. (2006). *Outsourcing your heart.* Time. Retrieved from http://www.time.com/time/magazine/article/0,9171,1196429,00.html

Koray, M. (2005). *Sosyal Politika, İmge Kitapevi, Güncellenmiş ve Gözden Geçirilmiş 3*. Ankara: Baskı.

Kornai, J., & Eggleston, K. (2001). *Welfare, choice and solidarity in transition: Reforming the health sector in Eastern Europe*. Cambridge University Press. doi:10.1017/CBO9780511492464

Labilloy, B. (2003). *European Insurance Regulation: New Opportunities for Insurers and Consumers*. Brussels: CEA.

Leibfried, S., & Pierson, P. (1992). Prospects for social Europe. *Politics & Society*, *20*(3), 333–366. doi:10.1177/003232929202000305

Malafronte, I., Porzio, C., & Starita, M. G. (2016). The nature and determinants of disclosure practices in the insurance industry: Evidence from European insurers. *International Review of Financial Analysis*, *45*, 367–382. doi:10.1016/j.irfa.2015.02.003

Mazgit, İ. (1998). *Ekonomik kalkınma sürecinde Türkiyede sağlık sektörünün yeniden yapılanması* [Doctoral dissertation]. DEÜ Sosyal Bilimleri Enstitüsü.

Mazzaschi, A. (2011). Surgeon and safari: Producing valuable bodies in Johannesburg. *Signs (Chicago, Ill.)*, *36*(2), 303–312. doi:10.1086/655941 PMID:21114075

Meryem, K., & Alper, T. (2000). *Sosyal Politika. Baskı*. Ekim.

Moran, M. (1999). Governing the health care state: a comparative study of the United Kingdom, the United States, and Germany. Manchester University Press.

Mossialos, E., Thomson, S., & World Health Organization. (2004). *Voluntary health insurance in the European Union*. Copenhagen: WHO Regional Office for Europe.

Noree, T., Hanefeld, J., & Smith, R. (2014). UK medical tourists in Thailand: They are not who you think they are. *Globalization and Health, 10*(1), 29. doi:10.1186/1744-8603-10-29 PMID:24885204

Noree, T., Hanefeld, J., & Smith, R. (2016). Medical tourism in Thailand: A cross-sectional study. *Bulletin of the World Health Organization, 94*(1), 30–36. doi:10.2471/BLT.14.152165 PMID:26769994

Olalı, H., & Timur, A. (1988). Turizmin Türk Ekonomisindeki Yeri, İzmir: Ofis Ticaret Matbaacılık San. Ltd. Şti.

Paleari, S. (2019). Disaster risk insurance: A comparison of national schemes in the EU-28. *International Journal of Disaster Risk Reduction, 35*, 101059. doi:10.1016/j.ijdrr.2018.12.021

Patients Beyond Borders. (2019). *Medical Tourism Statistics and Facts.* Retrieved from https://patientsbeyondborders.com/medical-tourism-statistics-facts

Pestieau, P. (2006). *The welfare state in the European Union: Economic and social perspectives.* Oxford University Press.

Pickering, J. F. & Matthews, D. (1997). The evolution of Rules for the Single European Market in Insurance. NIESR.

Rosenmöller, M., & Lluch, M. (2006). Meeting the needs of long-term residents in Spain. Patient Mobility in the European Union, 59.

Sağlık Bakanlığı. 2019. Sağlık Turizmi Nedir? Retrieved from http://www.saturk.gov.tr/index.phphttps://sagliktourizmi.saglik.gov.tr/TR,175/saglik-turizmi-hakkinda.html

Saltman, R. B. (2004). Social health insurance in perspective: the challenge of sustaining stability.

Şenkal, A. (2007). *Küreselleşme sürecinde sosyal politika.* Alfa Basım Yayım Dağıtım.

Şenkal, A., & Sarıipek, D. B. (2007). Avrupa Birliği'nin Karşılaştırmalı Refah Modelleri ve Sosyal Politikada Devletin Değişen Rolü. *Kocaeli Üniversitesi Sosyal Bilimler Dergisi*, (14), 146-175.

Snyder, J., & Crooks, V. A. (2010). Medical tourism and bariatric surgery: More moral challenges. *The American Journal of Bioethics, 10*(12), 28–30. doi:10.1080/15265161.2010.528510 PMID:21161839

Thaiwebsites.com. 2019. *Cost of Medical Treatment in Bangkok.* Retrieved from http://www.thaiwebsites.com/cost-medical-treatment.asp

The Guardian. 2014. Baby Gammy may be given Australian citizenship, government suggests. Retrieved from http://www.theguardian.com/world/2014/aug/04/baby-gammy-australian-citizenship-government-suggests

Thomas, R. K. (2003). *Society and health: sociology for health professionals.* Springer Science & Business Media.

Turner, L. (2008). Cross-border dental care:'dental tourism'and patient mobility. *British Dental Journal, 204*(10), 553–554. doi:10.1038j.bdj.2008.403 PMID:18500297

World Tourism Organization and European Travel Commission, UNWTO. (2018). *Exploring Health Tourism – Executive Summary.* Retrieved from https://www.e-unwto.org/doi/pdf/10.18111/9789284420308

UNWTO. (n.d.). [Conference Note]. In *Proceedings of the 22nd Session of the UNWTO General Assembly.* Academic Press.

Urry, J. (2002). *The tourist gaze.* London: Sage Publications.

Wasem, J., Greß, S., & Okma, K. G. (2004). The role of private health insurance in social health insurance countries.

Whittaker, A., & Speier, A. (2010). "Cycling overseas": Care, commodification, and stratification in cross-border reproductive travel. *Medical Anthropology, 29*(4), 363–383. doi:10.1080/01459740.2010.501313 PMID:21082483

World Health Organization. (2006). Constitution of the World Health Organization, 45th Edition of Basic Documents.

KEY TERMS AND DEFINITIONS

Health Tourism: (travel) Activity helps wellbeing. Health tourism covers both subtypes tourisms i.e. wellness and medical tourism. In other words, health tourism covers both mental and spiritual health via medical and wellness-based tourism.

Medical Tourism: The second subtype of tourism is the medical tourism, which covers diagnosis, cure, reatments, preventation etc.

Wellness Tourism: The first subtype of tourism is wellness tourism which covers items like healthy eating, fitness, relaxation, etc.

Section 2

Chapter 5
On Health Expenditure and Income Inequality

Orhan Torul
https://orcid.org/0000-0002-1251-1022
Boğaziçi University, Turkey

ABSTRACT

This study investigates the relationship between health care expenditure and income inequality empirically. Using data from a large panel of countries covering a sizeable period of time, how level and composition of health care expenditures correlate with income inequality is studied via the panel data fixed effects estimation methodology. These estimations yield several robust findings. First, there is a significant positive correlation between income inequality and reliance on private resources for health care financing. Second, there exists a significant negative correlation between health care expenditure per capita and income inequality. Third, there is a significant negative correlation between income inequality and health care expenditure as a share of GDP. Next, this study analyzes a select group of well-established democracies with developed economies to detect if health expenditure and income inequality variables correlate with public beliefs and preferences. Empirical analyses reveal that indeed belief and preferences accord well with policy choices.

INTRODUCTION

Since late 1970s, economic inequalities have been on the rise globally. A large body of literature has been discussing this upward trend via the evolution in income inequality measures.[1] Recent work by Piketty (2015) documents that the upward time trend in income inequality is not secular, but coupled with ever-increasing

DOI: 10.4018/978-1-7998-2329-2.ch005

wealth inequality. Figure 1 illustrates these developments by reporting the evolution of top income and wealth percentile share ratios in a select group of countries, and demonstrates that income and wealth concentration has already reached alarming levels in many different parts of the world.[2]

Advances in the study of economic inequality, along with higher-quality micro-level data sets have drawn considerable attention on the interaction between the distribution of economic variables, and numerous other economic and political subjects.[3] Access to health care is inherently affected by the rise in economic inequalities, since in most parts of the world households' private health care coverage is rather limited, either due to insufficient fiscal capacity and/or ideological health policy choices. As such, in order to have a comprehensive understanding of global analysis of universal health coverage, it is imperative to explore the historical and actual linkages between economic inequality and health care expenditure variables.

This study intends to contribute to research front on this end by investigating cross-country correlations between income inequality and the most objective and cross-country-comparable health care variable: expenditure on health care, along with its public versus private composition, share in GDP and its average per capita value. In particular, using a large panel data set covering over 150 countries and 20 years, I study associations between income inequality, and the level and composition of health expenditure variables, along with the fraction of GDP devoted to health care expenditure and health care expenditure per person. My estimations via panel-data fixed-effect regressions first reveal a robust and positive correlation between income inequality and reliance on private resources for health care financing: countries where health care provision is predominantly privately financed are also high-income inequality countries. Second, my estimation results document a robust negative correlation between health care expenditure per capita and income inequality: countries that engage in higher expenditure on health care services are also more frequently low-inequality countries, and as such, when low public health care provision is coupled with low overall health spending, higher income inequality emerges. Third, I document that the fraction of health care expenditure to GDP correlates negatively income inequality: low-inequality countries succeed in devoting a higher fraction of their GDP to health care provision. I verify that these findings are robust over variable specifications and methodological choices. These robust findings signal that if public health care provision is low in level, its dismal implications on more pronounced income inequality is more than probable.

The fact that these robust findings come from a large panel of countries covering a long time-span is of particular value, since previous studies on the subject tend to concentrate on variations in rather small samples: either via a limited spatial or time span. As such, the external validity of findings from these earlier studies are not without valid concern. The panel data set I rely on my econometric estimations cover a heterogeneous body of countries from all over the globe, and it does so for a broad period of time. Accordingly, the results from this heterogeneous cluster of countries and time series observations pave the way for a broader understanding on the link between health care spending level and composition and income inequality.

Next, I concentrate on a select group of well-established democracies to detect if health expenditure and income inequality variables correlate with public beliefs and preferences. My findings reveal that indeed this is the case, and belief and preferences accord well with policy choices. These findings indicate that a thorough understanding of health care expenditure variations is to be considered together with public beliefs and preferences. These novel findings shed light on why health expenditure variables exhibit the immense heterogeneity in the data.

The rest of the paper is organized as follows: in the Literature Review section, I review the related studies literature; in the Data and Methodology section, I describe the data and methodology I use throughout my analyses; in the Results section, I present and discuss my findings; in the Solutions and Recommendations section, I discuss methods to tackle observed problems; in the Future Research Directions section, I discuss ways to complement and improve my empirical results; and the Conclusion section offers my concluding remarks.

LITERATURE REVIEW

As discussed briefly, the rise in economic inequalities has resulted in a rich body of studies in the economics literature. These efforts resulted in several canonical books (Atkinson, 2015; Stiglitz, 2012; Milanovic, 2016; Piketty, 2015), technological and policy reports (Narayan et al., 2018; Alvaredo et al., 2018) and numerous top-notch academic articles (Abbott and Gallipoli, 2016; Aizer, 2014; Albanesi, 2007; Arawatari and Ono, 2013; Bavetta et al., 2017; Björklund et al., 2012; Blundell, 2014; Chetty et al., 2014; Chetty, et al, 2014; Fisher et al., 2014; Jerrim and Macmillan, 2015; Kerr, 2014; Rustichini and Vostroknutov, 2014). These studies explore underlying foundations of economic inequalities and attribute the rise in global economic inequality mainly to i) strong intergenerational transmission of education, income, and wealth; ii) public policy choices (e.g. taxation and redistribution, provision of public education and health care, …) and their resultant implications; iii) skill-biased technological progress and its resultant earnings premium; iv) assortative mating and its subsequent implications on the concentration of income and wealth; v) political connections between high-income agents, their lobbyists and public officers and representatives. These findings all point out to the fact that economic inequality is a multi-layered subject and is to be evaluated carefully and multidimensionally in order not to miss first-order channels and mechanisms.

Figure 1. Top 1% Income and wealth share by country

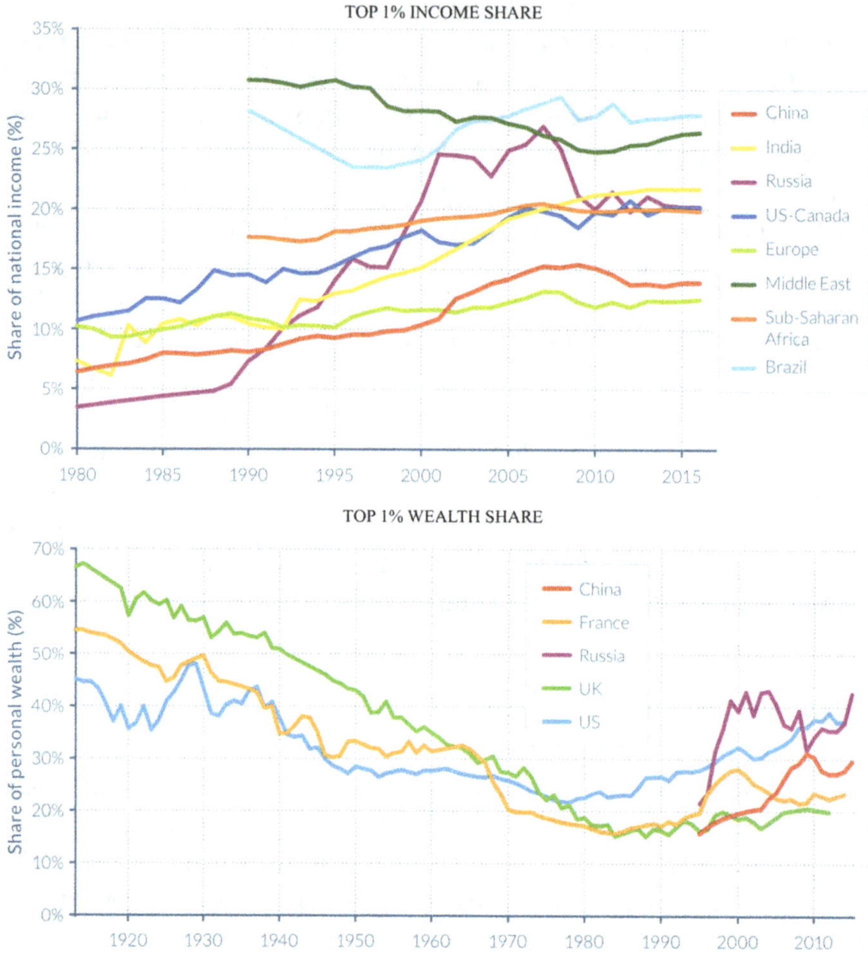

In order to consolidate findings by diverse analyses on different countries, a special issue at the *Review of Economic Dynamics* (*RED*): Cross-Sectional Facts for Macroeconomists thoroughly unveils cross-country similarities and differences in the evolution of economic inequalities by relying on cross-country comparable standardized methodology. In this special issue, Heathcote, et al. (2010), Brzozowski et al. (2010), Blundell and Etheridge (2010), Fuchs-Schündeln et al. (2010), Jappelli and Pistaferri (2010), Pijoan-Mas and Sánchez-Marcos (2010), Gorodnichenko et al. (2010), Binelli and Attanasio (2010), and Domeij and Flodén (2010) investigate inequality in the United States over 1980-2006, Canada over 1978-2006, the United Kingdom over 1978-2005, Germany over 1983-2003, Italy over 1987-2006, Spain over 1985-1996, Russia over 1998-2005, Mexico over 1989-2002 and Sweden over

1990-2001, respectively.[4] Most of these papers demonstrate increasing income inequality for these select group of countries.

Academic studies investigating the link between income inequality and health care are limited both in number and in content.[5] Among these rare attempts, Kawachi and Kennedy (1997) discuss socio-economic determinants of access to health care, and Kawachi and Kennedy (1999) study how income inequality relates to health quality, Shi and Starfield (2000) rely on surveys to explore the link between income inequality and primary care, along with individual morbidity as measured by self-rated health status, and Kondo et al. (2009) conduct a meta-analysis on income inequality and health quality. A burgeoning literature on health economics scrutinizes the link between individual health quality and care and income inequality (Wong et al., 2019), however none of these studies rely on cross-country data, and as such, the external validity of their findings is subject to concerns. This paper, by relying on up-to-date panel data estimation techniques aims to contribute to research frontier by delivering robust and cross-border-valid econometric findings.

DATA AND METHODOLOGY

Data

In order to investigate the interaction between health care spending and income inequality, I retrieve data from the World Bank Development Indicators data base. World Bank Development Indicators (WDI) is the World Bank's premier compilation of cross-country comparable data on numerous subjects, including but not limited to aggregate economic statistics, government statistics, education and health care spending statistics, and income inequality statistics. The data base contains 1,600-time series indicators for 217 economies and more than 40 country groups, spanning over 50 years for some of the variables. For my analyses, I rely on a number of different variables, though I pay particular attention to the following variables: i) Health Care Expenditure Per Capita (in Purchasing Power Parity (PPP) Adjusted International Dollars) to proxy for the how much per person health care spending different countries invest; ii) Private Health Care Expenditure to Total Health Care Expenditure Ratio to proxy for the composition of overall health care spending for countries of interest; iii) Health Care Expenditure to GDP ratio to proxy for what percentage of output is devoted to health care services, and iv) Gini Coefficient of Income Distribution to proxy for the degree of income inequality.[6] Especially cross-country comparable income inequality estimates for developing countries are only recent, and as such, instead of focusing on one country at a time, I rely only on panel data estimation techniques given data limitations.

In order to provide a general overview of the main variables of interest, in Table 1, 2, 3 and 4, I report summary statistics (in 2010) for total health care expenditure per capita, private health care expenditure to total health care expenditure ratio, total health care expenditure to GDP ratio and Gini coefficient, respectively.

Table 1 demonstrates that total health care expenditure per capita varies immensely over country groups in 2010: while average health care expenditure in Sub-Saharan Africa is a mere 243.06 PPP-adjusted international dollars, the same estimate in North America 6078.78, i.e. 25 times that of Sub-Saharan African countries.[7] As standard deviation estimates reveal, while within-group total health care expenditure per capita variations are limited mainly in low-spending country groups, country groups that spend more on average also exhibit high degrees of within-group variations. A comparison of North America or Europe and Central Asia with Sub-Saharan Africa or South Asia clearly demonstrates these patterns.

Table 2 shows that the way different country groups finance their health care expenditure also exhibits an immense variation.[8] While South Asian countries predominantly rely on private resources for health care expenditures (with an average of 59% and a median of 69%), East Asian and Pacific country rely substantially less on private resources for health care financing (with an average of 30% and a median of 26%). An investigation of within-group variations reveals that there is immense heterogeneity in all country groups, which does not necessarily depend either on average private-to-total spending ratio or total health care expenditure per capita. Instead, lowest within-group variation is exhibited in the Latin America and Caribbean country group. Accordingly, it is reasonable to conclude that there does not appear a single sufficient statistic to predict the reliance on private resources for health care financing.

Table 3 shows how much different country groups devote to the provision of health care services (as a share of their respective GDP). Table 3 shows that the North

Table 1. Descriptive statistics of total health care expenditure per capita

Region	*N*	Mean	Median	Std. Dev.	Minimum	Maximum
East Asia and Pacific	28	823.11	287.01	1048.90	63.21	3593.08
Europe and Central Asia	51	2227.17	1620.20	1662.56	120.51	6089.70
Latin America and Caribbean	32	752.69	680.14	400.16	150.35	1670.42
Middle East and North Africa	20	1099.71	1078.72	749.30	108.00	2290.24
North America	2	6078.78	6078.78	2646.15	4207.67	7949.90
South Asia	8	243.06	138.95	290.92	64.17	948.33
Sub-Saharan Africa	46	206.69	114.73	228.74	24.14	863.70
Total	187	1103.33	584.29	1384.34	24.14	7949.90

Table 2. Descriptive statistics of private to total health care expenditure ratio

Region	*N*	Mean	Median	Std. Dev.	Minimum	Maximum
East Asia and Pacific	28	0.30	0.26	0.22	0.03	0.79
Europe and Central Asia	48	0.33	0.29	0.17	0.15	0.76
Latin America and Caribbean	32	0.44	0.44	0.12	0.21	0.65
Middle East and North Africa	20	0.40	0.33	0.18	0.15	0.75
North America	2	0.39	0.39	0.17	0.27	0.51
South Asia	8	0.59	0.69	0.21	0.17	0.79
Sub-Saharan Africa	46	0.47	0.46	0.18	0.08	0.80
Total	184	0.40	0.37	0.19	0.03	0.80

America country group exhibits the highest percentage on health care services (with the United States devoting 16.50% and Canada devoting 10.56% of their respective GDPs), whereas the lowest percentage is devoted by the South Asian country group with only 4.70% on average, along with a median value of 3.23%. It is also noteworthy that within-group variations in the fraction of health care expenditure are also sizeable, particularly for the East Asia and Pacific country group.

Table 4 reports on income inequality by country groups via the Gini coefficient (in percentage terms). Formally, the most-frequently used inequality measure, the Gini coefficient is defined as follows:

$$\text{GiniCoefficient} = \frac{\sum_{i=1}^{I}\sum_{j=1}^{I}\left|x_i - x_j\right|}{2I^2\overline{x}} \tag{1}$$

Table 3. Descriptive statistics of health care expenditure to GDP ratio

Region	*N*	Mean	Median	Std. Dev.	Minimum	Maximum
East Asia and Pacific	28	6.30	4.70	4.26	1.34	19.30
Europe and Central Asia	51	7.77	7.80	2.21	2.33	12.16
Latin America and Caribbean	32	6.35	6.19	1.31	4.44	10.22
Middle East and North Africa	20	4.87	4.33	1.99	1.79	8.21
North America	2	13.48	13.48	4.13	10.56	16.40
South Asia	8	4.70	3.23	2.73	2.60	9.32
Sub-Saharan Africa	45	5.81	5.37	2.46	1.53	11.61
Total	186	6.45	6.08	2.83	1.34	19.30

The Gini coefficient is often calculated via the Lorenz curve, and it is twice the area between the Lorenz curve and the perfect equality (45 degree) line. It is possible to interpret the Gini coefficient of income as a measure of relative mean income difference, i.e. it is the mean of the income difference between every possible pair of individuals i and j, divided by the mean income, i.e. $\overline{x} = \sum_{i=1}^{I} x_i$. Table 4 demonstrates lower between-group variations in income inequality than the two former variables. This is so because while the Gini coefficient of income theoretically can take values between 0% (perfect equality of income) to 100% (maximum inequality of income), its *de facto* values globally are only between 20% and 65%. Table 4 reveals further that Latin America and Caribbean country group exhibits the highest degree of income inequality (with an average of 48.73% and a median of 47.55%), and Europe and Central Asia country group exhibits the lowest income inequality (with an average of 31.49% and a median of 31.00%). While economic development is argued to be one of the determinants of income inequality, taxation and redistribution also plays an instrumental role in governing distribution of income (Atkinson, 2015). The fact that income inequality in Europe and Central Asia is lower than that of North America is at least partially related to these taxation and redistribution differences.

A proper understanding of economic inequalities also requires a comprehension of the interaction between beliefs and perceptions, and economic inequalities. In particular, a specific strand of literature is interested in why developed countries with well-established democracies vary considerably over their public and private education and health care compositions, taxation and redistribution systems and their resultant economic inequalities. Specifically, the Transatlantic differences over developed economies have drawn considerable attention, and several explanations

Table 4. Descriptive Statistics of Income Inequality via Gini Coefficient

Region	*N*	Mean	Median	Std. Dev.	Minimum	Maximum
East Asia and Pacific	7	36.46	37.60	3.14	32.00	39.40
Europe and Central Asia	40	31.49	31.00	4.19	24.80	40.20
Latin America and Caribbean	12	48.03	47.55	3.89	43.00	54.80
Middle East and North Africa	6	34.65	34.50	4.64	29.00	42.60
North America	2	37.00	37.00	4.81	33.60	40.40
South Asia	3	31.57	32.10	1.57	29.80	32.80
Sub-Saharan Africa	10	46.66	46.35	9.97	30.80	63.40
Total	80	36.68	34.25	8.47	24.80	63.40

have been proposed. (Alesina et al, 2001; Alesina and Glaeser, 2004; Alesina and Angeletos, 2005; Alesina et al., 2011; Bénabou, 2000; Bénabou and Tirole, 2006). These differences, coined as the "American Exceptionalism" are shown to be relevant to Transatlantic differences in beliefs and perceptions.[9] In order to show how the "American Exceptionalism" is relevant in the case of health care expenditures, I retrieve and consolidate data from the World Values Survey (WVS) and merge it with the World Bank Development Indicators data. Several waves of the World Values Survey study how individual perceptions, beliefs, and tendencies vary at the individual-level globally. Due to its more appropriate structure, I concentrate on the World Values Survey in 2008 and report correlations on how different variables of interest correlate with country-specific average belief and perception scores in select European countries and the United States, i.e. developed countries with well-established democracies and comparable economic complexities.

Methodology

Given the structure of the data set, I rely on panel-data fixed-effects model for my econometric specifications. Consider the linear model for N country-specific observations (indexed with *i*) and T time periods ((indexed with *t* in years):

$$y_{it} = X_{it}\beta + \alpha_i + u_{it} \tag{2}$$

In the above expression, y_{it} denotes the dependent variable observed for country i at time t, y_{it} denotes the time-variant $T \times k$ regressor matrix, where k stands for the number of regressors, β denotes the $k \times 1$ matrix of parameters, α_i denotes the unobserved time-invariant individual effect, and u_{it} denotes the country-year specific the error term.

Under this specification, since country-fixed effect α_i is not directly observable, a transformation is required for capturing the country-fixed effect. The fixed-effect model does this transformation by eliminating the country-fixed effect α_i by de-meaning variables of interest:

$$y_{it} - \overline{y_i} = \left(X_{it} - \overline{X_i}\right)\beta + \left(\alpha_i - \overline{\alpha_i}\right) + \left(u_{it} - \overline{u_i}\right) \tag{3}$$

where $\overline{y_i} = \frac{1}{T}\sum_{t=1}^{T} y_{it}$, $\overline{\mathbf{X}_i} = \frac{1}{T}\sum_{t=1}^{T}\mathbf{X}_{it}$, and $\overline{u_i} = \frac{1}{T}\sum_{t=1}^{T} u_{it}$. Note that since α_i is just a constant, $\alpha_i = \overline{\alpha_i}$ and the country-fixed effect is eliminated.

Let $\widetilde{y_{it}} \equiv y_{it} - \overline{y_i}$, $\widetilde{\mathbf{X}_{it}} \equiv \mathbf{X}_{it} - \overline{\mathbf{X}_i}$ and $\widetilde{u_{it}} \equiv u_{it} - \overline{u_i}$. Then, the fixed-effects estimator $\hat{\beta}$ for β can be estimated by regressing $\widetilde{y_{it}}$ on $\widetilde{\mathbf{X}_{it}}$ via ordinary least squares (OLS) estimation, since the de-meaned model is of the form:

$$\widetilde{y_{it}} = \widetilde{X_{it}}\beta + \widetilde{u_{it}} \tag{4}$$

In order to investigate the role of health care expenditure on income inequality, in my benchmark estimations I set my dependent variable y_{it} as income inequality, and independent variables X_{it} as the vector of health care spending per capita, private to total health care expenditure ratio, GDP per capita, among other variables. Next, in order to study the role of income inequality on health care expenditure, I set my dependent variable y_{it} as total health care expenditure as a share of GDP, and for my independent variables X_{it}, I use the vector of income inequality as proxied by the Gini coefficient, private to total health care expenditure ratio, population share over 65 years old, GDP per capita (in PPP-adjusted international dollars), among other control variables.

RESULTS

Descriptive Analysis

Before reporting and discussing my econometric findings, I first demonstrate raw correlations between health care expenditure variables and income inequality. In Figure 2, I depict how income inequality correlates with private to total health care expenditure ratio, globally. The unit of analysis in Figure 2 is a country-year-specific observation, and as such, Figure 2 demonstrates how income inequality in a specific country i at a particular year t correlates with the private-to-total health care expenditure ratio for the same country-year it unit. In demonstrating the correlation between private-to-total health care expenditure ratio and income inequality, I also plot the linear fit, along with its 95% confidence interval.

The scatter plot in Figure 2 demonstrates a clear positive relationship between the two variables of interest: simple correlation analysis reveals that there is a significant positive relationship between the reliance on private resources for health care financing and the degree of income inequality. One way to interpret this correlation is that countries with more pronounced income inequality estimates tend to exhibit higher reliance on private resources for health care provision. Alternatively, another explanation is that higher reliance on private expenditure for health care practices

Figure 2. Private to total health care expenditure ratio

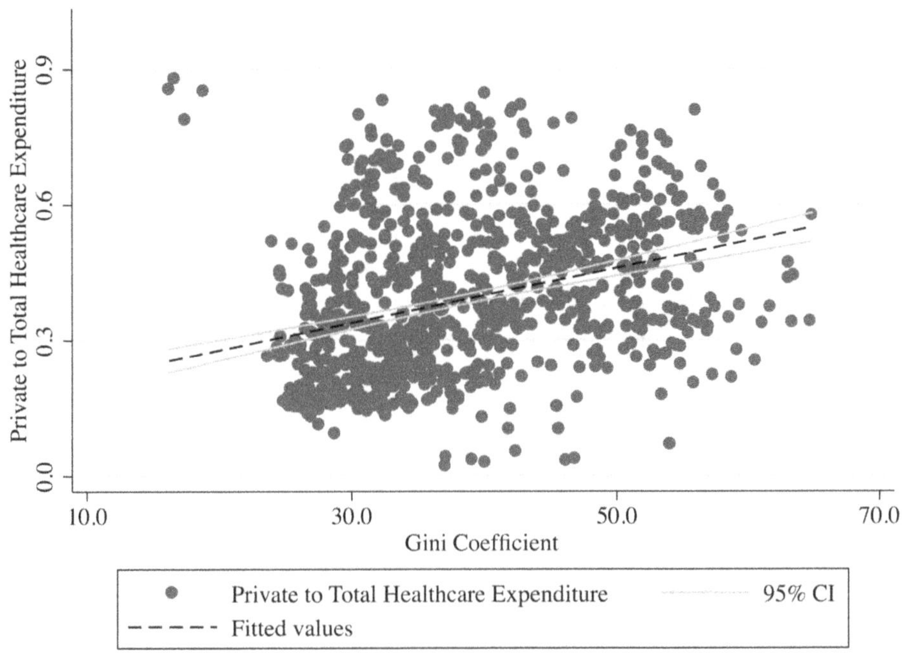

contributes to higher income inequality. My econometric estimation results via fixed-effects estimations favor both views, since private to total health care expenditure ratio is a significant and positive predictor of income inequality, and vice versa. The magnitude of the slope of the fitted line in Figure 2 is 0.0061 (with a standard error of 0.0006), suggesting that a 10% increase in the Gini coefficient is accompanied by a 6% higher reliance on private resources for health care financing.

One could suspect that the positive correlation in Figure 2 stems mainly from a specific cluster of countries. In order to demonstrate that this is actually not the case, in Figure 3, I repeat the same exercise only for the Europe and Central Asia, and the Latin America and Caribbean country groups.[10] Figure 3 demonstrates that the positive correlation between income inequality and private to total health care expenditure ratio is evident for both country groups, albeit at different rates: for the Europe and Central Asia subgroup, the slope of the fitted line is 0.0082 (with a standard deviation of 0.0016, whereas the same slope for the fitted line by the Latin America and Caribbean subgroup is 0.0054 (with a standard deviation of 0.0019), both significant at the 99% confidence interval. These findings indicate that the positive and significant correlation between income inequality and private to total

Figure 3. Private to total health care expenditure ratio by country group

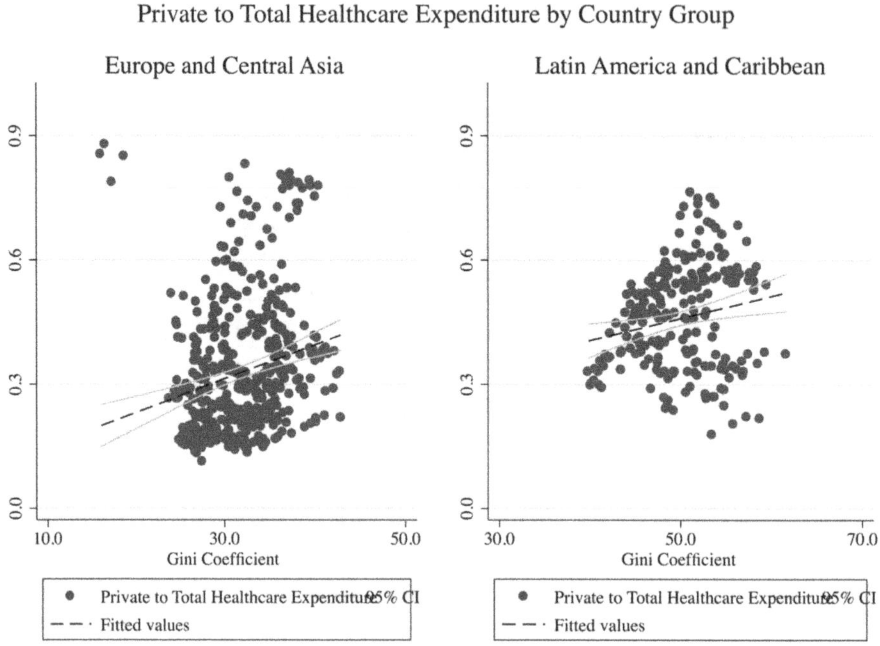

health care expenditure ratio does not stem only from geographical reasons, and is robust to the choice of country groups.

Next, I turn to demonstrating the raw correlation between income inequality and total health care expenditure per capita in PPP-adjusted international dollars, and depict my resultant findings in Figure 4. Again, I keep the unit of analysis in Figure 4 as a country-year-specific observation, and I report the linear fit, along with its 95% confidence interval. As in the case of Figure 2, Figure 4 displays a robust and significant correlation between the two variables of interest, however this time, the direction of the correlation is negative. This finding can possibly be interpreted as that higher income inequality contributes to lower total health care expenditure per capita. An alternative explanation could be that high average health care spending per capita results in the moderation in income inequality. My econometric findings favor the former explanation better: income inequality robustly and strongly predicts total health care expenditure per person, whereas total health care expenditure per capita has poor explanatory power over income distribution. The slope of the fitted line in Figure 4 is -76.9125 (with a standard deviation of 4.8498), indicating that a 10% increase in the Gini coefficient predicts a lower total health care per capita value of $769.25 PPP-adjusted international dollars.

Figure 4. Total health care expenditure per capita

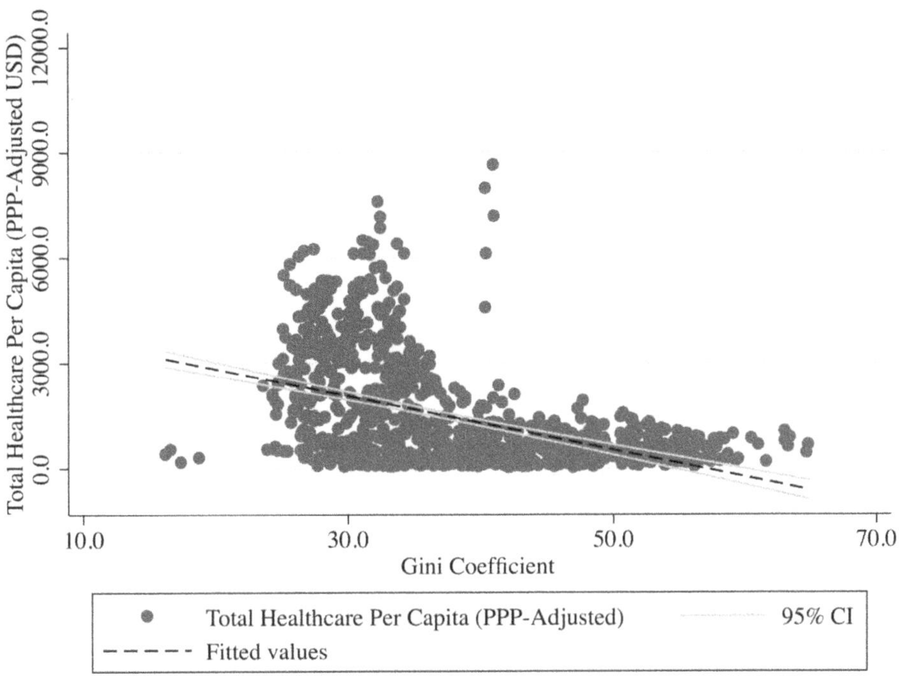

Next, I show the empirical relationship income inequality and total health care expenditure per capita by select groups in Figure 5. In doing so, I concentrate again on the Europe and Central Asia, and the Latin America and Caribbean country groups for the sake of brevity and comparability. Figure 5 illustrates that the negative correlation between income inequality and total health care expenditure per capita is present for both country groups, as well as for the omitted other groups. The slopes of the fitted lines by group are again at different magnitudes: for the Europe and Central Asia group, the predicted linear line has a slope of -96.7995 (with a standard deviation of 15.9878), whereas the same slope for the Latin America and Caribbean country group is -34.6943 (with a standard deviation of 5.1512). Albeit different at rates, both of the fitted lines are significant at the 99% confidence interval. These results by country groups depicted in Figure 5 reaffirm the robustness of the correlation between income inequality and total health care expenditure per capita.

Finally, I concentrate on the relationship between income inequality and total health care expenditure as a share of GDP, and I display the resultant scatter plot graph between the two variables of interest in Figure 6. As before, I keep the unit of analysis in Figure 6 as a country-year-specific observation, and I report the linear fit, along with its 95% confidence interval. As it is evident from Figure 6, cross-country

Figure 5. Total health care expenditure per capita by country group

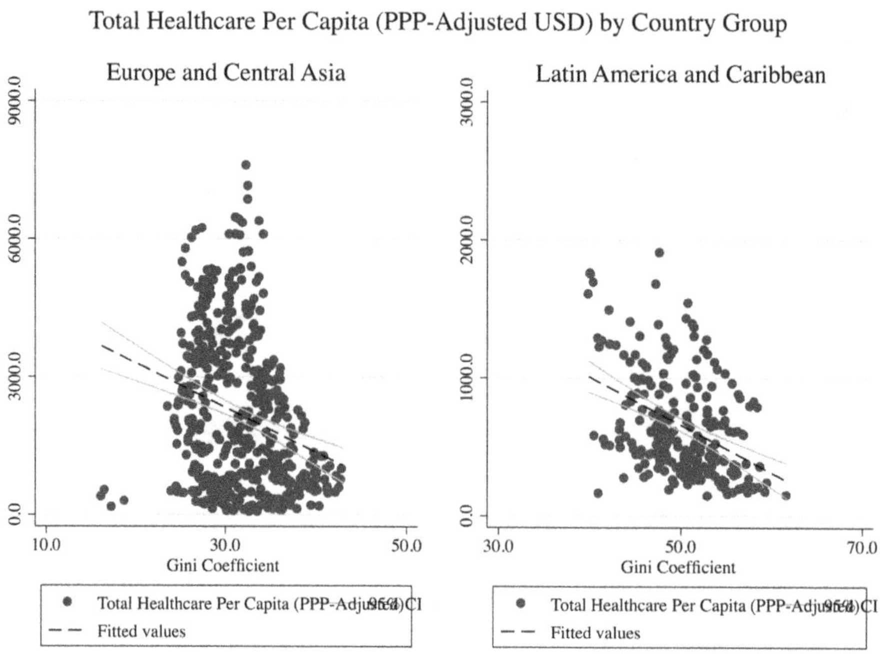

data suggests a negative and significant relationship between income inequality and health care expenditure as a share of GDP. One possible explanation behind this result is that higher economic inequality contributes to a reduction in the percentage of GDP devoted for the provision of health care services. Another possible explanation is that a higher GDP devoted to health care practices moderates income inequality. My econometric findings suggest that the direction of causality is likely to be bi-directional and that both mechanisms reinforce each other. The slope of the fitted line in Figure 6 is -0.0625 (with a standard deviation of 0.0074), indicating that a 10% increase in the Gini coefficient predicts a lower total health care to GDP ratio of 0.6%. While this slope is rather small in magnitude, it is statistically significant at the 99% confidence interval.

Next, I re-do the exercise in 6 for the same select country groups, and depict the correlation between income inequality and total health care expenditure as a share of GDP for the Europe and Central Asia, and Latin America and Caribbean country groups in Figure 7. This robustness exercise reaffirms that the negative correlation between the variables of interest is robust to the choice of country groups, and the resultant slope estimates for the Europe and Central Asia, and Latin America and Caribbean country groups are -0.0751 (with a standard deviation of 0.0188) and

Figure 6. Health care expenditure to GDP ratio

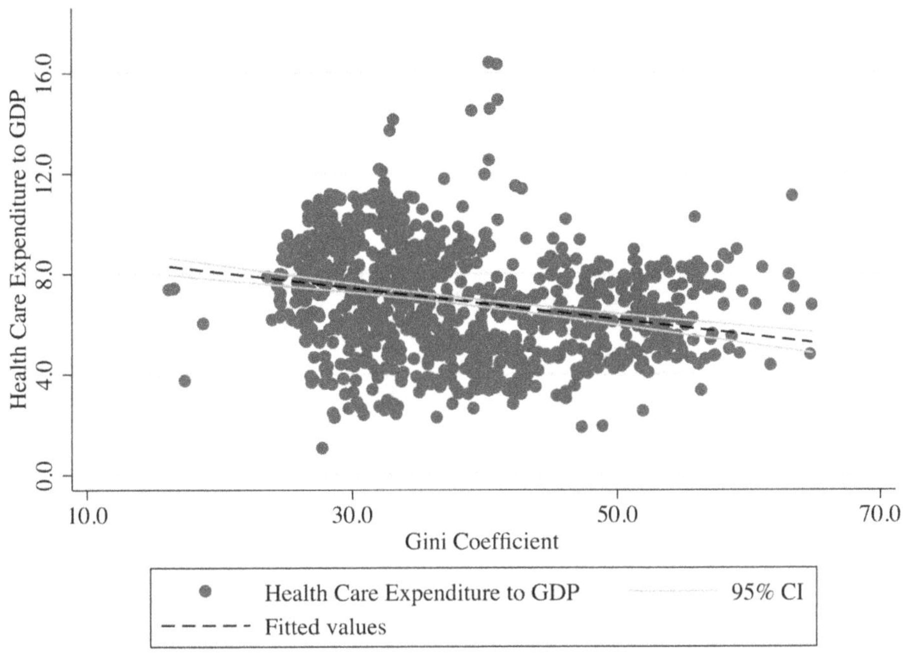

-0.0446 (with a standard deviation of 0.02013), respectively. Despite different in magnitude, both slope coefficients are statistically significant at the 99% confidence interval, thereby indicating rigor on the correlation of interest.

Econometric Results

In order to demonstrate that the correlations I documented so far are robust over econometric specifications, I next rely on the fixed-effects regression methodology I discussed in the previous section, and report my resultant estimation findings. In Table 5, I demonstrate the estimation results by regressing the income inequality variable (proxied by the Gini coefficient) on a number of control variables under competing econometric specifications. All results in Table 5 verify that the discussed findings are not due to spurious correlations, and are robust to econometric modelling choices.

The first model (1) in Table 5 reports the estimation results by regressing the Gini coefficient on the private to total health care expenditure ratio variable. The resultant positive coefficient of 13.517 before the private to total health care expenditure ratio variable is statistically significant at the 99% confidence interval, and reaffirms the positive association between income inequality and higher reliance

Figure 7. Total health care expenditure to GDP ratio by country group

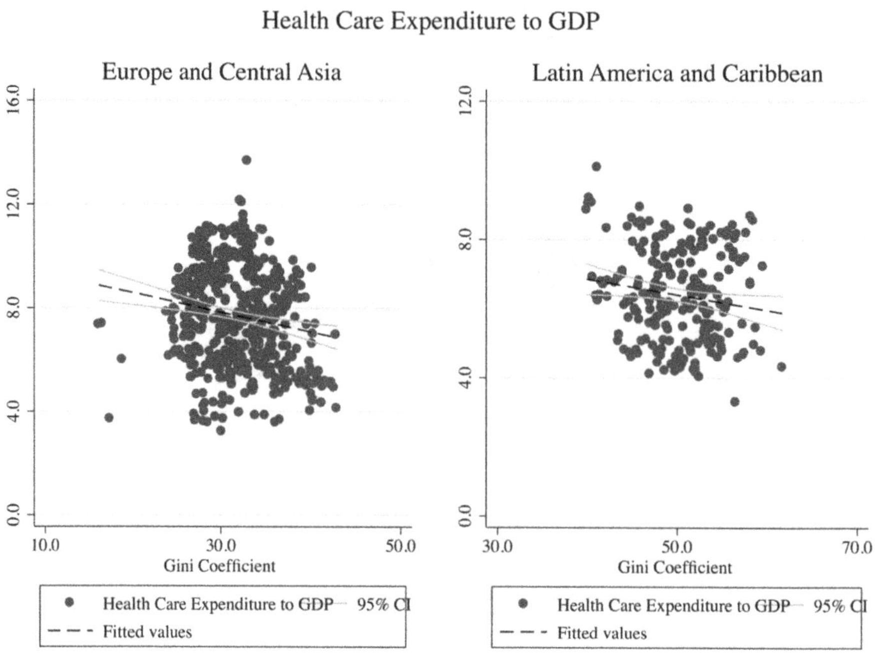

on private resources for health care financing.[11] The second model (2) in Table 5 reports the estimation results by regressing the Gini coefficient on the total health care expenditure to GDP ratio variable, while controlling for the private to total health care expenditure ratio. The resultant positive coefficient before the private to total health care expenditure variable is still statistically significant at the 99% confidence interval and is comparable in size, therefore reaffirms the positive association between income inequality and higher reliance on private resources for health care financing. The second model (2) in Table 5 further demonstrates that the health care expenditure as a share of GDP variable is a negative and significant predictor of income inequality, implying that low-inequality countries succeed better in devoting a higher percentage of their GDPs to the provision of health care services.

The third model (3) in Table 5 reports the estimation results by regressing the Gini coefficient on the total health care expenditure per capita (in PPP-adjusted international dollars) variable, while also controlling for the private to total health care expenditure ratio along with the total health care to GDP ratio. The resultant positive coefficient before the private to total health care expenditure variable is again statistically significant at the 99% confidence interval, and compares closely to the coefficient estimates by the two former models, therefore preserves its robustness

Table 5. Determinants of income inequality

VARIABLES	(1) Gini Coefficient	(2) Gini Coefficient	(3) Gini Coefficient	(4) Gini Coefficient
Private to Total Healthcare Expenditure Total Health Expenditure to GDP	13.517*** (1.658)	12.523*** (1.685) -0.344*** (0.104)	12.332*** (1.691) -0.280** (0.116)	11.245*** (1.670) -0.622*** (0.125)
Total Healthcare Per Capita (PPP-Adjusted)			-0.000	0.002***
GDP Per Capita (PPP-Adjusted USD) Constant	32.790***	35.545***	(0.000) 35.598***	(0.000) -0.000*** (0.000) 39.697***
	(0.646)	(1.065)	(1.065)	(1.226)
Observations	975	972	972	967
R-squared	0.075	0.088	0.090	0.141
Number of country id	152	151	151	149
Country Fixed-Effect Controls	Yes	Yes	Yes	Yes

Standard errors in parentheses
*** p<0.01, ** p<0.05, * p<0.1

over predicting income inequality positively. The coefficient before health care expenditure's share in GDP is still statistically significant, yet at the 95% confidence interval this time. Its magnitude is moderately lower than the estimate by the second model (2), suggesting that a fraction of the variation explained by the total health care per capita variable is captured by the inclusion of the total health care per person variable. Finally, the health care per capita variable is statistically insignificant, which is predominantly because of the inclusion of the health expenditure to GDP ratio, and its multicollinearity impact.[12]

The fourth model (4) in Table 5 reports the estimation results by regressing the Gini coefficient on the GDP per capita variable, while also controlling for the total health care expenditure per capita (in PPP-adjusted international dollars) variable, along with private to total health care expenditure and total health care to GDP ratios. The estimated positive coefficient before the private to total health care expenditure variable is statistically significant at the 99% confidence interval and is still quite comparable in magnitude. Further, its standard deviation is extremely similar to the ones by the three former models. As such, the four estimation results jointly reveal that private to total health care expenditure ratio is a very robust negative predictor of income inequality, and more reliance on private resources for health care financing contributes to worsening of income inequality. The total health care expenditure as a share of GDP variable is again negative and significant at the 99% confidence interval, reaffirming the robust adverse relationship between the share of expenditure devoted to health care provision and income inequality. While the inclusion of the GDP per capita variable improves the statistical significance of the total health care expenditure per capita, the multicollinearity problem as a result of the inclusion of linearly-dependent variables on the right-hand side results in spurious correlations, which are still not sizably different than zero in magnitude.

While estimating the role of health care expenditure variables on income inequality, next I turn to capturing the effect of time over. For this goal, I revise the econometric specifications reported in Table 5 by incorporating a year variable to control for the time trend. While valuable in documenting the time-series co-movements of variables of interest, this is a tedious exercise, and insights from this regression is to be taken with a grain of salt, since time trend also absorbs a large fraction of the co-movements by construction. I report my resultant findings in Table 6. The first model (1) in Table 6 demonstrates that when the private to total health care expenditure ratio is controlled for, there is a secular downward time trend in income inequality. This downward time trend, as exhibited by the negative and significant coefficient before the year variable is negative and statistically significant at the 99% confidence interval. The inclusion of the time trend variable does not affect the sign and statistical significance of the coefficient before the private to total health care ratio variable, and this coefficient of interest is still positive and significant at the 99% confidence interval.

The second model (2) in Table 6 displays the regression results when the Gini coefficient is regressed on the total health care expenditure to GDP ratio variable, while controlling for the time trend and the private to total health care expenditure ratio variable. The secular downward time trend in income inequality is repeated by the coefficient before the year variable, which is identical to the former model up to three decimals, and is statistically significant at the 99% confidence interval. The positive coefficient before the private to total health care expenditure ratio is comparable in size to its former model counterpart, and is still significant at the 99% confidence interval. As such, the positive predictive power of reliance on private resources for health care financing is robust to the inclusion of time trend and total health care expenditure as a share of GDP. While the coefficient before the total health care expenditure to GDP ratio is insignificant under this specification, it is significant when further control variables are incorporated into the econometric specification.

The third model (3) in Table 6 shows the regression results when the Gini coefficient is regressed on the total health care expenditure per capita (in PPP-adjusted international dollars) variable, while controlling for the time trend, and the private to total health care expenditure and total health care expenditure to

Table 6. Determinants of income inequality (year included)

VARIABLES	(1) Gini Coefficient	(2) Gini Coefficient	(3) Gini Coefficient	(4) Gini Coefficient
Year Private to Total Healthcare Expenditure	-0.202*** (0.019) 8.023*** (1.645)	-0.203*** (0.021) 8.138*** (1.654)	-0.297*** (0.025) 7.208*** (1.625)	-0.285*** (0.029) 7.687*** (1.623)
Total Health Expenditure to GDP		0.001	-0.210*	-0.266**
Total Healthcare Per Capita (PPP-Adjusted)		(0.104)	(0.108) 0.002*** (0.000)	(0.124) 0.002*** (0.000)
GDP Per Capita (PPP-Adjusted USD)				-0.000
Constant	440.099***	442.178***	631.184***	(0.000) 606.755***
	(38.957)	(41.124)	(50.744)	(58.175)
Observations	975	972	972	967
R-squared	0.184	0.185	0.221	0.231
Number of country id	152	151	151	149
Country Fixed-Effect Controls	Yes	Yes	Yes	Yes

Standard errors in parentheses
*** p<0.01, ** p<0.05, * p<0.1

GDP ratio variables. This regression output reiterates the statistical significance of the secular time trend in income inequality, as well as the positive predictive power of the private to total health care expenditure ratio. The inclusion of the total health care expenditure per capita variable corrects for the insignificance of the coefficient before the total health expenditure to GDP ratio, which now yields a negative and significant coefficient, as expected. However, the inclusion of per capita expenditure estimate also comes with its multicollinearity problems, and the linearly dependent right-hand side variables result in a spurious correlation for the per capita expenditure variable.

The fourth model (4) in Table 6 displays the regression results when income inequality the dependent variables in model (3), along with PPP-adjusted GDP per capita. The negative and significant coefficient before the year variable is recurrent, demonstrating the robust downward time trend in income inequality, when health expenditure variables are controlled for. Likewise, the positive and significant coefficient before the private to total health care expenditure ratio variable is again significant at the 99% confidence interval, and is comparable in magnitude, reaffirming the robustness of the positive predictive power of reliance on private resources for health care provision. The total health care expenditure as a share of GDP variable takes a negative and significant (at the 95% confidence interval) value, verifying the robust negative co-movement of a higher fraction of budget allocated for the provision of health care services and income inequality. The remaining coefficients are quite small in size, and suffer from the discussed multicollinearity issues, along with their resultant spurious correlations.

In order to examine the role of income inequality on what percentage of their GDP countries devote for the provision of health care services, I regress the share of total health expenditure in GDP to the Gini coefficient to proxy for income inequality, along with other controls. I report my fixed-effects panel data estimation results in Table 7. The first model (1) in Table 7 reports the regression result for only the Gini coefficient (along with country-fixed effects) as the regressor. The first model demonstrates that the income inequality variable negatively predicts health care expenditure as a share of GDP at the 99% confidence interval. The estimated coefficient of -0.055 suggests that a 10% increase in the Gini coefficient predicts a lower total health care to GDP ratio of 0.55%, which is comparable to the slope reported in Figure 6.

The second model (2) in Table 7 regresses the health care expenditure to GDP ratio to the private to total health care expenditure ratio, while controlling for the Gini coefficient. The resultant negative and significant (at the 99% confidence interval) coefficient before the private to total health care expenditure ratio variable indicates that higher reliance on private resources for the provision of health care services induces a lower fraction of the GDP to be devoted on health care expenditures, which accords well with my previously documented correlations. The negative and significant coefficient before the income inequality variable suggests that higher inequality still significantly predicts lower health care expenditure as a share of GDP when the decomposition of health care expenditure is controlled for.

One might expect that in an era of aging societies globally, what percentage of their GDP countries devote to the provision of health care services depends directly on the share of old population, i.e. when a sizable fraction of domestic residents are old in age (e.g. 65 years old or older), countries naturally spend more for the provision of health care services. As such, lacking old-age population fraction as a regressor could result in omitted variable bias. In order to address these concerns, the third model (3) in Table 7 regresses the health care expenditure to GDP ratio to the share of population older than 65 years, while controlling for the private to total health care expenditure ratio and the Gini coefficient. The resultant positive and statistically significant (at the 99% confidence interval) coefficient before the old population share accords well with these *a priori* expectations, and documents that the share of old population robustly predicts the percentage of GDP devoted for the provision of health care services. As such, data verifies that the upward time trend in the fraction of old population in developed (and some developing) countries is likely to be accompanied by higher shares of GDP devoted for the provision of health care services. The third model (3) in Table 7 further demonstrates that controlling for old age population fraction does not affect the statistical robustness of the other included variables, since the coefficient before the income inequality variable is still negative and statistically significant at the 95% confidence interval, and so is the coefficient before the private to total health care expenditure ratio, which is significant at a higher 99% confidence interval.

It is also possible that these estimated coefficients are affected by economic prosperity of countries of analysis, and as such failing to control for economic development induces omitted variable bias. In order to demonstrate that this is not the case, the fourth model (4) in Table 7 regresses the total health care expenditure to GDP ratio to the GDP per capita (in PPP-adjusted international dollars) variable to proxy for economic prosperity, while also controlling for the share old-age population, the private the total health care expenditure ratio and the Gini coefficient. The coefficient

Table 7. Determinants of Health Care Expenditure as a Share of GDP

VARIABLES	(1) Health Care Exp.	(2) Health Care Exp.	(3) Health Care Exp.	(4) Health Care Exp.
Gini Coefficient Private to Total Healthcare Expenditure Old (65+ Years) Population Share	-0.055*** (0.011)	-0.038*** (0.012) -2.703*** (0.573)	-0.026** (0.011) -2.119*** (0.556) 0.304*** (0.037)	-0.025** (0.011) -2.189*** (0.557) 0.290*** (0.046)
GDP Per Capita (PPP-Adjusted USD)				0.000
Constant	9.025***	9.404***	5.531***	(0.000) 5.613***
	(0.430)	(0.436)	(0.631)	(0.631)
Observations	998	972	971	966
R-squared	0.027	0.052	0.124	0.126
Number of country id	151	151	150	148
Country Fixed-Effect Controls	Yes	Yes	Yes	Yes

Standard errors in parentheses
*** $p < 0.01$, ** $p < 0.05$, * $p < 0.1$

before the GDP per capita variable is not statistically different than zero, suggesting the previously reported coefficients are not driven by failing to account for economic development. Indeed, the coefficients before the Gini coefficient, the private to total health care expenditure and the share of old-age populations by the fourth model (4) are statistically identical to their counterparts by the third model (3).[13] Accordingly, the four models in Table 7 jointly imply that the correlations between variables of interest are robust to different econometric specifications: income inequality and reliance on private resources for the provision of health care services positively and significantly predict the share of GDP devoted to health care expenditure, whereas the share of old population (over 65 years old) positively and significantly predicts what fraction of national output is devoted to health care expenditure.[14]

Table 5, 6 and 7 jointly suggest that income inequality is both an instrumental determinant and an immediate result of health care expenditure and composition. As such, in order to have a comprehensive understanding of the structure of the provision of health care services, it is imperative to bring income inequality into the picture, whose causality is documented to be bi-directional.

Health Care Expenditure Composition, Income Inequality and Transatlantic Differences

The econometric results I reported and discussed so far documents robust correlations between health care expenditure variables and income inequality estimates around the globe. One could expect that at least in well-established democracies that these health and inequality outcomes are to reflect public perceptions, beliefs and preferences.

In order to explore if indeed these variables of interest are correlated with public beliefs and perceptions, I focus on a select group of developed countries with high electoral scores and established democracies. As discussed, I retrieve belief, perception and preference data for feasible countries from the World Values Survey (WVS), and I merge this data with the income inequality and health expenditure estimates by the World Bank Development Indicators.

I start my discussion by depicting the share of public and private health care expenditures in GDP by country as of 2008 in Figure 8. The most striking observations between the United States and continental European countries with regards to health care expenditures are i) both the United States and continental European countries devote approximately 7% of their GDPs to the provision of public health care services, ii) the United States allocates a remarkable 9% more of its GDP for the provision of private health care services, whereas private health care provision accounts only for 2% of continental European country GDPs on average, iii) total health care expenditure in the United States accounts for more than 16% of overall GDP, whereas this figure is only 9% in the continental Europe on average.

Figure 8. Health Care expenditure and composition by country

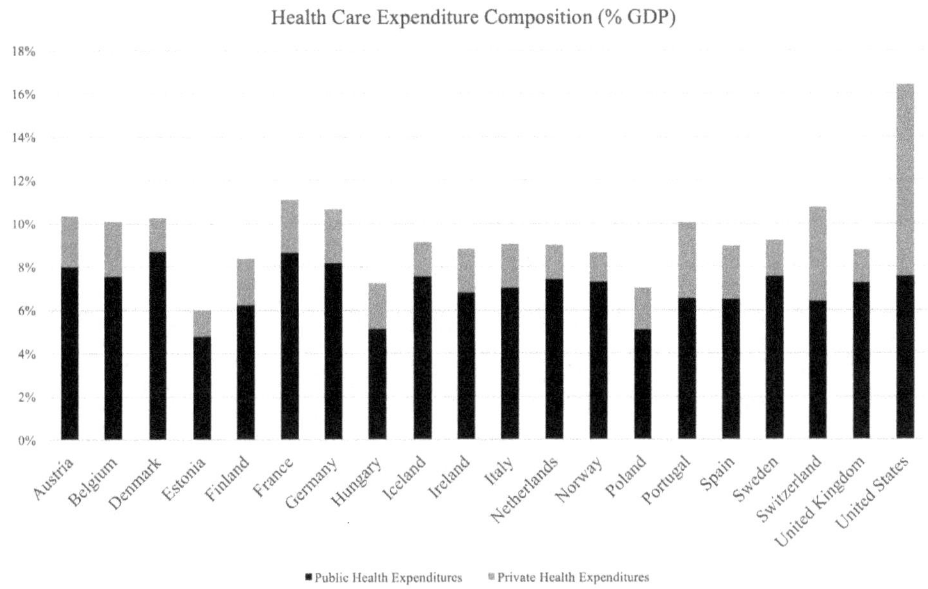

Accordingly, it is clear that while only 24% of health care services are provided via private resources in Europe on average, 54% of health care expenditure is financed by private resources in the United States.

The higher health expenditure (as a share of GDP) in the United States, along with its predominantly private financing is accompanied by higher income inequality. In Figure 9, I demonstrate income inequality in 2008 (via the Gini coefficient) by country. Figure 9 demonstrates that while the Gini coefficient in the continental European countries are within the 25.1% (Denmark) and 34.1% (the United Kingdom) interval, it is a remarkably higher (45%) in the United States.

Members of the more unequal and private-reliant United States economy predominantly believe that hard work usually brings a better life in the long run, whereas members of continental European countries believes that hard work does *not* generally bring success, and success is more a matter of luck and connections. These joint observations have been subject to a specific body of literature, as discussed (Alesina and Angeletos, 2005; Bénabou and Tirole, 2006), and the idiosyncrasy of the United States has often been coined as the "*American exceptionalism*". While the World Values Survey question on whether long run success depends on hard work versus luck and connections (coded e040) has been studied by a number of academic studies, how other questions correlate with income inequality and health

Figure 9. Income Inequality by Country

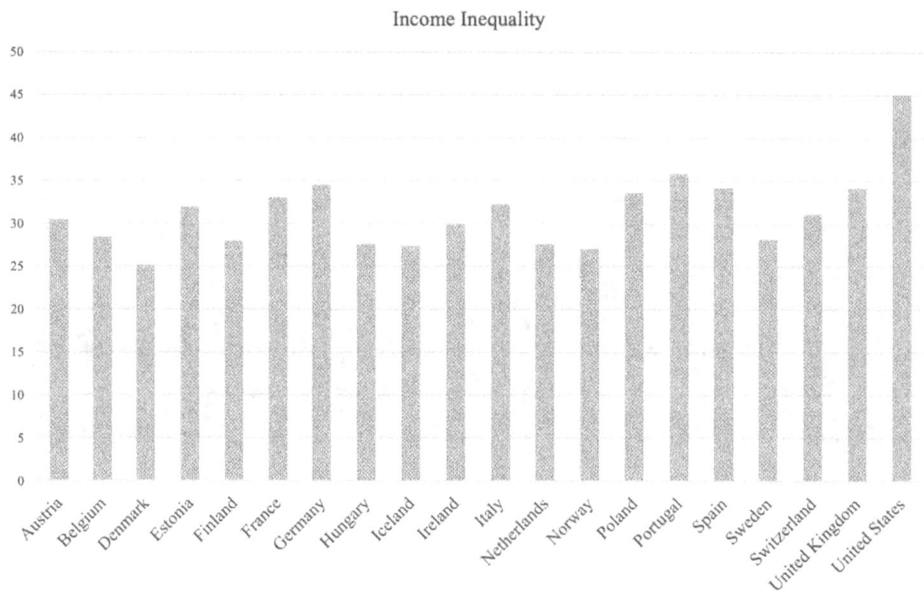

expenditure variables has yet remained unveiled. In this study, I analyze the following World Values Survey questions:

- **e040**: Hard work brings success {1, …, 10}
    - 1: In the long run, hard work usually brings a better life
    - 10: Hard work does not generally bring success - it is more a matter of luck and connections
- **e131**: Why are people in need? {1,2}
    - 1: Poor because of laziness and lack of will power
    - 2: Poor because of an unfair society
- **e132**: Chance to escape from poverty {1,2}
    - 1: They have a chance
    - 2: There is very little chance
- **e133**: How much is the government doing against poverty {1,2,3}
    - 1: Too much
    - 2: About the right amount
    - 3: Too little
- **e117**: Having a democratic political system {1,2,3,4}
    - 1: Very good
    - 2: Fairly good

    - 3: Fairly bad
    - 4: Very bad
- **e035**: Income equality {1, …, 10}
    - 1: Incomes should be made more equal
    - 10: We need larger income differences as incentives
- **e037**: Government responsibility to provide for people {1, ..., 10}
    - 1: People should take more responsibility
    - 10: The government should take more responsibility
- **g006**: How proud of nationality? {1,2,3,4}
    - 1: Very proud
    - 2: Quite proud
    - 3: Not very proud
    - 4: Not proud at all

For the above list of belief, perception and preference variables, I calculate country-specific averages, and investigate how these country averages correlate with i) total health expenditure as a percentage of GDP, ii) private to total health care expenditure ratio, and iii) the Gini coefficient for the list of countries in Figure 8 and 9 with available data. I report my resultant correlations in Table 8.

The first column of Table 8 demonstrates that countries with lower health care expenditure as a share of GDP, lower reliance on private expenditure financing and lower income inequality are also the ones whose residents attribute a more decisive role to luck and connections in success, although the correlation coefficients are small in magnitude.

The second column of Table 8 displays that countries where residents frequently believe that people are in need because of an unfair society (continental European countries with more extensive welfare states in particular) are also low-income inequality countries with low health care expenditure estimates, where health care provision is predominantly publicly financed. In the case of the question with the code e131, the correlation coefficient is high in magnitude and statistical significance.

The third column of Table 8 shows that the same low-inequality, low-health-expenditure countries with low private-reliance are also the ones where the public

Table 8. Correlation between health care expenditure, income inequality and beliefs

	e040	e131	e132	e133	e117	e035	e037	g004
Health Expenditure (%GDP)	-0.154	-0.655	-0.465	-0.920	-0.285	-0.260	-0.528	-0.066
Private to Total Health Exp.	-0.174	-0.704	-0.156	-0.762	-0.313	-0.264	-0.201	-0.332
Gini Coefficient	-0.124	-0.672	-0.109	-0.711	0.289	-0.083	-0.004	-0.362

prevalently believes that there is little chance in escaping poverty, albeit with low correlation statistics

The fourth column of Table 8 demonstrates that more unequal countries where health care expenditure as a share of GDP is higher and health care is more privately-financed are also the ones whose residents predominantly believe the government is already doing too much against poverty. As such, the limited public health care provision in these countries are not coincidental, but rather reflects public preferences. Evidently, these important correlations are significant and quite large in magnitude.

The fifth column of Table 8 shows that in countries where health care expenditure is sizable and financed mainly by private resources, the public favors democracy better. However, contrary to the correlations for the other belief and perception variables, democracy is favored among the more equal societies, as the sign of the correlation reverses in the last row.

The sixth column of Table 8 displays that countries with higher health care spending and higher private sector reliance for health care financing hosts residents who believe larger income differences are needed as incentives. As such, public preferences are again in accordance with policy choices. However, interestingly actual income inequality does not significantly correlate with preferences over income inequality.

The seventh column of Table 8 reports correlations on individualism versus collectivism, and demonstrates that countries where residents believe people should take more responsibility than the government, health care is predominantly privately financed, and as such, fractions of health care provision as a share of GDP are larger in size.

Finally, the last column of Table 8 reports correlations between pride in nationality, and shows that in more unequal countries where health care services are predominantly financed via private resources, residents are prouder of their nationalities.

These interesting correlations offer valuable lessons on the link between beliefs, perceptions and preferences, and level and composition of health care expenditure, as well as income inequality. The reported correlations in Table 8 illustrates that policy choices in well-established developed economies tend to reflect public preferences closely, and the cross-country variations in health care expenditure and income inequality estimates could very well stem mainly from electorates' choices.

SOLUTIONS AND RECOMMENDATIONS

In this study, I concentrate on the level and composition of health care expenditures, along with income inequality estimates and document that income inequality exhibits robust correlations: health care expenditure per capita decreases over income inequality, and more unequal countries rely more on private resources for health care financing. These results highlight that as expected, income inequality inherently affects the level of health care services. As such, policies to reduce income inequality, such as progressive taxation and redistribution, public provision of health care and education services, prevalent risk sharing devices by the state (e.g. unemployment benefits, social security transfers and social protection spending) are to contribute to reduce heterogeneity in access to health care services. I also document that health care expenditure per person and per capita increases over the private to total health care expenditure ratio. It is important also to evaluate the quality of health care services and how expenditure reflects on quality. Recent studies document that countries where public health care is prevalently state-funded, the same dollar spent on health care results in significantly higher-quality health services. (Ridic et al., 2012). As such, while privatization of the health care system and relying on the free market could boost health care expenditure per person, it does not necessarily translate into better access or quality of health services. This is particularly likely when the health industry lacks competitive markets and anti-trust regulations. When the health industry features monopolies or cartelized oligopolies, the resultant market prices and quantities are not welfare-enhancing, but profit maximizing. Accordingly, my results signal that privatization of health care expenditure requires limits and in addition to fighting against income inequality, the state is to play a central role in regulating and enhancing the health care industry.

FUTURE RESEARCH DIRECTIONS

In this study, I concentrate on cross-country panel data to infer the relationship between health care expenditure and income inequality. In doing so, I relied on macroeconomic country-specific estimates to examine the relationship between variables of interest. Future research consolidating both macro and micro-level data could improve the quality and external validity of the documented linkages.

The World Bank Research Department and the World Health Organization are conducting policy-relevant state-of-the-art research on universal health coverage globally. In particular, the 2017 United Health Care Global Monitoring Report studies how many people globally lack access to essential health services and how many are pushed into poverty or spending too much of their household budgets on out-of-pocket health expenses. While these attempts offer most valuable lessons, the incorporation of these attempts with income, consumption and wealth inequality is most central and instrumental for better policy devising.

CONCLUSION

Health care provision is a matter of substantial delicacy, as it directly affects the quality and well-being of lives of billions of world residents. The quality of health care provision naturally depends on expenditures associated with health care practices. Cross-country comparable data suggests there is an immense degree of heterogeneity both in the level and composition of health care expenditures. In many parts of the world, at least a certain degree of health care practices is provided publicly, i.e. without requiring major out-of-pocket costs and is accessibly regardless of personal finances. It is often coupled with private health care provision: patients are to finance their health care expenditures via their personal finances in the form of out-of-pocket costs. Especially in developing (and some developed) countries where public health care provision is limited and private health care spending is *de facto* required, income heterogeneity of patients matters considerably. As such, it is only natural to expect that health care expenditure levels and compositions are intertwined with income inequality. This study intends to contribute to the research front on this end, and aims to shed light on the link between health care expenditures and income inequality.

In this study, I try to address the link between income inequality and the most objective and cross-country-comparable health care variable: expenditure on health care, along with its public versus private composition, share in GDP and its average per capita value. In order to do so, relying on panel data fixed-effects methodology for a large body of countries covering a sizable time span, I estimate associations between income inequality, and the level and composition of health expenditure variables, along with the fraction of GDP devoted to health care expenditure and health care expenditure per capita. My estimation results first demonstrate that there is a robust positive correlation between income inequality and reliance on private resources for health care financing. These findings indicate that high income inequality is often coupled with higher reliance on private health care financing. Second, my estimation results document a robust negative correlation between health care expenditure per capita and income inequality, i.e. high inequality countries tend to have more limited resources per person for the provision of health care services. Third, my estimation results reveal that income inequality correlates negatively with the fraction of health care expenditure to GDP. In other words, high income inequality countries also face more hardship in allocating resources for health care provision as a share of their nation output. These correlations are robust over econometric specifications and variable definitions. These robust findings indicate that if public health care provision is low in level, its dismal implications on more pronounced income inequality is more than probable.

I also focus on a select group of well-established democracies with developed economies to detect if health expenditure and income inequality variables correlate with public beliefs and preferences. My empirical results demonstrate that indeed belief and preferences accord well with policy choices. These novel findings shed light on why health expenditure variables exhibit the immense heterogeneity that they preserve.

REFERENCES

Abbott, B., & Gallipoli, G. (2016). Human Capital Spill-Overs and the Geography of Intergenerational Mobility. *Review of Economic Dynamics*. doi:10.1016/j.red.2016.06.005

Aizer, A. (2014). Rising Inequality and Intergenerational Mobility: The Role of Public Investments in Human Capital. CESifo Group.

Albanesi, S. (2007). Inflation and Inequality. *Journal of Monetary Economics*, *54*(4), 1088–1114. doi:10.1016/j.jmoneco.2006.02.009

Alesina, A., Giuliano, P., Bisin, A., & Benhabib, J. (2011). Preferences for Redistribution. In Handbook of Social Economics (pp. 93-132). Academic Press.

Alesina, A. F., Glaeser, E.L., & Sacerdote, B. (2001). Why Doesn't the US Have a European-Style Welfare System? National Bureau of Economic Research.

Alesina, A.F., & Glaeser, E.L. (2004). *Fighting Poverty in the US and Europe*. Oxford University Press.

Alesina, A. F., & Angeletos, G.-M. (2005). Fairness and Redistribution. *The American Economic Review*, *95*(4), 960–980. doi:10.1257/0002828054825655

Alvaredo, F., Chancel, L., Piketty, T., Saez, E., & Zucman, G. (2018). *World Inequality Report 2018*. Belknap Press of Harvard University Press.

Arawatari, R., & Ono, T. (2013). Inequality, Mobility and Redistributive Politics. *Journal of Economic Theory*, *148*(1), 353–375. doi:10.1016/j.jet.2012.12.010

Atkinson, A. B. (2015). *Inequality*. Harvard University Press. doi:10.4159/9780674287013

Bavetta, S., Donni, P. L., & Marino, M. (2017). An Empirical Analysis of the Determinants of Perceived Inequality. *Review of Income and Wealth*. doi:10.1111/roiw.12351

Bénabou, R. (2000). Unequal Societies: Income Distribution and the Social Contract. *The American Economic Review, 90*(1), 96–129. doi:10.1257/aer.90.1.96

Bénabou, R., & Tirole, J. (2006). Belief in a Just World and Redistributive Politics. *The Quarterly Journal of Economics, 121*(2), 699–746. doi:10.1162/qjec.2006.121.2.699

Binelli, C., & Attanasio, O. (2010). Mexico in the 1990s: The Main Cross-Sectional Facts. *Review of Economic Dynamics, 13*(1), 238–264. doi:10.1016/j.red.2009.10.003

Björklund, A., Roine, J., & Waldenström, D. (2012). Intergenerational Top Income Mobility in Sweden: Capitalist Dynasties in the Land of Equal Opportunity? *Journal of Public Economics, 96*(5–6), 474–484. doi:10.1016/j.jpubeco.2012.02.003

Blundell, R. (2014). Income Dynamics and Life-cycle Inequality: Mechanisms and Controversies. *Economic Journal (London), 124*(576), 289–318. doi:10.1111/ecoj.12133

Blundell, R., & Etheridge, B. (2010). Consumption, Income and Earnings Inequality in Britain. *Review of Economic Dynamics, 13*(1), 76–102. doi:10.1016/j.red.2009.10.004

Brzozowski, M., Gervais, M., Klein, P., & Suzuki, M. (2010). Consumption, Income, and Wealth Inequality in Canada. *Review of Economic Dynamics, 13*(1), 52–75. doi:10.1016/j.red.2009.10.006

Chetty, R., Hendren, N., Kline, P., Saez, E., & Turner, N. (2014). Is the United States Still a Land of Opportunity? Recent Trends in Intergenerational Mobility. *The American Economic Review, 104*(5), 141–147.

Domeij, D., & Flodén, M. (2010). Inequality Trends in Sweden 19782004. *Review of Economic Dynamics, 13*(1), 179–208. doi:10.1016/j.red.2009.10.005

Fisher, J., Johnson, D. S., & Smeeding, T. M. (2015). Inequality of Income and Consumption in the US: Measuring the Trends in Inequality from 1984 to 2011 for the Same Individuals. *Review of Income and Wealth, 61*(4), 630–650.

Fuchs-Schündeln, N., Krueger, D., & Sommer, M. (2010). Inequality Trends for Germany in the Last Two Decades: A Tale of Two Countries. *Review of Economic Dynamics, 13*(1), 103–132. doi:10.1016/j.red.2009.09.004

Gorodnichenko, Y., Peter, K. S., & Stolyarov, D. (2010). Inequality and Volatility Moderation in Russia: Evidence from Micro-Level Panel Data on Consumption and Income. *Review of Economic Dynamics, 13*(1), 209–237. doi:10.1016/j.red.2009.09.006

Heathcote, J., Perri, F., & Violante, G. L. (2010). Unequal We Stand: An Empirical Analysis of Economic Inequality in the United States, 19672006. *Review of Economic Dynamics, 13*(1), 15–51. doi:10.1016/j.red.2009.10.010

Höchtl, W., Sausgruber, R., & Tyran, J.-R. (2012). Inequality Aversion and Voting on Redistribution. *European Economic Review, 56*(7), 1406–1421. doi:10.1016/j.euroecorev.2012.07.004 PMID:23564967

Jappelli, T., & Pistaferri, L. (2010). Does Consumption Inequality Track Income Inequality in Italy? *Review of Economic Dynamics, 13*(1), 133–153. doi:10.1016/j.red.2009.11.001

Jerrim, J., & Macmillan, L. (2015). Income Inequality, Intergenerational Mobility, and the Great Gatsby Curve: Is Education the Key? *Social Forces, 94*(2), 505–533. doi:10.1093fov075

Kawachi, I., & Kennedy, B. P. (1997). Socioeconomic Determinants of Health: Health and Social Cohesion: Why Care About Income Inequality? *British Medical Journal, 314*(7086).

Kawachi, I., & Kennedy, B. P. (1999). Income inequality and health: Pathways and mechanisms. *Health Services Research, 34*(1 Pt 2), 215.

Kerr, W. R. (2014). Income Inequality and Social Preferences for Redistribution and Compensation Differentials. *Journal of Monetary Economics*, (April), 1–41.

Kondo, N., Sembajwe, G., Kawachi, I., van Dam, R. M., Subramanian, S. V., & Yamagata, Z. (2009). Income inequality, mortality, and self rated health: Meta-analysis of multilevel studies. *BMJ (Clinical Research Ed.)*, ▪▪▪, 339.

Milanovic, B. (2016). *Global Inequality: A New Approach for the Age of Globalization.* Harvard University Press. doi:10.4159/9780674969797

Narayan, A., Van der Weide, R., Cojocaru, A., Lakner, C., Redaelli, S., Mahler, D. G., & Thewissen, S. (2018). *Fair Progress?: Economic Mobility Across Generations Around the World.* World Bank Publications.

Pijoan-Mas, J., & Sánchez-Marcos, V. (2010). Spain is Different: Falling Trends of Inequality. *Review of Economic Dynamics, 13*(1), 154–178. doi:10.1016/j.red.2009.10.002

Piketty, T. (2015). About Capital in the Twenty-First Century. *The American Economic Review, 105*(5), 48–53. doi:10.1257/aer.p20151060

Ridic, G., Gleason, S., & Ridic, O. (2012). Comparisons of health care systems in the United States, Germany and Canada. *Materia Socio-Medica, 24*(2), 112. doi:10.5455/msm.2012.24.112-120 PMID:23678317

Rueda, D., & Stegmueller, D. (2015). *Preferences That Matter: Inequality, Redistribution and Voting*. Mimeo.

Rustichini, A., & Vostroknutov, A. (2014). Merit and Justice: An Experimental Analysis of Attitude to Inequality. *PLoS One, 9*(12), e114512–e114525. doi:10.1371/journal.pone.0114512 PMID:25490094

Shi, L., & Starfield, B. (2000). *Primary Care, Income Inequality, and Self-Rated Health in the United States: A Mixed-Level Analysis. International Journal of Health Services, 30(3),* 541–555.

Stiglitz, J. E. (2012). *The Price of Inequality: How Today's Divided Society Endangers Our Future*. WW Norton & Company.

Tamkoç, M. N., & Torul, O. (2018). Cross Sectional Facts for Macroeconomists: Wage, Income and Consumption Inequality in Turkey. Bogaziçi University.

Torul, O., & Öztunalı, O. (2018). On Income and Wealth Inequality in Turkey. Central Bank Review, 18(3), 95-106. doi:10.1016/j.cbrev.2018.06.002

Wong, A., Mazumder, B., & Halliday, T. (2019). *The Intergenerational Transmission of Health in the United States: A Latent Variables Analysis*. University of Hawaii.

World Health Organization, (2017). Tracking universal health coverage: 2017 Global Monitoring Report.

KEY TERMS AND DEFINITIONS

Gini Coefficient: Gini index measures the extent to which the distribution of income (or, in some cases, consumption expenditure, wealth or education) among individuals or households within an economy deviates from a perfectly equal distribution. A Lorenz curve plots the cumulative percentages of total income received against the cumulative number of recipients, starting with the poorest individual or household. The Gini index measures the area between the Lorenz curve and a hypothetical line of absolute equality, expressed as a percentage of the maximum area under the line. A Gini index of 0 represents perfect equality, while an index of 100 implies perfect inequality. (World Bank Indicator Code: *SI.POV.GINI*)

Private Health Care Expenditure Per Capita: Domestic private expenditures on health per capita in international dollars at purchasing power parity (PPP). Estimates of current health expenditures include healthcare goods and services consumed during each year. (World Bank Indicator Code: *SH.XPD.PVTD.PP.CD*)

Private to Total Expenditure Ratio: Domestic private expenditures on health per capita in international dollars at purchasing power parity (PPP) divided by current expenditures on health per capita in international dollars at purchasing power parity (PPP).

Total Health Care Expenditure as a Ratio of GDP: Current total expenditures on health care services as a share of GDP. (World Bank Indicator Code: *SH.XPD.CHEX.GD.ZS*)

Total Health Care Expenditure Per Capita: Current expenditures on health per capita in international dollars at purchasing power parity (PPP). Estimates of current health expenditures include healthcare goods and services consumed during each year. (World Bank Indicator Code: *SH.XPD.CHEX.PP.CD*)

ENDNOTES

1. Among others, see Atkinson (2015), Stiglitz (2012), and Milanovic (2016) for recent advances in income inequality.
2. Tamkoç and Torul (2018) discusses in detail advances in wage, income and consumption inequality, and Torul and Öztunalı (2018) reviews the upward time trend in wealth inequality.
3. See Höchtl, et al. (2012) and Rueda and Stegmueller (2015) on redistributive preferences over economic inequalities and public policy choices.
4. In a recent paper, Tamkoç and Torul (2018) adhere to the same methodology and reports on the Turkish experience over the 2001-2016 period.
5. Further most of the studies from the health but not health economics literature.
6. I also use a number of different control variables (e.g. PPP-Adjusted GDP per capita to capture economic development, percentage of population over 65 years old so as to control for the effect of aging societies in health care spending trends, …)
7. The small number (2) of countries in the North America country group is due to the fact the the group consists only of the United States and Canada, and the careful reader could note that health care spending by the two countries differ considerably: while Canadians spend 4207.67 PPP-adjusted international dollars on average, Americans spend nearly double of this value on average: 7949.90. The high American spending on education and health care, along

with its predominant reliance on private resources is coined as the *American Exceptionalism*, which I discuss in detail in the next sections.

8 In this table, I report the private-to-total expenditure ratio, and one can infer state's involvement in health care (i.e. public health care expenditure to total health care expenditure ratio) by calculating the reported ratios' distances to 1.

9 Alesina and Angeletos (2005) and Bénabou and Tirole (2006) show that according to the World Values Survey (WVS) 54% of Americans believe skill and effort is decisive in final outcomes whereas only 29% of Europeans are in agreement with this belief, with the majority of Europeans believing that luck is more pivotal. Further authors argue for significant uni-directional causality from the perception of high decisiveness of luck to higher per-capita social protection spending, and they conclude that cross-country differences in perception of fairness endogenously lead to different levels of governmental intervention in the form of taxation and redistribution, which in turn induces a more unequal income distribution in the U.S. compared to Europe.

10 I omit other group-specific scatterplot graphs for the sake of brevity. These resultant omitted graphs are available upon request.

11 The countries whose data I use in my benchmark estimations are: Algeria, Angola, Argentina, Armenia, Australia, Austria, Azerbaijan, Bangladesh, Belarus, Belgium, Benin, Bhutan, Bolivia, Bosnia and Herzegovina, Botswana, Brazil, Bulgaria, Burkina Faso, Burundi, Cabo Verde, Cameroon, Canada, Central African Republic, Chad, Chile, China, Colombia, Comoros, Congo, Costa Rica, Cote d'Ivoire, Croatia, Cyprus, Czech Republic, Denmark, Djibouti, Dominican Republic, Ecuador, Egypt, El Salvador, Estonia, Eswatini, Ethiopia, Fiji, Finland, France, Gabon, Gambia, Georgia, Germany, Ghana, Greece, Guatemala, Guinea, Guinea-Bissau, Haiti, Honduras, Hungary, Iceland, India, Indonesia, Iran, Iraq, Ireland, Israel, Italy, Jamaica, Japan, Jordan, Kazakhstan, Kenya, Kiribati, Korea, Kyrgyz Republic, Lao PDR, Latvia, Lebanon, Lesotho, Liberia, Lithuania, Luxembourg, Macedonia, Madagascar, Malawi, Malaysia, Maldives, Mali, Malta, Mauritania, Mauritius, Mexico, Micronesia, Moldova, Mongolia, Montenegro, Morocco, Mozambique, Myanmar, Namibia, Nepal, Netherlands, Nicaragua, Niger, Nigeria, Norway, Pakistan, Panama, Papua New Guinea, Paraguay, Peru, Portugal, Romania, Russian Federation, Rwanda, Samoa, Sao Tome and Principe, Senegal, Seychelles, Sierra Leone, Slovak Republic, Slovenia, Solomon Islands, South Africa, Spain, Sri Lanka, Sudan, Sweden, Switzerland, Syrian Arab Republic, Tajikistan, Tanzania, Thailand, Timor-Leste, Togo, Tonga, Tunisia, Turkey, Tuvalu, Uganda, Ukraine, United Kingdom, United States, Uruguay, Uzbekistan, Vanuatu, Venezuela, Vietnam, Yemen, Zambia and Zimbabwe.

12 I verify that when the health expenditure to GDP ratio is omitted, the coefficient before the total health care expenditure per capita variable has a negative and insignificant coefficient.

13 The careful reader could notice that I omit total health care expenditure per capita as a regressor. I do so in order to avoid multicollinearity problems associated with the linear-dependence of the right-hand side variables.

14 I omit reporting the estimation results by incorporating time trend into the models in Table 7 for the sake of brevity. These results are also available upon request.

Chapter 6
Accessibility for Everyone in Health Communication Mobile Application Usage

Ihsan Eken
https://orcid.org/0000-0002-0401-8545
Istanbul Medipol University, Turkey

Basak Gezmen
Istanbul Medipol University, Turkey

ABSTRACT

With the development of new communication technologies and the change and transformation of mobile applications, communication styles also acquire a different dimension. Currently, individuals can access information about many health-related issues easily and quickly. Mobile applications also provide support to individuals in this area anywhere at any time. However, awareness about mobile applications and their availability is important at this point. While the transformation in the technological field makes life easier for users, not everyone (young, old, disabled, etc.) enjoys the advantages equally. In this study, user-based usability testing will be carried out on the axis of E-nabız application with female users above 65 years selected according to certain criteria. The E-nabız application is a platform for all citizens registered to the E-devlet system to access health information. In this context, besides pointing out the accessibility problems of the application, possible solutions will also be offered.

DOI: 10.4018/978-1-7998-2329-2.ch006

INTRODUCTION

Communication is a concept which has maintained its importance continuously from past to present. In every aspect of our lives, we are intertwined with the concept of communication. It is not possible for us to exist without communicating in our both daily lives and corporate lives. The subject of health always comes up so that individuals can adapt themselves to their environments, maintain a good life and have control over their lives. Topics such as health services, health communication, health literacy etc. are among the fields which are often discussed and studied today. It is very important to access information as a requirement of the information society, to exist in social life by using the devices created by information technologies and to ensure its continuity.

Nowadays, with the widespread use of the Internet and mobile phones, individuals are provided with facilities for many issues. McLuhan's argument "technology is an extension of the human being" is constantly reciprocated in our living space. Now, individuals maintain a life together with their smart phones at every moment of the day. Technology has become an indispensable element of individual life. Without smartphones, individuals feel isolated, lonely and secluded. They also carry out many life practices via smart phones. As in all the fields, the field of health continues to provide services by integrating itself with technology. Now, individuals carry out most of the health-related services, one of the most important elements of their lives, on the Internet. For example, for any date and hour, they can make an appointment online from any institution, access information about institutions in the field of health, also obtain information about prescription data, past analysis results, family medicine information etc. within the scope of person-specific private health information. Furthermore, many health-related mobile applications provide convenience to individuals. One of the most frequently used mobile applications in the recent period, E-nabız application is a platform where there are many links and sharing areas from reports containing all the health information of the people to prescription and medicine sections.

In the study, regarding the E-nabız application, the user-based usability test was applied to female users above 65 years of age, who were selected according to certain criteria, the situation will be assessed in terms of the accessibility issues of the application and suggestions will be proposed.

IMPORTANCE OF THE CONCEPT OF HEALTH IN COMMUNICATION PROCESS AND HEALTH COMMUNICATION

The concept of health, which may vary from society to society, from culture to culture, has come out of its static structure in the past, and today, it is dynamic and committed to the process. In the World Health Organization's definition of health, the concept of health is expressed not only as not being sick and disabled, but also as being comfortable and fine both physically and mentally and socially (Okay, A-2009, s. 13). The availability of all the biological health, social health and psychological health, which are known as the three basic components of health, in individuals is also used in the definitions of concept of health. The integrity of mental, physical and social health is important for the individual. Human being, which is physically an organism, is approached psychologically with his individuality and personality traits, attitudes and behaviors, and socially with his roles and interactions in the society as a group member. Successful holistic functioning of each of the elements which are possessed refers to the status of being healthy and functional impairment in any one of them indicates a disease. At this point, the ultimate duty of health services is to try to increase all these elements and to make the necessary effort in protecting and improving the individual health (Yakut, 2008, p. 23-24).

Instead of the word "communication", which was transferred from French to our language, the expression "informing each other" was often used in the past. Nowadays, communication can be defined as a comprehensive message exchange which includes the phenomenon of informing each other in general. However, as can be understood from the state of belonging to many people or objects within the meaning of communication, not only a simple message exchange, but an environment of social interaction is expressed. Here, the concepts of exchange and sharing are also important (Zıllıoğlu, 2003, p. 3).

The fact that the concept of communication is used in different areas leads to separate implications for its meaning. Communication, which emerged as a necessity in the process of existence of humanity, was used in order to meet and satisfy the needs with various primitive methods in primitive periods. The images drawn on the walls of the caves and the use of smoke with the fires burned can be stated as examples for the ways of communication and informing each other (Aziz, 2012, p. 25).

Initial investigations in the field of communication, which is said to have begun with Plato's early works, show the beginnings of general thoughts about communication and its effects. It is supposed that these thoughts paved the way for communication theories (Bourse & Yücel, 2012, p. 35). Technological, social, economic and political developments played a major role in the changes and transformations in the history of communication. The researches and theories about communication which entered the field of social sciences as a product of a certain period are shaped according to the important events and conditions in their periods. The reason why the issue of communication, which started to be on the agenda in the first periods of the 20th century, was emphasized in these periods was the political events involving great masses of people (Tüfekçioğlu, 1997, pp. 38-39).

Communication, which is a phenomenon that constantly interacts with nature like all living beings, is transformed and shaped according to the continuation of human existence, is also in connection with culture as long as nature is concerned. (Oskay, 1992, p. 7). Generally defined as the process of transferring information, thoughts and behaviors, communication (İlal, 1997, p. 9) is a mutual message exchange. It is a loop with no beginning and no end where sent messages can be received and interpreted at the same time and an inference can be made. Communication is a process that connects people to each other and enable them to live in a balanced and harmonious way. In order to exist in society, human beings have to communicate with each other. Human beings, who are constantly in communication throughout the process from birth to the moment of death, transfers many messages, verbal or non-verbal, to the other party. In this context, experiences, thoughts, feelings and shares are provided through the communication tool (Mısırlı, 2007, pp. 1-2).

Everyone can communicate. However, the important issue here is how and in which direction the correct communication should be established. Today, many institutions are organizing educational seminars, courses and programs on the subject due to the increasing importance of this matter. Trainers, who are experts in communication, explain the importance of communication in all areas of our life practices and try to provide the methods of establishing correct and effective communication in our daily and corporate lives in such programs. It is obvious that a life without communication cannot be imagined and an effective communication without corporate success cannot be achieved. The essential elements of communication consist of the transmitter receiver channel. In addition, it can be checked whether communication is achieved successfully through feedback, another element.

These elements need to be available for the achievement of communication, but in some cases, the phenomenon of communication may not occur despite the presence of these elements. This is explained by the concept of lack of communication or noise. During the communication process, when there are non-overlapping areas of perception on both sides, lack of communication emerges. At this point, the ambiguity needs to be settled. (Aziz, 2012, pp. 36-37)

Like individual communication, which is a sub-system of communication, health communication is also a sub-system and gaining importance increasingly. Health is among the most important issues of our time and efforts are made to make progress in this field continuously. At this point, the issue of health communication is one of the concepts that we frequently hear about and it remains on the agenda in the studies within this field. Rogers, who defines health communication as any kind of communication that includes health, primarily underlines the necessity of recognition of health services in these definitions. In addition, health communication is considered as a fundamental process in terms of ensuring and transferring right information flow, creating attitude changes related to health and developing policies that help with the adoption of healthy lifestyles. (Tabak, 2006, p. 29). The right to health is guaranteed by the constitutions of the states as a concept that is directly related to the right to life of each individual. A social state has to create economic and social conditions for its citizens to live in a sufficiently healthy, safe and clean environment and to secure the rights of its citizens with legal guarantee (Uğurlu, 2018, p. 15).

Scientific and technological developments are progressing in the field of health, and therefore, developments in health communication continue at the same pace. (Özkan, 2011, p. 21). In a modern society, health dynamics can be discussed under 6 main headings. These are the increase in life expectations, globalization and resulting new health risks, state expenditures on the field of health, stunning developments in the private health market, increasing sensitivity and importance for health, orientation of the health spectrum towards chronic diseases and prevention of some of these today (Okay, B-2014, pp. 3-4). Patient right, which is a complement of the right to health, one of the most fundamental rights of the individual, and started to be heard of after 1980s, is secured internationally through many agreements and declarations. In this sense, every individual has the right to access the health service, have medical treatment and make use of health services as the subjects of the right. Providing activities, trainings and counseling for the health development is also included in this scope (Yüksel et al., 2014, pp. 44-45).

The concept of health development is a process aiming at the individuals' control over their health and development on the basis of public health and preventive medicine. The process also provides organizational and economic environmental support including health education. (Yüksel et al., 2014, p. 48) The non-state institutions aiming at social utility should also target sharing the same responsibility in the activities for health development. While national health programs, developing health campaigns and public health plans are at the mass communication level of health communication, communication developing within the corporate culture is ensured in the organizational health communication. Interpersonal communication involves the interaction of employees with other employees and service receivers. Progress is made with developments and innovation in many fields such as health psychology, health sociology, behavioral medicine etc. (Tabak, 2006, p. 30). In a wide definition, health communication includes the issues such as the determination of the communication methods in the creation of awareness for individuals regarding health and any field-related matter and providing the necessary information flow, establishment and legitimization of health consciousness and health literacy, creation of consciousness about the right to health and to live in a healthy environment etc.

(Yüksel et al., 2014, p. 51). At this point, the main task of the media must be to give place to publications for raising awareness on health and developing the matter. In health publications, it is very important to keep the magazine aspect in the background and to transfer the right information within the information flow to the public.

USABILITY AND USER DIVERSITY

Usability is the ability of the users in the target group to be expressed in terms of the measurement of productivity, effectiveness, and satisfaction they exhibit during the performance of tasks in a given environment through the related tool (Çağıltay, 2011). User ideas have become very important nowadays and usability testing types and methods have emerged to learn users' opinions. The usability test is to examine whether the users meet their needs and expectations on real products, and to evaluate the usability of the product in terms of effectiveness, productivity and satisfaction, except for people's subjective opinions. Today, companies create their designs according to these tests and present them to users (Eken, 2017). Usability tests are divided into two groups according to the desired purpose, in other words, according to the test types and the source of the desired data or testing methods (Tübitak & Kalkınma Bakanlığı, p. 6). Due to the subject of the study, assessment will made over the user (experimental) based usability test in this section.

User (Experimental) Based: It aims to test the real interfaces by the real user group in specific laboratory or real environments and to analyze the data to be obtained from the test result. Certain criteria are created for usability tests, and the movements of the users are recorded by taking note of their speeches. This recorded information is used directly to improve the application or to eliminate its shortcomings. Once this application is made, a more usable application becomes available for everyone.

Different methods can be used for usability tests performed by real users. Body movements and behaviors of users can be recorded while using the application, and users may be asked to transfer them to usability experts through thinking aloud. In this way, the obtained video and audio recordings can be evaluated with previous test data (Çağıltay, 2011, p. 111). These user-based tests are the tests which present the most realistic data and are mostly used. On the other hand, these tests need to be elaborated very well and most of the mistakes are made in them. They are also very costly tests. The user-based method has advantages and disadvantages (Çağıltay, 2011, pp. 126-127).

Advantages of the user-based approach:

- Real usage data is obtained.

- The most important problems can be revealed.
- It can be used for both formative and summative tests.

Disadvantages of the user-based approach:

- It can be expensive and laborious, as each user needs to be assessed individually, tested individually, and the results to be reviewed and reported. In this respect, it is both very time-consuming and some expensive sources (such as the usability laboratory, devices for recording behaviors, eye movement monitoring device, etc.) may be needed due to the requirements of the test.
- It requires patience, as mentioned in the previous heading, it is necessary to work with each user individually. Tests should only be performed with the appropriate target group (such as the visually impaired, the elderly or children) and reaching appropriate subjects can be problematic.
- It should be planned very well. If useful data collection is required in the results of the tests, the entire usability test must be well designed and implemented from the beginning. It is extremely important to assign the most appropriate tasks to the most appropriate people and to present them in a specific scenario.
- The data obtained may not provide sufficient content for the redesign of the interface tested. For example, users may say they are not satisfied with the software, but information about how the software should be may not be obtained by testing. As a result, the new design needs to be retested.

User Diversity

Regardless of our social class, ethnicity, past or physical disabilities, everyone should have equal access to a service or product from which they can benefit. Access is directly related to human rights. (Rızvanoğlu, 2009, p. 21). According to Shneiderman (1999, p. 86), it is associated with the communication law including telephone, telegraph and radio services entering into force in the United States in 1934. This law was regulated "to provide the necessary facilities for reasonable costs" and entered into force in order "to prevent discrimination based on race, color, religion, national origin and gender" especially in rural areas. This law has been adapted to computer technologies over time and has become more important today thanks to mobile communication. Accessibility must be on equal terms for everyone. However, no user is the same; users may have diversities and differences depending on these diversities.

The first users that come to mind when we use the concept of user diversity are generally the specific target groups such as people with disabilities, different sexes, languages and cultures. However, almost all users can find a wide variety of environments and situations that affect their needs. According to Rızvanoğlu (2009, p. 47), even on a simple day, whether on the road, at home or in the office, any person will need different interfaces, as long as on the same device, against the varying demands and constraints of different environments or activities, in a process where they drive, travel, walk, run or do sports. Moreover, even within a single environment and activity, people can change their preferences. Therefore, diversity is not a feature to be attributed just to users. In addition to users, it can also be attributed to the environments and situations to which users may be exposed, and even to the limitations resulting from them. What is important is the quantity of the needs associated with the different user needs and the situation that can develop in parallel to these needs and the partnership of the solutions for both. For this reason, it is necessary to consider user diversity from a wider perspective.

User diversity is one of the most important problems to overcome, where it is also challenging to expand the participation. User diversity includes users with characteristics such as different skills, knowledge, age, gender, disability, preventing conditions (mobility, sunlight, noise), literacy, culture, income and so on (Shneiderman, 1999, p. 89). Due to the subject of the study, in this section, user diversity will be evaluated over the elderly and female users.

Considering personality differences in terms of user diversity, the gender factor can be regarded as one of the important variables. In the web design and mobile application interface studies, the gender-based differences in preference and usage between male and female users have constituted the subject of a very limited number of academic researches. From the past to the present, it is seen that applications regarding gender differences at the level of usage experience first appeared in the computer and video game design (Rızvanoğlu, 2009). However, it was determined that there were concrete differences between men and women in terms of access to computer technologies. In particular, women's socio-economic status draws attention as a fundamental justification for preventing their access to computer technology. In developing countries and Turkey, the factors such as the conservative culture, inequality of opportunity in education and a low-income level, which manifest themselves in rural areas, negatively affect the access of women to information technology (Törenli, 2005)

Considering personality differences in terms of user diversity, the age factor can be regarded as one of the important variables. Due to the widespread use of smart phones and the Internet among users over 65 years of age, the usage rate of computer technologies has increased. However, users over the age of 65 are still considered as limited-level users compared to users in younger age groups. According to the research on computer and the Internet usage conducted by Turkey Statistical Institute (TSI) according to age groups, differences are observed between women and men in terms of the rates of using computer and the Internet. Especially when Table 1 is examined according to certain age groups, it is found that the computer and Internet usage rates of female users between the ages of 65-74 are at the lowest level.

One of the most important reasons for users who are considered to be older than 65 years of age, that is, to be elderly is the usage of the computer technology for health and care purposes. Computer technologies and the Internet are thought to contribute positively especially to the living standards of the elderly. Today, with the development of mobile technologies, significant increases have been experienced in mobile applications. In particular, the information transmitted by healthcare professionals through artificial intelligence reaches users and makes their lives easier. Elderly users can easily access information such as prescriptions, medications, treatment information and controls through the mobile applications at hand.

RESEARCH: A HEALTH APP E-NABIZ

The E-nabız implementation put into effect by the Republic of Turkey Ministry of Health on January 1, 2015 (Sözcü, 2019) is a platform through which you can make online appointments on any day, at any hour, from any institution you like, can access information regarding the institutions in the field of health and also obtain data within the context of private health information such as prescription information, past analysis results, family practice information, etc.

E-nabız is an application that citizens and health professionals can access health data collected from health institutions via internet and mobile devices. It is a personal health record system where you can manage all your health information and access your medical background from a single spot, regardless of where your examinations and treatments are performed. It is the world's largest and most comprehensive health informatics sub-system, which you provide yourself, where your health records can be evaluated by physicians within the framework of an authority, the period and limits of which is determined, which in this way increases the quality and speed of the diagnosis and treatment process, enables the establishment of a strong communication network between you and your doctor and which you can reach safely through the internet (E-nabız).

There are many ways to log into the E-nabız application. All the users who have e-government password (E-devlet, 2019), which has over 43 million registered users can easily login to the system. Apart from this way, you can also log into the system

Table 1. Computer and internet usage by age groups

			2009	2010	2011	2012	2013	2014	2015	2016	2017	2018
25-34	PC	K	34,5	41,6	46,7	48,1	49,1	55,3	54,5	50,8	49,9	53,6
	NET	K	32,9	40,2	44,9	47,2	48,4	57,4	62	70,7	78,7	85,6
	PC	E	58,6	62,4	67,5	70	70	71,3	70,8	67,7	67,9	69,8
	NET	E	57,2	60,9	65,4	69,6	69,1	76,8	81,3	86,7	92,6	94,5
	PC	T	46,6	52	57,1	59,1	59,6	63,3	62,7	59,3	59	61,7
	NET	T	45,1	50,ü6	55,1	58,5	58,8	67,1	71,7	78,8	85,7	90,1
45-54	PC	K	11,6	12,7	13,9	17	15,9	20,6	22,8	22,7	22,6	23,2
	NET	K	10,5	12,9	13,2	16,2	15,1	20	24,2	30,6	40,9	51,1
	PC	E	28,9	33,6	34,3	36,3	36,2	40,5	41,2	39,7	41,1	42
	NET	E	26,7	31,9	32,1	34,8	34,7	40,7	43,7	51,8	62,5	71,8
	PC	T	20,2	23,2	24,1	26,7	26,1	30,6	32	31,2	31,9	32,6
	NET	T	18,6	22,4	22,7	25,5	24,9	30,4	34	41,3	51,7	61,5
65-74	PC	K	1,4	1,6	1,4	1,3	1,7	1,8	2,8	4,3	4,2	5,9
	NET	K	1,2	1,6	1,2	1,3	1,5	1,8	2,8	5,8	7,5	11,9
	PC	E	3,2	4,1	5	6,9	7,8	8,8	8,2	9,2	11,4	11,5
	NET	E	3,1	4,2	4,5	6,4	7,5	8,8	8,8	12,5	15,6	23
	PC	T	2,2	2,7	3	3,8	4,4	5	5,3	6,5	7,5	8,5
	NET	T	2	2,7	2,7	3,6	4,2	5	5,6	8,8	11,3	17

PC: Computer, Net: Internet, F: Female, M: Male, T: Total
Source: (dokuz8haber, 2018)

with a one time password, by having your e-signature, mobile signature and mobile number registered by your family doctor. (E-nabız)

The Aim and the Significance of the Research

As in any period, health is one of the most important issues approached sensitively today. Health, which is defined not only as the state of being sick and healthy but also as a state of social and psychological well-being, is of great importance in the group classified as elderly as in all age groups. Universal access is every human's common right without variables like age and gender. Mobile applications that are developed with the increase in the usage rate of mobile technology today make the lives of all the users easier in a certain way. However, the usability of the applications by the users from groups such as the ones with disabilities may not be as easy as in other user groups. The purpose of the usability test is to understand and research the usage of e-nabız applications on smartphones by female users above the age of 65, in other words, the accessibility status of e-nabız application. For this purpose, this study was conducted to measure the usability of these applications, evaluate the participation of the users in the applications and observe their experiences.

The Limitations of the Research

The study was conducted on female users above the age of 65. A survey was applied regarding the usability test before the study. The participants were selected according to the questions in the survey. All the participants in the study had E-devlet (e-government) memberships. Another limitation in the study is the fact that all the users had smartphones with the brand of iPhone. Another limitation for the users is that they had to apply to and were treated in/by hospitals, polyclinics or family physician because of their disease in the last year.

Methodology of the Study

When it came to the method, site and perspective of the study, the aim was to execute a study embodying the usability method, which is fed from the field of human-computer interaction, as both a method and a theoretical area. In the research, the user (experimental) based usability test was applied. The reason behind the execution of this test is its presentation of the most realistic data compared to other tests and its examination of real interfaces in specific real environments by the real user group and its analysis of the data to be obtained as a result of the test.

Determination of the ideal number of people needed for usability tests is one of the most argued matters. According to Nielsen, "the number of people needed to reveal the basic problems related to a system in usability tests must be at least five". Nielsen asserted that 75% of the problem can be revealed with five people in well-designed usability tests. Increasing the number of the users in the test, for example, increasing it from five to fifteen reveals about 15% of the problems (Çağıltay, 2011, p. 114). During the in-depth interviews with the firms working on usability in the sector, it was observed that these firms usually selected five people to conduct the test. Firms that apply the usability test increase the number of criteria rather than people and increase the number of people together with criteria. Thus, different results are researched for the test to be executed (Eken, 2017).

In the study, the purposive sampling technique was used. Another sampling technique which is not based on probability is purposive or judgment sampling. The sampling in which subjects with certain characteristics are thought to comply with the research problem through personal observations in the research is called purposive sampling (Gürbüz & Şahin, 2016, p. 135).

Three criteria were defined for user based usability tests. The usability test was conducted with fifteen people in total as five people for each criterion. The criteria defined for usability tests are the usage of smartphone at a low level, the usage of smartphone at a medium level and the usage of smartphone at a high level. The users selected for the usability test were chosen according to their levels of using a smartphone, which they provided after answering the certain survey questions. A certain amount of payment was made to all the visually impaired users who participated in the usability test for their attendance. Eight tasks were determined for the usability test.

Usability tests were conducted via iPhone 6S with the operating system of Apple IOS 12.3.1. Before the tests, the factory setting of the smartphone were restored and all the programs were removed. After this operation, E-nabız (2.5.2) application was installed on the smartphone which would be used by the female users above the age of 65. All the passwords in the smartphone that would be used in the test for the female users above the age of 65 were removed. When the screen lock was opened, a folder was created named as test next to the appearing programs and the application was placed in this folder.

Instead of a usability laboratory, the computer laboratory of Istanbul Medipol University Media Center was used so that the female users above the age of 65 could be comfortable during the test. In total, there are three attendants in the environment during the test: an attendant who follows the flow by asking questions, an attendant who takes note of the statements of the female users above the age of 65 and follows the task chart, and a cameraman who follows the tasks completed by the female users above the age of 65 on the smartphone. The female users above the age of 65 were requested to tell the tasks they performed during the test loudly. The performed tasks were both video and audio recorded. These user-based tests are the tests which present the most realistic data and are mostly used. On the other hand, these tests need to be elaborated very well and most of the mistakes are made in them.

The study was conducted in the computer laboratory of Istanbul Medipol University Media Center between July 1, 2019 and July 3, 2019. For the study, three criteria were determined; fifteen people were prepared in total as five people for each criterion. The criteria related to people were prepared according to their usage of smartphone at a low level, at a medium level and at a high level. Because the characteristics of each user were different from each other, the test durations also changed among the users. Among the users, the test durations changed between 45 minutes and 180 minutes.

Findings of the Research

Ten tasks were performed by fifteen different users on E-nabız application. On Table 2, ten tasks ranging from easy to difficult by women over the age of 65 and the data regarding these tasks are seen. Each task has a certain period of time and the number of buttons touched (steps) to be performed. In the table, the users between the 1st and the 5th were defined as those who can use the smartphone at a low level and the average of the users who use the smartphone at a low level was named as "Low (average)". In the table, the users between the 6th and the 10th were defined as the users who can use the smartphone at the intermediate level and the average of the users who used the smartphone moderately was named as "Medium (average)". In the table, users between the 11th and the 15th were defined as users who can use the smartphone at a good level and the average of the users who use it at a good level was named as "Good (average)". The average of all users was named as "General (average)". Each task requires a task duration and a number of steps to be performed. The optimal time and number of steps required for this time and number of steps is the overall average of all users.

E-nabız (2.5.2) application and 10 tasks were determined for mobile usability testing. For E-nabız application, the tasks determined were ""Being able to enter your age, height, weight and blood information from the tab "Edit Profile""", "Being able to record by writing the phrase "I am allergic to penicillin" in my emergency notes ","Finding the most recently visited hospital and being able to obtain the prescription written by the doctor, " "Being able to open the prospectus of the medicine you bought the latest," "Being able to find the hospital closest to your location, the address and the location of the hospital," "Opening the notices section and being able to display your log ins in the system," "Being able to make an appointment for the date July 31, 2019," "Being able to be a blood donor by entering the bone morrow section," "Being able to write and record the name İhsan Eken and the number 555 555 55 55, among the people to be called in stated of emergency," "Finding the recently registered disease among my diseases, display it and being able to monitor the procedures later."

It is observed that all users were able to complete the first task, which is "Being able to enter your information of age, height, weight and blood information from the tab of editing profile." The average time in which the users, who are between the 1th and 5th, that is who can use the smart phone at low levels can complete the task is 141.8 seconds and the average number of steps that they can complete the task is 25.75 steps. Within this group, the duration, which user 1, who is the fastest in the group completes the task is 120 seconds and the number of steps is 24. In this group, the duration of user 3, who completes the task the most slowly is 160 seconds and the number of steps is 28. The average time, that users who are between the 6th and

Table 2. The statistics of women over the age of 65, between their 1st and 5th tasks regarding the application of e-nabiz

	Task 1		Task 2		Task 3		Task 4		Task 5	
	Second	**Steps**	**Second**	**Steps**	**Second**	**Steps**	**Second**	**Steps**	**Second**	**Steps**
User 1	120	24	95	30	115	19	38	17	43	5
User 2	132	27	110	32	124	21	43	17	39	6
User 3	160	28	143	35	157	23	69	19	71	6
User 4	147	25	131	36	160	23	61	20	59	6
User 5	150	23	85	37	100	15	30	20	60	5
User 6	128	23	95	30	98	19	48	20	27	4
User 7	117	24	100	29	152	20	63	17	29	5
User 8	127	22	125	34	113	19	87	31	46	7
User 9	93	22	103	32	124	20	41	17	28	5
User 10	113	19	100	31	109	18	35	12	22	4
User 11	94	21	100	31	97	19	38	14	22	5
User 12	110	23	107	32	100	20	41	19	28	5
User 13	108	22	105	31	103	20	40	20	30	5
User 14	117	24	109	32	101	19	47	23	31	5
User 15	90	20	92	30	92	19	36	13	21	4
Low (av.)	141,80	25,75	112,80	34,00	131,20	20,20	48,20	18,25	54,40	5,75
Modarete (av.)	112,50	21,33	101,50	31,75	110,33	19,00	38,00	14,50	28,00	5,00
Good (av.)	103,80	22,00	102,60	31,20	98,60	19,40	39,71	17,25	26,40	5,00
General (av.)	119,37	23,03	105,63	32,32	113,38	19,53	41,97	16,67	36,27	5,25

10th user, that is who can use smart phone at moderate levels can complete the task is 112.5 seconds and their average number of steps in completing the task is 21.33 steps. Within this group, the duration of user 9, who completes the task the fastest is 93 seconds, and the number of steps is 22. Within this group, the duration of the user 6, who completes the task in the slowest way is 128 seconds and the number of steps is 23. The average time that the users between the 11th and 15th user, who can use the smart phone at a good level can complete the task is 103.8 seconds and the average number of steps that they can complete the task is 22. Within this group, the duration of user 15, who completes the task the fastest is 90 seconds, and the number of steps is 20. Within this group, the duration of the user 14, who completes the task in the slowest way is 117 seconds and the number of steps is 24. The number of users, between the 1st and 15th users, whose duration of completing the first task is below the average duration is 8 (user 7, user 9, user 10, user 11, user 12, user 13, user 14 and user 15) and the number of users, whose duration of completing the first task is above the average is 7 (user 1, user 2, user 3, user 4, user 5, user 6, and user 8). The number of users, between the 1st and the 15th users, who completed the first task with less than the average number of steps is 9 (user 5, user 6, user 8, user 9, user 10, user 11, user 12, user 13 and user 15) and the number of users, who completed the first task with more than the average number of steps is 6 (user 1, user 2, user 3, user 4, user 7 and user 14). When the average duration of users is examined, all of the users who can use the smart phone at moderate (6-10) and good (11-15) levels have been found to perform their tasks below average time. When the users' average number of steps was examined, users 7 and 14, who can use the smart phone at moderate (6-10) and good (11-15) levels were found to complete the task with a number of steps over the average. In addition, it was observed that even though the user 5 described him/herself as a user of smartphone at a low level, she completed the task with a smaller number of steps than the average.

It is seen that all users could complete the second task, which was being able to write the "I am allergic to penicillin," in the emergency notes and record it. The average time that the users between the 1st and the 5th, that is users who can use the smart phone at a low level could complete the task was 112.8 seconds, and the average number of steps that they could complete the task was 34. Within this group, the duration of user 5, who completed his/her task the fastest is 85 seconds, and his/her number of steps is 37. In this group, the duration of user 3, who completed his/her task the most slowly is 143 seconds and his/her number of steps is 35. The average time that users between the 6th and 10th user, that is those who can use the smart phone at a moderate level could complete the task was 101.5 seconds and their average number of steps was 31.75. Within this group, the duration of the user 6, who completed the task the fastest was 95 seconds and his/her number of steps was 30. Within this group, the duration of the user 8, who completed the task in the slowest way was 125 seconds and his/her number of steps was 34. The average duration, that the users between the 11th and the 15th users, that is those who can use the smart phone at a good level could complete the task was 102.6 seconds and their average number of steps was 31.2. . Within this group, the duration of the user 15, who completed the task the fastest was 92 seconds and his/her number of steps was 30. In this group, the duration of user 14, who completed his/her task the most slowly was 109 seconds and his/her number of steps was 32. The number of users, between the 1st and 15th user, who completed the second task below the average time is 9 (user 1, user 5, user 6, user 7, user 9, user 10, user 11, user 13 and user 15) and the number of users, who completed the task above the average time is 6 (user 2, user 3, user 4, user 8, user 12, and user 14). The number of users, between the 1st and 15th user, whose number of steps was below the average is 11 (user 1, user 2, user 6, user 7, user 9, user 10, user 11, user 12, user 13, user 14, and user 15) and the number of users, whose number of steps was above the average is 4 (user 3, user 4, user 5 and user 8). When the average duration of users was examined, it was seen that among the users who can use the smartphone at moderate (6-10) and good (11-15) levels, user 8, user 12 and user 14 performed their tasks above the average duration. Besides, even though users 1 and 5 described themselves as users of smart phones at a low level, they were found to complete their tasks under the average duration. When the users' average number of steps was examined, it was seen that all users who can use the smart phone at a good level (11-15) completed the task with a number of steps below the average. In addition, even though users 1 and 2 defined themselves as users of smart phone at a low level, they were found to complete the task with a number of steps below the average.

All the users were observed to complete the third task, which was "Finding the most recently visited hospital and being able to obtain the prescription written by the doctor." The average duration that the users between the 1st and the 5th, that is those who can use the smart phone at a low level could complete the task was 131.2 seconds and the average number of steps that they could complete the task was 20.2. Within this group, the duration of user 5, who completed his/her task the fastest was 100 seconds, and his/her number of steps was 15. Within this group, the duration of the user 4, who completed his/her task in the slowest way was 160 seconds and his/her number of steps was 23. The average duration, in which the users between the 6th and the 10th, that is those who can use the smart phone at a moderate level could complete the task was 110.33 seconds and the average number of steps with which they could complete the task was 19. Within this group, the duration of the user 6, who completed the task the fastest was 98 seconds and his/her number of steps was 19. In this group, the duration of user 7, who completed his/her task the most slowly was 152 seconds and his/her number of steps was 20. The average duration, that the users between the 11th and the 15th users, that is those who can use the smart phone at a good level could complete the task was 98.6 seconds and their average number of steps was 19.4. Within this group, the duration of the user 15, who completed the task the fastest was 92 seconds and his/her number of steps was 19. In this group, the duration of user 13, who completed his/her task the most slowly was 103 seconds and his/her number of steps was 20. The number of users, between the 1st and the 15th users, who completed the third task with a duration less than the average is 9 (user 5, user 6, user 8, user 10, user 11, user 12, user 13, user 14 and user 15) and the number of users, who completed the third task with a duration more than the average is 6 (user 1, user 2, user 3, user 4, user 7 and user 9). The number of users, between the 1st and the 15th user, who completed the third task with a number of steps less than the average is 8 (user 1, user 5, user 6, user

8, user 10, user 11, user 14 and user 15) and the number of users who completed the third task with a number of steps more than the average is 7 (user 2, user 3, user 4, user 7, user 9, user 12, and user 13). When the average duration of users is examined, all of the users who can use the smart phone at a good (11-15) level were found to perform their tasks below the average duration. Besides, even though users 5 defined him/herself as a user of smart phone at a low level, s/he was found to complete his/her task with a duration less than the average. When the average number of steps of users was examined, it was seen that none of the users who can use the smart phone at low (1-5), moderate (6-10) and good (11-15) levels could complete the task with a number of steps below the average.

It is seen that all the users were able to complete the fourth task, which is "Being able to open the prospectus of the medicine you bought most recently from the "my medicines" tab. The average duration in which the users between the 1st and the 5th, that is those who can use the smart phone at a low level could complete the task was 48.2 seconds and their number of steps was 18.25. Within this group, the duration of user 5, who completed his/her task the fastest was 30 seconds, and his/her number of steps was 20. In this group, the duration of user 3, who completed his/her task the most slowly was 69 seconds and his/her number of steps was 19. The average duration, in which the users between the 6th and the 10th, that is those who can use the smart phone at a moderate level could complete the task was 38 seconds and the average number of steps with which they could complete the task was 14.5. Within this group, the duration of user 10, who completed his/her task the fastest was 35 seconds, and his/her number of steps was 12. Within this group, the duration of the user 8, who completed his/her task in the slowest way was 87 seconds and his/her number of steps was 31. The average duration, that the users between the 11th and the 15th users, that is those who can use the smart phone at a good level could complete the task was 39.71 seconds and their average number of steps was 17.25. Within this group, the duration of the user 15, who completed the task the fastest was 36 seconds and his/her number of steps was 13. Within this group, the duration of the user 14, who completed his/her task in the slowest way was 47 seconds and his/her number of steps was 23. The number of users, between the 1st and 15th user, who completed the fourth task below the average duration is 8 (user 1, user 5, user 9, user 10, user 11, user 12, user 13 and user 15) and the number of users, who completed the task above the average duration is 7 (user 2, user 3, user 4, user 6, user 7, user 8, and user 14). The number of users, between the 1st and the 15th user who completed the fourth task with a number of steps below the average is 3 (user 10, user 11 and user 15) and the number of users who completed the fourth task with a number of steps above the average is 12 (user 1, user 2, user 3, user 4, user 5, user 6, user 7, user 8, user 9, user 12, user 13, and user 14). When the average time and steps of users are examined, the average of the users who can use the smart phone at the a moderate (6-10) level was found to be lower than the average of the users who can use the smart phone at a good level (11-15).

It is seen that all users could complete the fifth task, which is "Finding the nearest hospital to your location and being able to obtain the hospital address and location". The average duration in which the users between the 1st and the 5th, that is those who can use the smart phone at a low level could complete the fifth task was 54.4 seconds and the average number of steps with which they could complete the task was 5.75. Within this group, the duration of user 2, who completed his/her task the fastest was 39 seconds and his/her number of steps was 6. In this group, the duration of user 3, who completed his/her task the most slowly was 71 seconds and his/her number of steps was 6. The average duration, in which the users between the 6th and the 10th, that is those who can use the smart phone at a moderate level could complete the task was 28 seconds and the average number of steps with which they could complete the task was 5. Within this group, the duration of user 8, who completed his/her task the fastest was 22 seconds and his/her number of steps was 4. Within this group, the duration of user 8, who completed his/her task in the slowest way was 46 seconds and his/her number of steps was 7. The average duration, that the users between the 11th and the 15th users, that is those who can use the smart phone at a good level could complete the fifth task was 26.4 seconds and their average number of steps was 5. Within this group, the duration of the user 15, who completed the task the fastest was 21 seconds and his/her number of steps was 4. In this group, the duration of user 14, who completed his/her task the most slowly was 31 seconds and his/her number of steps was 5. The number of users, whose duration of completing the fifth task was below the average is 9 (user 6, user 7, user 9, user 10, user 11, user 12, user 13, user 14 and user 15) and the number of users, whose duration of completing the task was above the average is 6 (user 1, user 2, user 3, user 4, user 5 and user 8). The number of users, between the 1st and 15th users, who completed the fifth task with a number of steps below the average is 11 (user 1, user 5, user 6, user 7, user 9, user 10, user 11, user 12, user 13, user 14, and user 15) and the number of users, whose number of steps was above the average is 4 (user 2, user 3, user 4 and user 8). When the users' average duration and their number of steps is examined, all of the users who can use the smart phone at a good (11-15) level were found to complete their tasks below the average duration and number of steps.

It is seen that all the users were able to complete the sixth task, which was "Opening the notification section and being able to display your entries." The average duration, with which the users between the 1st and the 5th, that is that is those who can use the smart phone at a low level could complete the sixth task was 33.2 seconds and the average number of steps with which they could complete the task was 5.25 Within this group, the duration of the user 5, who completed the task

Table 3. The Statistics of women over the age of 65, between their 6st and 10th tasks regarding the application of e-nabiz

	Task 6		Task 7		Task 8		Task 9		Task 10	
	Second	Steps	Second	Steps	Second	Steps	Second	Steps	Second	Steps
User 1	54	7	312	103	89	31	78	39	41	5
User 2	43	6	290	98	85	32	70	37	39	6
User 3	21	3	267	90	74	23	61	32	34	6
User 4	29	4	279	93	77	21	69	32	35	6
User 5	19	4	261	87	70	21	64	31	25	6
User 6	15	3	267	88	51	16	63	37	20	6
User 7	17	3	257	82	51	15	53	30	20	6
User 8	18	4			71	34	73	34	43	4
User 9	41	7	278	86	70	14	50	31	37	4
User 10	13	5	275	95	65	20	53	35	15	3
User 11	16	3	260	80	45	12	48	30	21	3
User 12	19	4	254	81	60	15	51	31	29	4
User 13	17	3	263	84	59	15	50	30	30	4
User 14	22	4	271	89	63	14	52	32	23	3
User 15	15	3	250	80	46	14	47	30	17	3
Low (av.)	33,20	5,25	281,80	94,20	79,00	25,60	68,40	34,33	34,80	5,80
Modarete (av.)	22,75	4,75	269,25	87,75	68,67	19,80	53,00	35,00	27,00	4,60
Good (av.)	17,80	3,67	259,60	82,80	54,60	14,00	49,60	30,50	24,00	3,40
General (av.)	24,58	4,56	270,22	88,25	67,42	19,80	57,00	33,28	28,60	4,60

the fastest was 19 seconds and his/her number of steps was 4. In this group, the duration of user 2, who completed his/her task the most slowly was 43 seconds and his/her number of steps was 6. The average duration in which the users between the 6th and the 10th, that is those who can use the smart phone at a moderate level could complete the sixth task was 22.75 seconds and their average number of steps was 4.75. Within this group, the duration of user 10, who completed his/her task the fastest was 13 seconds, and his/her number of steps was 5. Within this group, the duration of user 9, who completed his/her task in the slowest way was 41 seconds and his/her number of steps was 7. The average time that the users between the 11th and 15th user, who can use the smart phone at a good level could complete the task was 18.8 seconds and the average number of steps with which they could complete the task was 3.67. Within this group, the duration of the user 15, who completed his/her task the fastest was 15 seconds and his/her number of steps was 3. Within this group, the duration of the user 14, who completed his/her task in the slowest way was 22 seconds and his/her number of steps was 4. The number of users, between the 1st and the 15th users, who completed the sixth task with a duration less than the average is 11 (user 3, user 5, user 6, user 7, user 8, user 10, user 11, user 12, user 13, user 14 and user 15) and the number of users, who completed the sixth task with a duration above the average is 4 (user 1, user 2, user 4 and user 9). The number of users, between the 1st and 15th users, who completed the sixth task with a number of steps below the average is 11 (user 3, user 4, user 5, user 6, user 7, user 8, user 11, user 12, user 13, user 14, and user 15) and the number of users, whose number of steps was above the average is 4 (user 1, user 2, user 9 and user 10). When the average duration of users was examined, it was determined that all users, except for the user 9, who can use the smart phone at a moderate (6-10) and good (11-15) level, completed their tasks below average duration. Besides, even though users 3 and 5 described themselves as users of smartphone at a low level, they completed their tasks in a duration below the average. When the users' average number of steps was examined, it was seen that all users who can use the smart phone at a good level (11-15) completed the task with a number of steps below the average. In addition, even though the users 3, 4 and 5 described themselves as users of smart phone at a low level, they were found to have completed their tasks with a number of steps below the average.

It is seen that all users, except user 8, could complete the seventh task which is "Being able to make an appointment for July 31, 2019." The average duration that the users between the 1st and the 5th, that is those who can use the smart phone at a low level could complete the task was 281.8 seconds and the average number of steps with which they could complete the task was 94.2. Within this group, the duration of user 5, who completed his/her task the fastest was 261 seconds, and his/her number of steps was 87. Within this group, the duration of the user 1, who completed the task in the slowest way was 312 seconds and his/her number of steps was 103. The average duration, in which the users between the 6th and the 10th, that is those who can use the smart phone at a moderate level could complete the seventh task was 269.71 seconds and the average number of steps with which they could complete the task was 87.75. Within this group, the duration of user 7, who completed his/her task the fastest was 257 seconds, and his/her number of steps was 82. Within this group, the duration of user 9, who completed his/her task in the slowest way was 278 seconds and his/her number of steps was 86. The average duration, that the users between the 11th and the 15th users, users, that is those who can use the smart phone at a good level could complete the task was 259.6 seconds and their average number of steps was 82.8. Within this group, the duration of user

15, who completed his/her task the fastest was 250 seconds, and his/her number of steps was 80. Within this group, the duration of user 14, who completed his/her task in the slowest way was 271 seconds and his/her number of steps was 89. The number of users, between the 1st and the 15th users, who completed the seventh task with a duration less than the average was 8 (user 3, user 5, user 6, user 7, user 8, user 11, user 12, user 13 and user 15) and the number of users, who completed the seventh task with a duration above the average is 6 (user 1, user 2, user 4, user 9, user 10 and user 14). The number of users, between the 1st and the 15th users, who completed the seventh task with a number of steps less than the average is 8 (user 5, user 6, user 7, user 8, user 9, user 11, user 12, user 13 and user 15) and the number of users, who completed the seventh task with a number of steps less than the average is 6 (user 1, user 2, user 3, user 4, user 10 and user 14).

It is seen that all users were able to complete the eighth task, which is "Being able to be a blood donor by entering the section of bone marrow". The average duration in which the users between the 1st and the 5th, that is those who can use the smart phone at a low level could complete the eighth task was 79 seconds and their number of steps was 25.6. Within this group, the duration of user 5, who completed his/her task the fastest was 70 seconds, and his/her number of steps was 21. Within this group, the duration of the user 1, who completed his/her task in the slowest way was 89 seconds and his/her number of steps was 31. The average duration, in which the users between the 6th and the 10th, that is those who can use the smart phone at a moderate level could complete the task was 68.67 seconds and the average number of steps with which they could complete the task was 19.8. Within this group, the duration of users 6 and 7, who completed their tasks the fastest was 51 seconds and their number of steps was 16 and 15. Within this group, the duration of the user 8, who completed his/her task in the slowest way was 71 seconds and his/her number of steps was 34. The average duration, that the users between the 11th and the 15th users, users, that is those who can use the smart phone at a good level could complete the eighth task was 54.6 seconds and their average number of steps was 14. Within this group, the duration of user 11, who completed his/her task the fastest was 45 seconds, and his/her number of steps was 12. Within this group, the duration of the user 14, who completed his/her task in the slowest way was 63 seconds and his/her number of steps was 14. The number of users, between the 1st and the 15th users, who completed the eighth task with a duration below the average is 8 (user 6, user 7, user 10, user 11, user 12, user 13, user 14 and user 15) and the number of users, whose duration of completing the task was above the average is 7 (user 1, user 2, user 3, user 4, user 5, user 8 and user 9). The number of users, between the 1st and the 15th users, who completed the eighth task with a number of steps less than the average is 8 (user 6, user 7, user 9, user 11, user 12, user 13, user 14 and user 15) and the number of users, who completed the eighth task with a number of steps above the average is 7 (user 1, user 2, user 3, user 4, user 5, user 8 and user 10). When the average duration of users was examined, it was found that all users who can use smart phone at a good level (11-15) completed their tasks within a duration below the average. When the users' average number of steps was examined, it was seen that all users who can use the smart phone at a good level (11-15) completed the task with a number of steps below the average.

It is seen that all users were able to complete the ninth task, which is "Being able to write and register the name İhsan Eken and the number 555 555 55 55, to be included among the people to be called in a state of emergency. The average duration in which the users between the 1st and the 5th, that is those who can use the smart phone at a low level could complete the ninth task was 68.4 seconds and the average number of steps with which they could complete the task was 34.33. Within this group, the duration of user 3, who completed his/her task the fastest was 61 seconds, and his/her number of steps was 32. Within this group, the duration of the user 1, who completed his/her task in the slowest way was 78 seconds and his/her number of steps was 39. The average duration, within which the users between the 6th and the 10th, that is those who can use the smart phone at a moderate level could complete the ninth task was 53 seconds and the average number of steps with which they could complete the task was 35. Within this group, the duration of user 9, who completed the task the fastest was 50 seconds, and his/her number of steps was 31. Within this group, the duration of user 8, who completed his/her task in the slowest way was 73 seconds and her number of steps was 34. The average duration, that the users between the 11th and the 15th, that is those who can use the smart phone at a good level could complete the fifth task was 49.6 seconds and their average number of steps was 30.5. Within this group, the duration of user 11, who completed his/her task the fastest was 45 seconds, and his/her number of steps was 12. Within this group, the duration of the user 15, who completed his/her task in the slowest way was 47 seconds and his/her number of steps was 30. The number of users, between the 1st and the 15th, whose duration of completing the ninth task is below the average is 8 (user 7, user 9, user 10, user 11, user 12, user 13, user 14 and user 15) and the number of users, whose duration of completing the task was above the average is 7 (user 1, user 2, user 3, user 4, user 5, user 6, and user 8). The number of users, between the 1st and 15th users, who completed the sixth task with a number of steps below the average is 10 (user 3, user 4, user 5, user 7, user 9, user 11, user 12, user 13, user 14 and user 15) and the number of users, whose number of steps was above the average is 5 (user 2, user 6, user 8 and user 10). When the average duration of users was examined, it was found that all users who can use smart phone at a good level (11-15) completed their tasks within a duration below the average. When the users' average number of steps was examined, it was seen that all users who can use the smart phone at a good level (11-15) completed the task with a number of steps below the average. In addition, even though the users 3, 4 and 5 described themselves as users, users of smart phone at a low level, they were found to have completed their tasks with a number of steps below the average.

It is seen that all users could complete the tenth task, which is "Finding and displaying your most recently registered disease from my illnesses and then being able to monitor the processes." The average duration that the users between the 1st and the 5th, that is those who can use the smart phone at a low level could complete the task was 34.8 seconds and the average number of steps with which they could complete the task was 5.8. Within this group, the duration of user 5, who completed his/her task the fastest was 25 seconds, and his/her number of steps was 6. Within this group, the duration of user 1, who completed his/her task in the slowest way was 41 seconds and his/her number of steps was 5. The average duration, within which the users between the 6th and the 10th10th, that is those who can use the smart phone at a moderate level could complete the tenth task was 27 seconds and the average number of steps with which they could complete the task was 4.6. Within this group, the duration of user 10, who completed his/her task the fastest was 15 seconds and his/her number of steps was 3. Within this group, the duration of user 8, who completed his/her task in the slowest way was 43 seconds and his/her number of steps was 4. The average duration, that the users between the 11th and the 15th users,, that is those who can use the smart phone at a good level could complete the tenth task was 24 seconds and their average number of steps was 3.4. Within this group, the duration of user 11, who completed his/her task the fastest was 45 seconds, and his/her number of steps was 12. Within this group, the duration of user 15, who completed his/her task the fastest was 17 seconds and his/her number of steps was 3. The number of users, between the 1st and 15th, who completed the tenth task within a duration below the average is 7 (user 5, user 6, user 7, user 10, user 11, user 14 and user 15) and the number of users who completed the task within a duration above the average is 8 (user 1, user 2, user 3, user 4, user 8, user 9, user 12 and user 13). The number of users, between the 1st and 15th, who completed the tenth task with a number of steps below the average is 8 (user 8, user 9, user 10, user 11, user 12, user 13, user 14 and user 15) and the number of users, who completed the task with a number of steps above the average is 7 (user 1, user 2, user 3, user 4, user 5, user 6 and user 7). When the users' average number of steps was examined, it was seen that all users who can use the smart phone at a good level (11-15) completed the task with a number of steps below the average.

When the ten tasks performed by women users over the age of 65 on E-nabız application were examined regarding duration on Table 2 and Table 3, it was found that the task finished within the longest duration in terms of general average is the seventh task. The average duration of the completion of this task is 270.22 seconds. The task completed by the users within the shortest period of time is the sixth task with an average of 24.58 seconds. If the duration of users' completion of tasks is to be ordered, the sorting will be as the 6th task (av. 24.58 sec.), the 10th task (av. 28.6 sec.), the 5th task (av. 36.27 sec.), the 4th task (av. 41.97 sec.), the 9th task (av. 57 sec.), the 8th task (av. 67.42 sec.), the 2nd task (av. 105.63 sec.), the 3rd task (av. 113.38 sec.), the 1st task (av. 119.37 sec.), the 7th task (av. 270.22 sec.). When the users' number of steps taken during the completion of the 10 tasks is examined, the task with the most number of steps was found to be the seventh task. The number of steps taken in this task is 88.25 in average. The task with the least number of user steps is the sixth task with an average of 4.56 steps. If the users' completion of task is ordered by the number of steps, the sorting will be as the 6th task (av. 4.56 steps), 10th task (av. 4.6 steps), 5th task (av. 5.25 steps), 4th task (av. 16.67 steps), 3rd task (av. 19.53 steps), 8th task (av. 19.8 steps, 1st task (av. 23.03 steps), 2nd task (av. 32.32 steps), 9th task (av. 33.28 steps), 7th task (av. 88.25 steps).

SOLUTIONS AND RECOMMENDATIONS

The concept of health is the leading topic among the topics, which the individuals are most sensitive about, not only in the world but also in our country. The digital world, which is constantly changing and transforming, has become an area where individuals spend time every minute without the concept of time. In this context, health services offerings have started to become more attractive and easy for users through the digital world. The development of technology does not only effect all kinds of fields such as media, finance, security, etc., but also transforms the forms of providing service. Concepts such as successful service delivery, health literacy, healthcare workers' communication and health communication often constitute the agenda of our day. At this point, it should be taken into consideration that being healthy is the basic freedom, and especially in public applications, universal design principles, accessibility and usability should be prioritized. The fact that every communication area in health communication is aimed at meeting the needs of the user is a matter of fundamental human rights rather than a necessity. The individual should be able to access any information s/he needs, any time, any minute, by him/herself without the help of anyone else. Digital transformation, which is one of the easing elements of life, shows itself in the field of health by constantly renewing itself. E-nabız, which is a public practice, enables individuals to make life easier at the point of health services, to make an online appointment at any day and time from the institution s/he likes to have access to information about institutions in the field of health, as well as prescription information, past analysis results, family practice information etc. Reproduction and development of such applications according to universal design principles, especially their being used by the disabled, elderly, etc., which are thought to be in need of help in the society without the help of others will allow them to act independently.

FUTURE RESEARCH DIRECTIONS

In line with the new technologies developed in the field of health as in all other fields, applications are being developed to provide benefits by accessing individuals more easily and faster. Health is one of the areas, which individuals prioritize the most in their lives. At this point, individuals want to be in a position where they can immediately access any information they need. Technological advances provide convenience to users with instant access to information, interactivity and recycling features. Health practices are also adapted to these areas by changing and transforming. Today, within the scope of health communication, many different applications are preferred by individuals, especially on the basis of smart phones. E-nabız is also vital for users in terms of providing individuals with instant access to relevant and necessary health information. The increase in the number of the E-nabız application and similar applications can help people to pursue their lives in a healthier way. At this point, the necessary studies should be carried out in order to increase such applications. Not all users have the same attributes or characteristics. Users are differentiated by age, gender and disability. Especially public applications should be designed in line with the universal design principles, for them to be used by all people. These applications should especially also be tested by user groups such as the disabled and the elderly and their use of these applications should be encouraged.

CONCLUSION

The concepts of being healthy, living in a healthy environment and health rights go back to the oldest periods of human existence. In the general definitions of the concept of health, non-sickness is indicated. However, considering current developments, the issue cannot be confined to disease or disability alone. In this context, physiological, psychological and social life concepts should also be considered. Each of these concepts forms a basic network in relation to each other. Many health care applications are on the agenda in terms of health promotion. These constantly evolving applications help individuals to access the information they want instantly. The aim is to ensure that the individuals in the society have the highest level of health and to provide high quality services. Here, the ultimate responsibility lies with the individual, but also the private sector, especially the state, has a number of duties to increase public and private practices. As new technologies, mobile devices and especially smart phones are constantly renewed and play a key role in our lives, health services have to be directed towards this field. Considering that each individual has different knowledge and skills, new applications adapted to the use of technology serve the majority of health services. Individuals often make use of these digital platforms.

E-nabız application, which is one of the most frequently used mobile applications in the recent period, is a platform where there are many links and sharing areas from reports containing all the health information of individuals to prescription and medicine sections. Within the scope of the research, mobile accessibility of female users over the age of 65 was investigated. Usability tests were conducted with women over 65 years of age according to their smartphone usage level. In the usability test, depending on the mobile applications, the statistical relationships between the application usage efficiency (task completion success), efficiency (task completion time and number of steps used) and satisfaction levels of the users have emerged.

Female users over the age of 65 (older) are also just one of the groups seen outside of general users. The fact that the individual can act alone and use the applications alone without needing anybody is very important in the current period when new communication technologies are developed. Female users over 65 years of age (elderly) can move more freely and more independently thanks to mobile applications.

Due to a number of financial concerns, websites or applications are made for general user groups. Elderly, disabled etc. user groups do not want a customary application to be made for them. Because, these types of practices, made for the small groups in the society are terminated after one or two updates, especially due to commercial concerns. In order to prevent this situation, the applications made for the users in the groups composed of the elderly, disabled, etc. may be designed in line with the universal design principles. Furthermore, if innovations in applications are subjected to usability test by various user groups, each user can use the application on equal terms. In this study, while accessibility problems of E-nabız mobile application were identified, solution offers for these accessibility problems were also presented and discussed.

E-nabız, which is one of the most important applications in the field of health in Turkey, is also studied academically by many researchers. Users can access the E-nabız application in many ways. More than 43 million E-devlet users are potentially also E-nabız users. In addition to entering the system with the e-government user code, you can also log into the system as a member of the E-nabız system.

In the E-nabız application, which was schemed as a plain and simple design when the application interface was examined, a design was formed with colorful boxes for the information it comprises by writing names on the boxes. Not all the people using E-nabız may be expected to use smartphone technology very well or they may not want to read all the boxes. If a search bar can be added to the top of your personal information in the application, this may also enable the elderly, disabled etc. to find the information they want to find more easily. For the information such as height and weight, which are in the first task to be entered, it is necessary to enter the profile editing option. It is not very easy for every user to find this option. If the search bar is made here, it may be easier for users to find the information they are looking for in the system.

In the third task, which is "Finding the hospital you visited most recently and being able to obtain the prescription written by the doctor," when you enter the hospital from my visits, you can see the information of hospital, doctor, etc. without displaying the details. If a prescription link can also be added here, it will save users time. When the user wants to see recipes from my visits, he or she will have to go to the home tab and search again to find the desired location.

In the fifth task, which is "finding the hospital closest to your location and being able to obtain the address and the location of the hospital," you can see all the hospitals in your district by marking them on the maps. However, when you click on the balloon marked on the map, you can only see the name of the hospital. With a link to be added here, when the user clicks on the balloon marked, the map application will be opened, and thanks to the navigation it may be easier for users to access the hospitals or polyclinics they want to reach, if they are provided with the route and the information by walking, by their personal cars or public transportation.

In the seventh task entitled "being able to make an appointment for the date July 31, 2019," you must first select the appointments option on the main page. When you select the option of "make an appointment from here," you are directed to a different system to make an appointment. You are confronted with the Republic of Turkey, Central Physician Appointment System. You must be a member here. Re-membership also affects the usability of the application. You must have a username and password to log in to the E-nabız application. The fact that there are two passwords in the application especially affects the usage of the application by users such as the disabled and the elderly. If the entire system can be accessed with a single password, the usability of the application can reach a better point.

The "OK" button in the top corner of the application design is particularly confusing to users. OK is a word used to confirm an event. When users click the OK button, the button removes the user from the system. Writing the output word instead of OK may be a factor that specifically improves the usability of the application.

The "<" and ">" marks at the bottom of the application design are used for backward or forward page orientation. Among these signs, only the "<" (backward) sign works. The ">" (forward) sign, which is next to this sign does not work.

This research has not only identified the accessibility problems of the E-nabız application, but also tried to to provide possible solutions to these accessibility problems. The aim here is to enable women over the age of 65 to continue their lives in a healthier way thanks to technological advances.

REFERENCES

Aziz, A. (2012). *İletişime Giriş*. İstanbul: Hiperlink Yayınları.

Bourse, M., & Yücel, H. (2012). *İletişim Bilimlerinin Serüveni*. İstanbul: Ayrıntı Yayınları.

Çağıltay, K. (2011). *İnsan Bilgisayar Etkileşimi ve Kullanılabilirlik Mühendisliği: Teoriden Pratiğe*. Ankara: ODTÜ Geliştirme Vakfı Yayıncılık.

dokuz8haber. (2018, December 13). *Verilerle Türkiye'de toplumun bilgisayar ve internet kullanımında değişim*. Retrieved from https://dokuz8haber.net/toplum-yasam/bilim-teknoloji/verilerle-turkiyede-toplumun-bilgisayar-ve-internet-kullaniminda-degisim/

E-devlet. (2019, August 15). *Ana Sayfa*. Retrieved from https://www.turkiye.gov.tr/

E-nabız. (n.d.). *E-NABIZ*. Retrieved from https://enabiz.gov.tr/Yardim/Index?page=a1&detail=b1

Eken, İ. (2017). *Herkes İçin Erişilebilir İletişim, Görme Engelli Kullanicilarin Mobil Erişebilirliği: Kullanilabilirlik Yaklaşimi İle Mobil Uygulamalarin Analizi*. İstanbul: İstanbul Ticaret Üniversitesi Sosyal Bilimler Enstitüsü Yayımlanmamış Doktora Tezi.

Gürbüz, S., & Şahin, F. (2016). *Sosyal Bilimlerde Araştırma Yöntemleri*. Ankara: Seçkin Yayıncılık.

İlal, E. (1997). *İletişim Yığınsal İletişim Araçları ve Toplum*. İstanbul: Der Yayınları.

Mısırlı, İ. (2007). *Genel ve Teknik İletişim Kavramlar,İlkeler ve Uygulamalar*. Ankara: Detay Yayıncılık.

Okay, A. (2009). *Sağlık İletişimi*. İstanbul: MediaCat Yayınları.

Okay, A. (2014). *Sağlık İletişimi*. İstanbul: Derin Yayınları.

Oskay, Ü. (1992). *İletişimin ABCsi*. İstanbul: Simavi Yayınları.

Özkan, Z. (2011). *66 Soruda Sağlıkta İletişimin Gücü*. İstanbul: Optimist Yayınları.

Rızvanoğlu, K. (2009). *Herkes İçin Web: Evrensel Kullanılabilirlik ve Tasarım*. İstanbul: Punto Yayınları.

Shneiderman, B. (1999). 7 31). Pushing Human-Computer Interaction Research to Empower Every Citizen: Universal Usability. *Communications of the ACM*, *43*(5), 85–91.

Sözcü. (2019, April 30). *E Nabız nedir? Nasıl kayıt olunur?* Retrieved from https:// www.sozcu.com.tr/2019/ekonomi/e-nabiz-nedir-nasil-kayit-olunur-szcu1-4612566/

Tabak, R. (2006). *Sağlık İletişimi*. İstanbul: Literatürk Yayıncıık.

Törenli, N. (2005). *Yeni Medya, Yeni İletişim Ortamı*. Ankara: Bilim ve Sanat Yayınları.

Tübitak, & Kalkınma Bakanlığı. (n.d.). *Kamu İnternet Siteleri Rehberi İnternet Sitelerinde Kullanılabilirlik*. Ankara: Tübitak. *Kalkınma Bakanlığı*.

Tüfekçioğlu, H. (1997). *İletişim Sosyolojisine Başlangıç*. İstanbul: Der Yayınları.

Uğurlu, M. (2018). *Sağlık Teknolojisi Değerlendirmesi Ülke Uygulamaları ve Türkiye İçin Model Önerisi*. Ankara: T.C Maliye Bakanlığı Strateji Geliştirme Başkanlığı Yayınları.

Yakut, İ. (2008). *Sağlık İletişiminde Katılımın İşlevi Hasta ve Hasta Yakınları Açısından*. İzmit: Umuttepe Yayınları.

Yüksel, E. at el. (2014). Check Up Sağlık İletişimi Kaynak İleti ve Hedef Kitle Bağlamında Sağlık Konulu Yayınların Analizi. Konya: Literatürk.

Zıllıoğlu, M. (2003). *İletişim Nedir?* İstanbul: Cem Yayınevi.

KEY TERMS AND DEFINITIONS

Accessibility: It is the state of each user to have access to any information at any time.

Availability: It is the use of web sites, programs or applications by people efficiently, effectively and satisfactorily.

E-nabız: It is an application developed by the Ministry of Health of the Republic of Turkey, which comprises the health information of all citizens of the Republic of Turkey.

Health: a state of psychological, physical and social well-being.

Health Communication: All applications for the protection and promotion of health.

Mobile Application: The applications, which have recently emerged with the Internet and smart phones and which enable people to obtain information in the areas of entertainment, business, education, etc. and spend time.

User-based Usability Testing: It is the testing of the application by various elements such as moderator and rapporteur, on real users, by assigning various tasks.

User Diversity: User groups divided into various factors such as age, gender and disability.

Chapter 7
Depression Rate, GDP Growth Rate, Health Expenditure, and Voice and Accountability:
Are There Co-Movements?

Ramesh Chandra Das
Vidyasagar University, India

Amit Chatterjee
MIT World Peace University, India

ABSTRACT

Existing studies on mental disorder reveal that, besides biological factors, major socioeconomic factors are responsible behind the ever-increasing prevalence of the part of population suffering from mental depression. The present study investigates whether depression rate has long run co-movements with growth of per capita GDP, health expenditure, and voice and accountability of the citizens for individuals as well as panels of four countries, USA, China, India, and Bangladesh, for the period 1995 to 2016. Using cointegration, error correction, and causality testing, the study observes that individual countries do not produce acceptable and robust results, but the panel data results produce long run relations among the four endogenous variables. The Wald test results show that all the two lagged values of depression rate, growth rate, health expenditure and voice and accountability are causing depression in the current period.

DOI: 10.4018/978-1-7998-2329-2.ch007

INTRODUCTION

Like some critical diseases mental disorder is also putting the world population under pressure as the number of people affected in any sort of mental illness is increasing day by day. Both the male and female sections of the society are almost equally affected by this disease (World Health Organization, 2014). Besides physiological and genetic causes, so many economic, social, political and environmental factors are getting responsible for the prevalence of the disease. From intuitive perspectives it can be said that increase in income makes people happy again increase in income may also cause mental disorder as because high income leads to uncontrolled lifestyle. Although a list of studies such as Murali and Oyebode (2004), Saxena et al. (2007), Jenkins et al. (2008), Lund et al. (2010) and Allen et al. (2014) reveals that poor income and unequal income distribution of countries have been one of the causes of mental depression. Globalization has mostly affected income and wellbeing of the people of a country and side by side it allows hazards of the effects of globalization like cybercrimes, internet account hacking, unlimited internet and smart phone uses, etc. Environmental pollution led to several changes in the neurological systems of human body and the ever-increasing magnitudes of pollution has been also one of the causes of mental disorder.

Good mental health is essential to human health and wellbeing. A person's mental health and many common mental disorders are formed by various social, economic, and physical environments operating at different stages of life. The occurrence and social distribution of mental disorders has been well recognized in high-income countries. While there is growing acknowledgment of the problem in low- and middle-income countries, a significant gap still exists in research to measure the problem, and in strategies, policies and programmes to avert mental disorders. There is a considerable need to raise the priority given to the deterrence of mental disorders and to the endorsement of mental health through action on the social determinants of health.

The World Health Organization describes mental health as "a state of well-being in which every individual realizes his or her own potential, can cope with the normal stresses of life, can work productively and fruitfully, and is able to make a contribution to her or his community". In this, the nonappearance of mental disorder does not necessarily mean the occurrence of good mental health. In another way to say, people living with mental disorder can also achieve good levels of wellbeing within the constraints of aching, worrying, or unbearable symptoms.

SURVEY OF LITERATURE

There is scanty literature on the associations between mental illness and socioeconomic factors. The present study has assembled a list of studies in the related research to justify its rationale to undertake.

Murali and Oyebode (2004) examined the direct and indirect effects of relative poverty on the development of emotional, behavioural and psychiatric problems, in the context of the growing inequality between rich and poor. They observed that children in the poorest households are three times more likely to have a mental illness than children in the best-off households. Besides, the study revealed that poverty and social disadvantage were most strongly associated with deficits in children's cognitive skills and educational achievements. The study recommended for reducing inequality both nationally and internationally to reduce the magnitude of mental illness.

Saxena et al. (2007) discussed the general availability of the resources such as mental health services, community resources, human resources, and funding, especially in low-income and middle-income countries upon mental health of people. The study mentioned that government funding is too low and inefficient to support for mental patients. The study thus observed that scarcity of available resources, inequities in their distribution, and inefficiencies in their use caused the three main obstacles to better mental health, especially in low-income and middle-income countries.

Jenkins et al. (2008) test the hypothesis that the association between low income and mental disorder is mediated by debt and its attendant financial hardship in a cross-sectional nationally representative survey of private households in England, Scotland and Wales, which assessed 8580 participants aged 16-74 years living in general households. The study reveals that those with low income were more likely to have mental disorder. Further that both low income and debt are associated with mental illness, but the effect of income appears to be mediated largely by debt.

In an extensive study Barry (2009) provides an overview of the existing concepts of positive mental health and its contribution to the health and well-being of society. The study reviews the determinants of positive mental health across the lifespan and identified the enhancing factors for promoting mental health at the structural, community and individual levels. The evidence recommends that policies focused on curing or preventing mental illness will not necessarily deliver improved mental health at population level. The increasing interest in positive mental health and well-being needs to be supplemented by investment in research on the determinants of positive mental health across the life course, as distinct from studies on the determinants of mental disorders.

In a wide review of works Lund et al. (2010) went through the epidemiological literature in low- and middle-income countries with the aim of examining this relationship between level of economic development and common mental diseases. Out of 115 studies reviewed, most reported positive associations between a range of poverty indicators and mental disorder. Besides a large part of the studies revealed positive associations between different dimensions of poverty and mental disorder.

Pointing out to the existence of a substantial research literature on policies that are effective in reducing or holding down rates of Alcohol, Patel et al. (2010), however, have commented that relatively a few interventions are designed to target social inequities within societies or between societies. The study thus recommended for an urgent need for a programme of strategically chosen demonstration projects on alcohol policy initiatives targeting health disparities in the context of developing societies and low-income populations paying close attention to measuring differences in effects by social class, income and other social differentiations.

In their widespread work Allen et al. (2014) identified several factors to mental disorders which are figured by various social, economic, and physical environments operating at different stages of life. Risk factors for many common mental disorders are heavily associated with social inequalities, whereby the greater the inequality the higher the inequality in risk. They recommend proper action throughout these life stages which would provide opportunities for both improving population mental health, and for reducing risk of those mental disorders that are associated with social inequalities.

Through the SMART Mental Health Project Kallakuri et al. (2018) have tried to provide technology based mental health services to the rural Indians. The project has covered more than 22000 respondents through primary survey in the age group of greater than equal to 18 years in Godavari District of Andhra Pradesh and the data was collected to find the prevalence of depression, anxiety and suicide risk. The study revealed that anxiety, depression and suicidal ideation affected 10.8, 14.4 and 3.5% of participants, respectively which were more common among women, and among those who were aged 30–59 years, uneducated, or divorced/ separated/ widowed. Stress due to financial loss was also found significant.

The studies in the survey so far we did lack in the attempt of discussing the long run relations among income, health expenditure and voice and accountability and mental disorder for the countries like USA, India, China and Bangladesh. The present study thus has attempted to fill the gap in research in the related area.

DATA SOURCE AND METHODOLOGY

Our important variable 'mental disorder' is taken as percentage of population of the countries affected in the disease. The mental disorders are schizophrenia (%), bipolar disorder (%), eating disorders (%), anxiety disorders (%), drug use disorders (%), depression (%) and alcohol use disorders (%). We have taken only the data on depression rate (male and female together) which is per cent of total population from Our World in Data base (https://ourworldindata.org/mental-health) for the period of 1995-2016. The data on per capita GDP (PCGDP) growth rate, health expenditure as per cent of GDP and Voice and Accountability (VA) from the data base of the World Bank. VA reflects perceptions of the extent to which a country's citizens are able to participate in selecting their government, as well as freedom of expression, freedom of association, and a free media. It is one of the six governance indicators estimated by the World Bank through several survey agencies. The standardized value for VA lies between +2.5 and -2.5. The +2.5 indicates the maximum value of VA indicator where there is no obstacle to expressing voice and -2.5 is the minimum values of VA where people has no way of expressing their voices. The value '0' is the average value of VA.

The data for VA is available from 1996 onwards with the data on 1997, 1999 and 2001 missing. We have interpolated the data of these three years and the initial year, 1995, by the average values of the data between the periods. The purpose of the interpolation is to extend the length of the study period as much as possible without losing the foundation of the data set to have acceptable results. The countries are USA, China, India and Bangladesh, the combination of developed, highly developing and developing economies.

Since the study has 22 data points in all the four indicators there may have stochastic trends and hence it is required to test for non-stationarity or unit roots of the four series for all the selected countries. We have tested for unit roots by Augmented Dickey-Fuller (ADF) (1979). The ADF test is based on the assumptions that the error term is serially independent and has a constant variance. For a data set of variables, y (y_t, t = 1, 2, ..., T), where t denotes time, let us consider the following linear regression set up for unit root test for two versions of the ADF(p) regression–viz.,

$$\Delta y_t = \alpha + \beta y_{t-1} + \sum_{j=1}^{p} \gamma_j \Delta y_{t-j} + u_t \qquad (1)$$

for the *without time trend case* and

$$\Delta y_t = \alpha + \delta t + \beta y_{t-1} + \sum_{j=1}^{p} \gamma_j \Delta y_{t-j} + u_t \quad (2)$$

for the *with time trend case.*

If β = 0 (or ρ = 1) is rejected by the ADF statistic, then we say that the series is stationary. If this property holds for all the series, Ment (stands for depression rate), PCGDP (stands for growth rate of per capita GDP), Health (stands for health expenditure as a ratio to GDP) and VA, then we can run regression without the possibility of getting counterfeit results. If any series is found to be non-stationary even at its first differences in any one of the three testing alternatives, intercept, trend and intercept and none, then execution of different time series objectives such as long run associations and short run dynamics will not be possible. In that case we can try for the panel of the countries data sets.

Panel Unit Roots

If there is time series data across the number of cross sections then running individual unit root tests suffer from power problem that would lead to spurious regression results. A panel unit root test overcomes this problem and provides results with more power. The system of equations required to test the objective of the study is given below-

For a data set of a variable 'y' ($y_{i,t}$, i = 1, 2, …., N (here N = 4) and t = 1, 2, ...,T (here T = 22), where t denotes time, let us consider the following linear regression model for panel unit root test in line with the ADF(p) (1979) regression–viz.,

$$\Delta y_{i,t} = (\rho_i - 1) y_{i,t-1} + \sum_{j=1}^{p} \gamma_j \Delta y_{i,t-j} + W'_{i,t}\alpha_i + u_{i,t} \quad (3)$$

where W_{it} represent the exogenous variables in the model, including any fixed effects or individual trends. The null hypothesis for this model is $\rho_i = 1$ against the alternative hypothesis $\rho_i < 1$. The above equation can be rewritten as-

$$\Delta y_{i,t} = \beta_i y_{i,t-1} + \sum_{j=1}^{p} \gamma_j \Delta y_{i,t-j} + W'_{i,t}\alpha_i + u_{i,t} \quad (4)$$

The null hypothesis for this model is $\beta_i = 0$ against the alternative hypothesis $\beta_i < 0$.

There are two approaches of testing panel unit roots depending on homogeneity or heterogeneity of the regression coefficients. Testing techniques where the coefficients (β_is) are restricted to be homogeneous across all units of the panel have been offered by Levin and Lin (1993) and Levin, Lin and Chu (2002), and testing techniques where the coefficients are heterogeneous have been by Im, Pesaran and Shin (1997, 2003), ADF - Fisher Chi-square and PP - Fisher Chi-square of Maddala and Wu (1999) and Choi (2001). The assumption of homogeneity (β_is = β, say) is clearly restrictive and subject to the possible homogeneity bias of the fixed effect estimator.

The Levin and Lin (1993) and Levin, Lin and Chu (2002) models are captured by the following equation (5) where β_is = β:

$$\Delta y_{i,t} = \beta y_{i,t-1} + \sum_{j=1}^{p} \gamma_j \Delta y_{i,t-j} + W'_{i,t} Z'_{i,t} \alpha + u_{i,t} \tag{5}$$

The test statistics proposed by Maddala and Wu (1999), based on the suggestion of Fischer, is of the form

$$\chi^2 = -2\sum_{i=1}^{N} (\log p_i) \tag{6}$$

(where i = 1, 2, …., N). It follows chi square distribution under the null hypothesis of $p_i=0$ for all the 'i_s'. The simulation suggests that the Maddala and Wu's Fisher test is more powerful than the Im, Pesaran and Shin test which is again more powerful than the Levin, Lin and Chu test in a variety of situations.

Panel Cointegration *Test*

In a panel data three tests are usually done for testing whether there are cointegrating relationships between/among the variables. The Pedroni (1999, 2004) and Kao (1999) tests are based on Engle-Granger (1987) two-step residual-based cointegration tests and Fisher test is a combined Johansen test. We apply all the three tests in our study.

The Engle-Granger (1987) test is based on the examination of the residuals of a counterfeit regression done upon I(1) variables. The variables will be cointegrated if the residuals capturing the linear combinations of both the variables turn out to be I (0). Pedroni puts forward several tests for cointegration that allow for heterogeneous intercepts and trend coefficients across cross-sections. Let us consider the following regression with no intercept and trends-

$$y_{i,t} = \beta_i x_{i,t} + u_{i,t} \tag{7}$$

for t = 1, 2, …, T and i = 1, 2, …, N; where y and x are assumed to be integrated of order one. Under the null hypothesis of no cointegration, the estimated residuals $\varepsilon_{i,t}$ will be I(1). The general approach is to obtain residuals from Equation (7) and then to test whether residuals are I(1) by running the auxiliary regression for each cross-section as-

$$\varepsilon_{i,t} = \rho_i \varepsilon_{i,t-1} + \sum_{j=1}^{p_i} \gamma_{ij} \Delta\varepsilon_{i,t-j} + e_{i,t} \tag{8}$$

Pedroni describes various methods of constructing statistics for testing for null hypothesis of no cointegration ($\rho_i = 1$). There are two alternative hypotheses: the homogenous alternative, ($\rho_i = \rho$) < 1 for all i (which Pedroni terms the within-dimension test or panel statistics test), and the heterogeneous alternative, ($\rho_i < 1$) for all i (also referred to as the between-dimension or group statistics test). The Pedroni panel cointegration statistic $\aleph_{N,T}$ is constructed from the residuals of Equation (8). A total of eleven statistics with varying degree of properties (size and power for different N and T are generated. Pedroni shows that the standardized statistic is asymptotically normally distributed, which is as follows-

$$\left[\aleph_{N,T} - \mu\sqrt{N}\right] / \sqrt{\upsilon} \Rightarrow N(0,\ 1) \tag{9}$$

where μ and υ are Monte Carlo generated adjustment terms.

Kao (1999), on the other hand, presents two tests for the null hypothesis of no cointegration in panel data: the DF and ADF type tests. He considers the special case where cointegration vectors are homogeneous between individuals. Kao presents two sets of specifications for the DF test statistics. The first set of test statistics depends directly on consistent estimation of long-run parameters. The second set of test statistics does not. Kao considers the model as depicted in equation (7) and (8). In order to test the null hypothesis of no cointegration, the set of hypotheses can be written as: H_0: ρ = 1 against the alternative H_A: ρ < 1. The OLS estimate of ρ is given by:

$$\hat{\rho} = \frac{\sum_{i=1}^{N}\sum_{t=2}^{T} \hat{\varepsilon}_{it}\, \hat{\varepsilon}_{i,t-1}}{\sum_{i=1}^{N}\sum_{t=2}^{T} \hat{\varepsilon}_{it}\, \hat{\varepsilon}^{2}_{i,t-1}} \tag{10}$$

The ADF test statistic for the null hypothesis of no cointegration is based on the above expression.

In a different testing specification, Johansen (1988) proposes two different statistics, one of them is the likelihood ratio trace statistics and the other one is maximum eigen value statistics, to determine the presence of cointegration vectors in the data with non-stationary time series. Using Johansen test for cointegration, Maddala and Wu (1999) consider Fisher's (1932) suggestion to combine individuals tests, to propose an alternative to the two previous tests, for testing for cointegration in the full panel by combining individual cross sections tests for cointegration.

Vector Error Correction Mechanism (VECM)

After proving the series as cointegrated or having long run relations between the variables, we need to test whether the errors in the short run deviations from the equilibrium relations are corrected and the series converge to the existing long run relation. Vector error correction mechanism (VECM) captures this phenomenon. VECM is a restricted Vector Autoregressive (VAR) model which is intended for using with cointegrated non-stationary series. The VECM has cointegration relations built into the specification so that it restricts the long-run behavior of the endogenous variables to converge to their cointegrating equilibrium relationships while allowing for short-run adjustment dynamics. The cointegration term is known as the *error correction* term since the deviation from long-run equilibrium is corrected gradually through a series of partial short-run adjustments.

Let us consider a two variable system with one cointegrating equation therein and no lagged difference terms to present the VECM. The cointegrating equation for no intercept and trend is given by the following equation:

$$y_t = \beta x_t \tag{11}$$

The estimated error term in first difference is given as-

$$\varepsilon_{t-1} = y_{t-1} - \beta x_{t-1} \tag{12}$$

Therefore, the corresponding VEC model is:

$$\Delta y_t = \alpha_y (y_{t-1} - \beta x_{t-1}) + e_y \\ \Delta x_t = \alpha_x (x_{t-1} - \beta y_{t-1}) + e_x \tag{13}$$

In the simple model, the only right-hand side term is the error correction (EC) term which is zero in the long run equilibrium. However, if 'y' and 'x' deviate from the long run relation, the error correction term will be nonzero and each variable adjusts to partially restore the equilibrium relation. The coefficient 'α' measures the speed of adjustment of the ith endogenous variable towards the equilibrium. If the error correction term is derived negative in sign and statistically significant then we say that the short-term errors have been corrected and the series are back to the long run relation. Additionally, we say that there is long run causality from 'y' to 'x' or vice versa.

At last the direction of causality for the short run can be tested in this VECM set up by applying Wald test.

RESULTS AND DISCUSSION

Before proceeding to econometric analyses, we present the series of data for the four indicators diagrammatically. Figure 1 presents the four trends of mental depression as per cent of total population of the four countries. It is observed that USA, being the only established developed economy in the selection, bears over 10 percent of its population suffering from mental depression. China's around 9 percent of population is also suffering from depression syndrome. India and Bangladesh have around 8 percent of such sufferings.

It is well known that the per capita GDP of USA is far above the per capita GDP of China, India and Bangladesh and so the trends of mental depression rate for the countries reveal that the high-income earning countries have higher rates of mental depression among the people.

Figure 2 depicts the trends of growth rates of PCGDP for the countries. It is observed that China leads the group in terms of growth rate followed by India, Bangladesh and the USA.

The insurgence of the global financial crisis has affected USA, China and India but Bangladesh is out of the outbreak so far as the growth of PCGDP is concerned.

Figure 3 illustrates the trends for health expenditure as the ratio to GDP of the four countries. The trends for all the countries except India show upward trend. The level as well as magnitude of the increase is highest for USA. On an average 16 per

Figure 1. Depression rate out of total population (%)
Source: Sketched by the authors

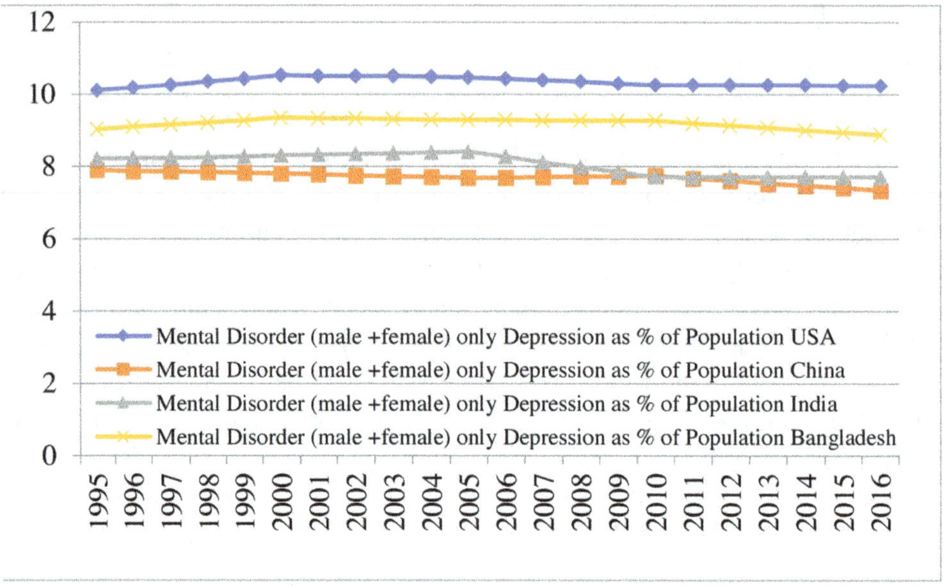

Figure 2. PCGDP growth rates
Source: Sketched by the authors

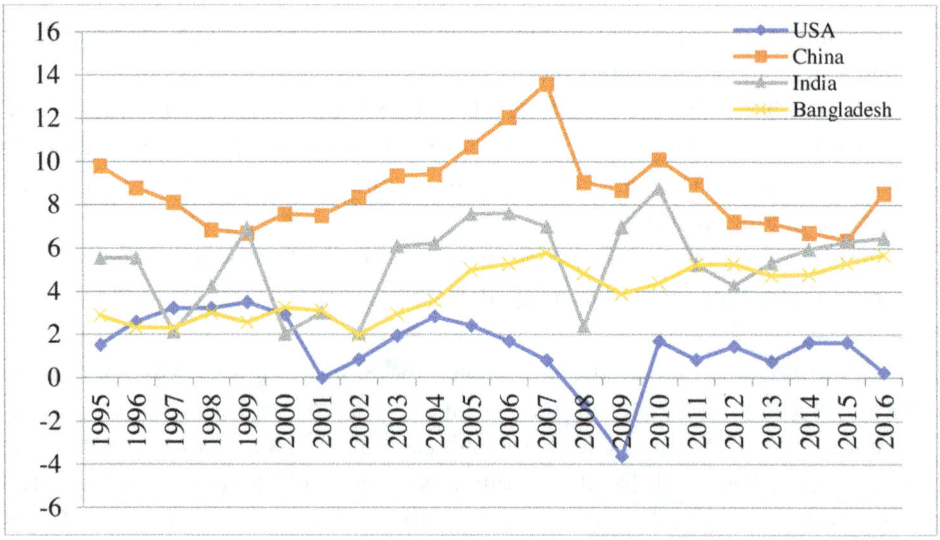

cent of the GDP of USA is spent on health purpose. There is mild decreasing trend for India hovering around four per cent of its GDP.

The indicator VA reflects perceptions of the extent to which a country's citizens are able to participate in selecting their government, as well as freedom of expression, freedom of association, and a free media. Figure 4 presents the series for VA of all the countries in the list.

It is observed from the figure that USA has the highest freedom offered to its citizens for expressing their views and selecting governments. On the other hand, China has worst scenario in VA which means its citizens are not opened to express their views and opinions publicly. India has relatively in better position compared to China. Even Bangladesh has superior position over China in this head.

Correlation Results

Prior to the discussion on whether there are co-movements of all the four indicators for the study period we have done a correlation analysis to have the understanding on the associations among all the four indicators. In all the cases depression rate has been taken as the key dependent variable and all the remaining three as independent variables. Table 1 presents the results.

It is revealed from the correlation results that depression rates of the countries have weak correlation with the growth rate of PCGDP. There are strong correlations between depression rate and health expenditure for China, India and Bangladesh

Figure 3. Health expenditure as per cent of GDP
Source: Sketched by the authors

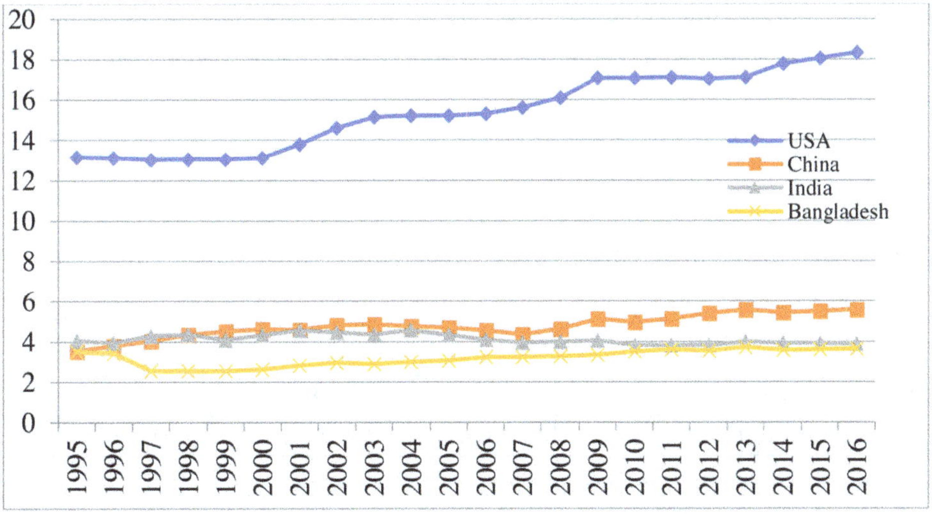

Figure 4. Voice and accountability
Source: Sketched by the authors

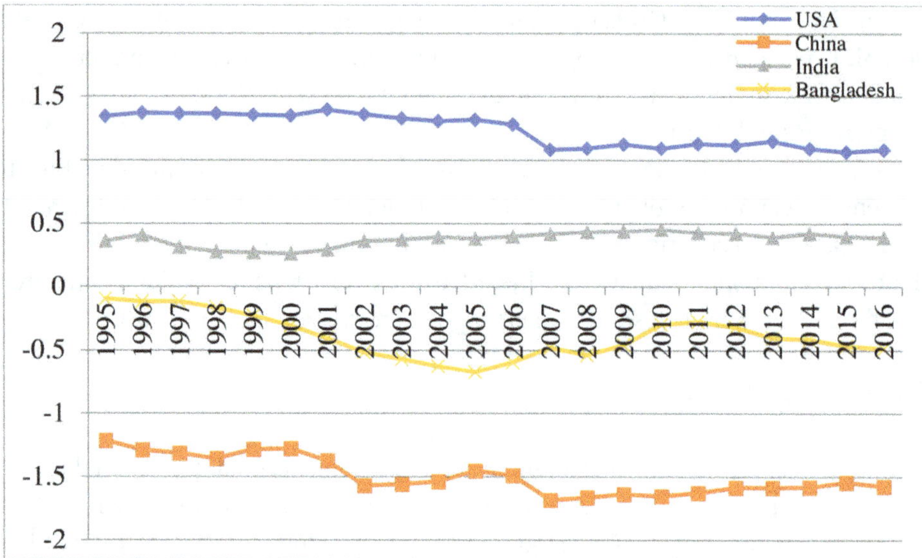

but India produces positive correlation and China and Bangladesh produce negative correlation results. India's negative trend of depression rate and negative trends of health expenditure have produced positive result which is unlike to that of China and Bangladesh. Finally there are positive and significant correlations observed for China and USA between depression rate and VA but positive result is obtained for India. Falling trend of VA for China may be the cause to mental disorder for its people but the reverse result is for India in the sense that its increasing VA makes possible of decreasing depression rate.

Table 1. Correlation results

	USA	China	India	Bangladesh
Depression-Growth	0.124275	0.197024	-0.22656	-0.3053578
Depression-Health	-0.30031	**-0.8577**	**0.82106**	**-0.6151991**
Depression-VA	**0.431853**	**0.574384**	**-0.59842**	-0.2626727

Note: Bold figures represent statistically significant results
Source: Computed by the authors

Unit Root Test Results for Individual Countries

Since the data used in the study is in a time series framework it is required to test whether all the four series are I(0). If not whether they are at least I(1). All the series are required to be in the same order of integration. We have tested the stationary properties of Depression Rate of the four countries. It is derived that the series are not stationary at levels. We have thus tested stationarity for the first difference series using equation (1 & 2). The results are given in Table 2.

It is observed that the series for Depression Rate for all the countries remain non stationary at their first differences in all the three alternative specifications (intercept, trend and intercept and none). So we did not proceed for testing stationarity of the three remaining series. Converting the series for Depression Rate into second difference we get stationary results for all the countries (results not shown). All the remaining three series are also second differenced stationary. Since multiple differencing leads to loss of information and low power of the tests we skipped for exercising short run dynamics among the four series in the second differenced series. As an alternative we have constructed the panel of all the series across four countries to get expected better results. Thus, the study has now (22*4=88) 88 panel data. The co-movements and short run dynamics of all the four variables in the panel data framework is analyzed below sequentially.

Panel Unit Roots Test Results

Estimating equation (3 to 6) the stationarity of the four panel series are tested. Again, all the series of the panels are found to be non-stationary at levels (results not shown) under common or individual unit root processes. We thus tested for their first differences in both the specifications. The results are given in Table 3.

Table 2. Unit root test results for depression rate for individual countries

ADF t Statistics First Differences								
	USA		China		India		Bangladesh	
	t statistics	Prob	t statistics	Prob	t statistics	Prob	t statistics	Prob
Intercept	-1.71	0.4	-1.35	0.58	-1.65	0.43	-1.64	0.44
Trend and Intercept	-1.47	0.8	-1.82	0.65	-1.51	0.78	-3.29	0.09
None	-1.83	0.06	-0.75	0.37	-1.56	0.1	-1.54	0.11

Source: Computed by the authors

The results show that all the four series in panel form are stationary at their first differences since the probability values given in the first brackets are well below 0.05 that reject the null hypothesis of unit root process. Next we test for panel cointegration.

Panel Cointegration Test Results

We have tested panel cointegration in three lines of measures. Table 4 describes Pedroni residual panel cointegration test results in three different specifications. With the null hypothesis of no cointegration in the panel the results for all the three specifications show that there is no cointegration among depression rate, PCGDP growth rate, health expenditure and VA for the four countries pooled together.

Table 5 illustrates the Kao residual cointegration test results. The results show that there are strong cointegrations among the four variables of the panel. The ADF value is too high to reject the null hypothesis of no cointegration.

Finally, Table 6 depicts the Johansen Fisher panel cointegration test results. Both the trace test and max-eigen test statistics show there are strong cointegrations among the variables of the panel with at least one cointegrating equations.

Table 3. Panel unit root test results at first differences of the indicators

Method	Null Hypothesis	Test Statistics with Intercepts (Prob.)			
		Depression Rate	**PCGDP Growth**	**Health Expd.**	**Voice & Account**
Levin, Lin and Chu	Unit root (under common unit root process)	-2.66 (0.00)	-5.92 (0.00)	-4.10 (0.00)	-8.25 (0.00)
Im, Pesaran and Shin	Unit root (under individual unit root process)	-3.83 (0.00)	-5.18 (0.00)	-3.59 (0.00)	-6.51 (0.00)
MW- ADF - Fisher Chi-square	Unit root (under individual unit root process)	18.96 (0.05)	40.05 (0.00)	27.84 (0.00)	50.71 (0.00)
MW- PP - Fisher Chi-square	Unit root (under individual unit root process)	21.10 (0.04)	108.96(0.00)	38.41 (0.00)	38.54 (0.00)

Source: Computed by the authors

Table 4. Pedroni residual panel cointegration test

Hypotheses→ / Test Criteria↓	*Null Hypothesis: No Cointegration*		Statistic (Prob)	Weighted Statistic (Prob)
No deterministic trend	Alternative hypothesis: common AR coefficients (within-dimension)	Panel v-Statistic	-0.23 (0.58)	-0.06 (0.52)
		Panel rho-Statistic	1.225 (0.88)	0.87 (0.80)
		Panel PP-Statistic	0.79 (0.78)	0.14 (0.55)
		Panel ADF-Statistic	-0.76 (0.22)	-1.28 (0.09)
	Alternative hypothesis: individual AR coefficients (between-dimension)	Group rho-Statistic	1.741 (0.95)	-
		Group PP-Statistic	0.654 (0.74)	-
		Group ADF-Statistic	-1.01 (0.15)	-
Deterministic intercept and trend	Alternative hypothesis: common AR coefficients (within-dimension)	Panel v-Statistic	-1.12 (0.86)	-0.88 (0.81)
		Panel rho-Statistic	2.11 (0.98)	1.77(0.96)
		Panel PP-Statistic	1.87 (0.96)	1.02 (0.84)
		Panel ADF-Statistic	-0.19 (0.42)	-1.21 (0.11)
	Alternative hypothesis: individual AR coefficients (between-dimension)	Group rho-Statistic	2.41 (0.98)	-
		Group PP-Statistic	0.981 (0.83)	-
		Group ADF-Statistic	-1.33 (0.09)	-
No deterministic intercept and trend	Alternative hypothesis: common AR coefficients (within-dimension)	Panel v-Statistic	0.17(0.43)	0.19 (0.42)
		Panel rho-Statistic	0.56 (0.71)	0.33 (0.63)
		Panel PP-Statistic	-0.09 (0.46)	-0.403 (0.34)
		Panel ADF-Statistic	-0.78 (0.21)	-1.06 (0.14)
	Alternative hypothesis: individual AR coefficients (between-dimension)	Group rho-Statistic	1.177 (0.88)	-
		Group PP-Statistic	-0.16 (0.43)	-
		Group ADF-Statistic	-1.37 (0.08)	-

Source: Computed by the authors

Table 5. Kao residual cointegration test results

Null Hypothesis: No cointegration		
Included observations: 88	t-Statistic	Prob.
ADF	-2.4577	0.007

Source: Computed by the authors

Combining the three test results for panel cointegration (Table 4, 5 & 6) there is long run association among the four variables in the panel data framework as two out of three test techniques provide significant results. Hence depression rate has long run relation with PCGDP growth rates, health expenditures and VA for the countries as a whole.

VECM Results

After getting the cointegration results, it is now required to investigate whether the errors due to short run deviations from the equilibrium relation are corrected and they converge to the equilibrium in the panel. The VECM results are presented in Table 7.

Table 6. Johansen Fisher panel cointegration test results

No. of CEs	Fisher Stat.	Included observations: 88	Fisher Stat.	
	(from trace test)	Prob.	(from max-eigen test)	Prob.
None	63.05	0.000	52.31	0.000
At most 1	20.5	0.008	18.15	0.051
At most 2	13.89	0.084	13.89	0.084

Source: Computed by the authors

Table 7. VECM results

Dependent Variables	EC terms	Probability	Whether errors corrected	Remarks
D(MENT)	C(1) = -0.008	0.11	No	No long run causality from All Variables to Depression Rate
D(MENT)	C(4) = 0.005 C(5) = 0.005	0.05 0.05	No	Long run causality from one and two periods lag values of PCGDP Growth to Depression Rate

Note: Optimum lag has been derived as 2 as most of the diagnostic sticks take lowest values at this lag. Exogenous variables stand for all the exogenous variables (PCGDP Growth, Health Exp. and Voice & Accountability) in two lag periods and one endogenous variable (MENT) in its two periods' lag values. C(4) and C(5) respectively stand for the regression coefficients of one and two periods lag values of PCGDP Growth to Depression Rate.

Source: Computed by the authors

Taking depression rate (MENT) as the endogenous variable and estimating equation (11 to 13) it is observed that the errors are not corrected and so there is no long run causality from all variables to Depression Rate in two lag periods as optimum lag value is 2. However, there is long run causality from one and two periods lag values of PCGDP Growth to Depression Rate (refer to last row of the table). This means income growth rate is the cause to depression rate for the panel of the economies in the long run.

Let us consider the short run dynamics which provide us the causal relations among the variables. The results of Wald test are given in Table 8. The value of Chi square statistic is too high (with very low probability) to reject the null hypothesis of no causality from all variables to depression rate. This means PCGDP growth rate, health expenditure share and VA together make a cause to mental depression rate in the short run.

All the diagnostic checking, serial correlation LM test, heteroskedasticity test and Histogram Normality Test produce acceptable results and so we infer that the derived results are robust and stable in statistical terms.

CONCLUDING OBSERVATIONS

The study is now in a position to conclude. We had fixed our objective to examine whether there are long run co-movements among depression rate, PCGDP growth rate, health expenditure and VA and short run dynamics in individual as well as panel of four countries, USA, China, India and Bangladesh for the period 1995-2016. The study reveals that individual country results do not produce acceptable and robust results, but the panel data results produce long run relations among the four endogenous variables. The Wald test results show that all the two lagged values of depression rate, growth rate, health expenditure and voice and accountability are making a cause to rate of depression in the current period. Further it reveals that the countries with higher per capita income like USA have higher rates of mental depression. Hence the claim of low income and un-equitable distribution of income being one of the discernible causes to mental disorder is not justified and even the

Table 8. Short run causality through Wald Test

Dependent Variable	Chi square	Probability	Remarks
D(MENT)	110.234	0.00	AV→MENTT

Note: AV stands for all the exogenous variables (PCGDP Growth, Health Exp. and Voice & Accountability) in two lag periods and one endogenous variable (MENT) in its two periods' lag values.

Source: Computed by the authors

high-income countries with high volume of health expenditure and good governance in terms of voice and accountability can also lead to high magnitudes of depression rate. Like destitution makes unhappy, affluence can also cause unhappy in the long run. Hence the countries should emphasize on thinking whether more liberty should be provided to the people in terms of earning income, free voice, uncontrolled life styles, etc. so far as controlling mental depression rate being the target.

REFERENCES

Allen, J., Balfour, R., Bell, R., & Marmot, M. (2014). *Social determinants of mental health*. Geneva: World Health Organization. doi:10.3109/09540261.2014.928270

Barry, M. M. (2009). Addressing the Determinants of Positive Mental Health: Concepts, evidence and practice. *International Journal of Mental Health Promotion*, *11*(3), 4–17. doi:10.1080/14623730.2009.9721788

Dickey, D. A., & Wayne, F. A. (1979). Distribution of the estimators for autoregressive timeseries with a unit root. *Journal of the American Statistical Association*, 74.

Engle, R. F., & Granger, C. W. (1987). Co-integration and error correction: Representation, estimation and testing. *Econometrica*, 55.

Granger, C. W. J. (1969). Investigating causal relations by econometric models and cross spectral methods. *Econometrica*, *37*(3), 424. doi:10.2307/1912791

Im, K. S., Pesaran, M. H., & Shin, Y. (2003). Testing for Unit Roots in Heterogeneous Panels. *Journal of Econometrics*, *115*(1), 53–74. doi:10.1016/S0304-4076(03)00092-7

Jenkins, R., Bhugra, D., Bebbington, P., Brugha, T., Farrell, M., Coid, J., ... Meltzer, H. (2008). Debt, income and mental disorder in the general population. *Psychological Medicine*, *38*(10), 1485–1493. doi:10.1017/S0033291707002516 PMID:18184442

Kallakuri, S., Devarapalli, S., Tripathi, A. P., Patel, A., & Maulik, P. K. (2018). Common mental disorders and risk factors in rural India: Baseline data from the SMART mental health project. *BJPsych Open*, *4*(4), 192–198. doi:10.1192/bjo.2018.28 PMID:29988932

Kao, C. (1999). Spurious Regression and Residual-Based Tests for Cointegration in Panel Data. *Journal of Econometrics*, *90*(1), 1–44. doi:10.1016/S0304-4076(98)00023-2

Levin, A., Lin, C. F., & Chu, C. S. J. (2002). Unit root tests in panel data: Asymptotic and finite-sample properties. *Journal of Econometrics*, *108*(1), 1–24. doi:10.1016/S0304-4076(01)00098-7

Lund, C., Breen, A., Flisher, A., Kakuma, R., Corrigall, J., Joska, J., ... Patel, V. (2010, August). Poverty and common mental disorders in low and middle income countries: A systematic review. *Social Science & Medicine*, *71*(3), 517–528. doi:10.1016/j.socscimed.2010.04.027 PMID:20621748

Maddala, G. S., & Wu, S. (1999). A Comparative Study of Unit Root Tests with Panel Data and A New Simple Test. *Oxford Bulletin of Economics and Statistics*, *61*(s1), 631–652. doi:10.1111/1468-0084.61.s1.13

Murali, V., & Oyebode, F. (2004). Poverty, social inequality and mental health. *Advances in Psychiatric Treatment*, *10*(3), 216–224. doi:10.1192/apt.10.3.216

Patel, V., Lund, C., Hatheril, S., Plagerson, S., Corrigall, J., & Funk, M. (2010). Mental disorders: equity and social determinants. In E. Blas & A. S. Kurup (Eds.), *Equity, social determinants and public health programmes* (pp. 115–134). Geneva: World Health Organization.

Pedroni, P. (1999). Critical Values for Cointegration Tests in Heterogeneous Panels with Multiple Regressors. *Oxford Bulletin of Economics and Statistics*, *61*(s1), 653–670. doi:10.1111/1468-0084.61.s1.14

Pedroni, P. (2004). Panel Cointegration: Asymptotic and Finite Sample Properties of Pooled Time Series Tests with an Application to the PPP Hypothesis. *Econometric Theory*, *20*(03), 597–625. doi:10.1017/S0266466604203073

Saxena, S., Thornicroft, G., Knapp, M., & Whiteford, H. (2007). Resources for mental health: Scarcity, inequity, and inefficiency. *Lancet*, *370*(9590), 878–889. doi:10.1016/S0140-6736(07)61239-2 PMID:17804062

KEY WORDS AND DEFINITIONS

Causality: It is the method used in time series econometrics where the short run interplays among two or more variables are studied. In a two variable model Granger causality test is run but in a VAR model Wald test is applied to test for causality.

Cointegration: It is an econometric tool applying in time series data sets for examining long run associations among the variables of concern. It is tested upon two or more variables which are non-stationary at levels but stationary at their first differences.

Growth Rate: It is the percentage change in aggregate or per capita income in a given year with respect to its base year value. For example growth rate of Y at time t is $(Y_t-Y_{t-1})/Y_{t-1})*100$.

Health Expenditure: Health is one of the most important indicators of human development and spending upon it makes a man physically and mentally fit. Health expenditure is the amount of money spent by citizens and public sector out of total income.

Mental Depression: It is the mood disorder that causes a persistent feeling of sadness and loss of interest and can interfere with your daily functioning. It is characterized by persistently depressed mood or loss of interest in activities, causing significant impairment in daily life. According to the source of the data, depression is one of the important contributors of mental disorders among people in any class of economies. Depression rate is the percentage of people out of total population suffering from that particular disease.

Per capita GDP: It is the gross domestic product per citizen. It is derived by dividing GDP (either in current or constant prices) with existing population of the country. Increase in its value leads to increase in standard of living of the citizens.

Voice and Accountability: It one of six component of governance indicator as stipulated by the World Bank. It reflects perceptions of the extent to which a country's citizens are able to participate in selecting their government, as well as freedom of expression, freedom of association, and a free media. The standardized value for VA lies between +2.5 and -2.5. The +2.5 indicates the situation where there is no obstacle to expressing voice and -2.5 is the situation where people have no way of expressing their voices. The value '0' is the average value of VA.

Chapter 8
Describing Health Ecosystem in NIS:
The Case of University Hospitals in Turkey

Işıl Çekçi
Istanbul Gelisim University, Turkey

Serhat Burmaoglu
https://orcid.org/0000-0002-5537-6887
Izmir Katip Celebi University, Turkey

Dilek Ozdemir Gungor
Izmir Katip Celebi University, Turkey

Levent B. Kidak
Izmir Katip Celebi University, Turkey

ABSTRACT

Technological innovation has been a key driving force for economic growth, industrial development, and increasing welfare. Two dominant streams of theories as market-failure and system-failure oriented the domain to reach development economy objectives for countries. In this case, national innovation systems have been recognized by the rising understanding of systems of innovation. National Innovation Systems have been considered as complex and multi-faceted. Therefore, for overcoming this complexity and make it simplified analytically, in this chapter only the healthcare field has been examined by considering University Hospital cases. It is aimed to understand cognitive contribution of university hospitals to health innovation system by examining scientific publications. It is found that regional perspective should be applied to create more applicable policies.

DOI: 10.4018/978-1-7998-2329-2.ch008

INTRODUCTION

Science, technology, and innovation are vital sources for countries in the so-called knowledge-economy era. All developed and developing countries created innovation policies for reaching these sources. Frenken (2017) asserted that there are two mainstreams for innovation policy development. These are market-failure and system-failure approaches. Based on Metcalfe's (1994) study, market-failure approach, which was contributed by Arrow (1962), Nelson (1959), and Usher (1964), was related to economic peculiarities of knowledge, its production, and dissemination; particularly indivisibilities, uncertainty, lack of appropriability, externalities and public good opportunities. Basically, market-failure may be deemed as a linear model and based on this perspective it is expected that firms underinvest in R&D, because, a part of the outputs of their investments spillover to other firms who imitate innovation without remunerating the originator (Arrow, 1962). Moreover, firms are not expected to raise investment in R&D because of risk and uncertainty about the future outcomes of their investments. Hence, governments with this approach put forward policies on protecting intellectual property rights and providing direct or indirect R&D subsidies to repair such market-failures. Other approach underlines an evolutionary perspective and adopts the behavioral theory of the firm and focuses upon learning processes and adaptive behavior based on Metcalfe's (1994) study. Systemic nature of this approach focuses on interaction and collaboration. Triple-helix concept is put forward by Etzkowitz and Leydesdorff (2000) in this approach and stressed the benefits of coordination and collaboration between actors.

With this collaborative perspective, discussions bred the systems of innovation idea and "national innovation systems-NIS" was put forward by scholars in innovation field (Lundvall, 2010; Freeman, 1995; Nelson, 1959). It was asserted that Christopher Freeman made his contribution on the systemic perspective of innovation with his innovation system concept by the end of the 1980s. According to Smith (2000) the underlying idea of Freeman could be traced back to List with its institutional aspect and Marx with its combination of a theory of technological change and a theory of development. Lundvall states that: "a national system encompasses elements and relationship, either located within or rooted inside the borders of a nation-state" (Lundvall, 2010, p. 2). Major components of a NIS include organizations (firms, universities, public research institutes), institutions (various laws, regulations, cultural norms), and governments. The main focus of NIS is on non-firm organizations, which provide a contextual background within which innovation can take place. Because of the complex nature of NIS, there were some integrated sub-systems. It can be stated that health innovation sub-system is the biggest component of the national innovation system. Consoli and Mina (2009) describe the health innovation system as in Figure 1.

Figure 1. Health Innovation System (Consoli and Mina, 2009)

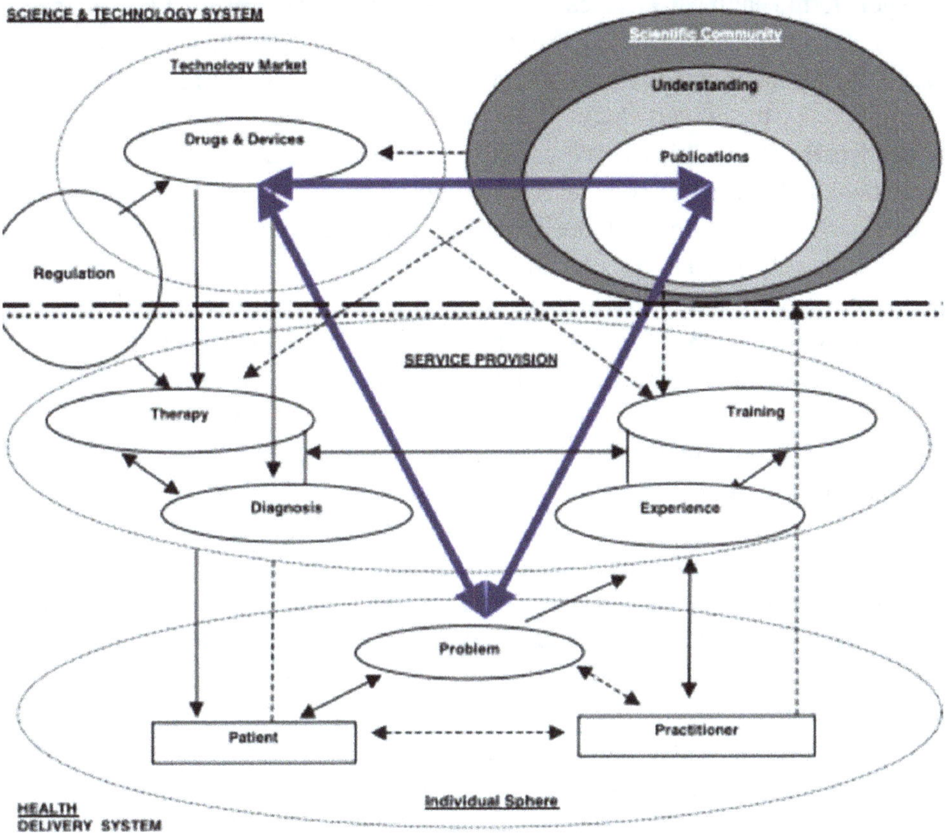

As sketched in Figure 1, there were interactions among relevant agents between interconnected layers. The bottom part was described as the practical domain of health innovation system in which the patient-practitioner relationship took place. Our focus is mainly on the upper part of figure 1 and especially the scientific production of research hospitals. It is clear that in this big picture, the scientific community is not limited to research hospitals in the health domain but for computational constraints, we focused on research hospitals and limited our study with these institutions.

Innovation is a necessity in order to reach a level of prosperity and to raise healthy individuals in our society. It is only possible to raise healthy individuals by prevention, diagnosis and treatment of diseases that may occur. The innovation structure of a hospital is possible by creating new products in all sectors that contribute to health (pharmaceutical, medical technology, information systems), creating a difference in the services provided and a new process of institutional structure (Hult & Hurley, 1998, p. 42).

According to WHO, hospitals are inpatient institutions that provide long-term or short-term health care services that can be grouped into observation, diagnosis, treatment and rehabilitation (Can & İbicioglu, 2008, p. 255). Hospitals are also directly and indirectly intertwined with education. The largest manpower of these organizations is provided by the universities providing medical and medical education and many other department faculties. Diseases that require many advanced specializations can only be found in the training and research hospitals of the universities. Hospitals, particularly, research hospitals are a component of health innovation systems, which can be conceptualized as distributed systems because of their extensive division of labor and complex collaborative approach to the application of beneficial knowledge (Coombs et al., 2003, p. 1145). Hospitals perform multiple functions in health innovation systems. They are the major providers of health-care services. They are adopters and users of new technologies. They are potential developers of processes and organizational innovations. Furthermore, hospitals can be an integral part of the education system in which new practitioners are trained, so they can be loci of clinical experimentation and large R&D performing institutions in their own right. All of them, they are key sites for the adoption, reproductive, and generation of medical knowledge (Mina &Thune, 2016: 1545). In Table 1 shows examples of the contributions of the faculties medicine of universities, which are academic health centers, to the health innovation system in order to improve health and improve the quality of life.

Abbreviations: *AHC indicates academic health center; *ECHO, Extension for Community Healthcare Outcomes; *RED, reengineered discharge; *CMP, Care-Management Program; *MGH, Massachusetts General Hospital. *"Health systems innovations" are defined as novel ideas, products, services, and processes—including new ways to promote healthy behaviors and better integrate health services with public health and other social services— which achieve better health outcomes and/or patient experience at equal or lower cost. Quality improvement efforts are included as a type of health systems innovation focused on process improvements.

Health Systems Innovation At Academic Health Centers (Ellner, Stout & Sullivan, 2015: 3)

Universities are an indispensable component in order to train qualified personnel for the sector by providing medical education as well as to provide technical personnel in all related fields and to carry out production supporting activities in order to form machinery and equipment. In addition to this, making science and creating publications and projects that support science is a criterion for its contribution to the health innovation system.

In this study, we discussed the health innovation system and particularly we examined the cognitive dimension of university hospitals quantitatively. Therefore, we aimed to review health innovation system by considering NIS literature and

Table 1. Examples of health innovation systems at AHCS, 2014

Institution	Innovation	Problem	Approach/ solution	Reported outputs and outcomes	Other potential measures of impact
University of California, San Francisco School of Medicine	eReferral	Limited access for primary care physicians and patients to specialists in San Francisco's safety net hospitals and clinics; problematic paperbased referral system	• Electronic review of specialist referral requests from primary care physicians • Facilitated communication between providers • Designated specialist "reviewer" who processed and evaluated incoming referrals	• Effective use of specialist time, only seeing complex cases • Reduced wait times for patients • Streamlined patient info allowed for accurate diagnosis and follow-up	• Collaboration across medical specialty areas, clinics, AHCs, and government agencies • Improved efficiency and work absenteeism among patients, by avoiding unnecessary visits
University of New Mexico School of Medicine	Project ECHO	Limited access to specialists and training opportunities for health care providers in rural and underserved areas	Physicians and health care staff connected with specialists via teleconferencing system in a "virtual clinic"	• Increased training/ collaboration opportunities for health professionals • Reduced patient travel times to access specialists • Effective way to treat hepatitis C	• Built a thought community within the network • "Demonopoliz(ed) medical knowledge" • Adopted by other AHCs; received multiple awards and other recognition • Model applied to other disease conditions
Boston University, Boston Medical Center	Project RED	High hospital readmission rates among patients with complex conditions; poor coordination of care between hospital and primary care physician	Patients assigned to discharge advocates who helped coordinate care; checklist outlined how to work with patient during discharge; use of "virtual patient advocates" to deliver discharge plan	• Primary care physicians able to address medical issues; decreased hospital readmission rates • Decreased costs related to hospital readmission	• Received numerous awards and recognition for patient safety and innovation • Adopted by other AHCs
Stanford University School of Medicine	Chronic Disease Self-Management Program	Patients lack self-efficacy support as they work to address their chronic diseases	Six-week course given by trained facilitators to patients in community settings; designed to create a space where patients supported each other as they worked toward better health	• Effective in helping patients control their chronic conditions • Reduced the number of readmissions and days spent in hospital	• Mobile app developed for participants to help them manage their progress • Delivered health programming in community settings; strengthened partnerships and collaboration • Replicated globally
Massachusetts General Hospital	Mass General CMP	Medicare patients with complex conditions were about 10% of the Medicare patient population and reflected about 70% of Medicare costs	Added nurse case managers to primary care groups to coordinate care for elderly patients enrolled in the program; these nurses helped with discharge plans, explained medications, and made sure patients had psychosocial supports	• Reduced hospital readmissions, emergency room visits, and mortality rates • Increased patient satisfaction • Reduced health care costs	• Centers for Medicaid and Medicare Services continued support after initial demonstration project, and program was successfully expanded to two other hospitals • Primary care providers reported having increased work–life satisfaction • A CMP icon was added to MGH's electronic medical record system that allowed for streamlined care coordination across the MGH system

examined scientific publications which were produced by university hospitals and indexed in PUBMED for understanding the cognitive contribution of these institutions in Turkey to health innovation system. One of the largest sources of medical scientific information is the PubMed / MEDLINE bibliographic database. PubMed / MEDLINE, web-based sources with excerpts and abstracts from approximately 5.516 up to date biomedicine and health-related journals from the US and more than 80 foreign countries in 39 languages, including medicine, nursing, dentistry, veterinary medical, healthcare system and preclinical sciences and includes regular professional updates, evidence-based patient care information and medical problem solutions (Mosa ve Yoo, 2013, p. 1).

Hospitals, in particular, university and research hospitals, are part of health innovation systems. They are not only served as health service providers but also, they are adopters and users of new technologies. Moreover, they are potential developers of new clinical processes and organizational innovations. Interaction of doctors and engineers is also considered as convergence of different fields to create product and service innovations.

We applied the scientometrics methodology for analysis. Scientometrics was originally introduced by Russian mathematicians Nalimov and Mul'chenko (1969) with the term "Naukometriya". Kinouchi (2014) further interpreted this notion as making ''science of science'' for creating better science policies and using a quantitative approach for evidence-based solutions. Science or bibliometric mapping produces a graphical representation of relations between disciplines, fields, documents, and authors (Small 1999). It has been widely used to show and uncover hidden key elements, such as documents, authors, institutions, and topics, in different research fields.

Turkey addressed publications were retrieved from PUBMED database and after applying preprocessing algorithms, data were analyzed to find the contribution of the universities, which have training and research hospitals, to the health innovation system. It was seen that study focuses of universities diverge from each other and it was interpreted as regional differences. Moreover, these differences also inspired us that regional innovation system approach may well-suit for health innovation system.

BIBLIOMETRIC METHODS

A bibliometric study can be defined as analyzes of well-structured scientific publications in order to derive hidden characteristics in the dataset. Although it is known for decades, its use has gained pace after the advancements in information and communication technologies. As the content has become digital, and scientific databases such as Web of Science, SCOPUS, PUBMED, and others are introduced data collection has gotten easier than ever. Data processing capacities of computers have increased considerably. A number of software to perform bibliometric analyzes have been launched. As a result of the developments, bibliometric has turned out to be available for researchers from different fields of study (Burmaoğlu, 2016; Zupic & Čater, 2015).

As an advantage, bibliometric brings a "measure of objectivity" into scientific fields by serving mainly for two reasons. It facilitates publication performance analyzes for both individuals and institutions. Performance metrics such as the number of citations, the number of publications introduce the quality of studies and performance of researchers. It produces structured maps and demonstrates conceptual, intellectual, and social networks within a field as well. Results of bibliometric analyzes demonstrate invisible networks or in other words "invisible colleges" within a research field (Cobo & Herrera, 2011; Zupic & Čater, 2015).

Bibliometric studies involve a number of steps; these are data retrieval, preprocessing, network extraction, normalization, and mapping. Bibliometric analyzes provide answers for different research questions. At network extraction step, researchers choose a suitable analysis for their research question. Co-word analysis is used in defining the conceptual structure. The output of co-author analysis demonstrates collaboration networks (Ravikumar, Agrahari, & Singh, 2015, p. 38). Researchers benefit from bibliographic coupling and co-citation analyzes to explain the intellectual base of the field (Chang, Huang, & Lin, 2015). In this study, cluster analysis is used in defining leading universities and their fields of expertise.

DATA RETRIEVAL AND PREPROCESSING

The outcome quality of bibliometric studies relies on the quality of data sources. In order to secure the quality, it is preferred to retrieve data from PubMed/MEDLINE database in which health-themed publications are indexed. PubMed/MEDLINE includes abstracts of scientific publications from more than 5200 journals in the areas such as medicine, nursing, dentistry, veterinary, health systems, pre-clinical sciences, and provides links to full papers (Mosa & Yoo, 2013, p. 1; US Dep. of Health and Human Services, 2019). It enables a structured search of papers by items such as title, language, abstract, publication type, and date, location, etc. The use of Medical Subject Headings (MeSH), which are continuously updated by the National Library of Medicine, simplifies the search procedure by subjects (Coletti & Bleich, 2001, p. 317; Ebbert, Dupras, & Erwin, 2003, p. 90).

Journal articles which are published by researchers from Medicine Faculties in Turkey in the period of 01.01.2006-31.12.2015 constitute the data set of the study. The query used in data retrieval is as follows:

"Turkey[ad] OR Turkei[ad] OR Turquie[ad] OR Turkiye[ad] OR Türkiye[ad] AND ([PDAT]: [PDAT])"

Among all the aforementioned steps, preprocessing is crucial. The output quality of the step directly determines the goodness of the results (Cobo & Herrera, 2011). Data retrieved from bibliographic databases necessitate a cleansing process before running analysis. In our case, the query returns 113.519 articles. In the dataset, 3000 repeating articles were defined and excluded from the set. 110.519 articles were used in the analysis.

Another common issue in datasets is the orthographical differences. For instance, "9 Eylül Üniversity" can be written as "Nine September University", "Dokuz Eylül University", or "Dokuz Eylül Üniversitesi". All these versions have to be collected under a single name. Similarly, medicine faculties and other faculties of health sciences can be named as "Tıp Fakültesi", "School of Medicine", "Medical Faculty", "Veterinerlik Fakültesi", "Veterinary Faculty", "Nursing Faculty", "Hemşirelik Fakültesi". Again, a standardization is essential. Authors gathered together all the alternative versions under the name of "medicine faculty".

Data grouping process was run parallel to the data cleansing process. The articles of the researchers working in different departments of the same university were grouped according to their universities. The final data set was restructured and prepared for bibliographic analysis in "Vantage Point" software.

2-Mode Datasets

In network analysis, "attributes of pairs of individuals", which are called as "dyadic attributes", are explored (Borgatti & Everett, 1997). 2-Mode nature is very common in real-world networks. In these networks, there are two classes, each containing a number of nodes, and links connecting two nodes from two classes. The two classes are distinct sets. A link can never exist between two nodes from the same class (Latapy, Magnien, & Vecchio, 2008).

In this paper, universities are linked to MeSH terms. In order to keep the analysis at an aggregate level, MeSH terms with a frequency less than 50 are excluded. The 2-Mode dataset includes 33.94% of the dataset. There are 70 universities and 500 MeSH terms.

Social Networks Analysis

Social network analysis (SNA) is used in identifying and interpreting information links in a particular area by analyzing relationships among actors such as authors or institutions (Karagöz & Kozak, 2014, p. 49; Valente, 2010, p. 4). There are different methods which are suitable to analyze networks according to different types of information. SNA makes visible major themes in a field (Leung, Sun, & Bai, 2017, p. 39). Therefore, scientists from different fields such as sociology, social psychology, anthropology, economics, and information technology benefit from SNA (Demir & Taktak, 2011, p. 8).

A social network has a dynamic structure due to appearing nodes, created by participating actors, and disappearing nodes originated from leaving actors (Karagöz & Kozak, 2014, p. 49). Thus, studying social networks provides clues about where to stand in a network.

Clustering Analysis

Within a homogeneous-looking network structure, there may be smaller but more homogeneous networks, which have some features in common with the large network (Girman & Newman, 2002, p. 7821). Clustering analysis enables the identification of these small networks. A commonly used quality measure for graph clustering is modularity value. It is a performance metric for clustering analysis (Brandes et al., 2008, p. 172; Newman, 2006, p. 8578). It is based on a comparison of a number of edges within a cluster and between clusters. The higher the modularity value points the better results obtained (Shiokawa, Fujiwara, & Onizuka, 2013). GEPHI, the visualization program used in analyzes, uses the Louvain algorithm to calculate a modularity value. Thus, Louvain modularity is used in the paper.

The next step is to define authorities and hub points in the clusters. Authorities are "the best source of information". The hubs are the "collection of links to authorities" (Zhang & Xu, 2008). HITS (hyperlink-induced topic search) algorithm returns two values as "authority" and "hub". It is used in defining specialized institutions and their level of specialization. The data of the relationships between MeSH terms and institutions are used in the analyzes.

Closeness-based centrality measure which is a distance-based measurement of centrality is used in prioritizing MeSH terms (Freeman, 1978).

RESULTS

Ten years of publication trend is visualized according to regions in Turkey in Figure 1. In the period of 2006-2013, a stable trend exists. In 2013, healthcare was defined as one of the priority fields. Ministry of Health put in practice the "Transformation in Health Policies," and improve the research opportunity in universities. Figure 1 reflects the effects of the policies as an upward trend in publication numbers.

Figure 2. ARABIC 1: Scientific publication trend by region

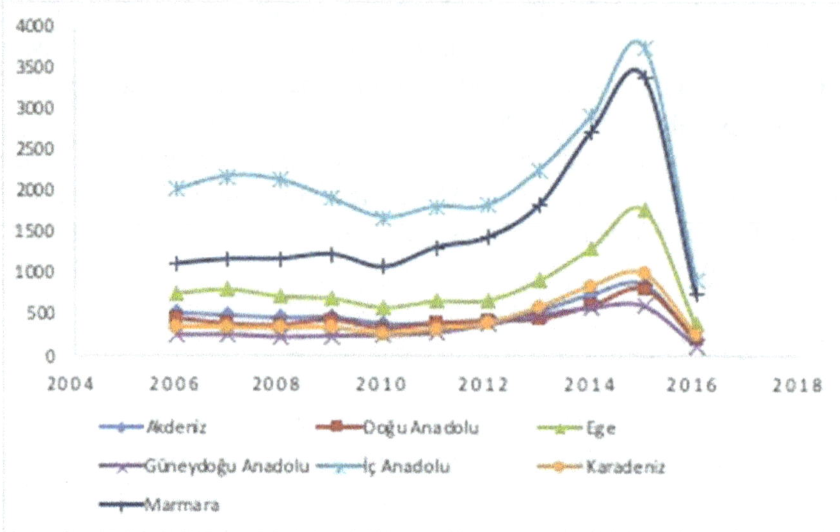

All regions show a similar trend but researchers in Marmara and Central Anatolia produced more publications than other researchers. It is worth to keep in mind that the figure demonstrates the total numbers, not average scores such as publication per researcher or publication per institution.

There are 16 institutions in Central Anatolia; Hacettepe University and Mevlana University are leading institutions in terms of publication quantity. The number of institutions in Marmara is larger than Central Anatolia, yet it takes place in the second order. Istanbul university outperforms other universities in the Marmara Region. Aegean region follows Marmara. Ege University is the leading university of the region. Other regions show relatively lower performance.

As Institution-MeSH terms relationships are visualized in a two-state network graph, eight clusters are defined. In the cluster definition, the aforementioned HITS algorithm and Louvain modularity values are used.

The first cluster, cluster 1, is given in Figure 2.

In cluster 1 genetic, surgical and therapeutic applications are the leading fields of study. Hacettepe University has the highest authority and hub scores. Universities from Eastern and Southeastern Anatolia do not exist in the cluster (see Table 2).

In Figure 3, cluster 2 exists. There are only four universities in the cluster. Gazi University appears as an authority.

In the second cluster, the prominent terms are the concepts related to renal transplantation and renal dialysis processes.

In cluster 3, as shown in Figure 4, only five universities exist.

Figure 3. ARABIC 2: Cluster 1

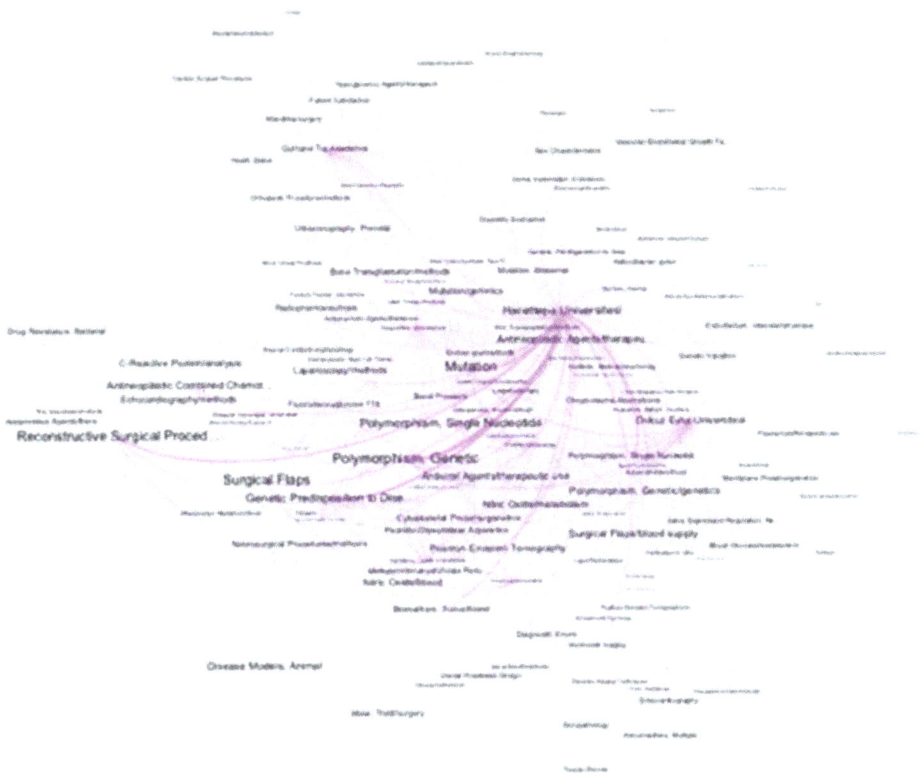

Ege University is the leading institution in the cluster. Regionally, there is only one university from the Aegean Region. There are two universities from Marmara and two universities from Central Anatolia in the cluster (see Table 3).

The first term MeSH studied in the third cluster is the concept of apoptosis, which means the death of cells, followed by homocysteine, an amino acid found in the blood. It can be said that the MeSH are directed towards different fields rather than a specific field.

There are a number of institutions in cluster 4 (see Figure 5). Institutions from the Marmara Region dominate the cluster. Yet, Ankara University has the highest authority and hub scores.

Quality of life and chemical for therapeutic purposes constitute the main fields of study in cluster 4. Health information and applications are the other concepts studied by the members of the cluster.

Cluster 5 is one of the crowded clusters. There is no dominant region, instead, each region has one or more representative institution in the cluster (see Figure 6).

Table 2. ARABIC 1: Authority, hub, and closeness centrality value scores in cluster 1

Universities in Cluster 1					
Institution Name	**Authority**	**Hub**	**Institution Name**	**Authority**	**Hub**
Hacettepe University	0.307785	0.099796	Gaziantep University	0.109416	0.035477
Dokuz Eylül University	0.202692	0.065721	Eskişehir Osmangazi U.	0.094946	0.030785
Gülhane Medical Acad.	0.201211	0.065241	Celal Bayar University	0.071928	0.023322
Uludağ University	0.133316	0.043226	Abant İzzet Baysal U.	0.064216	0.020821
Karadeniz Teknik U.	0.122356	0.039673	Medipol University	0.02698	0.008748
Çukurova University	0.113103	0.036673			
MeSH Terms in Cluster 1					
Mesh Terms	**CCV**	**Mesh Terms**	**CCV**		
Polymorphism, Genetic	0.501324	Genetic Predisposition to Disease	0.486718		
Surgical Flaps	0.49956	Antineoplastic Combined Chemotherapy Protocols/ therapeutic use	0.483404		
Mutation	0.497809	Antineoplastic Agents/ therapeutic use	0.483404		
Reconstructive Surgical Procedures/ methods	0.496938	Surgical Flaps/ blood supply	0.482583		
Polymorphism, Single Nucleotide	0.490078	Antiviral Agents/ therapeutic use	0.482583		
CCV: Closeness Centrality Value					

MeSH Terms of the cluster and the geographical distribution of institutions confirm that in each region there is at least one institution working on the pharmacological sciences that have a direct impact on human health (see Table 5).

Cluster 6 is another crowded cluster with 16 members. Başkent University has the highest authority and hub scores of the cluster. Similar to cluster 5, each region is represented by at least one institution.

Figure 4. ARABIC 3: Cluster 2

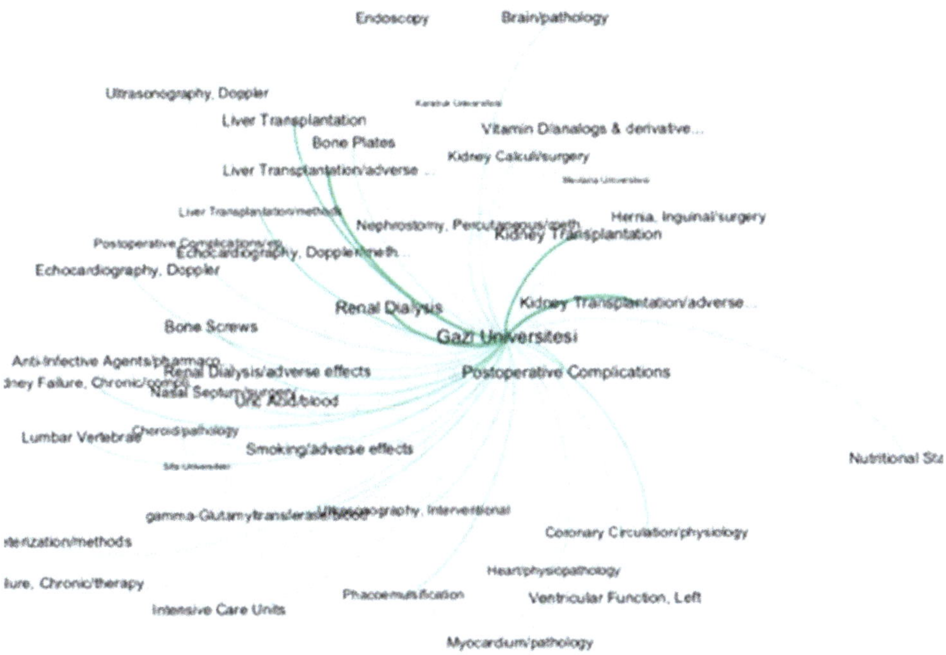

Table 3. ARABIC 2: Authority, hub, and closeness centrality value scores in cluster 2

Universities in Cluster 2					
Institution Name	**Authority**	**Hub**	**Institution Name**	**Authority**	**Hub**
Gazi University	0.25292	0.082007	Mevlana University	0.004935	0.0016
Şifa University	0.005439	0.001763	Karabük University	0.004787	0.001552
MeSH Terms in Cluster 2					
Mesh Terms	**CCV**	**Mesh Terms**	**CCV**		
Renal Dialysis	0.49607	Ventricular Function, Left	0.471369		
Postoperative Complications	0.486718	Renal Dialysis/ adverse effects	0.46981		
Kidney Transplantation	0.485056	Uric Acid/ blood	0.46981		
Kidney Transplantation/ adverse effects	0.477712	Nutritional Status	0.46981		
Bone Screws	0.477712	Liver Transplantation	0.469034		
CCV: Closeness Centrality Value					

Figure 5. ARABIC 4: Cluster 3

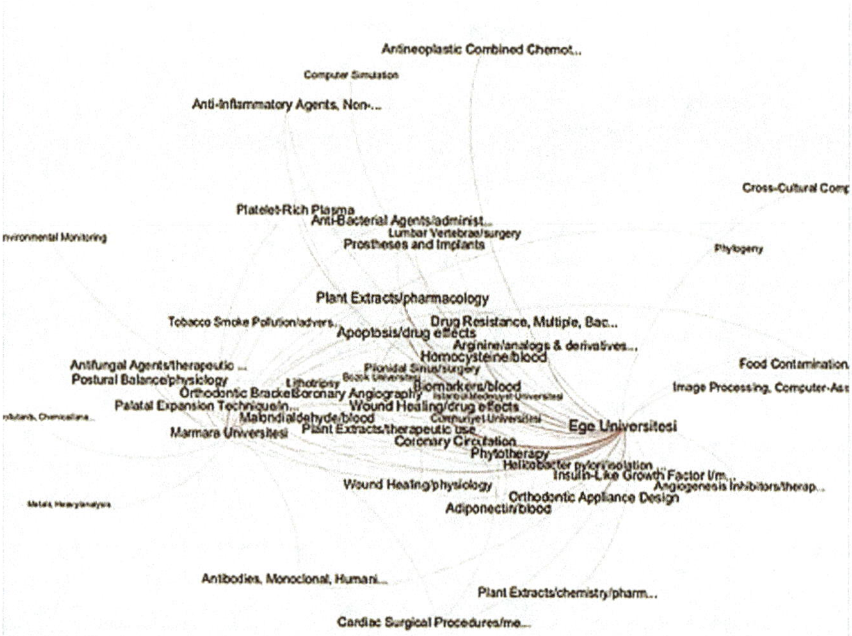

Table 4. ARABIC 3: Authority, hub, and closeness centrality value scores in cluster 3

Universities in Cluster 3					
Institution Name	**Authority**	**Hub**	**Institution Name**	**Authority**	**Hub**
Ege University	0.251528	0.081555	Istanbul Medeniyet University	0.026352	0.008544
Marmara University	0.183199	0.0594			
Cumhuriyet University	0.096431	0.031267	Bozok University	0.016745	0.005429
MeSH Terms in Cluster 3					
Mesh Terms	**CCV**	**Mesh Terms**	**CCV**		
Apoptosis/Drug Effects	0.497809	Coronary Circulation	0.477712		
Homocysteine/ Blood	0.493484	Phytotherapy	0.47691		
Biomarkers/Blood	0.493484	Adiponectin/ Blood	0.47452		
Wound Healing/ Drug Effects	0.490078	Malondialdehyde/ Blood	0.47452		
Plant Extracts/ Fharmacology	0.484228	Coronary Angiography	0.471369		
CCV: Closeness Centrality Value					

Figure 6. ARABIC 5: Cluster 4

In cluster 6, studies on imaging devices and medical devices leave behind the other fields of studies. All the institutions except the ones from the Mediterranean Region concentrate on these subjects (see Table 6).

As it is visible in Figure 8, institutions from four regions form cluster 7.

There are two universities that have authority and hub scores very close. Thus, there is no one dominant university in the cluster. Pharmacology (pharmaceutical science) and dentistry, physical methods in medical devices are the main fields of study in cluster 7. The studied subject of the cluster is wastes and water pollutants which have indirect effects on health (see Table 7).

The last cluster is an outstanding one (see Figure 9). There is only one institution, namely İstanbul Bilim University, working on molecular models, vibration, quantum theory, frequency analysis, spectrum analysis, and chemistry.

Table 5. ARABIC 4: Authority, Hub, and Closeness Centrality Value Scores in Cluster 4

Universities in Cluster 4					
Institution Name	**Authority**	**Hub**	**Institution Name**	**Authority**	**Hub**
Ankara University	0.230702	0.074803	Acıbadem University	0.042992	0.01394
Erciyes University	0.166459	0.053973	Çanakkale Onsekiz Mart U.	0.031322	0.010156
Yüzüncü Yıl University	0.112777	0.036567	Muğla Sıtkı Koçman U.	0.022447	0.007278
Düzce University	0.07835	0.025404	Maltepe University	0.014135	0.004583
MeSH Terms in Cluster-4					
Mesh Terms	**CCV**	**Mesh Terms**	**CCV**		
Quality of Life	0.504889	Rhinoplasty/ methods	0.479325		
Health Knowledge, Attitudes, Practice	0.49956	Models, Biological	0.459175		
Severity of Illness Index	0.494343	Suture Techniques	0.480948		
Attitude of Health Personnel	0.485885	Surveys and Questionnaires	0.483404		
Anti-Bacterial Agents/therapeutic use	0.501324	Quality of Life/ psychology	0.478517		
CCV: Closeness Centrality Value					

In reality, there is no network of the institutions in cluster 8, as there is only one institution. Therefore, the authority and hub scores of the institution are very low (see Table 8).

The analysis shows that most of the publications are produced in the Central Anatolia Region. Universities in the region mainly focus on surgical and genetic studies. Hacettepe University, with 4851 publications, has the highest number of publications in the region.

Marmara and Aegean follow Central Anatolia with 25.06% and 13.05% publication rates respectively. Mainly two fields of study dominate these regions; these are pharmacology and medical device technologies. Among the universities in these regions, Marmara University stands out with 5799 publications. Istanbul Bilim University attracts attention with its research on the effects of physical and chemical sciences on medical devices. Ege University is one the oldest and well-

Figure 7. ARABIC 6: Cluster 5

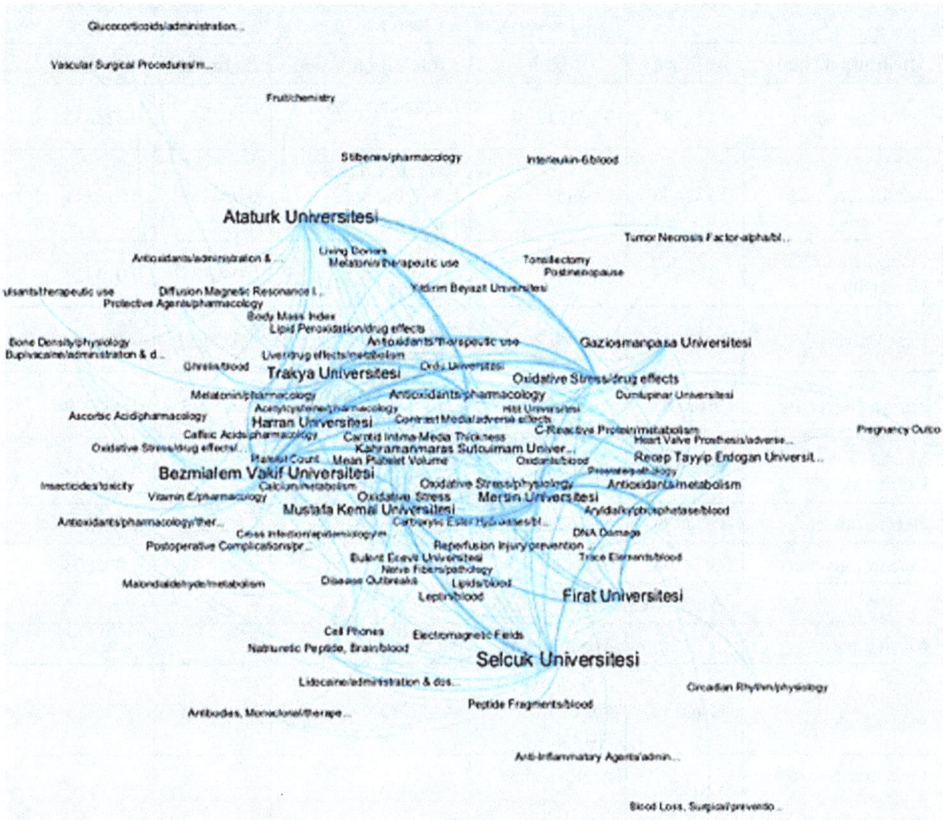

known universities in the Aegean Region. Researchers in Ege University focus on diseases related to cells. Treatment-purposed pharmacological studies are conducted in the university as well.

Mediterranean (8.10%), Black Sea (7.31%), and Eastern Anatolia (7.05%) regions produce 22.46% of all publications. Southeastern Anatolia Region has the least capacity of scientific publications in Turkey.

CONCLUSION

Reaching a level of development and prosperity under the conditions formed by global competition is only possible for countries which have healthy populations. Governments are responsible for improving health in societies. In order to achieve this duty, they need to establish health innovations systems strengthening the prevention

Table 6. ARABIC 5: Authority, hub, and closeness centrality value scores in cluster 5

Universities in Cluster 5					
Institution Name	**Authority**	**Hub**	**Institution Name**	**Authority**	**Hub**
Selçuk University	0.159794	0.051812	Gaziosmanpaşa University	0.067341	0.021835
Atatürk University	0.134406	0.04358	Kahramanmaraş Sütçü İmam University	0.056258	0.018241
Bezm-i Alem Vakıf University	0.109523	0.035512	Recep Tayyip Erdoğan University	0.040784	0.013224
Fırat University	0.105875	0.034329	Bülent Ecevit University	0.02572	0.008339
Trakya University	0.103862	0.033676	Yıldırım Beyazıt University	0.015233	0.004939
Mustafa Kemal University	0.075394	0.024446	Dumlupınar University	0.015613	0.005062
Harran University	0.077779	0.025219	Ordu University	0.013069	0.004237
Mersin University	0.074168	0.024048	Hitit University	0.008644	0.002803
MeSH Terms in Cluster 5					
Mesh Terms	**CCV**	**Mesh Terms**	**CCV**		
Antioxidants/ Pharmacology	0.510332	C-Reactive Protein/ metabolism	0.489233		
Oxidative Stress/ drug effects	0.507596	Antioxidants/ therapeutic use	0.489233		
Oxidative Stress	0.5031	Leptin/blood	0.484228		
Oxidative Stress/ physiology	0.498683	Natriuretic Peptide, Brain/ blood	0.482583		
Antioxidants/ metabolism	0.495205	Lipid Peroxidation/ drug effects	0.480135		
CCV: Closeness Centrality Value					

and treatment of diseases in a society which integrate all actors and factors, that are effective on the health of individuals directly or indirectly.

In our country, a number of attempts have been made to establish a national health innovation system. It can be said that the attempts after 2003 have accelerated improvements in the field. Turkish Government has managed to form a scientific and technological environment by using healthcare transformation policies and incentives. With the statutory decree in 2011, the Ministry of Health has reinforced education

Figure 8. ARABIC 7: Cluster 6

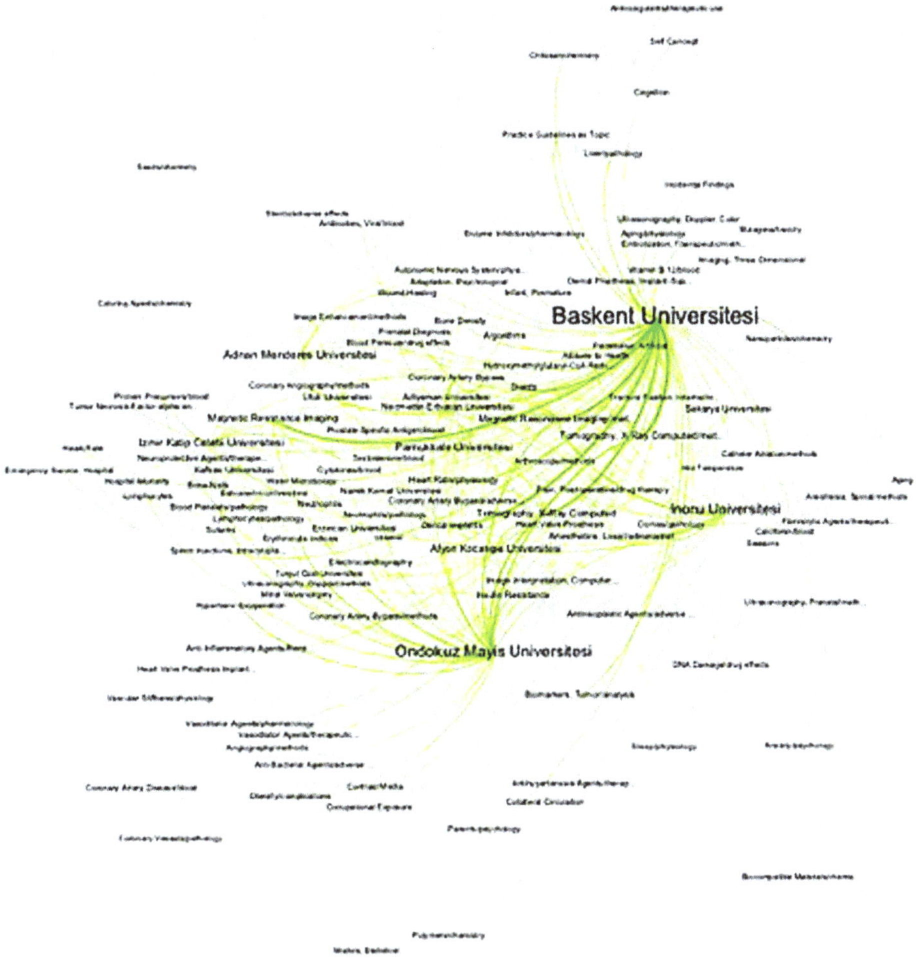

and research in healthcare. It has enabled access to cost-effective and reliable access to medications, medical devices, and other medical goods. New policies have been put in practice. As a result, an innovation ecosystem has become to emerge.

Universities, as institutions responsible for producing and disseminating scientific knowledge, gained importance after the improvement in science and technology in the nineteenth century. They have a similar role in the development of health innovation systems. In this study, the role of Turkish universities in the health innovation system is examined. It is aimed to analyze the status of universities in the national health innovation system and to present their contribution.

Table 7. ARABIC 6: Authority, hub, and closeness centrality value scores in cluster 6

Universities in Cluster 6					
Institution Name	**Authority**	**Hub**	**Institution Name**	**Authority**	**Hub**
Başkent University	0.291866	0.094635	Sakarya University	0.033998	0.011023
Ondokuz Mayıs University	0.169491	0.054956	Kafkas University	0.031225	0.010124
İnönü University	0.141495	0.045878	Ufuk University	0.031189	0.010113
Pamukkale University	0.083252	0.026994	Namık Kemal University	0.020724	0.006719
Adnan Menderes U.	0.088908	0.028827	Adıyaman University	0.021662	0.007024
Afyon Kocatepe U.	0.055864	0.018113	Turgut Özal University	0.004443	0.001441
İzmir Katip Çelebi U.	0.06483	0.021021	Erzincan University	0.020602	0.00668
Necmettin Erbakan U.	0.040037	0.012982	Bahçeşehir University	0.004186	0.001357
MeSH Terms in Cluster 6					
Mesh Terms	**CCV**	**Mesh Terms**	**CCV**		
Tomography, X-Ray Computed	0.508505	Stents	0.483404		
Magnetic Resonance Imaging/ methods	0.50221	Electrocardiography	0.484228		
Tomography, X-Ray Computed/methods	0.5031	Dental Implants	0.473728		
Algorithms	0.478517	Image Interpretation, Computer-Assisted/ methods	0.484228		
Magnetic Resonance Imaging	0.503993	Insulin Resistance	0.482583		
CCV: Closeness Centrality Value					

PubMed/MEDLINE is preferred as a data source as the database covers health-themed publications. Our bibliometric analyzes showed that the Central Anatolia Region is the leading region in terms of scientific publications. The region left behind Marmara and Aegean Regions which are considered as the most socio-economically developed regions. These two regions follow Central Anatolia.

Effects of transformation policies in healthcare are not visible right after their implementation. But, as healthcare is defined as one of the priority fields, a sharp

Figure 9. ARABIC 8: Cluster 7

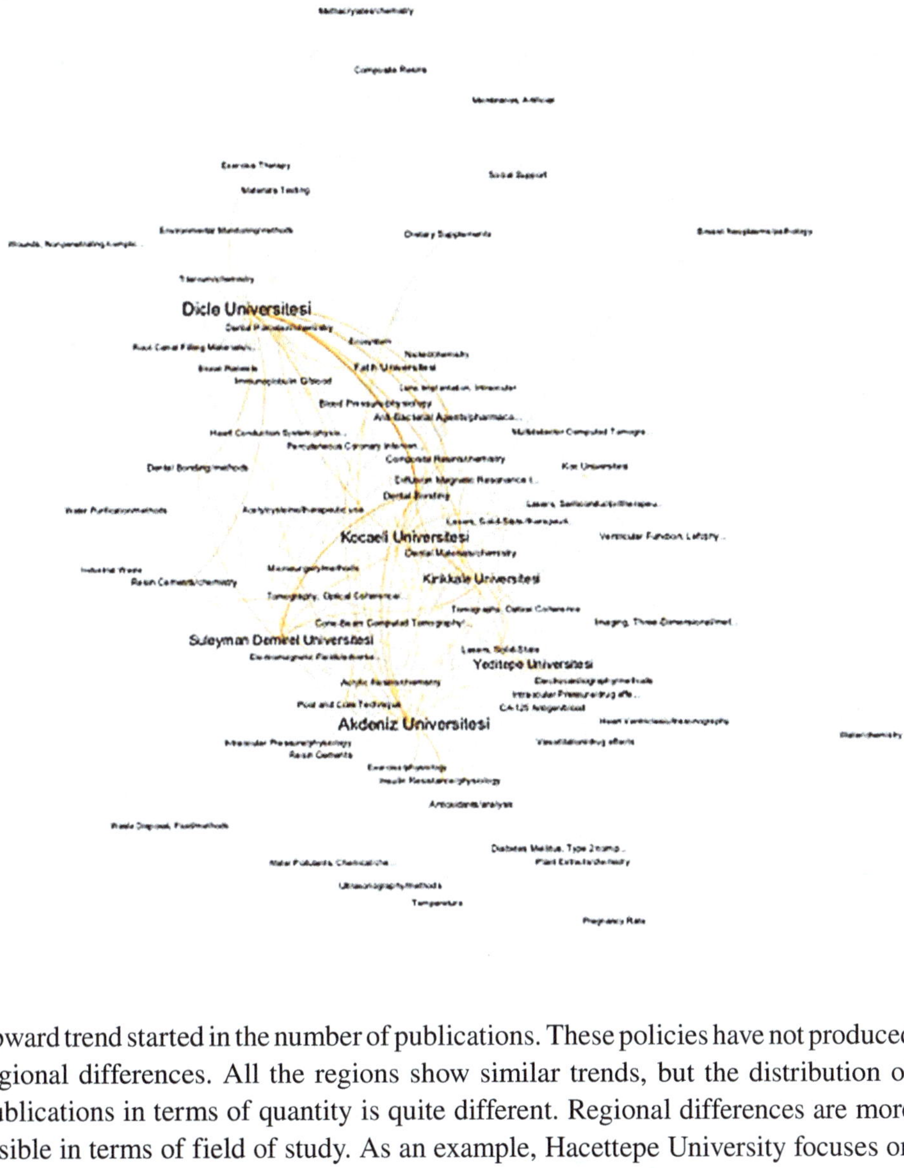

upward trend started in the number of publications. These policies have not produced regional differences. All the regions show similar trends, but the distribution of publications in terms of quantity is quite different. Regional differences are more visible in terms of field of study. As an example, Hacettepe University focuses on surgical treatment whereas Ege university concentrates on cytology.

Our results show where the field of study specific knowledge cumulates. Particularly, the fields of expertise for outstanding universities are defined. This information can be used in defining strategies in order to benefit from it in the most effective manner. We need to develop policies to use knowledge accumulation in creating regional development plans. Moreover, the need for qualified labor in healthcare is evident. Leading universities may serve as locomotives, and provide

Table 8. ARABIC 7: Authority, Hub, and Closeness Centrality Value Scores in Cluster 7

Universities in Cluster 7					
Institution Name	**Authority**	**Hub**	**Institution Name**	**Authority**	**Hub**
Dicle University	0.171791	0.055701	Yeditepe University	0.09817	0.031831
Akdeniz University	0.176715	0.057298	Kırıkkale University	0.091705	0.029735
Kocaeli University	0.123404	0.040012	Fatih University	0.05075	0.016455
Süleyman Demirel Uni.	0.112891	0.036604	Koç University	0.019038	0.006173
MeSH Terms in Cluster 7					
Mesh Terms	**CCV**	**Mesh Terms**	**CCV**		
Anti-Bacterial Agents/ pharmacology	0.488392	Dental Materials/ chemistry	0.477712		
Dental Bonding	0.485885	Composite Resins/ chemistry	0.47691		
Water Purification/ methods	0.292633	Diffusion Magnetic Resonance Imaging/ methods	0.484228		
Waste Disposal, Fluid/methods	0.292633	Dietary Supplements	0.473728		
Environmental Monitoring/methods	0.371485	Water Pollutants, Chemical/ chemistry	0.292633		
CCV: Closeness Centrality Value					

Figure 10. ARABIC 9: Cluster 8

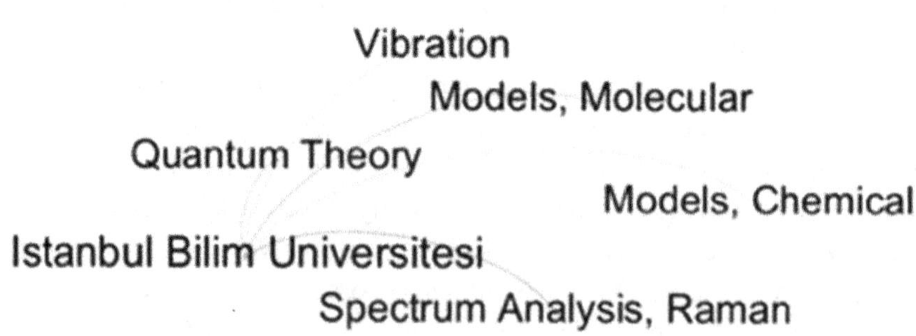

Table 9. ARABIC 8: Authority, hub, and closeness centrality value scores in cluster 8

Universities in Cluster 7			
Institution Name	**Authority**	**Hub**	
İstanbul Bilim University	0.01097	0.003557	
MeSH Terms in Cluster 7			
Mesh Terms	**CCV**	**Mesh Terms**	**CCV**
Models, Molecular	0.411296	Spectrum Analysis, Raman	0.325501
Vibration	0.397481	Models, Chemical	0.259954
Quantum Theory	0.325501		
CCV: Closeness Centrality Value			

high-quality education in their fields of expertise. In the long run, the increase in the qualified labor force may lessen the burden that excessive demand for healthcare service creates in university hospitals.

Besides that, the knowledge gap creates iniquity in terms of availability of healthcare service, and regional development. We have to develop sustainable and equitable ways to provide healthcare services to society while reducing the development gap among the regions. Supporting collaboration between the medical industry and universities may help to create competitive advantages. The government may increase direct R&D investment and subventions for health technology in order to expand the effectiveness of transformation policies.

Finally, authorities should consider regional differences and internal dynamics of the institutions while developing national innovation policies and plans. Collaboration and knowledge sharing between universities have to be supported. Knowledge gap has to be minimized without harming the scientific potential of leading universities.

REFERENCES

Arrow, K. (1962). Economic welfare and the allocation of resources for invention. In R. Nelson (Ed.), *The Rate and Direction of Inventive Activity: Economic and Social Factors*. Washington: NBER. doi:10.1515/9781400879762-024

Borgatti, S. P., & Everett, M. G. (1997). Network Analysis of 2-mode Data. *Social Networks*, *19*(3), 243–269. doi:10.1016/S0378-8733(96)00301-2

Brandes, U., Delling, D., Gaertler, M., Görke, R., Hefer, M., Nikoloski, Z., & Wagner, D. (2008). On Modularity Clustering. *IEEE Transactions on Knowledge and Data Engineering, 20*(2), 172–188. doi:10.1109/TKDE.2007.190689

Burmaoğlu, S. (2016). Sistem Yaklaşımı ve Sağlık Alanında Sistem Dinamikleri Uygulamaları : Bibliyometrik Bir Analiz. *Hacettepe Sağlık İdaresi Dergisi, 19*(4), 465–479. Retrieved from http://fs.hacettepe.edu.tr/saglikidaresidergisi/dosyalar/19.4.Makale 5.pdf

Can, A., & İbicioglu, H. (2008). Evaluation Of Unıversity Hospitals According To Management and Managership. *Suleyman Demirel University The Journal of Faculty of Economics and Administrative Sciences, 13*(3), 253–275.

Chang, Y. W., Huang, M. H., & Lin, C. W. (2015). Evolution of research subjects in library and information science based on keyword, bibliographical coupling, and co-citation analyses. *Scientometrics, 105*(3), 2071–2087. doi:10.100711192-015-1762-8

Chataway, J., Chaturvedi, K., Hanlin, R., Mugwagwa, J., Smith, J., & Wield, D. (2007). *Building the Case for National Systems of Health Innovation.* UK: ESRC Innogen Centre.

Cobo, M. J., & Herrera, F. (2011). Science Mapping Software Tools: Review, Analysis, and Cooperative Study Among Tools. *Journal of the American Society for Information Science and Technology, 62*(7), 1382–1402. doi:10.1002/asi.21525

Coletti, M. H., & Bleich, H. L. (2001). Medical Subject Headings Used to Search the Biomedical Literature. *Journal of the American Medical Informatics Association, 8*(4), 317–323. doi:10.1136/jamia.2001.0080317 PMID:11418538

Consoli, D., & Mina, A. (2009). An evolutionary perspective on health innovation systems. *Journal of Evolutionary Economics, 19*(2), 297–319. doi:10.100700191-008-0127-3

Coombs, R., Harvey, M., & Tether, B. S. (2003). Analysing distributed processes of provision and innovation. *Industrial and Corporate Change, 12*(6), 1125–1155. doi:10.1093/icc/12.6.1125

Demir, H., & Taktak, F. (2011). Konumsal Veri Üzerine Sosyal Ağ Analizi (SAA): Afyonkarahisar Örneği. *Teknolojik Araştırmalar, 3*(1), 7–16.

U.S. Dept. of Health and Human Services. (2019). MEDLINE: Description of the Database. Retrieved from https://www.nlm.nih.gov/bsd/medline.html

Ebbert, J. O., Dupras, D. M., & Erwin, P. J. (2003). Searching the Medical Literature Using PubMed: A Tutorial. *Mayo Clinic Proceedings*, *78*(1), 87–91. doi:10.4065/78.1.87 PMID:12528881

Ellner, A. L., Stout, S., Sullivan, E. E., Griffiths, E. P., Mountjoy, A., & Phillips, R. S. (2015). Health Systems Innovation at Academic Health Centers. *Academic Medicine*, *90*(7), 872–880. doi:10.1097/ACM.0000000000000679 PMID:25738387

Etzkowitz, H., & Leydesdorff, L. (2000). The Dynamics of Innovation: From National Systems and "Mode 2" to a Triple Helix of University-Industry-Government Relations. *Research Policy*, *29*(2), 109–123. doi:10.1016/S0048-7333(99)00055-4

Freeman, C. (1995). The 'National System of Innovation' in historical perspective. *Cambridge Journal of Economics*, *19*(1), 5–24.

Freeman, L. C. (1978). Centrality in Social Networks Conceptual Clarification. *Social Networks, 179*(1968), 215–239.

Frenken, K. (2017). A complexity-theoretic perspective on innovation policy. *Complexity, Innovation and Policy*, 35-47.

Girman, M., & Newman, E. J. (2002). Community structure in social and biological networks. In *Proceedings of The National Academy of Sciences* (*Vol. 99*, pp. 7821–7826). Academic Press. 10.1073/pnas.122653799

Hurley, R. F., & Hult, G. T. M. (1998). Innovation, market orientation, and organizational learning: An integration and empirical examination. *Journal of Marketing*, *62*(3), 42–54. doi:10.1177/002224299806200303

Karagöz, D., & Kozak, N. (2014). Anatolia Turizm Araştırmaları Dergisi'nin Bibliyometrik Analizi: Araştırma Konuları ve Kurumlar Arası İş Birliğinin Sosyal Ağ Analizi ile İncelenmesi. *Türk Kütüphaneciliği*, *28*, 47–61.

Kinouchi, R. R. (2014). Scentometrics: The project for a science of science transformed into an industry of measurements. *SCIENTLAE Studia*, *12*(1), 147–159. doi:10.1590/S1678-31662014000400008

Latapy, M., Magnien, C., & Del Vecchio, N. (2008). Basic notions for the analysis of large two-mode networks. *Social Networks*, *30*(1), 31–48. doi:10.1016/j.socnet.2007.04.006

Leung, X. Y., Sun, J., & Bai, B. (2017). Bibliometrics of social media research: A co-citation and co-word analysis. *International Journal of Hospitality Management*, *66*, 35–45. doi:10.1016/j.ijhm.2017.06.012

Lundvall, B. Å. (Ed.). (2010). *National systems of innovation: Toward a theory of innovation and interactive learning* (Vol. 2). Anthem press.

Metcalfe, J. S. (1994). Evolutionary economics and technology policy. *Economic Journal (London)*, *104*(425), 931–944. doi:10.2307/2234988

Mosa, A. S. M., & Yoo, I. (2013). A Study on Pubmed Search Tag Usage Pattern. Pdf. *Medical Informatics and Decision Making*, *13*(8), 1–14. PMID:23289362

Nalimov, V. V., & Mul'chenko, Z. M. (1969). *Naukometriya, The study of the development of science as an information process*. Moscow: Nauka.

Nelson, R. (1959). The simple economics of basic scientific research. *Journal of Political Economy*, *67*, 297-306.

Newman, M. E. J. (2006). Modularity and community structure in networks. *Proceedings of the National Academy of Sciences of the United States of America*, *103*(23), 8577–8582. doi:10.1073/pnas.0601602103 PMID:16723398

Prada, G. (2008). Exploring technological innovation in health systems: Is Canada measuring up? *Journal of Management & Marketing in Healthcare*, *1*(4), 362–374. doi:10.1179/mmh.2008.1.4.362

Ravikumar, S., Agrahari, A., & Singh, S. N. (2015). Mapping the intellectual structure of scientometrics: A co-word analysis of the journal scientometrics (2005–2010). *Scientometrics*, *102*(1), 929–955. doi:10.100711192-014-1402-8

Shiokawa, H., Fujiwara, Y., & Onizuka, M. (2013). Introduction to strong mixing conditions. In Fast Algorithm for Modularity-Based Graph Clustering Hiroaki (pp. 1170–1176). Academic Press.

Small, H. (1999). Visualizing science by citation mapping. *Journal of the American Society for Information Science*, *50*(9), 799–813. doi:10.1002/(SICI)1097-4571(1999)50:9<799::AID-ASI9>3.0.CO;2-G

Smith, K. (2000). Innovation as a systemic phenomenon: Rethinking the role of policy. *Enterprise and Innovation Management Studies*, *1*(1), 73–102. doi:10.1080/146324400363536

Thune, T., & Mina, A. (2016). Hospitals as innovators in the health-care system: A literature review and research agenda. *Research Policy*, *45*(8), 1545–1557. doi:10.1016/j.respol.2016.03.010

Usher, D. (1964). The welfare economics of invention. *Economica*, *31*(123), 279–287. doi:10.2307/2550623

Valente, T. W. (2010). *Social Networks and Health: Models*. Methods and Applications. doi:10.1093/acprof:oso/9780195301014.001.0001

Zhang, Y., & Xu, G. (2008). Using Web clustering for Web communities mining and analysis. In *Proceedings of the 2008 IEEE/WIC/ACM International Conference on Web Intelligence, WI 2008* (Vol. 1, pp. 20–31). IEEE. 10.1109/WIIAT.2008.415

Zupic, I., & Čater, T. (2015). Bibliometric Methods in Management and Organization. *Organizational Research Methods, 18*(3), 429–472. doi:10.1177/1094428114562629

Section 3

Chapter 9
Evaluating the Impact of Strategic Management and Strategic Thinking on Performance in the Public Health Sector

Zafer Adiguzel
https://orcid.org/0000-0001-8743-356X
Medipol Business School, Istanbul Medipol University, Turkey

ABSTRACT

In the 2000s, change in the business world and pioneering strategies that shape change are becoming the main conditions for superiority in competition. Until recently the traditional management and organization approaches that are in place are inadequate to meet the new expectations coming from change. The aim of this study is to reveal the extent to which the managers of health institutions have adopted the strategic management approach. In this study, it is explained whether the managers have knowledge about strategic management tools which are the basis of strategic management application methods, what strategic management tools they use, their level of satisfaction with these tools and what tools they intend to use in the future. In addition, the changes in the health management managers in the field of strategic management, the priorities in the selection of strategic management tools, the importance of strategic thinking and the effects of strategic management understanding on performance are examined.

DOI: 10.4018/978-1-7998-2329-2.ch009

INTRODUCTION

In today's world, rapid changes in the age of technology and information have made many of the classical competition assumptions in the business world obsolete. It is not enough for enterprises to benefit from new technologies in order to increase their success and competitiveness. At the same time, uniform distribution, competitiveness and access to consumers should be strengthened in their economies. All the efforts of the enterprises are aimed at establishing strategies for superiority in competition. In the 21st century, imagination is becoming the quality most needed by businesses. Within this framework, the primary purpose of the enterprises is to reach the future by defining strategies that will make a difference. In order for companies to gain a structure that is stronger and more competitive in business life and to enable them to compete, they should be put into practice by making use of different strategic methods. With this in mind, "Strategic Management Approach" can be considered as an application that will contribute to strengthening the competitive position of enterprises in their internal world.

The concept of strategic management has come to the forefront in the management of business organizations in the 1980s. With the increase in production, developments in the market began to intensify competition. Increasing pressure from competition has led businesses to set strategic goals for investment and market. Strategic management approaches that lead businesses to set goals are the main subject of the study. Effective management is based on long-term strategic strength as well as the involvement of the organization in decisions. In this context, the implementation of strategic decisions is important for organizations as well as for the country. An excellent structure and criteria of excellence are among the items to be sought in the future in terms of management. Today, participation principles, strategic management forms gain importance and weight.

Strategic management is an important concept for health institutions as well as for other institutions. Health institutions need the concept of strategic management in order to survive in a competitive environment, to analyze the internal and external environment of the institution, to identify the strengths and weaknesses of the institution, and to identify the threat elements of the institution and the aspects that will provide opportunities for the institution. In the face of globalization and the concept of competition that comes with this globalization, health institutions are beginning to give more strategic thinking, strategic decision making and strategic thinking as much as other institutions.

Although the concept of management is very old, the concept of business management is a concept that emerged about a century ago and is still being developed. The reason why the concept of business management is so new is the absence of large scale production-based enterprises until the industrial revolution that began in the 18th century. From this perspective, it is possible to characterize the time before the industrial revolution as the "pre-period" or "pre-period scientific". However, it is possible to say that the management activity existed in ancient times, even in the early ages, considering that there existed individuals and communities who came together to manage the same goal in the past.

Strategic Management is a concept obtained by combining the concepts of strategy and management (Thomas 1984). Therefore, it is necessary to give information about the concept of strategy. In the literature, it is stated that the strategy is based on two sources in terms of its origin. One of these; latin concept with stratum meaning road, line or bed. The second is related to the name of the former Greek General Strategos. It was used to indicate the art and knowledge of the general (Steiner 1971). The concept of strategic management has entered the business literature since 1980. Strategic management, planning the research, review, evaluation and selection efforts necessary for the planning of strategies, taking all kinds of structural and motivational measures within the organization for the implementation of these strategies, taking into force and implementing the strategies before and after the implementation of the top-level staff covering is the sum of the processes that concern their activities (Eren 2005).

STRATEGY

Strategy literally means "forwarding, directing, sending, taking and moving" The word is thought to have been used with reference to the knowledge and art of Strategos, one of the former Greek generals. In some sources, it is stated that the strategy comes from the Latin "stratum" which means road, line or river bed (Mütercimler 2006). Although there is controversy about the origin of the word, it can be said that both definitions have similar meanings in a general approach. This is related to direction (Dinçer 2007). The concept of strategy has been used as a military concept for centuries. According to Webster (1990)'s New International Dictionary, the strategy is the science and art of placing the military power of the parties in accordance with the conditions in order to reach a result in a war (Üzün 2000).

In general terms, the strategy is defined as the use of all kinds of instruments and measures in every field taken by an institution (or state) in order to achieve the objectives chosen in accordance with the politics pursued (Porter 1996). It is readily understood that the concept of general strategy can no longer remain within the framework of defense policy and cannot be distinguished from the general policy of each country (or institution). Since all kinds of political and economic activities are directed towards the welfare, demand and tendencies of the society, the current field of the strategy includes psychological, social, economic, ideological, military and administrative issues (Güçlü 2003). For the concept of strategy, it is possible to define definitions from different perspectives with complementary features. These definitions can be specified as follows (Akgemci 2013):

Strategy as a Plan: Orientation of actions and organizations in line with pre-defined and announced goals in a conscious and purposeful way.

Strategy as an Emerging Direction: The emergence of the direction of action as a result of the attitude and participation of the organizations within the sensitivity of the environment rather than the previously defined and announced target.

Strategy as Location: Explaining the position of organizations within the organization environment defined by the expectations and functions, and regulating the relationship between the organization and its environment.

Strategy as a Perspective: The perspective of the organizations meeting in the joint action, including the norms, values and behavior patterns they share due to their common missions.

As our world is facing large-scale technological and economic developments in the 21st century, the scales of all kinds of organizations are growing and turning to more complex structures and operating systems. Therefore, it is difficult to take measures to ensure the survival and development of enterprises and management of enterprises becomes difficult. As a result of these reasons, the ability of the business executives to anticipate the opportunities and dangers they may encounter in order to be successful and to have information about them leads to better and more reliable strategies. Therefore, they need to implement these strategies efficiently. The Strategy; importance is given to predicting the future direction of external variables and shaping alternative behaviors (Schelling 1980). The strategist demonstrates the ability to combine opposing forces in harmony by effectively identifying and testing strategies (Mintzberg 1987). Evaluating the possibilities of the person, what is being done, what is wanted to be done, and seeing the strengths and weaknesses of the enterprise, the values of the enterprise can be seen from a wide angle.

General Characteristics of Strategy

In today's complex and dynamic business environment, strategy is a tool that encourages and guides employees to survive and gain competitive advantage in the market. The characteristics of the strategy which acts as a compass for the activities of the enterprise, which takes the whole organization in harmony, can be summarized as follows (Eren 2002):

1. *An Art of Analysis:* This art is a method of thinking based on inter-factor logic principles and relationships in an open system, which is about making decisions

and removing obstacles in decisions and not aiming only one line or only one solution (Stockport 2010).

2. *Is A Factor Of Purpose:* The strategy of an enterprise serves the general objectives of that enterprise and ensures that the forces gather around them.
3. *Regulates Interaction Relations with the Business Environment:* It provides the opportunity to comprehend the environmental changes in economic, technological, political and social terms, to eliminate the negative effects on the enterprise and to make use of them by realizing the positive effects in a timely manner.
4. *It concerns a distant future system, in contrast to continuously repeated works:* Strategic choices are strictly separated from monotonous decisions and works since they are related to the policies that the enterprise will follow in a long time (Miles et al. 1978).
5. *Strategy is an Aspect That Manages and Activates All Financial and Human Resources of the Enterprise in Harmony:* The strategy is the guiding or compass of the events and decisions taken in the daily life of the enterprise. The strategy sets the rules of the game, reduces uncertainty and clarifies the paths and rules to be followed (Teece 2010).
6. *Strategy is a Tool for Encouraging and Mobilizing the Human Being in a Complex and Dynamic Organization:* Strategy is a motivating factor. People act more pessimistically in an uncertain environment. However, as they provide them with information to reduce or reduce uncertainty about the future and determine the goals to be achieved, their ambitions and courage will increase. Thus, employees and especially managers will be able to easily draft their tactical activities and easily determine the suitability of their personal activities for general purposes.
7. *Determines the Business Activity Areas in a Complex and Dynamic Environment:* It includes how to take advantage of the existing resources of the enterprise and how to distribute it over a long period of time.

Strategic Management Concept

The strategy, which was initially used as a military concept, has become an approach that businesses should apply in order to adapt to changing conditions and succeed in a competitive environment (Schendel and Hatten 1972; Bracker 1980). Just as plans are made after evaluating the status of the unity, the situation of the enemy and the possibilities at hand in order to achieve victory with the least loss in the minimum strategy, in challenging competition conditions, transmissions must follow the changing market conditions well in order to survive and prevent competitors and know the current characteristics of the competitors well. It should recognize. In the globalizing world, people's consumer awareness as well as their expectations have increased thanks to dizzying developing and changing transportation, information and communication technologies. Therefore, in order to adapt to rapid change and to maintain their existence in the long term, enterprises should adopt a strategic management style that will enable the direction of the future of transmission rather than traditional methods.

Strategic management enables the business to adapt to the environment, self-assessment and predict the future. It establishes a common goal at every level of the enterprise and ensures coordination and enables the establishment of target unity. Strategic management should be considered as a process in businesses and should be implemented (Gluck et al. 1982). The strategic management process should be considered as all of the information gathering, analysis, selection, decision and implementation activities aimed at sustaining the long-term life of the enterprise and providing sustainable competitive advantage (Shrivastava 1994; Ülgen and Mirze 2004).

Strategic management, planning the research, review, evaluation and selection efforts necessary for the planning of strategies, taking all kinds of structural and motivational measures within the organization for the implementation of these strategies, taking into force and implementing the strategies before and after the implementation of the top-level staff covering is the sum of the processes that concern their activities (Strickland and Thompson 1984; Eren 2005). Although there is no consensus on the definition of the concept of management, "management is to work through others" is the most accepted opinion (Koçel 2005). Strategic management, on the other hand, is a management technique that expresses the development of effective strategies, planning, implementation and control of an organization to achieve its objectives (Aktan 2008).

That the business world and the upper system it is a part of are constantly changing,

The institutions and competitors in the sector produce and implement various strategies in accordance with the changing environmental conditions,

To understand the necessity of new strategies that can respond to these strategies and even to make the company more productive states that they produce ideas and work on these issues (Ülgen and Mirze 2006).

Although strategic management is not a new concept, today many companies are unfamiliar with this concept. However, this is a fact that the necessity of enterprises to anticipate future uncertainties and to plan and manage them accordingly is an indispensable element. At this point, strategic management provides a competitive advantage to enterprises by being a dynamic management style, reacting to changes in its environment and eliminating uncertainty and shaping the future (Venkatraman and Camillus 1984). This is an indispensable desire for businesses in tough competitive conditions. Therefore, businesses should adopt the strategic management approach in a very good way by following the strategic management process mentioned in this study carefully and disciplined (Shrivastava 1986). Today, strategic management is tried to be applied in enterprises. However, it is seen that only the intuitive decisions based on experience are applied by the top management in the strategic decisions taken. The word strategy, which entered our literature as a military term in the early 20th century, was used in the sense of making a general plan and activating its own power when necessary to determine what the enemy could and could not do. For centuries, the art of war as a military concept and the military strategy to go to the conclusion of a military operation in the sense of the planning and implementation of the strategy used in the sense of the first, economists and mathematicians, two scientists, Neuman and Morgenstern used in the economic sense (Aytepe 2008).

Strategy; is a management tool that aims to keep the changes in progress under control in order to ensure innovation, progress, communication of the organization / institution with the environment and harmony with each other in parallel with the rapid changes experienced (Hussey 2007). It affects and shapes the decisions of managers and the behavior of employees. It is more about quality than quantity. It is not extroverted but extroverted. It is an organization-specific and distinctive claim (Güner 2005). Strategic management; It can be expressed as a participatory and flexible management approach that expresses the process of monitoring and evaluating their performances by establishing measurable criteria, as well as establishing a vision for the future based on the current situation, mission and basic principles of organizations, identifying the objectives and strategies that will enable them to reach these goals (Aytepe 2008). Strategic management not only creates strategies for the future, but also ensures that these strategies are implemented and the success of implementation is controlled (Erkan 2008).

Strategic management; research, review, evaluation and selection efforts necessary for planning strategies; It includes activities related to taking all kinds of measures within the organization and putting them into force in order to implement the planned strategies and to control the subsequent studies (Morden 2016). Strategic management is the process of systematically implementing various research, examination, evaluation, implementation, coordination and supervision steps for the most efficient implementation of plans by conducting internal and external analyzes in order to maintain an organization's long-term existence and achieve its objectives (Erdem 2006). Strategic management is a management technique that enables the determination of future goals and targets in all organizations and the determination of the procedures to be performed in order to achieve these goals (Atmaca 2007).

In forming strategies, it is important to have adequate and appropriate answers to What, Why, How, When, Where and Who questions. The analysis of these questions forms the basis of strategic management (Aktan 2008).

Strategic management, research, review, evaluation and selection efforts required for the planning of strategies, implementation of all planned and implemented structural and motivational measures for the implementation of these planned strategies, and then the implementation of the strategies once more in terms of compliance with the objectives of the business is the sum of the processes concerning the activities of the level staff (Ansoff et al. 2018). In order to achieve long-term organizational goals, senior managers shape the future of the organization through strategic management, which is a set of decisions and actions used in formulating and implementing strategies that will provide a superior harmony with the organization and its environment (Alpkan 2000).

Development of Strategic Management

In the 1970s, there were many uncontrollable and self-contained problems that would shake the economic and industrial foundations. Production had fallen, inflation, trade imbalance and cost competition had emerged. In addition, falling productivity, increasing regulation, low growth rate, technological obsolescence, rising debts of the III World, new technologies, fluctuations in money markets, serious global competition and socio-political problems affected all institutions and organizations trying to find a strategic direction. All these problems have led to a review of ongoing implementation and management methods (Gönüllü 2008).

Organizations have had to think more strategically in the face of globalization, rapid technological change, emerging markets, and the overwhelming competition resulting from changing customer expectations. Prior to the 1980s, strategic management was mostly implemented by a limited environment in the private sector, while today many organizations use strategic management as an important tool (Atmaca 2007).

If we take a short look at the history of management; It is seen that it is aimed to ensure compliance in every subject from classical management understanding to our time. The Classical Management Approach, which started in the 1900s, the Behavioral Approach in the 1930s and the Modern Management Approach that emerged in the 1960s, constitute the basic steps in the history of management. None of them has completed their mission and has not withdrawn from the application areas and examples of implementation are seen, if not on their own. Modern management approach includes system approach, management according to objectives, direction-action research, contingency approach and strategic management. Strategic management is a form of management that incorporates, synthesizes and manages these management processes and was developed to survive against changes (Erdem 2006).

Once upon a time, the Japanese were leading the whole market. It was a pioneer because it was able to produce and sell quality products that were intact for the customer. But every day all competitors have focused on quality service and production. As a result, there are many competitors in the same sector that do not differ from each other in terms of quality. As such, the size of the problem changed. Accordingly, the problem; total quality alone will not be enough, all competitors provide quality service if the customer is not the opponent, but what superiority of them to come to you, you must have the difference. The answer to this question can be explained with the concept of strategic management.

Towards the end of the 20th century, in parallel with globalization, a process of restructuring was initiated in public administration (Hunger and Wheelen 2003). In this structuring, the concept of social welfare state, including public ownership and broad public service, was abandoned. The most obvious aspect of this situation is the privatization of national industries and the abandonment of public services suitable for production and delivery by the private sector to market conditions (Güner 2005). With the change, organizations have had to apply various management techniques in order to increase their efficiency and effectiveness. In recent years, the economic, socio-social, health and political changes in the world due to the changes in the organizations to benefit from the changes, adapt to the differences in these changes in the environment, to be prepared for unexpected situations and to be least affected by them depends on the management technique to be implemented and continuous success.

The main tools used in the strategic management process are situation analysis (SWOT), portfolio analysis, Q sort analysis, vision-mission statements, scenario analysis, search conference, brainstorming, delphi technique and nominal group technique. Among the tools used, SWOT analysis is used to evaluate the internal and external environment of the organization, and to determine the fields of activity with the help of portfolio analysis matrices; Q sort analysis is used to identify the most important and the most important issues that determine the alternatives that can be used in the selection of the strategy, the mission and vision statements indicating the reason of existence of the organization, the transformation of the principles and values into written form; scenario analysis is used in predicting the future and determining alternative action styles, in-house communication in order to create a common mind in the organization of the call conference, and delphi technique is used in obtaining the opinions of experts in order to make predictions for the future, and the opinions of nominal group technique group members are taken without discussion. Apart from these techniques, open group discussions, quality circles, cost-benefit analyzes and risk analyzes are among the other tools that can be used in the strategic management process (Oyman 2009).

Characteristics of Strategic Management

Strategic management includes the characteristics of general management (Godet 1987). However, unlike these features, it is possible to mention some of the features of strategic management. In order to better understand the issue of strategic management, it is useful to reveal the basic features of strategic management.

Functional management and project or program management, distinguishing them from strategic management to distinguish these features are as follows (Paul 1982):

1. Strategic management is an issue that concerns mainly senior management. Strategic management is a function of top managers because it concerns the future of the enterprise as a whole and tries to determine a direction for it.
2. The future is oriented and related to the long-term goals of the business. Thinks about what the business will be in the determined time horizon and what needs to be done to achieve these results.
3. In strategic management, business is seen as a whole composed of interdependent and interdependent parts. Therefore, strategic management not only deals with the business as a whole, but also the components that make up it. When a decision is made for the whole or any of its components, its effects on the other components are taken into account (Best et al. 2007).
4. Strategic management defines enterprises as open systems. Businesses are in mutual interaction and dependence with their environment. Any changes in the environment also affect the business. Therefore, strategic management closely follows the environment (Wissema et al. 1981).
5. Strategic management considers the objectives of the enterprise and the interests of the society in integrity. In this respect, strategic management carries social responsibility towards its external environment.
6. Strategic management guides lower level managers. In other words, the objectives, decisions and activities determined by the strategic management constitute the common point of action of everyone up to the lowest units within the enterprise (Kolb et al. 1986).
7. Strategic management is about the most effective distribution of the company's resources. It distributes the necessary resources in accordance with the product or market compositions in order to realize the main objectives of the enterprise.
8. Strategic management emphasizes the importance of achieving the goals of the organization based on teamwork. The determination of the strategies is carried out with wide participation in the senior management and the most optimal decision-making techniques are selected for the company.

9. Strategic management helps to identify and solve the most effective problems in the organization. In this context, total quality methods are widely utilized (Bracker 1980).
10. Strategic management enables the planning, organization, coordination, implementation and control of the future activities of the organization.
11. Strategic management utilizes competition and portfolio analysis in the formation and selection of strategies. Portfolio analyzes are the techniques used in strategy selection. It is aimed to make a more rational decision on issues such as staying in the market or withdrawing from the market, merging with other companies and so on.
12. Strategic management helps to" think strategically". Within this framework, the most accurate strategies and tactics are tried to be determined and implemented (Franke et al. 1990).
13. The sources and data of the information used in decision making are different. Since strategic management is concerned with the effectiveness and efficiency of the business as a whole, the information sources and data on the subject are very diverse. Many businesses require a wealth of information and data on departments, functions and the environment (Brown 2005).

Strategic Management Process

Strategic management process can be considered as a special decision-making or problem-solving process (Dinçer and Fidan 1996). In this sense, we can define the strategic management process as all of the information gathering, analysis, selection, decision and implementation activities aimed at sustaining the organizations' long-term lives and achieving sustainable competitive advantage (Ülgen and Mirze 2010). The changing environmental conditions and the adaptation of the competitors have led the organizations to have strategic awareness. For this reason, in order to implement the process, it is necessary to select and appoint strategists to take part in the organization. While analyzing both the internal and external environment, the strategists employed determine the situation, reveal the current situation and question the future developments. After all these analyzes are made in the strategic orientation phase, the mission, vision, goals and objectives of the organization are determined. It is given the answer to how these objectives and targets determined in the strategy formation phase can be implemented according to which strategies. The quantitative and qualitative data obtained through the strategies applied after the studies on the structure of the organization and the decisions taken in the strategic implementation phase in which the prepared strategic plans will be applied are evaluated in the strategic control phase. The strategic management process, which can be reverted to the previous stages at every stage, is of great importance for the survival of the organizations.

Importance and Benefits of Strategic Management

Strategy is very important for businesses. Businesses that do not have a strategy cannot clearly and precisely determine their objectives. In addition, resources can not be used effectively and efficiently in enterprises without strategy (Eren 2005).

The benefits of strategic management can be summarized as follows (Glueck and Jauch 1989):

Strategic management allows organizations to anticipate changing situations.
Strategic management provides clear objectives and orientations.
Research in strategic management makes progress so that the process can help managers.
Things that perform strategic management are more effective.
Strategic management systemises business decisions.
Strategic management helps the communication of the enterprise, the coordination of individual projects, the allocation of resources and the development of short-term planning such as budget.

The phases of strategic management can be listed as follows (Ülgen and Mirze 2006): Selection and assignment phase of strategists, Strategic analysis phase: Determination of environmental opportunities and limitations, analysis of non-operating environment and analysis of internal environment, preparation of due diligence matrices,

Strategic steering phase: Determination of mission, vision and objectives, Strategy formation phase: Determination and selection of basic and sub-strategies, institutional, sectoral and functional strategies, determination of techniques to be used in their implementation,

Strategic implementation phase: Studies on organizational structure, information and decision systems to be used during the implementation of the strategy, appropriate leadership understanding, corporate culture and management styles,

Strategic control phase: Control of performance obtained through the implementation of strategies and techniques related to the control process.

In order to survive in the face of changing environmental conditions, today's enterprises must constantly change their balance and be prepared for new balance situations. The rapid and constant change that the world is experiencing affects all sectors to a great extent, renders existing goals and strategies invalid and inadequate in a short period of time, creates a ball of new problems and threatens its existence by dragging organizations into an environment of uncertainty. The fact that knowledge accumulation improves the technology and feeds the production and consumption of the developing technology increases the speed of change. The ability of the organization to survive in such an environment; to know the conditions of the environment in which it is located, to fulfill the necessity, to distinguish themselves from its competitors, to be more flexible and to adapt to changing conditions by responding to changes more quickly.

Strategic management is in a sense to manage environmental complexity and change (Coulter and Coulter 2002). In this sense, strategic management means meeting the future rather than waiting for the future, giving direction to the future and managing the future. This requires organizations to be managed in such a way that they can act as improvisations under very fast changing conditions. In terms of strategic management, predicting the future, which is a passive function in managing change as an improvisation (leading or creating change) is not sufficient, it is important to shape and manage the future, which is an active function, and that is what is desired. Because in an environment where only reaching the strategic goals of the future will never be enough; it is possible both to remain in the achieved goals and to make conscious and systematic leaps to further goals by managing the future (Karakaya 2004).

From a strategic point of view, enterprises capable of evaluating the environment and predicting the future provide orientation and consistency as a whole. In this way, businesses form a framework by referring and planning their activities to specific departments and evaluate themselves better. This improves the quality of business decisions and projects. Developing effective strategies for achieving predetermined or revised objectives, implementation is realized through concepts, methods, approaches and principles related to strategic management, planning, organizing, staffing, steering and auditing as a whole of decisions to evaluate and control the results (Rodoplu 2001).

Having Strategic Consciousness

The Strategic Management process starts with having 'strategic consciousness' (Ülgen and Mirze 2010). Consciousness is defined as man's ability to know himself and his environment, the process of viewing perceptions and information in the mind (Wheelen et al. 2010). Based on these definitions, we can say that strategic thinking is the first step in strategic management process in order to have strategic awareness. So if we define the definition of strategic thinking; According to Dess and Miller (1996), strategic thinking is the art of overcoming the opponent and doing this by keeping in mind that he is trying to apply the same to you. Strategic thinking starts with your basic skills and examines how they are best used. Strategic thinking sometimes means knowing when to avoid the game.

The main reason for drawing a strategy is to take long-term and rational actions; all actions carried out by reason are planned actions. Practical strategic thinking is all about planning future actions (Betz 2010).

Strategic management, which is a function of the top manager, is important for the organization to carry out its strategic actions with the decisions planned and made in the future. This is done with the support of senior management.

Therefore, Ülgen and Mirze (2010) emphasize the strategic awareness of managers in organizations;

- That the upper system in business and as a part of it is in constant change,
- Organizations and competitors in the sector produce and implement various strategies in line with the changing environmental conditions,
- They express the necessity of new strategies that can respond to these strategies and even make the organization more productive, understand, think about these issues, produce ideas and make studies (Ülgen and Mirze 2010).

STRATEGIC MANAGEMENT IN HEALTH INSTITUTIONS

Strategic management in health institutions consists of managerial decisions and practices for the health institution to continue its activities in harmony with its environment. In addition, strategic management in health institutions covers all applications related to the inspection, research, evaluation and elections required for the planning of strategies, taking all kinds of internal and external measures for the implementation of the planned strategies and putting them into operation after they are put into operation. It is also possible to see strategic management as a management technique in all organizations operating in the health sector and in all other sectors, which enables the determination of the goals and targets for the future and the determination of the actions to be taken in order to achieve these targets (Hitt et al. 2012). Strategic management is an important concept for the health sector as it is for all organizations. With strategic planning, health institutions can design futures and draw a direction for the unknown future. With strategic management, health institutions can determine their goals and objectives for the future. In addition, strategic management enables health institutions to determine the path to be followed in order to achieve their goals and objectives.

Definition of Strategic Management in Health Institutions

Strategic management in health institutions is divided into three main headings. These three main headings are as follows:

- Series of decisions
- Corporate behavior
- Plan

The concept of strategic management, known as a series of decisions, means a collection of decisions to determine the position of the health institution within the environment. Strategic management, which is expressed as corporate behavior, is seen as activities aimed at reacting and adapting to changes in the external environment. In addition, strategic management can be seen as a plan. The strategy is related to the future and expresses the results the organization wants to achieve in the future (Pearce et al. 2000). These three concepts are known as common features of strategic management. The series of decisions, corporate behavior and plan are important concepts for health institutions to be oriented towards the external environment or to provide competitive advantage. The concept of strategic management is a very important concept for health institutions in terms of superiority over competitors and ideas that direct the behaviors of the institution. The concept of strategic management is defined as a continuous and repetitive process that enables the health institution to work in harmony with its environment. There are three main concepts that are important in the strategic management process for health institutions. These concepts are as follows:

- **Environment:** Strategic management focuses on the external environment. Health institutions operate in a variable environment. In this respect, environmental changes create both opportunities and threats. A health institution will be able to survive to the extent that it can benefit from environmental opportunities and be protected from environmental threats.
- **Continuity:** Strategic management is not a process that starts and ends; Since the environment in which it is constantly changing, the institution must always adapt to these changes successfully.
- **Duplicate Process:** As discussed in the following section, strategic management is a process involving more than one stage. Strategic management starts with the analysis of the external environment, but does not end with the stage of strategic control. The process starts again with the analysis of the external environment and this cycle is repeated continuously (Freeman 2010). Strategic management process is an important concept

in health institutions. This concept includes environment, continuity and repetitive process concepts. Health institutions operate in a constantly changing environment. For health institutions, environmental changes can pose both threats and opportunities. In this context, health institutions can continue their lives and provide quality services as long as they can benefit from environmental opportunities and be protected from environmental threats. Strategic management is not a concept for health institutions, but a continuous concept because of the continuous change in its environment. In addition, strategic management is a continuous process for health institutions. Strategic management in health institutions starts with external environment analysis and ends with the audit of strategies. It is possible to say that it is a recurring process because it is repeated in the same way.

Functions of Strategic Management in Health Institutions

The functions of strategic management in health institutions are defined as performance-based budget, e-government, accountability, performance management, governance and total quality management (TQM). For health institutions to become more effective, managers need to use the concept of strategic management as a useful tool. Strategic management in health institutions contributes in particular to the vision, mission, goals and objectives of the institution. In this way, health institutions can have an idea about predetermining their future and directing their works in this direction. Public managers view their activities through strategic management from a long-term perspective. Strategic management contributes to public organizations, especially in terms of vision, mission and values. Thus, public institutions have the opportunity to determine their future in advance and to direct their activities accordingly. Strategic management has many side functions as well as the main function of securing long-term permanence in the public sector. These; coordination function, change function, reflection and explanation function, integration function (Elma 2010). Strategic management in health institutions is defined as the process of reviewing, researching, selecting and evaluating necessary for the planning of corporate strategies and taking all internal and external structural and motivational measures in order to implement the planned strategies. In addition, strategic management includes the process of examining these strategies applied to health institutions both before and after implementation and performing supervisory procedures.

All of the decisions and actions used in determining and implementing the strategies that can adapt to both the internal and external environment of the health institution in order to reach the long-term institution goals considered in health institutions can direct the future of the managers in the health institution through the strategic management. In addition to its relationship with the environment, strategic management gives a new meaning to the administrative functions in the long run by taking holistic functions and functions of the institution in order to create the future of the institution. Strategic management is an important management technique which aims to define the goals of the health institutions about what they are doing and where they want to reach as a result and integrates all efforts in this field, including the creation of strategies, the implementation of the activities and the control of the activities.

Development of Strategic Management in Health Institutions

Due to the rapidly changing technology, globalization, changing expectations of service users and the competition resulting from emerging markets, health institutions need to think more strategically. While strategic management was used in some areas in the private sector until the 2000s, many organizations today use the concept of strategic management. Strategic management has been used as an important tool in health institutions after the 2000s. If we take a short look at the history of management; It is seen that it is aimed to ensure compliance in every subject from classical management understanding to our time. The Classical Management Approach, which started in the 1900s, the Behavioral Approach in the 1930s and the Modern Management Approach that emerged in the 1960s, constitute the basic steps in the history of management. None of them has completed their mission and has not withdrawn from the application areas and examples of implementation are seen, if not on their own. Modern management approach includes system approach, management according to objectives, direction-action research, contingency approach and strategic management. Strategic management is a form of management that incorporates, synthesizes and manages these management processes and was developed to survive against changes (Erdem 2006). Due to technological change and the creation of new markets, health institutions have had to find and apply new management techniques to keep their effectiveness and efficiency at the highest levels. As a result of the changes in social, health, economic and political fields in recent years, health institutions need to apply new management techniques in order to benefit from these changes and adapt to the differences in the environment as a result of these changes. The most important of these management techniques is strategic management.

The Importance of Strategic Management in Health Institutions

Strategic management is very important for health institutions to form the vision of the organization based on the current situation, mission and basic principles and to determine the objectives and appropriate targets and strategies in line with this vision. In addition, strategic management is defined as a flexible and participatory management approach that expresses the process of monitoring and evaluating the performance of the institution by establishing measurable criteria for health institutions by various methods. Strategic management in health care institutions is not only a way to determine and formulate future-oriented strategies, but also to implement these strategies and to check the success at the end of the implementation. Strategic management; research, review, evaluation and selection efforts necessary for planning strategies; It includes activities related to taking all kinds of measures within the organization and putting them into force in order to implement the planned strategies and to control the subsequent studies (Kavaler and Spiegel 2003). Strategic management is the process of systematically implementing various research, examination, evaluation, implementation, coordination and supervision steps for the most efficient implementation of plans by conducting internal and external analyzes in order to maintain an organization's long-term existence and achieve its objectives (Teece et al. 1997). It is a management that will create a strategic management mission in health institutions and will enable the determination of the vision, goals and targets for the future and the actions that can be taken to reach these targets. Strategic management in health institutions is a management technique that helps the organization to work more effectively, efficiently and with high performance.

Purpose of Strategic Management in Health Institutions

The purpose of strategic management in health organizations is to determine the future of the organization and act in line with the objectives of the organization. Strategic management is an important concept not only for businesses but also within countries. Political existence is an important fact for countries. Today, being politically required now requires economic strength, and countries need to act with project-based plans due to factors such as economic change constantly, countries looking for new resources, development of space technologies, and information technology showing itself in every field. The goals of strategic management are as follows for health institutions:

1. To create a vision to guide the health institution,
2. To set goals based on this vision,
3. Setting a strategy to achieve the objectives,
4. To implement the selected strategy effectively and efficiently,
5. The strategy is to start implementing its objectives and long-term implementation instructions correctly with the vision, in the light of new opportunities, new

ideas, changing conditions and experiences, and to evaluate performance (David and David 2013).

One of the most important objectives of strategic management in health institutions is to determine the dangers or opportunities that may occur within the organization and to act accordingly. With the strategic management, health institutions can achieve the level of patient satisfaction that the quality of service they provide. In health institutions, a solid framework is established for strategic management, plans and budgets to be made for the organization, internal communication is strengthened, the goals and objectives of the organization are put forward in a more realistic manner and all activities carried out within the institution are carried out at a better and higher level.

Characteristics of Strategic Management in Health Institutions

Strategic management, which is an important concept for all organizations, has the same importance among health institutions. It is possible to say that strategic management is the most effective way for health institutions to follow in the light of the existing opportunities and conditions in the environment in order to achieve their future goals and objectives. Therefore, the concept of strategic management has several features. In this sense, the basic features of the concept of strategic management applied in health institutions are as follows:

1. Strategic management in health institutions is a method of analysis and thinking. Therefore, strategic management is related to decision processes based on inter-factor logic principles and relationships in an open system.
2. Strategic management in health institutions ensures that forces are gathered around goals.
3. Strategic management in health institutions ensures that environmental changes are monitored and the organization evaluates external factors effectively.
4. The strategic management process in health institutions is a long-term process. This character is distinguished from routine decisions and jobs.
5. Strategic management in health institutions is an element that ensures that the resources of the institution are managed in harmony.
6. Strategic management in health institutions determines the areas in which the organization can operate with its existing resources and clearly shows how its resources will be utilized and its long-term distribution.
7. Strategic management in health institutions is defined as a guiding and motivating factor. Because it is possible to say that the uncertainty about the future is relieving or reducing (Martin and Singer 2003).

These characteristics are expressed as the general content of strategic management in health institutions. It is possible to say that these features are the backbone of strategic management to be implemented in health institutions. In order to implement a successful strategy in health institutions, these features should be taken into consideration and all strategies to be implemented should be built on these features. Because of the increasing competition and changing technology, it is not important for health institutions to have a successful strategy, but to have a successful and optimal strategy and to implement this strategy.

Strategic Thinking

Strategic thinking requires a series of decisions about what actions the company wants to take to achieve its goals more quickly and more successfully (Schoemaker 1995). Companies should try to make strategic thinking not during the interim periods, but throughout the whole process in which they operate. At the heart of strategic thinking is the ability to identify and exploit opportunities that arise by anticipating significant gaps in the competitive market. Strategic thinking helps managers make crucial choice decisions and makes a vision contribution to the organization. In other words, strategic thinking involves seeing and thinking of the future (Hartmann and Rosche 2003). Strategic thinking, which is interested in balancing the environment, opportunities, value and culture, is a continuous method. Strategic thinking is a fundamental necessity and a useful first move for strategic management that seeks to achieve its goals (Tampoe and Macmillan 2000). Strategic thinking requires early action to keep pace with future variability. Strategic thinking is beneficial for the business as it enables being targeted. Because the employees who focus on the target offer all their powers cumulatively. Another benefit of strategic thinking is the ability to think at the right moment (Heinrichs 2001).

Having strategic thinking helps businesses to minimize the risks of choosing decisions they will regret later (Eren 2002). Organizational activities reduce the risks and make it easier to solve the problems that arise during these activities thanks to the plans that enterprises make in order to achieve their goals and targets. In addition, the higher the level of strategic thinking in enterprises, the higher the synergy associated with it (Pablo and Javidan 2009). Synergy is a sign that will determine in which areas the existing tools or elements of the enterprise will be successful and in which areas they will fail (Timuroğlu 2010). Therefore, synergy is a key element in the choice of strategic decisions.

According to Heracleous (1998), strategic thinking primarily enables a manager to determine how to use the limited resources he / she has in the most efficient way and to advance the company towards its goals. At the same time, the emerging competitive threats enable the company to be prepared by making various plans for the situations that may arise as a result of changes in the national and local economy. Companies with strategic thinking skills are strengthening the hand of managers on the right time and the best tools to attack opponents, as they continually evaluate the strengths and weaknesses of their businesses and the strengths and weaknesses of the major competitors. On the other hand, it prefers to survive and grow by renewing by contributing to the innovation of all aspects of the business. Finally, it enables managers who make strategic thinking a central element of management philosophy and become strategic thinkers in time as it enables them to use improved decision making methods.

According to Liedtka (1998), strategic thinking can be a critical factor in the success of companies as it helps managers to recognize and take advantage of opportunities by chance, but also allows them to identify and evaluate lost opportunities. In addition, since it encourages business managers and employees to think critically about the rooted causes of the problems, it offers different recommendations for focusing on problem solving about the company's business model and operations. In the same way, it enables the formation of an internal strategic mentality set and makes the company active in creating a clearer strategy. Finally, it takes the company forward to be proactive, as it requires working on programs to show early signs of how to be successful in current business conditions and in more difficult times.

Creative Thinking and Strategic Thinking

Edward Mead Earl defines strategy as "a state or a community of states to take control of the resources and armed forces to take advantage of them to develop and secure their vital interests" (Luecke 2010). The strategy is about understanding what you are doing, looking at long-term looking to determine what you want to be, and - most importantly - focusing on how you plan to get there (Fogg 2010).

Strategy is an art because it requires creative thinking or thinking, both the ability to identify alternative positions for the future, to inspire people to implement the strategy, and strong communication skills to connect them; it is a science because it requires managers or interested persons to collect and analyze the information they can then put into action (Fogg 2010). In short, strategy can be expressed as a blend of art and science. Strategic thinking, in its most basic sense, is about analyzing opportunities and problems from a broad perspective and understanding the possible impact your actions may have on others (Collis 2011).

Strategic thinkers envision what might happen and take holistic approaches to everyday challenges and challenges; and they do this as a process that goes on rather than a one-off event (Collis 2011). In this process, strategic thinkers have to be clever in areas where we already feel stupid / ignorant (Gilhooly 1988). Individuals with strategic thinking or strategic thinkers have a sense of the future, are at risk, perceive and identify patterns and tendencies, make concessions, think holistically, see the "big picture", activate their intuition, rely on the validity of these intuitions, engage in complexity, think and visualize with metaphor they derive meaning from smoke or a handful of air, collect complex and sometimes ambiguous data and interpret them effectively and accurately, identify strategic goals effectively, are creative and have creative thinking, analyze information and prioritize demand and competing priorities (Collis 2011).

One of the specific steps in the process of strategic thinking, or in other words, an important component of strategic thinking, is expressed as having creative and creative thinking skills (Collis 2011). It should be remembered immediately that effective strategic planning requires effective and very strong strategic thinking or "strategic thinkers", but the number of experts or strategic thinkers with strategic thinking skills is very small (Mumford et al. 2012). No doubt, some of the award-winning work (Bademci 2007) As can be seen, Vahid Bademci, "strategy" and "strategic thinking" stands out as the most important and valuable names in the Turkey issues (Korkmaz 2010).

Performance in Strategic Management Process

The concept of performance is related to the execution or realization of a specific purpose, task or function (Akal 1992). Each economic unit converts the resources (inputs) it obtains from its external environment into outputs in the form of goods and services by using a certain production technology in order to realize its aims. Evaluating the performance of enterprises in a certain period of time is the examination of how rationally they behave while converting the inputs they use to outputs (Tetik 2003; Yürüşen 2011). The performance of a system is the output or run result at a given time. This result is the degree to which business objectives or tasks are fulfilled. In this sense, business performance can be defined as the evaluation of all efforts made to achieve business objectives (Zerenler 2005). When the concept of performance is analyzed on an organizational basis, it expresses the ability of the organization to reach its predetermined goals by using its resources in the most effective way (Nutt and Backoff 1987). The performance of an enterprise is defined as the evaluation of the results obtained at the end of a certain period of time and the efforts made for the realization of the business objectives (Simsek and Nursoy 2002). Corporate performance is the definition of the degree of fulfillment of the business purpose or task according to the output / result obtained at the end of a certain period (in a certain period of time) (Öztek 2005; Turunç 2006). Performance at the enterprise level is the total result obtained by the interaction of all components of the organization, machines, employees, management and environment (Çakmak and Ocakli 2006).

Performance in terms of health institutions can be defined as the quantitative or qualitative determination of the results of the activities and the activities of the personnel and the activities they undertake to realize the strategic objectives determined by the Ministry of Health, thus determining the overall success of health institutions (Alptekin 2007). In order to determine the performance, the results of the activities should be evaluated. The values that emerge after the performance is measured constitute the performance indicators. Individual business performance is very important for the organization. The organization is also affected by the strong or weak performance of individual employees. Since increasing the performance of the organization is the duty of the manager, it is the responsibility of the manager to increase the performance of the employees (Wooldridge and Floyd 1990). Every behavior an employee performs to fulfill his or her task is part of his / her performance. The scope of performance; to produce a certain number of parts / goods, to solve a problem, to carry out a project, to do a job, such as doing any job-oriented. It is a function of performance, motivation and skill from an individual perspective. In terms of organization, performance can be expressed as the degree of approaching the expected goals and behaviors in compliance with pre-determined standards as a requirement of any task (Arslan 2007).

In order for the performance appraisal system to be successful, firstly the task and job analysis should be done and the work and tasks should be defined. Afterwards, the process of defining the criteria which are the evaluation dimensions that employees will be measured can be started. Among the data to be evaluated for the criteria observed in employee performance; subordinates, peers and customers are also very important (Paksoy 2006). It provides the information needed in management processes such as performance measurement, planning, budgeting, performance management, process improvement and comparison, and plays a critical role in achieving corporate objectives by showing the priorities of the organization and the activities that personnel should focus on in order to realize these priorities. Establish a comprehensive performance measurement process; to define the performance, in other words, to clarify the objectives of the programs, to establish the relationship between inputs, processes and results, to clearly determine how to measure performance, to overcome technical problems related to the performance measurement system, to provide information on realizations and planned performance in a regular manner, and performance information should be created in a structure suitable for use in strategic decisions.

SOLUTIONS AND RECOMMENDATIONS

Today, the rapid changes experienced in social, economic, political and technological aspects necessitate renewal and adaptation to these changes. Regardless of the sector, enterprises also need effective strategic management in order to exist and sustain these assets despite environmental changes. Strategic management in general can be expressed as the process of using the production resources effectively and efficiently in order to realize the objectives of the organization (Ülgen and Mirze 2010). Health institutions are highly complex, full-time and vitally important healthcare providers, technology and labor intensive, affected by legal regulations and include many different occupational groups. Each of these features causes health institutions to face internal and external changes at any time. Therefore, the fact that the health sector has an ever changing and developing environment increases the importance of strategic management in the field of health and it becomes a subject that strategic management managers should emphasize in both private and public sector (Swayne et al. 2006). Hospital managers also benefit from strategic management tools as well as other business executives within the scope of the strategic management approach required for health institutions to adapt to all the changes and developments that are experienced today, to anticipate the opportunities and threats that may occur, to make the necessary organizational changes and to sustain their lives in short.

Given that the health sector is built on human life and health, it is thought to be more complex and more difficult to manage than other sectors. However, it can be difficult to implement the strategic management which can bring success in a systematic way in the health sector where different professional groups, physicians and managers operate together, whose common aim is to provide health services and both groups have a say in its management. Therefore, all managers in the health institution, who are responsible for both administrative and medical services, need to be knowledgeable and effective in strategic management. Therefore, all managers in health institutions are expected to be actively using strategic management tools with the awareness of strategic management practices. Strategic management tools are all techniques, methods, models, frameworks, approaches and methodologies that help managers make strategic decisions (Preble 1997). The right strategies can only be realized with the help of strategic management tools which are of great importance in order to prevent the gap between theory and practice and to realize the strategic management effectively (Key and Popkin 1998)

In the international literature, there are studies conducted in various sectors for the use of strategic management tools. Among these studies, Bain & Company, a global management consulting firm, has been conducting regular research every year since 1993. On behalf of Bain & Company, Rigby and Bilodeau update this study every year and use the 25 management tools they have developed to manage the world's leading companies and publish their results, revealing the management trend in the world and annual changes in this trend (Rigby and Bilodeau 2013). However, such a study investigating the level of knowledge and use of health care managers about strategic management tools is not found in the literature.

FUTURE RESEARCH DIRECTIONS

Today's health services are becoming more expensive in parallel with the developments in rapidly changing technology and service provision, the share of the amount spent on treatment services in total health expenditures increases and social security institutions face payment problems. This situation necessitates the reduction of the cost of the treatment services consuming a significant portion of the resources in our country and the efficient use of the resources. To this end, efforts are underway to make public hospitals autonomous, self-sufficient and to provide services in a competitive environment with private hospitals in accordance with the principle of efficiency. These studies aim to ensure that public and private hospitals produce better quality and efficient services together and under competitive conditions in the sector and this necessitates competition in the health sector.

Where there is scarcity, there is always competition. However, the peculiar characteristics of health care markets make this competition different from most other markets (Morrisey 2001). Therefore, health institutions have to take into account the characteristics of health services in determining their competitive strategies. Because the basis of determining a competitive strategy is to be successful in a competitive environment. Determining appropriate competitive strategies for an enterprise requires, first of all, an examination of the sector in which the entity operates and its competitive status. To be successful in every sector, different needs must be met. At the same time, there may be various differences between sectors depending on factors such as concentration, economies of scale, product differentiation and entry barriers.

In this case, developing a competitive strategy means developing a general formula on how a company will compete, what its goals should be and what policies are needed to achieve these goals (Porter and Locations 2000). Therefore, an enterprise should examine the market and develop a competitive strategy before developing a competition strategy. The aim of the competition strategy is to find a place where the business can best defend itself against the competitive forces in the sector. This defense can be realized by examining the structure of the market and competitive forces (Pollard and Hotho 2006). More precisely, the development of a product or service should be based not only on the capabilities of the organization, but also on the competitive situation or external risks. Therefore, position strategies should be selected considering internal requirements and external risks (Ginter et al. 2018). So the essence of strategy formation is to overcome competition. The competition situation in a sector is based on the five forces. The power of the sum of these forces determines the ultimate profit potential of the sector (Porter 1998).

CONCLUSION

Today, when the waves created by globalization have changed the perception of time and space and radically changed society and social structures, restructuring has become a necessity in public health and management. Turkey, the health sector in its geography, is destined to become a reference center in the health sector. In line with this objective, radical changes and developments are experienced in the sector. On the one hand, the number of private health institutions is increasing rapidly and therefore competition has intensified, and on the other hand, the regulations have paved the way for patients to receive health care services from both private hospitals and public health institutions. Also; Providing service providers in health institutions affiliated to the Ministry of Health to benefit from the revolving fund revenues of the institution brought a different dimension to the competition. Service quality and patient satisfaction have gained importance for healthcare providers in order to gain and maintain superiority in such an environment. Targeted with the quality of health services; it is not only a longer life, but an improvement in the quality of life.

It is important to provide equal, continuous and adequate service in the health sector, to create the necessary infrastructure for these services, to meet the need of manpower and financial resources, and to use the physical infrastructure and manpower effectively. Health is one of the most important tools and indicators of development. Since health care is an abstract product that transfers value to the recipient at the time of production, it is difficult to define and measure the output. The quality of health services provided by health institutions requires patient satisfaction. The high level of patient satisfaction causes the patients to choose the same health institution or recommend it to others in their subsequent needs and consequently to become a loyal customer of that health institution.

In the context of globalization and overwhelming competition, organizations have to renew and change their management structures, systems, processes, human and information resources. Especially in the health sector, the concept of strategic management is one of the most important concepts to be considered. Although strategic management has emerged primarily in the private sector, it has found application in public institutions as well. It is important to implement strategic management of public organizations not for profit as private sector organizations, but for the principle of effective service, and for citizen-oriented applications rather than customer-oriented organizations such as private sector organizations.

Planning of a realistic reform according to the advantages and weaknesses, opportunities and dangers of the internal and external environment analysis of public administration, institutionalization and continuity of change can only be ensured by the understanding of strategic management. Another important concept for institutions is performance evaluation. In order for organizations to obtain the expected benefits from performance measurement, the performance measurement system must be in harmony with the organizational strategy, the information obtained as a result of performance measurement should be reliable, the selected performance indicators should have the capacity to reflect all aspects of performance and the obtained performance information should be used in the decision process. Use of strategic management and performance measurement in the public sector, It is important for public institutions to require that they evaluate their internal processes and external environmental conditions, to determine the objectives and strategies to achieve these objectives by clarifying them, and to be the basis for the evaluation of implementation results and accountability.

Modern management approach requires employees to be rewarded according to their success. The most common of these rewarding methods is the performance-based remuneration system. In other words, performance-based remuneration systems are the means used to reward and appreciate employees in proportion to the achievement of an organization's goals or individual performance goals. The basic starting point of these systems is to determine a part of the wages or the additional payment given with the fixed wage according to the performance of the employee. Wages paid based on performance are variable and are often a reflection of their performance. These wages depend on the performance of the employee in the specified period and vary depending on the performance of the organization, the performance of the department in which he / she works, the individual's performance or the combination of these within the specified unit time period.

REFERENCES

Akal, Z. (1992). *İşletmelerde performans ölçüm ve denetimi*. Ankara: Milli Prodüktivite Yayınları.

Akgemci, T. (2013). *Stratejik Yönetim (3. Baskı)*. Ankara: Gazi Kitapevi.

Aktan, C. C. (2008). Stratejik yönetim ve stratejik planlama. *Çimento İşveren Dergisi, 22*(4), 4-21.

Alpkan, L. (2000). *Stratejik Yönetimin Kapsamlılığı. Stratejik Tercihler ve Yönetici Özellikleri Arasındaki İlişkiler (Basılmamış Doktora Tezi), Gebze Yüksek Teknoloji Enstitüsü, Sosyal Bilimler Enstitüsü.* Gebze.

Alptekin, C. (2007). *Sağlık Kurumlarında Performans Yönetimi: İkinci Basamağa İlişkin Bir Uygulama.* İzmir: Yayınlanmamış Yüksek Lisans Tezi, Dokuz Eylül Üniversitesi Sosyal Bilimler Enstitüsü.

Ansoff, H. I., Kipley, D., Lewis, A. O., Helm-Stevens, R., & Ansoff, R. (2018). *Implanting strategic management.* Springer.

Arslan, F. (2007). *Kamuda Performansa Dayalı Ücret Sistemleri* [Doctoral dissertation]. Yüksek Lisans Tezi, Sivas.

Atmaca, L. (2007). *Türk Kamu Yönetiminde Stratejik Düşünme Ve Reform Çalışmalarının Stratejik Düşünce Bakış Açısıyla İncelenmesi. Yayınlanmamış Yüksek Lisans Tezi, Kocaeli Üniversitesi Sosyal Bilimler Enstitüsü.* Kocaeli.

Aytepe, T. (2008). *Türk Kamu Yönetiminde Stratejik Yönetim ve Stratejik Planlamanın Uygulanabilirliği: Ordu Emniyet Müdürlüğü Model Önerisi.* Ankara: Polis Akademisi Güvenlik Bilimleri Enstitüsü.

Bademci, V. (2007). *Tehlike (risk) altındaki çocuklar. In Okullarda şiddet ve çocuk suçluluğu* (pp. 171–186). Ankara: HEGEM.

Best, R., de Valence, G., & Langston, C. (2007). Strategic management. In *Workplace Strategies and Facilities Management* (pp. 91–102). Routledge. doi:10.4324/9780080521299

Betz, F., & Şensoy, Ü. (2010). *Yönetim stratejisi: stratejik yönetim ve enformasyon teknolojisi.* TÜBİTAK Popüler Bilim Kitapları.

Bianca, A. (2014). Why Is Strategic Thinking Important To The Success of Business? Azcentral. Retrieved from http://yourbusiness.azcentral.com/strategic-thinkingimportant-success-business-9612.html

Bracker, J. (1980). The historical development of the strategic management concept. *Academy of Management Review, 5*(2), 219–224. doi:10.5465/amr.1980.4288731

Bracker, J. (1980). The historical development of the strategic management concept. *Academy of Management Review, 5*(2), 219–224. doi:10.5465/amr.1980.4288731

Brown, P. (2005). The evolving role of strategic management development. *Journal of Management Development, 24*(3), 209–222. doi:10.1108/02621710510584035

Çakmak, N., & Ocakli, E. (2006). Performans değerlendirmesi gerekli midir? Neden? *UNAK*, *6*, 406–418.

Collis, D. J. (2011). *Stratejik Düşünmek. Çev: Melis İnan*. İstanbul: Optimist.

Coulter, M. K., & Coulter, M. K. (2002). *Strategic management in action*. Upper Saddle River, NJ: Prentice Hall.

David, F. R., & David, F. R. (2013). *Strategic management: Concepts and cases: A competitive advantage approach*. Pearson.

Dess, G. G., & Miller, A. (1996). *Strategic management* (Vol. 2). McGraw-Hill.

Dinçer, Ö. (2007). *Stratejik yönetim ve işletme politikası (8. Baskı)*. İstanbul: Alfa Yayınları.

Dinçer, Ö., & Fidan, Y. (1996). *İşletme Yönetimi, Beta Basım Yayım Dağıtım AŞ*. İstanbul: Baskı.

Elma, R. (2010). *Kamu yönetiminde kurumsal dönüşüm ve stratejik liderlik* [Master's thesis]. Karamanoğlu Mehmetbey Üniversitesi Sosyal Bilimler Enstitüsü.

Erdem, A. (2006). *Stratejik Yönetim ve Kamu Örgütlerine Uygulanabilirliği (Basılmamış Yüksek Lisans Tezi)*. Mersin: Mersin Üniversitesi Sosyal Bilimler Enstitüsü.

Eren, E. (2002). *Stratejik yönetim ve işletme politikası*. İstanbul: Beta Yayınları.

Eren, E. (2005). İşletmelerde stratejik yönetim ve işletme politikası. *BETA Bulletin of Experimental Treatments for AIDS*.

Erkan, V. (2008). *Kamu kuruluşlarında stratejik planlama: Türkiye uygulaması ve kuruluşlarda başarıyı etkileyen faktörler. Devlet Planlama Teşkilatı Yayınları, Yayın*, (2759).

Erkut, H. (1998). *Strateji ve Senaryo Tekniği*. İstanbul: İrfan Yayımcılık.

Fogg, C. D. (2010). *Stratejiyi Uygulamak, Çev: Melis İnan*. İstanbul: Optimist.

Franke, R. H., Edlund, T. W., & Oster, F. III. (1990). The development of strategic management: Journal quality and article impact. *Strategic Management Journal*, *11*(3), 243–253. doi:10.1002mj.4250110306

Freeman, R. E. (2010). *Strategic management: A stakeholder approach*. Cambridge university press. doi:10.1017/CBO9781139192675

Gilhooly, K. J. (1988). *Thinking: Directed, undirected and creative*. Academic Press.

Ginter, P. M., Duncan, W. J., & Swayne, L. E. (2018). *The strategic management of health care organizations*. John Wiley & Sons.

Gluck, F., Kaufman, S., & Walleck, A. S. (1982). The four phases of strategic management. *The Journal of Business Strategy*, *2*(3), 9.

Glueck, W. F., & Jauch, L. R. (1989). *Manajemen strategis dan kebijakan perusahaan. Edisi Kedua*. Jakarta: Penerbit Erlangga.

Godet, M. (1987). *Scenarios and strategic management* (p. 210). London: Butterworths.

Gönüllü, A. (2008). *Kamu Yönetiminde Stratejik Planlamaya Geçiş: Mersin Milli Eğitim Müdürlüğü Örneği*. Yayımlanmamış Yüksek Lisans Tezi.

Güçlü, N. (2003). Stratejik yönetim. *Gazi Üniversitesi Gazi Eğitim Fakültesi Dergisi*, *23*(2).

Güner, S. (2005). Stratejik yönetim anlayışı ve kamu yönetimi. *Türk İdare Dergisi*, *446*, 61–78.

Hartmann, A. L., & Whiteman, R. (2003). Personality Correlates of Strategic Thinking. In *An Organizational Context. Yayınlanmamış Doktora Tezi*. California: Alliant International University.

Heinrichs, J. H. (2001). *Interaction effects of strategic decision models and business intelligence tools on knowledge generation in manufacturing firms*. The University of Toledo.

Heracleous, L. (1998). Strategic thinking or strategic planning? *Long Range Planning*, *31*(3), 481–487. doi:10.1016/S0024-6301(98)80015-0

Hill, B. (n.d.). Why Is Strategic Thinking Important To The Success of Business? Chron. Retrieved from http://smallbusiness.chron.com/strategic-thinking-important-success-business4661.html

Hitt, M. A., Ireland, R. D., & Hoskisson, R. E. (2012). *Strategic management cases: competitiveness and globalization*. Cengage Learning.

Hunger, J. D., & Wheelen, T. L. (2003). *Essentials of strategic management* (Vol. 9). NJ: Prentice Hall.

Hussey, D. E. (2007). *Strategic management: from theory to implementation*. Routledge. doi:10.4324/9780080498287

Karakaya A. (2004). Stratejik Yönetim Sisteminin Kriz Yönetimine Katkısı Üzerine Bir Araştırma. *Teknoloji*, *7*(2).

Kavaler, F., & Spiegel, A. D. (2003). *Risk management in health care institutions: a strategic approach*. Jones & Bartlett Learning.

Key, S., & Popkin, S. J. (1998). Integrating ethics into the strategic management process: Doing well by doing good. *Management Decision*, *36*(5), 331–338. doi:10.1108/00251749810220531

Koçel, T. (2005). *İşletme Yöneticiliği, Yönetim ve Organizasyonlarda Davranış Klasik-Modern-Çağdaş ve Güncel Yaklaşımlar. Baskı*. İstanbul: Beta Yayınları.

Kolb, D., Lublin, S., Spoth, J., & Baker, R. (1986). Strategic management development: Using experiential learning theory to assess and develop managerial competencies. *Journal of Management Development*, *5*(3), 13–24. doi:10.1108/eb051612

Korkmaz, A. (2010). *Vahit Bademci'nin Paradigma Değişikliği Üzerine Bir Araştırma. Testler Değil, Ölçümler Güvenilirdir"". Yayımlanmamış Yüksek Lisans Tezi*. Zonguldak: Zonguldak Karaelmas Üniversitesi, Sosyal Bilimler Enstitüsü.

Liedtka, J. M. (1998). Strategic thinking: Can it be taught? *Long Range Planning*, *31*(1), 120–129. doi:10.1016/S0024-6301(97)00098-8

Luecke, R. (2010). *Strateji, Çev: Turan Parlak*. İstanbul: Türkiye İş Bankası Kültür Yayınları.

Martin, D., & Singer, P. (2003). A strategy to improve priority setting in health care institutions. *Health Care Analysis*, *11*(1), 59–68. doi:10.1023/A:1025338013629 PMID:14510309

Miles, R. E., Snow, C. C., Meyer, A. D., & Coleman, H. J. Jr. (1978). Organizational strategy, structure, and process. *Academy of Management Review*, *3*(3), 546–562. doi:10.5465/amr.1978.4305755 PMID:10238389

Mintzberg, H. (1987). The strategy concept I: Five Ps for strategy. *California Management Review*, *30*(1), 11–24. doi:10.2307/41165263

Morden, T. (2016). *Principles of strategic management*. Routledge. doi:10.4324/9781315602172

Morrisey, M. A. (2001). Competition in hospital and health insurance markets: A review and research agenda. *Health Services Research*, *36*(1 Pt 2), 191. PMID:11327174

Mumford, M. D., Medeiros, K. E., & Partlow, P. J. (2012). Creative thinking: Processes, strategies, and knowledge. *The Journal of Creative Behavior*, *46*(1), 30–47. doi:10.1002/jocb.003

Mütercimler, E. (2006). *Yüksek Stratejiden Etki Odaklı Harekâta Geleceği Yönetmek*. İstanbul: İkinci Baskı, Alfa Basım.

Nutt, P. C., & Backoff, R. W. (1987). A strategic management process for public and third-sector organizations. *Journal of the American Planning Association*, *53*(1), 44–57. doi:10.1080/01944368708976634

Oyman, S. (2009). *Stratejik yönetim sürecinde performans ölçümü ve dengeli sonuç kartı uygulaması: Türkiye Cumhuriyet Merkez Bankası için bir değerlendirme*. Ankara: Uzmanlık Yeterlilik Tezi, Türkiye Cumhuriyet Merkez Bankası.

Öztek, M. Y. (2005). Performans Ölçümünde Esas Alınan Ölçütler. *Öneri Dergisi*, *6*(23), 19-22.

Pablo, A. L., & Javidan, M. (Eds.). (2009). *Mergers and acquisitions: Creating integrative knowledge*. John Wiley & Sons.

Paksoy, A. (2006). *Performansa Dayalı Ücretleme: Bir Alan Araştırması*. Kahramanmaraş: Yayınlanmamış Yüksek Lisans Tezi, Kahramanmaraş Sütçü İmam Üniversitesi Sosyal Bilimler Enstitüsü.

Paul, S. (1982). *Strategic management of development programmes: guidelines for action (No. 19)*. International Labour Organization.

Pearce, J. A., Robinson, R. B., & Subramanian, R. (2000). *Strategic management: Formulation, implementation, and control*. Columbus, OH: Irwin/McGraw-Hill.

Pollard, D., & Hotho, S. (2006). Crises, scenarios and the strategic management process. *Management Decision*, *44*(6), 721–736. doi:10.1108/00251740610673297

Porter, M. E. (1996). What is strategy.

Porter, M. E. (1998). Clusters and the new economics of competition. *Harvard Business Review*, *76*(6), 77–90.

Porter, M. E., & Locations, C. (2000). Company strategy. In *The Oxford handbook of economic geography* (pp. 253–274). Oxford press.

Preble, J. F. (1997). Integrating the crisis management perspective into the strategic management process. *Journal of Management Studies*, *34*(5), 769–791. doi:10.1111/1467-6486.00071

Rigby, D., & Bilodeau, B. (2013). Management Tools & Trends 2013. Bain & Company. Retrieved from http://www.bain.com/consulting-services/strategy/fundamentals-of-growth.aspx

Rodoplu, D. (2001). *Stratejik Yönetim Düzeyinde Zaman Yönetimi ve Yetki Devri". Yayımlanmamış Yüksek Lisans Tezi, TC Kocaeli Üniversitesi, Sosyal Bilimler Enstitüsü*. Kocaeli.

Schelling, T. C. (1980). *The strategy of conflict*. Harvard university press.

Schendel, D. E., & Hatten, K. J. (1972). Business policy or strategic management: A broader view for an emerging discipline. In Academy of management proceedings (No. 1, pp. 99-102). Briarcliff Manor, NY: Academy of Management. doi:10.5465/ambpp.1972.4981324

Schoemaker, P. J. (1995). Scenario planning: A tool for strategic thinking. *Sloan Management Review*, *36*(2), 25–50.

Shrivastava, P. (1986). Is strategic management ideological? *Journal of Management*, *12*(3), 363–377. doi:10.1177/014920638601200305

Shrivastava, P. (1994). *Strategic management: Concepts & practices*. South-Western Publishing Company.

Simsek, M., & Nursoy, M. (2002). *Toplam Kalite Yönetiminde Performans Olçümü*. Istanbul: Hayat Yayınları.

Steiner, G. A. (1971). *Business and society*.

Stockport, G. J. (2010). Semco: Cultural transformation and strategic leadership. *International Journal of Technology Marketing*, *5*(1), 67–78. doi:10.1504/IJTMKT.2010.033297

Strickland, A. J., & Thompson, A. A. (1984). *Strategic management: concepts and cases*. Plano, Tex.: Business Publications.

Swayne, L. E., Duncan, W. J., & Ginter, P. M. (2006). *Strategic Management of Health Care Organizations (5. bs.)*. Cornwall: Blackwell Publishing.

Tampoe, M., & Macmillan, H. (2000). *Strategic management, process, content and implementation*. Oxford University Press.

Teece, D. J. (2010). Business models, business strategy and innovation. *Long Range Planning*, *43*(2-3), 172–194. doi:10.1016/j.lrp.2009.07.003

Teece, D. J., Pisano, G., & Shuen, A. (1997). Dynamic capabilities and strategic management. *Strategic Management Journal*, *18*(7), 509–533. doi:10.1002/(SICI)1097-0266(199708)18:7<509::AID-SMJ882>3.0.CO;2-Z

Tetik, S. (2003). İşletme performansını belirlemede veri zarflama analizi. *Yönetim ve Ekonomi: Celal Bayar Üniversitesi İktisadi ve İdari Bilimler Fakültesi Dergisi*, *10*(2), 221–230.

Thomas, H. (1984). Strategic decision analysis: Applied decision analysis and its role in the strategic management process. *Strategic Management Journal*, *5*(2), 139–156. doi:10.1002mj.4250050205

Timuroğlu, M. K. (2010). *Stratejik Düşünce, Öğrenme Yönlülük Ve Yenilik. Yayınlanmamış Doktora Tezi*. Erzurum: Atatürk Üniversitesi, Sosyal Bilimler Enstitüsü, İşletme Anabilim Dalı.

Turunç, Ö. (2006). Bilgi Teknolojileri Kullaniminin İşletmelerin Örgütsel Performansina Etkisi Hizmet Sektöründe Bir Araştirma. *Toros Üniversitesi İİSBF Sosyal Bilimler Dergisi*, *3*(5), 225–247.

Ülgen, H., & Mirze, K. (2006). *İşletmelerde Stratejik Yönetim, Literatür Yayınları, 3*. İstanbul: Basım.

Ülgen, H., & Mirze, S. K. (2004). Isletmelerde stratejik yonetim. İstanbul: Literatür yayıncılık.

Ülgen, H., & Mirze, S. K. (2010). *İşletmelerde stratejik yönetim (5. Baskı)*. İstanbul: Beta Basım Yayım Dağıtım.

Üzün, C. (2000). *Stratejik yönetim ve halkla ilişkiler*. Dokuz Eylül Yayıncılık.

Venkatraman, N., & Camillus, J. C. (1984). Exploring the concept of "fit" in strategic management. *Academy of Management Review*, *9*(3), 513–525.

Webster, P. R. (1990). Creativity as creative thinking. *Music Educators Journal*, *76*(9), 22–28. doi:10.2307/3401073

Wheelen, T. L., Hunger, J. D., Hoffman, A. N., & Bamford, C. E. (2010). *Strategic management and business policy*. New Jersey: Prentice Hall.

Wissema, J. G., Brand, A. F., & Van Pol, H. D. (1981). The incorporation of management development in strategic management. *Strategic Management Journal*, *2*(4), 361–377. doi:10.1002mj.4250020405

Wooldridge, B., & Floyd, S. W. (1990). The strategy process, middle management involvement, and organizational performance. *Strategic Management Journal, 11*(3), 231–241. doi:10.1002mj.4250110305

Yürüşen, S. (2011). *Veri zarflama analizi ile bayi performansının hesaplanması: otomotiv sektöründe bir uygulama* [Doctoral dissertation]. Fen Bilimleri Enstitüsü.

Zerenler, M. (2005). *Performans ölçüm sistemleri tasarımı ve üretim sistemlerinin performansının ölçümüne yönelik bir araştırma*. Ekonomik ve Sosyal Araştırmalar Dergisi.

Chapter 10
Evaluation of the Broken Windows Theory in Terms of Patient Safety

Erkan Turan Demirel
https://orcid.org/0000-0001-7754-774X
Firat University, Turkey

Eda Emul
https://orcid.org/0000-0002-9649-9971
Firat University, Turkey

ABSTRACT

The broken windows theory introduces an approach applicable to different fields of discipline insofar as it explains how disorder (crime, etc.) occurs in a community and provides a basis from which solutions can be developed to prevent it. Considering the complexity of healthcare systems, irregularities, and rule violations that commonly mark them and put human health at risk, it is important to produce more effective solutions by taking advantage of different perspectives. This study evaluates the applicability of the broken windows theory to patient safety. As this theory can be an effective solution to the medical errors, neglect and rule violations that commonly occur in the delivery of health services, it is important that further research on this subject be performed.

DOI: 10.4018/978-1-7998-2329-2.ch010

INTRODUCTION

Based on current conditions, the following developments seem to be leading the health sector: Types of service and diversity in provision are increasing. Health informatics and technology are developing. In society, the rate of health literacy is increasing. Patients and their relatives have access to a broad level of knowledge about their rights and are more conscious about their rights. With the impact of these developments, interest in the quality of healthcare is increasing.

The concept of patient safety is one of the first concepts among the primary factors in the quality of healthcare. In general terms, it is expressed as the precautions taken by the healthcare institution and its personnel to prevent harm to the patient. Healthcare personnel cannot usually agree on how to evaluate various factors of benefit and harm because of a lack of concrete evidence about the benefits and harms (Ersoy and Aydın, 1994). It is possible to eliminate this conflict by using the ethical values that have been adopted and implemented by institutions and healthcare personnel.

Practices aimed at ensuring and maintaining patient safety are the most important indicators of healthcare quality. Patient safety refers to all kinds of measures taken by health institutions and their employees to prevent potentially negative effects of health services on individuals (Güven, 2007). At a conference in Geneva in 2007, the World Health Organization (WHO) noted that each year around ten million people worldwide are injured or killed by preventable medical errors, a fact which points to the need for further studies on patient safety (WHO, 2007: cited in Aydemir, 2015).

A healthcare system built on quality and reliability is one defined by patient safety and the prevention of medical errors at every step of the health services delivery process. Therefore, patient safety has been the focus of recent studies and clinical care practices. The idea of patient safety can be described as the development of practices aimed at eliminating the damages to patients and healthcare workers derived from procedural medical errors and the measures taken for ensuring that the errors are identified, reported, and corrected before they cause damages. In effect, patient safety aims to eliminate preventable medical errors and to take precautions against unexpected events at every stage of the healthcare delivery system (Emül, 2017).

While health workers used to be at the center of health service delivery, the focus has now switched to patient satisfaction and patient rights in line with the effects of modernization and social development on the healthcare sector. Factors such as the increased interest in diversity and quality of health service delivery, which emerged as a result of technological and pharmacological developments, the decrease in trust and confidence in health institutions due to errors made by health professionals operating in this complex system, the increased amount of pressure on health professional and health institutions, and the deterioration in the peaceful atmosphere of healthcare environments have prompted the need for studies on patient safety (Emül, 2017).

Certain approaches, accreditation and standardization practices help to ensure and maintain patient safety. In addition, concepts like patient safety culture, ethical climate and ethical leadership, all of which are reported to have a cause-effect relationship with patient safety, are present in the literature. However, one concept that has met with little discussion and that has been the subject of only limited research in studies on patient safety is "the broken windows theory". This theory was originally developed in the field of sociology to explain the phenomenon and prevention of crime. The broken windows theory, which is based on the basic claim that "even minor offenses can pave the way for crime, thereby necessary measures should be taken against the factors that will prepare a ground for crimes", seems adaptable to health services in the context of patient safety and protection.

The main purpose of this study is to evaluate whether "the broken windows theory is adaptable to patient safety". Its adaptability to patient safety is evaluated after first presenting an outline of the conceptual framework on "medical errors, patient safety and broken windows theory".

Medical Errors

Scientific and technological developments have made the healthcare field both labor and technology intensive and has increased the complexity of healthcare services, which in turn has increased the number of undesirable conditions, like medical errors. It is inevitable for human beings to fall into error and cause accidents; yet, the main purpose of medicine, since the time of Hippocrates, is to prevent harm and heal people. To achieve this primary objective, it is necessary to be highly attentive to medical errors (Kohn et al., 2000; cited: Avcı & Aktan, 2015).

For a long time, humanity has viewed medical errors as being a natural phenomenon. Following the publication of the report titled "To Err Is Human" by the US Institute of Medicine in November 1999, medical errors have become a subject of increasing importance and have started to draw attention. The report states that between 44,000 and 98,000 people die annually in the United States due to medical errors; these figures are higher than those caused by cancer or traffic accidents. In another study, it was report that disability and deaths caused by preventable medical errors lead to the need of additional health services and loss of income, adding an annual burden of 17-29 billion dollars to the US budget (Akalın, 2005).

According to a report by the Institute of Medicine published in 1999, a medical error is defined as "the failure of a planned action to be completed as intended or the use of a wrong plan to achieve an aim". Medical errors can occur in hospitals, polyclinics, physician offices, nursing services, pharmacies, nursing homes, and even in patients' homes (Akalın, 2005).

Medical intervention errors refer to errors ranging from those which deteriorate the normal course of the disease and increase recovery time, to those which cause patient death, as a result of suggestions and practices of health workers, such as physicians, nurses, physiotherapists, psychologists, dietitians and other health professionals who are entitled to make interventions on patients in accordance with applicable legislation for providing health services (Hancı, 2002, p. 28; cited in Tansüyer, 2010).

In its 44th General Assembly held in 1992, the World Medical Association defined medical malpractice as "the loss incurred due to failure of a physician to provide proper standard treatment or the lack of physician skill in providing standard treatment". According to one of the US teachings medical malpractice is defined as follows: "medical malpractice (error/health worker error) refers to an act of negligence or executive act committed by a healthcare professional that causes harm to the patient or complications" (Can et al., 2011).

Although the concepts of malpractice and medical error are used interchangeably, there is a fine line between them. Malpractice refers to "a concept used for situations that are definitely expected to cause harm to the patient"; whereas medical errors refer to "situations that sometimes do not cause harm to the patient or in which damage may not occur even if they do harm to the patient". It can be understood that malpractice is a medical error, but there are also medical errors that are not considered malpractice because no harm occurs (Karataş and Yakıncı, 2010).

The Concept of Patient Safety

The definition of patient safety is based on the principle of primum non nocere – "first, to do no harm". This principle means that all practices in all types of healthcare institutions should be protected from factors that may adversely affect patients' existing conditions (Hansen et al., 2003; cited: Cengiz, 2014). According to Pronovost et al. (2005), patient safety includes the measures taken to create a safe environment for every patient who comes to the hospital and the continuity of care. The most important priority in delivery of health services should be to provide the service without harming the patient. According to Budak (2008), healthcare providers witness many incidents that have a negative impact on patients. These incidents, most of which are caused by medical errors, should not be ignored, rather, they should be reported, analyzed and improved by taking necessary measures. In this way, the principle of "first, to do no harm" will gain meaning and be reflected in the practice.

Patient safety is elsewhere defined as "the measures taken by health institutions and their employees to avoid adverse events that may occur due to medical care and medical errors and adversely affect patients and their relatives, and the prevention of any adverse events by health services that could harm individuals" (Çiçek, 2012).

In addition to being a concept directly related to human life, health services form a multi-dimensional, complex and continuous structure that is sensitive to uncertainties and does not accept errors. Therefore, patient safety, which is a basic condition of providing effective and efficient health care services today, should be adopted with a determined attitude by health managers and workers. Patient safety is ensured when health professionals create a service environment free from errors and work with a spirit of teamwork with effective communication (Yardımcı & Başbakkal, 2012).

The spread of healthcare services and the increasing awareness of those receiving these services have helped to make the concept of patient safety gain importance in the health sector. Ensuring patient safety at every stage of the health service delivery and thus preventing medical errors are among the priorities of healthcare institutions. The provision of health services, which over time has become gradually more complicated due to the rapid changes seen in the field of health, aims to make people healthy, to protect their health, and to raise the health standards of society by taking measures against diseases. For this purpose, disruptions in the implementation of treatment and care procedures (for example, the decrease in the number of qualified health workers) adversely affect patient safety (Yıldız et al., 2012).

Adverse events regarding patient safety can generate harmful consequences for patients who visit health institutions to benefit from their services, and they also generate additional costs to these institutions. The harm suffered by the patient may lead to more serious injuries, prolonged hospital stays, disability or even death (Karaca & Aslan, 2014).

The nature of healthcare systems has become increasingly complex due to continuous technological developments. This complexity is one of the reasons more studies need to be conducted on patient safety. Patient safety has become a global problem, one faced by all countries, regardless of their development levels. Patient safety problems can result in injury or death to many patients on account of unsafe medical care practices, especially in developing countries. The most common medical errors include hospital-acquired infections, misdiagnosis, delays in treatment, incompetent use of medical devices, medication errors, blood products, errors in the care of specific groups (pregnant women, newborns and the elderly), fall-related injuries, and adverse events in surgical and anesthetic practices (WHO, 2009).

Violations of patient safety rules result from willful deviations from standard procedures. However, it is not always easy to identify nonconformity. The level of compliance or non-compliance, that is, interpretation of the violation, may vary depending on the type of instruction, the nature of the work, and the social and organizational environment. Violations, which may occasionally have positive aspects, can, in some situations, actually generate effects that serve to increase system performance and individual satisfaction. When it comes to the negative sides of medical errors, the response is usually to put forth efforts to eliminate them. However, system dynamics make errors inevitable. Although it is not possible to eliminate all violations, it is possible to manage them. For example, despite there being very serious and guiding standards for implementations in healthcare services, violations can nonetheless occur (Amalberti et al., 2006).

Violations can be seen even in sectors with very good security records. Moreover, while violations are often attributed to economic reasons, they can also be based on social and organizational processes as well as individual motivation. Therefore, violations constitute a complex and multifaceted phenomenon. Some violations may be preferred insofar as they can be useful for individuals and the system, can be tolerated by teams, and can serve to alleviate workload. The existence of violations requires some of the following inquiries in terms of healthcare services (Amalberti et al., 2006):

- Should the violation be accepted if it did not cause any danger or harm?
- Is it possible to distinguish between acceptable and unacceptable violations?
- Is there tolerance to standards? If so, what are the criteria?
- Is there a need for different security approaches to violations?

Since evaluations of violations in health services are rarely open to the public, the available data are limited (Leape et al., 1991; Baker et al., 2004). Three reasons can be suggested to explain the relative absence of information on violations in health services. First, the rules governing the healthcare sector have less clarity than the rules of other industries where there are high levels of risk. Although there are many protocols and guidelines, it can't be said that there is flexibility in the health sector. Therefore, violations can be difficult to explain. Second, most of the information related to security problems in healthcare services is obtained from incident reporting systems. It is, therefore, difficult to accurately assess whether there are violations from the summary narrative data on errors. Third, a system in which violations are reported voluntarily cannot be established in healthcare. In addition, even if there is no explicit intention to harm, reporting violations can open a gateway to professional abuse (Lawton, 1997; Marx, 2001). All these reasons prevent adequate investigation of violations in healthcare services and increase the likelihood of further errors (Amalberti, 2006).

Although health and care services focus on quality and safety, there has been no significant decrease in the rate of inadvertent and harmful errors to patients

[Classen et al., 2011; Chassin & Loeb, 2013). This could be because health care professionals work in a cultural setting that normalizes their non-standard, i.e. substandard, behaviors (Waring et al., 2016).

Violations of service delivery standards in hospitals are often tolerated by healthcare providers. The reason behind this attitude is that such violations provide some benefits, such as productivity, personal development and patient-centered care (Amalberti et al., 2006; Debono et al., 2013; Alper et al., 2012).

Ethical climate and culture of patient safety are also needed to achieve patient safety. It should be mentioned that there are some expectations in the context of social exchange theory that there is a strong relationship between ethical climate and patient safety culture. Accordingly, health institutions should clearly define their ethical principles, top management should lead the implementation of these principles unreservedly, and staff should be rewarded for behaving in accordance with ethical principles. Naturally, employees will also exhibit the ethical behaviors required by this environment. Since ethical principles are part of the culture, it can be said that ethical principles are among the factors contributing to the formation of patient safety culture. Top management's positive attitude about patient safety culture (for example, the development of award mechanisms to protect patient safety) will encourage employees to adopt patient safety culture. The belief and support of top management need to be both strong and sustainable. In this sense, with the synergy that can be created by the improvements, it is possible to see improvements in other factors (Emül and Demirel, 2018).

Dimensions of Patient Safety

Patient safety is generally examined under six dimensions, namely, patient safety culture, education, communication, personnel, organizational structure and leadership. These concepts, which serve as a guide to health institutions being more efficient and effective, are explained below (Derin & Demirel, 2011).

Patient Safety Culture: All health institutions should have a patient safety culture in which all health workers who are in direct communication and interaction with patients and their relatives receiving health services must respect, protect and take care of patient rights (Durmaz, 2016).

Education for Improving Patient Safety: One of the building blocks used for ensuring patient safety is education practices. The lack of in-service training on safety and the issues related to patient safety, which plays an important role in healthcare, cause health workers to feel a sense of inadequacy. Practical education is key to making health workers learn applicable standards in health institutions and to changing their wrong behaviors (Akalın, 2005). Patient safety is directly proportional to the education, skills and attention of health service providers (Murray et al., 2000).

Personnel in Improving Patient Safety: Adequate environment, equipment and technical staff are needed to provide healthcare services (Murray et al., 2000). Health workers operating in health institutions where working conditions are intense and complex aim to provide successful health services by following the rules and methods. Therefore, creative, competent health professionals who keep up with technology, like their jobs and integrate with the system are required for achieving this target (Pedreira & Marin, 2004).

Communication in Improving Patient Safety: One of the factors that jeopardizes safety in health institutions is the lack of communication. Errors in identifying patients, errors in referring patients, and errors in transferring medical information result from inefficient communication. An environment in which accurate and complete information is transparently communicated to and shared, discussed and analyzed with health workers should be created in order to improve institutional performance (Mcfadden et al., 2009).

Organizational Structure: Failures in patient safety are based on both personal-related problems and system-related errors. An organizational structure equipped with the necessary safety measures should be established by making improvements in the workflows of the system, creating a supportive organization in line with technological developments, and identifying system-related problems (Anderson et al., 2006). A good (effective) management structure with accurate information and effective communication is required (Murray et al., 2000).

Effective Leadership in Patient Safety (Transformational Leadership): The managers of health institutions, that is, their leaders, should support employees in pursuing patient safety, allocate financial resources to patient safety, and share this safety culture without condemning or exerting pressure on them. They should establish an organizational culture that prioritizes teamwork (Russell, 2005).

Broken Windows Theory

The broken windows theory is one of the theories used by sociologists to explain the phenomenon of crime. It was developed through the experiments of Zimbardo (1969) and used by Wilson and Kelling (1982) to explain the sources of crime. Wilson and Kelling's study was the first study to suggest that tolerated irregularities prepare the ground for crimes. Their study also argued that tolerated and uncorrected irregularities cause people to believe that control mechanisms are ineffective.

In one of Zimbardo experiments, an automobile without license plates was parked with its hood up on a street in a suburban area. A similar vehicle was also left in a central place where people with high levels of education and income lived. The first vehicle was attacked by "vandals" within ten minutes of its "abandonment". However, the second vehicle sat untouched for more than a week. A week later, the researcher smashed part of it with a sledgehammer. Soon, passersby joined in and the car ended up being turned upside down and utterly destroyed within only a few hours. The same experiment was repeated using two buildings that appeared to be abandoned. Soon, the building with broken windows was looted and became a place for the homeless. The other building with no broken windows suffered the same fate after several windows were broken by the researchers. At the conclusion of these experiments, the main idea governing the broken windows theory was that "untended environments, property and individuals can become fair game for people who out for fun or plunder". If the first broken window is tolerated and no precautions are taken to fix it and prevent further attacks, then a small-scale disorder can develop into a major source of crime. This is why it seems possible to prevent crimes in environments where the rules of conduct are clearly defined and security measures are sufficiently taken and adequately controlled (Altuntop, 2015).

The broken windows theory reveals that places which seem abandoned, uncontrolled, neglected, untended and uncared for can produce crimes and suggests that necessary measures should be taken against such places. In this context, it is possible to say that avenues and streets without sufficient lighting, a situation frequently seen in cities, as well as unrepaired derelict buildings, uncontrolled vehicle parking areas and workplaces with insufficient physical security can encourage potential criminals by creating proper areas for committing crimes (Doğan & Sevinç, 2011).

The broken windows theory also suggests that well-ordered public urban environments should be monitored to maintain the order and prevent more serious crimes and vandalism. Here, the goal is to maintain law and order by fixing even small things that are broken. The theory can be projected to social or working life as follows. For example, a failure to enforce the decision taken at a meeting or assuming an attitude of "just one time won't hurt" towards any error can cause employees to question the seriousness of subsequent meetings and to ignore errors, and thus can significantly increase the number of these errors (Broken Windows Theory, Internet: 02.10.2017). In this context, the broken windows theory suggests that one of the best ways to combat crimes is to combat irregularities that precede crimes and prepare the ground for them (Beşe, 2006).

There are studies that have tested the legitimacy of the broken windows theory. Two of these studies found a statistically significant and important negative relationship between number of misdemeanor arrests and crime rates (Kelling & Sousa, 2001; Corman & Mocan, 2005). However, not all studies looking at this subject have been able to gather evidence supporting the theory; that is, there are also studies suggesting that irregularities weakly affect or do not affect crime rates at all (Sampson & Raudenbush, 1999).

Although studies on the broken windows theory have conflicting results, they all suggest that irregularities occurring in public spheres will increase if they are not fixed quickly. If irregularities in social settings are not eliminated, people perceive that the social body (public authority, society or related groups) does not care about the order or rules, and people naturally start to feel that these irregularities create a suitable environment for individuals who are prone to crime or who hope to benefit from these irregularities. In this respect, the broken windows theory suggests that the relevant authority acts as insurance for the maintenance of public order (Wilson & Kelling, 1982).

The theory suggests that visible negativities, like broken windows and garbage laying around, are particularly effective in increasing crime rates in certain environments. Physical elements feed on each other insofar as they supported by cyclic (successive) violations of rules. Physical disorders bring about rule violations, which in turn cause physical disorders to continue to increase. This cycle feeds the rise in crime rates, normalizes the violation of social norms and rules, and ultimately leads to criminal offenses. Minor and invisible disorders gradually enter into a cycle whose elements feed off each other and eventually turn into physical disorders and rule violations, as this situation does not impose any cost (material, moral, social) on those who create disorders and violate rules, while at the same time, it indicates poor-functioning social control mechanisms (Keuschnigg et al., 2015; Sampson & Raudenbush, 1999).

Patient Safety and Broken Windows Theory

It is also possible to assess health services within the framework of the views described above. In effect, if "those who commit crimes and break windows" is replaced by "any element that threatens patient safety and medical error", then the broken windows theory becomes an exemplary theory for any effort that requires patient safety or the well-functioning of the healthcare system. The broken windows theory is known as a criminological theory, but it has been applied in different disciplines. Nevertheless, the examples of using the theory for handling issues of healthcare services and patient safety are new and rare (Kayral, internet: 02.10.2017). From this perspective, the applicability of the principles of the broken windows theory to ensure the continuity of patient safety seems realistic (Emül & Demirel, 2018).

There are several other reasons why the broken windows theory is adaptable to healthcare:

Providing health care is a high risk job. Unlike other sectors, guidelines, protocols and policies are implemented flexibly in the field of healthcare. Medical staff generally work independently and have the freedom to conduct clinical judgements (Braithwaite et al., 2013). However, there is little likelihood to control behaviors of employees in such environments formally or informally. Temporary solutions may conflict with institutional purposes (Debono et al., 2013; Debono et al., 2017).

Ensuring safe care for patients, the timely provision of healthcare services, the absence of noise, lighting or ventilation problems, compliance with hygiene rules, and the presence of physical elements (apparent aspects of the service), such as keeping work areas tidy, all tend to keep employees in compliance with safe working procedures. As the broken windows theory explains the relationship between behaviors and physical environment, it can be adapted to health services.

Physical proof of the service is one of the basic elements for the service quality. Phenomena such as physical properties of the service environment (color, design, lighting, heating, cleanliness, regularity, aesthetics, etc.), physical appearance of the personnel, and suitability of the equipment to requirements of the moment and the service all serve to indicate the presence of the concrete (visible) effects of the service. For example, the visible effects of a hospital's diagnostic and treatment services can be listed as follows: compliance with patient rights and patient safety; appropriate physical appearance of health workers; use of state-of-the-art technology devices; and compliance of the hospital building with lighting, heating, ventilation, noise and hygiene standards. This dimension also explains the psychological and social situation of the service environment. The nature of the relationship between employees and the organizational culture is evaluated within this framework (Buttle, 1996).

The broken windows theory seems to be adaptable to health care to the extent that it can provide solutions to physical problems associated with providing safe care to patients. By arranging physical conditions and paying attention to the small things, it seems possible to strengthen patient safety and increase patient satisfaction. However, this is not based on zero tolerance. On the contrary, it involves a dynamic balancing act in a complex adaptive system instead of over-control and burdensome regulations that lead to the normalization of unsafe practices.

Therefore, studies are needed to test the applicability of the broken windows theory to healthcare services. It should be noted that the studies to be performed for this purpose will encounter the difficulties of monitoring whether the employees behave according to the rules. Furthermore, although the relationship between regularity/irregularity and patient outcomes may be suggestive, the measurements on this issue may be difficult.

The broken windows theory could emerge to be one of the new ways of providing safe patient care and of examining hospitals and healthcare professionals in this context. In terms of recognition of the context and the culture, it can be accepted that there are aspects compatible with other approaches to this issue, and further studies can be done from this perspective.

Considering the identification of risks to patient safety and the possibility of the harm these risks can cause to patients, the main question to be asked in hospitals from the perspective of the broken windows theory is: "What are the underlying factors of disorders?" It will not be enough to evaluate the errors occurring in such a complex system as healthcare and the irregularities leading to these errors on the basis of physical elements alone. Furthermore, an agreement will be needed to reveal the nature of the error within the hospital culture (Bosk, 2003).

From the perspective of the broken windows theory, it is of course not easy to define the relationship between physical disorders and staff violations and health care outcomes. However, despite the challenge, the theory should nonetheless still first focus on identifying the relationship between the health outcomes of the patients and the degree of order/disorder (Churruca et al., 2018)

In a system where the relationship between health outcomes and irregularities is correctly defined, the broken windows theory can be put into practice by detecting the visible signs of irregularities and violations. Otherwise, if irregularities are visible and ignored in an institutional environment, then simple rule violations, such as violations of hand hygiene rules, inadequate/incorrect management of hospital wastes, and inappropriate use of medical equipment, will become widespread and gradually turn into behavioral patterns. Eventually, these irregularities and systemic breakdowns will give rise to a reinforcing relationship with irreparable rule violations; after a while, this situation will normalize the events that harm patients in a routine state of "deviance" (Amalberti et al., 2006).

SOLUTIONS AND RECOMMENDATIONS

In the light of the aforementioned views, the adaptability of the broken windows theory to the healthcare field in terms of patient safety seems realistic. If it were to be adapted to the field, then it would be necessary to consider and discuss its holistic adaptation to health services. In this sense, it would be useful to look at the horizon opened by the broken windows theory and to develop measures against unwanted events, neglects and violations in all areas related to patient and employee rights, as well as the inputs and outputs of health services and health service delivery processes. From this point of view, it is important that new studies that are able to make original contributions to both practice and the literature be carried out. It is worth noting that measures to address risks to patient safety should be taken before "the first window is broken", in order not to "allow all windows to be broken" and avoid bearing costs that cannot be recovered.

FUTURE RESEARCH DIRECTIONS

From this point of view, it is important that new studies that are able to make original contributions to both practice and the literature be carried out. It is worth noting that measures to address risks to patient safety should be taken before "the first window is broken", in order not to "allow all windows to be broken" and avoid bearing costs that cannot be recovered.

CONCLUSION

As healthcare services develop and patients learn their rights, the interest in diverse healthcare provision and quality is also increasing. In general terms, the concept of patient safety, which is among the main quality factors in healthcare, is expressed as the precautions taken by the healthcare institution and its personnel to prevent harm to the patient. At this point, the "principle of beneficence" manifests itself in terms of medical ethics. The principle of beneficence can be defined as the state in which the "first do no harm, non-maleficence" principle has become "give priority to the benefit of the patient under all conditions". Without prejudice to the decision of the patient himself, it is possible that healthcare staff decisions about the patient may lead to ethical dilemmas or problems. The principle of beneficence introduces ethical obligations to healthcare professionals in terms of "being absolutely beneficial (prevents harm, removes harm, improve wellness)" and "providing a benefit–harm balance". Healthcare professionals often do not agree on what to focus on when balancing various factors relating to benefit and harm. Because of the lack of objective evidence regarding what the benefits and harm are, the subject of what to focus on often leads to discussions. In the clinic, similar contradictions arise as a result of different assessments of occupational obligation by healthcare professionals and patients (Ersoy and Aydin, 1994).

It is thought that the patient safety can also be evaluated in the context of the broken windows theory. The broken windows theory claims that if an environment is prepared to prevent the occurrence of a crime, the crime will go away. However, if a crime is committed, the guilty must be punished appropriately without delay. Otherwise, the perception that the crime will be ignored will lead to undesirable environments, such as vandalism. When the factors that cause crime are replaced with "all factors and medical errors that threaten patient safety", the applicability of the principles proposed by the broken window theory seems realistic in order to ensure continuity of patient safety. Accordingly, in the case of the struggle with ethical violations and events that could impair patient safety patient safety will not be easily damaged. In addition, when a medical error or an event that impairs patient safety occurs, it is immediately reported, discussed, and solved, and if the employees who were involved this situation are not labeled, patient safety will be strengthened.

Efforts to establish or strengthen patient safety are likely to mediate the reduction of medical errors and consequently the reduction of material and moral losses. This development will also result in positive effects on the economy by contributing to reducing additional costs borne by institutions and patients.

An important part of the studies on healthcare delivery and patient safety focuses on minimizing unwanted events and preventable errors. Despite being developed under a different discipline, the broken windows theory offers a different perspective in the sociology literature of crime in urban life, which seeks solutions to the problems and yields significant results in practice. Applying this approach in healthcare services may also bring about interdisciplinary opportunities in developing different solutions to the problems.

As healthcare delivery requires high performance and low tolerance for error, standards and employee training alone will not be sufficient to ensure patient safety. In this context, based on the fact that hospitals are social structures, designing, in advance, appropriate measures to address irregularities caused by failures to comply with applicable standards and trainings will contribute to the solution. In particular, specifying priorities to address the most serious adverse events and errors that can adversely affect patient outcomes and then instituting these priorities will ensure efficient use of the resources.

REFERENCES

Akalın, H. E. (2005). Yoğun Bakım Ünitelerinde Hasta Güvenliği. *Yoğun Bakım Dergisi.*, *5*(3), 141–146.

Alper, S. J., Holden, R. J., Scanlon, M. C., Patel, N., Kaushal, R., Skibinski, K., ... Karsh, B.-T. (2012). Self-reported violations during medication administration in two paediatric hospitals. *BMJ Quality & Safety*, *21*(5), 408–415. doi:10.1136/bmjqs-2011-000007 PMID:22447818

Altuntop, S. (2015). Kırık Camlar. In S. Altuntop (Ed.), Suçla Mücadele ve Güvenlik: Klasik ve Çağdaş Metinler (pp. 231-245). Ankara: Siyasal Kitabevi

Amalberti, R., Vincent, C., Auroy, Y., & de Saint, M. G. (2006). Violations and migrations in health care: A framework for understanding and management. *Quality & Safety in Health Care*, *15*(1suppl_1), 66–71. doi:10.1136/qshc.2005.015982 PMID:17142612

Anderson, J. G., Ramanujam, R., Hensel, D., Anderson, M. M., & Sirio, C. A. (2006). The Need for Organizational Change in Patient Safety Initiatives. *International Journal of Medical Informatics*, *75*(12), 809–817. doi:10.1016/j.ijmedinf.2006.05.043 PMID:16870501

Avcı, K. ve Aktan, T. (2015). Bir Sistem Sorunu Olarak Tıbbi Hatalar ve Hasta Güvenliği. *Düzce Üniversitesi Sağlık Bilimleri Enstitüsü Dergisi*, *5*(2), 48–54.

Aydemir, A. (2015). *Acil Serviste Çalışan Hemşirelerde Hasta güvenliği Kültürü ve Tutumunu Etkileyen Faktörler*. Samsun: Ondokuz Mayıs Üniversitesi Sağlık Bilimleri Enstitüsü Yayınlanmamış Yüksek Lisans Tezi.

Beşe, E. (2006). Kırık Pencereler Teorisi Bağlamında Kentsel Yaşamda Suç ve Güvenlik. *Polis Bilimleri Dergisi.*, *8*(1), 1–24.

Bosk, C. L. (2003). *Forgive and remember: managing medical failure* (2nd ed.). Chicago: University of Chicago Press. doi:10.7208/chicago/9780226924687.001.0001

Braithwaite, J., Wears, R. L., & Hollnagel, E. (2015). Resilient health care: Turning patient safety on its head. *International Journal for Quality in Health Care*, *27*(5), 418–420. doi:10.1093/intqhc/mzv063 PMID:26294709

Budak, M. (2008). Hasta Güvenliği Kültürü. *Sağlık Düşüncesi ve Tıp Kültürü Dergisi*, *7*, 54–57.

Buttle, F. (1996). Servqual: Review, Critique, Research Agenda. *European Journal of Marketing*, *30*(1), 8–32. doi:10.1108/03090569610105762

Can, Ö.İ., & Özkara, E., & Can, M. (2011). Yargıtay'da Karara Bağlanan Tıbbi Uygulama Hatası Dosyalarının Değerlendirilmesi. *Dokuz Eylül Üniversitesi Tıp Fakültesi Dergisi*, *25*, 69–76.

Cengiz, C. (2014). *Hasta Güvenliğinde Kimlik Doğrulama, Hastaların Doğru Tanımlanmasının Önemi, Karşılaşılan Sorunlar ve Çözüm Önerileri ve Bir Üniversite Hastanesi Uygulaması*. Ankara: Gazi Üniversitesi Sosyal Bilimler Enstitüsü Yayınlanmamış Yüksek Lisans Tezi.

Chassin, M. R., & Loeb, J. M. (2013). High-reliability health care: Getting there from Here. *The Milbank Quarterly*, *91*(3), 459–490. doi:10.1111/1468-0009.12023 PMID:24028696

Churruca, K., Ellis, L. A., & Braithwaite, J. (2018). 'Broken hospital windows': Debating the theory of spreading disorder and its application to healthcare organizations. MC. *Health Services Research*, *18*(1), 201. doi:10.118612913-018-3012-2 PMID:29566697

Çiçek, A. (2012). *Hemşirelerin Hasta Güvenliğine Yönelik Görüş ve Tutumlarının İncelenmesi*. İzmir: Ege Üniversitesi Sağlık Bilimleri Enstitüsü Yayınlanmamış Yüksek Lisans Tezi.

Classen, D. C., Resar, R., Griffin, F., Federico, F., Frankel, T., Kimmel, N., ... James, B. C. (2011). 'global trigger tool' shows that adverse events in hospitals may be ten times greater than previously measured. *Health Affairs (Project Hope)*, *30*(4), 581–589. doi:10.1377/hlthaff.2011.0190 PMID:21471476

Corman, H., & Mocan, N. (2005). Carrots, sticks, and broken windows. *The Journal of Law & Economics*, *48*(1), 235–266. doi:10.1086/425594

Debono, D., Taylor, N., Lipworth, W., Greenfield, D., Travaglia, J., Black, D., & Braithwaite, J. (2017). Applying the theoretical domains framework to identify barriers and targeted interventions to enhance nurses' use of electronic medication management systems in two Australian hospitals. *Implementation Science; IS*, *12*(1), 42. doi:10.118613012-017-0572-1 PMID:28347319

Debono, D. S., Greenfield, D., Travaglia, J. F., Long, J. C., Black, D., Johnson, J., & Braithwaite, J. (2013). Nurses' workarounds in acute healthcare settings: A scoping review. *BMC Health Services Research*, *3*(1), 175. doi:10.1186/1472-6963-13-175 PMID:23663305

Debono, D. S., Greenfield, D., Travaglia, J. F., Long, J. C., Black, D., Johnson, J., & Braithwaite, J. (2013). Nurses' workarounds in acute healthcare settings: A scoping review. *BMC Health Services Research*, *13*(1), 175. doi:10.1186/1472-6963-13-175 PMID:23663305

Derin, N. & Demirel, E.T. (2011). Hastanelerde Verimlilik Artışı İçin Hasta Güvenliği Uygulamaları ve Hasta Güvenliğinin Sağlanmasında Dönüşümcü Liderliğin Etkisi. *Verimlilik Dergisi*, *3*, 51–82.

Doğan, H.İ. & Sevinç, B. (2011). Suç Teorileri ve Şehir Güvenliği: Bitlis İliyle İlgili Genel Bir Değerlendirme. *Polis Bilimleri Dergisi*, *13*(4), 27–53.

Durmaz, G. (2016). *Cerrahi Hemşirelerinde Hasta Güvenliği Kültürü Algısını Etkileyen Faktörlerin Belirlenmesi*. Yeditepe Üniversitesi Sağlık Bilimleri Enstitüsü Yayınlanmamış Yüksek Lisans Tezi.

Emül, E. (2017). *Etik İklim Algısının Hasta Güvenliği Kültürü Üzerine Etkisi: Elazığ Örneği*. Elazığ: Fırat Üniversitesi Sosyal Bilimler Enstitüsü Yayınlanmamış Yüksek Lisans Tezi.

Emül, E. & Demirel, E.T. (2018). Etik İklim Algısının Hasta Güvenliği Kültürü Üzerine Etkisi: Elazığ Örneği. *Turkish Studies - International Periodical For The Languages. Literature and History of Turkish or Turkic, 13*(7), 83–122.

Ersoy, N. & Aydın, E. (1994). Tıbbi Etik'te Yararlılık İlkesi. *Türkiye Klinikleri J Med Ethics, 2*(2), 57–60.

Güven, R. (2007). *Dezenfeksiyon ve Sterilizasyon Uygulamalarında Hasta Güvenliği Kavramı*. Antalya: Ulusal Sterilizasyon Dezenfeksiyon Kongresi Bildirileri.

Hancı, Ş. H. (2002). *Malpraktis: Tıbbi Girişimler Nedeniyle Hekimin Ceza ve Tazminat Sorumluluğu*. Ankara: Seçkin Yayıncılık.

Hansen, M. M., Durbin, J., Sinkowitz-Cochran, R., Vaughn, A., Langowski, G. S., & Gleason, S. (2003). Do No Harm. Provider Perceptions of Patient Safety. *The Journal of Nursing Administration, 33*(10), 507–508. doi:10.1097/00005110-200310000-00004 PMID:14551467

Karaca, A. & Arslan, H. (. (2014). Hemşirelik Hizmetlerinde Hasta Güvenliği Kültürünün Değerlendirilmesine Yönelik Bir Çalışma. *Sağlık ve Hemşirelik Yönetimi Dergisi., 1*(1), 9–18. doi:10.5222/SHYD.2014.009

Karataş, M. & Yakıncı, C. (2010). Tıbbi Hata Nedenleri ve Çözüm Yolları. *İnönü Üniversitesi Tıp Fakültesi Dergisi, 17*(3), 233-236.

Kayral, İ. (2017). *Hasta Güvenliği ve Kırık Pencereler Kuramı*. Retrieved from http://www.ibrahimkayral.com/wp/2015/10/hasta-guvenligi-ve-kirik-pencereler-kurami/

Kelling, G. L., & Sousa, W. H. (2001). *Do police matter? An analysis of the impact of New York City's police reforms*. New York, NY: The Manhattan Institute.

Keuschnigg, M., & Wolbring, T. (2015) Disorder, social capital, and norm violation: three field experiments on the broken windows thesis. *Ration Soc., 27*(1), 96–126.

Kırık Cam Teorisi. (2017). Retrieved from http://isletmeyonetimiuzerineyazilar.blogspot.com.tr/2017/01/krk-cam-teorisi.html

Kohn, L. T., Corrigan, J. M., & Donaldson, M. S. (2000). Errors in healthcare: A leadingcause of dealthandinjury. In L. T. Kohn, J. M. Corrigan, & M. S. Donaldson (Eds.), *Toerr is human: building a safer health system* (pp. 26–48). Washington, DC: Institute of Medicine National Academy Press.

Lawton, R. (1998). Not working to rule: Understanding procedural violations at work. *Safety Science, 28*(2), 75–95. doi:10.1016/S0925-7535(97)00073-8

Marx, D. (2001). Patient safety and the 'just culture': a primer for health care executives. In *MERS: Medical event reporting system for transfusion medicine.* Washington, DC: AHRQ.

McFadden, K. L., Henagan, S. C., & Gowen, C. R. III. (2009). The Patient Safety Chain: Transformational Leadership's Effect on Patient Safety Culture, Initiatives, and Outcomes. *Journal of Operations Management, 27*(5), 390–404. doi:10.1016/j.jom.2009.01.001

Murray, W. B., & Foster, P. A. (2000). Crisis Resource Management Among Strangers: Principles of Organizing a Multidisciplinary Group for Crisis Resource Management. *Journal of Clinical Anesthesia, 12*(8), 633–638. doi:10.1016/S0952-8180(00)00223-3 PMID:11173002

Pedreira, M. L., & Marin, H. F. (2004). Patient Safety Initiatives in Brazil: A Nursing Perspective. *International Journal of Medical Informatics, 73*(7-8), 563–567. doi:10.1016/j.ijmedinf.2004.05.001 PMID:15246036

Pronovost, P., Weast, B., Rosenstein, B., Sexton, B., Holzmueller, C. G., Paine, L., ... Rubin, H. R. (2005). Implementing and Validating a Comprehensive Unit-Based Safety Program. *Journal of Patient Safety, 1*(1), 33–40. doi:10.1097/01209203-200503000-00008

Russel, T. (2005). Special Address To The Midwest Surgical Association on Surgical Outcome Analysis and Patient Safety. *American Journal of Surgery, 189*(3), 264–267. doi:10.1016/j.amjsurg.2004.11.011 PMID:15792747

Sampson, R. J., & Raudenbush, S. W. (1999). Systematic social observation of public spaces: A new look at disorder in urban neighborhoods. *American Journal of Sociology, 105*(3), 603–651. doi:10.1086/210356

Tansüyer, T. (2010). *Hasta Güvenliği ve Tıbbi Hatalar Konusunda Sağlık Personelinin Görüşlerini Belirlemeye Yönelik Bir Alan Araştırması.* Ankara: Gazi Üniversitesi Sosyal Bilimleri Enstitüsü Yayınlanmamış Yüksek Lisans Tezi.

Baker, G. R., Norton, P. G., Flintoft, V., Blais, R., Brown, A., Cox, J., ... & O'Beirne, M. (2004). The Canadian Adverse Events Study: The incidence of adverse events among hospital patients in Canada. *Canadian Medical Association Journal, 170*(11), 1678–1686. doi:10.1503/cmaj.1040498 PMID:15159366

Leape, L. L., Brennan, T. A., Laird, N., Lawthers, A. G., Localio, A. R., Barnes, B. A., ... Hiatt, H. (1991). The nature of adverse events and negligence in hospitalized patients: Results of the Harvard Medical Practice Survey study II. [PubMed]. *The New England Journal of Medicine, 324*(6), 377–384. doi:10.1056/NEJM199102073240605

Waring, J., Allen, D., Braithwaite, J., & Sandall, J. (2016). Healthcare quality and safety: A review of policy, practice and research. *Sociology of Health & Illness*, *38*(2), 198–215. doi:10.1111/1467-9566.12391 PMID:26663206

Wilson, J. Q., & Kelling, G. L. (1982). Broken windows: The police and neighborhood safety. *Atlantic Monthly*, *211*, 29–38.

World Health Organization. (2007), European Regional Patients for Patient Safety Workshop Report. Dublin.

World Health Organization. (2009) World Alliance for Patient Safety Forward Programme, France.

Yardımcı, F., Başbakkal, Z., Beytut, D., & Muslu, G. & Ersun, A. (2014). Bir Devlet Hastanesinde Sağlık Çalışanlarının Hasta Güvenliği Kültürü Algısının İncelenmesi. *Anadolu Tıbbi Araştırmalar Dergisi*, *8*(4), 173–179.

Yıldız,, T., Eriten,, G., Erdem,, İ., Gökay,, N.S., & Kulaç,, M., & Alp, R. (2012). Mezuniyetin ve Profesyonel Sağlık Personeli Olarak Çalışmanın Hasta Güvenliği Bilinci Üzerine Etkileri. *Kafkas J Med Sci*, *2*(3), 94–98. doi:10.5505/kjms.2012.03511

Chapter 11
Identifying the Relationship Between Health Expenditures and Life Expectancy at Birth:
A Cointegration Analysis for MENA Countries

Halim Baş
Istanbul Medipol University, Turkey

Muhammed Erkam Kocakaya
Istanbul University, Turkey

ABSTRACT

In this study, 16 countries in the MENA region (United Arab Emirates, Bahrain, Djibouti, Algeria, Egypt, Iran, Jordan, Kuwait, Lebanon, Morocco, Malta, Oman, Qatar, Saudi Arabia, Tunisia, and Yemen) were included to the sample and was analyzed, by using a panel data method Pedroni Cointegration test, that relationship between "health expenditures" and "life expectancy at birth" in 2000-2016 period these countries. As a result of the analysis, there was no relationship between health expenditures and life expectancy at birth. Although health expenditures do not have a direct impact on life expectancy at birth, If the MENA region countries take needed measures (such as; to attach importance to institutionalization and functionality in health, focusing on disadvantaged groups, and to encourage investments of hospital and personnel), the inequalities in health outcomes would be reduced.

DOI: 10.4018/978-1-7998-2329-2.ch011

INTRODUCTION

Health expenditures are becoming an increasingly important item in countries where both the free market system is strong, and the public economy and public service concept is effective. In this sense, health expenditures consist of both public and private expenditure items. However, the effectiveness of health expenditures cannot be explained only by the large amount of expenditure (Dinçer and Yüksel, 2019; Shi et al., 2019). The MENA region consists of countries with different levels of social, economic and political development and stability. For this reason, there is no similar and common health expenditure policy for all MENA countries. However, in Lebanon, which has one of the highest life expectancies in the region, health care is provided through a private sector-dominated system, which is largely dependent on public sector funding. Lebanon spends 8% of GDP on health care. For example, as the poorest countries in the MENA region, the health system in Djibouti and Yemen is inadequate in providing basic health services and "mother and child deaths" and "malnutrition" are priority areas for health expenditures in these countries. However, in Qatar, another MENA country, traffic accidents are seen more frequently than other countries in the world, and accordingly, to do policies and expenditures for "reducing accidents and preventing injuries" have priority for the health system. Overall, countries in the MENA region lag behind developed countries such as the United Kingdom, Germany, and the USA, in terms of hospital capacity, the number of doctors, and medical staff. When the health expenditures are taken into consideration, the average health expenditure of the MENA region is quite lower than the world average.

Different domestic and foreign economic, social and political structures and problems of MENA countries result in different conclusions in the studies conducted on these countries. Health expenditures and life expectancy at birth are also observed to reach these different results. The insufficiency of health expenditures compared to other parts of the world forces citizens to pay a high rate of out-of-pocket payments. The increasing share of out-of-pocket payments exposes citizens to the risk of poverty and leads to imbalances in health access, leading to an increase in health outcomes. However, the increasing burden of health systems in MENA countries and the contraction of per capita health spending due to the decline in oil revenues since 2014 are likely to reflect the potential consequences for health spending and future labor productivity (Yazbeck et al., 2017). For example, Hamidi and Akinci (2016) emphasize in their study that the increase in health expenditures in the MENA region will increase the "life expectancy at birth" in this region. However, in our study, no relation was found between health expenditures in the MENA region and life expectancy at birth. Firstly, socio-economic outcomes of 16 countries in the MENA region (United Arab Emirates, Bahrain, Djibouti, Algeria, Egypt, Iran,

Jordan, Kuwait, Lebanon, Morocco, Malta, Oman, Qatar, Saudi Arabia, Tunisia, and Yemen) were reviewed and it was handle data regarding health expenditures and life expectancy at birth. Secondly, similar studies were evaluated by reviewing the literature on health expenditures and life expectancy at birth. Thirdly, an empirical application was developed on the relationship between health expenditures and life expectancy at birth, and the Pedroni cointegration test was performed with a panel data method. Finally, empirical findings were evaluated, and the conclusion written.

OUTLOOK OF HEALTH EXPENDITURES AND LIFE EXPECTANCY AT BIRTH IN MENA COUNTRIES

The most valuable treasure for human beings is health. Being healthy is one of the most important goals in human life. In this respect, not only the illness during the life of the individual, but also efforts to improve the quality of life are considered important gains on the basis of the individual and society (Lustig, 2006). Creating a healthy society is one of the most important social policies for all countries. Because individual and community health have direct and indirect effects on the social-economic welfare of countries. When the developments in health conditions are taken into consideration since the last century when the human population increased and the whole world opened to communication and transportation with the help of technology, the 1940s is considered a turning point. Because, during the period of nearly a century between 1850 and 1940s, "life expectancy at birth" was also affected by the high rates of infectious diseases and child mortality. Since the 1940s, a new era has begun with the developments in the fields of science and medicine and the new discoveries and treatment methods in the field of health and this transition period has been called "epidemiological transition". Thus, "life expectancy at birth" has gained an increasing trend in the world. (Acemoğlu and Johnson, 2006).

Despite national and international policies and strategic investments to improve the health system, there are inequalities between health expenditures and their outcomes at the level of countries and sub-populations. These inequalities stem from the failure to implement preventive and remedial measures for the factors determining health and disease status. When the lack of resources, which is the main problem of health systems, is added to this problem, the expenditure - outcome balance deteriorates. All these difficulties make us think of the functionality of the coordination between the dynamics of health and social development. (Ogden et al., 2013, 1076). At this point, the effectiveness of social policies is important for making health systems functional and strong. The content of social policies is different according to the classification of Esping-Andersen (1990), which classifies social welfare regimes.

The basis of these differences is determined by economic factors. In MENA countries, social welfare regimes have emerged under different conditions after the second half of the twentieth century. This social welfare regime could only have existed within a very narrow framework and an authoritarian form of governance in the places where modern institutions exist. Within this framework, the "authoritarian corporatist" social policy approach developed in MENA countries between 1950 and 1970. At that time, however, the social welfare regime seemed to be economically unrealistic. The most important priority in the 1950s and 1960s was the establishment of the social and economic infrastructure necessary for a modern economy to cope with adverse conditions for social development. Because the countries of the region were governed by economic systems under the control of the public, where the free market system was not sufficiently established. Life expectancy in most MENA countries was under 50 years at that time, while the mortality rate under 5 was over 300 per 1000 live births. In the 1960s and 1970s, the health indicators of the region had a negative outlook compared to other countries with similar income levels. (Karshenas et al., 2014; Sayım, 2011). Today, although the health expenditures of the countries of the region are becoming increasingly important in the public economy, the outlook in the field of social welfare does not seem very heartwarming. Significant changes have taken place in the last five years in terms of social and economic development, especially in terms of long-term refugee situations and large migration flows. However, since the region is demographically, politically and economically heterogeneous, the reflection of social dynamics is not the same or similar for each country. However, as a common problem, difficulties in reaching the most basic needs of the society are increasing, poverty is deepening, and the number of dysfunctional and unstable institutions in which hinder economic development and prosperity is increasing. (Ministry fo Foreign Affairs Sweden, 2016, 3) There are also significant economic differences between the countries in the region, particularly the health system and access conditions. For example, the gross domestic product is only 944 USD in Yemen and 63 222 USD in Qatar. Likewise, many health problems (infectious diseases) can cause serious harm due to the lack of qualified physicians. In Iraq, there are approximately 0.85 doctors per thousand people, while in the United Kingdom it is about 2.83 (Borthwcik and Horton, 2006; World Bank, 2019). Although there have been limited economic developments in MENA countries since the 1990s, there have been significant improvements in the health status of citizens. In the same period, there has been a significant decrease in the deaths of mothers and children under the age of five, and substantial improvements have been made in the health status of individuals as well as other developments observed in the health system. Life expectancy at birth in the region increased from 59 to 74 years in the period from 1980 to 2017. (Borthwcik and Horton, 2006). Figure 1 shows the expected life expectancy at birth from 1960 to 2017 across countries in the MENA region.

Figure 1 shows that the life expectancy at birth is estimated to increase by approximately 50% when the average MENA countries' from the 1960's (47 years) to 2000's (70 years) is examined. However, this upward trend has continued meek since 2000 and as of 2017, life expectancy at birth was recorded as 74 years. In Figure 2 below, life expectancy at birth is classified according to gender.

When the data in Figure 2 is taken as a reference, it is determined that the life expectancy at birth women and men in MENA countries increased from the 1960s to 2017 and that the life expectancy of women was longer than men. According to the 2017 data, the expected life expectancy at birth is 75 for women and 72 for men.

When the expenditures on improving health status in the countries of the region are taken into consideration, it is seen that it occupies a small area within the economies. Since the shares allocated to health expenditures are considered as an indicator, for example, total health expenditures accounted for 4.5% of the gross domestic product in 2000, which increased to 5.6% in 2017. (World Bank, 2019) However, in the same period, the average in the MENA region is well below the global average. When the general government health expenditures are examined, a similar picture can be seen. While the share of general government health expenditures in 2000 was 2.5% in gross domestic product, it increased to 3.3% in 2017. An important item in the calculation of total health expenditures and general government expenditures is

Figure 1. Life expectancy at birth (years), MENA region, (1960- 2017)
Source: The World Bank, World Development Indicators Database (https://databank.worldbank.org/source/world-development-indicators/preview/on), access date 20.08.2019.

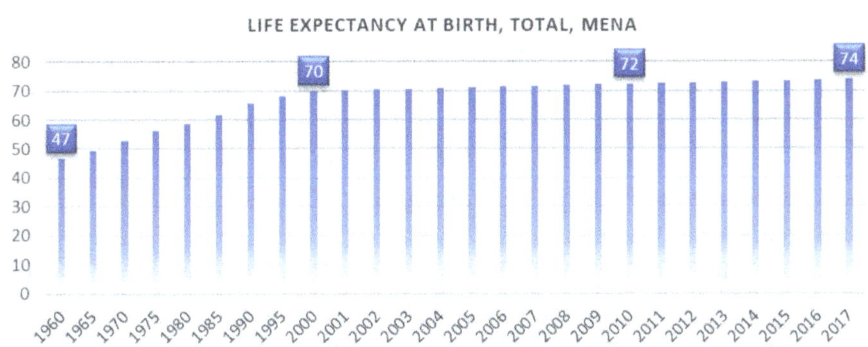

Figure 2. Life expectancy at birth(years), MENA region, (1960 -2017)
Source: The World Bank, World Development Indicators Database (https://databank.worldbank.org/source/world-development-indicators/preview/on), access date 20.08.2019.

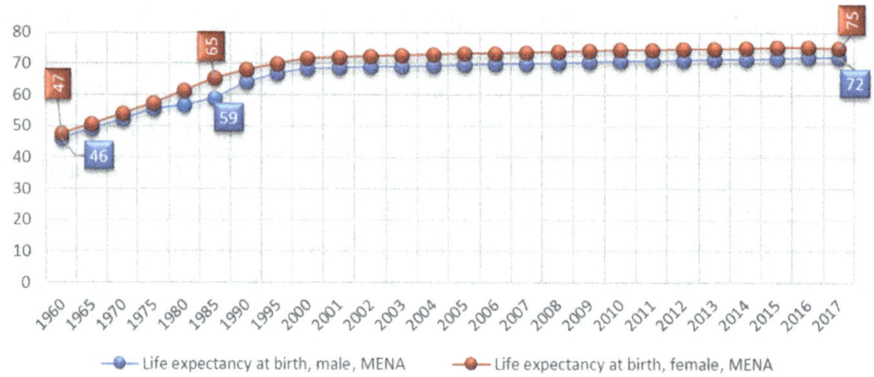

out-of-pocket expenditures. Because out-of-pocket spending in a country has to do with the level of economic development, any increase or decrease may be direct or indirect in proportion to the government's overall health expenditure. Accordingly, the share of out-of-pocket spending has decreased slightly in total health expenditures. Out-of-pocket expenditures accounted for 38% of total health expenditures in 2000, while they accounted for 30% in 2014 (Asbu et al., 2017), (World Bank, 2019).

In 2000, MENA governments signed the Millennium Development Goals (Millennium Development Goals), and most MENA countries are implementing policies in line with the targets. However, in the poorest countries, the situation is much lower than in the richest countries. These countries are more vulnerable to non-communicable disease burdens. According to the estimates of the World Health Organization, by 2020, 60% of the burden of disease will be non-communicable diseases. According to the findings of the Global Burden of Disease Project, early mortality rates from non-communicable diseases are higher than those of countries with high mortality, low incomes and industrialized populations (Borthwcik and Horton, 2006).

Figure 3 shows the ratio of health expenditures in GDP (gross domestic product) across MENA countries by years. Accordingly, in 1960, 4.49% of GDP was allocated to health expenditures, while the lowest level in 2008 was 3.97%. While the share of health expenditures in GDP, which increased to 5.04% in 2009, showed a downward trend until 2014, it increased again since 2014 and reached 5.59% as of 2016.

When data on the Table 1 taken as a reference in which shows "Health expenditures" and "life expectancy at birth" of countries in MENA region between 2000 - 2016/2017,

Figure 3. Current health expenditure (%gdp), MENA, (2000 – 2016)
Source: The World Bank, World Development Indicators Database (https://databank.worldbank.org/source/world-development-indicators/preview/on), access date 20.08.2019.

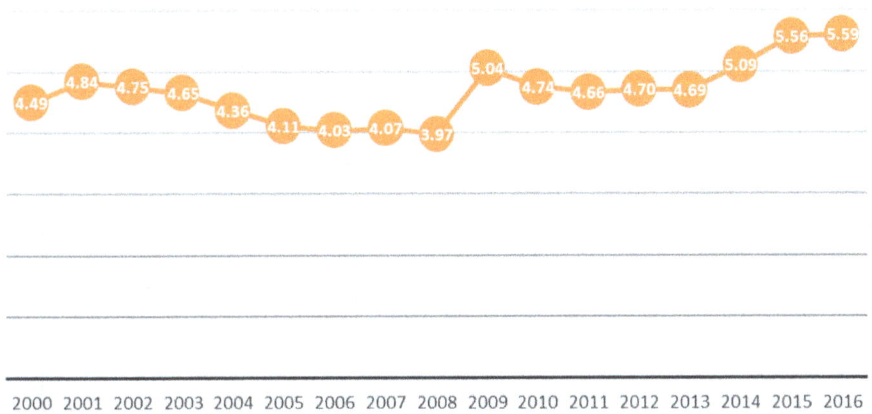

in Egypt, Lebanon, Jordan and Djibouti, the share of total health expenditures in GDP has decreased but the expected life expectancy at birth continues to increase. On the other hand, Malta (9,30%), Iran (8,10%) and Lebanon (8,01%) had the highest share of health expenditures in GDP as of 2016.

When Table 1 is examined in terms of life expectancy at birth, the countries with the highest year as of 2017 are as follows; Malta (82 years), Lebanon (80 years), Qatar (78 years), while the countries with the lowest year were identified as Djibouti (63 years) and Yemen (65 years).

BACKGROUND

There are results of studies examining the relationship between health expenditures and life expectancy at birth in different times and countries. The following table shows these different studies.

In Linden and Ray (2016) studies, the effect of private and public health expenditures on life expectancy was examined. In this study, 34 OECD countries were taken into consideration in the period of 1970-2012 and VAR method was used. As a result of this study, private and public sector expenditures are positively correlated with expected life expectancy in the long term.

Table 1. Middle East & North Africa countries "current health expenditure (% of GDP)" and "life expectancy at birth (years)"", (2000 – 2017)

Country	Indicator	2000	2005	2010	2011	2012	2013	2014	2015	2016	2017
Middle East & North Africa	Current health expenditure (% of GDP)	4,49	4,11	4,74	4,66	4,70	4,69	5,09	5,56	5,59	-
	Life expectancy at birth, total (years)	70	71	72	73	73	73	73	73	74	74
Algeria	Current health expenditure (% of GDP)	3,49	3,24	5,12	5,27	6,00	6,04	6,55	6,98	6,65	-
	Life expectancy at birth, total (years)	70	73	75	75	75	75	76	76	76	76
Egypt, Arab Rep.	Current health expenditure (% of GDP)	4,92	4,92	4,15	4,36	4,55	4,65	4,69	4,62	4,64	-
	Life expectancy at birth, total (years)	69	69	70	71	71	71	71	71	71	72
Lebanon	Current health expenditure (% of GDP)	10,69	7,55	7,44	8,15	8,00	7,76	7,97	7,83	8,02	-
	Life expectancy at birth, total (years)	74	77	78	79	79	79	79	79	80	80
Morocco	Current health expenditure (% of GDP)	3,98	4,76	5,86	5,73	5,75	5,65	5,68	5,41	5,84	-
	Life expectancy at birth, total (years)	69	71	74	74	75	75	75	76	76	76
Saudi Arabia	Current health expenditure (% of GDP)	4,21	3,42	3,66	3,71	4,02	4,47	5,23	6,00	5,74	-
	Life expectancy at birth, total (years)	72	73	74	74	74	74	74	74	75	75
United Arab Emirates	Current health expenditure (% of GDP)	2,37	2,32	3,88	3,67	3,42	3,59	3,63	3,59	3,52	-
	Life expectancy at birth, total (years)	74	75	76	76	77	77	77	77	77	77
Oman	Current health expenditure (% of GDP)	3,06	2,59	2,74	2,55	2,55	2,79	3,53	4,31	4,29	-
	Life expectancy at birth, total (years)	72	74	76	76	76	76	77	77	77	77
Iran, Islamic Rep.	Current health expenditure (% of GDP)	4,74	5,31	6,75	6,61	6,64	5,99	6,91	7,76	8,10	-
	Life expectancy at birth, total (years)	70	72	74	74	75	75	75	76	76	76
Jordan	Current health expenditure (% of GDP)	9,63	8,86	8,39	8,34	7,99	7,35	7,41	6,28	5,47	-
	Life expectancy at birth, total (years)	72	73	73	74	74	74	74	74	74	74
Bahrain	Current health expenditure (% of GDP)	3,56	3,18	3,84	3,58	4,11	4,31	4,41	4,98	4,87	-
	Life expectancy at birth, total (years)	74	75	76	76	76	76	77	77	77	77
Yemen, Rep.	Current health expenditure (% of GDP)	4,67	5,21	5,16	4,77	5,20	4,96	4,84	5,60	-	-
	Life expectancy at birth, total (years)	60	62	64	64	64	64	65	65	65	65

continued on following page

Table 1. Continued

Country	Indicator	2000	2005	2010	2011	2012	2013	2014	2015	2016	2017
Tunisia	Current health expenditure (% of GDP)	5,05	5,40	5,88	6,43	6,61	6,86	6,81	7,01	6,95	-
	Life expectancy at birth, total (years)	73	74	75	75	75	75	75	76	76	76
Qatar	Current health expenditure (% of GDP)	2,01	2,57	1,79	1,60	1,75	2,08	2,42	3,10	3,08	-
	Life expectancy at birth, total (years)	76	77	77	77	78	78	78	78	78	78
Malta	Current health expenditure (% of GDP)	6,54	8,69	8,21	8,55	9,00	9,54	9,42	9,36	9,30	-
	Life expectancy at birth, total (years)	78	79	81	81	81	82	82	82	82	82
Kuwait	Current health expenditure (% of GDP)	2,51	2,38	2,76	2,62	2,57	2,59	3,20	4,01	3,90	-
	Life expectancy at birth, total (years)	73	74	74	74	74	74	74	75	75	75
Iraq	Current health expenditure (% of GDP)	-	2,90	3,23	2,79	2,69	2,81	2,79	3,11	3,31	-
	Life expectancy at birth, total (years)	69	68	68	69	69	69	69	70	70	70
Djibouti	Current health expenditure (% of GDP)	4,13	4,53	4,30	4,74	4,63	4,10	4,14	4,39	3,50	-
	Life expectancy at birth, total (years)	57	58	60	61	61	62	62	62	62	63

Source: (The World Bank, World Development Indicators Database (https://databank.worldbank.org/source/world-development-indicators/preview/on), access date 20.08.2019)

* Syria, Israel, and Palestine countries are not included in this table.

Tüylüoğlu and Tekin (2009) examined the effects of variables of international income and health expenditures on infant mortality and life expectancy at birth. Regression analysis was performed on the data of 176 countries based on 2003. According to the results of the analysis, it was found that health expenditures had more effect on life expectancy at infant mortality and birth according to income level.

Nixon and Ullman (2006), taking into account the 1980-1995 period, have assumed that increases in health expenditures for 15 OECD countries are largely related to infant mortality but may have a marginal effect on life expectancy.

Barlow and Yissandjie (1999) examined the effects of direct and indirect determinants of life expectancy at birth by regression analysis in 77 countries based on 1990 data. It has been observed that variables such as per capita health expenditure and urbanization rate have low impact on life expectancy at birth.

Crémieux et al., (1999) in their study of the relationship between health expenditures and health outcomes are discussed. The study was conducted in different Canadian provinces and was based on 15 years of data. As a result, the low health care expenditures have a negative impact on infant mortality and life expectancy in Canada.

Authors	Scope	Period	Method	Results
(Linden, Mikael & Rayb, Deb, 2017)	34 OECD Countries	1970 -2012	VAR Analysis	There is a positive relationship between public health expenditures and life expectancy.
(Tüylüoğlu, Şevket & Tekin, Mustafa, 2009)	176 Countries	2003	Regression Analysis	Health expenditures effect life expectancy at birth and infant mortality rates
(Nixon, John &Ullman, Phil ippe 2006)	The Former 15 Members of the European Union	1980 - 1995	Panel Data Analysis	Supposition that increases in health spending were largely related to infant mortality but only have a marginal impact on life expectancy.
(Barlow, Robin & Yissandjie, Bilkis, 1999)	77 Countries	1990	Regression Analysis	It has been observed that variables such as per capita health expenditure and urbanization rate have low impact on life expectancy at birth.
(Crémieux, P. Y., Ouellette, P., & Pilon, C. 1999)	Canada	1978 - 1992	Regression Analysis	Low health care expenditures have a negative impact on infant mortality and life expectancy in Canada.
(Elola, J., Daponte, A., & Navarro, V., 1995)	17 Western European Countries	-	Regression Analysis	In countries where infant mortality rates are less common, national health system is found to be more effective than social security system.
(Babazono, A., & Hillman, A. L., 1994)	21 OECD Countries	1988	Multiple Regression Models	Total health expenditure per capita are not related to health outcomes.
(Jaba, E., Balan, C. B., & Robu, I. B., 2014)	175 World Countries	1995 - 2010	Panel Data Analysis	As a result of the analysis, a significant relationship was found between health expenditures and life expectancy at birth.
(Shaw, J. W., Horrace, W. C., & Vogel, R. J., 2005)	19 OECD Countries	2000	Log-Linear Model Analysis	Per capita pharmaceutical expenditures, has a positive effect on population life expectancy at various ages.
(Or, Z., 2000)	21 OECD Countries	1972 - 1992	Fixed-Effects Model Panel Data Analysis	In this study, which analyzed the effects of health expenditures on health outcomes, it was found to be negative and significant for women and not statistically significant for men.
(Nketiah-Amponsah, E. 2019).	46 Sub -Saharan African Countries	2000 - 2015	-	As a result of the analysis, it was found that health expenditures had a positive and significant effect on health outcomes such as life expectancy, under-five deaths and maternal deaths, and stable increases in health expenditures tended to improve health outcomes in 46 sub-Saharan African countries.
(Novignon, J., Olakojo, S. A., & Nonvignon, J., 2012)	44 Sub -Saharan African Countries	1995 - 2010	Panel Regression Analysis: Fixed And Random Effects	It has been found that health expenditures are related to the increase in life expectancy at birth and decrease in mortality and infant mortality rates. On the other hand, public health expenditures have a relatively larger impact on private health expenditures.
(Ssozi, J., & Amlani, S., 2015)	43 Sub -Saharan African Countries	1995 - 2011	Panel Data Analysis: General Method of Moments (GMM)	It has been found that Development Assistance for Health to Government and Development Assistance for Health to Non-Government Entities improves all three health measures (infant, child mortality rates and life expectancy)
(Mathers, C. D., Sadana, R., Salomon, J. A., Murray, C. J., & Lopez, A. D., 2001)	191 Countries	1999	Sullivan's method	As average levels of health expenditure per capita increase, healthy life expectancy increases at a greater rate than total life expectancy.
(Bein, M. A., Unlucan, D., Olowu, G., & Kalifa, W., 2017)	8 East African countries	2000 – 2014	Panel Data Analysis	There is a strong, positive association between total healthcare expenditures and total life expectancy. In addition, while identified a positive relationship between healthcare expenditures and female and male life expectancy, healthcare had a stronger effect on improving life expectancy in females than in males. Besides, there is a negative relationship between healthcare expenditures and the number of neonatal, infant, and under-five deaths.

continued on following page

Table 2. Continued

Authors	Scope	Period	Method	Results
(Ziesemer, T., 2016)	65 Low-İncome Countries	1960 - 2010	Panel Data Analysis: General Method of Moments (GMM) and FMOLS	The growth rates of aid per capita have significantly favorable effects on the growth rates of life expectancy
(Van den Heuvel, W. J., & Olaroiu, M., 2017)	31 European Countries	2013	Linear Regression Analysis	It has been found that health care expenditures are not the main determinant of life expectancy at birth, but social protection expenditures are.
(Ventelou, B., & Abu-Zaineh, M., 2016)	18 MENA Countries	1995 - 2012	Panel Data Analysis	As a result, increasing health care expenditure in the MENA region is a necessary but not sufficient condition for health outcomes improvements. However, institutional quality has a important role on the association between health expenditure and health outcomes in the MENA region.
(Dreger, C., & Reimers, H. E., 2005)	21 OECD Countries	1975 - 2001	Panel Cointegration Methods	Health expenditures are not only determined by income. Other factor are life expectancy, infant mortality and the share of elderly.
(Kabir, M., 2008)	91 Developing Countries	1992 - 2002	Multiple Regression Probit Regressions	As a result of the analysis, the effect of socio-economic factors such as per capita income, education, health expenditures, access to safe water and urbanization on life expectancy was insignificant.

Elola et al., (1995), in their study, 17 Western European countries discussed health expenditures and the structure of health systems. The scope of the study, which was initially thought to be 80 countries, was finally compared with the Regression analysis over 17 countries and as a result of this analysis, it was found that the national health system was more effective than the social security system in countries where infant mortality rates were less common.

Babazono, A., & Hillman (1994) examined the impact of health expenditure indicators of 21 OECD countries on health outcomes by considering Multiple Regression model and 1988 data. According to the findings of the study, it was found that health expenditures per capita were not related to health outcomes, but health care expenditure affect only female life expectancy at birth.

Jaba, E., Balan, C. B., & Robu, I. B. (2014) measured the relationship between the inputs and outputs of the health care system using panel data analysis method. In this analysis covering a 16 year period between 1995 and 2010, per capita health expenditures in 175 world countries classified according to their geographical location and income level were evaluated as the input of the health system and life expectancy at birth as the output of the health system. As a result of the analysis, a significant relationship was found between health expenditures and life expectancy at birth.

Shaw, J. W., Horrace, W. C., & Vogel, R. J. (2005) analyzed 19 OECD countries using the Log-linear model with reference to 2000 data and per capita drug expenditures have a positive effect on the life expectancy of the population at various ages.

Or, Z. (2000), taking into account the data of 21 OECD countries for the years 1972 - 1992, analyzed the effects of health expenditures on health outcomes by using

Fixed-Effects model panel data analysis method. In this study, it was found that my health expenditures were negative and significant for women and not statistically positive and significant for men.

Nketiah-Amponsah, E. (2019) examined the main macroeconomic and social determinants of health expenditures in sub-Saharan Africa (SSA), and the impact of health expenditures on health outcomes such as life expectancy, under-five deaths and maternal deaths. Data on 46 sub-Saharan African countries for the period 2000-2015 were used. As a result of the analysis, it was found that health expenditures had a positive and meaningful effect on all three health outcomes and that the steady increases in health expenditures tended to improve the health outcomes in 46 sub-Saharan African countries.

Novignon, J., Olakojo, S. A., & Nonvignon, J. (2012) applied Panel Regression Analysis in 44 Sub-Saharan African countries to determine the effects of health expenditures from 1995 to 2010 on health outcomes. As a result of this analysis, it was found that health expenditures were related to the increase in life expectancy at birth and decrease in mortality and infant mortality rates. On the other hand, public health expenditures have a relatively larger impact on private health expenditures.

Mathers, C. D., Sadana, R., Salomon, J. A., Murray, C. J., & Lopez, A. D. (2001) analyzed the data of 191 countries in 1999 with Sullivan's method in order to estimate healthy life expectancy. As a result of this analysis, as the average health expenditure per capita increases, the health expectancy increases more than the total life expectancy.

In their study, Ssozi, J., & Amlani, S. (2015) analyzed the effectiveness of health spending in 43 countries of Sub-Saharan Africa from 1995 to 2011 using the General Moments Method. It has been found that Development Assistance for Health to government and Development Assistance for Health to Non-Government Entities improves all three health measures (infant, child mortality rates and life expectancy)

Bein, M. A., Unlucan, D., Olowu, G., & Kalifa, W. (2017) discuss the relationship between health expenditure and health outcomes for 8 East African countries. These countries; Burundi, Eritrea, Ethiopia, Kenya, Rwanda, Sudan, Tanzania and Uganda. Using panel data analysis, it was found that there was a strong and positive relationship between total health expenditures and total life expectancy. In addition, while it was observed that there was a positive relationship between health expenditures and life expectancy of men and women, health service had a stronger effect on increasing life expectancy in women than men. Another conclusion reached is that there is a negative relationship between health expenditures and the number of newborn, infant and under-five deaths.

Ziesemer (2016), examines 65 low-income countries from 1960 to 2010 with Panel Data Analysis: General Method of Moments (GMM) and FMOLS, and finds that the growth rates of aid per capita have significantly favorable effects on the growth rates of life expectancy.

Van den Heuvel, W. J., & Olaroiu, M. (2017) examined the 2013 national data of 31 European countries by linear regression analysis and analyzed the relationship between life expectancy at birth and health care expenditures. As a result of this analysis, it was found that health expenditures are not social determinants of life expectancy at birth but social protection expenses.

Ventelou, B., & Abu-Zaineh, M. (2016) examined the impact of health expenditures on health outcomes by creating a panel data set of 18 countries from the Middle East and North Africa region for the period 1995-2012. As a result of this analysis, it was found that the increase in health expenditures in MENA region is not a necessary but sufficient condition for improvements in health outcomes. Nevertheless, it has been stated that institutional quality has an important role in the relationship between health expenditures and health outcomes in MENA region.

Dreger, C., & Reimers, H. E. (2005) examined the long-term relationship between health expenditures and GDP of 21 OECD countries using panel co-integration methods from 1975-2001 data. The analysis found that health expenditures were not only determined by income but also various variables such as life expectancy, infant mortality and the share of the elderly were influential in this relationship. Life expectancy or the share of the elderly are also mentioned as the main factors for the increase in health expenditures in the future.

Kabir, M. (2008), using multiple regression and probit models with the data of 1992-2002, related socio-economic factors such as per capita income, education, health expenditure, access to safe water and urbanization over the life expectancy period of 91 developing countries were discussed. As a result of the analysis, the effect of socio-economic factors was negligible.

EMPIRICAL PRACTICE

Data Set and Methodology

In this study, the period between 2000-2016 was examined in order to examine the relationship between life expectancy at birth and health expenditures in MENA countries. 16 countries (UAE, Bahrain, Djibouti, Algeria, Egypt, Iran, Jordan, Kuwait, Lebanon, Morocco, Malta, Oman, Qatar, Saudi Arabia, Tunisia and Yemen) have been selected from the World Bank. The variables used in the study are explained in Table 3 below. Accordingly, GDP percentages of expected life expectancy at birth" and" health expenditures "data were obtained from world bank data. Pedroni cointegration analysis was used to measure the relationship between these two variables. Unit root tests were used for the variables before the analysis.

Unit Root Test

Unit root test is used to determine whether the series are stationary. If there is no stasis in a time series, it is formulated as ΔX = X_t-X_ (t-1) and the difference is taken until it becomes stable. When the time series becomes stagnant, this series Δ. is integrated at the level, the stability of the series is shown as X_t ~ I (Δ).

To investigate the presence of unit root in panel data analysis, both DF (Dickey – Fuller) and ADF (Augmented Dickey – Fuller) tests were extended for panel data analysis, and in panel data analysis, many unit root tests are based on the expansion of the ADF test. (Gülmez, 2015: 21) In the literature, Levin et al. (2002), Im et al. (2003), Maddala and Wu (1999), Choi (2001) are generally accepted. Fisher Type tests recommended by Maddala and Wu (1999) and Choi (2001), Breitung (2000), Levin, Lin and Chu (LLC) (2002) and Im, Pesaran and Shin (IPS) (2003) to perform unit root testing in panel data models.

As shown in Equation 1, LLC is based on the Augmented Dickey-Fuller-ADF test and is based on the assumption that the autoregressive (ρ) coefficient of the variable is homogeneous. In the model with constant parameters, ε_it, ie the error process, is distributed independently between the variables (Levin vd., 2002).

$$\Delta y_{it} = \alpha_{0i} + \rho y_{it-1} + \varepsilon_{it} \quad (1)$$

In addition, starting from equation 1, the unit root test hypotheses are established below. In the hypothesis, if the coefficient ρ is equal to 0, the hypothesis H_0 is accepted and y_ (it-1) in equation 1 has a unit root, that is, the series is not stationary. In this case, the difference must be obtained for the series to become stable

$$H_0 : \rho = 0 \, ve \, H_1 : \rho \neq 0$$

Table 3. Variable names and resources

Variable name	Definition	Data Source
LifeExpectancy	Life expectancy at birth, total (years)	World Bank[1]
HealthExp	Current health expenditure (% of GDP)	World Bank [2]

In Levin, Lin and Chu (LLC) (2002) test, the autoregressive ρ coefficient is homogeneous for all units, whereas in the Im, Pesaran and Shin (IPS) (2003) test, the ρ coefficient is allowed to be heterogeneous. In IPS test, unit root test is applied to time series separately for each unit without combining the data and IPS test statistic is obtained by averaging the obtained statistics. (Im, Pesaran, Shin, 2003). Maddala and Wu (1999) and Choi (2001) alternatively proposed Fisher's type test based on the combination of unit root test statistics for each non-parametric cross-section (Güven & Mert, 2016).

Pedroni Cointegration

Cointegration analysis is a test method that provides information about the long-term relationship between the series. Stating that linear combinations of two or more non-stationary series may be stationary, Engle and Granger (1987) made an important contribution to the literature with cointegration analysis. In panel cointegration analyzes, the method that we often encounter in the literature is developed by Pedroni. This method is expressed in Equation (2) below. The existence of the relationship between x and y in this equation depends on the stability of the error term e_it residue. If the error term is stationary, there is a long-term relationship between x and y (Pedroni, 2001).

$$y_{it} = \alpha_i + \delta_i t + \beta_{1i} X_{2it} + \beta_{2i} X_{2it} + \ldots + \beta_{Mi} X_{Mit} + e_{it} \quad (2)$$

Pedroni tests are indicated to allow multiple regressors, variation of the cointegration vector across different parts of the panel, as well as allowing heterogeneity of errors across cross-sectional units. Two different panel cointegration tests, Kao (1999) and Pedroni (1999), are used to test for cointegration in panel data. Pedroni (1999) uses two-variable model for cointegration analysis. Pedroni panel cointegration analysis, panel v-statistic, panel rho-statistic, panel Philips-Peron (PP) -statistic, panel ADF-statistic, group rho-statistic, group PP-statistic and group ADF-statistic has 7 different tests. It is possible to divide these different tests into two categories. The first category includes four tests pooled in the "within" dimension. The second category includes three other tests in the "between" dimension (Asteriou and Hall, 2007). The first three of the four tests in the first category are non-parametric tests. The first test is a variance rate type statistic. The second one is similar to Phillips-Peron (PP) (rho) statistics and the third one is similar to PP (t) statistics. The fourth statistic is a parametric statistic similar to the Augmented Dickey Fuller (ADF) (t) statistic. In the second category, the first of the three tests was similar to the PP (rho) statistics, while the other two were similar to the PP (t) and ADF (t) statistics (Güvenek and Alptekin, 2010; Dinçer et al., 2019a,b,c).

This methodology seems appropriate when evaluating using panel methods. In this test, the probability values of all 7 tests were calculated. If the probability values of 4 or more tests are less than 0.05, it means that there is cointegration between the variables. In other words, it can be said that these variables involve long term relationships.

EMPIRICAL FINDINGS

Unit Root Test Results

The prerequisite for panel cointegration and panel causality analyzes is that the series are stationary. In order to stabilize the series, variables are subjected to unit root test. The unit root test results of the variables are presented in Table 4. As shown in Table 4, there are 5 unit root test methods. Stability of variables is accepted at 1% and 5% significance levels. If the result of at least 4 of the 5 methods is significant at the level of 5% for the stability of the variables in Table 4, the variable is considered to be stationary. The first difference of the lifeexp variable was taken to make the stasis stronger.

Levels, Lin & Chu, Im, Pesaran and Shin W-stat, and ADF - Fisher Chi-square, were found to be static at the level of "lifeexp" representing the expected life expectancy at birth, other methods were not considered static. The first difference of the series is taken as we consider stasis in at least 4 methods. Except for the first aware PP-Fisher Chi-square of the lifeexpancy variable where only the constant value was taken into account, the variable became stable in other methods. The healthex variable, which represents health expenditures, appears to be stationary and trendy only in Levin, Lin & Chu, but not in other methods. When we take the first difference of the HealthExp variable as a constant, we see that the variable becomes stagnant in all methods. After stabilizing the variables, the cointegration test may be involved.

Panel Cointegration Test

Cointegration is a method that provides information about the relationship between two variables. After the variables used in the study were stabilized, the panel was subjected to cointegration test. According to the test results in Table 5, there is no relationship between health expenditures and life expectancy at birth. In other words, since the significance of the statistical values of the relationship in question

Table 4. Panel unit root test results

	LifeExpectancy			
	Constant and Trend		Constant	
	t-statistics I(0)	Probability I(0)	t-statistics I(1)	Probability I(1)
Levin, Lin & Chu	-29.1007	0.0000	-18.4842	0.0000
Breitung t-stat	-0.14469	0.4425	-	-
Im, Pesaran and Shin W-stat	-36.4790	0.0000	-15.3822	0.0000
ADF - Fisher Chi-square	250.381	0.0000	224.273	0.0000
PP - Fisher Chi-square	28.5350	0.6427	34.0037	0.3713
	HealthExp			
	Constant and Trend		**Constant**	
	t-statistics I(0)	**Probability I(0)**	**t-statistics I(1)**	**Probability I(1)**
Levin, Lin & Chu	-2.25560	0.0120	-6.96594	0.0000
Breitung t-stat	0.65970	0.7453	-	-
Im, Pesaran and Shin W-stat	0.32656	0.6280	-5.10506	0.0000
ADF - Fisher Chi-square	34.9431	0.3300	82.7668	0.0000
PP - Fisher Chi-square	17.4681	0.9827	127.942	0.0000

in Table 5 is greater than 0.05 in 4 of the 7 methods, the relationship between the variables is not accepted.

When the findings were evaluated, no relationship was found between life expectancy at birth and health expenditures in MENA countries. In general, countries make a choice to increase health expenditures per capita in order to be least affected by the economic and social effects of demographic transformations. So much so that besides the economic and social care burden of a healthy society, many factors can correspond to a significant proportion of the public budget. For this reason, MENA countries need to review health expenditures both in order to minimize this financial burden as well as to active working life.

Table 5. Pedroni cointegration test

Relationship Type	Test Method	Statistic	Prob.	Weighted Statistic	Prob.
Relationship between life expectancy at birth and health expenditure	Panel v-Statistic	-2.200769	0.9861	-2.053921	0.9800
	Panel rho-Statistic	-2.580222	0.0049	1.897844	0.9711
	Panel PP-Statistic	-13.93624	0.0000	0.912783	0.8193
	Panel ADF-Statistic	-10.14263	0.0000	2.070656	0.9808
	Grup rho-Statistic	3.736058	0.9999	-	-
	Grup PP-Statistic	2.105659	0.9824	-	-
	Grup ADF-Statistic	2.823625	0.9976	-	-

SOLUTIONS AND RECOMMENDATIONS

From this point of view, the importance of the institutionalization and functionality of health in the countries of the region encourages investments such as hospitals, clinics and health personnel, and effective results can be obtained if focusing on preventive public health investments and priority groups, and reducing the inequalities in health outcomes among regional countries as in the world. Policies will be in place for.

FUTURE RESEARCH DIRECTIONS

In the future studies, other country groups can be taken into consideration.

CONCLUSION

Health expenditures are mentioned among the most important expenditure items allocated by government administrations from public budgets. Because states are obliged to protect human health in terms of compliance with laws and international conventions and norms. In this context, the health of the society is among the main duties of the states. However, health expenditures are not of equal importance or priority for each country. The most important reasons for this are due to the economic preferences of countries and their priorities for spending due to their strategic and political positions. It is known that health expenditures affect economic development and growth in a society. At the same time, health expenditures are expected to increase life expectancy at birth. In this study, the effect of health expenditures on life expectancy at birth was examined within the framework of MENA countries. While examining the literature for the study, studies focusing on the economic development context of health expenditures were found, but this study was deemed necessary because the issue was not examined directly in the context of MENA countries. In this study, it is thought that the relationship between health expenditures and life expectancy at birth with Pedroni cointegration will contribute to the literature.

The relationship between UAE, Bahrain, Djibouti, Algeria, Egypt, Iran, Jordan, Kuwait, Lebanon, Morocco, Oman, Qatar, Saudi Arabia, Tunisia and Yemen in MENA countries In our study which examined by panel data method, Pedroni cointegration test was applied. In the cointegration test, no correlation was found between health expenditures and life expectancy at birth. When we compare the results of the study with similar studies, the increase in the health expenditures of Ventelou and Abu-Zaineh (2016) in MENA region is in line with the conclusion that it is not a necessary but sufficient condition for improvements in health outcomes. There is also emphasis on the role of institutional quality in health systems on health outcomes. Wang and Yazbeck (2017) found findings related to the focus of the study. Some of these findings have lower expected life expectancy, although some countries spend less on health. Health expenditure is less than expected, with countries with higher life expectancy and less spending and higher performance in terms of expected health status. Again Heuvel et al. (2017) analyzed the relationship between life expectancy at birth and health care expenditures. As a result of this analysis, it is significant according to the findings obtained in our study that health expenditures are not the main determinants of life expectancy at birth. However, contrary to the findings in the study, results are also possible. A strong and positive relationship was found between total health expenditure and total life expectancy in 8 East African countries, and a negative relationship between the deaths of newborns and five or six children. As can be seen, health expenditures may have a positive or negative relationship with respect to different countries and geographies, as well as the absence of any relationship to the outcome of our study. Again, based on the findings of the study, the impact of economic power on health institutionality or functionality is important. As a matter of fact, the overall effect of the fact that the number of doctors per capita in Iraq is very low can be considered meaningful for the period (2000-2017). Or there may be a significant relationship between Yemen's lowest per capita income in selected countries and Qatar and Lebanon's highest per capita income and expected life expectancy. But above all, there is no single factor in determining the health outcomes per capita income, and health expenditures do not have a direct impact on life expectancy at birth.

REFERENCES

Acemoglu, D., & Johnson, S. (2006). Disease and Development: The Effect of Life Expectancy on Economic Growth. MIT. Retrieved from https://economics.mit.edu/files/4478

Asbu, E. Z., Masri, M. D., & Kaissi, A. (2017). Health status and health systems financing in the MENA region: roadmap to universal health coverage. *Global health research and policy, 2*(1), 25.

Asteriou, D., & Hall, S. G. (2007). *Applied Econometrics: a modern approach* (rev. ed.). Hampshire: Palgrave Macmillan.

Babazono, A., & Hillman, A. L. (1994). A comparison of international health outcomes and health care spending. *International Journal of Technology Assessment in Health Care, 10*(3), 376–381. doi:10.1017/S0266462300006619 PMID:8071000

Barlow, R., & Vissandjee, B. (1999). Determinants of national life expectancy. *Canadian Journal of Development Studies. Canadian Journal of Development Studies, 20*(1), 9–29. doi:10.1080/02255189.1999.9668787

Bein, M. A., Unlucan, D., Olowu, G., & Kalifa, W. (2017). Healthcare spending and health outcomes: Evidence from selected East African countries. *African Health Sciences, 17*(1), 247–254. doi:10.4314/ahs.v17i1.30 PMID:29026399

Borthwick, J., & Horton, R. (2006). The Middle East and health. *Lancet, 367*(9515), 961. doi:10.1016/S0140-6736(06)68401-8 PMID:16564342

Choi, I. (2001). Unit root tests for panel data. *Journal of International Money and Finance, 20*(2), 249–272. doi:10.1016/S0261-5606(00)00048-6

Crémieux, P. Y., Ouellette, P., & Pilon, C. (1999). Health care spending as determinants of health outcomes. *Health Economics, 8*(7), 627–639. doi:10.1002/(SICI)1099-1050(199911)8:7<627::AID-HEC474>3.0.CO;2-8 PMID:10544328

Dinçer, H., & Yüksel, S. (2019). Identifying the causality relationship between health expenditure and economic growth: An application on E7 countries. *Journal of Health Systems and Policies, 1*(1), 5–23.

Dinçer, H., Yüksel, S., & Adalı, Z. (2019c). Determining the Effects of Monetary Policies on Capital Markets of the Emerging Economies: An Evidence from E7 Countries. In The Impacts of Monetary Policy in the 21st Century: Perspectives from Emerging Economies. Emerald Publishing Limited.

Dinçer, H., Yüksel, S., & Canbolat, Z. N. (2019b). A Strategic Approach to Reduce Energy Imports of E7 Countries: Use of Renewable Energy. In Handbook of Research on Economic and Political Implications of Green Trading and Energy Use (pp. 18-38). Hershey, PA: IGI Global.

Dinçer, H., Yüksel, S., Pınarbaşı, F., & Çetiner, İ. T. (2019a). Measurement of Economic and Banking Stability in Emerging Markets by Considering Income Inequality and Nonperforming Loans. In Maintaining Financial Stability in Times of Risk and Uncertainty (pp. 49–68). Hershey, PA: IGI Global. doi:10.4018/978-1-5225-7208-4.ch003

Dreger, C., & Reimers, H. E. (2005). Health care expenditures in OECD countries: a panel unit root and cointegration analysis.

Elola, J., Daponte, A., & Navarro, V. (1995). Health indicators and the organization of health care systems in western Europe. *American Journal of Public Health*, *85*(10), 1397–1401. doi:10.2105/AJPH.85.10.1397 PMID:7573624

Engle, R. F., & Granger, C. W. (1987). Co-integration and error correction: Representation, estimation, and testing. *Econometrica*, *55*(2), 251–276. doi:10.2307/1913236

Gülmez, A. (2015). OECD ülkelerinde ekonomik büyüme ve hava kirliliği ilişkisi: Panel veri analizi. *Kastamonu Üniversitesi İktisadi ve İdari Bilimler Fakültesi Dergisi*, *9*(3), 18–30.

Güven, S., & Mert, M. (2016). Uluslararası Turizm Talebinin Eşbütünleşme Analizi: Antalya İçin Panel Ardl Yaklaşımı. *Cumhuriyet Üniversitesi İktisadi ve İdari Bilimler Dergisi*, *17*(1), 133–152.

Güvenek, B., & Alptekin, V. (2010). Enerji tüketimi ve büyüme ilişkisi: OECD Ülkelerine İlişkin bir panel veri analizi. *Enerji. Piyasa ve Düzenleme*, *1*(2), 172–193.

Im, K. S., Pesaran, M. H., & Shin, Y. (2003). Testing for unit roots in heterogeneous panels. *Journal of Econometrics*, *115*(1), 53–74. doi:10.1016/S0304-4076(03)00092-7

Jaba, E., Balan, C. B., & Robu, I. B. (2014). The relationship between life expectancy at birth and health expenditures estimated by a cross-country and time-series analysis. *Procedia Economics and Finance*, *15*, 108–114. doi:10.1016/S2212-5671(14)00454-7

Kabir, M. (2008). Determinants of life expectancy in developing countries. *Journal of Developing Areas*, *41*(2), 185–204. doi:10.1353/jda.2008.0013

Kao, C. (1999). Spurious regression and residual-based tests for cointegration in panel data. *Journal of Econometrics*, *90*(1), 1–44. doi:10.1016/S0304-4076(98)00023-2

Karshenas, M., Moghadam, V. M., & Alami, R. (2014). Social policy after the Arab Spring: States and social rights in the MENA Region. *World Development*, *64*, 726–739. doi:10.1016/j.worlddev.2014.07.002

Kronfol, N., Khalife, J., Romanos, J., Makouk, J., Noun, P., & Ammar, W. (2014). Observations on the Ministry of Public Health program of support to the hospitalization of patients in Lebanon. *Lebanese Medical Journal*, *103*(1006), 1–7. PMID:24684124

Levin, A., Lin, C. F., & Chu, C. S. J. (2002). Unit root tests in panel data: Asymptotic and finite-sample properties. *Journal of Econometrics*, *108*(1), 1–24. doi:10.1016/S0304-4076(01)00098-7

Linden, M., & Ray, D. (2017). Life expectancy effects of public and private health expenditures in OECD countries 1970–2012: Panel time series approach. *Economic Analysis and Policy*, *56*, 101–113. doi:10.1016/j.eap.2017.06.005

Lustig, N. (2007). Investing in health for economic development: The case of Mexico. In *Advancing Development* (pp. 168–182). London: Palgrave Macmillan. doi:10.1057/9780230801462_10

Maddala, G. S., & Shaowen, W. (1999). Comparative Study of Unit Root Tests With Panel Data and a New Simple Test. *Oxford Bulletin of Economics and Statistics*, *61*(Special Issue), 631–652. doi:10.1111/1468-0084.61.s1.13

Mathers, C. D., Sadana, R., Salomon, J. A., Murray, C. J., & Lopez, A. D. (2001). Healthy life expectancy in 191 countries, 1999. *Lancet*, *357*(9269), 1685–1691. doi:10.1016/S0140-6736(00)04824-8 PMID:11425392

Ministry for Foreign Affairs Sweden. (2016). Regional Strategy for Sweden's Development Cooperation with the Middle East and North Africa (MENA) 2016-2020.

Nixon, J., & Ulmann, P. (2006). The relationship between health care expenditure and health outcomes. *The European Journal of Health Economics*, *7*(1), 7–18. doi:10.100710198-005-0336-8 PMID:16429295

Nketiah-Amponsah, E. (2019). The Impact of Health Expenditures on Health Outcomes in Sub-Saharan Africa. *Journal of Developing Societies*, *35*(1), 134–152. doi:10.1177/0169796X19826759

Novignon, J., Olakojo, S. A., & Nonvignon, J. (2012). The effects of public and private health care expenditure on health status in sub-Saharan Africa: New evidence from panel data analysis. *Health Economics Review*, *2*(1), 22. doi:10.1186/2191-1991-2-22 PMID:23232089

Ogden, J., Morrison, K., & Hardee, K. (2013). Social capital to strengthen health policy and health systems. *Health Policy and Planning*, *29*(8), 1075–1085. doi:10.1093/heapol/czt087 PMID:24277736

Or, Z. (2000). Determinants of health outcomes in industrialised countries: a pooled, cross-country, time-series analysis. *OECD Economic Studies*.

Pedroni, P. (1999). Critical values for cointegration tests in heterogeneous panels with multiple regressors. *Oxford Bulletin of Economics and Statistics*, *61*(1), 653–670. doi:10.1111/1468-0084.61.s1.14

Pedroni, P. (2001). Fully modified OLS for heterogeneous cointegrated panels. In *Nonstationary panels, panel cointegration, and dynamic panels* (pp. 93–130). Emerald Group Publishing Limited.

Sayım, F. (2011). Mena Ülkelerinde Sağlık Ekonomisi. In H. Genç & F. Sayım (Eds.), *Ortadoğu ve Afrika Ülkelerinin Ekonomik Yapısı MENA Ülkeleri Ekonomisi* (pp. 151–175). Bursa: MKM Yayınları.

Shaw, J. W., Horrace, W. C., & Vogel, R. J. (2005). The determinants of life expectancy: An analysis of the OECD health data. *Southern Economic Journal*, *71*(4), 768–783. doi:10.2307/20062079

Shi, X., Li, J., Wang, F., Dinçer, H., & Yüksel, S. (2019). A Hybrid Decision-Making Approach for the Service and Financial-Based Measurement of Universal Health Coverage for the E7 Economies. *International Journal of Environmental Research and Public Health*, *16*(18), 3295. doi:10.3390/ijerph16183295 PMID:31500288

Ssozi, J., & Amlani, S. (2015). The effectiveness of health expenditure on the proximate and ultimate goals of healthcare in Sub-Saharan Africa. *World Development*, *76*, 165–179. doi:10.1016/j.worlddev.2015.07.010

(2006). The Lancet. *Middle East Health*, *367*, 961–964.

The World Bank. (n.d.). World Health Organization's Global Health Workforce Statistics Database. Retrieved from https://data.worldbank.org/indicator/SH.MED.PHYS.ZS

The World Bank. (n.d.). World Development Indicators Database. Retrieved from https://databank.worldbank.org/source/world-development-indicators/preview/on.

Tüylüoğlu, Ş., & Tekin, M. (2009). Gelir Düzeyi ve Sağlık Harcamalarının Beklenen Yaşam Süresi ve Bebek Ölüm Oranı Üzerindeki Etkileri. *Çukurova Üniversitesi İktisadi ve İdari Bilimler Fakültesi Dergisi, 13*(1), 1-31.

Van den Heuvel, W. J., & Olaroiu, M. (2017). How important are health care expenditures for life expectancy? A comparative, European analysis. *Journal of the American Medical Directors Association, 18*(3), 276–289. doi:10.1016/j.jamda.2016.11.027 PMID:28131720

Ventelou, B., & Abu-Zaineh, M. (2016). Medicine and democracy: The importance of institutional quality in the relationship between health expenditure and health outcomes in the MENA region. *Health Policy (Amsterdam), 120*(8), 928–935. doi:10.1016/j.healthpol.2016.06.005 PMID:27370915

Wang, H., & Yazbeck, A. S. (2017). Benchmarking health Systems in Middle Eastern and North African Countries. *Health Systems & Reform, 3*(1), 7–13. doi:10.1080/23288604.2016.1272983 PMID:31514711

Yazbeck, A. S. (2017). *Tamer S. Rabie & Aaka Pande*. Health Sector Reform.

Ziesemer, T. (2016). The Impact of Development Aid on Education and Health: Survey and New Evidence for Low-income Countries from Dynamic Models. *Journal of International Development, 28*(8), 1358–1380. doi:10.1002/jid.3223

ENDNOTES

1 World Bank Data, https://data.worldbank.org/indicator/SP.DYN.LE00.IN?locations=SY-TR

2 World Bank Data, https://data.worldbank.org/indicator/SH.XPD.CHEX.GD.ZS

Chapter 12
Improving Health and Efficiency With Strategic Social Media Use in Health Organizations:
A Critical Review of the Status Quo

Gokhan Aydin
https://orcid.org/0000-0002-5652-8694
Istanbul Medipol University, Turkey

ABSTRACT

The emergence of social networking systems as mainstream applications and an inherent element of daily life is a phenomenon observed throughout the world as the worldwide social media users exceeds 2.7 billion. Similar to other sectors, healthcare organizations have also started benefiting from social media in distinct ways such as collecting feedback, educating, communicating and supporting patients and citizens. Social networks can act as remarkable channels for healthcare providers, governmental institutions, pharmaceutical companies, hospitals and others to educate, communicate to, listen, connect to and engage existing and potential customers, patients, physicians and healthcare professionals. Despite the various benefits offered, health institutions, health professionals and stakeholders are reluctant to utilize social media due to several barriers and lack of expertise. This chapter aims to provide a better understanding on the ways healthcare companies can utilize social networks in detail to overcome use barriers and obtain related benefits.

DOI: 10.4018/978-1-7998-2329-2.ch012

INTRODUCTION

Currently the Internet has become an important and integral part of daily life throughout the world. In line with decreasing cost of communication and rapidly growing population with access to the Internet, new opportunities have arisen, new economies have been devised and current ones have been transformed. Even small-sized organizations now have the ability to directly reach millions of individual citizens and potential customers. This ability to reach millions was only available through the use of intermediaries and was commonly a unique capability of larger, well-established institutions (Palmer & Koenig-Lewis, 2009). The developments in the last decade regarding enabling technologies such as the Internet, communication technologies, Web 2.0 and social networking sites (SNS) have transformed the daily lives of billions of consumers and companies alike. Among the most significant developments, the emergence of SNS as mainstream applications is a phenomenon observed not only in developed countries but also globally. The estimated number of global users of social media have exceeded 2.7 billion in 2018 and is expected to reach to 2.95 billion in 2020 (Clement, 2018). On the other hand, the increase in number of people interacting with each other and companies and creating content themselves have led to an exponential increase of data available to institutions and consumers. It has become particularly difficult to process and evaluate all the data available to individuals and organizations alike to acquire relevant information. Web 2.0 technologies have been diffusing to the healthcare arena as well. Social media use in healthcare is becoming a significant issue in a variety of ways. Effective use of SNS can enable cost-effective healthcare professional (physician) - patient communication and exchange of relevant information and experience among patients. Moreover, it is possible for companies (e.g. pharmaceutical) to collect data from patients to explore new medical knowledge or confirm existing knowledge. Moreover, epidemic trend detection and education of citizens are promising areas that governmental bodies and Non-Governmental Organizations (NGOs) can utilize via social networks to improve and sustain public health.

Despite all the benefits offered, health institutions, professionals and stakeholders are reluctant to utilize social media fully. There are several barriers and lack of expertise in the healthcare industry on effective social media use. This chapters aims to highlight the distinct ways social networking sites can be utilized to benefit all stakeholders of healthcare industry. The barriers that are hindering wider adoption of social media in healthcare organizations and recommendations for relevant healthcare institutions, professionals and governmental bodies are provided in the following pages of this chapter.

BACKGROUND

Origin of Health 2.0: From Web 1.0 to Web 2.0

It is argued that the most successful period for technology companies was experienced after 2001. This coincides with the emergence of Web 2.0, whose most important aspect is the interaction capability provided to users. Individuals can conveniently interact and communicate with the companies and other users and through the content everyone create. Web 2.0 offers not a read-only system that users access to get informed but an editable platform that can be used in distinct ways by users. Unlike its predecessor, Web 2.0 facilitates the interaction between users and websites, and provides an abundance of interactivity, participation, and sharing. Countless successful enterprises such as YouTube, Facebook and Skype emerged after 2001 and benefited from Web 2.0 technologies. Furthermore, the general social networking sites (SNS) such as Facebook and Twitter that are positioned to reap the benefits offered by Web 2.0 have also emerged during this period. Before furthering the discussion it is best to define the social networks as “a group of internet-based applications that were built on the ideological and technological foundations of Web 2.0 and that allow creation and exchange of user generated content” (Kaplan & Haenlein, 2010).

Web 2.0 technologies connect people with each other mainly through SNS, which have created opportunities and challenges for managers and marketers. Within the changing digital environment, the online and offline strategies are being integrated and multi-channel approaches are becoming more common as online media and social networks are used more commonly for sharing information rapidly. The power is shifting from sellers to buyers as information transparency increases and consumers’ trust in each other exceeds their trust in companies. Following the media fragmentation (increasing number of channels to reach information), online connections are becoming more critical as everyone is a becoming a content producer.

Through the Web 2.0, not only a limited technologically savvy portion of the population, but a large majority of users obtained the ability to create and share content online conveniently. Ranging from short text comments to long videos, creation and sharing of content became commonplace with the enabling technologies and proliferating social networking services. In general these systems are also called social media and have become an integral part of daily life. They are used in many different ways from entertainment to information gathering and learning. Among these, a significant area of information seeking is focused on healthcare and well-being of consumers. SNS offer various ways to help users in reaching the health related information and support they seek online (Sarasohn-Kahn, 2008).

Commonly, Web 2.0, social media and social networking sites are used interchangeably, moreover, this concept is also called the “new media” from a communication professional's perspective. A comparison of social media to traditional media provided in Table 1 may help in exploring the concept in more detail. As can be seen from this table, social media is focused on sharing, interactivity and collaboration whereas traditional media is a more inflexible system that focuses on one-way communication.

In the Web 2.0 era, the Internet has progressed from a one-way broadcasting medium to a participatory, and collaborative platform which allows people to easily share the content they generate (Thevenot, 2007). The emergence of SNS as mainstream applications is a phenomenon observed not only in developed countries but also globally. The estimated number of global users of social media have exceeded 2.3 billion in 2016 and is expected to reach to 2.95 billion in year 2020 (Clement, 2018). Parallel to their popularity, social networks have proliferated and several types of sites that have become an integral part of daily lives of consumers and professionals have emerged. These different social network types are pondered in the following section.

Social Networking Sites

To explore social network sites in a more systematic way, the following Table 2 developed upon a categorization by Constantinides and Fountain (2008) identifies basic principal categories of social network types.

Table 1. Properties of traditional and social media, developed upon (Stokes, 2011, p. 125)

Traditional Media	Social Media
Fixed system	Instantly updateable system
Limited commentary and interactivity	Unlimited commentary and interactivity
Feedback/commentary not in real-time	Real-time commentary and interactivity
Limited, time-delayed bestseller/popularity lists	Instant popularity gauge
Hard to measure	Easy to measure
Access to archives is hard & limited	Archives easily accessible
Limited media mix	Different types of media can be mixed
Committee / institutional publishers	Individual publishers
Finite communication	Infinite communication
Sharing not encouraged	Sharing and participation encouraged
Controlled environment	Free environment

Among the more commonly accepted category of social networks is the general social network sites, which is also termed as social media sites. Facebook is currently the most popular SNS in the world with more than 1.4 billion active members, 82% of whom are living outside its birthplace, the U.S. (Socialbakers, 2018). Twitter,

Table 2. Social network types

Social Network	Definition
Blogs & Microblogs	Web-logs, the first type of Web 2.0 applications that are considered as "social media" were developed before the year 2000. Web-logs are commonly referred as blogs currently. They can be considered as journals that individuals' or institutions publish online. A blog is a quick and easy way to publish and share content online. Posts can be text only or enriched with audio or visual content and podcasts. It is still a popular way to establish a basic presence online. Another version of blogs is the micro-blogs pioneered by Twitter. Microblogs are used for quick information distribution, fast / real-time communication and social networking. Twitter is a blog service that allows networks of users to send short updates to each other.
General Social networking sites	General SNS are applications that provide their users the ability to build personal online spaces accessible to other users. These sites are used to connect, communicate, interact and stay in touch with friends and family and offer convenient two-way communication and interaction (Steinfield, Ellison, & Lampe, 2008). Facebook, the most popular social networking site throughout the world is a good example of this category.
Thematic & Professional Networking Sites	Thematic networking sites are social network services that are specialized on a certain topic such as health. Thus, they are preferred by a subset of Internet users with specific needs. Professional networking sites are a subset of these thematic SNS that focus on communication and interactions between professionals and business executives (e.g. Linkedin). Sites that provide a discussion and communication platform for health professionals are among the examples of this SNS category (e.g. Sermo, Doximity etc.).
Content sharing sites & communities	Content sharing sites are SNS that systematically organize and classify information (e.g. specific types of content) and share it on their own platform. Online sites/ services that provide individuals to create galleries of graphical content (photos / videos) or other content such as presentations are categorized in this category. The service provider stores and makes the content available to other users publicly or privately (e.g. Flickr, 5oopx).
Forums/bulletin boards	Forums are websites that are devoted to exchanging ideas and information on special interests. They can be related to hobbies, shopping, or more significant topics such as healthcare. They are valuable sources of information through discussions and questions and answers.
Content aggregators & & collaborative filtering sites	Websites/online services in this category allow their members to customize the web content they wish to access in various ways. A website where information is filtered or collected according to patterns such as StumbleUpon and del.icio.us are examples of this category. Different practices to enable collaboration among multiple agents, viewpoints, and data sources are often used in these sites.
Instant Messaging Apps	The popularity of instant messaging apps increased in the last decade rapidly and with the novel attributes they've become popular applications considered under the larger SNS category. WhatsApp, WeChat, Snapchat are among the examples of this category that enable quick messaging and content shares among closed groups of friends. They offer better prospects in rapid two way communication than e-mail.

acting as a micro-blogging site and a general social networking site is among the most popular SNSs with 330 million monthly active users, 79% of which are located outside the US (Statista, 2019b). Twitter is used by the companies and marketing professionals as a real-time marketing and guerrilla marketing platform as well. With an open structure, large, distributed conversations going on throughout the world, Twitter offers a plethora of information to both companies and users (Twitter Inc., 2017). To highlight the other popular SNS, the number of estimated active users for the largest social networks are provided in Figure 1.

Web 2.0 and Healthcare = Health 2.0

The so-called Web 2.0 technologies that enable instant two-way communication and easy content creation parallel to the emergence of SNS are empowering consumers by educating them and helping them in providing and getting feedback and recommendations. From a wide perspective, social media can be used to collect and/or relay information by carrying out conversations. Information on various trends on products, consumption, brands, diseases, symptoms and customer feedback (including complaints) can be collected.

The use of social media in health care is termed as Health 2.0, which can be defined as: "the use of social software and its ability to promote collaboration

Figure 1. Major social networks' number of active users (Statista, 2019a)

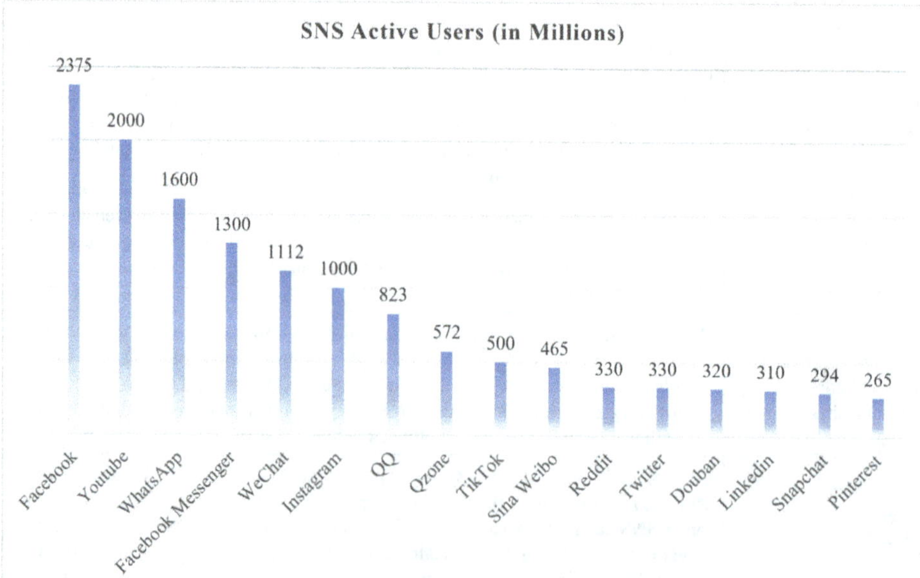

between patients, their caregivers, medical professionals, and other stakeholders in health" (Sarasohn-Kahn, 2008, p. 2). Within the Health 2.0 setting, consumers with chronic health conditions can share their experiences with each other. This is helpful for informational purposes also for providing emotional support for the receiver of this experience. Gaining insights of similar patients with comparable health backgrounds that can be found in social networks and online communities may offer valuable feedback to patients. On the other hand of the spectrum, physicians and health professionals are also utilizing social media as well. Health professionals can share their views on problems and recent developments in healthcare, try to solve challenging cases with their peers and try to come up with efficient solutions to problems at hand.

Health 2.0 enables interaction between the physicians, organizations and consumers, which may lead to beneficial outcomes for all parties involved. Social networks can act as a great channel for pharmaceutical companies, healthcare providers, hospitals and many others to educate, communicate to, listen, connect and engage with existing and potential customers, patients, physicians and healthcare professionals (Jorner, 2018). Researchers and physicians can learn about patients' experiences, side-effects, follow their recovery and collect feedback. Organizations can follow trends, analyze the feedback they have received and provide support over social networks. Not surprisingly thousands of hospitals and health institutions are using social media actively through their own accounts (Li, Wang, Lin, & Hajli, 2018). The ways healthcare companies can utilize social networks is categorized and contemplated in the following sections of this chapter to offer a good understanding of each potential activity.

Word of Mouth (WOM)

Before the emergence of the Internet and social media, many organizations valued the traditional word of mouth highly and used it to gain loyal customers in a cost-effective way. In the current age of Web 2.0, traditional ways of creating buzz is enhanced in a substantial way. Creating word of mouth online, which is termed as online WOM or "e-WOM", was made possible with the emergence of new technologies and ways to share content (Hennig-Thurau & Walsh, 2003). The ease of sharing comments, opinions and various types of content instantly on SNS is the basis of the significance of e-WOM. The content generated by organizations and users will spread rapidly if it can get the attention of large groups of users (e.g. shares, re-tweets etc.) and will reach to a much larger group than traditional word-of-mouth. As e-WOM can be established rapidly, it can act as a double-edged sword. The considerably greater reach made possible through the use of SNS and the relative ease of use to create and share content creates this powerful yet hard to control tool. A simple comment made on a social media site can influence thousands or even millions in certain circumstances. Consequently, an organization has to manage social media carefully and systematically by establishing a strategy and related sharing policies and reputation management systems that can quickly respond to criticisms and negative e-WOM. Online reputation management systems basically utilizes SNS and similar digital channels to monitor and analyze a brand's reputation and engage in conversation to improve its reputation (Stokes, 2011, pp. 420–421). This is also a noteworthy topic for public health professionals. Promoting content to create positive-WOM yet preventing the spread of misinformation (e.g. public display of unhealthy behavior and promotion of harmful products) is not straightforward. There's almost no control on e-WOM even for governmental organizations. The significance of e-WOM is further elaborated in recommendations section of this chapter.

SOCIAL MEDIA USE IN HEALTHCARE

Issues and Problems

Given the abundance of platforms considered under the larger SNS categorizations, there are numerous relevant use cases for consumers, organizations and health professionals. For instance, clinician to patient communication, patient to patient communication, online health information search, sharing healthcare experiences, dissemination of health information, chronic disease management, marketing communication, professional training of healthcare personnel are among the major areas that attract interest of researchers, policy makers and practitioners (Zhou, Zhang, Yang, & Wang, 2018). Each distinct way of using SNS has its own benefits, issues and barriers that are pondered in detail in this section.

Social Networks for Consumers (motives / uses, benefits & barriers)

The power owned by organizations in the 1900s has shifted towards the consumers in the new millennia. The empowerment of consumers is related to increased information availability and the content that users generate themselves. The open democracy culture and the ability to share information quickly using Web 2.0 technologies have decreased information asymmetry (Leung, 2013; Strauss & Frost, 2013). Thus, SNS have become popular platforms consumers utilize for a variety of reasons. They can be used to stay in touch with friends, family and colleagues, to interact with brands and organizations. Social networks provide up-to-date information on current events promptly and it is possible to share opinions and thoughts on various subjects. Moreover, they are good platforms to meet other people, do networking and even to pass idle time and get entertained.

Consumers are increasingly utilizing the Internet and social networks to search for health information. According to a study carried out by Pew Internet Project in US, over 70% of Internet users seek health information online (Zhou et al., 2018). The basic motives for consumers utilizing social networks in a healthcare context are as follows (Antheunis, Tates, & Nieboer, 2013; Li et al., 2018; Lin, Zhang, Song, & Omori, 2016; Moorhead et al., 2013):

- Increasing knowledge on health problems / symptoms / diseases.
- Expressing one's thoughts and emotions on a health problem / disease / adverse effects.
- Sharing one's experience on a health problem / disease and its treatment (medicines, therapies, etc.).
- Giving advice to patients with similar problems.
- Getting advice / consultation from health professionals or other patients with similar problems.
- Providing personal information on one's current health and updating friends and others.

On specialized social networks such as PatientsLikeMe, HealthBoards, MedHelp, HealthUnlocked, patients from several countries assemble to share their personal experiences on medicine use, side effects they have experienced, and their treatment histories for a wide range of conditions. Special interest group pages on Facebook also offer a similar and convenient way to access and share health information and experiences, also to get emotional support from community members. These specialized SNS are becoming a preferred avenue to reach information by citizens (Greene, Choudhry, Kilabuk, & Shrank, 2011; Lin et al., 2016). As their number of members increase, the SNS's effectiveness also increases through positive network effects. The more participants there are in a social network — the foundation of Health 2.0 — the more value they create.

Despite the benefits of social networking systems, the vast amount of available information which is of questionable quality, makes it hard for citizens and patients to find useful and relevant information. Moreover, there are several limitations posed by SNS and certain barriers exist to use them effectively. The barriers that consumers face and the limitations they perceive in using social networks may be summarized as follows (Antheunis et al., 2013; Bates, Romina, Ahmed, & Hopson, 2006; Li et al., 2018; Lin et al., 2016; Moorhead et al., 2013):

- Lack of confidentiality & privacy.

- Patients are not fully aware of the risks of disclosing information online.
- Unreliability and unknown quality of information.
- Inefficiency of systems.
- Lack of trust to the SNS.
- Risks associated with communicating harmful or incorrect advice using social media.
- Information overload in using SNS.
- Amount of time required to seek and find relevant information.
- Not sure how to correctly apply information found online to their personal health situation.
- Adverse health consequences and potential negative health behaviors.

The privacy concern is related to the fact that the patients want to stay anonymous and do not want to be known as patients on the social networks.

Social Networks for Healthcare Professionals (Motives / Uses, Benefits and Barriers)

As mentioned during discussing social network types, SNS are not focused only on consumers but also cater to professionals as well. These networks that have been set up to exchange information about a specific area of interest offer opportunities to professionals that are harder to establish on general SNS. For instance, LinkedIn can be used to reach professionals working in a specific field such as healthcare, with certain expertise and are of a certain managerial level. Moreover, social networks that are catered for physicians such as Sermo and Doximity offer their members platforms for learning, personal development and collaboration. These sites, along with closed groups on general SNS (e.g. Facebook) are popular among medical doctors, but also cater to pharmacists, nurse practitioners and physician assistants. Specialized SNS platforms and groups such as these enable and encourage discussion of cases with other healthcare providers and staying up to date with the current developments and advancements in medicine in a convenient way. When healthcare professionals share their expertise with each other on SNS, the results they get usually go well beyond an individual interchange of clinical experiences and insights thanks to the collective wisdom (Sarasohn-Kahn, 2008). Technically, the value created by networks increase with the increasing number of members due to the positive network effects.

Considering the examples provided and the academic studies on SNS use of health professionals, several noteworthy motives emerge, which may be listed as follows (Moorhead et al., 2013):

- Providing health information on a range of conditions to promote and improve health.
- Provide general or specific answers to medical questions raised by patients and other healthcare professionals.
- Facilitate one-to-one dialogue with patients and other healthcare professionals.
- Collecting feedback and data on patient experiences and opinions from patients and healthcare professionals.
- Providing and getting online consultations and medical experience of peers and experts.
- For health intervention, health promotion and health education.
- For reducing stigma.

Despite the wide breadth of available ways to utilize social media, SNS use is limited among health professionals. First of all, when utilizing social media sites, health care professionals are obligated to adhere to ethical and professional conduct standards of their relevant profession, similar to other types of communication that they carry out. Moreover, institutional guidelines may limit or suppress the use of social media among their employees to overcome possible problems related to privacy, confidentiality and reputations. In addition to these barriers, several studies provide insights on further use barriers that health professionals perceive in adopting SNS for professional use (Antheunis et al., 2013; Moorhead et al., 2013):

- Privacy concerns & lack of confidentiality.
- Not feeling a need for using it.
- Legal grounds.
- Inefficiency of SNS systems.
- Lack of relevant skills to use social media effectively.
- Social media may act as a deterrent for patients from visiting health professionals.
- Lack of proper compensation provided for giving advice on SNS.
- Lack of reliability.
- Quality concerns.

Moreover, using social media ethically and without creating adverse legal consequences is not straightforward. To prevent possible issues, the medical associations throughout the world have started publishing guidelines for health professionals in using social media (Australian Medical Association Council, 2010; British Medical Association, 2019) in addition to the institutional guidelines prepared by large healthcare providers such as MayoClinic (Gagnon & Sabus, 2015).

Social Networks for Organizations (Motives / Uses, Benefits and *Barriers)*

SNS can act as a great channel for companies such as health tracking device manufacturers, pharmaceutical companies, hospitals and many others to educate, communicate to, listen, connect and engage with their existing and potential customers, patients, physicians and healthcare professionals. Various ways healthcare companies can use social networks is contemplated in this section to provide a good understanding of popular possible activities.

Organizations in healthcare industry may benefit from social networks in a multitude of ways such as:

- Collecting feedback and information.
- Relaying information to educate patients.
- Public relations.
- Improving physician-patient communication.
- Improving internal communication, discussion and problem solving.
- Data collection and trend detection.

Social media can be used as a platform to find new customers also to help consumers in finding organizations. Existing customers, potential ones and influencers can all be engaged using social media to obtain various positive outcomes. Creating a bond, increasing loyalty, attracting talent can all be obtained using social networks effectively. In addition, engagement with customers and influencers may lead to actionable insights and intelligence by utilizing data on SNS. Using social media systematically can lead to strategic value for organization if it is used to produce solutions for issues at hand and to strategically developing innovative ideas.

Using conversations and two-way communication, the organizations can collect feedback to understand and attract more customers and retain them by answering their needs rapidly. Various consumption trends, diseases, or customer feedback can be collected via social media. This information can help in segmenting and targeting consumers in a better way. Listening consumers on social networks is less intrusive than actively communicating with them on these platforms. In social networks, the users feel a sense of ownership of the network and its community, so consumers may be resentful of intrusion into their own perceived community space by companies (Palmer & Koenig-Lewis, 2009). In this way, effective use of social media as a customer relationship tool that can help improving brand loyalty is possible (D. Leung, Law, van Hoof, & Buhalis, 2013). The term "social media listening" defining the continuous process of identifying and monitoring what's being said about a company/brand or a topic of interest online have become a popular one in the last decade. However, a thorough analysis of massive amounts of data published on SNS requires significant investments, which only a small percentage of companies are willing to, in arriving at actionable outcomes. For instance, SouthWest Airlines has a "listening center" to centrally manage all the data coming from social networks, online industry and their internal operations. This center monitors what customers are talking about the company, industry, or a specific topic of interest to the company. Keyword-based listening is used to collect data in terms of mentions from social networks such as Twitter and blogs. Integrating this data with operational information, real-time insights can be generated to identify issues and opportunities to engage customers rapidly (Dupre, 2014).

Another way social networks can be used is for marketing communication and public relations. As a communication tool, social media can help companies in increasing conversations and their exposure (Bermúdez-Tamayo et al., 2013). These conversations may be on products, services trends, problems, suggestions and can be carried out with customers, potential customers, admirers of the brand, suppliers, influencers, employees and even competitors. As the trust in the advertisements are falling, SNS offer more promising avenues to establish trust in marketing communication. It has been found that customers find their friends and colleagues' as more credible sources than company's own communication such as advertising. This is a relevant phenomenon validated for professional and personal services providers (Cheung, Luo, Sia, & Chen, 2009; Harrison-Walker, 2001; Zichermann & Cunningham, 2011). Relatedly, the trust in WOM (both offline and online) is on the rise as evidenced by global research company Nielsen on a study on 28,000 people living in 56 countries. The 83% of the respondents indicated that the recommendations they get from their family, friends and colleagues is the most credible source of information. The second most reliable source of information appeared as the online WOM with 66% of respondents indicating that online comments in various social networks are the most reliable in this study (Nielsen, 2015). Another study carried out in the US and Canada demonstrated that 88% of consumers find online comments as credible as comments from personally acquainted sources (Murphy, 2018). These studies highlight the critical role of SNS as a communication medium and a way to relay messages in a more credible manner. Using social media effectively can also lower the costs of communication, customer relationship management, complaint handling and idea generation through crowdsourcing (Arora & Predmore, 2013).

Albeit the prospects of using social media, there are certain risks involved for the companies and they are faced with a dilemma when planning their SNS strategies. Increasing two-way communication to reach consumers and get feedback is a lucrative opportunity, however, if not managed effectively and timely, it can lead to problems that have significant impacts due to the open-to-all nature of content shared through SNS. Organizations use as many communication channels as possible to reach a wider audience, yet this is set-back by the resources they can put into managing all these channels. Making sure that the communication created by the company provides high-quality and consistent messages to target audiences require resources such as time, effort and careful planning. The content created by SNS users regarding each organization is virtually impossible to control. On the other hand, these communications can be handled through careful and timely responses that support the brand promise and company values when needed. These factors may be among the reasons that not all healthcare institutions embrace social media. As evidenced in a study by Bermúdez-Tamayo et al. (2013) in Spain, SNS are used more often by larger hospitals that have access to more resources.

Social Networks for Policy Makers and Governmental Institutions

A good way for governmental institutions in utilizing SNS is for public health surveillance and tracking epidemic diseases (Chunara, Andrews, & Brownstein, 2012; McGough, Brownstein, Hawkins, & Santillana, 2017). Moreover, attitudes of the public towards specific public health issues may be analyzed via sentiment analysis using SNS data (Yang, Lee, & Kuo, 2016). Utilizing the data available online on SNS, disease trend prediction with good predictive accuracy is possible as evidenced by several researchers (Denecke et al., 2013; Hors-Fraile et al., 2016; Signorini, Segre, & Polgreen, 2011; Velasco, Agheneza, Denecke, Kirchner, & Eckmanns, 2014; M. Yang, Kiang, & Shang, 2015). For instance, Sickweather, a start-up focusing on social networks was able to use the online conversations to predict flu season in the US. Listening (monitoring conversation) about flu symptoms online, Sickweather saw a 30% increase of flu chatter in October compared to the previous year, which led them to predict that the flu season have started earlier (Sass, 2012). By using SNS, public health professionals may get more valuable and timely health information on different geographical levels, which may be used to improve health outcomes.

Moreover, discovering adverse drug reactions and drug-drug interactions are possible utilizing the online SNS data (Correia, Li, & Rocha, 2016; Nguyen et al., 2017). To carry out such studies, text mining and information extraction has been widely used in the literature. Drug and disease names, common symptoms of adverse drug reactions and interactions are among the major types of textual content mined from SNS such as blogs. These approaches can be either lexicon (dictionary) and knowledge- based methods or machine learning methods (Zhou et al., 2018). Further information on methodologies may be found in the aforementioned studies as it is beyond the scope of this chapter.

RECOMMENDATIONS

The rapid adoption of social media worldwide and the level of popularity among users have not yet been matched by most organizations in healthcare. A large fraction of stakeholders such as physicians, healthcare institution managers, academic institutions and governmental bodies are unacquainted with the power of social media and entire potential applications. Their use in communication, information gathering, customer relations and daily operations are not pondered in detail. Moreover, the risks involved in using these networks, crises management and reputation management are not well thought of (Grajales, Sheps, Ho, Novak-Lauscher, & Eysenbach, 2014). The following subsections offer best practices derived from social media research and industry reports that may help in overcoming barriers and solving relevant problems in a variety of SNS use cases. Moreover, various types of social media applications in healthcare are listed as follows to offer a concise list for practitioners (Chew & Eysenbach, 2010; Eysenbach, 2011; Kapp, Peters, & Oliver, 2013; Li et al., 2018; Seeman, Ing, & Rizo, 2010):

- Marketing communication aimed at existing and potential customers.
- Creating online communities to connect with patients/customers and collecting direct feedback.
- Enabling patient interaction in online communities to establish psychological benefits.
- Educating customers and patients by sharing relevant content and answering questions (Li et al., 2018).
- Providing access to educational resources to clinicians by establishing blogs and micro-sites (Eysenbach, 2011).
- Establishing discussion platforms to healthcare professionals to share medical expertise and collaborate.
- Establishing reference resources that is content rich and focused on healthcare aiming public and patients (specialized wikis).
- Public health surveillance, evaluation of real-time epidemic disease trends (Seeman et al., 2010),
- Increasing outreach and engagement of public health campaigns (Chew & Eysenbach, 2010).
- Recruitment to clinical trials and online healthcare studies (Kapp et al., 2013).
- Uncovering disease trends by social listening of social networks such as Twitter (Denecke et al., 2013).
- Improving internal communication and employee empowerment in organizations (Arora & Predmore, 2013).

Public Health Monitoring

Parallel to the increasing SNS use, a growing number of patients utilize online platforms and SNS to describe and their healthcare experiences and emotions. As a consequence, it is possible to obtain information regarding poor quality healthcare service, epidemics, disease trends, drug use etc. utilizing the publicly available SNS data (Greaves, Ramirez-Cano, Millett, Darzi, & Donaldson, 2013; Velasco et al., 2014). Broadly four different sources of data are available for carrying out relevant analysis: rating and feedback websites (Greaves et al., 2013), patient networks, discussion platforms, blogs and general social media (Facebook, Twitter). Among these platforms, information in the form of rating scores, text descriptions of healthcare providers and patients' experiences with them, comments on health provider pages and public messages send to healthcare providers are the major data that can be utilized. Yet, this data does not always reflect the reality fully. The data collected in this manner may not be representative of all target groups and a bias towards higher education and income group may be evident especially in underdeveloped regions. Another issue is that the content shared on review sites are open to manipulation and may be uploaded by employees, agencies or paid individuals. Lastly, the posts on Facebook, Twitter and similar platforms are short, and it is not very common to share details of health-related issues on these platforms, making it hard to arrive at deep and detailed insights.

Educating Patients and Citizens

It was observed that SNS may be used in protecting citizens from public health threats as a convenient and effective communication channel during epidemics (Hors-Fraile et al., 2016; Velasco et al., 2014). Disease-specific or health service/ product specific educational information can be relayed to customers/citizens. This communication can present non-biased information on diseases and help patients understand their symptoms and get into touch and engage with their healthcare providers to improve outcomes. It was discussed by Gagnon & Sabus (2015) that creating a social media presence to provide credible and high-quality health care information on fitness, wellness, and rehabilitation is an obligation for healthcare professionals. For instance, Johnson & Johnson worked together with an organization aiming for an "AIDS Free Generation" to create a social media campaign to educate customers on AIDS. Johnson & Johnson donated one dollar to the Global Fund to fight AIDS for every share or tweet of an informative AIDS infographic on social media (Olenski, 2013). Thus, increasing awareness and fund-raising was realized together over social media.

Yet, the power of SNS and the open structure of these systems may also lead to dissemination of disinformation. There are several cases of misinformation against vaccination, promoting anorexia etc. that has been circulating on various online platforms such as YouTube (Madathil, Rivera-Rodriguez, Greenstein, & Gramopadhye, 2015). Moreover, SNS such as YouTube are used for promoting controversial and unscientific drugs and ineffective / harmful therapies (Madathil et al., 2015). In a study by Lau, Gabarron, Fernandez-luque and Armayones (2012), five problematic areas for citizens regarding healthcare on YouTube use were identified as follows:

- Harmful product promotion (tobacco or drug advertising)
- Public display of unhealthy behavior (self-injury or hurting others)
- Tainted public health messages (e.g. anti-vaccination)
- Psychological impact of inappropriate, offensive content
- Distorting policy and research funding agendas

There are several ways to overcome these problems. First, activity of online bloggers, influencers and related company accounts (e.g. uncertified drug promoters etc.) on SNS may be listened and real time counter-marketing strategies and activities may be carried out to limit the adverse effects on public health (Seeman et al., 2010). Higher participation and better promotion of content from credible sources such as healthcare professionals, relevant NGOs and governmental bodies may help in decreasing the effect of misleading buzz created on SNS. Thus, tracking and analyzing the health-related information and shares on SNS and incentivizing and promoting credible sharers may both be beneficial for public health.

Utilizing Patient Communities

Another way to better utilize SNS in healthcare is by creating patient support communities. Patients with certain diseases / conditions can be allowed to connect to each other, communicate and interact to discuss the benefits or side effects of a particular treatment, physician or healthcare facility to help and support each other. It was found that supportive traditional social networks (offline) improves health outcomes for individuals with several conditions such as depression, preoperative pain and anxiety (Hopkins & Campbell, 2008; Mitchinson, Kim, Geisser, Rosenberg, & Hinshaw, 2008). Moreover, patients with rare diseases are faced with several difficulties such as extensive travelling in diagnosis and finding similar patients that have experienced the same problems as them. SNS helps patients in obtaining information on a rare disease and develop a close-knit community to ease their emotional burden (Zhou et al., 2018).

Online social networks have also been found to lead to improvements in health literacy (Benetoli, Chen, & Aslani, 2018). When patients managing the same chronic condition share observations with each other, their collective wisdom can yield clinical insights well beyond the understanding of any single patient. Misleading health and treatment related information on SNS can be overcome by self-correcting through attracting a high number of active members that contribute to discussions (Sarasohn-Kahn, 2008). Yet patients are more eager in reading about health information on SNS than posting about their health (Weaver, Lindsay, & Gitelman, 2012).

Communicating with Healthcare Professionals

In a systematic review by Smailhodzic, Hooijsma, Boonstra and Langley (2016) on social media use in healthcare, patient-healthcare professional relationship was found to be affected by SNS use. They have indicated that more equal communication between the patient and healthcare professional, harmonious relationships yet increased physician switching, and suboptimal interactions between the patient and healthcare professional were encountered in their review. Similarly, in a recent study, SNS use was found to have a positive impact on patients' health literacy and on communication with healthcare providers as patients feel more empowered and competent in relevant decision-making (Benetoli et al., 2018).

In a separate vein, social media can be used to communicate with physicians-the main target audience of pharmaceutical companies-as an effective way of education and reducing costs of frequent visits. A decrease in the drug representatives' visits may be beneficial for the physician as well, by means of fewer disruptions in physicians' daily schedule. One-to-many and many-to-many communication capabilities offered by social media platforms denotes that pharmaceutical companies can reach and interact with a group of physicians easily. It is also possible to bring together high-profile researchers and best sales representatives in the company with physicians' online, who cannot visit everyone using physical means (Belbey, 2016).

Utilizing Healthcare Professional Communities

Connecting with colleagues worldwide through SNS can be a noteworthy source of learning for health professionals. Professional networks such as LinkedIn should be utilized to a greater extent to get in touch with relevant colleagues and follow the up-to-date content. Yet more specialized communities offer even more value as they can be used to communicate on a special topic more easily without losing focus in a large network. A convenient way to establish such closed communities is using invitation only Facebook groups where health professionals can exchange information regarding specific conditions (Weaver et al., 2012).

Moreover, physicians should educate themselves on the policies of their employers and adhere to the standards set by their employing institution and other professional bodies to overcome any future problems (Gagnon & Sabus, 2015). These two points are valid in communication with the patients and other healthcare professionals as well.

In addition to the general SNS, establishing and utilizing organization-wide internal social networks also offer several benefits. For instance, employees may contribute to solving daily internal issues or future strategy development by providing comments, feedback and starting their own discussions on company-wide social networking systems. Creating a platform for open discussion regardless of seniority or managerial level in an organization helps empowerment of employees motivate them to share and to own projects and initiatives being carried out in the company (Arora & Predmore, 2013). Another role of social media as an internal communication tool and a way to increase motivation, engagement and loyalty among employees is evident.

Clinical Trial Enrollment and Crowdsourcing

Yet another proven way to utilize social media is to use it for crowdsourcing and clinical trial enrollments. Attracting and recruiting individuals to participate in online research initiatives and clinical trials is a major barrier that limits rapid execution of these studies. It is estimated that almost 30% of time is spent on recruitment in these studies. Social media can be used as a good way to increase enrollment and can decrease time and expense devoted to this process (Belbey, 2016; Wisk, Nelson, Magane, & Weitzman, 2019). It was found out that Facebook is among the major SNS with the highest yield recruitment source (Wisk et al., 2019). Given that Facebook is the largest SNS, this finding is not surprising. Facebook ads emerge as a promising tool for recruiting participants for clinical trial studies. Information and guidelines on optimizing the recruitment and enrollment via creating a Facebook presence, designing ads, planning advertising campaigns to attract potential participants is provided by Akers and Gordon (2018).

In addition, category / product managers or product development teams may benefit from crowdsourcing platforms in coming up with improvements and modifications of existing products and new product ideas (Arora & Predmore, 2013). For instance, several companies utilize crowdsourcing in improving both simple and complex products/services they offer and coming up new ones (Starbucks, 2017; Wortman Vaughan, 2018).

Communicating with Customers and Patients

Managing all the online communities and SNS effectively is not a straightforward job. There should be a careful balance established between the control of the content that is steered through the posts of sponsors/companies and the posts of community members. Trying to control the information flow to guide the community and user generated content towards the company's own interests directly may pose problems in engagement and sustainability of these communities (Muniz & O'Guinn, 2001). An indirect approach with minimum perceived intrusion may create a higher sense of belonging among the members of the community (Brown, Broderick, & Lee, 2007). Retail brands such as Starbucks have benefited from online communities they have sponsored to get customer feedback to improve their operations, products and services. Starbucks have gained insights on the current trends and changing customer needs and wants using a crowdsourcing platform named MyStarbuckIdeas that allows customers to see, share, discuss and vote on ideas (Starbucks, 2017).

Actively managing and steering communities may not be the best solution for every institution in all social platforms. The underlying promise of social media for marketers is achieving positive word of mouth and earned media for a brand / company through conversations of consumers. Consequently, an indirect approach without direct intervention of companies may be preferred. This goal may be hard to reach if the intervention of the company that actively tries to direct the buzz about themselves.

In establishing a presence in online communities, it is best to set clear goals beforehand. As discussed throughout this chapter, the ways that SNS can be utilized are numerous and clear goals help in choosing the best ones that fit the organization. To use the social media effectively proper strategic planning should be carried out on which channels to use. The chosen social media should be a good match with the brand values and personality and also a proper platform to reach the target audience.

FUTURE RESEARCH DIRECTIONS

Future research into the use of SNS in healthcare have several promising avenues. Firstly, the increasing data available created by the users on several SNS platforms may be better utilized by the policy makers and pharmaceutical companies and health device/application developers. Yet the quality and accuracy of this data is questionable. Studies that focus on developing methodologies to improve / filter accurate, genuine data and improving the data quality is called for. Another interesting line of research may focus on the effect of privacy of personal information and related legislations on healthcare professionals and institutions social media use behavior.

Collecting and protecting personal information of each patient / customer, storing them securely or deleting them after a certain time limit are not straightforward tasks yet the legislations call for. The changing legal environment on the use of personal information online and the related ethical dilemmas and problems faced by healthcare professionals may be assessed in a variety of legislative settings.

CONCLUSION

Social media use in healthcare from a variety of perspectives ranging from health professionals to organizations and governmental bodies have been pondered in detail throughout this chapter. It is evident that from each stakeholder's perspective, there are abundant opportunities to benefit from SNS use. Yet each use case is utilized in a limited way compared to the total online population and organizations that have a means to access SNS. There is still a long way to go before utilizing the possibilities offered by SNS and the data available in them in healthcare for consumers, organizations and governmental bodies. Relevant use barriers and risks associated with SNS use for each stakeholder should be handled one by one and ways to overcome or lessen the impact of each barrier should be put forward. Future research focusing on the aforementioned issues should help to understand the rapidly changing user behavior, effect of legislations and standards put in force and new technological developments.

REFERENCES

Akers, L., & Gordon, J. S. (2018). Using Facebook for Large-Scale Online Randomized Clinical Trial Recruitment: Effective Advertising Strategies. *Journal of Medical Internet Research*, *20*(11), e290. doi:10.2196/jmir.9372 PMID:30409765

Antheunis, M. L., Tates, K., & Nieboer, T. E. (2013). Patients' and health professionals' use of social media in health care: Motives, barriers and expectations. *Patient Education and Counseling*, *92*(3), 426–431. doi:10.1016/j.pec.2013.06.020 PMID:23899831

Arora, P., & Predmore, C. E. (2013). Social media as a strategic tool: Going beyond the obvious. In *Social Media in Strategic Management* (Vol. 11, pp. 115–127). Emerald Group Publishing Limited; doi:10.1108/S1877-6361(2013)0000011010

Australian Medical Association Council. (2010). A guide to online professionalism for medical practitioners and medical students. Retrieved from https://ama.com.au/article/social-media-and-medical-profession

Bates, B. R., Romina, S., Ahmed, R., & Hopson, D. (2006). The effect of source credibility on consumers' perceptions of the quality of health information on the Internet. *Medical Informatics and the Internet in Medicine, 31*(1), 45–52. doi:10.1080/14639230600552601 PMID:16754366

Belbey, J. (2016). 6 Ways Pharma May Use Social Media. Forbes. Retrieved from https://www.forbes.com/sites/joannabelbey/2016/03/09/6-ways-pharma-may-use-social-media/

Benetoli, A., Chen, T. F., & Aslani, P. (2018). How patients' use of social media impacts their interactions with healthcare professionals. *Patient Education and Counseling, 101*(3), 439–444. doi:10.1016/j.pec.2017.08.015 PMID:28882545

Bermúdez-Tamayo, C., Alba-Ruiz, R., Jiménez-Pernett, J., García Gutiérrez, J.-F., Traver-Salcedo, V., & Yubraham-Sánchez, D. (2013). Use of Social Media by Spanish Hospitals: Perceptions, Difficulties, and Success Factors. *Telemedicine Journal and e-Health, 19*(2), 137–145. doi:10.1089/tmj.2012.0066 PMID:23368890

British Medical Association. (2019). Social media guidance for doctors. Retrieved from https://www.bma.org.uk/advice/employment/ethics/social-media-guidance-for-doctors

Brown, J., Broderick, A. J., & Lee, N. (2007). Word of mouth communication within online communities: Conceptualizing the online social network. *Journal of Interactive Marketing, 21*(3), 2–20. doi:10.1002/dir.20082

Cheung, M. Y., Luo, C., Sia, C. L., & Chen, H. (2009). Credibility of Electronic Word-of-Mouth: Informational and Normative Determinants of On-line Consumer Recommendations. *International Journal of Electronic Commerce, 13*(4), 9–38. doi:10.2753/JEC1086-4415130402

Chew, C., & Eysenbach, G. (2010). Pandemics in the Age of Twitter: Content Analysis of Tweets during the 2009 H1N1 Outbreak. *PLoS One, 5*(11), e14118. doi:10.1371/journal.pone.0014118 PMID:21124761

Chunara, R., Andrews, J. R., & Brownstein, J. S. (2012). Social and news media enable estimation of epidemiological patterns early in the 2010 Haitian cholera outbreak. *American Journal of Tropical Medicine and Hygiene*. Retrieved from http://www.ajtmh.org/content/86/1/39.full.pdf+html%5Cnhttp://ovidsp.ovid.com/ovidweb.cgi?T=JS&PAGE=reference&D=emed10&NEWS=N&AN=2012026627

Clement, J. (2018). Number of social media users worldwide from 2010 to 2021. Statista. Retrieved from https://www.statista.com/topics/1164/social-networks/

Constantinides, E., & Fountain, S. J. (2008). Web 2.0: Conceptual foundations and marketing issues. *Journal of Direct. Data and Digital Marketing Practice*, *9*(3), 231–244. doi:10.1057/palgrave.dddmp.4350098

Correia, R. B., Li, L., & Rocha, L. M. (2016). Monitoring potential drug interactions and reactions via network analysis of instagram user timelines. In Biocomputing 2016 (pp. 492–503). WORLD SCIENTIFIC. doi:10.1142/9789814749411_0045

Denecke, K., Krieck, M., Otrusina, L., Smrz, P., Dolog, P., Nejdl, W., & Velasco, E. (2013). How to exploit twitter for public health monitoring? *Methods of Information in Medicine*, *52*(4), 326–339. doi:10.3414/ME12-02-0010 PMID:23877537

Dupre, E. (2014). Southwest Airlines Takes Customer Listening to New Heights. DM News. Retrieved from http://www.dmnews.com/southwest-airlines-takes-customer-listening-to-new-heights/article/375950/

Eysenbach, G. (2011). Infodemiology and Infoveillance. *American Journal of Preventive Medicine*, *40*(5), S154–S158. doi:10.1016/j.amepre.2011.02.006 PMID:21521589

Gagnon, K., & Sabus, C. (2015). Professionalism in a Digital Age: Opportunities and Considerations for Using Social Media in Health Care. *Physical Therapy*, *95*(3), 406–414. doi:10.2522/ptj.20130227 PMID:24903111

Grajales, F. J., Sheps, S., Ho, K., Novak-Lauscher, H., & Eysenbach, G. (2014). Social media: A review and tutorial of applications in medicine and health care. *Journal of Medical Internet Research*, *16*(2). doi:10.2196/jmir.2912 PMID:24518354

Greaves, F., Ramirez-Cano, D., Millett, C., Darzi, A., & Donaldson, L. (2013). Harnessing the cloud of patient experience: Using social media to detect poor quality healthcare. *BMJ Quality & Safety*, *22*(3), 251–255. doi:10.1136/bmjqs-2012-001527 PMID:23349387

Greene, J. A., Choudhry, N. K., Kilabuk, E., & Shrank, W. H. (2011). Online social networking by patients with diabetes: A qualitative evaluation of communication with Facebook. *Journal of General Internal Medicine*, *26*(3), 287–292. doi:10.100711606-010-1526-3 PMID:20945113

Harrison-Walker, L. J. (2001). The Measurement of Word-of-Mouth Communication and an Investigation of Service Quality and Customer Commitment As Potential Antecedents. *Journal of Service Research*, *4*(1), 60–75. doi:10.1177/109467050141006

Hennig-Thurau, T., Walsh, G., & Walsh, G. (2003). Electronic Word-of-Mouth: Motives for and Consequences of Reading Customer Articulations on the Internet. *International Journal of Electronic Commerce*, *8*(2), 51–74. doi:10.1080/10864415.2003.11044293

Hopkins, J., & Campbell, S. B. (2008). Development and validation of a scale to assess social support in the postpartum period. *Archives of Women's Mental Health*, *11*(1), 57–65. doi:10.100700737-008-0212-5 PMID:18317709

Hors-Fraile, S., Atique, S., Mayer, M. A., Denecke, K., Merolli, M., & Househ, M. (2016). The Unintended Consequences of Social Media in Healthcare: New Problems and New Solutions. *Yearbook of Medical Informatics*, *25*(01), 47–52. doi:10.15265/IY-2016-009 PMID:27830230

Jorner, J. (2018). 4 Industries That Will Dominate Social Media in 2018. ADWeek. Retrieved from https://www.adweek.com/digital/4-industries-that-will-dominate-social-media-in-2018/

Kaplan, A. M., & Haenlein, M. (2010). Users of the world, unite! The challenges and opportunities of Social Media. *Business Horizons*, *53*(1), 59–68. doi:10.1016/j.bushor.2009.09.003

Kapp, J. M., Peters, C., & Oliver, D. P. (2013). Research Recruitment Using Facebook Advertising: Big Potential, Big Challenges. *Journal of Cancer Education*, *28*(1), 134–137. doi:10.100713187-012-0443-z PMID:23292877

Lau, A. Y. S., Gabarron, E., Fernandez-luque, L., & Armayones, M. (2012). Social media in health – what are the safety concerns for health consumers? *The HIM Journal*, *41*(2), 30–35. doi:10.1177/183335831204100204 PMID:23705132

Leung, D., Law, R., van Hoof, H., & Buhalis, D. (2013). Social Media in Tourism and Hospitality: A Literature Review. *Journal of Travel & Tourism Marketing*, *30*(1–2), 3–22. doi:10.1080/10548408.2013.750919

Leung, R. C. (2013). Increasing Dynamic Capabilities of Health Organizations with Social Media. In *Social Media in Strategic Management* (Vol. 11, pp. 129–142). Emerald Group Publishing Limited; doi:10.1108/S1877-6361(2013)0000011011

Li, Y., Wang, X., Lin, X., & Hajli, M. (2018). Seeking and sharing health information on social media: A net valence model and cross-cultural comparison. *Technological Forecasting and Social Change*, *126*, 28–40. doi:10.1016/j.techfore.2016.07.021

Lin, W. Y., Zhang, X., Song, H., & Omori, K. (2016). Health information seeking in the Web 2.0 age: Trust in social media, uncertainty reduction, and self-disclosure. *Computers in Human Behavior*, *56*, 289–294. doi:10.1016/j.chb.2015.11.055

Madathil, K. C., Rivera-Rodriguez, A. J., Greenstein, J. S., & Gramopadhye, A. K. (2015). Healthcare information on YouTube: A systematic review. *Health Informatics Journal*, *21*(3), 173–194. doi:10.1177/1460458213512220 PMID:24670899

McGough, S. F., Brownstein, J. S., Hawkins, J. B., & Santillana, M. (2017). Forecasting Zika Incidence in the 2016 Latin America Outbreak Combining Traditional Disease Surveillance with Search, Social Media, and News Report Data. *PLoS Neglected Tropical Diseases*, *11*(1), e0005295. doi:10.1371/journal.pntd.0005295 PMID:28085877

Mitchinson, A. R., Kim, H. M., Geisser, M., Rosenberg, J. M., & Hinshaw, D. B. (2008). Social Connectedness and Patient Recovery after Major Operations. *Journal of the American College of Surgeons*, *206*(2), 292–300. doi:10.1016/j.jamcollsurg.2007.08.017 PMID:18222382

Moorhead, S. A., Hazlett, D. E., Harrison, L., Carroll, J. K., Irwin, A., & Hoving, C. (2013). A new dimension of health care: Systematic review of the uses, benefits, and limitations of social media for health communication. *Journal of Medical Internet Research*, *15*(4), 1–16. doi:10.2196/jmir.1933 PMID:23615206

Muniz, A. M. J. Jr, & O'Guinn, T. C. (2001). Brand Community. *The Journal of Consumer Research*, *27*(4), 412–432. doi:10.1086/319618

Murphy, R. (2018). Local Consumer Review Survey. Bright Local. Retrieved from https://www.brightlocal.com/research/local-consumer-review-survey/

Nguyen, T., Larsen, M. E., O'Dea, B., Phung, D., Venkatesh, S., & Christensen, H. (2017). Estimation of the prevalence of adverse drug reactions from social media. *International Journal of Medical Informatics*, *102*, 130–137. doi:10.1016/j.ijmedinf.2017.03.013 PMID:28495341

Nielsen. (2015). Winning Strategies for an Evolving Media Landscaping. Retrieved from https://www.nielsen.com/sa/en/insights/report/2015/global-trust-in-advertising-2015/

Olenski, S. (2013). How Johnson & Johnson Is Using Social Media To Save Lives. Forbes. Retrieved from https://www.forbes.com/sites/steveolenski/2013/07/10/how-johnson-johnson-is-using-social-media-to-save-lives/#7f371b81d773

Palmer, A., & Koenig-Lewis, N. (2009). An experiential, social network-based approach to direct marketing. *Direct Marketing: An International Journal*, *3*(3), 162–176. doi:10.1108/17505930910985116

Sarasohn-Kahn, J. (2008). The Wisdom of Patients: Health Care Meets Online Social Media. *Medical Benefits, 25*(13), 12. Retrieved from http://search.ebscohost.com/login.aspx?direct=true&db=bth&AN=32816528&site=ehost-live&scope=site

Sass, E. (2012). Social Health Site Sickweather Predicts Early Flu Season. Retrieved from https://www.mediapost.com/publications/article/190027/social-health-site-sickweather-predicts-early-flu.html

Seeman, N., Ing, A., & Rizo, C. (2010). Assessing and Responding in Real Time to Online Anti-vaccine Sentiment during a Flu Pandemic. *Healthcare Quarterly, 13*(sp), 8–15. doi:10.12927/hcq.2010.21923

Signorini, A., Segre, A. M., & Polgreen, P. M. (2011). The Use of Twitter to Track Levels of Disease Activity and Public Concern in the U.S. during the Influenza A H1N1 Pandemic. *PLoS One*, *6*(5), e19467. doi:10.1371/journal.pone.0019467 PMID:21573238

Smailhodzic, E., Hooijsma, W., Boonstra, A., & Langley, D. J. (2016). Social media use in healthcare: A systematic review of effects on patients and on their relationship with healthcare professionals. *BMC Health Services Research*, *16*(1), 1–14. doi:10.118612913-016-1691-0 PMID:27562728

Socialbakers. (2018). Facebook statistics directory. Retrieved from https://www.socialbakers.com/statistics/facebook/

Starbucks. (2017). Share. Vote. Discuss. See. Retrieved from https://www.starbucks.com/coffeehouse/learn-more/my-starbucks-idea

Statista. (2019a). Most popular social networks worldwide as of July 2019, ranked by number of active users (in millions). Retrieved from https://www.statista.com/statistics/272014/global-social-networks-ranked-by-number-of-users/

Statista. (2019b). Number of monthly active Twitter users worldwide from 1st quarter 2010 to 1st quarter 2019 (in millions). Retrieved from https://www.statista.com/statistics/282087/number-of-monthly-active-twitter-users/

Steinfield, C., Ellison, N. B., & Lampe, C. (2008). Social capital, self-esteem, and use of online social network sites: A longitudinal analysis. *Journal of Applied Developmental Psychology*, *29*(6), 434–445. doi:10.1016/j.appdev.2008.07.002

Stokes, R. (2011). The Essential Guide to Digital Marketing (4th ed.). Quirk e-marketing Pty Ltd.

Strauss, J., & Frost, R. (2013). *E-Marketing: Pearson New* (International Edition). Essex, UK: Pearson Education Limited.

Thevenot, G. (2007). Blogging as a social media. *Tourism and Hospitality Research*, *7*(3–4), 287–289. doi:10.1057/palgrave.thr.6050062

Twitter Inc. (2017). Twitter Usage & Company Facts. Retrieved from https://about.twitter.com/company

Velasco, E., Agheneza, T., Denecke, K., Kirchner, G., & Eckmanns, T. (2014). Social media and internet-based data in global systems for public health surveillance: A systematic review. *The Milbank Quarterly*, *92*(1), 7–33. doi:10.1111/1468-0009.12038 PMID:24597553

Weaver, B., Lindsay, B., & Gitelman, B. (2012). Communication technology and social media: Opportunities and implications for healthcare systems. *Online Journal of Issues in Nursing*, *17*(3). doi:10.3912/OJIN.Vol17No03Man03 PMID:23036059

Wisk, L. E., Nelson, E. B., Magane, K. M., & Weitzman, E. R. (2019). Clinical Trial Recruitment and Retention of College Students with Type 1 Diabetes via Social Media: An Implementation Case Study. *Journal of Diabetes Science and Technology*, *13*(3), 445–456. doi:10.1177/1932296819839503 PMID:31010315

Wortman Vaughan, J. (2018). Making Better Use of the Crowd: How Crowdsourcing Can Advance Machine Learning Research. *JMLR, 18*(193), 1–46. Retrieved from https://www.microsoft.com/en-us/research/publication/making-better-use-of-the-crowd-how-crowdsourcing-can-advance-machine-learning-research/

Yang, F. C., Lee, A. J. T., & Kuo, S. C. (2016). Mining Health Social Media with Sentiment Analysis. *Journal of Medical Systems*, *40*(11), 236. doi:10.100710916-016-0604-4 PMID:27663246

Yang, M., Kiang, M., & Shang, W. (2015). Filtering big data from social media - Building an early warning system for adverse drug reactions. *Journal of Biomedical Informatics*, *54*, 230–240. doi:10.1016/j.jbi.2015.01.011 PMID:25688695

Zhou, L., Zhang, D., Yang, C. C., & Wang, Y. (2018). Harnessing social media for health information management. *Electronic Commerce Research and Applications*, *27*, 139–151. doi:10.1016/j.elerap.2017.12.003 PMID:30147636

Zichermann, G., & Cunningham, C. (2011). *Gamification by Design: Implementing Game Mechanics in Web and Mobile Apps*. Sebastopol, CA: O'Reilly & Associates Inc. doi:10.1093/intimm/dxs132

KEY TERMS AND DEFINITIONS

Crowdsourcing: The practice of obtaining input into a task by enlisting the services of a large number of people mainly via online channels such as the Internet and SNS.

e-WOM: Any positive or negative statement made by consumers / patients about a product or organization, that is made available to a multitude of people and institutions via the Internet and SNS.

Health 2.0: The use of social networking sites and relevant technologies to promote collaboration between patients, their caregivers, health professionals, and other related stakeholders in health.

Online Communities: Groups of online people that have common interests and get together in SNS and similar platforms to communicate, exchange ideas / experiences, work together and pursue their interests.

Social Networking Sites: A group of internet-based applications built on the Web 2.0 technological foundations that enable creation and easy exchange of user generated content.

Use Barriers: The factors that affect to continuous use of a certain service or technology.

Web 2.0: Web technologies that facilitate the easy interaction between users and companies via two way communication, interactivity and sharing.

Word of Mouth (WOM): All informal communications towards other users/ consumers with regards to the usage, or characteristics of certain products / services and their sponsors /owners.

Section 4

Chapter 13
Public-Private Partnerships and Its Reflections to the Health Sector

Yeter Demir Uslu
Istanbul Medipol University, Turkey

Emre Yılmaz
Istanbul Medipol University, Turkey

ABSTRACT

The purpose of this study is to define the concept of public-private cooperation, to talk about its advantages and disadvantages and to examine its reflections on the health sector. In this context, the main features of the Public Private Partnership and the financing models applied throughout the world have been mentioned by making extensive literature review. In addition to this, the effects of public-private cooperation on health sector practices are discussed and the benefit of the synergy created as a result of cooperation is emphasized. In the literature review, the creation of Public Private Partnerships for various purposes together with various financing models, the services public and private sector provide for a common purpose, the risk sharing resulting from all these factors have been discussed. It is stated that the provision of compulsory public services by the government in cooperation with the private sector adds value to projects both in terms of innovation and time cost.

DOI: 10.4018/978-1-7998-2329-2.ch013

INTRODUCTION

The term PPP emerged in the 1950s and began to be used in the United States, education and other sectors as the joint undertaking of public and private sectors to finance the services to be provided (Atasever, 2018). Up to the end of the 90s, about ten countries are using this model, while today, it is known that most states use it (Boz, 2013). Among the fundamental aims of the state is to provide the services that the public needs. The services to be provided include different services such as hospitals, roads, schools, infrastructure services, and prisons. Debates on how and how each service item will be made available to the public, and how to manage it effectively and efficiently, have existed from the past to the present (Teker, 2008).

The Public-Private Partnership (PPP) model can be defined as a model that undertakes the financing of large-scale infrastructure activities and projects, collaborates with the public and private sectors to provide public service, and shares the risks that may occur in all processes in order to ensure public service provision and sustainability (Yaşar, 2015). The PPP model in the health sector has a history of nearly a quarter-century. There are two main reasons why the PPP model is preferred. These are to utilize the financing capacity of the private sector and to benefit from the private sector's operational ability and competencies in the organization of public services (OECD, 2010).

Within the scope of the globalization process, organizations and administrations in all sectors have become more affected by the dynamics experienced in their internal and external environments and have grown sensitive systems and have tended to direct their strategies in this direction. One of the essential concepts that stand out at this point is the managerial and process sustainability. Considering that the impacts of both public and private sectors are equal in the structuring of the City Hospital, where the strategic importance of sustainability concept is on the agenda again, it is inevitable that both areas will come together and be evaluated within the scope of a strategic partnership in terms of both the management and the sustainability of the enterprise. In this context, it is critical to determine the strategic objectives of hospitals, to ensure that the enterprise allocates resources correctly and effectively in the vital planning phase, to understand the priorities and preferences of all concerned, to demonstrate the transfer of responsibilities and accountability within the framework of the results.

PUBLIC-PRIVATE PARTNERSHIP

Basic Concepts and Development

The primary responsibilities of the state include the provision of public services. How and when these types of services will be offered has been among the topics discussed in each period. One of the biggest problems in public service provision is the narrowing of the share allocated to investment due to budget deficits. Reducing the share of investment in some public services, failure, the expected level of quality, or worse, the service cannot be caused at all. Above all, the state needs to find its solution to all the risks that may arise at all stages of the public service (including planning, design, construction, and operation) of the state monopoly. Privatization is another way to provide public project and activity financing. The benefits of privatization; the creation of a competitive economy by increasing competitor firms in the market, alleviating the state budget burden, strengthening the capital market and restoring the savings to the economy, and transferring the funds obtained to the public infrastructure services through this method (Teker, 2008).

With the Public-Private Cooperation Model, a significant portion of the risks in project development, construction, financing, and operation are transferred to contractor companies. However, the fact that a substantial part of the risks is attributed to entrepreneurs invests in this area less prefer for the private sector. In this context, contractor companies prepare scenarios against all risks that are likely to occur. To mitigate these drawbacks, public procurement of goods and services produced or minimum usage and price guarantee practices are implemented. Since the lifetime of the projects in question is expressed in decades, in terms of various guarantees for the future there may be problems between the public and the private sector (Teker et al., 2013). However, if the PPP Model is implemented under the right projects and conditions, a win-win situation can be created for the public and private sectors. The reason why PPP Model is chosen instead of a traditional tender method to constitute an important point here; if the public sector suffers from finding funding for the investments it has to make, compulsorily the best alternatives will come to the fore.

The most significant benefit of the PPP model to the public sector is that the financing of the services to be provided by the state does not put a substantial burden on the state budget in the short term. In this way, the realization of public resources can be directed to more critical areas (PPIAF, 2009). For this reason, the PPP model is widely used in the world and is preferred in other public services, especially in infrastructure investments. Thus, countries can reduce their costs in public expenditures, ensure that private sector service quality is formation in public service and that risk is shared (Uygun, 2013).

Besides this, the PPP model creates several disadvantages for the public sector. Covering the investment in the projects by the private sector may increase borrowing costs. Also, the long term of the investment and operation period of the project tries to reflect the possible risks of the contractor companies to the price as much as possible. Especially during the execution of city hospitals as both public and private sectors are new in this area, the solution of the problems progresses slowly and creates the need for new legislation. There is a company established will be the addressee of the tender and for private purposes during the 25-year contract period by contractor firms in the city hospitals constructed with PPP model (Atasever, 2018).

The necessity of establishing new units/organizations, employing personnel and providing many services from the market in countries with past and experience in the model implementation reveals that PPP causes public expenditures with these characteristics (Koray, 2011). While the PPP model can be used in various infrastructure investments of the health system, it has gained a lot of place in the establishment and operation of the hospital. For the PPP model to be implemented successfully, it must complete the process involving some activities respectively. The process of the hospital set up the PPP model; needed investment will meet what needs and to what extent and the starts with the determination of hospital services in the current area.

The roles of stakeholder and stakeholders are defined. To meet the needs, risks and opportunities are evaluated, and strategies are determined within the scope of the tender to be held. Preliminary acceptance is realized by evaluating the proposals made to the project. As a result of the negotiations with the companies that have received pre-acceptance, the tender is made. An agreement is reached with the private sector entrepreneur who wins the bid. As a result of the signed contract, the investments begin, and the contractor firm establishes the health facility by using its resources within the conditions determined by the Ministry of Health. With the transfer of the completed health facility to the Ministry of Health, the service delivery phase begins with the PPP application.

With the start of service delivery; The Ministry of Health pays rent for the amount specified in the period defined in the contract with the contractor company. Contractor firms can generate commercial income from commercial areas other than excluding those specified in the contract stated area and health services area. Except those, it may be requested that the contractor covers the procurement of services. The contractor companies must cover all maintenance and renewals specified in the contract. Upon expiry of the contract period (at the end of 25 years), the health facility is delivered to the Ministry of Health (Atasever, 2014).

Properties

Generally, the main role of the public sector in Public Private Partnership models is known as determining the nature of the work, identifying priorities, objectives and outputs, and creating performance assessment methods for measuring the services provided by the private sector. The public side aims to make the service available at the optimum level and to provide the service at the most favorable price for the users. The private sector strives to provide these services in the best possible way and aims to make a profit as a result of this service.

Partnership with long-term contracts, which are mostly inherent in projects, requires the private sector to make long and detailed feasibility studies. The private sector wants to measure the likelihood of investing the project at its net present value by calculating the return on all investment over the contract period.

Considering the traditional attitudes of the public and private sectors towards each other, the process of construction of the Public Private Partnership projects is becoming longer and more difficult. However, despite all these difficulties, factors such as the fact that the public has to provide infrastructure investment and that the private sector provides the public sector with a long-term contract increase the desire to make projects on both sides. For a successful PPP model, public institutions and the private sector must adopt each other's needs in a spirit of partnership without compromising each other's needs and acting in line with common goals (Klein, 2015).

In PPP projects, public and contractor firms cooperate on issues such as investment costs, risk sharing, financing and sustainability, responsibility, and profit/loss. The primary purpose of such cooperation is to benefit from the advantages of both sides in a joint project. Roles of projects may vary on both sides compared to financing models. In some cases, the contractor may be responsible for the provision of the service, and sometimes it may only be involved in carrying out construction activities and providing financial support (Booth and Starodubtseva, 2015).

Through such collaborations, efficiency and effectiveness are ensured both in terms of design and financing in public service delivery and infrastructure project investments, as well as in maintenance and repair works of the operation and facility. The main objective of the PPP model is to design, finance, and co-operate with the private sector in the construction and operation of any project under the responsibility of the public sector. The public undertakes the risks that may arise in all these activities with the contractor company and the profit and loss to be obtained is shared between the two parties. The factors that make the cooperation of public and private sectors attractive can be evaluated in two different dimensions in terms of service quality and cost advantages (David, 2003):

Quality of Service Provided: It is often difficult for the public to have expertise in all sectors and services, to carry out the necessary feasibility studies on the activities and to be an efficient enterprise with financial sustainability. The quality of services provided is often low due to lack of expertise and for the reasons mentioned. One of the essential advantages of the PPP model is that it can provide public service by utilizing the power of knowledge of the private sector.

Cost Advantage: The costs of the public sector are higher than the private sector due to inefficiencies in the provision of services. Taking advantage of the power of expertise in the private sector, while increasing the quality of service delivery, the construction and operation of the facility is also the responsibility of the private sector, which will provide significant cost advantages. According to Bettignies and Ross (De Bettignies and Ross, 2004), PPP has three main characteristics. The first is that the majority of the PPP agreement consists of more than one employment contract. The second key feature is the collection of responsibility from a single party or the release of more than one business to the burden of one party.

To explain this situation; for example, when considering a bridge construction, any of the partners can undertake both financing and installation and maintenance of the bridge. The last main feature is the allocation of the funding to private sector responsibility. The characteristics of PPP, which has application models in most sectors with its various models and methods, can be listed as follows in the literature (IFSL 2003; Akintoye et al., 2003; Karahanoğluları, 2012; Klijn and Teisman, 2003; Bult-Spiering et al., 2006). These:

- With the PPP model, pre-determined service items are purchased from the private sector.
- Public-private cooperation can be combined into a common denominator around the interests of the health service provider, the user requesting the service and the creditors providing the financing.
- Public-Private Cooperation creates a coherent relationship between the public and private sectors rather than cooperation with opposing views.
- To ensure the sustainability of quality products and services, qualified training is determined for employees and motivation, and rewarding of employees is ensured.
- Although the Public-Private Partnership is mostly used for large scale infrastructure activities and projects that require high costs, nowadays its small size applications are increasing.
- The most important feature that distinguishes Public-Private Partnership projects is the financing provided by the private sector. Public-Private Partnership is not a financing model or concession agreement such as outsourcing.
- In most Public-Private Partnership projects, financing, building design, construction, and maintenance are intertwined. The most common purpose

known for assigning design or operation to the responsibility of the contractor is due to the merger within a single contractor (or consortium). The goal of combining these functions is to ensure the minimization of all related sub-service costs as a result of the service delivery of the consortium (De Bettignies and Ross, 2004).

- The fact that the state provides compulsory public services together with private sector cooperation adds value to the projects both in terms of innovation and time costs.
- In PPP projects, there may be project companies with more than one private sector representatives on the contractor side.
- It is of utmost importance to ensure the sustainability of the product or service produced at Kau Special Cooperation projects at the specified quality level.
- The Public-Private Partnership project contracts are concluded on a long-term basis for 25-49 years.
- The quality and quantity of the product or service in PPP projects are determined around the criteria set by the public.
- The main task of the public in PPP projects is to provide a global organization. The authority to audit is in the hands of the public. Therefore, the public project plays an active role at every stage during the contract period.
- Both public and contractor firms should show the necessary incentives when investing in the material and intangible resources of the product or service produced.
- All actors involved in such projects should assume responsibility for the results of their activities.
- Most of the cost items in PPP projects consist of payments made to the building management.
- In PPP projects, the facility is transferred to the public at the end of the contract.

In addition to the basic features of PPP projects, the basic principles of PPP should be mentioned. These basic principles can be grouped under four headings (Rosenau, 1999). These:

- Actors (parties, stakeholders)
- Network
- Project
- Relationship

Today, the planning and development of PPP projects are complicated for the public, private and civil society groups. Each sector has its own economic and social characteristics. While the public sector is moving towards the social benefit and environmental awareness, the private sector can focus on making profits by acting more dynamic and creative.

The third sector, the civil society sector, operates with feelings of responsibility and pity. But the activities and objectives of each area, the changing roles of the public and the increasingly blurred boundary line between them and the private sector intersect these sectors at most points. But the activities and objectives of each area, the changing roles of the public and the increasingly blurred boundary line between them and the private sector intersect these sectors at most points. When industries that have different structures and objectives act for everyday purposes, they establish a network and work in cooperation. PPPs are the most significant representatives of this network (Bult-Spiering et al., 2006).

Risk Sharing

To provide public services such as health, infrastructure, transportation and education, facility design, construction, financing, and operation needs to be passed. Each item requires a high level of investment and expertise to oversee the workflow processes. However, due to the budget deficits and the lack of knowledge of the public in different areas, the provision of the necessary services may not be realized. Furthermore, due to the cost-benefit advantage, it may not be available at expected service quality standards.

Different methods are applied to provide these services to the public in a fast, effective, efficient and sustainable manner. Privatization is a model that includes these methods. With the privatization, all public goods or services are left to the private sector for an unlimited period. Although privatization is often seen as a useful alternative for the provision of public services, it is criticized by many for the loss of state control over the goods and services. The provision of public services in the state monopoly is inadequate in terms of budget deficiencies, lack of expert knowledge and control losses. Public-Private Partnership (PPP-PPP) models that eliminate disadvantages (Grimsey and Lewis, 2002).

There are multiple derivative models in public-private cooperation projects. In these projects, it is generally the principle that the project should be financed and operated by the private sector without any burden of investment cost to the state. The risks that may occur throughout the whole process are shared jointly by public and contractor companies. Thanks to the cooperation, the sustainability of the services to be provided to the public and the expected quality level are ensured, and this process continues under state control. To sum up, PPP projects are based on a win-win approach on both sides (Teker, 2008).

The project may face different risks during its economic life. PPP projects are examined in three primary stages according to possible threats. These phases are the design phase, construction phase and operation phase of the project. During the design and development phase, the cost-benefit analysis is carried out by including the feasibility study of the whole process.

As a result of this analysis, risk analyses are made by making calculations in various items including possible risks of the project, construction and operational costs, maintenance and repair costs, logistics costs (ship, aircraft, truck), expropriation costs, economic life, indirect and direct income, and taxes of the project. With all these calculations, the contractor company should be able to recover the opportunity cost of the capital put into the project to accept the PPP project and accept the risks (Lonsdale, 2005).

Financing Models

Project financing is defined as the design and construction of a project or the creation of enough and appropriate resources to develop an existing plan. Project finance is the financing used for the activation of investments requiring significant scale capital. The private sector institutions that are demanding to finance the projects are strictly related to the income generation power to be obtained from the project and the use of project assets as collateral (Teker, 2008). PPP projects have been used extensively in the US, Australia, and most European countries since the early 1990s. According to a study conducted in America at the beginning of 2000; Among the reasons for applying to PPP models of the states, it has been shown that the private sector can provide high-quality services with cost savings, expertise, flexibility and ability to make quick decisions and to implement them (Esty Benjamin, 2004).

To realize public investments requiring a long-term process and high investment costs, companies in the private sector were used. In the 1970s, financing models aiming to benefit from their experience and efficiency and efficiency in business management, especially financing sources, became famous. Since the early 1980s, it has been used widely in the world. To solve the financing problems of the projects, different financing models have been implemented. Since the 1990s, various financing models have been used in the Private Public-Private Partnership (PPP)" system (OECD, 2012). PPP models vary in terms of the responsibilities undertaken by the private sector in project planning. Contractors in the private area can make the design, construction, management, and ownership of projects for public service.

The PPP project financing models commonly used by States are as follows:

- Build Transfer (IT)
- Build Lease Operate Transfer (BLOT)

- Build Transfer Operate (BTO)
- Build Operate Transfer (BOT)
- Build Own Operate Transfer (BOOT)
- Build Own Operate (BOO)

In the Build Transfer (IT) model, the public sets quality standards in the design and construction process. Perform cost analysis and form performance criteria. Controls the practices of the contractor company in which the private sector cooperates. After the completion of the project construction, it is transferred to the government for the operation. The model often considers ownership of the public. It is based on benefiting from the expertise of the private sector only in plant design and construction stages. The main advantages of the model are; the possible risks during the construction process are on the contractor firm, the design process proceeds with the expertise of the contractor firm, and therefore the creation of a higher quality facility structure is the completion of the plant construction period in a shorter time.

In Build Lease Operate Transfer (BLOT) model, the contractor company in the private sector wing completes the construction of the facility and delivers the ownership to the public. In some cases, the project leases the project itself and sometimes the related units for a specified period. This type of financing model is generally used when the private sector should not own the project. For example; the tunnel, motorway, and bridges remain in the public domain.

In the Build Transfer Operate (BTO) model, the public finds a partner for the project's financial resources and construction processes. When the project construction is completed, ownership is transferred to the public. In exchange for development, the public gives the contractor the right to operate the plant until it has a predetermined income. The most important advantage of the model; to benefit from the experience of construction and operation of the private collaborator of the public sector and to save costs with this method. The property is entirely public. The

Table 1. Public-private partnership models

<table>
<tr><th>Government Finance</th><th colspan="6">Public Private Partnership Models</th><th>Privatization</th></tr>
<tr><td>-The project is financed and operated by the state.
-Risk and income belong to the country.</td><td>BT</td><td>BLOT</td><td>BTO</td><td>BOT</td><td>BOOT</td><td>BOO</td><td>-Public service is owned and operated by the private sector.
-Risk and income belong to the private sector.</td></tr>
</table>

public has the authority to control the flow of income and expenses on the facility. The public audit the company's performance and service quality standards. The contractor may be changed if the specified criteria are not met.

The Build Operate Transfer (BOT) model is a collaboration made as a result of the support of a private contractor for public infrastructure services that require high technology and financial support. The contractor firm sells the goods or services to the public institutions and organizations by taking into consideration the proposed tariffs. At the end of the process, the contractor company completes the maintenance of the project or facility it operates and transfers it entirely to the public. If we give an example to this model; The Scissors Bridge between England and Wales, Shajao power plant in China can be shown.

In the Build Own Operate Transfer (BOOT) model, it is a financing model used in infrastructure works (roads, bridges, dams, etc.) which require high budget costs in many developing countries, especially Australia. In this model, the contractor provides funding support for the construction of the facility, designs and builds it and owns and operates the facility for the specified period. The period is usually 15 to 30 years. After expiry of the period, the facility is transferred to the public. Worldwide, the World Bank, the Asian Development Bank, and the European Development Bank support the model. For example; The Mangawhai Port wastewater plant, established in New Zealand, can be given to the Sydney Harbor Tunnel in Australia.

Build Own Operate (BOO) is similar to the build-own-operate-transfer model in terms of plant design, construction, and financing. The most crucial difference is that the facility is not transferred to the public at the end of a specified operating period. (indefinite operating rights). However, the state may set some standards for the operation of the plant and make arrangements. For example, the public may have a say on pricing policies. To give a model throughout the world; a $ 400 million power plant planned to be built in Lithuania in cooperation with American Calenergy, Duke Energy and German Siemens can be shown.

In all public-private cooperation models, the risk-sharing levels of the private sector and the degree of contribution to the management of the facility vary. for each financing model, private sector contribution, and the degree of risk undertaken are shown (David, 2003). PPP models are frequently used today in most countries, particularly in the UK, America, the Netherlands, and Australia. Table to lists the countries where the PPP models are widely used and their usage areas.

Development of Public-Private Partnership in Health

The PPP model in the health sector has a history of nearly a quarter-century. There are two main reasons for preferring PPP model. These are to benefit from the in the organization of public services, the private sector's financing power in the process

Table 2. Usage areas of public-private sector cooperation models in other countries

Country	Usage Areas
Finland	Transportation, school and university construction
France	Water and waste plants
Greece	Road construction and train transport
Ireland	Transportation, training and wastewater facilities
Italy	Hospital, transportation, and waste facilities
Portugal	Airport and road construction
Spain	Highway and wastewater plants
Japan	Hospital, nursing home, informatics and transportation
Australia	Road construction, hospital, and prison
South Africa	Prison, water and wastewater facilities, hospital and school construction

of public investments, operation capacity, and competencies (OECD, 2010). In this field, the model of PPPs throughout the world implement mainly in England, France, Italy, Spain, Germany, Australia, Hungary, Romania, Poland, South Africa Portugal, Japan, Canada, Mexico countries. Although countries continue to invest in PPP, they still constitute a small portion of total public investments (OECD, 2012).

The Public-Private Cooperation Model may vary according to the specific characteristics of each country. OECD stated in this the report that it is necessary to establish a separate unit to carry out this cooperation (tender process, budget calculations, audit, etc.) of the countries implementing the PPP model. It is emphasized that the fact that this unit is a separate unit affiliated to ministries, an autonomous structure of supreme board type or a public legal entity or a private legal entity should be determined according to the characteristics of the countries (OECD, 2012). There are various advantages and disadvantages of the City Hospitals that are introduced

Table 3. Public-Private Cooperation Practices in Health in the World

Countries	Start Year	Number of Projects	Project Budget
Britain	1990	130	$ 15 Billion
Italy	1999	50	$ 6.5 Billion
Germany	2002	21	$ 3 Billion
France	2002	50	$ 5 Billion
Portugal	2002	6	$ 1 Billion
Canada	2003	92	$ 26 Billion
Turkey	2009	34	$ 20 Billion

to our country with the PPP model in the health system. These are: (Atasever, 2018; PPIAF, 2009; Koray, 2011; Acartürk and Keskin, 2012; Tekin, 2007).

Advantages:

- Encourages reform in the public sector.
- Public service can be performed in better quality and cost-effective manner.
- It provides an alternative solution to the problems experienced in the financing of public services.
- It is easier to implement projects that require great financial resources.
- Increases the quality level of the service provided by creating a competitive environment.
- Enables the use of private sector capacity in the provision of public services.
- It reduces the state's participation in economic activities and the burden of responsibility of management.
- Ensures that project risk is shared.
- Prevents budget deficits due to investment costs.
- The penalty shall be imposed for each minute in which the defects and obstacles which cause the disruption of the health service delivery process due to the project error, etc., reasons caused by the contractor company are not eliminated or corrected. The penalty is deducted from the usage fee.
- The rapid process management of the private sector in hospitals and the absence of problems such as insufficient funds in public hospitals allow the application of advanced technology structures.
- Hospitals in terms of technological infrastructure; green hospital systems, trigeneration, earthquake isolators, increase in world standards in indoor bedside areas, indoor parking and so on. Provides a systematic and structural gain.
- At the end of 25 years, the hospitals are well maintained and in working condition and will be transferred to the Ministry of Health without paying the price.
- It also provides advantages such as spreading treatment diversity throughout the country, increasing service quality, using new technologies, and increasing the quality of bed capacity.

Disadvantages:

- Large-scale projects limit the capital offered to a specific size and prevent the creation of a competitive environment during the tender stage.
- Costs may increase due to limitations in the domestic market.

- The long-term term of the investment and operation period of the project will try to reflect the possible risks of the contractor companies to the price as much as possible.
- Professionals must do contract design, implementation, and management. Otherwise, the lack of prioritization of risks and incomplete or inadequate sanctions may create long-term problems.
- Since it is indebted to the private sector, more resource costs are increasing.
- The fact that the contracts are long-term necessitates long-term payment to the source. This situation reduces the overall budget flexibility of the public sector.
- As the public and private sectors are new in this area, the solution of the problems progresses slowly and creates the need for new legislation in the operation of the City Hospitals.
- The long-term nature of contracts may arise from differences in understanding of the guidelines/legislation of staff (both public and private) that change through the operational process.

The large and complex structures of city hospitals bring about the intensification and increasing of services, as well as the organizational and managerial complexity. This situation will inevitably increase the scale growth when the financial dimensions are considered. It would not be right to design an organization chart according to the management mechanism of the other hospitals in this hospital.

The size of the hospitals and the number of managers and their distribution should be designed specifically to these hospitals. There is a coordination board including the contractor company in the management of city hospitals. The contractor firm also has a say in the management levels of the hospital as a stakeholder (Koray, 2011). The fact that the coordination board creates a perfect synergy between both the public side and the contractor side will bring the success of the city hospitals (Atasever, 2018).

SOLUTIONS AND RECOMMENDATIONS

The implementation and partnership of projects in cooperation between public and private sectors requires managing a very complex structure. In order to further increase the project capability and institutionalism of the public; It is necessary to ensure effective coordination in all project processes and to gather these experiences in a common pool. Thanks to the information and experience gathered in this direction, it will be ensured that Public Private Partnership standards are established and implemented in many projects in a sustainable manner. Correct and effective management of Public Private Partnership will be possible through the effective use of the management skills of the contractor firm to be identified and the stakeholders have a common objective among themselves in a transparent, equitable and equal perspective (EU Commission Report, 2011).

If the risks are correctly identified and controlled in a cost-effective manner in PPP projects, their manageability will be easy. Project tenders must be held between the designated parties in accordance with the principles of openness and transparency in a competitive environment in accordance with the tender procedure (Grimsey and Lewis, 2004).

PPP is basically a financing model. However, for the availability of financing, projects must be creditable. Otherwise, the financing and sustainability of the project cannot be ensured. Therefore, reducing the risk posed by the inflation and exchange rates to the contractors; it will enable the project to be financed under easier and more feasible conditions. In addition to the PPP projects, the projects requiring major investment and infrastructure such as roads, tunnels, hospitals and sewerage that are required by the State continue to be realized in cooperation with the private sector. Such projects should be implemented in an environment in which authorities and responsibilities, costs and risks, revenues and public and private sectors are shared at optimum rates (Booth and Starodubtseva, 2015; UNECE, 2009).

The state is personally responsible for the provision of public health services. The bureaucrats and other public personnel authorized by the state shall execute the contracts on behalf of the state. In this respect, contractor firms should have the necessary power to supervise the business processes in detail. However, many projects in the health sector have been put into practice before the public has gained enough knowledge and experience to carry out the activities correctly and effectively.

Therefore, the public sector could not prepare the basis for enough managerial skills in terms of contract management and service supervision. For the projects to be operated for 25 years, the number of personnel who know the PPP procedures and contract standards in detail is insufficient.

It is necessary to increase the capacity of public institutions based on their expertise in managerial processes in PPP projects, identify future roadmaps and make strategic planning, and collect legislation within the general framework. This will strengthen the coordination of PPP projects and help to create a monitoring and evaluation system that can measure the impact of risk factors on project budgeting. In order to ensure the sustainability and effectiveness of the process in PPP projects, all the processes from the preparation of feasibility reports to the operation and re-transfer of the facility to the public need to be improved. Stakeholders in the processes should be analyzed and evaluated according to internationally determined standards (Tony, 2015).

To summarize, in order to achieve successful results of PPP projects; structural arrangements should be developed, contracts should be prepared and examined in detail, financial statements should be formed and analyzed correctly. The legal basis of the project needs to be designed in an appropriate way, the services to be given priority should be determined correctly and finally the whole process should be managed correctly.

FUTURE RESEARCH DIRECTIONS

In the future studies, this analysis can be performed with a different econometric methodology.

CONCLUSION

Public-Private Partnership is based on the principle of carrying out infrastructure works and providing public services by bringing together the knowledge, experience, and opportunities of the public and private sectors for a common purpose. It aims to alleviate the financial burden of infrastructure investments and provide a high-quality, sustainable, customer-oriented approach to citizens with a high level of satisfaction. Considering all of its benefits, it has been used as important financing and public service execution model for political governments. Among the reasons that are attracted by the private sector are the advantages that PPP enables new investment areas and demand is guaranteed. This has led to its implementation in many different areas.

In general, public-private cooperation refers to the sharing of the costs, risks, and revenues of certain contractual service items between the public and private sectors. Another important feature that distinguishes this method from other traditional methods is that the cooperation with the private sector is not only realized during the construction of the facility but also during the operation phase. This contributes to the establishment of operational synergies between public and private. While the traditional understanding of public services and the production of certain goods by the public is dominant, the participation of the private sector in these activities has been increasing in recent years.

The private sector can participate in these activities in various ways. These practices, in which the private sector supports the production of goods and services of the public under various models, are called Public-Private Partnership. Build-Transfer, Build-Lease-Operate-Transfer, Build-Transfer-Operate, Build-Operate-

Transfer, Build-Own-Operate-Transfer, Build-Own-Operate models are examples of public-private cooperation practices.

The model was initially seen to provide the financing needed to meet the country's infrastructure investments. Today, however, it is accepted as a model in which the private sector will benefit from efficient management skills and the public will focus on areas such as coordination of investments, general planning, supervision, and policymaking. The advantages of Public-Private Partnership are; to have new market opportunities in the sector, to ensure economic growth, to have a broad choice and decision-making authority of the public authority, to the contractor firm in the project, to have positive effects on society and other stakeholders, to allow risk-sharing and to provide effective public service delivery.

PPP practices, which have emerged with the understanding of the inclusion of the private sector in the provision of public services, are increasingly increasing. In addition to the PPP models, problems arising from the structure and function of the public sector such as qualified experts and labor force, experience and legislation infrastructure are solved through the cooperation of the private sector. For the state, which has to meet the expectations of the public with limited funding sources, PPP is a good alternative service execution model.

ACKNOWLEDGMENT

This study was derived from Emre Yılmaz's master thesis written in İstanbul Medipol University.

REFERENCES

Acartürk, E., & Keskin, S. (2012). Türkiye'de Sağlık Sektöründe Kamu Özel Ortaklığı Modeli. *Süleyman Demirel Üniversitesi İktisadi ve İdari Bilimler Fakültesi Dergisi.*, *17*(3), 25–51.

ADB. (2013). *Guidebook on Public-Private Partnership in Hospital Management*. Philippines: Asian Development Bank.

Akintoye, A., Hardcastle, C., Beck, M., Chinyio, E., & Asenova, D. (2003). D. Achieving best value in private finance initiative project procurement. *Construction Management and Economics*, *21*(5), 461–470. doi:10.1080/0144619032000087285

Atasever, M. (2014). Türkiye Sağlık Hizmetlerinin Finansmanı ve Sağlık Harcamalarının Analizi 2002-2013 Dönemi. Ankara: Bakanlık Yayın.

Atasever, M. (2018). *Şehir Hastaneleri Araştırması*. Ankara: Sağlık-Sen Stratejik Araştırmalar Merkezi Enstitüsü.

Bayar, M. (2017). *Küresel Ekonomik Gelişmelerin Sağlık Sektörüne Etkileri: Sağlık Kamu Özel İşbirliği (KÖİ) Programı*. OHSAD Konferansı.

Booth, L., & Starodubtseva, V. (2015). *PFI: costs and benefits, House of Commons Library*. Briefing.

Boz, S. S. (2013). Kamu Özel İşbirliği (PPP) Modeli. *İnönü Üniversitesi Hukuk Fakültesi Dergisi*, *4*(2), 279-332.

Bult-Spiering, M., Dewulf, GP., Blanken A., Bult-Spiering, W.D., & Dewulf, G.P.M.R. (2006). The future of Public-Private Partnerships. In *Strategic Issues in Public-Private Partnerships: An international perspective* (pp. 176-202). Academic Press.

David, H. (2003). Value for Money tests and accounting treatment in PFI schemes. *Accounting and Accountability Journal*, *16*(3), 342–371. doi:10.1108/09513570310482291

De Bettignies, J. E., & Ross, T. W. (2004). The economics of public-private partnerships. *Canadian Public Policy*, *30*(2), 135–154. doi:10.2307/3552389

Esty Benjamin, C. (2004). *Modern Project Finance* (International Edition). Wiley.

EU Commission. (2011). EU Public Procurement Legislation Evaluation Report Executive Summary.

Grimsey D. & Lewis K., (2004). Public Private Partnerships: the Worldwide Revolution in Infrastructure Provision and Project Finance.

Grimsey, D., & Lewis, M. K. (2002). Evaluating Risks of Public Private Partnerships for Public Infrastructure Projects. *International Journal of Project Management*, *20*(2), 107–118. doi:10.1016/S0263-7863(00)00040-5

Ibanez Tony, G. (2015). *Vfm Analysis of PPP*. World Bank.

International Financial Services London (IFSL). (2003). *Public Private Partnerships – UK Expertise for International Markets 2003*. Retrieved from http://www.ifsl.org.uk/uploads/PPP%20report%202002.pdf

Karahanoğluları Y., (2012). Kamu Özel Ortaklığı Modelinin Mali Değerlendirmesi. *Ankara Üniversitesi SBF Dergisi*, *67*(2).

Klein, M. (2015). *Fundamental of PPP*. World Bank.

Klijn, E. H., & Teisman, G. R. (2003). Institutional and strategic barriers to public-private partnership: An analysis of Dutch cases. *Public Money & Management, 23*(3), 137–146. doi:10.1111/1467-9302.00361

Koray, K. (2011). Sağlık Hizmetlerinin Örgütlenmesinde Kamu-Özel Ortaklığı. *Ankara Üniversitesi Sağlık Bilimleri Fakültesi Dergisi, 66*(3), 217–262.

Lonsdale, C. (2005). Post-contractual lock-in and the UK private finance initiative (PFI): The cases of National Savings and Investments and the Lord Chancellor's Department. *Public Administration, 83*(1), 67–88. doi:10.1111/j.0033-3298.2005.00438.x

OECD. (2010). *Dedicated Public-Private Partnership Units: A Survey of Institutional and Governance Structure*. Paris: OECD Publishing.

OECD. (2012). *Dedicated Public-Private Partnership Units: A Survey of Institutional and Governance Structure*. Paris: OECD Publishing.

PPIAF. (2009). Toolkit for Public-Private Partnerships. In *Roads & Highways*. Public-Private Infrastructure Advisory Facility.

Prats, J., Demaestri, E., & Chiara, J. (2018). *Public–Private Partnership Databases*. Inter-American Development Bank.

Rosenau, PV. (1999). *Introduction: The strengths and weaknesses of public-private policy partnerships.*

Teker, D.L. (2008). Sağlık Sektöründe Proje Finansman Modelleri: Türkiye İçin Bir Model Önerisi ve Bir Hastane Projesinin Fizibilite Analizi. *Muhasebe ve Finansman Dergisi*, (37), 1-18.

Teker, S. Teker, D., & Çimen M. (2013). Ulaştırma projeleri finansmanı için bir model önerisi: kamu-özel sektör ortaklığı ile yap-işlet-devret. *İşletme Araştırmaları Dergisi, 5*(1), 116-129.

Tekin, AG. (2007). Kamu-Özel Sektör İşbirlikleri-Kamu-Özel Ortaklıkları. *İdarecinin Sesi Dergisi, 21*(122), 10-14.

United Nations–Economic Commission for Europe. (2000). *Guidelines on Public-Private Partnerships for Infrastructure Development.*

Uygun, B. (2013). Yeni Bir İlişki Türü: Kamu Özel Ortaklığı. *Hukuk Gündemi*, 24-27.

Yaşar, M. F. (2015). *Şehir Hastaneleri ve Kamu Özel İşbilirği (PPP).* Modeli.

Chapter 14
The Effects of Health Expenditures to Decrease Infant Mortality Rates in OECD Countries

Funda Kara
Independent Researcher, Turkey

İrfan Ersin
https://orcid.org/0000-0002-7407-3654
Istanbul Medipol University, Turkey

ABSTRACT

There is a positive relationship between the health level of the society and its economic development. The main reason is that improving quality of the lives and increasing lifetime has lead to higher economic performance. This evaluates the relationship between health expenditure and infant mortality rate in OECD countries. In the analysis process, 20 different countries in the OECD are selected and annual data of these countries for the years between 1980 and 2017 is evaluated with the help of Kao panel cointegration and Dumitrescu-Hurlin causality analysis. The findings show that there is long term relationship between health expenditure and infant mortality rates in OECD countries. Another important conclusion is that there is a causality analysis from health expenditure to the infant mortality rate. While considering these results, it is recommended that OECD countries should take some actions in order to increase health expenditure so that it can be possible to decrease infant mortality rate.

DOI: 10.4018/978-1-7998-2329-2.ch014

INTRODUCTION

Health expenditures are an important indicator of the development of developed and developing countries. There is a positive relationship between health expenditures and the level of development of economies. The increase in the health expenditures increases the life expectancy of a country's population and thus the life expectancy and economic growth are positively affected in the long term. Increasing the economic growth and welfare of countries in the long term is measured by the importance they attach to health expenditures.

In many countries of the world, new applications and system changes are being made to improve the health sector. Today, health indicators of countries are now accepted as the main factors determining the level of development. Therefore, health services need to be developed and expanded both nationally and internationally. The increase in health expenditures in recent years, as in many countries, leads to also a discussion of health policies in OECD countries. OECD countries are making rapid progress not only in terms of health expenditures but also in terms of prolongation of and quality of life with a reduction in infant mortality rates. Therefore, testing the effect of health expenditures on infant mortality is an issue to be investigated.

In our study, the effect of health expenditures on infant mortality rates in OECD countries was tested with panel cointegration and panel causality analyzes. 20 OECD countries with data between 1980 and 2017 were selected and analyzed. In the first part of our study, the development of health expenditures in the world was mentioned, in the second part, the literature study related to the subject is given and in the third part, the findings of the study are discussed. In the last part, the study was also completed with results and evaluation.

DEVELOPMENT OF HEALTH EXPENDITURES IN THE WORLD

The amount a country spends on health can be influenced by a wide array of social and economic determinants. In addition, the financing of the health system, organizational structure and organizational structure can also affect. There is a close relationship between the income level of a country and the amount of expenditure of its population on health care (OECD/EU, 2018).

Health expenditures have been in an increasing trend all over the world in recent years. Health expenditures in developed countries are affected by the adoption of new medical technologies to treat chronic diseases. In developing countries are directed to cost-effective technologies to treat infectious diseases (Çelik et al., 2016).

Health expenditures are one of the important issues of discussion all over the world. In the historical process, health expenditures are generally seen to be in an upward trend. In the 1970s, the share of OECD countries in GNP for health was around 6% on average. This share has increased over the years (Martin et al., 2011).

Prior to 2009, average health expenditures were realized by 4-6% annually as a result of rising prices in the health sector. Moreover, health expenditures are closely following economic growth since 2012. For example, health expenditures per capita in Greece in 2017 (at 2010 prices) remained below the 2009 level of approximately 30%. In Portugal, Italy and Spain, per capita expenditure has reached pre-crisis levels. Health expenditures in Latvia and Estonia also declined significantly in the early periods of the crisis, but health expenditures continued to rise rapidly after this period. For these two countries, health expenditure in 2017 is about 40% of the 2009 level. Excluding Europe as well the rate of increase in health expenditures slowed down during the economic crisis. Health expenditures in Korea have increased by 6% on average since 2009. This shows that expenditure per capita in 2017 is 55% higher than in 2009. Australia, Canada and the United States have also increased steadily in this period, and expenditure per capita levels were 10-20% higher than in 2009. Health expenditures constituted 8.9% of gross domestic product (GDP) in 2016 (OECD, 2018)

Health expenditures in the United States (17.2% of GDP) represent a much larger part of the economy, followed by Switzerland (12.3%) and France (11.5%) as the second and third highest expenditure countries. Countries such as Turkey (4.2%) and Mexico (5.4%) have accounted for less than 6% of GDP. Each one of those country's (Mexico, Turkey and Colombia) health expenditure is around one-tenth of the United States (approximately USD 1,000 per person) (OECD, 2018).

Negative health expenditure growth across Europe following the economic crisis in 2008, growth rates picked up again in almost all countries in recent years. Across the European Union, health expenditure per capita increased by around 1.9% each year in real terms between 2013 and 2017, compared with an annual growth rate of only 0.6% between 2009 and 2013. During the subsequent four-year period, there has been a large-scale turnaround with all but two EU countries seeing some growth in health expenditure, albeit growth has remained slow in some countries (OECD/EU, 2018).

In the models established for the future of health expenditures, the increase in health expenditures is expected to continue in the following years. Various policies are being developed to increase the value of health expenditure in the world and various improvements are being made at the health level of the community (Hadad et al., 2013).

According to the Human Development Index (2017), the life expectancy at birth in countries such as Canada, Australia, USA, Switzerland, Denmark, Belgium, Japan, Italy, which allocates a significant portion of GDP to health expenditures is over 80 years; in countries such as Pakistan, Syria, Philippines, Turkmenistan and

Indonesia, the economic development level is lower than 70 years. In countries like Turkey, Thailand, Tunisia and Bulgaria, the expected life expectancy was 75 years on average (TUIK, 2018).

Health expenditures are made primarily with pooled funds raised through taxes and employee benefit plans. Decisions about how much to spend on each person from that pool will be based on individual medical needs. Insurance and government financing are ways to make sure that a person's ability to pay or family income does not limit the care they receive when they need it. Yet collectively the ability of everyone to pay, their aggregate prior contributions in taxes and insurance premiums, puts an absolute limit on how much can be spent in total on all the individulals treated. As the focus shifts from micro to macro allocation, the signicant determinant of expenditure shifts from medical need to avaliable income (Table 1) (Getzen, 2013).

There is a close correlation between the economic development of a society and its health level. The budget allocated for health in countries whose economic development has reached a certain level shows an increase. However, the level of knowledge and awareness of individuals regarding health will also increase. Otherwise, the improvement in health conditions supports the economic development of the country. Therefore, studies show that economic indicators and health indicators positively affect each other. The source allocated to health services in the world is in parallel with the increase in the level of development (Ersoz, 2008). Moreover, the life expectancy and expectations of individuals are increasing with the effect of the increase in health expenditures (Kelly, 1997).

Health care and health care expenditures are focused on the future like other sectors. Focusing on the future is a fact that is at the core of the concept of investment. Therefore, health expenditures are not much different from resources allocated to major infrastructure projects. The potential return on investments to health is not seen as fast other sectors. Investments in basic health services are subject to prejudice in society. Countries should consider long-term analysis in the planning of investments. Thus, investments in health care can be handled more carefully in economic development plans (Suhrcke et al., 2005, p. 85).

Table 1. Micro and macro determinants of health expenditure

Micro	→	Macro
Health Status	←	**GDP per capita**
Individual differences in medical expenditure are determined mostly by differences in health status, i.e., whether or not the person is sick		National differences in expenditure per person are largely determined by differences in income.

Source: Getzen, T.E. (2013). Health Economics and Financing, Temple University and İHEA, Wiley, Fifth Edition, 376.

LITERATURE REVIEW

A summary of the current studies in the literature on our subject is included in Table 2.

In the literature, there are studies on the relationship between health expenditures and income. Liang and Tussing (2019) investigate in their research the extent to which population health outcomes are affected by responses of GHE to business cycles, i.e., cyclicality of GHE. They estimate GHE cyclicality by regressing detrended GHE on detrended gross domestic product (GDP). Jabaa et al. (2014) have investigated the influence of health resources on health outcomes for groups of countries defined according to the income level and geographic position. Their study revealed that inequalities in health care expenditures explain the different outcomes of health care systems. The results of this research show that the variation of health expenditures per capita is also more important among the developed and developing or less developed countries, and this difference is growing in time. Heuvel and Olaroiu (2017) in their study show that in countries that spend a high percentage of their GDP on social protection, that have fewer curative beds and low infant mortality, whose citizens report fewer unmet health care needs and drink less alcohol, citizens have a significant longer life expectancy. According to Kovacı et al. (2018) life expectancy, population, prices, and global crisis are effective factors on health care expenditures except for per capita income in developed countries and developing countries, while prices are only efficient factor in underdeveloped countries. Lee and Miller (2002) in their study develop stochastic forecasts of Medicare expenditures over the next 75 years. They find a 95 percent probability that Medicare expenditure in 2075 will fall between 4 percent and 18 percent of GDP, indicating a wide band of uncertainty. Karasoy and Demirtaş (2018) stated that income, life expectancy, improvements in governance and dependency ratio significantly and positively affect health expenditures. Ersöz (2009) stated that the first 20 countries participating in OECD are developed countries and are high income countries that transmit enough resources for health expenditures. According to this, Turkey is within the 10 countries and middle-income groups that joined the OECD later and is similar to the health indicators of these countries. Reynolds and Avendano (2018) stated that the U.S. life expectancy lag could be fairly smaller if U.S. expenditures on education and incapacity programs were comparable with those in other high-income countries.

There are a variety of studies examining the relationship between health expenditures and life expectancy for the main theme of the study. For example Lubitz et al. (2003) in their study show that for the elderly better health results in longer life but not in higher health care expenditures. Obrizan and Wehby (2008) in their study suggest that increasing health expenditure in countries withlow life expectancy may have important returns to life expectancy and significantly diminish

Table 2. Literature Review

Author	Method	Period	Result
Liang, Tussing, (2019)	Economic Time Series	1995-2014	The present research investigates the extent to which population health outcomes are affected by responses of government health expenditure (GHE) to business cycles, i.e., cyclicality of GHE. They estimate GHE cyclicality by regressing detrended GHE on detrended gross domestic product (GDP).
Alptekin, Yeşilaydın, (2016)	Fuzzy Data Envelopment Analysis	2012	This study aims to determine health efficiencies of OECD countries. 34 member countries of the OECD were taken into consideration and the number of the most suitable cluster was five; three countries in the first cluster, nine in the second cluster, nine in the third cluster, six in the fourth cluster, and seven in the fifth cluster. Turkey is located in the fourth cluster.
Bayın, (2016)	Regression Analysis	2013	As a result of the research, it was concluded that the most influential variable in the life expectancy expected in both men and women was the infant mortality rate. Health expenditures per person and health service usage levels are among the variables that have the most impact on the life expectancy expected at the age of 65.
Teker et al., (2012)	Unit Root Test, Cointegration Test, Vector Error Correction Model	1975-2009	Demographic and economic factors, such as the rate of national income of health expenditures, the rate of workable population of the elderly population, the number of beds per thousand persons per thousand, the number of doctors per thousand patients and the ability of men and women to affect their lives were analyzed. It has been found that each factor studied has a significant effect on the life expectancy of men and women.
Fayissa, Gutema, (2005)	Panel Data Analyses	1990-2000	The results of the study, which has a health production function in Africa with socioeconomic factors showed that per capita income, literacy and food availability variables play a positive and significant role in life expectancy.
Lubitz, Cai, Kramarow, Lentzner, (2003)	Using Medicare Current Beneficiary Survey	1992-1998	By developing a model to illustrate the relationship between health, longevity and health expenditures, they realized life expectancy estimates. Their study show that for the elderly better health results in longer life but not in higher health care expenditures.
Kabir (2008)	Multiple Regression, Probit Models	UNDP (2004, 1994), UNCTAD (2004), World Bank (2003)	In the model which was created using many variables such as per capita income, education, health expenditures and urbanization, it was concluded that none of these variables were effective in determining the expected living time.
Obrizan, Wehby, (2008)	Using Guantile Regression Model	2006-2011	The results suggest that increasing health expenditure in countries withlow life expectancy may have important returns to life expectancy and significantly diminish globalinequalities in longevity and development by reducing the spread of the world's life expectancy distribution.
Tüylüoğlu, Tekin, (2009)	Multiple Regression Method	2003	The conclusions from analyses suggest that life expectancy at birth and infant mortality rates are affected more by health expenditures than income levels denoting that increasing income level is not only a reliable factor. This result is consistent with the arguments of development economics.

continued on following page

Table 2. Continued

Author	Method	Period	Result
Şamkar, Güner (2018)	The Least Squared Method, Biased Estimation Techniques Ridge and Liu Estimators	2013	It was found that among the parameter estimations calculated using both Ridge and Liu estimators, the variables of number of births, health expenditures and total population were statistically significant variables for explaining the number of deaths of children under five years old and that the biggest contribution for explaining variation in the dependent variable belonged to the variable of number of births a negative relationship was found between the health expenditures and the number of deaths in children under five years of age.
Kızılkaya, Dağ, Kızılkaya, (2017)	Cointegration Test, FMOLS Method.	1975-2014	There was a positive and statistically significant correlation between life expectancy and health expenditures at birth, and a negative and statistically significant correlation between infant mortality and health expenditures. There was a negative and statistically significant correlation between mortality rate and health expenditures under the age of 5 years.
Yalçın, Çakmak (2016)	Durbin-Watson Testi, White Testi, Regression Analysis	1991-2013	It has been concluded that public health expenditure during the period had a significant impact on human progress and impatient treatment organizations and health staff are more needed because both total health expenditure and public health expenditure are under the OECD average.
Kovacı, Belke, Bolat, (2018)	Panel Data Model	2008-2015	The results of the panel data analysis show that health care expenditures are necessity goods in developed countries, and luxury goods in developing and underdeveloped countries. Life expectancy, population, prices, and global crisis are effective factors on health care expenditures except for per capita income in developed countries and developing countries, while prices are only efficient factor in underdeveloped countries.
Howdona, Rice, (2018)	Panel Data Model	2005-2006 2011-2012	Their study show that health care expenditures is determined by proximity to death rather than age and that proximity to death is itself a proxy for morbidity.
Linden, Ray, (2017)	Panel VAR Models and Impulse Response Analys	1970-2012	The results stress the importance of the positive relationship between public health expenditures and life expectancy. Additional results based on private health expenditure as a share of GDP show also the importance of private expenditures for life expectancy, although these are at the same time also drive nup by public health expenditures.
Heuvel, Olaroiu (2017)	Bivariate Correlation, Linear Regression Analysis	-	The regression analysis shows that in countries that spend a high percentage of their GDP on social protection, that have fewer curative beds and low infant mortality, whose citizens report fewer unmet health care needs and drink less alcohol, citizens have a significant longer life expectancy.
Shang, Goldman (2008)	Hazard Models, Regression Analyses	1992-1999	They show that using life expectancy rather than age results in lower projections of future health care expenditures. This result suggests that increases in longevity might be less costly than models based on the current age profile of expenditure would predict.
Ersöz (2009)	The Hierarchical Method and Two Non-hierarchical Methods, the K-Means and Medoid Clustering Method.	2004	The most significant variables among health indicators in 2004 (such as health expenditures per capita, life expectation at birth and death number per 1000 births) were used in the analysis. In conclusion Turkey clusters with Poland, Slovak Republic, Czech Republic, Hungary, Mexico, Korean Republic, according to non-hierarchical (K-means) clustering, with Portugal, Poland, Slovak Republic, Hungary, Czech Republic, Mexico, and Korean Republic and according to Medoid clustering, only with Mexico.

continued on following page

Table 2. Continued

Author	Method	Period	Result
Öngel, Altındağ, Öngel (2014)	T Test, One Way Anova	2007-2012	For BRIC ve MINT countries, the relationship between health expenditure percapita and life expectancy at birth time and mortality rates of children under age 1 are analyzed retrospectively. It has been observed that the longest life expectancy was 77 years in Mexico and that Turkey and China were behind this country. Turkey ranks third in per capita health expenditures after Brazil and Russia, and has the lowest rates of child deaths under 1 year old with China after Russia.
Khosroshahi (2018)	New Generation Dynamic Panel Data Analysis, Durbin-Hausman Method, panel ARDL Method	1990-2015	The determinants of infant mortality rates are per capita health expenditure, per capita national income and inflation. The most important determinants of the coarse birth rate and life expectancy at birth are; per capita health expenditure, per capita national income and unemployment rate.
Arslanhan (2010)	Comparison and Evaluation	1980-2008	Health expenditures and basic health indicators have been examined in relation to EU-15 and other countries and Turkey's expenditures and indicators have been observed to be closer to the EU-15 average. While health expenditures increased and life expectancy increased rapidly during the 1980-2008 period, the infant mortality rate decreased significantly.
Lee, Miller (2002)	Stochastic Time Series Models	2002	Stochastic time series models are estimated for historical variations in fertility, mortality, and health expenditure per capita in the United States, and used to generate stochastic simulations of the growth of Medicare expenditures. They find a 95 percent probability that Medicare expenditure in 2075 will fall between 4 percent and 18 percent of GDP, indicating a wide band of uncertainty.
Burner, Waldo, McKusick, (1992)	Trend Analysis	1990-2030	It is estimated that US national health expenditures will increase by 8.3% annually from 1990 to 2030. However, it suggests that population aging increases annual health expenditures by 0.06% and the effect is low.
Getzen (1992)	Cross Section, Time Series	1960-1988	There is a positive and meaningful relationship between population ageing and health expenditures.
Karasoy, Demirtaş (2018)	Panel Data Analysis	2000-2015	The determinants of health expenditures were examined by taking into consideration the data of 2000-2015 period for selected 27 OECD countries. In all four models, which correspond to each pollutant employed; income, life expectancy, improvements in governance and dependency ratio significantly and positively affect health expenditures.
Riumallo-Herl, Canning, Salomon (2018)	Sullivan's method.	2010-2015	They propose poverty-free life expectancy (PFLE) as a new metric that uses widely available data to provide a composite measure of population health and economic wellbein. In 67 of 90 countries, the difference between life expectancy and PFLE was greater for females than for males, indicating that women generally live more years of life in poverty than men do.
Halicioglu (2011)	Time Series Data, Cointegration Framework	1965-2005	Empirical results suggest that nutrition and food availability along with health expenditures are the main positive factors for improving longevity whereas smoking seems to be the main cause for mortality.

continued on following page

Table 2. Continued

Author	Method	Period	Result
Wang, (2002)	Instrumental Variable (IV)	1990-1999	DHS data from over 60 low-income countries between 1990 and 1999 reveal two interesting observations. First is the observed negative association between the level and inequality in child mortality. Second is the significant gap in child mortality between urban and rural areas, with rural population having a much slower reduction in mortality compared with their urban counterpart. They find that, at the national level, access to electricity, vaccination in the first year of life and public health expenditure can significantly reduce child mortality.
Nixon, Ulmann (2006)	Panel Data Analysis	1980-1995	The findings show that increases in health care expenditure are significantly as sociated with large improvements in infant mortality but only marginally in relation to life expectancy. They make only a marginal contribution to the improvement of male and female life expectancy.
Behr, Theune (2017)	Data Envelopment Analysis (DEA)	2012	The results of analysis hinted strongly that absolute income and health expenditure per capita have no proportional effect on life expectancy. They sighted very moderate effects of relative health care expenditure and equality on life expectancy in their study.
Rahman, Khanam, Rahman (2018)	Panel Data Analysis	1995–2014	Total health expenditure, public health expenditure and private health expenditure significantly reduced infant mortality rates and the extent of effect of private health expenditure was greater than that of public health expenditure. Private health expenditure also had a significant role in reducing the crude death rate. Per capita income growth and improved sanitation facilities also had significant positive roles in improving population health in the region.
Bein, Unlucan, Olowu, Kalifa (2017)	Panel Regression	2000-2014	First, they documented that there is a strong, positive relationship between total healthcare expenditures and total life expectancy. They found that healthcare had a stronger effect on improving life expectancy in females than in males. Moreover, they found a negative relationship between healthcare expenditures and the number of neonatal, infant, and under-five deaths.
Lichtenberg (2000)	Time Series Analysis	1960-1997	It estimates longevity models using annual U.S. time-series data on life expectancy, health expenditure and medical innovation. The empirical analysis provides strong support for the hypothesis that both medical innovation and expenditure on medical care contributed to longevity increase during the period 1960-1997.
Barlow, Vissandjée (1999)	Multivariate Cross-National Analysis of National Life Expectancy at Birth, Purchasing Power Parity Method	1990	Health expenditure fails to have much impact on national life expectancy. But it is unclear whether this result is due to real impotence or to multicolinearity. It is found that literacy, per capita income, and access to safe water supplies have significantly positive effects on life expectancy.
Kim, Lane (2013)	Linear Mixed Model, Mixed-Effect Model	1973-2000	The findings showed a negative relationship between government health expenditure and infant mortality rate and a positive relationship between government health expenditure and life expectancy at birth. The results suggest that higher government expenditure on medical goods and services can be shown to provide better overall health results for individuals.

continued on following page

Table 2. Continued

Author	Method	Period	Result
Gallet, Doucouliagos (2017)	Meta-Regression Analysis (MRA)	1969-2014	Healthcare expenditure is found to have the greatest impact on the mortality rate compared to life expectancy. MRA results reveal that the expenditure elasticity for the mortality rate is particularly sensitive to data aggregation, the specification of the health production function, and the nature of healthcare expenditure.
Sayılı, Sayman, Vehid, Köksal, Erginöz (2017)	Shapiro-Wilk Test Single Sample T test	2013, 2015	In their study, Turkey is statistically significantly lower according to the OECD countries average in the life expectancy in women and men, healthy life expectancy; and statistically significantly higher in neonatal mortality rate, under-five mortality rate and maternal mortality rate.
Reynolds, Avendano (2018)	Fixed Effects Models	1980-2010, 2016	The U.S. life expectancy lag could be considerably smaller if U.S. expenditures on education and incapacity programs were comparable with those in other high-income countries.
Jakovljevic, Vukovic, Fontanesi (2015)	Data Envelopment Analysis	1989-2012	The strongest expenditure growth was recorded in EU 2004 followed by SEE and the CIS. A surprisingly similar longevity increase was present in SEE and EU 2004. In 1989, countries that joined EU in 2004 were relatively inefficient in the number of life-years gained yet had a lower life expectancy than the SEE region and was only slightly higher than the CIS region (DEA). By 2012 the revenue spent was roughly linear to additional life-year expectancies.
Jabaa, Balana, Robu (2014)	Panel Data Analysis	1995-2010	In this investigation, the aim was to assess the relationship between life expectancy at birth and health expenditure per capita by groups of countries with different development levels and geographic positions. The results of the panel data analysis using the fixed effects model revealed that inequalities in health care expenditures explain the different outcomes of health care systems, by groups of countries defined according to income level and geographic region.

global inequalities in longevity and development by reducing the spread of the world's life expectancy distribution. Şamkar and Güner (2018) in their study it was stated that the variables of number of births, health expenditures and total population were significant variables for explaining the number of deaths of children under five years old. Moreover, the most important contribution for explaining variation in the dependent variable was belonged to the variable of number of births. Linden and Ray (2017) stated that private and public health expenditures had a similar positive impact on life expectancy on the highest public share cluster in their study. They stressed that the private expenditures are important for life expectancy. Shang and Goldman (2008) in their study stated that age has very little additional predictive power over health expenditures after life expectancy was checked. On the other hand, when health status measures are included in the model, predictive power of life expectancy is reduced. Öngel et al. (2014) analyzed retrospectively the relationship between health expenditure per capita and life expectancy at birth time and mortality rates of children under age 1 for BRIC and MINT countries. It was stated the longest expected life expectancy was in Mexico (77 years), Turkey and China were behind Mexico. Yalçın and Çakmak (2016) stated that public health expenditure during the period between 1991-2013 years had a significant impact on human progress in their study and impatient treatment organizations and health staff are more needed. Burner et al. (1992) stated that by the year 2030, as the babies of America entered the seventies and eighties, health expenditures will be 32 per cent of GDP. Getzen (1992) in his study stated that aging is not an important cause of rising health care costs, can help to lessen the frequent and misleading blaming of elderly persons. Behr and Theune (2017) in their study sighted very moderate effects of relative health care expenditure and equality on life expectancy. Jakovljevic et al. (2015) stated that EU 2004 members were the best performers in terms of balanced longevity increase following the rise in health expenditure. Bein et al. (2017) in their study stated that there was positive relationship between total healthcare expenditures and total life expectancy. They also indicated a negative association between healthcare expenditures and the number of neonatal, infant, and under-five deaths. Lichtenberg (2000) in his study estimated the longevity model on life expectancy, health expenditure and medical innovation for the period 1960-1997. Analysis results showed that medical innovation and medical care expenditures contributed to increase length of life in the period of 1960-1997. Barlow and Visandjée (1999) carried out a multivariate cross national analysis of life expectancy at birth in 1990. Literacy, income per capita and access to safe water resources have had a positive impact on life expectancy, while health expenditure per capita and urbanization have had a poor impact. Kim and Lane (2013) it has shown that there is a positive relationship between government health expenditure and life expectancy at birth. In contrast they stated that there is a negative relationship between government health expenditure and infant mortality rate.

Howdona and Rice (2018) in their study stated that health care expenditures is determined by proximity to death rather than age and that proximity to death is itself a proxy for morbidity.

Depending on this, studies on the relationship between infant mortality rate and health expenditures are also observed in the literature. Wang's (2002) study showed that factors affecting child mortality significantly differ in urban and rural areas. Demographic and Health Survey (DHS) data from over 60 low-income countries between 1990-1999 showed that was negative association between the level and inequality in child mortality. There is also important difference in child mortality between urban and rural areas, with rural population having a much slower reduction in mortality. Gallet and Doucouliagos (2017) stated that health expenditures have a significant effect on mortality compared to life expectancy. Sayılı et al. (2017) in their study suggested that Turkey is quite lower compared to the OECD countries average in the life expectancy in women and men. Moreover it is higher in neonatal, maternal and under-five mortality rates. In Bayın's (2016) study was concluded that the most influential variable in the life expectancy expected in both men and women was the infant mortality rate. Health expenditures per person and health service usage levels are among the variables that have the most impact on the life expectancy expected at the age of 65. Tüylüoğlu and Tekin (2009) shows that life expectancy at birth and infant mortality rates are more affected than health expenditures. It is also states that the increase in income is not only a reliable factor. Kızılkaya et al. (2017) found a positive correlation between lifestyle and health expenditures at birth. According to this, 1 percentage point increase in the percentage of health expenditures in GDP will increase the life expectancy at birth by 0.53 units. In addition, a negative correlation was found between infant mortality and health expenditures. According to Arslanhan (2010), Turkey converges to the EU-15 average considering health expenditures. It also converges, including basic health indicators. While health expenditures and life expectancy increased in Turkey during the 1980-2008 period, infant mortality rate decreased significantly. Nixon and Ulmann (2006) in their study showed that increases in health care expenditure are considerably as sociated with majör improvements in infant mortality however only marginally in relation to life expectancy. Rahman (2018) stated that total health expenditure, public health expenditure and private health expenditure importantly reduced infant mortality rates, in addition the scope of effect of private health expenditure was greater than that of public health expenditure.

Finally, we can approach the studies on the factors affecting the life expectancy in the literature. For example, Kabir (2008) in his study stated that none of the factors such as income per capita, education, health expenditures and urbanization were effective in determining expected life expectancy. Halicioglu (2011) in his study suggest that nutrition and food availability along with health expenditures are the main positive factors for improving longevity whereas smoking seems to be the main cause for mortality. Teker et al. (2012) in their study, the relationship between life expectancy of men and women in Turkey and socio-economic variables are examined. The effect of demographic and economic factors such as the ratio of health expenditures to GDP, the ratio of elderly to employable population, the number of hospital beds per thousand people, the number of doctors per thousand patients are analyzed. It has been found that each factor studied has a significant effect on the life expectancy of men and women. Fayissa and Gutema (2005) in their study examines the determinants of health status in SSA based on the Grossman (1972) theoretical model which considers the economic, social and environmental factors. Results showed that a decrease in illiteracy rate and an increase in the food availability index are well positively associated with improvements in life expectancy at birth. Khosroshahi's (2018) study stated that the most important determinants of rough birth rate and expected life expectancy were per capita health expenditures, per capita income and unemployment rate. Riumallo-Herl et al. (2018) proposed that poverty-free life expectancy (PFLE) as a new metric. They said that differences in PFLE between countries are considerably greater than differences in life expectancy. Also, in 67 countries, the difference between life expectancy and PFLE was greater for females and women usually live more years of life in poverty.

Alptekin and Yeşilaydin in their study aims to determine health efficiencies of OECD countries. The data of 34 countries and Turkey have been compared in order to determine the current status of Turkey in relation to the variables identified. Among the results; Turkey is health expenditure per capita is at least the first (according to the purchasing power parity, usd), the expected life expectancy at birth is the second lowest; the maternal mortality rate is the fourth highest.

EMPIRICAL APPLICATION

Data and Methodology

The variable names and resources used in our study are given in Table 3. In addition, 22 OECD (Organization for Economic Co-operation and Development) countries with data from 1980-2017 were analyzed in this study. In this context, the ratio of infant mortality rates and health expenditures in GDP was taken as a variable from OECD statistics (OECD, 2019). In the literature, it is assumed that the attitudes and behaviors of the people about health and the policies implemented by the states towards health will increase the life expectancy of the individuals (average life expectancy) and decrease the infant mortality rates (Bayın, 2016; Tüylüoğlu and Tekin, 2009). In this respect, life expectancy at birth and infant mortality rates are frequently used as health indicators in the literature. In addition, in the literature, variables such as the share of health expenditures in GDP, per capita health expenditures, population growth rate, birth rate, death rate, total fertility rate are also used (Kızılkaya et al., 2017). Based on the literature, our study assumed that healthy individuals would live longer and accepted that infant mortality rates are an important indicator for a healthy population. Therefore, infant mortality rates were used as a variable in our study.

Our study examines the relationship between health expenditures and infant mortality rates in the dimension of causality and cointegration. In order for causality or cointegration, variables have to be subjected to unit root test. The unit root test of the variables is given in Table 4. In this study, as the Panel Causality Test, Dumitrescu-Hurlin Panel Causality and Cointegration Test were also taken as Kao-Cointegration test.

Table 3. Definition of variables used and data sources

Variable	Definition	Data Source
Health Expenditure (HEXP)	Ratio of Health Expenditures in GDP	OECD (https://data.oecd.org/healthres/ health-spending.htm
Infant Mortality Rates (INFMOR)	The infant mortality rate is defined by OECD as the number of deaths of children under one year of age, expressed per 1 000 live births.	OECD (https://data.oecd.org/healthstat/ infant-mortality-rates.htm)

Unit Root Test

The unit root test is a test that gives result about whether any series is stationary. If there is no stability in a time series, then it is formulated as a serial $\Delta = X_t - X_{t-1}$ and is taken different until it becomes stable. If there is no stationarity in a time series, then it is formulated as a serial KX and is taken different until it becomes stationarity. When the time series becomes stationary, it is stated that this series is integrated at a level Δ. In addition, the stability of the series is shown in $X \sim I(\Delta)$ format. In the literature, Levin et al. (2002), Im at hand. (2003), Maddala and Wu (1999), Choi (2001) 's work is generally accepted in measuring the stability tests in panel data models. In our study, LLC unit root test was used. As seen in Equation 1, LLC is basically based on the ADF test and is based on the assumption that the coefficient of autoregressive (ρ) is homogeneous. In the fixed parameter model, X, ie the error process, show to distributed independently between the variables (Levin et al., 2002; Sirvan & Alp, 2017).

$$\Delta y_{it} = \alpha_{0i} + \rho y_{it-1} + \varepsilon_{it} \quad (1)$$

In addition, based on equation 1, our unit root test hypotheses have established below. In the hypotheses, if the coefficient ρ is equal to 0, then the hypothesis H_0 is accepted and in Equation 1 emerge that y_{it-1} has a unit root. So, it is seen that the series is not stationary. In this case, the difference of series must be taken for series to be stationary.

$$H_0 : \rho = 0 ve H_1 : \rho \neq 0$$

Panel Cointegration Test

Cointegration analysis is a test method that provides information about the existence of long-term relationships among serieses. Engle and Granger (1987), who stated that linear combinations of two or more non-stationary series could be stationary, made a significant contribution to the literature with co-integration analysis. Cointegration analysis can also be performed using panel data. In the panel cointegration analysis, a method developed by Pedroni, which we often encounter in literature, was used. This method is expressed in Equation (2) below. The existence of the relationship between x and y in this equation depends on the stationary of the Q residue, which is the error term. If the term error is stationary, there is a long-term relationship between x and y (Pedroni, 1999).

$$y_{i,t} = \alpha_i + \delta_i t + \beta_{1i} X_{2i,t} + \beta_{2i} X_{2i,t} + \ldots + \beta_{Mi} X_{Mi,t} + e_{i,t} \tag{2}$$

$t = 1, 2, \ldots, M$; $i = 1, 2, \ldots, N$; $m = 1, 2, \ldots$, M

In the equation above, α denotes the constant effect parameter, δ deterministic time trend, β slope coefficients, t observation number, i horizontal number, m variable number. In the Pedroni cointegration analysis, the cointegration relationship between Y and X variables is tested by the stationarity analysis for Q error terms. Pedroni (1999) developed seven different cointegration statistics be on the point of being four of the tests were in the group and three of the tests were between groups.

Kao (1999), which extends the cointegration analysis by using the method of Pedroni, has entered the literature. Kao (1999), using Dickey Fuller (DF) and Augmented Dickey Fuller (ADF) type tests, discussed the cointegration tests in panel data in two ways. A cointegration test was developed by applying Augment Dickey fuller (ADF) and Dickey Fuller (DF) stationary tests to the error terms mentioned in Model 3. Here, the null hypothesis is established in the form there is no cointegration (H0: $\rho = 1$)

$$y_{i,t} = x_{i,t}\beta + y_{i,t}\delta + \varepsilon_{i,t} \tag{3}$$

Panel Causality Test

The causality test is a more powerful version of the cointegration test. Indicates a strong relationship between two or more variables. Dumitrescu Hurlin (2012) had been measured the causality test with the panel data and had been ensured that the literaround entered. Dumitrescu-Hurlin panel causality is a methodology for understanding the causal relationship between variables. Granger is considered to be an advanced version of causality analysis. The Dumitrescu-Hurlin panel causality analysis is shown below in Equation (4).

$$Y_{i,t} = a_i + \sum_{k=1}^{K} Y_i^k Y_{i,t-k} + \sum_{k=1}^{K} B_i^k X_{i,t-k} + \varepsilon_{i,t} \tag{4}$$

In this equation X and Y represent the variables. Therefore, the purpose of this method is to determine whether X is the main cause of Y. In addition, B is the coefficient of the variable and a constant term. Besides, Q symbol gives reference to error term and K gives information about optimal delay interval (Dumitrescu & Hurlin, 2012).

This method used in the panel data approach was also used in similar studies. Boubtane et al. (2013) conducted a panel causality analysis between unemployment and GDP in OECD countries. Menard and Weill (2016, p. 270) used panel causality analysis and examined the relationship between help and poverty. In the study of Hartwig (2010), panel causality was used to examine the relationship between health capital and economic growth. Dincer et al. (2018), the relationship between defense spending and growth was analyzed by Dumitrescu - Hurlin causality test. Adalı and Yüksel (2017) conducted the relationship between foreign direct investment and economic development in developing economies with Dumitrescu - Hurlin causality analysis. The same test application was used performed by Dinçer et al. (2018) for the relationship among inefficient credit, industry and economic growth. The validity of Okun's law for countries with different levels of development were analysis by Yüksel and Oktar (2017) with this method. İn the study of Ersin (2018), the effect of exports on growth in MINT countries was analyzed with the causality test. Ersin and Ergeç (2018) 's relation between expenditure components and sectoral employment was also used in the causality test. In addition, Ersin and Baş (2019) examined the relationship between growth and social expenditure with causality. This method has also been taken into consideration in the effectiveness of research and development expenditures and efficiency of the banking sector (Yüksel, 2017; Dinçer et al., 2017; Dinçer et al., 2019a, 2019b, 2019c). Moreover, in the literature, the panel data method was used in many similar studies (Eroğlu & Kara, 2017; Yıldırım, 2016a; Yıldırım, 2016b; Kalkavan & Ersin, 2019).

Empirical Findings

Unit Root Test Results

The precondition for panel cointegration and panel causality analysis is that the series are stationary. In the Table 4 are shown the unit root test results of the series. In order to accept the series as stationary, at least three of the 4 unit root tests were considered as stationary. According to the results, health expenditures were stationary at the level in all panel unit root tests. In the unit root test, intercept and Trend measurement was performed at the level. When we look at the infant mortality rates, while the series level was only stationary according to LLC and PP, in others the unit root problem occurred. To eliminate this problem, the first differences of the series were taken, and the series became stationary.

Table 4. Panel Unit Root Test Results

Health Expenditure (HEXP)				
	Intercept and Trend			
	t- statistic I(0)	Probabilty I(0)	t- statistic I(1)	Probabilty I(1)
Levin, Lin & Chu	-1.93052	0.0268**	-	-
Im, Pesaran and Shin W-stat	-1.93157	0.0267**	-	-
ADF - Fisher Chi-square	61.2125	0.0170**	-	-
PP -Fisher Chi-square	63.2384	0.0110**	-	-
Infant Mortality Rate (INFANT)				
	İntercept and Trend		İntercept	
	t- statistic I(0)	Probabilty I(0)	t- statistic I(1)	Probabilty I(0)
Levin, Lin & Chu	-4.16464	0.0000	-7.71833	0.0000
Im, Pesaran and Shin W-stat	0.98637	0.8380	-13.8699	0.0000
ADF - Fisher Chi-square	35.4667	0.6744	265.111	0.0000
PP - Fisher Chi-square	104.762	0.0000	543.305	0.0000

Table 5. Kao Panel Cointegration Test Results

Kao Panel Cointegration Test Result		
	t- statistic	**Probabilty**
	-15.81340*	0.0000
ADF		
Residual variance	0.738369	
HAC variance	0.343039	

Kao Cointegration Test Results

Cointegration is a method that gives information about the relationship between two variables. In our study, Kao cointegration analysis was taken into consideration. Because Kao is the more advanced version of Pedroni. The results of Kao cointegration are shown in Table 5. According to the results, there is a long-term cointegration relationship between health expenditures and infant mortality rates. That is, the H_0 hypothesis (no cointegration between series) was rejected. Therefore, the alternative hypothesis (cointegration between series) was accepted.

Dumitrescu-Hurlin Panel Causility Test Results

Dumitrescu - Hurlin causality analysis, an advanced version of Granger causality analysis, gives information about the causality of the relationship between variables. Table 6 shows the causality results.

When we examine the causality relationship between the health expenditures and the infant mortality rates in Table 6, the probability value of all the lag values emerged less than 0.05 and the test statistics were found to be statistically significant.

Table 6. Panel causality test results

The Direction of Causal Relationship	Lag Value	Prob.	H_0	Result
From Health Expenditures to Infant Mortality	1	0.0000	Health Expenditure does not homogeneously cause İnfant Mortality	Accept
	2	0.0000		Accept
	3	0.0473		Accept
From Infant Mortality to Health Expenditures	1	0.4911	İnfant Mortality does not homogeneously cause Health Expenditure	Reject
	2	0.9528		Reject
	3	0.4157		Reject

The null hypothesis from health expenditures to infant mortality rates was rejected. The fact that all three of the lag values are meaningful also reinforces the reliability of the results. Thus, it is concluded that health expenditures are the cause of infant mortality rates.

When the causality relationship between health expenditures in infant mortality rates is examined in Table 6, the probability values in all of the lag values were higher than 0.05 and test statistics were meaningless. Infant mortality rates did not emerge as a cause of health expenditure.

CONCLUSION

The increase in health expenditures positively affects the life expectancy and quality of individuals. The economic situation in the country is a factor determining the importance given to health development and the resources to be allocated. In this context, the development of health expenditures in the world may show differences among countries. While health expenditures are realized at a higher rate in developed countries, it is seen that health expenditures are realized at a low rate in less developed and developing countries. When the health expenditures of OECD countries are analyzed, the share of health expenditures in GDP increased from 6% to 9% from 1970 to the present. This means that OECD countries increase health expenditures and the health status of society increases.

One of the important indicators of health expenditures is infant mortality rates. In this study, the effect of health expenditures on infant mortality rates was examined and 20 OECD countries with data between 1980 and 2017 were analyzed. In the study using Kao Cointegration and Dumitrescu-Hurlin Causality tests, a long-term relationship was found between health expenditures and infant mortality rates in OECD countries. In addition, the causality relationship was determined from health expenditures to infant mortality rates. According to these results, the increase in health expenditures in OECD countries reduces infant mortality rates. Therefore, the continuation of health investments is important in reducing infant mortality rates in terms of the formation of a healthy population. To further reduce infant mortality in OECD countries, it is important to invest in healthcare in the light of long-term analysis. This will undoubtedly contribute to economic growth and development.

REFERENCES

Adalı, Z., & Yüksel, S. (2017). Gelişmekte Olan Ekonomilerde Doğrudan Yabancı Yatırım ve Ekonomik Gelişme Arasındaki Nedensellik İlişkisi. *Marmara İktisat Dergisi*, *1*(2), 109–118.

Akgül, O. (2018). *Türkiye'de Asgari Ücret Sisteminin Uluslararası Standartlar Açısından Değerlendirilmesi*. İstanbul: Harf Yayınları.

Alptekin, N., & Yeşilaydın, G. (2016). Bulanık Veri Zarflama Analizi ile OECD Ülkelerinin Sağlık Alanındaki Etkinliklerinin Değerlendirilmesi. *Sosyoekonomi*, *24*(30), 207–224. doi:10.17233e.2016.10.013

Arslanhan, S. (2010). How Does the Increase in Health Expenditures Affect Main Health Indicators? *Economy Policy Research Foundation of Turkey*.

Barlow, R., & Vissandjée, B. (1999). Determinants of National Life Expectancy. *Canadian Journal of Development Studies*, *20*(1). doi:10.1080/02255189.1999.9668787

Baş, H. (2017). Türkiye'de Yerel Yönetimlerin Aileye Yönelik Sosyal Politikaları Üzerinden Bir Değerlendirme. *MCBÜ Sosyal Bilimler Dergisi*, *15*(2), 165–196.

Baş, H., & Çetin, B. I. (2017). Bir Sosyal Belediyecilik Uygulaması Olarak İstanbul Esenler Belediyesi Gençlik Merkezi Örneği. *AİBÜ Sosyal Bilimler Enstitüsü Dergisi*, *17*(1), 149–175.

Bayın, G. (2016). Doğuşta ve İleri Yaşta Beklenen Yaşam Sürelerine Etki Eden Faktörlerin Belirlenmesi. *Türkiye Aile Hekimliği Dergisi*, *20*(3), 93–103. doi:10.15511/tahd.16.21693

Behr, A., & Theune, K. (2017). Health System Efficiency: A Fragmented Picture Based on OECD Data. *PharmacoEconomics-Open*, *1*(3), 203–221. doi:10.100741669-017-0010-y PMID:29441492

Bein, M. A., Unlucan, D., Olowu, G., & Kalifa, W. (2017). Healthcare Expenditure and Health Outcomes: Evidence from Selected East African Countries. *African Health Sciences*, *17*(1), 247–254. doi:10.4314/ahs.v17i1.30 PMID:29026399

Boubtane, E., Coulibaly, D., & Rault, C. (2013). Immigration, Unemployment and GDP in the Host Country: Bootstrap Panel Granger Causality Analysis on OECD Countries. *Economic Modelling*, *33*, 261–269. doi:10.1016/j.econmod.2013.04.017

Burner, T. S., Waldo, D. R., & Mckusık, D. R. (1992). National Health Expenditures Projections Through 2030. *Health Care Financing Review*, *14*(1), 1–29. PMID:10124432

Çelik, Y., Khan, M., & Hikmet, N. (2016). Achieving Value for Money in Health: A Comparative Analysis of OECD Countries and Regional Countries. *The International Journal of Health Planning and Management*. doi:10.1002/hpm.2375 PMID:27510835

Dinçer, H., Hacıoğlu, Ü., & Yüksel, S. (2018). Conflict Risk and Defense Expenses and Their Impact on the Economic Growth. In Handbook of Research on Military Expenditure on Economic and Political Resources (pp. 1–23). Hershey, PA: IGI Global. doi:10.4018/978-1-5225-4778-5.ch001

Dinçer, H., Yüksel, S., & Adalı, Z. (2017). Identifying Causality Relationship between Energy Consumption and Economic Growth in Developed Countries. *International Business and Accounting Research Journal*, *1*(2), 71–81. doi:10.15294/ibarj.v1i2.9

Dinçer, H., Yuksel, S., & Adalı, Z. (2018). Relationship Between Non-Performing Loans, Industry, and Economic Growth of the African Economies and Policy Recommendations for Global Growth. In Globalization and Trade Integration in Developing Countries (pp. 203–228). Hershey, PA: IGI Global. doi:10.4018/978-1-5225-4032-8.ch009

Dinçer, H., Yüksel, S., Adalı, Z., & Aydın, R. (2019). Evaluating the Role of Research and Development and Technology Investments on Economic Development of E7 Countries. In Organizational Transformation and Managing Innovation in the Fourth Industrial Revolution (pp. 245-263). Hershey, PA: IGI Global.

Dinçer, H., Yüksel, S., Eti, S., & Tula, A. (2019c). Effects of Demographic Characteristics on Business Success: An Evidence From Turkish Banking Sector. In Handbook of Research on Business Models in Modern Competitive Scenarios (pp. 304–324). Hershey, PA: IGI Global. doi:10.4018/978-1-5225-7265-7.ch016

Dinçer, H., Yüksel, S., Pınarbaşı, F., & Çetiner, İ. T. (2019b). Measurement of Economic and Banking Stability in Emerging Markets by Considering Income Inequality and Nonperforming Loans. In Maintaining Financial Stability in Times of Risk and Uncertainty (pp. 49–68). Hershey, PA: IGI Global. doi:10.4018/978-1-5225-7208-4.ch003

Dumitrescu, E. I., & Hurlin, C. (2012). Testing for Granger Non-Causality in Heterogeneous Panels. *Economic Modelling*, *29*(4), 1450–1460. doi:10.1016/j.econmod.2012.02.014

Engle, R. F., & Granger, C. W. (1987). Co-integration and Error Correction: Representation Estimation, and Testing. *Econometrica*, *55*(2), 251–276. doi:10.2307/1913236

Eroğlu, N., & Kara, F. (2017). Türkiye'de Makro İhtiyati Para Politikası Araçlarının Makroekonomik Değişkenlere Etkisinin Var Analizi ile İncelenmesi. *İstanbul İktisat Dergisi/Istanbul. Journal of Economics*, *67*(2), 59–88.

Ersin, İ. (2018). İhracata Dayalı Büyüme Hipotezinin Test Edilmesi: MINT Ülkeleri Örneği. *Ekonomi, İşletme ve Maliye Araştırmaları Dergisi*, *1*(1), 26–38.

Ersin, İ., & Baş, H. (2019). Güney Avrupa Refah Ülkelerinde Sosyal Harcamalar ve Ekonomik Büyüme Arasındaki İlişkinin İncelenmesi. *Sosyal Güvenlik Dergisi*, *9*(1), 193–213. doi:10.32331gd.582752

Ersin, İ. & Ergeç, E.H. (2018), Harcama Bileşenleri ve Sektörel İstihdam Arasındaki Nedensellik İlişkisi. *Yönetim ve Ekonomi Araştırmaları Dergisi*, *16*(1), 161-180.

Ersöz, F. (2008). Türkiye ile OECD Ülkelerinin Sağlık Düzeyleri ve Sağlık Harcamalarının Analizi. *İstatistikçiler Dergisi*, *1*(2), 95- 104.

Ersöz, F. (2009). OECD'ye Üye Ülkelerin Seçilmiş Sağlık Göstergelerinin Kümeleme ve Ayırma Analizi ile Karşılaştırılması: Türkiye Klinikleri. *Journal of Medical Science*, *29*(6), 1650–1659.

Fayissa, B., & Gutema, P. (2005). The Determinants of Health Status in Sub-Saharan Africa (Ssa). *The American Economist*, *49*(2), 900207. doi:10.1177/056943450504900207

Gallet, C. A., & Doucouliagos, H. (2017). The Impact of Healthcare Expenditure on Health Outcomes: A Meta-Regression Analysis. *Social Science & Medicine*, *179*, 9–17. doi:10.1016/j.socscimed.2017.02.024 PMID:28237460

Getzen, T. E. (1992). Population Ageing and Growth of Health Expenditures. *The Journals of Gerontology. Series B, Psychological Sciences and Social Sciences*, *47*(3), 97–104.

Getzen, T. E. (2013). Health Economics and Financing, Temple University and İHEA, Wiley, Fifth Edition. Globalization and Health, 14(113). doi:10.118612992-018-0430-1

Hadad, S., Hadad, Y., & Tuva, T. S. (2013). Determinants of Healthcare System's Efficiency in OECD Countries. *The European Journal of Health Economics*, *14*(2), 253–265. doi:10.100710198-011-0366-3 PMID:22146798

Halicioglu, F. (2011). Modeling Life Expectancy in Turkey. *Economic Modelling*, *28*(5), 2075–2082. doi:10.1016/j.econmod.2011.05.002

Hartwig, J. (2010). Is Health Capital Formation Good for Long-term Economic Growth?- Panel Granger-Causality Evidence for OECD Countries. *Journal of Macroeconomics*, *32*(1), 314–325. doi:10.1016/j.jmacro.2009.06.003

Heuvel, W. J., & Olaroiu, M. (2017). How Important Are Health Care Expenditures for Life Expectancy? A Comparative, European Analysis. *JAMDA Online*, *18*(3), 276.e9–276.e12. doi:10.1016/j.jamda.2016.11.027 PMID:28131720

Howdona, D., & Rice, N. (2018). Health Care Expenditures Age Proximity to Death and Morbidity: Implications for An Ageing Population. *Journal of Health Economics*, *57*, 60–74. doi:10.1016/j.jhealeco.2017.11.001 PMID:29182935

Im, K. S., Pesaran, M. H., & Shin, Y. (2003). Testing for Unit Roots in Heterogeneous Panels. *Journal of Econometrics*, *115*(1), 53–74. doi:10.1016/S0304-4076(03)00092-7

Jabaa, E., Balana, C. B., & Robu, I. B. (2014). The Relationship Between Life Expectancy at Birth and Health Expenditures Estimated by A Cross-Country and Time-Series Analysis. *Procedia Economics and Finance*, *15*, 108–114. doi:10.1016/S2212-5671(14)00454-7

Jakovljevic, M. B., Vukovic, M., & Fontanesi, J. (2015). Life Expectancy and Health Expenditure Evolution in Eastern Europe-DiD and DEA Analysis. *Expert Review of Pharmacoeconomics & Outcomes Research*, *16*(4), 537–546. doi:10.1586/14737167.2016.1125293 PMID:26606654

Kabir, M. (2008). Determinants of Life Expectancy in Developing Countries. *Journal of Developing Areas*, *41*(2), 185–204. doi:10.1353/jda.2008.0013

Kalkavan, H., & Ersin, I. (2019). Determination of Factors Affecting the South East Asian Crisis of 1997 Probit-Logit Panel Regression: The South East Asian Crisis. In Handbook of Research on Global Issues in Financial Communication and Investment Decision Making (pp. 148–167). Hershey, PA: IGI Global. doi:10.4018/978-1-5225-9265-5.ch008

Kao, C. (1999). Spurious Regression and Residual-Based Tests for Cointegration In Panel Data. *Journal of Econometrics*, *90*(1), 1–44. doi:10.1016/S0304-4076(98)00023-2

Karasoy, A. & Demirtaş G. (2018). Sağlık Harcamalarının Belirleyicileri Üzerine Bir Uygulama: Çevre Kirliliği ve Yönetişimin Etkilerinin İncelenmesi, *İnsan ve Toplum Bilimleri Araştırmaları Dergisi*, *7*(3), 1917-1939.

Kelly, T. (1997). Public Expenditures and Growth. *The Journal of Development Studies, 34*(1), 60–84. doi:10.1080/00220389708422503

Kim, T. K., & Lane, S. R. (2013). Government Health Expenditure and Public Health Outcomes: A Comparative Study Among 17 Countries and Implications for US Health Care Reform. *American International Journal of Contemporary Research, 3*(9), 8–13.

Kızılkaya, O., Dağ, M., & Kızılkaya, F. (2017). *Türkiye'de Sağlık Harcamalarının Sağlık Göstergeleri Üzerindeki Etkisi: Ekonometrik Bir Analiz*. Uluslararası Sosyal Bilimler ve Eğitim Araştırmaları Sempozyumu.

Kosroshahi, N. H. (2018). *Sosyo-Ekonomik Değişkenlerin Sağlık Göstergeleri Üzerindeki Etkisi*. Atatürk Üniversitesi Sosyal Bilimler Enstitüsü, Doktora Tezi.

Kovacı, S., Belke, M. & Bolat, S. (2018). Ülke Gruplarına Göre Ekonomik Gelişme ve Sağlık Harcamaları İlişkisi. In *Uluslararası Sosyal Bilimler ve İnovasyon Kongresi* (pp. 165-179). Academic Press.

Lee, R., & Miller, T. (2002). An Approach to Forecasting Health Expenditures with Application to the U.S. Medicare System, *Heatlh Servies Research.* 37(5), 1365-1386. Retrieved from http://onlinelibrary.wiley.com/wol1/doi/10.1111/1475-6773.01112/full

Levin, A., Lin, C. F., & Chu, C. S. J. (2002). Unit Root Tests In Panel Data: Asymptotic and Finite-Sample Properties. *Journal of Econometrics, 108*(1), 1–24. doi:10.1016/S0304-4076(01)00098-7

Liang, L. L., & Tussing, A. D. (2019). The Cyclicality of Government Health Expenditure and Its Effects on Population Health. *Health Policy (Amsterdam), 123*, 96–103. doi:10.1016/j.healthpol.2018.11.004

Lichtenberg, F. R. (2000). Sources of U.S. Longevity Increase 1960-1997. *CESifo*. Retrieved from https://www.econstor.eu/bitstream/10419/75781/1/cesifo wp405.pdf

Linden, M., & Ray, D. (2017). Life Expectancy Effects of Public and Private Health Expenditures in OECD Countries 1970–2012: Panel Time Series Approach. *Economic Analysis and Policy, 56*, 101–113. doi:10.1016/j.eap.2017.06.005

Lubitz, J., Cai, L., Kramarow, E., & Lentzner, H. (2003). Health, Life Expectancy, and Health Care Expenditure Among the Elderly. *The New England Journal of Medicine, 349*(11), 1048–1055. doi:10.1056/NEJMsa020614 PMID:12968089

Maddala, G. S., & Wu, S. (1999). Comparative study of unit root tests with panel data and a new simple test. *Oxford Bulletin of Economics and Statistics, 61*(Special Issue), 631–652. doi:10.1111/1468-0084.61.s1.13

Martin, M. J., Gonzalez, M. P. L., & Garcia, M. D. G. (2011). Review of the literature on the determinants of healthcare expenditures. *Applied Economics, 43*(1), 19–46. doi:10.1080/00036841003689754

Nixon, J., & Ulmann, P. (2006). The Relationship Between Health Care Expenditure and Health Outcomes: Evidence and Caveats for a Causal link. *The European Journal of Health Economics, 7*(1), 7–18. doi:10.100710198-005-0336-8 PMID:16429295

Obrizan, M. & Wehby, G.L. (2018). Health Expenditures and Global Inequalities in Longevity, *World Development, 101*, 28-36. doi:.08.003 doi:10.1016/j.worlddev.2017

OECD. (n.d.). Health spending. Retrieved from https://data.oecd.org/healthres/health-spending.htm

OECD. (n.d.). Infant mortality rates. Retrieved from https://data.oecd.org/healthstat/infant-mortality-rates.htm

OECD/EU. (2018). *Health at a Glance: Europe 2018: State of Health in the EU Cycle*. Paris: OECD Publishing. doi:10.1787/health_glance_eur-2018-

Öngel, V., Altındağ, E., & Öngel, Ö. (2014). Kişi Başına Sağlık Harcamalarının Sağlık Göstergeleri Üzerindeki Etkileri: MINT ve BRIC Ülkelerinin Karşılaştırmalı Analizi. In *Proceedings of the International Conference on Eurasian Economies* (pp. 1-5). Academic Press.

Pedroni, P. (1999). Critical Values for Cointegration Tests in Heterogeneous Panels with Multiple Regressors. *Oxford Bulletin of Economics and Statistics, 61*(1), 653–670. doi:10.1111/1468-0084.61.s1.14

Rahman, M. M., Khanam, R., & Rahman, M. (2018). Health Care Expenditure and Health Outcome Nexus: New Evidence from the SAARC-ASEAN Region.

Reynolds, M. M., & Avendano, M. (2018). Social Policy Expenditures and Life Expectancy in High-Income Countries. *American Journal of Preventive Medicine, 54*(1), 72–79. doi:10.1016/j.amepre.2017.09.001

Riumallo-Herl, C., Canning, D. & Salomon, J.A. (2018). Measuring Health and Economic Wellbeing in the Sustainable Development Goals Era: Development of a Poverty-Free Life Expectancy Metric and Estimates for 90 Countries. *The Lancet Global Health, 6*(8), e843-e858.

Şamkar, H., & Güner, D. (2018). OECD Ülkelerindeki Beş Yaş Altı Çocuk Ölüm Sayılarının Yanlı Tahmin Teknikleriyle Modellenmesi. *Ulikidince, 11*(21), 273–284. doi:10.18092/ulikidince.398068

Sayılı, U., Sayman, Ö. A., Vehid, S., Köksal, S. S., & Erginöz, E. (2017). Türkiye ve OECD Ülkelerinin Sağlık Göstergeleri ve Sağlık Harcamalarının Karşılaştırılması. *Online Türk Sağlık Bilimleri Dergisi, 2*(3), 1–12.

Shang, B., & Goldman, D. (2008). Does Age or Life Expectancy Better Predict Health Care Expenditures? *Health Economics, 17*(4), 487–501. doi:10.1002/hec.1295 PMID:17935199

Şirvan, N., & Alp, Ö. S. (2017). Türev Piyasa Araçlarının Türk Bankacılık Sektöründe Riske Olan Etkileri1. *Başkent Üniversitesi Ticari Bilimler Fakültesi Dergisi, 1*(1), 130–157.

Suhrcke, M., Mckee, M., Arce, R. S., Tsolova, S., & Mortensen, J. (2005). The Contribution of Health to the Economy in the European Union. *Health & Consumer Protection Directorate-General.* Retrieved fromhttps://ec.europa.eu/health/archive/ph_overview/documents/health_economy_en.pdf

Teker, D., Teker, S., & Sönmez, M. (2012). *Ekonomik Değişkenlerin Kadın ve Erkeğin Yaşam Süresine Etkisi. İşletme Araştırmaları Dergisi, 4*(3), 118–126.

TUIK. (n.d.). Uluslararası Seçilmiş Göstergeler. Retrieved from https://biruni.tuik.gov.tr/secilmisgostergeler/tabloOlustur.do.

Tüylüoğlu, Ş., Tekin (2009). Gelir Düzeyi ve Sağlık Harcamalarının Beklenen Yaşam Süresi ve Bebek Ölüm Oranı Üzerindeki Etkileri, *Çukurova Üniversitesi İktisadi ve İdari Bilimler Fakültesi Dergisi*, 13(1), 1-31.

UNDP. (n.d.). İnsani Gelişme Endeksleri ve Göstergeleri: 2018 İstatistiksel Güncellemesi Türkiye. Retrieved fromhttp://www.tr.undp.org/content/dam/turkey/hdr2018/tr/Turkey%20Briefing%20NoteTurkey%20Briefing%20NoteTRv01.pdf

Wang, L. (2002). Health Outcomes in Low-Income Countries: Empirical Findings from Demographic and Health Surveys. *World Bank.*

Yalçın, A. Z., & Çakmak, F. (2016). Türkiye'de Kamu Sağlık Harcamalarının İnsani Gelişim Üzerindeki Etkisi. *Atatürk Üniversitesi İktisadi ve İdari Bilimler Dergisi, 30*(4), 705–723.

Yıldırım, C. (2016a). Patent Başvurusu ve İhracat Arasındaki İlişki: Panel Veri Analizi. *Bartın Üniversitesi İİ BF Dergisi, 7*(13), 226–249.

Yıldırım, C. (2016b). Tüketici Fiyat Endeksi ile Faiz Oranı İlişkisinin Ekonometrik Bir İncelemesi. *Kastamonu Üniversitesi İktisadi ve İdari Bilimler Fakültesi Dergisi*, *12*(2), 431–445. doi:10.21180/kuiibf.20161218337

Yüksel, S. (2017). The Impacts of Research and Development Expenses on Export and Economic Growth. *International Business and Accounting Research Journal*, *1*(1), 1–8. doi:10.15294/ibarj.v1i1.1

Yüksel, S., & Oktar, S. (2017). Okun Yasasının Farklı Gelişme Düzeyindeki Ülkelere İlişkin Ekonometrik Analizi. *Marmara Üniversitesi İktisadi ve İdari Bilimler Dergisi*, *39*(1), 323–332. doi:10.14780/muiibd.329945

Chapter 15
The Mediating Role of Self-Efficacy and Leadership in Pygmalion Perception of the Workers:
Trb1 Region Health Worker Research

Eray Ekin Sezgin
Munzur University, Turkey

Muhammet Düşükcan
https://orcid.org/0000-0001-5742-1787
Fırat University, Turkey

ABSTRACT

The main objective of the chapter was to examine the effect on the motivations of Pygmalion perception of health workers working in public-private hospitals operating in TRB1 region (Elazığ, Malatya, Tunceli, and Bingöl) and to analyze the mediator role of self-efficacy and leadership in this effect. For this purpose, employees of all public and private sector hospitals in the region were accepted as main mass and data was collected. A total of 12,939 health workers are employed in these hospitals. The sample of the study consisted of 414 health workers. In this study, the quantitative research method has been used and data was obtained through a face-to-face survey technique. The main analyses used in this study were descriptive statistics, validity and reliability, regression and mediating role analyzes. Pygmalion perception can be effective at a rate of 11% on motivation (r = 0.329; r2 = 0.108; p<0.001). In addition, it was found that leadership and self-efficacy had a partial mediating role in the effect of Pygmalion perception on motivation.

DOI: 10.4018/978-1-7998-2329-2.ch015

INTRODUCTION

It is the human that forms the basis of all businesses. The effective, productive and willing work of the person would be possible with increasing motivation levels and performances. Every employee with high performance and motivation levels rides his/her organization high. From the perspective of hospital businesses, although there is a need for professional staff specialized in today's hospital management, it is an undeniable reality that the manager and health worker, who are fully aware of their duties, powers and responsibilities, integrate with the hospital where they work, fully aware of their duties and increase the performance and efficiency of the institution they work for. For this reason, methods that would contribute to the relationship between the manager and the health worker and hospital performance are gaining importance day by day. In the manager-health worker interaction, employee perceptions about the expectations of managers affect the motivation of health workers. In order to achieve success, one must first be aware of him/herself, believe in what he/she can do, and convince those who follow him/her about what they can do about themselves. Thus, a new understanding of management, "Perception of Pygmalion" would be realized.

The perception (effect) of Pygmalion, which has been found in many different disciplines inspired by mythology, is an effect that enables the target person to meet the expectation as a result of a person's positive or high expectations directed towards the target person and his approach towards these expectations, that is, the fulfillment of the prophecy (Ülgen, 2016, pp. 141-142). In short, the perception of Pygmalion is that the positive and high expectations of an authority figure result in high performance and motivation.

The aim of this study is to determine the effect of Pygmalion perception on the motivation of employees. Another aim of the study is to test whether self-efficacy and leadership play a mediating role in this effect. In this context, in the first part of the study, a theoretical framework about the perception of Pygmalion has been established and the relationship between the concept and motivation, self-efficacy and leadership issues has been explained. In the second part, the aim, importance, method, limits and scales of the study were given and the findings were evaluated, and the necessary analyzes were made for the hypotheses. Finally, the results were stated and suggestions were given.

THEORETICAL FRAMEWORK

The Concept of Pygmalion and the Perception (effect) of Pygmalion

The term Pygmalion, put forward by Rosenthal and Jacobson (1968), is based on a sculptor named Pygmalion, who fell in love with a sculpture that he made, called Galatea in Greek mythology (Kierein & Gold, 2000, p. 914). If we look at Pygmalion mythology in more detail, we can say:

Thanks to the mythology of Hamilton, we know that the Pygmalion myth was described in the Metamorphoses of Roman Publius Ovidius Naso, one of the most important poets of ancient Greek mythology (B.C.33-A.D.18) (Dörtkulak, 2009, p. 69). As Ovidius describes in his work, Pygmalion, a Cypriot sculptor, is a man who does not believe in love, rejects love, hates women, and vows that he would not marry for life. One day, Pygmalion began to make a statue of a woman out of ivory (Hamilton, 2006), and Pygmalion repeatedly corrected and reformed the statue in order to make the most beautiful woman sculpture ever made by working day and night. This woman sculpture, which he has worked diligently on for days and named Galetea, is so beautiful that Pygmalion falls in love with the statue and begs the goddess Venus to give her life. Eventually Venus accepted his wish, gave life to the statue, and Pygmalion and Galetea got married, and had a daughter named Paphos (Grimall, 1997, p. 702). Rumor has it that Paphos, a port city in Cyprus, was named after Paphos, the daughter of Pygmalion and Galetea (Ülgen, 2016, p. 143). This story is also the basis of the Irish classic film George Bernard Shaw's Pygmalion. This film was later transformed into the musical "My Fair Lady" (http://www.artfulliving.com.tr).

Pygmalion, a myth states that something that people desire or perceive as real, would happen sooner or later (Gürel & Muter 2007: 561), is very important in terms of the recognition and fixation of a judgement that still maintains its validity on the existential level by the society (Connerton, 1999, p. 89).

The perception of Pygmalion is defined as the behavior of the person after a while that corresponds to the expectations of others (especially those whom he/she regards as superior to himself or herself) (Psikoloji Sözlüğü, 2000, p. 622). The perception of Pygmalion is the effect of interpersonal expectations, that is, what one person expects can serve as a self-fulfilling prophecy to another (Friedrich et al., 2015, p. 2).

In the psychological literature, the myth of Pygmalion is used as a metaphor. The high expectations of a manager bring special attention to his subordinate and the performance of the subordinate improves. This is called "Pygmalion Perception". The emphasis is on "the manager". Secondly, the subordinate perceives these high expectations of the manager and the performance of the subordinate who perceives the high expectations of the manager improves (Yücel, 2013, p. 23).

Pygmalion is one of mythology-inspired stories that have been included in our lives. Pygmalion is a source of inspiration for the stories of falling in love with the character and person it creates, raised, transformed, changed and even gave life.

Models on the Perception of Pygmalion

In this section, we look at the 4 models that are frequently seen in the literature. These are Rosenthal's Four Factor Model, Rosenthal's Sense-Effort Model, Darley and Fozio's Model, and Reynolds' Pygmalion Model.

Rosenthal's Four Factor Model

In 1968, Rosenthal and Jacobson carried out the Pygmalion in the Classroom, which was highly influential at that time and focused on teacher-student interaction. The researchers who applied a widely used intelligence test to primary school students asked teachers at school to choose a random student and to indicate that a randomly selected group of students who did not differ from their classmates that they would show a significant mental development within 8 months according to the test results. At the end of the semester, the same test was applied to the same students again and it was revealed that the children who were told that they would show mental development, showed a remarkable mental development. According to the findings of this research, this difference stems entirely from the expectations formed in the minds of teachers. Teachers were more patient and encouraging in line with the positive expectations they had developed, and conveyed their expectations to them with voice tone, facial expression and similar gestures and facial expressions. This situation positively affected the students' perceptions about themselves and conditioned them to work more (Rosenthal & Jacobson, 1968). In line with the results of this study, Rosenthal developed the Four Factor Model.

Rosenthal explains the verbal and nonverbal forms of communication with these four factor models and describes the behavior of people with positive Pygmalion perceptions (Brodersen, 2001, p. 12). These four factors can be shaped in Rosenthal's work and in business organizations:

Climate: Climate refers to the socio-emotional environment (Reynolds, 2000, p. 35). It consists of verbal and non-verbal meanings. This factor is associated with high managerial expectations and expresses the confidence that managers have in their subordinates' ability to accomplish the tasks assigned to them (McNatt, 2001, p. 4).

Leaders or managers who say that business organizations do not require a socio-emotional mood or a climate in which the climate is recognized and encouraged, stated that they would be able to provide this situation with sincerity, honest attention, a smile from the heart, nodding with pleasure, covering all forms of communication while maintaining eye contact and emotional support (Brodersen, 2001, p. 12).

In short, in this study, teachers who created a much warmer socio-emotional environment for the students they thought were special, argued that this situation was manifested by non-verbal communication methods such as making eye contact and smiling sincerely (Demirtaş, 2004, p. 47).

Input: Input consists of all the information and resources that managers provide to their employees. Giving extra time to their employees, giving them ideas to realize their projects and providing sufficient resources are examples of good behavior of a manager with high expectations from their employees. Not giving important information about the job, not guiding, not giving enough guidance to the employees, waiting too long to give support when needed, giving limited and sloppy information and acting as inadequate can be given as an example of the bad behaviors that low expectation managers can exhibit (McNatt, 2001: 4). In Rosenthal's experiment, teachers' willingness to teach more and more difficult materials to their "special" students was associated with this factor (Rosenthal, 1994, p. 178).

It is possible to relate the place of the concept in the management of the organization to the managers' approaches that are more supportive, have more material and information towards their employees that those managers have high expectations.

Output: The concept of output refers to approaches that increase the likelihood of success of the other party (Ülgen, 2016, p. 154).

In the research, teachers selected these special students more to answer the questions and offered a longer period of time to them than others (Demirtaş, 2004, p. 48).

In another study, they argued that in order to ask more questions and give more answers, the experimental group should be encouraged more and given more time to do the work correctly (Brodersen, 2001, p. 13).

Feedback: Although many definitions of feedback have been made, Kluger and DeNisi (1996) made the most known and common definition. According to this definition, feedback is activities that provide information about one's performance (Kluger & DeNisi, 1996).

It has been demonstrated that employees in the experimental group need more verbal cues, more responses, more praise, and sometimes even more criticism to learn what they need for their development in order to improve their performance (Brodersen, 2001, p. 13).

In the research, teachers gave feedback that is more detailed to these students about their behaviors (Demirtaş, 2004, pp. 47-48).

Rosenthal's Sense-Effort Model

The four-factor model underwent some changes in 1989 and was renamed as the "sense-effort model" (Demirtaş, 2004, p. 48). According to the model, expectations affect the sensor behavior towards the target through two main factors. The first one includes nonverbal behaviors related to the sense of feelings, like or dislike. The other element, effort, refers to the level of time and interest devoted to the goal. All these behaviors and approaches create a positive effect on the target and provide parallel behaviors when the sensor transmits his / her positive expectations about the target by making closer, relevant, frequent eye contact, spends more time, gives more chance to compensate for errors, and establishes a closer and open communication (Ülgen, 2016, p. 155).

The positive increase in emotion is interpreted as an increase in the love and respect towards the student for many possible reasons. The increase in the teaching effort is considered as a reflection of the increase in the teacher's belief in the adequacy of the student's learning capacity (Demirtaş, 2004, p. 48).

Darley and Fazio's Model

In Darley and Fazio's highly cognitive model, they listed the realization stages of the self-fulfilling prophecy process as follows (Darley & Fazio, 1980):

Establishment of the expectations of the sensor about the target person: The sensor develops expectations about the target person from the experiences he / she has spent with the target person or the social class that the target person is a member. These expectations are also pronounced as target-based and class-based.

Compliance with the expectation of the behavior of the sensor: In this model, the sensor reacts to the target person in a way that is consistent with his expectation.

Interpretation of the target person about this behavior: The target person assigns a meaning to the behavior coming from the sensor.

Reaction of the target person: The target person responds to the sensor in accordance with the meaning it gives to its behavior.

Interpretation of the sensor regarding this response: The sensor makes sense of this response.

Interpretation of the target person's own response: The target person assigns and interprets a meaning to his or her own behavior before the sensor responds.

Reynolds' Pygmalion Model

This model, which is the most recently developed model in the literature, consists of four steps. The distinctive feature of the model is that it does not include the self-expectations of the employees. According to Reynolds, self-efficacy in predicting performance is a better predictor than self-expectations (Leppink, 2010, p. 70).

According to this model, the first factor for the formation of Pygmalion perception is the positive expectations of the managers about their employees. On the other hand, these expectations are meaningful as long as they are conveyed to the employees through behavior. In this context, the second factor is the manager's behavior in accordance with their expectations. Managers' approach to their employees in communicating their expectations and the way of communication they use would create or strengthen the third factor, the self-efficacy beliefs of the employees, and as a result, employees would behave in accordance with the expectations of the manager. In addition, employees' beliefs in self-efficacy would create an increase in managers' expectations (Reynolds, 2000, p. 46).

Undoubtedly, it is possible to see in the literature that many new models have been proposed other than those mentioned so far. However, these new models are not very different from the others, i.e. they repeat other models. For this reason, if we are going to list the sensor's, that is present in all of these models, common points of the stages related to the target person, the following can be expressed (Jussim & Fleming, 1996, p. 165):

- Generally creates unfounded expectations.
- These expectations of the sensor affect his/her behavior towards the target person
- The target person reacts to this behavior in a way that adapts to the expectations of the sensor.

RELATİONSHİP BETWEEN VARİABLES

Relation of Pygmalion Perception with Motivation

David C. McClelland of Harvard University and John W. Atkinson of the University of Michigan demonstrated the relationship between motivation and expectation with the help of a bell curve. Accordingly, the degree of motivation and effort increases until the expectation of success reaches 50 percent, and then begins to decline even if the expectation of success continues to increase. No motivation or reaction arises when it is seen that reaching the goal is either almost certain or almost impossible (Livingston, 1988, p. 127).

Eden argued that there might be a way to set difficult goals, increase expectations, and trigger prophecies in organizations. In his study published in 1988, he stated that expectation plays an effective role in business motivation. The increase in the expectation of the manager affects the motivation and performance of the employee in a direct proportion (Eden, 1988, p. 645). In his study, Dov Eden (1984) stated that the motivation scale had an effect on measuring this effect in the model he established in business organizations on the perception (effect) of Pygmalion. In addition, in his study published in 1988, he stated that expectation plays an effective role in business motivation. He stated that the increase in the expectations of the manager affected the motivation of the employee in direct proportion.

In 1971, King looked for the ways to motivate employees who lack basic social rights. The results of the research show that employees who are deprived of basic social rights can be motivated by making them aware that more responsibility, more competence and more success are expected of them (King, 1971, p. 378).

Relation of Pygmalion Perception with Self-Efficacy

Self-efficacy, derived from social cognitive theory (Bandura, 1968), is a theory that sets out a triple causality model in which the behavior, cognition and environment dynamically influence each other (Gist & Mitchell, 1992, p. 184). Self-efficacy is a concept that strongly influences one's belief in the ability to achieve desired results, people's behavior, motivation and ultimately their success or failure (Bandura, 1977).

An employee with high self-efficacy expectations tries to accomplish tasks that are more difficult and tries to find solutions that are more effective when faced with difficulties. Knowledge about the tools (machinery, equipment, technology, etc.), human resources (managers, teams and employees), organizational characteristics (management style, organizational structure, etc.) and the adequacy of environmental conditions affect the self-efficacy belief. The individual makes an assessment of the tools available in terms of functionality. This phenomenon, called vehicle competence, expresses the individual's belief in the availability and adequacy of the available tools to achieve the desired performance. Even if the individual is very confident in their own abilities, if they do not believe in the resources they have and the competence of the people they work with, they would have doubts that they can achieve the desired results (Yücel, 2013, p. 70).

Pygmalion can influence self-efficacy with the convincing effect of others with positive expectations. Persuasion is an important source of knowledge of activity.

Bandura stated that the types of information, such as the reliability and expertise of the resource, the consensus among multiple sources, and the familiarity of the resource with the task demands, affect the persuasion success. While the expectations of a leader can be seen as a powerful input to the perceptions of subordinates, it is possible that persuasion can be influenced by the reliability of the leader. Therefore, organizational processes related to identifying, evaluating and improving high performances can be influenced by the interaction between the leader's expectations and the subordinate's self-efficacy. It is clear that there is a need for research that controls preferential treatment to clarify the extent that one's expectations can affect self-efficacy perceptions and performance (Gist, 1987, pp. 477-478).

In short, since the Pygmalion Effect is based on the individuals' achievement of the goal they want with high expectations, the high expectations of individuals about themselves are closely related to how advanced their self-efficacy is. There is no doubt that increasing the beliefs of individuals about what they can do would positively affect the business success of both leaders and subordinates.

Relation of Pygmalion Perception with Leadership

A leader who does not hesitate to have strong colleagues and subordinates undoubtedly knows that he is ultimately responsible. An active leader wants strong colleagues and is a person who enjoys their encouragement and emboldening, that is, their presence. He does not see their victories as a threat to himself and sees himself as the ultimate responsible for their mistakes (Drucker, 2000, p. 131).

The role of the employee learning is increasingly important to sustain organizational effectiveness in businesses. Therefore, it should be noted that managing and supporting learning activities is a necessary part of leader responsibilities (Bezuijen et al., 2009, p. 1249). In order for leaders to be effective, their subordinates must strive to develop, become strong and successful employees and leaders must give them the opportunity to learn and practice. The Pygmalion Effect can be used as a correct method in this development process.

Eden (1992), in his study, argued that the manager's expectations about subordinates affect the motivation and performance of the subordinates. According to Eden, managers should be effective leaders and encourage their subordinates to achieve goals that are more challenging, provide constructive feedback on their performance and support them to improve their performance. When subordinates realize their managers' high expectations of themselves, they would make more efforts to perform better. With this process, while competence over the leadership of the managers increases, the performance of the subordinates would improve further. In the study of Priyabhashini and Krishnan (2005), it was found that the perception of the leader's expectations by the followers had a significant positive effect on the motivation of the followers.

METHODOLOGY

Purpose and Contributions of the Research

The aim of the study is to examine the mediating role of self-efficacy and leadership in the effect of the perception of Pygmalion on the motivation of health workers working in public-private hospitals operating in TRB1 region.

The contribution of the study to the application is that the number of the studies related to Pygmalion perception in Turkey is limited. In addition, the absence of a study in the field of health makes this study a pioneer.

The theoretical contribution of the study is that Pygmalion Attitude Index, Self-Efficacy Scale, Leadership Scale and Motivation Scale are used together for the first time and examined in a holistic model.

Universe and Sampling

The universe of the research consists of public and private hospitals operating in TRB1 (Elazığ, Malatya, Bingöl, Tunceli) Region. There are 6031 health workers in Elazığ, 4723 in Malatya, 1697 in Bingöl and 488 in Tunceli (no private hospitals). These figures are based on the information obtained from hospital administrations as of April 2018.

When the universe size (N) is taken as 12939, the sample size (n), also known as the Cochran Formula, should be at least 374. In our study, 414 health workers constitute the sample size. With this number, it will be possible to say that the sample size has the power of representing the Universe at 95% confidence level (Demirel, 2009).

$$SampleSize(n) = \frac{N \times t^2 \times p \times q}{\left((N-1) \times d^2\right) + \left(t^2 \times p \times q\right)}$$

N: universe (12939); t: ∞ theoretical t table value at degree of freedom (1,96); p: probability of occurrence of the examined event (0,5); q: probability of event not being examined (0,5); pxq: variance (0,25) d: accepted sampling error (0,05).

Data Collection and Analysis Method

The data in this study was collected by questionnaire method which is a widely used method in first degree data collection. Health workers in hospitals were reached directly. The aim of the study and the content of the questionnaires were explained to health workers who will participate in the study with face to face interviews.

The questionnaire form used in the study consists of five parts. The first part contains the "Pygmalion attitude index", which includes ten questions. The scale was developed by Eden (1990). The scale, which consists of one dimension, was translated into Turkish by Yücel (2013); it was used in a study conducted by Bayram (2014). The reliability and validity of the scale were tested and found to be acceptable. Cronbach's Alpha (internal consistency coefficient) was determined as 0.659 by Yücel (2013) and as 0.779 by Bayram (2014).

The second part of the questionnaire contains the "Self-Efficacy Scale", which was developed by Chen, Gully and Eden (2001) and translated into Turkish by Yücel (2013). This scale consists of 8 questions and one dimension. Cronbach's Alpha (internal consistency coefficient) was determined as 0.815 by Yücel (2013); 0.824 by Bayram (2014), and 0.892 by Mushtaq and Khalidi (2016).

In the third part of the questionnaire contains the "Motivation Scale", which was developed by Priyabhashini and Krishnan (2005). This scale consists of 5 questions and one dimension. Cronbach's Alpha (internal consistency coefficient) was determined as 0.71 by Priyabhashini and Krishnan (2005).

The fourth part of the questionnaire includes Multifactor Leadership Questionnaire developed by Avolio and Bass (1995) to measure leadership. This scale consists of 45 items; the first 36 items measure leadership dimensions and the remaining 9 items measure leadership output. Since no hypothesis has been developed regarding the outcomes of leadership within the context of this study, the last 9 items in the scale were not included in the questionnaire. In this scale, 5 items that are assumed to measure the dimensions of mental incentive, inspirational leadership, individual interest, charismatic and laissez faire leadership dimensions are included (Tosunoğlu, 2014). These four scales are rated according to a five-point Likert scale. In the final part of the questionnaire, there are 7 questions to determine the demographic characteristics of health workers.

SPSS 20.0 statistical package program was used to evaluate the data. The main analyzes used in the study are descriptive statistics, validity and reliability, regression and mediator variable analysis.

Problem Sentence, Hypothesis and Model of Research

The problem statement of the Research has been determined as; "Does Pygmalion Perception (Effect), affect the motivation of the workers? Does this effect become meaningful by means of the perception of leadership and self-efficacy? The following hypotheses have been put forward based on this problem statement:

H_1: There is the effect of Pygmalion perception of the workers on worker motivation.
H_2: There is the effect of Pygmalion perception of the workers on workers leadership behavior perception level.
H_3: There is the effect of Pygmalion perception of the workers on worker self-efficacy.
H_4: There is the effect of leadership behavior perception level of the workers on worker motivation.
H_5: There is the effect of self-efficacy of the worker on worker motivation.
H_6: Leadership has a mediating role in the relation between Pygmalion perception of the workers and worker motivation.
H_7: Self-efficacy has a mediating role in the relation between Pygmalion perception of the workers and worker motivation.

Starting from the researches in the literature, the research models developed in this study as a result of the concepts explained are shown below (figure 1 and figure 2):

Assumptions and Limitations of the Research

The assumptions of the research are as follows:

Figure 1. Model of the research-I

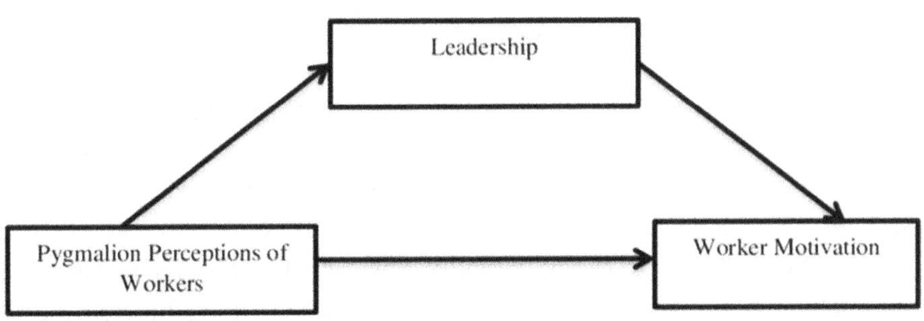

Figure 2. Model of the research-II

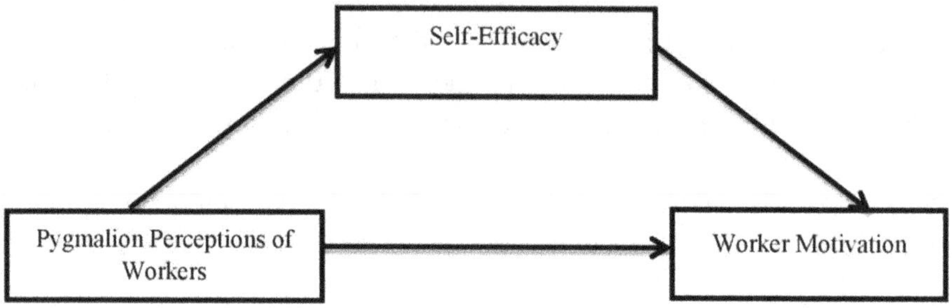

- Through operating hospitals, it is thought that Pygmalion perception of health workers regarding the emotions in the organizational management of public-private hospitals in TRB1 region will be realistically determined.
- It is assumed that the scales to be used cover all the details related to the subject.
- It is thought that health workers have a positive effect on the achievement of the goals of the people within the scope of Pygmalion perception and in terms of improving the management functions of hospitals.

The limitations of the study are as follows:

- The subject will be approached within the framework of health institutions and organization management.
- The fact that the study was carried out in a certain period and on certain hospitals in TRB1 region comes out to be a limitation of the study.
- Although the results obtained from the study are enough to make generalization, different results can be obtained in different fields, different regions and/or different hospitals considering the limitations of the study.

Reliability and Validity of Research

At this stage, validity and reliability analysis was performed for the scales used within the scope of Pygmalion Perception used in the research part of the study. Cronbach's Alpha coefficient was used for the reliability and validity of the questionnaire questions.

Table 1 shows the results of the reliability analysis of Pygmalion attitude index, self-efficacy, motivation and leadership. As it is seen in the chart, the results are

Table 1. Results of reliability / validity analysis of scales

Name of Scale	Cronbach's Alpha
Pygmalion Attitude İndex	0,842
Self-Efficacy	0,882
Motivation	0,680
Leadership	0,833

quite reliable and highly reliable, and so these coefficients are enough for the study (Erdoğruca, 2011).

Confirmatory Factor Analysis has been used to crosscheck the factor structure of the scales. The results of the confirmatory factor analysis are presented in the following table:

Confirmatory factor analysis was applied to Pygmalion attitude index, self-efficacy and leadership scales. The data obtained show that the structure is validated, ie the model fit index values are acceptable (Pygmalion attitude index, self-efficacy and leadership) and at a very good level (motivation).

ANALYSIS OF DATA

Distribution of Health Workers by Demographic Characteristics

The demographic distribution of health workers working in Public-Private hospitals in TRB1 region is shown in the table below.

41.8% of the health workers are male and 58.2% are female. It is seen that women's weight in public-private hospitals in TRB1 Region is reflected in our survey. 52.9% of the health workers are married category and 47.1% of are unmarried. 45.9% of

Table 2. Confirmatory factor analysis model fit indexes of scale

	Uyum İndeksleri								
	$\chi 2$	sd	$\chi 2$ / sd	p	AGFI	GFI	CFI	NFI	RMSEA
Pygmalion Attitude İndex	132,078	32	**4,127**	0,000	0,901	0,943	0,920	0,898	**0,080**
Self-Efficacy	51,792	19	**2,726**	0,000	0,940	0,968	0,976	0,963	**0,065**
Motivation	9,168	5	**1,184**	0,103	0,974	0,991	0,988	0,974	**0,045**
Leadership	15,861	5	**3,172**	0,007	0,956	0,985	0,985	0,979	**0,073**

Table 3. Demographic distribution of health workers (n=414)

Variable	Demographic	Frequency	%
Gender	Male	173	41.8
	Female	241	58.2
Marital Status	Married	219	52.9
	Unmarried	195	47.1
Age	≤ 29	190	45.9
	30-39	171	41.3
	40-49	42	10.1
	≥ 50	11	2.7
Education Level	Secondary School	3	0.7
	High School	41	9.9
	Associate Degree	49	11.8
	Undergraduate	269	65.0
	Postgraduate	52	12.6
Position	Doctor	164	39.6
	Nurse/Midwife	164	39.6
	Health Officer	65	15.7
	Health Technician	21	5.1
Professional Experience	1-5 years	167	40.3
	6-10 years	131	31.6
	11-15 years	49	11.8
	16-20 years	54	13.0
	≥ 21 years	13	3.1
Duty Periods in Available Hospital	1-5 years	214	51.7
	6-10 years	96	23.2
	11-15 years	49	11.8
	16-20 years	44	10.6
	≥ 21 years	11	2.7

the health workers are health workers under the age of 29. 41.3% of health care workers are health workers between the ages of 30-39. 10.1% of health workers are health workers between the ages of 40-49. 2.7% of the health workers are health workers over the age of 50. 0.7% of health workers are secondary school, 9.9% are high school, 11.8% are associate degree, 65% are undergraduate and 12.6% are postgraduate education. 39.6% of the health workers are doctors, 39.6% are nurses

/ midwives, 15.7% are health officers and 5.1% are health technicians. 40.3% of the health workers have been experiencing for 1-5 years, 31.6% for 6-10 years, 11.8% 11-15 years, 13% for 16-20 years and 3.1% for 21 years or more. 51.7% of the health workers have been working in the current hospital for 1-5 years, 23.2% for 6-10 years, 11.8% for 11-15 years, 10.6% for 16-20 years and 2.7% for 21 years or more.

REGRESSION ANALYSIS BETWEEN VARIABLES

The Effect Pygmalion Perception of the Workers on Worker Motivation

Regression analysis was performed to determine whether Pygmalion perceptions of health workers had an effect on worker motivation and the results indicated in Table 4 were obtained.

As seen in Table 4, the analyzed regression model is statistically significant at a significance level of 0.05 and the R^2 value have been found to be 0.108. Accordingly, the motivation of the health worker can explain the Pygmalion perception of health workers only by 10.8%. Pygmalion attitude index (β= 0.329: $p < 0.05$), which is one of the variables in the model, was found to have an effect on the motivation scale. In the context of the above results, the H_1 hypothesis was supported.

The Effect Pygmalion Perception of the Workers on Workers Leadership Behavior Perception Level

Regression analysis was performed to determine whether Pygmalion perceptions of health workers had an effect on leadership behavior perception level and the results indicated in Table 5 were obtained.

Table 4. Effect of Pygmalion perception on motivation

Variables	Motivation			Correlations			Collinearity Statistics	
	Beta	t	p	Zero-Order	Partial	Part	Tolerance	VIF
Pygmalion Attitude Index	0.329	7.080	0.000	0.329	0.329	0.329	1.000	1.000
R	0.329							
R^2	0.108							
Adjusted R^2	0.106							

As seen in Table 5, the analyzed regression model is statistically significant at a significance level of 0.05 and the R^2 value have been found to be 0.094. Accordingly, the leadership of the health worker can explain the Pygmalion perception of health workers only by 9.4%. Pygmalion attitude index (β= 0.306: p<0.05), which is one of the variables in the model, was found to have an effect on the leadership scale. In the context of the above results, the H_2 hypothesis was supported.

The Effect Pygmalion Perception of the Workers on Worker Self-Efficacy

Regression analysis was performed to determine whether Pygmalion perceptions of health workers had an effect on worker self-efficacy and the results indicated in Table 6 were obtained.

As seen in Table 6, the analyzed regression model is statistically significant at a significance level of 0.05 and the R^2 value have been found to be 0.144. Accordingly, the self-efficacy of the health worker can explain the Pygmalion perception of health

Table 5. Effect of Pygmalion perception on leadership behavior perception level

Variables	Leadership			Correlations			Collinearity Statistics	
	Beta	t	p	Zero-Order	Partial	Part	Tolerance	VIF
Pygmalion Attitude Index	0,306	6,525	0,000	0,306	0,306	0,306	1.000	1.000
R	0,306							
R^2	0,094							
Adjusted R^2	0,091							

Table 6. Effect of Pygmalion perception on self-efficacy

Variables	Self-Efficacy			Correlations			Collinearity Statistics	
	Beta	t	p	Zero-Order	Partial	Part	Tolerance	VIF
Pygmalion Attitude Index	0,380	8,340	0,000	0,380	0,380	0,380	1.000	1.000
R	0,380							
R^2	0,144							
Adjusted R^2	0,142							

workers only by 14.4%. Pygmalion attitude index (β= 0.380: $p<0.05$), which is one of the variables in the model, was found to have an effect on the self-efficacy scale. In the context of the above results, the H_3 hypothesis was supported.

The Effect Leadership Behavior Perception Level of the Workers on Worker Motivation

Regression analysis was performed to determine whether leadership behavior perception level of health workers had an effect on worker motivation and the results indicated in Table 7 were obtained.

As seen in Table 7, the analyzed regression model is statistically significant at a significance level of 0.05 and the R^2 value have been found to be 0.075. Accordingly, the motivation of the health worker can explain the leadership behavior perception level of health workers only by 7.5%. Leadership Behavior Perception Level (β = 0.274: $p < 0.05$), which is one of the variables in the model, was found to have an effect on the motivation scale. In the context of the above results, the H_4 hypothesis was supported.

The Effect Self-Efficacy of the Workers on Worker Motivation

Regression analysis was performed to determine whether self-efficacy of health workers had an effect on worker motivation and the results indicated in Table 8 were obtained.

As seen in Table 8, the analyzed regression model are statistically significant at a significance level of 0.05 and the R^2 value have been found to be 0.201. Accordingly, the motivation of the health worker can explain the Self-efficacy of health workers only by 20.1%. Self-Efficacy (β = 0.448: $p < 0.05$), which is one of the variables

Table 7. Effect of leadership behavior perception level on motivation

Variables	Motivation			Correlations			Collinearity Statistics	
	Beta	t	p	Zero-Order	Partial	Part	Tolerance	VIF
Leadership	0,274	5,790	0,000	0,274	0,274	0,274	1.000	1.000
R	0,274							
R^2	0,075							
Adjusted R^2	0,073							

Table 8. Effect of self-efficacy on motivation

Variables	Motivation			Correlations			Collinearity Statistics	
	Beta	t	p	Zero-Order	Partial	Part	Tolerance	VIF
Self-Efficacy	0,448	10,172	0,000	0,448	0,448	0,448	1.000	1.000
R	0,448							
R^2	0,201							
Adjusted R^2	0,199							

in the model, was found to have an effect on the motivation scale. In the context of the above results, the H_5 hypothesis was supported.

Mediating Effect of Leadership Between Pygmalion Perception of the Workers and Worker Motivation

The motivation of the health worker was considered as dependent variable, pygmalion perceptions as independent variable and leadership behavior perception level as mediating variable. The results obtained are presented in Table 9.

When Table 9 is examined, it is seen that the conditions of Baron and Kenny are fulfilled. The first condition was that there was a significant effect between the independent variable (Pygmalion perceptions of health worker) and the mediator variable (leadership between Pygmalion perception of health worker) and this is realized (β=0.306, p=0.000). The second condition was that the independent variable (Pygmalion perceptions of health workers) had a significant effect on the dependent variable (Worker Motivation). This effect was statistically significant (β = 0.329, p= 0.000). Finally, the independent variable and the intermediate variable were included together in the model and the dependent variable was tried to be explained. After this step, the significant effect's becoming insignificant (absolute mediating effect) or decline in the effect level of the significant effect (partial mediating effect) will give clues about the existence of mediating effect. When the third step is examined, it can be seen that the relation between Pygmalion perceptions of the health workers and worker motivation (compared to second step) has not become insignificant, yet the effect level has declined (β=0.271, p=0.000). This may result in a partial mediating effect leadership behavior perception level of worker between the Pygmalion perception of health workers and worker motivation. However, this is not sufficient to talk about mediating effect. The significance of the amount of the decline in Beta (β) values is to be determined to obtain an exact result. The

Table 9. Mediating effect of leadership between Pygmalion perception and motivation

	Variable	B	Standard Error $_B$	β	t	p	Double r	Partial r	Tolerance	VIF
Model 1	Constant	2.182	0.249		8.769	0.000				
	Worker Perception	0.387	0.059	0.306	6.525	0.000	0.306	0.306	1.000	1.000
	$R = 0.306; R^2 = 0.094; F_{(1.413)} = 42.575; p = .000$									
	Leadership = 2.182 + 0.387* Worker Perception									
Model 2	Constant	3.384	0.157		21.576	0.000				
	Worker Perception	0.264	0.037	0.329	7.080	0.000	0.329	0.329	1.000	1.000
	$R = 0.329; R^2 = 0.108; F_{(1.413)} = 50.122; p = .000$									
	Motivation = 3.384 + 0.264* Worker Perception									
Model 3	Constant	3.118	0.168		18.580	0.000				
	Worker Perception	0.217	0.039	0.271	5.640	0.000	0.268	0.258	0.906	1.103
	Leadership	0.122	0.031	0.191	3.988	0.000	0.193	0.182	0.906	1.103
	$R = 0.376; R^2 = 0.142; F_{(2.411)} = 33.921; p = .000$									
	Motivation = 3.118 + 0.217*Worker Perceptions + 0.122*Leadership									

significance level of the amount of decline in Beta values was found out by using Sobel Test. According to the results of Sobel Test; Z = 4.344 and p = 0.000 values were obtained with the inputs a = 0.387, b = 0.174, Sa = 0.059 and Sb = 0.030. According to these results, the decrease in the values is significant. From this point on, it can be said that the leadership behavior perception level between Pygmalion perceptions of health workers and worker motivation have partial mediating effect. In the context of the above results, the H_6 hypothesis was supported.

Mediating Effect of Self-Efficacy Between Pygmalion Perception of the Workers and Worker Motivation

The motivation of the health worker was considered as dependent variable, Pygmalion perceptions as independent variable and self-efficacy as mediating variable. The results obtained are presented in Table 10.

When Table 10 is examined, it is seen that the conditions of Baron and Kenny are fulfilled. The first condition was that there was a significant effect between the independent variable (Pygmalion perceptions of health worker) and the mediator variable (self-efficacy of health worker) and this is realized (β=0.380, p=0.000). The second condition was that the independent variable (Pygmalion perceptions

Table 10. Mediating effect of self-efficacy between Pygmalion perception and motivation

	Variable	B	Standard Error $_B$	β	t	p	Double r	Partial r	Tolerance	VIF
Model 1	Constant	2.955	0.177		16.704	0.000				
	Worker Perception	0.351	0.042	0.380	8.340	0.000	0.380	0.380	1.000	1.000
	$R = 0.380$; $R^2 = 0.144$; $F_{(1.413)} = 69.553$; $p = .000$									
	Self-Efficacy = 2.955 + 0.351* Worker Perceptions									
Model 2	Constant	3.384	0.157		21.576	0.000				
	Worker Perception	0.264	0.037	0.329	7.080	0.000	0.329	0.329	1.000	1.000
	$R = 0.329$; $R^2 = 0.108$; $F_{(1.413)} = 50.122$; $p = .000$									
	Motivation = 3.384 + 0.264* Worker Perceptions									
Model 3	Constant	2.415	0.189		12.783	0.000				
	Worker Perception	0.149	0.038	0.186	3.974	0.000	0.192	0.172	0.856	1.169
	Self-Efficacy	0.328	0.041	0.377	8.066	0.000	0.370	0.349	0.856	1.169
	$R = 0.480$; $R^2 = 0.230$; $F_{(2.411)} = 61.491$; $p = .000$									
	Motivation = 2.415 + 0.149* Worker Perceptions + 0.328*Self-Efficacy									

of health workers) had a significant effect on the dependent variable (Worker Motivation). This effect was statistically significant ($\beta = 0.329$, $p = 0.000$). Finally, the independent variable and the intermediate variable were included together in the model and the dependent variable was tried to be explained. After this step, the significant effect's becoming insignificant (absolute mediating effect) or decline in the effect level of the significant effect (partial mediating effect) will give clues about the existence of mediating effect. When the third step is examined, it can be seen that the relation between Pygmalion perceptions of the health workers and worker motivation (compared to second step) has not become insignificant, yet the effect level has declined ($\beta = 0.186$, $p = 0.000$). This may result in a partial mediating effect self-efficacy of worker between the Pygmalion perception of health workers and worker motivation. However, this is not sufficient to talk about mediating effect. The significance of the amount of the decline in Beta (β) values is to be determined to obtain an exact result. The significance level of the amount of decline in Beta values was found out by using Sobel Test. According to the results of Sobel Test; $Z = 6.473$ and $p = 0.000$ values were obtained with the inputs $a = 0.351$, $b = 0.389$, $Sa = 0.042$ and $Sb = 0.038$. According to these results, the decrease in the values is significant. From this point on, it can be said that the self-efficacy between Pygmalion perceptions of health workers and worker motivation have partial mediating effect. In the context of the above results, the H_7 hypothesis was supported.

SOLUTIONS AND RECOMMENDATIONS

Hospitals need to manage their human resources effectively and efficiently in order to compete and maintain their competitive advantage. Hospitals should use their human resources in the most effective and efficient way to make a difference in the global world where they can reach all the resources more easily. It is possible for the enterprises to be productive with the high level of motivation of the employees. From this point of view, managers have a big role to make employees have higher motivation. Managers need to develop high expectations about health workers. The motivation of healthcare workers, who perceive high managerial expectations, would increase. In summary, the expectations of the manager and the perception of these expectations by the health workers affect the motivation of the health worker.

- It is important that the communication between the managers and healthcare workers who take part in the system, as a part of the system is realized correctly. In this process, which is co-operative in terms of work process flow in hospitals, the ability of managers to direct health workers as leaders is of great importance for the success of hospitals in the health industry market. Therefore, managers need to be aware of their self-efficacy and make efforts to develop them further.
- High expectations have the chance to be realized only if they are compatible with the capacities of health workers. Having high expectations without knowing the individuals and having an idea about their self-efficacy can disappoint both managers and healthcare workers. Therefore, managers should try to get to know the health workers they work with and be aware of their capacities.
- As a result of the study, it is seen that the perception of Pygmalion can be realized in the health workers in hospitals. Hospitals have a complex organizational structure and include many businesses with different characteristics. However, if hospital managers have knowledge about the subject and include this practice in the hospital system, the motivation of health workers and their perceptions about their managers would improve in a positive way, which would contribute to decrease employee turnover and increase organizational commitment.

- Pygmalion trainings can be given not only for the health sector but also for increasing the performance, self-efficacy and motivation of the employees in many other sectors.
- The research was conducted on health workers working in public-private hospitals in TRB1 Region (Elazığ, Malatya, Bingöl, and Tunceli). The generalization of the research results on all health workers would not be correct. Therefore, conducting similar researches covering different provinces and districts would contribute to the comparison and evaluation of the results.
- Likewise, the study of Pygmalion Perception on the employees of different sectors would make an additional contribution to the notion of this concept and the literature.

FUTURE RESEARCH DIRECTIONS

The empirical and conceptual results of this study, combined with the abovementioned limitations, reveal a number of interesting future research opportunities. One of the accepted limitations of this study is that the study was conducted on some hospitals in the TRB1 Region within a certain period of time. Health sector has a very changeable structure depending on its dynamic structure. Policies, procedures and practices change over time. Therefore, it would be useful to compare the findings of our study with the researchers at a different time in the future.

This study is limited to the hospitals operating in TRB1 region. Research is also required in different areas, different regions and / or different hospitals. In addition, in other studies, different variables (performance etc.) can be added to the analysis by expanding the scope. It is also thought that other investigations would have the advantage of discovering potential mediator roles and moderators for these links. In this respect, it is important to conduct new studies that can contribute to both practice and literature.

CONCLUSION

This study was conducted to investigate the effects of the perception of Pygmalion on motivation of health workers working in public and private hospitals of TRB1 Region. The answers to the questions of "Does the perception of Pygmalion affect the motivation of employees? Does this effect make sense through the perceptions of leadership and self-efficacy?" were sought. The study reveals that the expectations (Pygmalion perception) of healthcare workers' managers have a positive effect on their motivation. It is important for the health worker to have a positive place in the expectations of the managers. The motivation of a health worker who thinks that he/she creates a positive perception would also increase.

In addition, it was found that self-efficacy and leadership had a partial mediating role in the relationship between employees' perceptions of Pygmalion and their motivation. The presence of a partial mediation effect indicates that another variable can mediate between the dependent variable and the independent variable (Baron & Kenny, 1986). From this point of view, it can be concluded that the relationship between Pygmalion perceptions of health workers and employee motivation can be mediated by other variables besides employee self-efficacy and leadership behaviors.

In Turkey, the limited research on the perception of Pygmalion, and in particular the lack of a work previously done in the health field, makes this study a pioneer. Therefore, it is hoped that it would make a modest contribution to the field. In addition, it is thought that it would be a belief and practice that could be used to benefit from the perception of Pygmalion, in other words to direct people in line with expectations, not only in the health sector, but also in other sectors where human relations are intense and in cases of business success. In short, the perception of Pygmalion draws attention to the relationship between healthcare workers in hospitals from a different perspective and positively affects individual and organizational performance and provides an important benefit to both people-oriented management and organization management. It is estimated that this perception would play an important role in the motivation of employees in health enterprises and would emerge as a management approach that creates change and value in order to survive in the global competitive environment.

REFERENCES

Bandura, A. (1977). Self-efficacy: Toward a Unifying Theory of Behavioral Change. *Psychological Review*, *84*(2), 191–215. doi:10.1037/0033-295X.84.2.191 PMID:847061

Baron, R. M., & Kenny, D. A. (1986). The Moderator-Mediator Variable Distinction in Social Psychological Research: Conceptual, Strategic, And Statistical Considerations. *Journal of Personality and Social Psychology*, *51*(6), 1173–1182. doi:10.1037/0022-3514.51.6.1173 PMID:3806354

Bayram, Ü. (2014). *Turizm Sektörü Yönetici ve İşgörenleri Arasında Pygmalion Etkisi: Otel İşletmelerinde Bir Uygulama*. Ankara: Gazi Üniversitesi Eğitim Bil. Ens. Doktora Tezi.

Bezuijen, X. M., Berg, P. T., Dam, K., & Thierry, H. (2009). Pygmalion and Employee Learning: The Role of Leader Behaviors. *The Netherlands Journal of Management, 35*(5), 1248–1267.

Brodersen, R. B. (2001). Can Woman Leaders in Organizational Settings in The United States Produce the Pygmalion Effect? [Doctoral thesis]. Nova Southeastern University, FL.

Chen, G., Gully, S. M., & Eden, D. (2001). Validation of a New General Self- Efficacy Scale. *Organizational Research Methods, 4*(1), 62–83. doi:10.1177/109442810141004

Connerton, P. (1999). *Toplumlar Nasıl Anımsar? Çev. Alâeddin Şenel.* İstanbul: Ayrıntı Yayınları.

Darley, J. M., & Fazio, R. H. (1980). Expectancy Confirmation Processes Arising in The Social Interaction Sequence. *The American Psychologist, 35*(10), 867–881. doi:10.1037/0003-066X.35.10.867

Demirel, E. T. (2009). *İşletmelerin Kalite ve Sistem Belgelendirme İle İlgili Bilgi Düzeylerinin ve Karşılaştıkları Sorunların Tespiti: Doğu ve Güneydoğu Anadolu Bölgelerinde Faaliyet Gösteren İhracatçı İmalat Sanayi İşletmelerinde Bir Araştırma, İnönü Üniversitesi Sos.* Malatya: Bil.Ens. Doktora Tezi.

Demirtaş, A. (2004). *Sosyal Sınıflandırma. Kişilerarası Beklentiler ve Kendini Gerçekleştiren Kehanet, İletişim Araştırmaları, 2*(2), 33–53.

Dörtkulak, F. (2009). Maturation Of Shavian Women: A Study Of The Maturation Processes Of Female Pratogonists. In *George Bernard Shaw's Pygmalion and Mrs Warren's Profession, Ortadoğu Teknik Üniversitesi Sos.* Ankara: Bil.Ens. Yüksek Lisans Tezi.

Drucker, P. F. (2000). *Gelecek için yönetim: 1990'lar ve sonrası. (F. Üçcan, Çev.).* Ankara: Türkiye İş Bankası Kültür Yayınları.

Eden, D. (1988). Pygmalion, Goal Setting, and Expectancy: Compatible Ways to Boost Productivity. *Academy of Management Review, 13*(4), 639–652. doi:10.5465/amr.1988.4307530

Eden, D. (1990). *Pygmalion in Management: Productivity as Self-Fulfilling Prophecy.* Lexington, MA: Lexington Books.

Eden, D. (1992). Leadership and Expectations: Pygmalion Effects and Other Self-Fulfilling Prophecies in Organizations. *The Leadership Quarterly, 3*(4), 271–305. doi:10.1016/1048-9843(92)90018-B

Erdoğruca, P. (2011). *Dönüşümcü (Transformasyonel)*. Konya: Liderlik ve Örgütsel Bağlılık Arasındaki İlişki, Selçuk Üniversitesi Sos.Bil.Ens. Yüksek Lisans Tezi.

Friedrich, A., Flunger, B., Nagengast, B., Jonkmann, K., & Trautwein, U. (2015). Pygmalion Effects in The Classroom: Teacher Expectancy Effects On Students' Math Achievement. *Contemporary Educational Psychology*, *41*, 1–12. doi:10.1016/j.cedpsych.2014.10.006

Gist, M. E. (1987). Self-Efficacy: Implications for Organizational Behavior and Human Resource Management. *Academy of Management Review*, *12*(3), 472–485. doi:10.5465/amr.1987.4306562

Gist, M. E., & Mitchell, T. R. (1992). Self-Efficacy: A Theoretical Analysis of Its Determinants and Malleability. *Academy of Management Review*, *17*(2), 183–211. doi:10.5465/amr.1992.4279530

Grimall, P. (1997). *Mitoloji Sözlüğü, Çev. Sevgi Tamgüç*. İstanbul: Sosyal Yayınlar.

Gürel, E. ve Muter, C. (2007). Psikomitolojik Terimler: Psikoloji Literatüründe Mitolojinin Kullanılması. *Anadolu Üniversitesi Sosyal Bilimler Dergisi*, *7*(1), 537–569.

Hamilton, E. (2006). *Mitologya, Çev. Ülkü Tamer*. İstanbul: Varlık Yayınları.

Jussim, L., & Fleming, C. (1996). *Self-Fulfilling Prophecies and The Maintenance of Social Stereotypes: The role of dyadic interactions and social forces. In Stereotypes and stereotyping* (pp. 161–193). NY: The Guilford Press.

Kierein, N. M., & Gold, M. A. (2000). Pygmalion in Work Organizations: A Meta-Analysis. *Journal of Organizational Behavior*, *21*(8), 913–928. doi:10.1002/1099-1379(200012)21:8<913::AID-JOB62>3.0.CO;2-#

King, A. S. (1971). Self-Fulfilling Prophecies in Training The Hard-core: Supervisors' Expectations and The Underprivileged Workers' Performance. *Social Science Quarterly*, *52*(2), 369–378.

Kluger, A. N., & DeNisi, A. (1996). The Effects of Feedback Interventions on Performance: A Historical Review, Meta-Analysis, and A Preliminary Feedback Intervention Theory. *Psychological Bulletin*, *119*(2), 254–284. doi:10.1037/0033-2909.119.2.254

Leppink, C. K. (2010). Pygmalion Training in a For-Profit Organization: The Nondeceptive Creation of the Pygmalion Effect [Doctoral Thesis]. Regent University, Virginia.

Livingston, J. S. (1988). Pygmalion in Management. *Harvard Business Review*, 121–130. PMID:12545926

McNatt, B. (2001). *The Pygmalion Effect Managing The Power of Expectations: Leader's Guide*. CRM Learning.

Mushtaq, Y., & Khalidi, M. (2016). A Study on Pygmalion Effect: A Case of Academic Training in a Military Unit. *Market Forces*, *11*(1), 35–48.

Priyabhashini, A., & Krishnan, V. R. (2005). Transformational Leadership and Follower's Career Advancement: Role of Pygmalion Effect. *Indian Journal of Industrial Relations*, *40*(4), 482–499.

Psikoloji Sözlüğü. (2000). Rol karışıklığı. In *"Rol haritası", "Rol mesafesi", "Stereotip", "Pygmalion etkisi", "Pygmalionizm", "Toplum yanlısı saldırganlık", "Özdeşim teorisi". S. Budak (haz.)*. Ankara: Bilim ve Sanat Yayınları.

Reynolds, D. E. (2000). Pygmalion in Management: Understanding Supervisory Expectations As an Antecedent of Managerial Self-Efficacy [Doctoral Thesis]. Cornell University, NY.

Rosenthal, R. (1994). Interpersonal Expectancy Effects: A 30-year perspective. *Current Directions in Psychological Science*, *3*(6), 176–179. doi:10.1111/1467-8721.ep10770698

Rosenthal, R., & Jacobson, L. (1968). *Pygmalion in the classroom*. New York: Holt, Rinehart &Winston Inc. doi:10.1007/BF02322211

Tosunoğlu, H. (2014). *Liderlik Tarzı Algısının Örgütsel Bağlılık Üzerindeki Etkisinde Örgüte Güvenin Aracı Rolü: Bir Örnek Olay İncelemesi, Hacettepe Üniversitesi Sos.* Ankara: Bil.Ens. Yüksek Lisans Tezi.

Ülgen, B. (2016). *Örgüt Yönetiminde Duygular, Nobel Dağıtım, 1*. Ankara: Baskı.

Yücel, D. (2013). Pygmalion Etkisi Kapsamında Yönetici Beklentilerinin Astlar Tarafından Algılanmasının Astların Performansı Üzerindeki Etkileri ve Bir Araştırma [Doktora Tezi]. Marmara Üniversitesi Sos.Bil.Ens., İstanbul. Retrieved from http://www.artfulliving.com.tr/kultur-ve-yasam/pygmalion-bir-kadin-yaratmak-ve-onunla-aska-dusmek-i-6059

Chapter 16
What Drives the Convergence of Per-Capita Health Expenditures in the EU Member Countries?
A Geographically-Weighted Regression Analysis

Gönül Yüce Akinci
Ünye Faculty of Economics and Administrative Sciences, Ordu University, Turkey

Merter Akinci
Ünye Faculty of Economics and Administrative Sciences, Ordu University, Turkey

ABSTRACT

One of the most important issues in economic development is the examination of the convergence phenomenon. The convergence analysis has been enhanced with the efforts of various economists and the convergence trends in all areas of the economic system have been determined with the help of applied analysis. As well as income convergence analysis among countries, the convergence dynamics in health expenditures have become popular in recent years. Therefore, the main motivation of this study is to examine the convergence process of health expenditures in the European Union member countries using a geographically weighted regression analysis of the period 1970 to 2017. The results of the analysis indicate that a statistically strong convergence is valid in "the Six" and the Eurozone, while there is not any statistically significant convergence in non-member states of the Eurozone. Also, the findings of the panel cross-country analysis also point out the nonexistence of the convergence. Finally, the analysis is extended to examine convergence by adding some control variables.

DOI: 10.4018/978-1-7998-2329-2.ch016

INTRODUCTION

The concept of convergence that emerges with the neoclassical school is developed under the pioneering work of Solow (1956) and convergence process is defined as follows: underdeveloped or developing countries will grow faster than developed countries and the per capita income level differences in these country groups will close. Besides, convergence hypothesis is defined as the coming back of a country to its own steady state by growing or shrinking at a certain rate. The basis of the convergence hypothesis is that there is a negative relationship between per capita income and the growth rate of per capita income. Neoclassical theory states that underdeveloped countries with lower capital/labor ratio and lower per capita income will grow faster than developed countries due to the fact that capital is subject to diminishing returns to scale. The fact that capital is subject to diminishing returns reflects that the return generated by an additional unit of capital will be higher in poorer countries than in rich countries. Therefore, the convergence hypothesis suggests that economic growth will be slower in countries with higher per capita income than that of in other countries (Mbaku and Kimenyi, 1997, p. 121; Akıncı, 2017, p. 340).

The convergence hypothesis is based on three theories. These are can be noted as “Beta (β)Convergence”, “Sigma (σ) Convergence” and “Log-Per Capita Income Convergence.” Beta convergence is a phenomenon within the concept of unconditional convergence, which is based on the assumption that all countries have the same structural characteristics, in other words, all countries have the same steady state equilibrium. The relationship between average growth rate of per capita income and per capita income level in the beginning year can be expressed with the help of equation numbered (1) (Arbia and Piras, 2005, p. 13):

$$\frac{y_{it} - y_{it-1}}{y_{it-1}} = \alpha + \beta y_{it-1} + \varepsilon_{it} \qquad (1)$$

where y_{it} indicates the level of output per capita in country i, y_{it-1} means the per capita income level of the beginning year, the left side of the equation reflecting the dependent variable is the level of income growth, α is constant term; β is the convergence coefficient and ε_{it} is the error term. It is mentioned that there is convergence process if β coefficient takes a statistically significant negative value and divergence process if β coefficient takes a statistically significant positive value.

The sigma convergence demonstrates the distribution of per capita income over a given period of time and assumes that the differences in per capita income distributions of the economies will decrease over time (Sala-i-Martin, 1996, p. 1020). Standard deviation (σ) is the main criterion which is taken into consideration to measure sigma convergence. If standard deviation tends to decrease in a given period of time, convergence is mentioned; otherwise it is possible to say the validity of divergence process (Valdes, 1999, p. 41). Sigma convergence can be expressed with the help of equation numbered (2) (Gündem, 2010, p. 3094):

$$\sigma_t = \sqrt{I^{-1}\sum_{i=1}^{I}\left(y_{it} - \overline{y_t}\right)^2} \tag{2}$$

where I refers to the country considered in the analyzes, y_{it} reflects the income level of country i in period t and $\overline{y_t}$ points out the average income level of all other countries in period t.

Log-per capita convergence hypothesis examines whether different countries share a common deterministic or stochastic trend. Log-per capita convergence process can be expressed with the help of equation numbered (3) (Young et al., 2008, p. 1086):

$$log\left(\frac{y_{it}}{y_{i,t-1}}\right) = \alpha - \beta log\left(y_{i,t-1}\right) + u_{it} \tag{3}$$

With the help of the equation numbered (3) which is similar to the equation of beta convergence, comments can be made about whether there is any convergence trends depending on the sign of beta coefficient.

Due to its wide scope, convergence analyzes is used not only in terms of per capita income but also in all areas of the macroeconomic relations. Both the importance it has for economic development process and the rapid increase in health care expenditures in the developed countries in the recent years have raised the significance of convergence analyzes in the field of health economics. Therefore, increases in health care expenditures are of particular interest for policymakers in the health sector. In this context, economic studies are directed not only to detecting the determinants of health care expenditures, but also to determine whether health care expenditure differences between countries diminish over time. Detecting the determinants of health care expenditures and eliminating expenditure differences between countries can play a key role in determining the path dependence of countries' development policies. Therefore, the main motivation of this study is to examine the convergence process of health care expenditures in the European Union member countries using Geographically Weighted Regression analysis in the period of 1970-2017. For this purpose, the study consists of five chapters. In the second section, the literature review about the issue of health care convergence is discussed. The method, data and econometric model belonging to the empirical researches of the study are described in the third section and research findings are shown in the fourth section. The study concludes with the fifth section, where a general evaluation is conducted.

LITERATURE REVIEW

The economic development, which took its place in the discipline of economics with the Great Depression of 1929, became increasingly stronger within the world economy following the World War II and the problems specific to the countries were tried to be solved within the context of development economics. Since then, although development economics is generally considered as a discipline for underdeveloped and developing countries, it is essential to examine the social, political, cultural and demographic development processes of all world countries regardless of their development level. In this context, the phenomenon of health care expenditures, which is one of the most fundamental issues of the discipline of economic development, has attracted the attention of both economists and policy makers for 40 years. In the economic literature, the determinants of health care expenditures, the relationship between health care expenditures and economic growth/development, and the convergence process of health care expenditures are frequently examined. These studies have reached different theoretical and econometric results because of different methodology, variables, time period and country groups, and therefore the proposed policy preferences differ depending on the econometric results obtained. Therefore, in this part of the study, the results of various econometric studies examining the convergence process in health care expenditures are examined and summary information of these studies is presented in Table 1.

DATA SET, METHODOLOGY AND ECONOMETRIC MODEL

In this study, the convergence process of the health care expenditures is examined in the European Union member countries using Geographically Weighted Regression (GWR) analysis in the period of 1970-2017. The main feature making this study superior to the other studies in the literature is that it covers the EU member countries with the highest level of health care expenditures in the world and uses a new spatial

Table 1. The Summary of literature review

Author	Country	Time Span	Method	Result	
				Convergence	Divergence
Nixon (2000)	15 EU Countries	1960-1995	Panel Data Analysis	✓	
Okunade et al. (2004)	25 OECD Countries	1968-1997	Panel Data Analysis	✓	
Spitzer et al. (2006)	20 Western European Countries	1990-2001	Panel Data Analysis	✓	
Narayan (2007)	The UK, Canada, Japan, Switzerland, Spain and the USA	1960-2000	Unit Root Tests and Panel Data Analysis	✓	
Kerem et al. (2008)	23 EU Countries	1992-2004	Panel Data Analysis	✓	
Chou and Wang (2009)	28 Provinces of China	1978-2004	Cross-Section Regression Analysis and Cluster Analysis		✓
Wang (2009)	The US States	1980-2004	Panel Data Analysis	✓	
Schmitt and Starke (2011)	21 OECD Countries	1980-2005	Error Correction Model	✓	
Fallahi (2011)	OECD Countries	1960-2006	Unit Root Tests with Structural Breaks	✓	
Panopoulou and Pantelidis (2012)	OECD Countries	1972-2006	Panel Data Analysis		✓
Panopoulou and Pantelidis (2013)	The US States	1980-2004	Panel Data Analysis	✓	
Lau and Fung (2013)	14 EU Countries	1975-2008	Panel Unit Root Test		✓
Lau et al. (2014)	14 EU Countries	1970-2008	Panel Unit Root Test		✓
Odhiambo et al. (2015)	41 Sub-Saharan African Countries	2000-2011	GMM Analysis	✓	
Noy and McManus (2015)	26 Latin America and Caribbean Countries	1995-2009	Panel Data Analysis	✓	
Payne et al. (2015)	19 OECD Countries	1972-2008	LM and RALS-LM Unit Root Tests	✓	
Pekkurnaz (2015)	22 OECD Countries	1980-2012	Panel Unit Root Tests	✓	
Apergis (2015)	50 US States	1966-2009	Panel Unit Root Tests	✓	
Oyedele and Adebayo (2015)	15 ECOWAS Countries	1995-2011	Panel Unit Root Tests and Panel GMM Analysis		✓
Zeren et al. (2016)	81 Provinces of Turkey	2002-2010	Spatial Quantile Method	✓	
Kulyk and Augustowski (2017)	12 EU and 4 Visegrad Countries	2002-2015	Panel Data Analysis		✓
Nghiem and Connelly (2017)	OECD Countries	1975-2004	Panel Data Analysis		✓
Goli-Srinivas et al. (2019)	193 Countries	1950-2015	Panel Data Analysis	✓	

econometric analysis method, GWR. With the help of GWR analysis, both the convergence process of health care expenditures can be investigated and the effects of spatial differences of the countries on the convergence process can be examined. In addition, applying GWR method with a large data set provides additional support for the robustness of the analysis. The study done by Panopoulou and Pantelidis (2012) will be followed while employing the analysis. Table 2 presents the main information about the dataset.

While examining the convergence process of health care expenditures, the analyses assuming that all of the EU member countries have similar structural characteristics can bring about relatively fallacious findings. Therefore, it is important to investigate the convergence process by locally differentiating parameters. GWR is one of the main techniques based on the econometric estimation of locally differentiating parameters. In this study, in order to examine the convergence process of health care expenditures in the EU member countries, the methodology developed by Öcal and Yıldırım (2010) is utilized.

GWR analysis incorporating non-parametric spatial modeling process is based on local linear regression tests to estimate each point in space. This approach takes into account the distance-based weighting process and allows parameter estimates for each parameter and geographic region. With the help of GWR analysis, local parameter estimates can be made for each country in the data set and this analysis is considered as a superior method compared to other econometric models that do not make any distinction between countries. In GWR analysis, individual regressions for each country are weighted according to their spatial proxy levels. Hence, the spatial changes in the parameters are smoothed to the extent of the spatial weights and the regional differences in the parameters are removed (Öcal and Yıldırım, 2010, p. 483).

The GWR analysis, which weighted the observation values as a function of the distance between coefficient estimates of the regions, can be described as an extended version of the OLS analysis. In this context, parameter estimates turn out more specific for each space *i* as expressed by Fotheringham et al. (1997). Generally, GWR model can be explained as follows;

$$Y_{it} = \alpha_{it0} + \sum_{k=1}^{p} \alpha_{itk} X_{itk} + \varepsilon_{it} \tag{4}$$

In the regression equation numbered (4), *Y* is a dependent variable and comes out of combinations of X_{itk} independent variables ranging from 1 to *p*, $k = 1,..., p$. ε_{it} is the white noise error term. α_{itk} points out the coefficients of the regression for every location *i* and variable *k*. α_{it0} shows the constant term. The local estimates obtained by the regression model numbered (4) are determined using weighted

Table 2. The main information about the variables and the dataset

Variable	Definition	Time Span	Data Source
Health Care Variables			
Growth of Health Care Expenditure	Growth of Total Health Care Expenditure as a Percent of GDP	1970-2017	OECD
Per Capita Health Care Expenditure	Total Health Care Expenditure in US Dollar PPP	1970-2017	OECD
Life Expectancy (Females, Males, Total)	Life Expectancy at Birth by Year	1970-2016	OECD
Year of Life Lost	Potential Loss of Life per 100000 People	1970-2016	OECD
Mortality Rate	Total Death All Causes per 100000 People	1979-2016	World Health Organization
Infant Mortality	Infant Mortality per 1000 Live Births	1970-2016	OECD
Hospital Beds	Number of Hospital Beds per 1000 People	1970-2016	OECD
Immunization	The percentage of children ages 12-23 months who received DPT vaccinations before 12 months	1990-2017	World Bank
Prevalence of Undernourishment	Prevalence of Undernourishment as a Percent of Total Population	2000-2016	World Bank
Economic Variables			
Per Capita GDP	Per Capita GDP in US Dollar PPP	1972-2017	World Bank
Income Equality	Labour Compensation Rate as a Percent of Gross Value Added	1970-2017	OECD
Inflation	Percent Change in Average Consumer Prices	1980-2017	IMF
Savings	Gross National Savings as a Percent of GDP	1980-2017	IMF
Investment	Total Investments as a Percent of GDP	1980-2017	IMF
Public Health Care Expenditure	Government Expenditure on Health Care as a Percent of Total Government Expenditure	1970-2017	OECD
Labour Productivity	Annual Growth Rate of Labour Productivity	1971-2017	OECD
Employment Rate	Employment to Population Ratio in Total Population 15 and over	1991-2017	World Bank
Demographic Variables			
Age Dependency Ratio	Age Dependency Ratio as a Percent of Working-Age Population	1970-2017	World Bank
Population Ages 0-14	Population under 14 as a Percent of Total Population	1970-2017	World Bank
Population Ages 15-64	Population between 15 and 64 as a Percent of Total Population	1970-2017	World Bank
Population Ages 65+	Population 65 and over as a Percent of Total Population	1970-2017	World Bank
Population Growth	Annual Population Growth Rate	1970-2017	World Bank
Schooling Rate	Average Years of Total Schooling in Total Population 15 and over	1990-2010	World Bank
Education Rate	Government Expenditure on Education as a Percent of Total Government Expenditure	1980-2017	World Bank
Behavioral Variables			
Alcohol Consumption	Per Capita Alcohol Consumption in Population 15 and over (Litres/Capita)	1970-2016	OECD
Tobacco Consumption	Per Capita Tobacco Consumption in Population 15 and over (Grams/Capita)	1970-2016	OECD

regression models. Weighted regression models are created with the help of weighted observations expressed as a function of the distance between location *i* and other locations. The vectors of parameters in location *i* can be noted as,

$$\hat{\alpha}_{it} = \left(X^T W_{it} X\right)^{-1} X^T W_{it} Y, \quad i = 1,...,n \tag{5}$$

where W_{it} points out the locally weighted spatial matrix for every observation. The most important consideration for GWR analysis is the formation of a weighted matrix representing each observation between locations. In spatial analysis, it is assumed that location *i* get under the influence of the location closest to it. In the process of estimating the parameters at location *i*, more weight should be given to locations that are closer to location *i*. In this context, the basic way to obtain the weighting matrix is to run the 1/d process called the reverse distance criterion. *d* symbolizes the weight between locations, namely *i* and *j*.

The weighting matrix for location *i* can be obtained by externalizing farther location observations. If the distance *i* to *j* is longer than the parameter distance that takes the threshold value of *d*, the weight value of 0 should be given to observation *j*: (Öcal and Yıldırım, 2010, p. 484)

$$\text{For Every } i, j = 1,...,n \begin{cases} W_{ij} = 1 \text{ if } d_{ij} \leq d \\ W_{ij} = 0 \text{ if } d_{ij} > d \end{cases}$$

Once the weighting matrix is obtained, the GWR parameters can be estimated using different α parameters which make the sum of the error squares minimum:

$$\sum_{i=1}^{n} \left[Y_{it} - Y_{it}^{*}(\alpha)\right]^2 \tag{6}$$

$Y_{it}^{*}(\alpha)$ in the regression numbered (6) presents the locally weighted values of Y_{it} at location *i*. Because the locally weighted values of Y_{it}^{*} are the linear combinations of X_{it} and $\hat{\alpha}_{itk}$, α_{itk} should be estimated at each location (Öcal and Yıldırım, 2010, p. 484).

In order to investigate the convergence process of health care expenditures in the EU member countries, the regression equation numbered (7) is used:

$$Growth_{HCE_{it}} = \beta_0 + \beta_1 HCE_{PCit} W_{it} + \beta_2 X'_{it} W_{it} + \varepsilon_{it} \tag{7}$$

where *HCE* implies the health care expenditures, β_0 is constant term, β_1 and β_2 represent the gradient parameters, X'_{it} expresses the vector of control variables, W_{it} represents the geographical weighing of location *i* and ε_{it} points out the white noise error term. β_1 coefficient is expected to be negative and statistically significant for the convergence process in health care expenditures.

RESULTS OF THE ECONOMETRIC ANALYSIS

GWR analysis is applied in order to examine the convergence process of health care expenditures in the EU member countries using Geographically Weighted Regression analysis in the period of 1970-2017. In parallel with this objective, Table 3 represents the panel analysis results regarding the convergence process of health care expenditures and Figure 1 and Figure 2 represent the spatial distribution of the coefficient of $Growth_{HCE}$ variable in the context of individual countries.

Figure 1 and Figure 2, where the effects of previous values of $Growth_{HCE}$ variable on the growth of health care expenditure in current period are shown, indicates that the values of $Growth_{HCE}$ range between -0.097 and -0.407 for "the Six", whereas it ranges between -0.059 and -0.206 for the member countries of the Eurozone. These figures

Figure 1. Spatial distribution of beginning period $growth_{hce}$ coefficient in "the six"

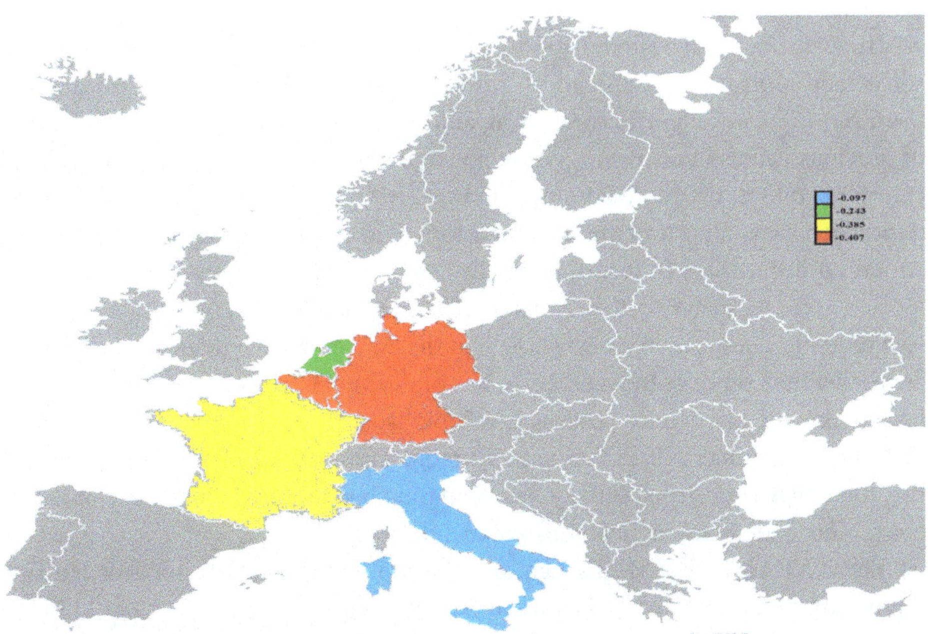

Figure 2. Spatial Distribution of Beginning Period $Growth_{HCE}$ *Coefficient in the Eurozone Countries and Non-Member of the Eurozone Countries*

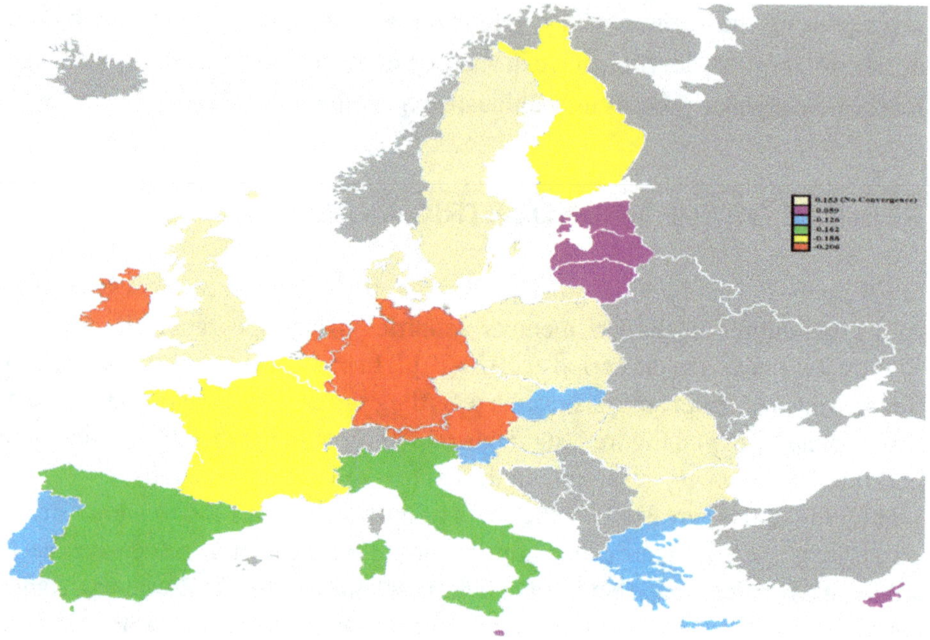

reflect that the countries in the east and south-east regions exhibit lower parameter estimates than those in the west and north regions in the context of convergence coefficients. As it can be understood, Figure 1 and Figure 2 are important indicators, since they represent the spread of convergence coefficients in the EU member countries in western, northern, eastern, and southern locations. Spatial distribution of previous values of $Growth_{HCE}$ variable indicates that convergence trend in health care expenditures are more dominant in western and northern Europe, whereas this trend decreases in eastern and south-eastern Europe. This result reflects the large structural differences in terms of health care expenditures between the countries located in the west and north regions and the countries located in the east and south-east regions. These figures also show that the convergence tendencies in "the Six" are higher than those of the member states of the monetary union. In addition, it can be said that the divergence process is valid in health care expenditures in countries that are not members of the monetary union. These results reflect the possibility that there may be a strong linkage between membership in the monetary union and convergence tendency in health care expenditures.

The GWR analysis findings regarding the convergence results presented in Table 3 point out that the convergence trend of health care expenditures is valid in "the

Table 3. The convergence results of the health care expenditures (GWR analysis)

Unconditional Convergence Findings	Country Groups							
	The Six		The Member of the Eurozone		Non-Member of the Eurozone		All Countries	
	$\hat{\beta}_1$	Prob $(\hat{\beta}_1)$	$\hat{\beta}_1$	Prob $(\hat{\beta}_1)$	$\hat{\beta}_1$	Prob $(\hat{\beta}_1)$	$\hat{\beta}_1$	Prob $(\hat{\beta}_1)$
$Growth_{HCE_{it}} = \beta_0 + \beta_1 HCE_{PC_{it}} W_{it}$	-0.403***	0.000	-0.202**	0.033	0.149*	0.065	0.153*	0.079
Conditional Convergence Findings (Equation Numbered 7)								
Health Care Variables								
Life Expectancy (Females)	-0.443**	0.016	-0.281**	0.027	0.112	0.885	0.056	0.911
Life Expectancy (Males)	-0.312**	0.028	-0.201**	0.033	0.083	0.901	0.028	0.952
Life Expectancy (Total)	-0.388**	0.023	-0.252**	0.019	-0.014*	0.086	-0.203*	0.072
Year of Life Lost	0.119*	0.062	0.151*	0.077	0.224**	0.027	0.622**	0.033
Mortality Rate	0.171	0.557	0.200*	0.062	0.119**	0.038	0.229**	0.016
Infant Mortality	0.226	0.519	0.109	0.765	0.029*	0.077	0.111**	0.038
Hospital Beds	0.336	0.404	0.227	0.660	-0.159	0.764	0.137	0.615
Immunization	-0.108*	0.061	-0.096*	0.071	-0.044*	0.086	0.155	0.646
Prevalence of Undernourishment	0.097	0.889	0.113	0.864	0.166*	0.066	0.437**	0.022
Economic Variables								
Per Capita GDP	-0.357**	0.021	-0.313**	0.024	-0.017*	0.081	-0.129	0.677
Income Equality	-0.160**	0.028	-0.121*	0.085	0.155	0.744	0.258	0.573
Inflation	0.220*	0.057	0.252**	0.044	0.243**	0.026	0.466***	0.000
Savings	0.265	0.561	0.227	0.656	0.138	0.773	0.013	0.951
Investment	0.188	0.672	0.086	0.899	0.048	0.855	0.057	0.897
Public Health Care Expenditure	-0.336***	0.003	-0.307**	0.021	-0.111	0.886	0.143	0.701
Labour Productivity	-0.119*	0.053	-0.100*	0.065	0.226	0.661	0.202	0.669
Employment Rate	-0.097*	0.084	-0.062**	0.032	0.130	0.716	0.097	0.873
Demographic Variables								
Age Dependency Ratio	0.114*	0.073	0.247**	0.026	0.337***	0.004	0.404***	0.000
Population Ages 0-14	0.083*	0.088	0.147*	0.082	0.224**	0.021	0.262**	0.015
Population Ages 15-64	-0.223**	0.013	-0.133*	0.073	0.441	0.484	0.333	0.529
Population Ages 65+	0.106*	0.074	0.330**	0.029	0.363***	0.000	0.119*	0.074

continued on following page

Table 3. Continued

Unconditional Convergence Findings	Country Groups							
	The Six		The Member of the Eurozone		Non-Member of the Eurozone		All Countries	
	$\widehat{2}_1$	*Prob* $(\widehat{2}_1)$	$\widehat{2}_1$	*Prob* $(\widehat{2}_1)$	$\widehat{2}_1$	*Prob* $(\widehat{2}_1)$	$\widehat{2}_1$	*Prob* $(\widehat{2}_1)$
Population Growth	0.131*	0.067	0.286*	0.068	0.300**	0.015	0.456***	0.000
Schooling Rate	-0.282***	0.006	-0.161**	0.019	0.016	0.903	-0.151	0.720
Education Rate	-0.303***	0.002	-0.250**	0.014	-0.029*	0.078	-0.037**	0.026
Behavioural Variables								
Alcohol Consumption	-0.413***	0.000	-0.216*	0.064	-0.551**	0.022	-0.443***	0.000
Tobacco Consumption	-0.363***	0.000	-0.227*	0.056	-0.212*	0.064	-0.293*	0.053

Note: The coefficient of each independent variable reflects the new value of convergence or divergence coefficient as a result of adding the relevant independent variable to the regression equation numbered 7. ***, ** and * indicate significance at 1%, 5% and 10%, respectively.

Six" and the member countries of the monetary union. However, it is observed that the convergence dynamism emerged in "the Six" is more dominant (-0.403) than that of the member countries of the monetary union (-0.202). It is also understood that the converge dynamism is generally driven by life expectancy, per capita income, public health care expenditures, education rate and alcohol/tobacco consumption in "the Six" and the member countries of the monetary union. Analysis findings showing that the convergence dynamism gains momentum due to the increase in life expectancy reflect that convergence process emerges as a result of increasing immunization in both country groups. Nevertheless, the divergence tendency is observed due to the increase in loss of life years and the mortality rates in both country groups. Besides, findings reflecting that per capita income growth and income equality accelerate the convergence process show that the increase in public sector investments in health care expenditures, labour productivity and employment rates pave the way for convergence dynamism in both country groups. Analysis findings showing that inflation supports the divergence process also point out that savings and investment expenditures do not have a statistically significant effect on the convergence process. On the other hand, three out of the seven demographic variables exhibit the convergence tendency in the health care expenditures. These variables are population ages between 15 and 64 years, schooling rate and education rate. This finding emphasizes the importance of the presence of the working group and the level of education in determining the convergence process. On the other hand, it can be observed that the increase in age dependency ratios and population growth rates triggers the divergence process in health care expenditures. Finally, two behavioural variables are added into the analysis in order to examine the effect of consumption habits on the convergence process. The findings reflecting that consumption behaviours may have an effect on the convergence tendency represent that convergence emerges due to increases in alcohol and tobacco consumption in both country groups.

In the countries not members of the monetary union and the panel group, the divergence process in health care expenditures has emerged. It is observed that the divergence coefficients of these two groups are similar (0.149 and 0.153). In terms of health care variables, convergence is found in two out of nine variables in the member states of the monetary union. Increases in life expectancy (total) and immunization levels lead to convergence tendencies in the member states of the monetary union, whereas in panel countries, the convergence process results only from the increase in life expectancy. It is determined that the increase in loss of life years, mortality rates and undernourishment level causes divergence in health care expenditures in both groups of countries. In the case of economic variables, it can be said that only the per capita income level has a tendency to converge in health care expenditures in the member states of the monetary union. On the other hand, it is observed that none of the economic variables have an effect on the convergence process in health care expenditures in the panel group of countries. In addition, it is also determined that the divergence process manifested itself only in terms of inflation variable in both country groups. These results reflect that convergence/divergence tendencies in health care expenditures are not determined by economic variables in two country groups. Besides, in terms of demographic variables, it is seen that only investments in education expenditures trigger the convergence process in health care expenditures. On the other hand, it is found that divergence process emerges in parallel with the increase in age dependency rates, and the working class has no ability to reverse this divergence process. This result is interesting in showing whether the transition from divergence to convergence is possible by the contribution of the working class. The finding constitutes one of the main differences in convergence between the member states of the monetary union and the non-member states of the monetary union. In addition, divergence process is triggered by the increase in the population growth. Lastly, when behavioural and life-style variables are taken into consideration, it is observed that alcohol and tobacco consumption habits lead to convergence process in health care expenditures in each country group.

CONCLUSION

The main purpose of this study is to reconsider the phenomenon of health care expenditures, which has attracted the great interest of policy makers and economists for nearly 40 years, in the context of convergence analysis. Therefore, the main motivation of this study is to examine the convergence process of health care expenditures in the EU member countries using GWR analysis in the period of 1970-2017.

The results of the analysis indicate that a statistically strong convergence trend is valid in "the Six" and the Eurozone, while there are not any statistically significant convergence trends in non-member states of the monetary union. Besides, the findings of the panel cross-country analysis also point out the nonexistence of the convergence trends. In addition, the analysis findings show that various control variables added to econometric models directly affect convergence results. In other words, health care, economic and demographic variables have had significant effects on convergence results in "the Six" and the member states of the monetary union, while they have had very limited effects in the non-member countries of the monetary union and the panel cross-countries. That the divergence dynamics prevail in countries that are not members of the monetary union in terms of health care variables necessitates the determination and implementation of common policies with countries that are members of the monetary union in the health sector. In particular increasing the life expectancy rates, reducing the loss of life years, decreasing the mortality rates and eliminating the health problems due to prevalence of undernourishment should be at the forefront of urgent health policies. On the other hand, achieving higher economic cooperation and the coordination of economic policies between the member states and the non-member states of the monetary union may accelerate the convergence dynamism in terms of health care expenditures. Particularly, increasing per capita income, implementing policies that will ensure income equality, meeting Maastricht criteria in inflation rates, accelerating public health care expenditures and increasing labor productivity by raising labor productivity are of great importance in terms of convergence dynamism. Besides, the convergence dynamism should be increased by raising the quality and quantity of the working class with the help of effective employment policies and the divergence process that manifests itself due to high age dependency rates should be prevented. Consequently, as a result of the implementation of quality-oriented population policies, the divergence process may be prevented on the one hand, and on the other hand the convergence process can be accelerated depending on the harmonization of education policies. These results indicate that convergence in health care expenditures can be determined not only with the help of health variables, but also with the help of economic and social variables. Therefore, for a stronger development perspective of the European continent, it should include harmonization of economic policies, as well as social, demographic and behavioral policies.

REFERENCES

Akıncı, M. (2017). Türkiye Ekonomisinde Yakınsama Dinamiği Üzerine. *Marmara Üniversitesi İktisadi ve İdari Bilimler Dergisi*, *39*(2), 339–360.

Apergis, N., Chang, T., Christou, C., & Gupta, R. (2015). Convergence of Health Care Expenditures across the US States: A Reconsideration. *University of Pretoria*.

Arbia, G., & Piras, G. (2005). Convergence in Per-Capita GDP Across European Regions Using Panel Data Models Extended to Spatial Autocorrelation Effects. *ISAE*.

Chou, W. L., & Wang, Z. (2009). Regional Inequality in China's Health Care Expenditures. *Health Economics*, *18*(S2), 137–146. doi:10.1002/hec.1511 PMID:19548323

Fallahi, F. (2011). Convergence of Total Health Expenditure as a Share of GDP: Evidence from Selected OECD Countries. *MPRA*.

Fotheringham, A. S., Charlton, M. E., & Brunsdon, C. (1997). Measuring Spatial Variations in Relationships with Geographically Weighted Regression. In M.M. Fisher & A. Getis (Eds.), Recent Developments in Spatial Analysis (pp. 60-85). Berlin: Springer. doi:10.1007/978-3-662-03499-6_4

Goli-Srinivas, M., Chakravorty, S., & Rammohan, A. (2019). World Health Status 1950-2015: Converging or Diverging. *PLoS One*, *14*(3), 1–20. PMID:30889208

Gündem, F. (2010). Avrupa Birliği ve Türkiye Finans Piyasalarının Bütünleşmesi. *Journal of Yasar University*, *5*(18), 3091–3096.

Kerem, K., Püss, T., Viies, M., & Maldre, R. (2008). Health and Convergence of Health Care Expenditure in EU. *International Business & Economics Research Journal*, *7*(3), 29–44.

Kulyk, P., & Augustowski, L. (2017). Convergence of Health Expenditure in EU 12 and V4 States. *Copernican Journal of Finance & Accounting*, *6*(2), 33–43. doi:10.12775/CJFA.2017.009

Lau, M. C. K., & Fung, K. W. T. (2013). Convergence in Health Care Expenditure of 14 EU Countries: New Evidence from Non-Linear Panel Unit Root Test. *MPRA*.

Lau, M. C. K., Fung, K. W. T., & Pugalis, L. (2014). Is Health Care Expenditures Across Europe Converging? Findings from the Application of a Nonlinear Panel Unit Root Test. *Eurasian Business Review*, *4*(2), 137–156. doi:10.100740821-014-0014-9

Mbaku, J. M., & Kimenyi, M. S. (1997). Macroeconomic Determinants of Growth: Further Evidence on the Role of Political Freedom. *Journal of Economic Development*, *22*(2), 119–132.

Narayan, P. K. (2007). Do Health Expenditures 'Catch-Up'? Evidence from OECD Countries. *Health Economics*, *16*(10), 993–1008. doi:10.1002/hec.1196 PMID:17238220

Nghiem, S. H., & Connelly, L. B. (2017). Convergence and Determinants of Health Expenditures in OECD Countries. *Health Economics Review*, *7*(1), 1–11. doi:10.118613561-017-0164-4 PMID:28819772

Nixon, J. (2000). Convergence of Health Care Spending and Health Outcomes in the European Union, 1960-95. *The University of York Centre for Health Economics.*

Noy, S., & McManus, P. A. (2015). Modernization, Globalization, Trends and Convergence in Health Expenditure in Latin America and the Caribbean. *Social Development*, *1*(2), 321–346. doi:10.1525od.2015.1.2.321

Öcal, N., & Yıldırım, J. (2010). Regional Effects of Terrorism on Economic Growth in Turkey: A Geographically Weighted Regression Approach. *Journal of Peace Research*, *47*(4), 477–489. doi:10.1177/0022343310364576

Odhiambo, S. A., Wambugu, A., & Kriti-Ng, T. (2015). Convergence of Health Expenditure in Sub-Saharan Africa: Evidence from a Dynamic Panel. *Journal of Economics and Sustainable Development*, *6*(6), 185–205.

Okunade, A. A., Karakuş, M. C., & Okeke, C. (2004). Determinants of Health Expenditure Growth of the OECD Countries: Jackknife Resampling Plan Estimates. *Health Care Management Science*, *7*(3), 173–183. doi:10.1023/B:HCMS.0000039380.42784.20 PMID:15648560

Oyedele, O., & Adebayo, A. (2015). Convergence of Health Expenditure and Health Outcomes in Ecowas Countries. *International Journal of Economics Financial Management*, *4*(2), 46–53.

Panopoulou, E., & Pantelidis, T. (2012). Convergence in Per Capita Health Expenditures and Health Outcomes in the OECD Countries. *Applied Economics*, *44*(30), 3909–3920. doi:10.1080/00036846.2011.583222

Panopoulou, E., & Pantelidis, T. (2013). Cross-State Disparities in US Health Care Expenditures. *Health Economics*, *22*(4), 451–465. doi:10.1002/hec.2816 PMID:22473657

Payne, J. E., Anderson, S., Lee, J., & Cho, M. H. (2015). Do Per-Capita Health Care Expenditures Converge Among OECD Countries? Evidence from Unit Root Tests with Level and Trend-Shifts. *Applied Economics*, *47*(52), 5600–5613. doi:10.1080/00036846.2015.1054070

Pekkurnaz, D. (2015). Convergence of Health Expenditure in OECD Countries: Evidence from a Nonlinear Asymmetric Heterogeneous Panel Unit Root Test. *Journal of Reviews on Global Economics*, *4*, 76–86. doi:10.6000/1929-7092.2015.04.07

Sala-i-Martin, X. X. (1996). The Classical Approach to Convergence Analysis. *Economic Journal (London)*, *106*(437), 1019–1036. doi:10.2307/2235375

Schmitt, C., & Starke, P. (2011). Explaining Convergence of OECD Welfare States: A Conditional Approach. *Journal of European Social Policy*, *21*(2), 120–135. doi:10.1177/0958928710395049

Solow, R. (1956). A Contribution to the Theory of Economic Growth. *The Quarterly Journal of Economics*, *70*(1), 65–94. doi:10.2307/1884513

Spitzer, A., Camus, D., Desaulles, C., & Kuhne, N. (2006). The Changing Context of Western European Healthcare Systems: Convergence versus Divergence in Nursing Problematics. *Social Science & Medicine*, *63*(7), 1796–1810. doi:10.1016/j.socscimed.2006.03.023 PMID:16782252

Valdes, B. (1999). *Economic Growth: Theory, Empirics and Policy*. USA: Edward Elgar.

Wang, Z. (2009). The Convergence of Health Care Expenditures in the US States. *Health Economics*, *18*(1), 55–70. doi:10.1002/hec.1343 PMID:18273915

Young, A. T., Higgins, M. J., & Levy, D. (2008). Sigma Convergence versus Beta Convergence: Evidence from U.S. County-Level Data. *Journal of Money, Credit and Banking*, *40*(5), 1083–1093. doi:10.1111/j.1538-4616.2008.00148.x

Zeren, F., Özcan, B., & Menteşe, E. Y. (2016). Health Care Convergence Analysis in Turkey on the Province Level: Spatial Quantile Method. *Procedia Economics and Finance*, *38*, 90–97. doi:10.1016/S2212-5671(16)30181-2

Compilation of References

(2006). The Lancet. *Middle East Health, 367*, 961–964.

Abbott, B., & Gallipoli, G. (2016). Human Capital Spill-Overs and the Geography of Intergenerational Mobility. *Review of Economic Dynamics*. doi:10.1016/j.red.2016.06.005

Abualigah, L. M., Khader, A. T., & Hanandeh, E. S. (2018). A combination of objective functions and hybrid Krill herd algorithm for text document clustering analysis. *Engineering Applications of Artificial Intelligence, 73*, 111–125. doi:10.1016/j.engappai.2018.05.003

Acartürk, E., & Keskin, S. (2012). Türkiye'de Sağlık Sektöründe Kamu Özel Ortaklığı Modeli. *Süleyman Demirel Üniversitesi İktisadi ve İdari Bilimler Fakültesi Dergisi., 17*(3), 25–51.

Acemoglu, D., & Johnson, S. (2006). Disease and Development: The Effect of Life Expectancy on Economic Growth. MIT. Retrieved from https://economics.mit.edu/files/4478

Adalı, Z., & Yüksel, S. (2017). Gelişmekte Olan Ekonomilerde Doğrudan Yabancı Yatırım ve Ekonomik Gelişme Arasındaki Nedensellik İlişkisi. *Marmara İktisat Dergisi, 1*(2), 109–118.

ADB. (2013). *Guidebook on Public-Private Partnership in Hospital Management*. Philippines: Asian Development Bank.

Aditya, R., & Hause, R. J. (2002). Interpersonal acumen and leadership across cultures: Pointers from the GLOBE study. In *Proceedings of the 9th Kravis-de Roulet Leadership Conference*. Lawrence Erlbaum Associates Publishers.

Aizer, A. (2014). Rising Inequality and Intergenerational Mobility: The Role of Public Investments in Human Capital. CESifo Group.

Akalın, H. E. (2005). Yoğun Bakım Ünitelerinde Hasta Güvenliği. *Yoğun Bakım Dergisi., 5*(3), 141–146.

Akal, Z. (1992). *İşletmelerde performans ölçüm ve denetimi*. Ankara: Milli Prodüktivite Yayınları.

Akça, H. (2015). Beşeri Sermaye Harcamaları: Türkiye'de Yaşanan Gelişmeler Ve Sonuçlar Üzerine Bir İnceleme. *Ekonomi Bilimleri Dergisi, 7*(2), 33–57.

Akers, L., & Gordon, J. S. (2018). Using Facebook for Large-Scale Online Randomized Clinical Trial Recruitment: Effective Advertising Strategies. *Journal of Medical Internet Research, 20*(11), e290. doi:10.2196/jmir.9372 PMID:30409765

Akgemci, T. (2013). *Stratejik Yönetim (3. Baskı)*. Ankara: Gazi Kitapevi.

Akgül, O. (2018). *Türkiye'de Asgari Ücret Sisteminin Uluslararası Standartlar Açısından Değerlendirilmesi*. İstanbul: Harf Yayınları.

Akın, C. S. (2007). *Sağlık ve sağlık harcamalarının ekonomik büyüme üzerine etkisi: Türkiye'de sağlık sektörü harcamaları*. Çukurova Üniversitesi Sosyal Bilimler Enstitüsü, İktisat Anabilim Dalı, Yayınlanmamış Yüksek Lisans Tezi.

Akıncı, M. (2017). Türkiye Ekonomisinde Yakınsama Dinamiği Üzerine. *Marmara Üniversitesi İktisadi ve İdari Bilimler Dergisi, 39*(2), 339–360.

Akıncı, Z. (2002). Turizm sektöründe işgören iş tatminini etkileyen faktörler: Beş yıldızlı konaklama işletmelerinde bir uygulama. *Akdeniz Üniversitesi İktisadi ve İdari Bilimler Fakültesi Dergisi, 4*, 1–25.

Akintoye, A., Hardcastle, C., Beck, M., Chinyio, E., & Asenova, D. (2003). D. Achieving best value in private finance initiative project procurement. *Construction Management and Economics, 21*(5), 461–470. doi:10.1080/0144619032000087285

Aktan, C. C. (2008). Stratejik yönetim ve stratejik planlama. *Çimento İşveren Dergisi, 22*(4), 4-21.

Aktan, C. C., & Işık, A. K. (2010). *Sağlık Hizmetlerinin Sunumu ve Alternatif Yöntemler*. Retrieved from http://www.canaktan.org/ekonomi/saglik-degisim-caginda/pdf-aktan/sunum-alternatif.pdf

Al Omar, A., Bhuiyan, M. Z. A., Basu, A., Kiyomoto, S., & Rahman, M. S. (2019). Privacy-friendly platform for healthcare data in cloud based on blockchain environment. *Future Generation Computer Systems, 95*, 511–521. doi:10.1016/j.future.2018.12.044

Albanesi, S. (2007). Inflation and Inequality. *Journal of Monetary Economics, 54*(4), 1088–1114. doi:10.1016/j.jmoneco.2006.02.009

Alesina, A. F., Glaeser, E.L., & Sacerdote, B. (2001). Why Doesn't the US Have a European-Style Welfare System? National Bureau of Economic Research.

Alesina, A., Giuliano, P., Bisin, A., & Benhabib, J. (2011). Preferences for Redistribution. In Handbook of Social Economics (pp. 93-132). Academic Press.

Alesina, A.F., & Glaeser, E.L. (2004). *Fighting Poverty in the US and Europe*. Oxford University Press.

Alesina, A. F., & Angeletos, G.-M. (2005). Fairness and Redistribution. *The American Economic Review, 95*(4), 960–980. doi:10.1257/0002828054825655

Aljarah, I., Mafarja, M., Heidari, A. A., Faris, H., & Mirjalili, S. (2019). Clustering analysis using a novel locality-informed grey wolf-inspired clustering approach. *Knowledge and Information Systems*, 1–33.

Allard, S., Qayyum, M. A., & Mehra, B. (2017). Intercultural leadership toolkit for librarians: Building awareness to effectively serve diverse multicultural populations. *Education Libraries*, *30*(1), 5–12. doi:10.26443/el.v30i1.231

Allen, J., Balfour, R., Bell, R., & Marmot, M. (2014). *Social determinants of mental health*. Geneva: World Health Organization. doi:10.3109/09540261.2014.928270

Allison, I. (2017). Gem shows off first blockchain application for health claims. International Business Times. Retrieved from https://www.ibtimes.co.uk/gem-shows-off-first-blockchain-application-health-claims-1622574

Alpar, R. (2017). *Uygulamalı çok değişkenli istatistiksel yöntemler*. Detay Yayıncılık.

Alper, S. J., Holden, R. J., Scanlon, M. C., Patel, N., Kaushal, R., Skibinski, K., ... Karsh, B.-T. (2012). Self-reported violations during medication administration in two paediatric hospitals. *BMJ Quality & Safety*, *21*(5), 408–415. doi:10.1136/bmjqs-2011-000007 PMID:22447818

Alpkan, L. (2000). *Stratejik Yönetimin Kapsamlılığı. Stratejik Tercihler ve Yönetici Özellikleri Arasındaki İlişkiler (Basılmamış Doktora Tezi), Gebze Yüksek Teknoloji Enstitüsü, Sosyal Bilimler Enstitüsü*. Gebze.

Alptekin, C. (2007). *Sağlık Kurumlarında Performans Yönetimi: İkinci Basamağa İlişkin Bir Uygulama*. İzmir: Yayınlanmamış Yüksek Lisans Tezi, Dokuz Eylül Üniversitesi Sosyal Bilimler Enstitüsü.

Alptekin, N., & Yeşilaydın, G. (2016). Bulanık Veri Zarflama Analizi ile OECD Ülkelerinin Sağlık Alanındaki Etkinliklerinin Değerlendirilmesi. *Sosyoekonomi*, *24*(30), 207–224. doi:10.17233e.2016.10.013

Altuntop, S. (2015). Kırık Camlar. In S. Altuntop (Ed.), Suçla Mücadele ve Güvenlik: Klasik ve Çağdaş Metinler (pp. 231-245). Ankara: Siyasal Kitabevi

Aluko, O. O., & Marvelous, A. I. (2018). Public health expenditure and economic growth in Nigeria: An error correction model. *Journal of Economics, Management and Trade*, 1-11.

Alvaredo, F., Chancel, L., Piketty, T., Saez, E., & Zucman, G. (2018). *World Inequality Report 2018*. Belknap Press of Harvard University Press.

Amalberti, R., Vincent, C., Auroy, Y., & de Saint, M. G. (2006). Violations and migrations in health care: A framework for understanding and management. *Quality & Safety in Health Care*, *15*(1suppl_1), 66–71. doi:10.1136/qshc.2005.015982 PMID:17142612

Anderson, J. G., Ramanujam, R., Hensel, D., Anderson, M. M., & Sirio, C. A. (2006). The Need for Organizational Change in Patient Safety Initiatives. *International Journal of Medical Informatics*, *75*(12), 809–817. doi:10.1016/j.ijmedinf.2006.05.043 PMID:16870501

Angeletti, F., Chatzigiannakis, I., & Vitaletti, A. (2017, September). The role of blockchain and IoT in recruiting participants for digital clinical trials. In *Proceedings of the 2017 25th International Conference on Software, Telecommunications and Computer Networks (SoftCOM)* (pp. 1-5). IEEE. 10.23919/SOFTCOM.2017.8115590

Angraal, S., Krumholz, H. M., & Schulz, W. L. (2017). Blockchain technology: Applications in health care. *Circulation: Cardiovascular Quality and Outcomes, 10*(9), e003800. doi:10.1161/CIRCOUTCOMES.117.003800 PMID:28912202

Ang, S., & Van Dyne, L. (2008). *Handbook of Cultural Intelligence: Theory. Measurement and Application.* Routledge.

Ang, S., & Van Dyne, L. (2015). *Handbook of cultural intelligence.* Routledge. doi:10.4324/9781315703855

Ansoff, H. I., Kipley, D., Lewis, A. O., Helm-Stevens, R., & Ansoff, R. (2018). *Implanting strategic management.* Springer.

Antheunis, M. L., Tates, K., & Nieboer, T. E. (2013). Patients' and health professionals' use of social media in health care: Motives, barriers and expectations. *Patient Education and Counseling, 92*(3), 426–431. doi:10.1016/j.pec.2013.06.020 PMID:23899831

Apergis, N., Chang, T., Christou, C., & Gupta, R. (2015). Convergence of Health Care Expenditures across the US States: A Reconsideration. *University of Pretoria.*

Arawatari, R., & Ono, T. (2013). Inequality, Mobility and Redistributive Politics. *Journal of Economic Theory, 148*(1), 353–375. doi:10.1016/j.jet.2012.12.010

Arbia, G., & Piras, G. (2005). Convergence in Per-Capita GDP Across European Regions Using Panel Data Models Extended to Spatial Autocorrelation Effects. *ISAE.*

Argon, T., & Eren, A. (2004). İnsan Kaynakları Yönetimi. Nobel Yayın Dağıtım.

Arora, P., & Predmore, C. E. (2013). Social media as a strategic tool: Going beyond the obvious. In *Social Media in Strategic Management* (Vol. 11, pp. 115–127). Emerald Group Publishing Limited; doi:10.1108/S1877-6361(2013)0000011010

Arrow, K. (1962). Economic welfare and the allocation of resources for invention. In R. Nelson (Ed.), *The Rate and Direction of Inventive Activity: Economic and Social Factors.* Washington: NBER. doi:10.1515/9781400879762-024

Arslan, F. (2007). *Kamuda Performansa Dayalı Ücret Sistemleri* [Doctoral dissertation]. Yüksek Lisans Tezi, Sivas.

Arslanhan, S. (2010). How Does the Increase in Health Expenditures Affect Main Health Indicators? *Economy Policy Research Foundation of Turkey.*

Asbu, E. Z., Masri, M. D., & Kaissi, A. (2017). Health status and health systems financing in the MENA region: roadmap to universal health coverage. *Global health research and policy, 2*(1), 25.

Aslan, A., Menegaki, A. N., & Tugcu, C. T. (2016). Health and economic growth in high-income countries revisited: Evidence from an augmented production function for the period 1980–2009. *Quality & Quantity, 50*(2), 937–953. doi:10.100711135-015-0184-2

Asteriou, D., & Hall, S. G. (2007). *Applied Econometrics: a modern approach* (rev. ed.). Hampshire: Palgrave Macmillan.

Atasever, M. (2014). Türkiye Sağlık Hizmetlerinin Finansmanı ve Sağlık Harcamalarının Analizi 2002-2013 Dönemi. Ankara: Bakanlık Yayın.

Atasever, M. (2018). *Şehir Hastaneleri Araştırması*. Ankara: Sağlık-Sen Stratejik Araştırmalar Merkezi Enstitüsü.

Atilgan, E., Kilic, D., & Ertugrul, H. M. (2017). The dynamic relationship between health expenditure and economic growth: Is the health-led growth hypothesis valid for Turkey? *The European Journal of Health Economics, 18*(5), 567–574. doi:10.100710198-016-0810-5 PMID:27260182

Atkinson, A. B. (2015). *Inequality*. Harvard University Press. doi:10.4159/9780674287013

Atmaca, L. (2007). *Türk Kamu Yönetiminde Stratejik Düşünme Ve Reform Çalışmalarının Stratejik Düşünce Bakış Açısıyla İncelenmesi. Yayınlanmamış Yüksek Lisans Tezi, Kocaeli Üniversitesi Sosyal Bilimler Enstitüsü.* Kocaeli.

Australian Medical Association Council. (2010). A guide to online professionalism for medical practitioners and medical students. Retrieved from https://ama.com.au/article/social-media-and-medical-profession

Avcı, K. ve Aktan, T. (2015). Bir Sistem Sorunu Olarak Tıbbi Hatalar ve Hasta Güvenliği. *Düzce Üniversitesi Sağlık Bilimleri Enstitüsü Dergisi, 5*(2), 48–54.

Aydemir, A. (2015). *Acil Serviste Çalışan Hemşirelerde Hasta güvenliği Kültürü ve Tutumunu Etkileyen Faktörler*. Samsun: Ondokuz Mayıs Üniversitesi Sağlık Bilimleri Enstitüsü Yayınlanmamış Yüksek Lisans Tezi.

Ayobami, O. T., & Ayinla, A. A. (n.d.). Government expenditure, Economic Growth and Poverty Level in Nigeria: A Disaggregated Approach.

Aytepe, T. (2008). *Türk Kamu Yönetiminde Stratejik Yönetim ve Stratejik Planlamanın Uygulanabilirliği: Ordu Emniyet Müdürlüğü Model Önerisi*. Ankara: Polis Akademisi Güvenlik Bilimleri Enstitüsü.

Azaria, A., Ekblaw, T. V., & Lippman, A. (2016). MedRec: Using Blockchain for Medical Data Access and Permission Management. In *Proceedings of the 2016 2nd International Conference on Open and Big Data (OBD)* (pp. 25-30). Academic Press. 10.1109/OBD.2016.11

Aziri, B. (2011). Job Satisfaction: A Literature Review. *Management Research & Practice, 3*(4).

Aziz, A. (2012). *İletişime Giriş*. İstanbul: Hiperlink Yayınları.

Babazono, A., & Hillman, A. L. (1994). A comparison of international health outcomes and health care spending. *International Journal of Technology Assessment in Health Care, 10*(3), 376–381. doi:10.1017/S0266462300006619 PMID:8071000

Bademci, V. (2007). *Tehlike (risk) altındaki çocuklar. In Okullarda şiddet ve çocuk suçluluğu* (pp. 171–186). Ankara: HEGEM.

Bakan, İ., & Büyükbeşe, T. (2010). Liderlik "türleri" ve "güç kaynakları" na ilişkin mevcut-gelecek durum karşılaştırması. *Karamanoğlu Mehmetbey Üniversitesi Sosyal ve Ekonomik Araştırmalar Dergisi,* (2), 73-84.

Baker, G. R., Norton, P. G., Flintoft, V., Blais, R., Brown, A., Cox, J., ... & O'Beirne, M. (2004). The Canadian Adverse Events Study: The incidence of adverse events among hospital patients in Canada. *Canadian Medical Association Journal, 170*(11), 1678–1686. doi:10.1503/cmaj.1040498 PMID:15159366

Bandura, A. (1977). Self-efficacy: Toward a Unifying Theory of Behavioral Change. *Psychological Review, 84*(2), 191–215. doi:10.1037/0033-295X.84.2.191 PMID:847061

Barlow, R., & Vissandjee, B. (1999). Determinants of national life expectancy. *Canadian Journal of Development Studies. Canadian Journal of Development Studies, 20*(1), 9–29. doi:10.1080/02255189.1999.9668787

Baron, R. M., & Kenny, D. A. (1986). The Moderator-Mediator Variable Distinction in Social Psychological Research: Conceptual, Strategic, And Statistical Considerations. *Journal of Personality and Social Psychology, 51*(6), 1173–1182. doi:10.1037/0022-3514.51.6.1173 PMID:3806354

Barreto, S., Ferreira, C., Paixao, J., & Santos, B. S. (2007). Using clustering analysis in a capacitated location-routing problem. *European Journal of Operational Research, 179*(3), 968–977. doi:10.1016/j.ejor.2005.06.074

Barry, M. M. (2009). Addressing the Determinants of Positive Mental Health: Concepts, evidence and practice. *International Journal of Mental Health Promotion, 11*(3), 4–17. doi:10.1080/14623730.2009.9721788

Bartolo, K., & Furlonger, B. (2000). Leadership and job satisfaction among aviation fire fighters in Australia. *Journal of Managerial Psychology, 15*(1), 87–93. doi:10.1108/02683940010305324

Başar, S., Künü, S., & Bozma, G. (2016). Eğitim ve Sağlık Harcamalarının Ekonomik Büyüme Üzerine Etkisi: Türkiye Üzerine Bir Uygulama. *Igdir University Journal of Social Sciences*, (10).

Başaran, İ. E. (1991). *Örgütsel Davranış İnsanın Üretim Gücü.* Ankara: Gül Yayınevi.

Baş, H. (2017). Türkiye'de Yerel Yönetimlerin Aileye Yönelik Sosyal Politikaları Üzerinden Bir Değerlendirme. *MCBÜ Sosyal Bilimler Dergisi, 15*(2), 165–196.

Baş, H., & Çetin, B. I. (2017). Bir Sosyal Belediyecilik Uygulaması Olarak İstanbul Esenler Belediyesi Gençlik Merkezi Örneği. *AİBÜ Sosyal Bilimler Enstitüsü Dergisi, 17*(1), 149–175.

Bass, B. M., & Stogdill, R. M. (1990). *Bass & Stogdill's handbook of leadership: Theory, research, and managerial applications*. Simon and Schuster.

Bates, B. R., Romina, S., Ahmed, R., & Hopson, D. (2006). The effect of source credibility on consumers' perceptions of the quality of health information on the Internet. *Medical Informatics and the Internet in Medicine*, *31*(1), 45–52. doi:10.1080/14639230600552601 PMID:16754366

Bavetta, S., Donni, P. L., & Marino, M. (2017). An Empirical Analysis of the Determinants of Perceived Inequality. *Review of Income and Wealth*. doi:10.1111/roiw.12351

Bayar, M. (2017). *Küresel Ekonomik Gelişmelerin Sağlık Sektörüne Etkileri: Sağlık Kamu Özel İşbirliği (KÖİ) Programı*. OHSAD Konferansı.

Bayın, G. (2016). Doğuşta ve İleri Yaşta Beklenen Yaşam Sürelerine Etki Eden Faktörlerin Belirlenmesi. *Türkiye Aile Hekimliği Dergisi*, *20*(3), 93–103. doi:10.15511/tahd.16.21693

Bayram, Ü. (2014). *Turizm Sektörü Yönetici ve İşgörenleri Arasında Pygmalion Etkisi: Otel İşletmelerinde Bir Uygulama*. Ankara: Gazi Üniversitesi Eğitim Bil.Ens. Doktora Tezi.

Bedir, S. (2016). Healthcare expenditure and economic growth in developing countries. *Advances in Economics and Business*, *4*(2), 76–86. doi:10.13189/aeb.2016.040202

Behr, A., & Theune, K. (2017). Health System Efficiency: A Fragmented Picture Based on OECD Data. *PharmacoEconomics-Open*, *1*(3), 203–221. doi:10.100741669-017-0010-y PMID:29441492

Bein, M. A., Unlucan, D., Olowu, G., & Kalifa, W. (2017). Healthcare spending and health outcomes: Evidence from selected East African countries. *African Health Sciences*, *17*(1), 247–254. doi:10.4314/ahs.v17i1.30 PMID:29026399

Belbey, J. (2016). 6 Ways Pharma May Use Social Media. Forbes. Retrieved from https://www.forbes.com/sites/joannabelbey/2016/03/09/6-ways-pharma-may-use-social-media/

Bénabou, R. (2000). Unequal Societies: Income Distribution and the Social Contract. *The American Economic Review*, *90*(1), 96–129. doi:10.1257/aer.90.1.96

Bénabou, R., & Tirole, J. (2006). Belief in a Just World and Redistributive Politics. *The Quarterly Journal of Economics*, *121*(2), 699–746. doi:10.1162/qjec.2006.121.2.699

Benchoufi, M., & Ravaud, P. (2017). Blockchain technology for improving clinical research quality. *Trials*, *18*(1), 335. doi:10.118613063-017-2035-z PMID:28724395

Benetoli, A., Chen, T. F., & Aslani, P. (2018). How patients' use of social media impacts their interactions with healthcare professionals. *Patient Education and Counseling*, *101*(3), 439–444. doi:10.1016/j.pec.2017.08.015 PMID:28882545

Bermúdez-Tamayo, C., Alba-Ruiz, R., Jiménez-Pernett, J., García Gutiérrez, J.-F., Traver-Salcedo, V., & Yubraham-Sánchez, D. (2013). Use of Social Media by Spanish Hospitals: Perceptions, Difficulties, and Success Factors. *Telemedicine Journal and e-Health*, *19*(2), 137–145. doi:10.1089/tmj.2012.0066 PMID:23368890

Bertinato, L., & Canapero, M. (n.d.). *Health Tourism-the Growth Phenomenon.* Asian HHM. Retrieved at https://www.asianhhm.com/healthcare-management/health-tourism

Beşe, E. (2006). Kırık Pencereler Teorisi Bağlamında Kentsel Yaşamda Suç ve Güvenlik. *Polis Bilimleri Dergisi., 8*(1), 1–24.

Best, R., de Valence, G., & Langston, C. (2007). Strategic management. In *Workplace Strategies and Facilities Management* (pp. 91–102). Routledge. doi:10.4324/9780080521299

Betz, F., & Şensoy, Ü. (2010). *Yönetim stratejisi: stratejik yönetim ve enformasyon teknolojisi.* TÜBİTAK Popüler Bilim Kitapları.

Bezuijen, X. M., Berg, P. T., Dam, K., & Thierry, H. (2009). Pygmalion and Employee Learning: The Role of Leader Behaviors. *The Netherlands Journal of Management, 35*(5), 1248–1267.

Bianca, A. (2014). Why Is Strategic Thinking Important To The Success of Business? Azcentral. Retrieved from http://yourbusiness.azcentral.com/strategic-thinkingimportant-success-business-9612.html

Bilgili, Ö. (2008). *Özel Sağlık Kurum ve Kuruluşları Personeli: İstihdamı ve Sosyal Güvenlikleri.* Unpublished doctoral dissertation, Dokuz Eylül Üniversitesi, İzmir, Turkey.

Binelli, C., & Attanasio, O. (2010). Mexico in the 1990s: The Main Cross-Sectional Facts. *Review of Economic Dynamics, 13*(1), 238–264. doi:10.1016/j.red.2009.10.003

Björklund, A., Roine, J., & Waldenström, D. (2012). Intergenerational Top Income Mobility in Sweden: Capitalist Dynasties in the Land of Equal Opportunity? *Journal of Public Economics, 96*(5–6), 474–484. doi:10.1016/j.jpubeco.2012.02.003

Blackhurst, J., Rungtusanatham, M. J., Scheibe, K., & Ambulkar, S. (2018). Supply chain vulnerability assessment: A network based visualization and clustering analysis approach. *Journal of Purchasing and Supply Management, 24*(1), 21–30. doi:10.1016/j.pursup.2017.10.004

Blundell, R. (2014). Income Dynamics and Life-cycle Inequality: Mechanisms and Controversies. *Economic Journal (London), 124*(576), 289–318. doi:10.1111/ecoj.12133

Blundell, R., & Etheridge, B. (2010). Consumption, Income and Earnings Inequality in Britain. *Review of Economic Dynamics, 13*(1), 76–102. doi:10.1016/j.red.2009.10.004

Boles, M., Pelletier, B., & Lynch, W. (2004). The relationship between health risks and work productivity. *Journal of Occupational and Environmental Medicine, 46*(7), 737–745. doi:10.1097/01.jom.0000131830.45744.97 PMID:15247814

Bonnes, M., & Secchiaroli, G. (1995). Environmental psychology: A psycho-social introduction. *Sage (Atlanta, Ga.).*

Bookman, M. (2007). *Medical tourism in developing countries.* Springer. doi:10.1057/9780230605657

Booth, L., & Starodubtseva, V. (2015). *PFI: costs and benefits, House of Commons Library.* Briefing.

Borgatti, S. P., & Everett, M. G. (1997). Network Analysis of 2-mode Data. *Social Networks, 19*(3), 243–269. doi:10.1016/S0378-8733(96)00301-2

Borowski, A., & Daya, U. (2014). Employee motivation tools. In *Human capital without borders: Knowledge and learning for quality of life. Proceedings of the management, knowledge and learning international conference*. Academic Press.

Borthwick, J., & Horton, R. (2006). The Middle East and health. *Lancet, 367*(9515), 961. doi:10.1016/S0140-6736(06)68401-8 PMID:16564342

Bosk, C. L. (2003). *Forgive and remember: managing medical failure* (2nd ed.). Chicago: University of Chicago Press. doi:10.7208/chicago/9780226924687.001.0001

Boubtane, E., Coulibaly, D., & Rault, C. (2013). Immigration, Unemployment and GDP in the Host Country: Bootstrap Panel Granger Causality Analysis on OECD Countries. *Economic Modelling, 33*, 261–269. doi:10.1016/j.econmod.2013.04.017

Bourse, M., & Yücel, H. (2012). *İletişim Bilimlerinin Serüveni*. İstanbul: Ayrıntı Yayınları.

Boz, S. S. (2013). Kamu Özel İşbirliği (PPP) Modeli. *İnönü Üniversitesi Hukuk Fakültesi Dergisi, 4*(2), 279-332.

Bracker, J. (1980). The historical development of the strategic management concept. *Academy of Management Review, 5*(2), 219–224. doi:10.5465/amr.1980.4288731

Braithwaite, J., Wears, R. L., & Hollnagel, E. (2015). Resilient health care: Turning patient safety on its head. *International Journal for Quality in Health Care, 27*(5), 418–420. doi:10.1093/intqhc/mzv063 PMID:26294709

Brandes, U., Delling, D., Gaertler, M., Görke, R., Hefer, M., Nikoloski, Z., & Wagner, D. (2008). On Modularity Clustering. *IEEE Transactions on Knowledge and Data Engineering, 20*(2), 172–188. doi:10.1109/TKDE.2007.190689

Breemhaar, B., & Van den Borne, H. W. (1991). Effects of education and support for surgical patients: The role of perceived control. *Patient Education and Counseling, 18*(3), 199–210. doi:10.1016/0738-3991(91)90129-S

Brennan, B. (2017). Healthcoin – blockchain-enabled platform for diabetes prevention. *Blockchain Healthcare Review.* Retrieved from https://blockchainhealthcarereview.com/healthcoin-blockchain-enabled-platform-for-diabetes-prevention/

Briggs, A. (1961). The welfare state in historical perspective. *European Journal of Sociology. Archives Européennes de Sociologie, 2*(2), 221–258. doi:10.1017/S0003975600000412

British Medical Association. (2019). Social media guidance for doctors. Retrieved from https://www.bma.org.uk/advice/employment/ethics/social-media-guidance-for-doctors

Brittan, L. (1990). European insurance in a single market. *Tijdschrift voor Economie en Management, 35*(4), 411–423.

Brodersen, R. B. (2001). Can Woman Leaders in Organizational Settings in The United States Produce the Pygmalion Effect? [Doctoral thesis]. Nova Southeastern University, FL.

Brodersen, C., Kalis, B., Leong, C., Mitchell, E., Pupo, E., Truscott, A., & Accenture, L. (2016). *Blockchain: Securing a New Health Interoperability Experience*. Accenture LLP.

Brouwer, W., Van Exel, J., Hermans, B., & Stoop, A. (2003). Should I stay or should I go? Waiting lists and cross-border care in the Netherlands. *Health Policy (Amsterdam)*, *63*(3), 289–298. doi:10.1016/S0168-8510(02)00120-3 PMID:12595128

Browne, J. H. (2000). Benchmarking HRM practices in healthy work organizations. *American Business Review*, *18*(2), 54.

Brown, J., Broderick, A. J., & Lee, N. (2007). Word of mouth communication within online communities: Conceptualizing the online social network. *Journal of Interactive Marketing*, *21*(3), 2–20. doi:10.1002/dir.20082

Brown, P. (2005). The evolving role of strategic management development. *Journal of Management Development*, *24*(3), 209–222. doi:10.1108/02621710510584035

Brzozowski, M., Gervais, M., Klein, P., & Suzuki, M. (2010). Consumption, Income, and Wealth Inequality in Canada. *Review of Economic Dynamics*, *13*(1), 52–75. doi:10.1016/j.red.2009.10.006

Budak, M. (2008). Hasta Güvenliği Kültürü. *Sağlık Düşüncesi ve Tıp Kültürü Dergisi*, *7*, 54–57.

Bult-Spiering, M., Dewulf, GP., Blanken A., Bult-Spiering, W.D., & Dewulf, G.P.M.R. (2006). The future of Public-Private Partnerships. In *Strategic Issues in Public-Private Partnerships: An international perspective* (pp. 176-202). Academic Press.

Burmaoğlu, S. (2016). Sistem Yaklaşımı ve Sağlık Alanında Sistem Dinamikleri Uygulamaları : Bibliyometrik Bir Analiz. *Hacettepe Sağlık İdaresi Dergisi*, *19*(4), 465–479. Retrieved from http://fs.hacettepe.edu.tr/saglikidaresidergisi/dosyalar/19.4.Makale 5.pdf

Burner, T. S., Waldo, D. R., & Mckusık, D. R. (1992). National Health Expenditures Projections Through 2030. *Health Care Financing Review*, *14*(1), 1–29. PMID:10124432

Burns, J. P. (2001). Complexity science and leadership in healthcare. *JONA: The Journal of Nursing Administration*, *31*(10), 474–482. doi:10.1097/00005110-200110000-00011 PMID:11676217

Busse, R., Wismar, M., & Berman, P. C. (Eds.). (2002). *The European Union and health services: the impact of the single European market on member states* (Vol. 50). IOS Press.

Buttle, F. (1996). Servqual: Review, Critique, Research Agenda. *European Journal of Marketing*, *30*(1), 8–32. doi:10.1108/03090569610105762

Çağıltay, K. (2011). *İnsan Bilgisayar Etkileşimi ve Kullanılabilirlik Mühendisliği: Teoriden Pratiğe*. Ankara: ODTÜ Geliştirme Vakfı Yayıncılık.

Çakmak, N., & Ocakli, E. (2006). Performans değerlendirmesi gerekli midir? Neden? *UNAK*, *6*, 406–418.

Can, A., & İbicioglu, H. (2008). Evaluation Of Unıversity Hospitals According To Management and Managership. *Suleyman Demirel University The Journal of Faculty of Economics and Administrative Sciences*, *13*(3), 253–275.

Candoğan, A. K. C. A., & Erigüç, G. (2006). Hastane çalışanlarının yöneticileri ve çalışma arkadaşları ile yaşadıkları çatışma nedenlerine yönelik bir araştırma. *Hacettepe Sağlık İdaresi Dergisi*, *9*(2), 126–153.

Can, Ö.İ., & Özkara, E., & Can, M. (2011). Yargıtay'da Karara Bağlanan Tıbbi Uygulama Hatası Dosyalarının Değerlendirilmesi. *Dokuz Eylül Üniversitesi Tıp Fakültesi Dergisi*, *25*, 69–76.

Capgemini. (2017). Blockchain: A healthcare endustry review. Retrieved from https://www.capgemini.com/wp-content/uploads/2017/07/blockchain-a_healthcare_industry_view_2017_web.pdf)

Carrera, P. M., & Bridges, J. F. (2006). Globalization and healthcare: Understanding health and medical tourism. *Expert Review of Pharmacoeconomics & Outcomes Research*, *6*(4), 447–454. doi:10.1586/14737167.6.4.447 PMID:20528514

Cebeci, E., & AY, A. (2016). The Effects Of Health Expendıtures On Economıc Growth: A Panel Regressıon Analysıs On Brıcs Countrıes And Turkey. *Dumlupinar University Journal of Social Science/Dumlupinar Üniversitesi Soysyal Bilimler Dergisi.*

Çelik, Y., Khan, M., & Hikmet, N. (2016). Achieving Value for Money in Health: A Comparative Analysis of OECD Countries and Regional Countries. *The International Journal of Health Planning and Management*. doi:10.1002/hpm.2375 PMID:27510835

Cengiz, C. (2014). *Hasta Güvenliğinde Kimlik Doğrulama, Hastaların Doğru Tanımlanmasının Önemi, Karşılaşılan Sorunlar ve Çözüm Önerileri ve Bir Üniversite Hastanesi Uygulaması*. Ankara: Gazi Üniversitesi Sosyal Bilimler Enstitüsü Yayınlanmamış Yüksek Lisans Tezi.

Çetin, M., & Ecevit, E. (2010). Sağlık harcamalarının ekonomik büyüme üzerindeki etkisi: OECD ülkeleri üzerine bir panel regresyon analizi.

Çetin, S. (2009). Vizyon yönetimi. *Selçuk Üniversitesi Sosyal Bilimler Enstitüsü Dergisi*, (22), 95-103.

Chakroun, M. (2010). Health care expenditure and GDP: An international panel smooth transition approach. *International Journal of Economics*, *4*(1), 189–200.

Chang, Y. W., Huang, M. H., & Lin, C. W. (2015). Evolution of research subjects in library and information science based on keyword, bibliographical coupling, and co-citation analyses. *Scientometrics*, *105*(3), 2071–2087. doi:10.100711192-015-1762-8

Chan, S. H. (2010). The influence of leadership expertise and experience on organizational performance: A study of Amanah Ikhtiar Malaysia. *Asia Pacific Business Review*, *16*(1-2), 59–77. doi:10.1080/13602380802503566

Chassin, M. R., & Loeb, J. M. (2013). High-reliability health care: Getting there from Here. *The Milbank Quarterly*, *91*(3), 459–490. doi:10.1111/1468-0009.12023 PMID:24028696

Chataway, J., Chaturvedi, K., Hanlin, R., Mugwagwa, J., Smith, J., & Wield, D. (2007). *Building the Case for National Systems of Health Innovation.* UK: ESRC Innogen Centre.

Chen, G. M., & An, R. (2009). A Chinese model of intercultural leadership competence. In The SAGE handbook of intercultural competence (pp. 196-208). Sage.

Chen, C. M. (2006). Citespace II: Detecting and visualizing emerging trends and transient patterns in scientific literature. *Journal of the American Society for Information Science and Technology*, *57*(3), 359–377. doi:10.1002/asi.20317

Chen, G., Gully, S. M., & Eden, D. (2001). Validation of a New General Self- Efficacy Scale. *Organizational Research Methods*, *4*(1), 62–83. doi:10.1177/109442810141004

Chetty, R., Hendren, N., Kline, P., Saez, E., & Turner, N. (2014). Is the United States Still a Land of Opportunity? Recent Trends in Intergenerational Mobility. *The American Economic Review*, *104*(5), 141–147.

Cheung, M. Y., Luo, C., Sia, C. L., & Chen, H. (2009). Credibility of Electronic Word-of-Mouth: Informational and Normative Determinants of On-line Consumer Recommendations. *International Journal of Electronic Commerce*, *13*(4), 9–38. doi:10.2753/JEC1086-4415130402

Chew, C., & Eysenbach, G. (2010). Pandemics in the Age of Twitter: Content Analysis of Tweets during the 2009 H1N1 Outbreak. *PLoS One*, *5*(11), e14118. doi:10.1371/journal.pone.0014118 PMID:21124761

Choi, I. (2001). Unit root tests for panel data. *Journal of International Money and Finance*, *20*(2), 249–272. doi:10.1016/S0261-5606(00)00048-6

Chou, W. L., & Wang, Z. (2009). Regional Inequality in China's Health Care Expenditures. *Health Economics*, *18*(S2), 137–146. doi:10.1002/hec.1511 PMID:19548323

Chunara, R., Andrews, J. R., & Brownstein, J. S. (2012). Social and news media enable estimation of epidemiological patterns early in the 2010 Haitian cholera outbreak. *American Journal of Tropical Medicine and Hygiene*. Retrieved from http://www.ajtmh.org/content/86/1/39.full.pdf+html%5Cnhttp://ovidsp.ovid.com/ovidweb.cgi?T=JS&PAGE=reference&D=emed10&NEWS=N&AN=2012026627

Churruca, K., Ellis, L. A., & Braithwaite, J. (2018). 'Broken hospital windows': Debating the theory of spreading disorder and its application to healthcare organizations. MC. *Health Services Research*, *18*(1), 201. doi:10.118612913-018-3012-2 PMID:29566697

Çiçek, A. (2012). *Hemşirelerin Hasta Güvenliğine Yönelik Görüş ve Tutumlarının İncelenmesi.* İzmir: Ege Üniversitesi Sağlık Bilimleri Enstitüsü Yayınlanmamış Yüksek Lisans Tezi.

Clark, B. D., & Matze, M. G. (1999). A core of global leadership: Relational competence. *Advances in global leadership, 1*, 127-161.

Classen, D. C., Resar, R., Griffin, F., Federico, F., Frankel, T., Kimmel, N., ... James, B. C. (2011). 'global trigger tool' shows that adverse events in hospitals may be ten times greater than previously measured. *Health Affairs (Project Hope), 30*(4), 581–589. doi:10.1377/hlthaff.2011.0190 PMID:21471476

Clauson, K. A., Breeden, E. A., Davidson, C., & Mackey, T. K. (2018). *Leveraging blockchain technology to enhance supply chain management in healthcare. Blockchain in Healthcare Today.* doi:10.30953/bhty.v1.20

Clement, J. (2018). Number of social media users worldwide from 2010 to 2021. Statista. Retrieved from https://www.statista.com/topics/1164/social-networks/

Cobo, M. J., Lopez-Herrera, A. G., Herrera-Viedma, E., & Herrera, F. (2011). Science mapping software tools: Review, analysis, and cooperative study among tools. *Journal of the American Society for Information Science and Technology, 62*(7), 1382–1402. doi:10.1002/asi.21525

Cocir. (2017) Beyond the hype of blockchain in healthcare. Retrieved from http://www.cocir.org/uploads/media/17069_COC_Blockchain_paper_web.pdf

Code, S., & Langan-Fox, J. (2001). Motivation, cognitions and traits: Predicting occupational health, well-being and performance. *Stress and Health: Journal of the International Society for the Investigation of Stress, 17*(3), 159–174. doi:10.1002mi.897

Coleman, J. A. (1997). Authority, power, leadership: Sociological understandings. *New Theology Review, 10*(3).

Coletti, M. H., & Bleich, H. L. (2001). Medical Subject Headings Used to Search the Biomedical Literature. *Journal of the American Medical Informatics Association, 8*(4), 317–323. doi:10.1136/jamia.2001.0080317 PMID:11418538

Collard, J., & Wang, T. (2005). Leadership and intercultural dynamics. *Journal of School Leadership, 15*(2), 178–195. doi:10.1177/105268460501500205

Collis, D. J. (2011). *Stratejik Düşünmek. Çev: Melis İnan.* İstanbul: Optimist.

Conger, J. A., & Kanungo, R. N. (1998). *Charismatic leadership in organizations.* Sage Publications.

Connell, J. (2006). Medical tourism: Sea, sun, sand and… surgery. *Tourism Management, 27*(6), 1093–1100. doi:10.1016/j.tourman.2005.11.005

Connell, J. (2013). Contemporary medical tourism: Conceptualisation, culture and commodification. *Tourism Management, 34*, 1–13. doi:10.1016/j.tourman.2012.05.009

Connerton, P. (1999). *Toplumlar Nasıl Anımsar? Çev. Alâeddin Şenel.* İstanbul: Ayrıntı Yayınları.

Consoli, D., & Mina, A. (2009). An evolutionary perspective on health innovation systems. *Journal of Evolutionary Economics, 19*(2), 297–319. doi:10.100700191-008-0127-3

Constantinides, E., & Fountain, S. J. (2008). Web 2.0: Conceptual foundations and marketing issues. *Journal of Direct. Data and Digital Marketing Practice*, *9*(3), 231–244. doi:10.1057/palgrave.dddmp.4350098

Coombs, R., Harvey, M., & Tether, B. S. (2003). Analysing distributed processes of provision and innovation. *Industrial and Corporate Change*, *12*(6), 1125–1155. doi:10.1093/icc/12.6.1125

Corman, H., & Mocan, N. (2005). Carrots, sticks, and broken windows. *The Journal of Law & Economics*, *48*(1), 235–266. doi:10.1086/425594

Correia, R. B., Li, L., & Rocha, L. M. (2016). Monitoring potential drug interactions and reactions via network analysis of instagram user timelines. In Biocomputing 2016 (pp. 492–503). WORLD SCIENTIFIC. doi:10.1142/9789814749411_0045

Cortez, N. (2008). Patient without borders: The emerging global market for patients and the evolution of modern health care. *Industrial Law Journal*, *83*, 71.

Coulter, M. K., & Coulter, M. K. (2002). *Strategic management in action*. Upper Saddle River, NJ: Prentice Hall.

Cousins, M. (Ed.). (2007). *Welfare Policy and Poverty*. Combat Poverty Agency.

Crémieux, P. Y., Ouellette, P., & Pilon, C. (1999). Health care spending as determinants of health outcomes. *Health Economics*, *8*(7), 627–639. doi:10.1002/(SICI)1099-1050(199911)8:7<627::AID-HEC474>3.0.CO;2-8 PMID:10544328

Crush, J., Chikanda, A., & Maswikwa, B. (2012). Patients without borders: Medical tourism and medical migration in Southern Africa.

Culver, K. (2016). Blockchain Technologies: A whitepaper discussing how the claims process can be improved. In *Proceedings of the ONC/NIST Use of Blockchain for Healthcare and Research Workshop*. ONC/NIST.

Daft, R. L. (2014). *The leadership experience*. Cengage Learning.

Darley, J. M., & Fazio, R. H. (1980). Expectancy Confirmation Processes Arising in The Social Interaction Sequence. *The American Psychologist*, *35*(10), 867–881. doi:10.1037/0003-066X.35.10.867

Das, R. (2017). Does Blockchain Have A Place In Healthcare? *Pharma&Healthcare*. Retrieved from https://www.forbes.com/sites/reenitadas/2017/05/08/does-blockchain-have-a-place-in-healthcare/#552cb0c91c31

Daştan, İ., & Çetinkaya, V. (2015). OECD Ülkeleri ve Türkiye'nin Sağlık Sistemleri, Sağlık Harcamaları ve Sağlık Göstergeleri Karşılaştırması. *SGD-Sosyal Güvenlik Dergisi*, *5*(1), 104–134.

David, F. R., & David, F. R. (2013). *Strategic management: Concepts and cases: A competitive advantage approach*. Pearson.

David, H. (2003). Value for Money tests and accounting treatment in PFI schemes. *Accounting and Accountability Journal*, *16*(3), 342–371. doi:10.1108/09513570310482291

De Arellano, A. B. R. (2007). Patients without borders: The emergence of medical tourism. *International Journal of Health Services*, *37*(1), 193–198. doi:10.2190/4857-468G-2325-47UU PMID:17436992

De Bettignies, J. E., & Ross, T. W. (2004). The economics of public-private partnerships. *Canadian Public Policy*, *30*(2), 135–154. doi:10.2307/3552389

De Haan, J., Oosterloo, S., & Schoenmaker, D. (2009). *European financial markets and institutions*. Cambridge University Press. doi:10.1017/CBO9780511806230

Debono, D. S., Greenfield, D., Travaglia, J. F., Long, J. C., Black, D., Johnson, J., & Braithwaite, J. (2013). Nurses' workarounds in acute healthcare settings: A scoping review. *BMC Health Services Research*, *3*(1), 175. doi:10.1186/1472-6963-13-175 PMID:23663305

Debono, D., Taylor, N., Lipworth, W., Greenfield, D., Travaglia, J., Black, D., & Braithwaite, J. (2017). Applying the theoretical domains framework to identify barriers and targeted interventions to enhance nurses' use of electronic medication management systems in two Australian hospitals. *Implementation Science; IS*, *12*(1), 42. doi:10.118613012-017-0572-1 PMID:28347319

Deci, E. L., & Ryan, R. M. (2008). Self-determination theory: A macrotheory of human motivation, development, and health. *Canadian Psychology*, *49*(3), 182–185. doi:10.1037/a0012801

Deloitte. (2018). Blockchain to blockchains in life sciences and health care-What broader integration is making possible today. Retrieved from https://www2.deloitte.com/content/dam/Deloitte/us/Documents/life-sciences-health-care/us-lshc-tech-trends2-blockchain.pdf

Demirel, E. T. (2009). *İşletmelerin Kalite ve Sistem Belgelendirme İle İlgili Bilgi Düzeylerinin ve Karşılaştıkları Sorunların Tespiti: Doğu ve Güneydoğu Anadolu Bölgelerinde Faaliyet Gösteren İhracatçı İmalat Sanayi İşletmelerinde Bir Araştırma, İnönü Üniversitesi Sos*. Malatya: Bil.Ens. Doktora Tezi.

Demir, H., & Taktak, F. (2011). Konumsal Veri Üzerine Sosyal Ağ Analizi (SAA): Afyonkarahisar Örneği. *Teknolojik Araştırmalar*, *3*(1), 7–16.

Demirtaş, A. (2004). *Sosyal Sınıflandırma. Kişilerarası Beklentiler ve Kendini Gerçekleştiren Kehanet, İletişim Araştırmaları*, *2*(2), 33–53.

Denecke, K., Krieck, M., Otrusina, L., Smrz, P., Dolog, P., Nejdl, W., & Velasco, E. (2013). How to exploit twitter for public health monitoring? *Methods of Information in Medicine*, *52*(4), 326–339. doi:10.3414/ME12-02-0010 PMID:23877537

Deng, L., & Gibson, P. (2008). A qualitative evaluation on the role of cultural intelligence in cross-cultural leadership effectiveness. *International journal of leadership studies, 3*(2), 181-197.

Deniz, M., & Çolak, M. (2008). Örgütlerde çatışmanın yönetiminde gücün kullanımı ve bir araştırma. *Elektronik Sosyal Bilimler Dergisi*, *7*(23), 304–332.

Dennis, R. S., Kinzler-Norheim, L., & Bocarnea, M. (2010). Servant leadership theory. In *Servant leadership* (pp. 169–179). London: Palgrave Macmillan. doi:10.1057/9780230299184_14

Derin, N. & Demirel, E.T. (2011). Hastanelerde Verimlilik Artışı İçin Hasta Güvenliği Uygulamaları ve Hasta Güvenliğinin Sağlanmasında Dönüşümcü Liderliğin Etkisi. *Verimlilik Dergisi*, *3*, 51–82.

Dess, G. G., & Miller, A. (1996). *Strategic management* (Vol. 2). McGraw-Hill.

Dias, J. P., Reis, L., Ferreira, H. S., & Martins, Â. (2018). Blockchain for access control in e-health scenarios.

Dickey, D. A., & Wayne, F. A. (1979). Distribution of the estimators for autoregressive timeseries with a unit root. *Journal of the American Statistical Association*, 74.

Dickson, M. W., Den Hartog, D. N., & Mitchelson, J. K. (2003). Research on leadership in a cross-cultural context: Making progress, and raising new questions. *The Leadership Quarterly*, *14*(6), 729–768. doi:10.1016/j.leaqua.2003.09.002

Dinan, D. (2005). *Ever closer union: an introduction to European integration*. Palgrave Macmillan.

Dinçer, H., Hacıoğlu, Ü., & Yüksel, S. (2018c). Conflict Risk and Defense Expenses and Their Impact on the Economic Growth. In Handbook of Research on Military Expenditure on Economic and Political Resources (pp. 1–23). Hershey, PA: IGI Global. doi:10.4018/978-1-5225-4778-5.ch001

Dinçer, H., Yuksel, S., & Adalı, Z. (2018a). Relationship Between Non-Performing Loans, Industry, and Economic Growth of the African Economies and Policy Recommendations for Global Growth. In Globalization and Trade Integration in Developing Countries (pp. 203–228). Hershey, PA: IGI Global. doi:10.4018/978-1-5225-4032-8.ch009

Dinçer, H., Yüksel, S., & Adalı, Z. (2019c). Determining the Effects of Monetary Policies on Capital Markets of the Emerging Economies: An Evidence from E7 Countries. In The Impacts of Monetary Policy in the 21st Century: Perspectives from Emerging Economies. Emerald Publishing Limited.

Dinçer, H., Yüksel, S., & Canbolat, Z. N. (2019b). A Strategic Approach to Reduce Energy Imports of E7 Countries: Use of Renewable Energy. In Handbook of Research on Economic and Political Implications of Green Trading and Energy Use (pp. 18-38). Hershey, PA: IGI Global.

Dinçer, H., Yüksel, S., Adalı, Z., & Aydın, R. (2019). Evaluating the Role of Research and Development and Technology Investments on Economic Development of E7 Countries. In Organizational Transformation and Managing Innovation in the Fourth Industrial Revolution (pp. 245-263). Hershey, PA: IGI Global.

Dinçer, H., Yüksel, S., Adalı, Z., & Aydın, R. (2019a). Evaluating the Role of Research and Development and Technology Investments on Economic Development of E7 Countries. In Organizational Transformation and Managing Innovation in the Fourth Industrial Revolution (pp. 245-263). Hershey, PA: IGI Global.

Dinçer, H., Yüksel, S., Eti, S., & Tula, A. (2019c). Effects of Demographic Characteristics on Business Success: An Evidence From Turkish Banking Sector. In Handbook of Research on Business Models in Modern Competitive Scenarios (pp. 304–324). Hershey, PA: IGI Global. doi:10.4018/978-1-5225-7265-7.ch016

Dinçer, H., Yüksel, S., Pınarbaşı, F., & Çetiner, İ. T. (2019a). Measurement of Economic and Banking Stability in Emerging Markets by Considering Income Inequality and Nonperforming Loans. In Maintaining Financial Stability in Times of Risk and Uncertainty (pp. 49–68). Hershey, PA: IGI Global. doi:10.4018/978-1-5225-7208-4.ch003

Dinçer, H., & Yüksel, S. (2019). Identifying the causality relationship between health expenditure and economic growth: An application on E7 countries. *Journal of Health Systems and Policies*, *1*, 5.

Dinçer, H., Yüksel, S., & Adalı, Z. (2017). Identifying Causality Relationship between Energy Consumption and Economic Growth in Developed Countries. *International Business and Accounting Research Journal*, *1*(2), 71–81. doi:10.15294/ibarj.v1i2.9

Dinçer, H., Yüksel, S., Korsakienė, R., Raišienė, A. G., & Bilan, Y. (2019b). IT2 hybrid decision-making approach to performance measurement of internationalized firms in the baltic states. *Sustainability*, *11*(1), 296. doi:10.3390u11010296

Dincer, H., Yüksel, S., & Martinez, L. (2019c). Balanced scorecard-based Analysis about European Energy Investment Policies: A hybrid hesitant fuzzy decision-making approach with Quality Function Deployment. *Expert Systems with Applications*, *115*, 152–171. doi:10.1016/j.eswa.2018.07.072

Dinçer, H., Yüksel, S., & Şenel, S. (2018b). Analyzing the global risks for the financial crisis after the great depression using comparative hybrid hesitant fuzzy decision-making models: Policy recommendations for sustainable economic growth. *Sustainability*, *10*(9), 3126. doi:10.3390u10093126

Dinçer, Ö. (2007). *Stratejik yönetim ve işletme politikası (8. Baskı)*. İstanbul: Alfa Yayınları.

Dinçer, Ö., & Fidan, Y. (1996). *İşletme Yönetimi, Beta Basım Yayım Dağıtım AŞ*. İstanbul: Baskı.

Doğan, H.İ. & Sevinç, B. (2011). Suç Teorileri ve Şehir Güvenliği: Bitlis İliyle İlgili Genel Bir Değerlendirme. *Polis Bilimleri Dergisi*, *13*(4), 27–53.

dokuz8haber. (2018, December 13). *Verilerle Türkiye'de toplumun bilgisayar ve internet kullanımında değişim*. Retrieved from https://dokuz8haber.net/toplum-yasam/bilim-teknoloji/verilerle-turkiyede-toplumun-bilgisayar-ve-internet-kullaniminda-degisim/

Domeij, D., & Flodén, M. (2010). Inequality Trends in Sweden 19782004. *Review of Economic Dynamics*, *13*(1), 179–208. doi:10.1016/j.red.2009.10.005

Dörnyei, Z., & Ushioda, E. (2013). *Teaching and researching: Motivation*. Routledge.

Dörtkulak, F. (2009). Maturation Of Shavian Women: A Study Of The Maturation Processes Of Female Pratogonists. In *George Bernard Shaw's Pygmalion and Mrs Warren's Profession, Ortadoğu Teknik Üniversitesi Sos.* Ankara: Bil.Ens. Yüksek Lisans Tezi.

Drabbe, H. (1994). The Internal Market for Insurance: A Reality? *The Geneva Papers on Risk and Insurance. Issues and Practice, 19*(2), 135–143. doi:10.1057/gpp.1994.11

Dreger, C., & Reimers, H. E. (2005). Health care expenditures in OECD countries: a panel unit root and cointegration analysis.

Drucker, P. F. (2000). *Gelecek için yönetim: 1990'lar ve sonrası. (F. Üçcan, Çev.).* Ankara: Türkiye İş Bankası Kültür Yayınları.

Dubovitskaya, A., Xu, Z., Ryu, S., Schumacher, M., & Wang, F. (2017). Secure and Trustable Electronic Medical Records Sharing using Blockchain. In *Proceedings of the AMIA 2017 Annual Symposium Proceedings*. Academic Press.

Dubrin, A. J. (2010). *Impression management in the workplace: Research, theory and practice.* Routledge. doi:10.4324/9780203865712

Dulebohn, J. H., Bommer, W. H., Liden, R. C., Brouer, R. L., & Ferris, G. R. (2012). A meta-analysis of antecedents and consequences of leader-member exchange: Integrating the past with an eye toward the future. *Journal of Management, 38*(6), 1715–1759. doi:10.1177/0149206311415280

Dumitrescu, E. I., & Hurlin, C. (2012). Testing for Granger Non-Causality in Heterogeneous Panels. *Economic Modelling, 29*(4), 1450–1460. doi:10.1016/j.econmod.2012.02.014

Dupre, E. (2014). Southwest Airlines Takes Customer Listening to New Heights. DM News. Retrieved from http://www.dmnews.com/southwest-airlines-takes-customer-listening-to-new-heights/article/375950/

Durmaz, G. (2016). *Cerrahi Hemşirelerinde Hasta Güvenliği Kültürü Algısını Etkileyen Faktörlerin Belirlenmesi.* Yeditepe Üniversitesi Sağlık Bilimleri Enstitüsü Yayınlanmamış Yüksek Lisans Tezi.

Duygulu, S. (2007). *Servis sorumlu hemşirelerine yönelik hazırlanan transformasyonel liderlik eğitim programının liderlik uygulamaları üzerine etkisi* [Doctoral dissertation]. Hacettepe Üniversitesi Sağlık Bilimleri Enstitüsü.

Dwivedi, A. D., Srivastava, G., Dhar, S., & Singh, R. (2019). A decentralized privacy-preserving healthcare blockchain for iot. *Sensors (Basel), 19*(2), 326. doi:10.339019020326 PMID:30650612

Earley, P. C., & Ang, S. (2003). *Cultural intelligence: Individual interactions across cultures.* Stanford University Press.

Earley, P. C., & Mosakowski, E. (2004). Cultural intelligence. *Harvard Business Review, 82*(10), 139–146. PMID:15559582

Ebbert, J. O., Dupras, D. M., & Erwin, P. J. (2003). Searching the Medical Literature Using PubMed: A Tutorial. *Mayo Clinic Proceedings, 78*(1), 87–91. doi:10.4065/78.1.87 PMID:12528881

Eden, D. (1988). Pygmalion, Goal Setting, and Expectancy: Compatible Ways to Boost Productivity. *Academy of Management Review, 13*(4), 639–652. doi:10.5465/amr.1988.4307530

Eden, D. (1990). *Pygmalion in Management: Productivity as Self-Fulfilling Prophecy*. Lexington, MA: Lexington Books.

Eden, D. (1992). Leadership and Expectations: Pygmalion Effects and Other Self-Fulfilling Prophecies in Organizations. *The Leadership Quarterly, 3*(4), 271–305. doi:10.1016/1048-9843(92)90018-B

E-devlet. (2019, August 15). *Ana Sayfa*. Retrieved from https://www.turkiye.gov.tr/

Egan, M. (2010). The single market. *European Union Politics, 3*, 258–274.

Eggoh, J., Houeninvo, H., & Sossou, G. A. (2015). Education, health and economic growth in African countries. *Journal of Economic Development, 40*(1), 93–111. doi:10.35866/caujed.2015.40.1.004

Eken, İ. (2017). *Herkes İçin Erişilebilir İletişim, Görme Engelli Kullanicilarin Mobil Erişebilirliği: Kullanilabilirlik Yaklaşimi İle Mobil Uygulamalarin Analizi*. İstanbul: İstanbul Ticaret Üniversitesi Sosyal Bilimler Enstitüsü Yayımlanmamış Doktora Tezi.

Eling, M., & Schaper, P. (2017). Under pressure: How the business environment affects productivity and efficiency of European life insurance companies. *European Journal of Operational Research, 258*(3), 1082–1094. doi:10.1016/j.ejor.2016.08.070

Ellner, A. L., Stout, S., Sullivan, E. E., Griffiths, E. P., Mountjoy, A., & Phillips, R. S. (2015). Health Systems Innovation at Academic Health Centers. *Academic Medicine, 90*(7), 872–880. doi:10.1097/ACM.0000000000000679 PMID:25738387

Elma, R. (2010). *Kamu yönetiminde kurumsal dönüşüm ve stratejik liderlik* [Master's thesis]. Karamanoğlu Mehmetbey Üniversitesi Sosyal Bilimler Enstitüsü.

Elmi, Z. M., & Sadeghi, S. (2012). Health care expenditures and economic growth in developing countries: Panel co-integration and causality. *Middle East Journal of Scientific Research, 12*(1), 88–91.

Elola, J., Daponte, A., & Navarro, V. (1995). Health indicators and the organization of health care systems in western Europe. *American Journal of Public Health, 85*(10), 1397–1401. doi:10.2105/AJPH.85.10.1397 PMID:7573624

Elstad, J. I. (1998). The psycho-social perspective on social inequalities in health. *Sociology of Health & Illness, 20*(5), 598–618. doi:10.1111/1467-9566.00121

Emül, E. & Demirel, E.T. (2018). Etik İklim Algısının Hasta Güvenliği Kültürü Üzerine Etkisi: Elazığ Örneği. *Turkish Studies - International Periodical For The Languages. Literature and History of Turkish or Turkic, 13*(7), 83–122.

Emül, E. (2017). *Etik İklim Algısının Hasta Güvenliği Kültürü Üzerine Etkisi: Elazığ Örneği.* Elazığ: Fırat Üniversitesi Sosyal Bilimler Enstitüsü Yayınlanmamış Yüksek Lisans Tezi.

E-nabız. (n.d.). *E-NABIZ.* Retrieved from https://enabiz.gov.tr/Yardim/Index?page=a1&detail=b1

Engelhardt, M. A. (2017). Hitching Healthcare to the Chain: An Introduction to Blockchain Technology in the Healthcare Sector. *Technology Innovation Management Review.*, *7*(10), 22–34. doi:10.22215/timreview/1111

Engle, R. F., & Granger, C. W. (1987). Co-integration and error correction: Representation, estimation and testing. *Econometrica*, 55.

Engle, R. F., & Granger, C. W. (1987). Co-integration and error correction: Representation, estimation, and testing. *Econometrica*, *55*(2), 251–276. doi:10.2307/1913236

Ennsfellner, K. C., & Dorfman, M. S. (1998). The Transition to a Single Insurance Market in the European Union. *Risk Management & Insurance Review*, *1*(2), 35–53. doi:10.1111/j.1540-6296.1998.tb00071.x

Erdem, A. (2006). *Stratejik Yönetim ve Kamu Örgütlerine Uygulanabilirliği (Basılmamış Yüksek Lisans Tezi).* Mersin: Mersin Üniversitesi Sosyal Bilimler Enstitüsü.

Erdem, R., & Yıldırım, H. H. (2003). Sağlık hizmetlerinde vekalet ilişkisi ve arzın talep yaratması problemi. *Hacettepe Sağlık İdaresi Dergisi*, *6*(2), 3–26.

Erdoğan, İ. (1996). *İşletme Yönetiminde Örgütsel Davranış.* İstanbul: Beta Yayınları.

Erdoğruca, P. (2011). *Dönüşümcü (Transformasyonel).* Konya: Liderlik ve Örgütsel Bağlılık Arasındaki İlişki, Selçuk Üniversitesi Sos.Bil.Ens. Yüksek Lisans Tezi.

Eren, E. (1993). *Yönetim psikolojisi. 4. Baskı* (pp. 193–255). İstanbul: Beta Basım Yayım Dağıtım.

Eren, E. (2002). *Stratejik yönetim ve işletme politikası.* İstanbul: Beta Yayınları.

Eren, E. (2005). İşletmelerde stratejik yönetim ve işletme politikası. *BETA Bulletin of Experimental Treatments for AIDS.*

Erkan, V. (2008). *Kamu kuruluşlarında stratejik planlama: Türkiye uygulaması ve kuruluşlarda başarıyı etkileyen faktörler. Devlet Planlama Teşkilatı Yayınları, Yayın*, (2759).

Erkut, H. (1998). *Strateji ve Senaryo Tekniği.* İstanbul: İrfan Yayımcılık.

Eroğlu, N., & Kara, F. (2017). Türkiye'de Makro İhtiyati Para Politikası Araçlarının Makroekonomik Değişkenlere Etkisinin Var Analizi ile İncelenmesi. *İstanbul İktisat Dergisi/Istanbul. Journal of Economics*, *67*(2), 59–88.

Ersin, İ. & Ergeç, E.H. (2018), Harcama Bileşenleri ve Sektörel İstihdam Arasındaki Nedensellik İlişkisi. *Yönetim ve Ekonomi Araştırmaları Dergisi*, *16*(1), 161-180.

Ersin, İ. (2018). İhracata Dayalı Büyüme Hipotezinin Test Edilmesi: MINT Ülkeleri Örneği. *Ekonomi, İşletme ve Maliye Araştırmaları Dergisi*, *1*(1), 26–38.

Ersin, İ., & Baş, H. (2019). Güney Avrupa Refah Ülkelerinde Sosyal Harcamalar ve Ekonomik Büyüme Arasındaki İlişkinin İncelenmesi. *Sosyal Güvenlik Dergisi*, *9*(1), 193–213. doi:10.32331gd.582752

Ersin, İ., & Eti, S. (2017). Measuring the Waste-Conscious and Saving Habits of the Youth in Turkey: The Sample of Istanbul Medipol University. *Uluslararası İslam Ekonomisi ve Finansı Araştırmaları Dergisi*, *3*(3), 41–49.

Ersoy, N. & Aydın, E. (1994). Tıbbi Etik'te Yararlılık İlkesi. *Türkiye Klinikleri J Med Ethics*, *2*(2), 57–60.

Ersöz, F. (2008). Türkiye ile OECD Ülkelerinin Sağlık Düzeyleri ve Sağlık Harcamalarının Analizi. *İstatistikçiler Dergisi*, *1*(2), 95- 104.

Ersöz, F. (2009). OECD'ye Üye Ülkelerin Seçilmiş Sağlık Göstergelerinin Kümeleme ve Ayırma Analizi ile Karşılaştırılması: Türkiye Klinikleri. *Journal of Medical Science*, *29*(6), 1650–1659.

Ertek, T. A. (2007). Temel ekonomi: (Basından örneklerle). *BETA Bulletin of Experimental Treatments for AIDS*.

Ertürk, M. (2000). *İşletmelerde Yönetim ve Organizasyon (3. Baskı)*. İstanbul: Beta Yayınevi.

Eryigit, S. B., Eryigit, K. Y., & Selen, U. (2012). The long-run linkages between education, health and defence expenditures and economic growth: Evidence from Turkey. *Defence and Peace Economics*, *23*(6), 559–574. doi:10.1080/10242694.2012.663577

Esping-Andersen, G., Gallie, D., Hemerijck, A., & Myles, J. (2002). *Why we need a new welfare state*. USA: Oxford University Press. doi:10.1093/0199256438.001.0001

Esty Benjamin, C. (2004). *Modern Project Finance* (International Edition). Wiley.

Eti, S. (2019). The Use of Quantitative Methods in Investment Decisions: A Literature Review. In Handbook of Research on Global Issues in Financial Communication and Investment Decision Making (pp. 256–275). Hershey, PA: IGI Global. doi:10.4018/978-1-5225-9265-5.ch013

Etzkowitz, H., & Leydesdorff, L. (2000). The Dynamics of Innovation: From National Systems and "Mode 2" to a Triple Helix of University-Industry-Government Relations. *Research Policy*, *29*(2), 109–123. doi:10.1016/S0048-7333(99)00055-4

EU Commission. (2011). EU Public Procurement Legislation Evaluation Report Executive Summary.

European Council. (2008). Commission staff working document - Accompanying document to the proposal for a Directive of the European Parliament and of the Council on the application of patients' rights in cross-border healthcare - Impact assessment. Retrieved from https://eur-lex.europa.eu/legal-content/EN/ALL/?uri=CELEX:52008SC2163

Evanoff, B. (1994). Psychophysiologic stressors and work organization. In L. Rosenstock & M.R. Cullen (Eds.), *Textbook of clinical occupational and environmental medicine*. Academic Press.

Eysenbach, G. (2011). Infodemiology and Infoveillance. *American Journal of Preventive Medicine, 40*(5), S154–S158. doi:10.1016/j.amepre.2011.02.006 PMID:21521589

Fallahi, F. (2011). Convergence of Total Health Expenditure as a Share of GDP: Evidence from Selected OECD Countries. *MPRA*.

Faragher, E. B., Cass, M., & Cooper, C. L. (2005). The relationship between job satisfaction and health: A meta-analysis. *Occupational and Environmental Medicine, 62*(2), 105–112. doi:10.1136/oem.2002.006734 PMID:15657192

Fayissa, B., & Gutema, P. (2005). The Determinants of Health Status in Sub-Saharan Africa (Ssa). *The American Economist, 49*(2), 900207. doi:10.1177/056943450504900207

Fisher, J., Johnson, D. S., & Smeeding, T. M. (2015). Inequality of Income and Consumption in the US: Measuring the Trends in Inequality from 1984 to 2011 for the Same Individuals. *Review of Income and Wealth, 61*(4), 630–650.

Flower, J. (2006). Five-star hospitals. *Strategy and Business, 42*, 66.

Fogg, C. D. (2010). *Stratejiyi Uygulamak, Çev: Melis İnan*. İstanbul: Optimist.

Fotheringham, A. S., Charlton, M. E., & Brunsdon, C. (1997). Measuring Spatial Variations in Relationships with Geographically Weighted Regression. In M.M. Fisher & A. Getis (Eds.), Recent Developments in Spatial Analysis (pp. 60-85). Berlin: Springer. doi:10.1007/978-3-662-03499-6_4

Franke, R. H., Edlund, T. W., & Oster, F. III. (1990). The development of strategic management: Journal quality and article impact. *Strategic Management Journal, 11*(3), 243–253. doi:10.1002mj.4250110306

Frawley, J., & Fasoli, L. (2012). Working together: Intercultural leadership capabilities for both-ways education. *School Leadership & Management, 32*(4), 309–320. doi:10.1080/13632434.2012.708328

Freeman, L. C. (1978). Centrality in Social Networks Conceptual Clarification. *Social Networks, 179*(1968), 215–239.

Freeman, C. (1995). The 'National System of Innovation' in historical perspective. *Cambridge Journal of Economics, 19*(1), 5–24.

Freeman, R. (2000). *The politics of health in Europe*. Manchester University Press.

Freeman, R. E. (2010). *Strategic management: A stakeholder approach*. Cambridge university press. doi:10.1017/CBO9781139192675

French, J., & Raven, B. (1968). The bases of social power. *Studies in Social Power*, 150-167.

Frenken, K. (2017). A complexity-theoretic perspective on innovation policy. *Complexity, Innovation and Policy*, 35-47.

Fried, H. O., Schmidt, S. S., & Yaisawarng, S. (1999). Incorporating the operating environment into a nonparametric measure of technical efficiency. *Journal of Productivity Analysis, 12*(3), 249–267. doi:10.1023/A:1007800306752

Friedrich, A., Flunger, B., Nagengast, B., Jonkmann, K., & Trautwein, U. (2015). Pygmalion Effects in The Classroom: Teacher Expectancy Effects On Students' Math Achievement. *Contemporary Educational Psychology, 41*, 1–12. doi:10.1016/j.cedpsych.2014.10.006

Fries, A. (2009). *Daydreams at work: Wake up your creative powers*. Capital Books.

Frost and Sullivan. (2017). Blockchain Technology in Global Healthcare, 2017–2025. Retrieved from http://www.frost.com/sublib/display-report.do?searchQuery=blockchain&id=K1DB-01-00-00-00&bdata=aHR0cHM6Ly93d3cuZnJvc3QuY29tL3NyY2gvY2F0YWxvZy1zZWFyY2guZG8%2FcGFnZVN pemU9MTImcXVlcnlUZXh0PWJsb2NrY2hhaW4mbWFya2V0Q29kZXM9SEMmZmlsdGVyU3dpdG NoPWZhbHNlQH5AU2VhcmNoIFJlc3VsdHNAfkAxNTE1MjU0MDg1NDk3

Fuchs-Schündeln, N., Krueger, D., & Sommer, M. (2010). Inequality Trends for Germany in the Last Two Decades: A Tale of Two Countries. *Review of Economic Dynamics, 13*(1), 103–132. doi:10.1016/j.red.2009.09.004

Fugate, M., Kinicki, A. J., & Ashforth, B. E. (2004). Employability: A psycho-social construct, its dimensions, and applications. *Journal of Vocational Behavior, 65*(1), 14–38. doi:10.1016/j.jvb.2003.10.005

Gagnon, K., & Sabus, C. (2015). Professionalism in a Digital Age: Opportunities and Considerations for Using Social Media in Health Care. *Physical Therapy, 95*(3), 406–414. doi:10.2522/ptj.20130227 PMID:24903111

Gallet, C. A., & Doucouliagos, H. (2017). The Impact of Healthcare Expenditure on Health Outcomes: A Meta-Regression Analysis. *Social Science & Medicine, 179*, 9–17. doi:10.1016/j.socscimed.2017.02.024 PMID:28237460

Gallo, C., Faccilongo, N., & La Sala, P. (2018). Clustering analysis of environmental emissions: A study on Kyoto Protocol's impact on member countries. *Journal of Cleaner Production, 172*, 3685–3703. doi:10.1016/j.jclepro.2017.07.194

Getzen, T. E. (2013). Health Economics and Financing, Temple University and İHEA, Wiley, Fifth Edition. Globalization and Health, 14(113). doi:10.118612992-018-0430-1

Getzen, T. E. (1992). Population Ageing and Growth of Health Expenditures. *The Journals of Gerontology. Series B, Psychological Sciences and Social Sciences, 47*(3), 97–104.

Gezici, A. (2007). *Yöneticilerin liderlik stillerinin çalışanların iş tatmini üzerindeki etkileri: özel eğitim kurumlarında öğretimsel liderlik ve bir uygulama. Yayınlanmamış Yüksek Lisans Tezi.* Kütahya: Dumlupınar Üniversitesi SBE.

Ghahari, A., Kumar, S. R., & Badea, T. C. (2018). Identification of Retinal Ganglion Cell Firing Patterns Using Clustering Analysis Supplied with Failure Diagnosis. *International Journal of Neural Systems*, *28*(8), 1850008. doi:10.1142/S0129065718500089 PMID:29631502

Gilhooly, K. J. (1988). *Thinking: Directed, undirected and creative*. Academic Press.

Gimson, A., Moskaliuk, J., & Kimmerle, J. (2009). Using wikis for organizational learning: functional and psycho-social principles. *Development and Learning in Organizations: An International Journal*.

Ginter, P. M., Duncan, W. J., & Swayne, L. E. (2018). *The strategic management of health care organizations*. John Wiley & Sons.

Girman, M., & Newman, E. J. (2002). Community structure in social and biological networks. In *Proceedings of The National Academy of Sciences* (*Vol. 99*, pp. 7821–7826). Academic Press. 10.1073/pnas.122653799

Gist, M. E. (1987). Self-Efficacy: Implications for Organizational Behavior and Human Resource Management. *Academy of Management Review*, *12*(3), 472–485. doi:10.5465/amr.1987.4306562

Gist, M. E., & Mitchell, T. R. (1992). Self-Efficacy: A Theoretical Analysis of Its Determinants and Malleability. *Academy of Management Review*, *17*(2), 183–211. doi:10.5465/amr.1992.4279530

Glinos, I. A., & Baeten, R. (2006). A literature review of cross-border patient mobility in the European Union. *Observatoire social européen, Europe for patients*.

Gluck, F., Kaufman, S., & Walleck, A. S. (1982). The four phases of strategic management. *The Journal of Business Strategy*, *2*(3), 9.

Glueck, W. F., & Jauch, L. R. (1989). *Manajemen strategis dan kebijakan perusahaan. Edisi Kedua*. Jakarta: Penerbit Erlangga.

Godet, M. (1987). *Scenarios and strategic management* (p. 210). London: Butterworths.

Gökbunar, R., Özdemir, H., & Uğur, A. (2008). Küreselleşme kıskacındaki refah devletinde sosyal refah harcamaları.

Goli-Srinivas, M., Chakravorty, S., & Rammohan, A. (2019). World Health Status 1950-2015: Converging or Diverging. *PLoS One*, *14*(3), 1–20. PMID:30889208

Gong, L., Li, H., & Wang, D. (2012). Health investment, physical capital accumulation, and economic growth. *China Economic Review*, *23*(4), 1104–1119. doi:10.1016/j.chieco.2012.07.002

Gönüllü, A. (2008). *Kamu Yönetiminde Stratejik Planlamaya Geçiş: Mersin Milli Eğitim Müdürlüğü Örneği*. Yayımlanmamış Yüksek Lisans Tezi.

Goodwin, N. (2000). Leadership and the UK health service. *Health Policy (Amsterdam)*, *51*(1), 49–60. doi:10.1016/S0168-8510(99)00072-X PMID:11010225

Gordon, R. D. (2010). Dispersed leadership: Exploring the impact of antecedent forms of power using a communicative framework. *Management Communication Quarterly*, *24*(2), 260–287. doi:10.1177/0893318909360213

Gordon, W. J., & Catalini, C. (2018). Blockchain technology for healthcare: Facilitating the transition to patient-driven interoperability. *Computational and Structural Biotechnology Journal*, *16*, 224–230. doi:10.1016/j.csbj.2018.06.003 PMID:30069284

Gorodnichenko, Y., Peter, K. S., & Stolyarov, D. (2010). Inequality and Volatility Moderation in Russia: Evidence from Micro-Level Panel Data on Consumption and Income. *Review of Economic Dynamics*, *13*(1), 209–237. doi:10.1016/j.red.2009.09.006

Grajales, F. J., Sheps, S., Ho, K., Novak-Lauscher, H., & Eysenbach, G. (2014). Social media: A review and tutorial of applications in medicine and health care. *Journal of Medical Internet Research*, *16*(2). doi:10.2196/jmir.2912 PMID:24518354

Granger, C. W. J. (1969). Investigating causal relations by econometric models and cross spectral methods. *Econometrica*, *37*(3), 424. doi:10.2307/1912791

Greaves, F., Ramirez-Cano, D., Millett, C., Darzi, A., & Donaldson, L. (2013). Harnessing the cloud of patient experience: Using social media to detect poor quality healthcare. *BMJ Quality & Safety*, *22*(3), 251–255. doi:10.1136/bmjqs-2012-001527 PMID:23349387

Greene, J. A., Choudhry, N. K., Kilabuk, E., & Shrank, W. H. (2011). Online social networking by patients with diabetes: A qualitative evaluation of communication with Facebook. *Journal of General Internal Medicine*, *26*(3), 287–292. doi:10.100711606-010-1526-3 PMID:20945113

Griffin, M. A., Patterson, M. G., & West, M. A. (2001). Job satisfaction and teamwork: The role of supervisor support. *Journal of Organizational Behavior: The International Journal of Industrial. Occupational and Organizational Psychology and Behavior*, *22*(5), 537–550. doi:10.1002/job.101

Griggs, K. N., Ossipova, O., Kohlios, C. P., Baccarini, A. N., Howson, E. A., & Hayajneh, T. (2018). Healthcare Blockchain System Using Smart Contracts for Secure Automated Remote Patient Monitoring. *Journal of Medical Systems*, *42*(7), 130. doi:10.100710916-018-0982-x PMID:29876661

Grimall, P. (1997). *Mitoloji Sözlüğü, Çev. Sevgi Tamgüç*. İstanbul: Sosyal Yayınlar.

Grimsey D. & Lewis K., (2004). Public Private Partnerships: the Worldwide Revolution in Infrastructure Provision and Project Finance.

Grimsey, D., & Lewis, M. K. (2002). Evaluating Risks of Public Private Partnerships for Public Infrastructure Projects. *International Journal of Project Management*, *20*(2), 107–118. doi:10.1016/S0263-7863(00)00040-5

Groves, K. S., & Feyerherm, A. E. (2011). Leader cultural intelligence in context: Testing the moderating effects of team cultural diversity on leader and team performance. *Group & Organization Management*, *36*(5), 535–566. doi:10.1177/1059601111415664

Güçlü, N. (2003). Stratejik yönetim. *Gazi Üniversitesi Gazi Eğitim Fakültesi Dergisi, 23*(2).

Gülmez, A. (2015). OECD ülkelerinde ekonomik büyüme ve hava kirliliği ilişkisi: Panel veri analizi. *Kastamonu Üniversitesi İktisadi ve İdari Bilimler Fakültesi Dergisi, 9*(3), 18–30.

Gündem, F. (2010). Avrupa Birliği ve Türkiye Finans Piyasalarının Bütünleşmesi. *Journal of Yasar University, 5*(18), 3091–3096.

Güner, S. (2005). Stratejik yönetim anlayışı ve kamu yönetimi. *Türk İdare Dergisi, 446*, 61–78.

Güney, S. (2000). *Davranış Bilimleri (2. Baskı)*. Ankara: Nobel Yayın Dağıtım.

Gün, İ., & Aslan, Ö. (2018). Liderlik Kuramları ve Sağlık İşletmelerinde Liderlik. *Journal of Health and Nursing Management, 5*(3), 217–226.

Gürbüz, S., & Şahin, F. (2016). *Sosyal Bilimlerde Araştırma Yöntemleri*. Ankara: Seçkin Yayıncılık.

Gürel, E. ve Muter, C. (2007). Psikomitolojik Terimler: Psikoloji Literatüründe Mitolojinin Kullanılması. *Anadolu Üniversitesi Sosyal Bilimler Dergisi, 7*(1), 537–569.

Güven, R. (2007). *Dezenfeksiyon ve Sterilizasyon Uygulamalarında Hasta Güvenliği Kavramı*. Antalya: Ulusal Sterilizasyon Dezenfeksiyon Kongresi Bildirileri.

Güvenek, B., & Alptekin, V. (2010). Enerji tüketimi ve büyüme ilişkisi: OECD Ülkelerine İlişkin bir panel veri analizi. *Enerji. Piyasa ve Düzenleme, 1*(2), 172–193.

Güven, S., & Mert, M. (2016). Uluslararası Turizm Talebinin Eşbütünleşme Analizi: Antalya İçin Panel Ardl Yaklaşımı. *Cumhuriyet Üniversitesi İktisadi ve İdari Bilimler Dergisi, 17*(1), 133–152.

Güzel, A., Okur, A. R., & Caniklioğlu, N. (2002). Sosyal güvenlik hukuku.

Gyimah-Brempong, K., & Wilson, M. (2004). Health human capital and economic growth in Sub-Saharan African and OECD countries. *The Quarterly Review of Economics and Finance, 44*(2), 296–320. doi:10.1016/j.qref.2003.07.002

Hadad, S., Hadad, Y., & Tuva, T. S. (2013). Determinants of Healthcare System's Efficiency in OECD Countries. *The European Journal of Health Economics, 14*(2), 253–265. doi:10.100710198-011-0366-3 PMID:22146798

Hair, J. F., Black, W. C., Babin, B. J., & Anderson, R. E. (2014). *Multivariate data analysis: Pearson new international edition*. Essex: Pearson Education Limited.

Halicioglu, F. (2011). Modeling Life Expectancy in Turkey. *Economic Modelling, 28*(5), 2075–2082. doi:10.1016/j.econmod.2011.05.002

Halıcı-Tülüce, N. S., Doğan, İ., & Dumrul, C. (2016). Is income relevant for health expenditure and economic growth nexus? *International Journal of Health Economics and Management, 16*(1), 23–49. doi:10.100710754-015-9179-8 PMID:27878709

Hamilton, E. (2006). *Mitologya, Çev. Ülkü Tamer*. İstanbul: Varlık Yayınları.

Hancı, Ş. H. (2002). *Malpraktis: Tıbbi Girişimler Nedeniyle Hekimin Ceza ve Tazminat Sorumluluğu*. Ankara: Seçkin Yayıncılık.

Hanefeld, J., Horsfall, D., Lunt, N., & Smith, R. (2013). Medical tourism: A cost or benefit to the NHS? *PLoS One*, *8*(10), e70406. doi:10.1371/journal.pone.0070406 PMID:24204556

Hansen, M. M., Durbin, J., Sinkowitz-Cochran, R., Vaughn, A., Langowski, G. S., & Gleason, S. (2003). Do No Harm. Provider Perceptions of Patient Safety. *The Journal of Nursing Administration*, *33*(10), 507–508. doi:10.1097/00005110-200310000-00004 PMID:14551467

Hanson, W. R., & Ford, R. (2010). Complexity leadership in healthcare: Leader network awareness. *Procedia: Social and Behavioral Sciences*, *2*(4), 6587–6596. doi:10.1016/j.sbspro.2010.04.069

Hargreaves, A., & Fink, D. (2012). *Sustainable leadership* (Vol. 6). John Wiley & Sons.

Harrison-Walker, L. J. (2001). The Measurement of Word-of-Mouth Communication and an Investigation of Service Quality and Customer Commitment As Potential Antecedents. *Journal of Service Research*, *4*(1), 60–75. doi:10.1177/109467050141006

Hartley, J., & Benington, J. (2010). *Leadership for healthcare*. Policy Press.

Hartley, J., & Fletcher, C. (2008). Leading with political awareness: Leadership across diverse interests inside and outside the organisation. In *Leadership perspectives* (pp. 163–176). London: Palgrave Macmillan. doi:10.1057/9780230584068_12

Hartmann, A. L., & Whiteman, R. (2003). Personality Correlates of Strategic Thinking. In *An Organizational Context. Yayınlanmamış Doktora Tezi*. California: Alliant International University.

Hartwig, J. (2010). Is health capital formation good for long-term economic growth? –Panel Granger-causality evidence for OECD countries. *Journal of Macroeconomics*, *32*(1), 314–325. doi:10.1016/j.jmacro.2009.06.003

Hay, C., Watson, M., & Wincott, D. (1999). *Globalisation, European integration and the persistence of European social models*. Sussex European Institute, University of Sussex.

Heathcote, J., Perri, F., & Violante, G. L. (2010). Unequal We Stand: An Empirical Analysis of Economic Inequality in the United States, 19672006. *Review of Economic Dynamics*, *13*(1), 15–51. doi:10.1016/j.red.2009.10.010

Heinrichs, J. H. (2001). *Interaction effects of strategic decision models and business intelligence tools on knowledge generation in manufacturing firms*. The University of Toledo.

Hennig-Thurau, T., Walsh, G., & Walsh, G. (2003). Electronic Word-of-Mouth: Motives for and Consequences of Reading Customer Articulations on the Internet. *International Journal of Electronic Commerce*, *8*(2), 51–74. doi:10.1080/10864415.2003.11044293

Heracleous, L. (1998). Strategic thinking or strategic planning? *Long Range Planning*, *31*(3), 481–487. doi:10.1016/S0024-6301(98)80015-0

Hermans, H. E. (2000). Cross-border health care in the European Union: Recent legal implications of 'Decker and Kohll'. *Journal of Evaluation in Clinical Practice*, *6*(4), 431–439. doi:10.1046/j.1365-2753.2000.00250.x PMID:11133126

Herrick, D. M. (2007). *Medical tourism: Global competition in health care*. Heal Wheel India. Retrieved from http://www.heal-wheel-india.com/white-pappers/Medical-Tourism-Global-Competition-in-Health-Care-NCPA-Report.pdf

Hersey, P., Blanchard, K. H., & Natemeyer, W. E. (1979). Situational leadership, perception, and the impact of power. *Group & Organization Studies*, *4*(4), 418–428. doi:10.1177/105960117900400404

Hervey, T. K., & McHale, J. V. (2004). *Health law and the European Union*. Cambridge University Press. doi:10.1017/CBO9780511617553

Herzberg, F. (2017). *Motivation to work*. Routledge. doi:10.4324/9781315124827

Heshmati, A. (2001). On the causality between GDP and health care expenditure in augmented Solow growth model. SSE/EFI.

Heung, V. C., Kucukusta, D., & Song, H. (2011). Medical tourism development in Hong Kong: An assessment of the barriers. *Tourism Management*, *32*(5), 995–1005. doi:10.1016/j.tourman.2010.08.012

Hill, B. (n.d.). Why Is Strategic Thinking Important To The Success of Business? Chron. Retrieved from http://smallbusiness.chron.com/strategic-thinking-important-success-business4661.html

Hitt, M. A., Ireland, R. D., & Hoskisson, R. E. (2012). *Strategic management cases: competitiveness and globalization*. Cengage Learning.

Höchtl, W., Sausgruber, R., & Tyran, J.-R. (2012). Inequality Aversion and Voting on Redistribution. *European Economic Review*, *56*(7), 1406–1421. doi:10.1016/j.euroecorev.2012.07.004 PMID:23564967

Hodgkinson, L., & Partington, G. H. (2008). The Motivation for Takeovers in the UK. *Journal of Business Finance & Accounting*, *35*(1-2), 102–126. doi:10.1111/j.1468-5957.2007.02063.x

Hofstede, G. (1980). Motivation, leadership, and organization: Do American theories apply abroad? *Organizational Dynamics*, *9*(1), 42–63. doi:10.1016/0090-2616(80)90013-3

Hofstede, G. (1993). Cultural constraints in management theories. *The Academy of Management Perspectives*, *7*(1), 81–94. doi:10.5465/ame.1993.9409142061

Hogan, R., Curphy, G. J., & Hogan, J. (1994). What we know about leadership: Effectiveness and personality. *The American Psychologist*, *49*(6), 493–504. doi:10.1037/0003-066X.49.6.493 PMID:8042818

Hölbl, M., Kompara, M., Kamišalić, A., & Nemec Zlatolas, L. (2018). A systematic review of the use of blockchain in healthcare. *Symmetry*, *10*(10), 470. doi:10.3390ym10100470

Hopkins, J., & Campbell, S. B. (2008). Development and validation of a scale to assess social support in the postpartum period. *Archives of Women's Mental Health, 11*(1), 57–65. doi:10.100700737-008-0212-5 PMID:18317709

Hopkins, L., Labonté, R., Runnels, V., & Packer, C. (2010). Medical tourism today: What is the state of existing knowledge? *Journal of Public Health Policy, 31*(2), 185–198. doi:10.1057/jphp.2010.10 PMID:20535101

Hors-Fraile, S., Atique, S., Mayer, M. A., Denecke, K., Merolli, M., & Househ, M. (2016). The Unintended Consequences of Social Media in Healthcare: New Problems and New Solutions. *Yearbook of Medical Informatics, 25*(01), 47–52. doi:10.15265/IY-2016-009 PMID:27830230

House, R. J., Hanges, P. J., Javidan, M., Dorfman, P. W., & Gupta, V. (Eds.). (2004). *Culture, leadership, and organizations: The GLOBE study of 62 societies*. Sage publications.

Howdona, D., & Rice, N. (2018). Health Care Expenditures Age Proximity to Death and Morbidity: Implications for An Ageing Population. *Journal of Health Economics, 57*, 60–74. doi:10.1016/j.jhealeco.2017.11.001 PMID:29182935

Hudson, N., Culley, L., Blyth, E., Norton, W., Rapport, F., & Pacey, A. (2011). Cross-border reproductive care: A review of the literature. *Reproductive Biomedicine Online, 22*(7), 673–685. doi:10.1016/j.rbmo.2011.03.010 PMID:21498121

Hughes, R. L. (1993). *Leadership: Enhancing the lessons of experience. Burridge, IL* : Richard D. Irwin, Inc.

Hunger, J. D., & Wheelen, T. L. (2003). *Essentials of strategic management* (Vol. 9). NJ: Prentice Hall.

Hunt, J. G. (1991). *Leadership: A new synthesis*. Sage Publications, Inc.

Hurley, R. F., & Hult, G. T. M. (1998). Innovation, market orientation, and organizational learning: An integration and empirical examination. *Journal of Marketing, 62*(3), 42–54. doi:10.1177/002224299806200303

Hussey, D. E. (2007). *Strategic management: from theory to implementation*. Routledge. doi:10.4324/9780080498287

Ibanez Tony, G. (2015). *Vfm Analysis of PPP*. World Bank.

IBM. (2016). Blockchain: The Chain of Trust and its Potential to Transform Healthcare – Our Point of View. Retrieved from https://www.healthit.gov/sites/default/files/8-31-blockchain-ibm_ideation-challenge_aug8.pdf

İlal, E. (1997). *İletişim Yığınsal İletişim Araçları ve Toplum*. İstanbul: Der Yayınları.

Im, K. S., Pesaran, M. H., & Shin, Y. (2003). Testing for Unit Roots in Heterogeneous Panels. *Journal of Econometrics, 115*(1), 53–74. doi:10.1016/S0304-4076(03)00092-7

International Financial Services London (IFSL). (2003). *Public Private Partnerships – UK Expertise for International Markets 2003*. Retrieved from http://www.ifsl.org.uk/uploads/PPP%20report%202002.pdf

Irving, G., & Holden, J. (2016). How blockchain-timestamped protocols could improve the trustworthiness of medical science. *F1000 Research*, 5. PMID:27239273

Jaba, E., Balan, C. B., & Robu, I. B. (2014). The relationship between life expectancy at birth and health expenditures estimated by a cross-country and time-series analysis. *Procedia Economics and Finance*, *15*, 108–114. doi:10.1016/S2212-5671(14)00454-7

Jaffe, D. T. (1995). The healthy company: Research paradigms for personal and organizational health.

Jakovljevic, M. B., Vukovic, M., & Fontanesi, J. (2015). Life Expectancy and Health Expenditure Evolution in Eastern Europe-DiD and DEA Analysis. *Expert Review of Pharmacoeconomics & Outcomes Research*, *16*(4), 537–546. doi:10.1586/14737167.2016.1125293 PMID:26606654

Jappelli, T., & Pistaferri, L. (2010). Does Consumption Inequality Track Income Inequality in Italy? *Review of Economic Dynamics*, *13*(1), 133–153. doi:10.1016/j.red.2009.11.001

Jasper, M., & Jumaa, M. (Eds.). (2008). *Effective healthcare leadership*. John Wiley & Sons.

Javidan, M., & House, R. J. (2001). Cultural acumen for the global manager: Lessons from project GLOBE. *Organizational Dynamics*, *29*(4), 289–305. doi:10.1016/S0090-2616(01)00034-1

Jenkins, R., Bhugra, D., Bebbington, P., Brugha, T., Farrell, M., Coid, J., ... Meltzer, H. (2008). Debt, income and mental disorder in the general population. *Psychological Medicine*, *38*(10), 1485–1493. doi:10.1017/S0033291707002516 PMID:18184442

Jerrim, J., & Macmillan, L. (2015). Income Inequality, Intergenerational Mobility, and the Great Gatsby Curve: Is Education the Key? *Social Forces*, *94*(2), 505–533. doi:10.1093fov075

Jiménez-Murcia, S., Granero, R., Fernandez-Aranda, F., Stinchfield, R., Tremblay, J., Steward, T., ... Perales, J. C. (2019). Phenotypes in Gambling Disorder Using Sociodemographic and Clinical Clustering Analysis: An Unidentified New Subtype? *Frontiers in Psychiatry*, 10.

Johnson, N. (1987). *The welfare state in transition: The theory and practice of welfare pluralism*. Univ of Massachusetts Press.

Johnson, T. J., & Garman, A. N. (2010). Impact of medical travel on imports and exports of medical services. *Health Policy (Amsterdam)*, *98*(2-3), 171–177. doi:10.1016/j.healthpol.2010.06.006 PMID:20619919

Jorens, Y. (2002). The right to health care across borders. In *The impact of EU law on health care systems* (Vol. 39, pp. 83–122). Peter Lang.

Jorner, J. (2018). 4 Industries That Will Dominate Social Media in 2018. ADWeek. Retrieved from https://www.adweek.com/digital/4-industries-that-will-dominate-social-media-in-2018/

Judge, T. A., Bono, J. E., & Locke, E. A. (2000). Personality and job satisfaction: The mediating role of job characteristics. *The Journal of Applied Psychology*, *85*(2), 237–249. doi:10.1037/0021-9010.85.2.237 PMID:10783540

Jussim, L., & Fleming, C. (1996). *Self-Fulfilling Prophecies and The Maintenance of Social Stereotypes: The role of dyadic interactions and social forces. In Stereotypes and stereotyping* (pp. 161–193). NY: The Guilford Press.

Kabir, M. (2008). Determinants of life expectancy in developing countries. *Journal of Developing Areas*, *41*(2), 185–204. doi:10.1353/jda.2008.0013

Kâhya, C. (2013). *Dönüştürücü ve etkileşimci liderlik anlayışları ile örgütsel sessizlik arasındaki ilişkide örgütsel güvenin rolü*. Erzurum: Atatürk Üniversitesi Sosyal Bilimler Enstitüsü Yayımlanmamış Doktora Tezi.

Kalkavan, H., & Ersin, I. (2019). Determination of Factors Affecting the South East Asian Crisis of 1997 Probit-Logit Panel Regression: The South East Asian Crisis. In Handbook of Research on Global Issues in Financial Communication and Investment Decision Making (pp. 148–167). Hershey, PA: IGI Global. doi:10.4018/978-1-5225-9265-5.ch008

Kallakuri, S., Devarapalli, S., Tripathi, A. P., Patel, A., & Maulik, P. K. (2018). Common mental disorders and risk factors in rural India: Baseline data from the SMART mental health project. *BJPsych Open*, *4*(4), 192–198. doi:10.1192/bjo.2018.28 PMID:29988932

Kamacı, A., & Yazıcı, H. U. (2017). OECD Ülkelerinde Sağlik Harcamalarinin Ekonomik Büyüme Üzerindeki Etkisinin Ekonometrik Analizi. *Sakarya İktisat Dergisi*, *6*(2), 52–69.

Kanfer, R. (1990). Motivation theory and industrial and organizational psychology. In Handbook of industrial and organizational psychology (pp. 75-130). Academic Press.

Kao, C. (1999). Spurious Regression and Residual-Based Tests for Cointegration in Panel Data. *Journal of Econometrics*, *90*(1), 1–44. doi:10.1016/S0304-4076(98)00023-2

Kaplan, A. M., & Haenlein, M. (2010). Users of the world, unite! The challenges and opportunities of Social Media. *Business Horizons*, *53*(1), 59–68. doi:10.1016/j.bushor.2009.09.003

Kapp, J. M., Peters, C., & Oliver, D. P. (2013). Research Recruitment Using Facebook Advertising: Big Potential, Big Challenges. *Journal of Cancer Education*, *28*(1), 134–137. doi:10.100713187-012-0443-z PMID:23292877

Karaca, A. & Arslan, H. (. (2014). Hemşirelik Hizmetlerinde Hasta Güvenliği Kültürünün Değerlendirilmesine Yönelik Bir Çalışma. *Sağlık ve Hemşirelik Yönetimi Dergisi.*, *1*(1), 9–18. doi:10.5222/SHYD.2014.009

Karagöz, D., & Kozak, N. (2014). Anatolia Turizm Araştırmaları Dergisi'nin Bibliyometrik Analizi: Araştırma Konuları ve Kurumlar Arası İş Birliğinin Sosyal Ağ Analizi ile İncelenmesi. *Türk Kütüphaneciliği*, *28*, 47–61.

Karahan, A. (2008). Hastanelerde liderlik ve örgütsel bağlılık arasındaki ilişkinin incelenmesi. *Sosyal Bilimler Dergisi, 10*(1).

Karahanoğluları Y., (2012). Kamu Özel Ortaklığı Modelinin Mali Değerlendirmesi. *Ankara Üniversitesi SBF Dergisi, 67*(2).

Karakaya A. (2004). Stratejik Yönetim Sisteminin Kriz Yönetimine Katkısı Üzerine Bir Araştırma. *Teknoloji, 7*(2).

Karakuzu, A. (2013). *Sağlık Çalışanlarında Motivasyon ve Motivasyonu Etkileyen Faktörler (Kırklareli Örneği).* İstanbul: Beykent Üniversitesi Sosyal Bilimler Enstitüsü Yüksek Lisans Tezi.

Karasoy, A. & Demirtaş G. (2018). Sağlık Harcamalarının Belirleyicileri Üzerine Bir Uygulama: Çevre Kirliliği ve Yönetişimin Etkilerinin İncelenmesi, *İnsan ve Toplum Bilimleri Araştırmaları Dergisi, 7*(3), 1917-1939.

Karataş, M. & Yakıncı, C. (2010). Tıbbi Hata Nedenleri ve Çözüm Yolları. *İnönü Üniversitesi Tıp Fakültesi Dergisi, 17*(3), 233-236.

Karlıdağ, R., Ünal, S., & Yoloğlu, S. (2000). Hekimlerde iş doyumu ve tükenmişlik düzeyi. *Türk Psikiyatri Dergisi, 11*(1), 49–57.

Karshenas, M., Moghadam, V. M., & Alami, R. (2014). Social policy after the Arab Spring: States and social rights in the MENA Region. *World Development, 64*, 726–739. doi:10.1016/j.worlddev.2014.07.002

Katrougalos, G., & Lazaridis, G. (2003). *Southern European welfare states.* New York: Problems, Challenges and Prospects. doi:10.1057/9780230523722

Katuwal, G. J., Pandey, S., Hennessey, M., & Lamichhane, B. (2018). Applications of Blockchain in Healthcare: Current Landscape & Challenges.

Katzell, R. A., & Thompson, D. E. (1990). Work motivation: Theory and practice. *The American Psychologist, 45*(2), 144–153. doi:10.1037/0003-066X.45.2.144

Kavaler, F., & Spiegel, A. D. (2003). *Risk management in health care institutions: a strategic approach.* Jones & Bartlett Learning.

Kawachi, I., & Kennedy, B. P. (1997). Socioeconomic Determinants of Health: Health and Social Cohesion: Why Care About Income Inequality? *British Medical Journal, 314*(7086).

Kawachi, I., & Kennedy, B. P. (1999). Income inequality and health: Pathways and mechanisms. *Health Services Research, 34*(1 Pt 2), 215.

Kayral, İ. (2017). *Hasta Güvenliği ve Kırık Pencereler Kuramı.* Retrieved from http://www.ibrahimkayral.com/wp/2015/10/hasta-guvenligi-ve-kirik-pencereler-kurami/

Keenan, K. (1996). *Yöneticinin kılavuzu, zamanı doğru kullanma. Translation: E. Koparan.* İstanbul: Remzi Kitabevi.

Kelling, G. L., & Sousa, W. H. (2001). *Do police matter? An analysis of the impact of New York City's police reforms*. New York, NY: The Manhattan Institute.

Kelly, T. (1997). Public Expenditures and Growth. *The Journal of Development Studies*, *34*(1), 60–84. doi:10.1080/00220389708422503

Kerem, K., Püss, T., Viies, M., & Maldre, R. (2008). Health and Convergence of Health Care Expenditure in EU. *International Business & Economics Research Journal*, *7*(3), 29–44.

Kerr, W. R. (2014). Income Inequality and Social Preferences for Redistribution and Compensation Differentials. *Journal of Monetary Economics*, (April), 1–41.

Keuschnigg, M., & Wolbring, T. (2015) Disorder, social capital, and norm violation: three field experiments on the broken windows thesis. *Ration Soc.*, *27*(1), 96–126.

Key, S., & Popkin, S. J. (1998). Integrating ethics into the strategic management process: Doing well by doing good. *Management Decision*, *36*(5), 331–338. doi:10.1108/00251749810220531

Kher, U. (2006). *Outsourcing your heart.* Time. Retrieved from http://www.time.com/time/magazine/article/0,9171,1196429,00.html

Kierein, N. M., & Gold, M. A. (2000). Pygmalion in Work Organizations: A Meta-Analysis. *Journal of Organizational Behavior*, *21*(8), 913–928. doi:10.1002/1099-1379(200012)21:8<913::AID-JOB62>3.0.CO;2-#

Kılınçarslan, Ş., İnce, E. Y., Tuncay, E. B., & Yağmurlu, F. (2018). Clustering Analysis of Normal Strength Concretes Produced with Different Aggregate Types. *Open Chemistry*, *16*(1), 918–922. doi:10.1515/chem-2018-0100

Kim, T. K., & Lane, S. R. (2013). Government Health Expenditure and Public Health Outcomes: A Comparative Study Among 17 Countries and Implications for US Health Care Reform. *American International Journal of Contemporary Research*, *3*(9), 8–13.

King, A. S. (1971). Self-Fulfilling Prophecies in Training The Hard-core: Supervisors' Expectations and The Underprivileged Workers' Performance. *Social Science Quarterly*, *52*(2), 369–378.

Kinouchi, R. R. (2014). Scentometrics: The project for a science of science transformed into an industry of measurements. *SCIENTLAE Studia*, *12*(1), 147–159. doi:10.1590/S1678-31662014000400008

Kırık Cam Teorisi. (2017). Retrieved from http://isletmeyonetimiuzerineyazilar.blogspot.com.tr/2017/01/krk-cam-teorisi.html

Kızılkaya, O., Dağ, M., & Kızılkaya, F. (2017). *Türkiye'de Sağlık Harcamalarının Sağlık Göstergeleri Üzerindeki Etkisi: Ekonometrik Bir Analiz*. Uluslararası Sosyal Bilimler ve Eğitim Araştırmaları Sempozyumu.

Klein, M. (2015). *Fundamental of PPP*. World Bank.

Klijn, E. H., & Teisman, G. R. (2003). Institutional and strategic barriers to public-private partnership: An analysis of Dutch cases. *Public Money & Management, 23*(3), 137–146. doi:10.1111/1467-9302.00361

Kluger, A. N., & DeNisi, A. (1996). The Effects of Feedback Interventions on Performance: A Historical Review, Meta-Analysis, and A Preliminary Feedback Intervention Theory. *Psychological Bulletin, 119*(2), 254–284. doi:10.1037/0033-2909.119.2.254

Koçak, O., Arslan, H., & Eti, S. (2017). Belediyelerde sosyal politika uygulamaları ve Pendik belediyesi örneği. *Uluslararası Toplum Araştırmaları Dergisi, 7*(12), 119–144. doi:10.26466/opus.311278

Koçak, O., Beki, A., & Eti, S. (2018). The Effects of the Different Activities on the Depression Level of Older People. *OPUS Uluslararası Toplum Araştırmaları Dergisi, 8*(15), 1241–1266.

Koçak, R. D., & Özüdoğru, H. (2012). Yöneticilerin liderlik özelliklerinin çalışanların motivasyonu ve performansı üzerindeki etkileri: Kamu ve özel hastanelerinde bir uygulama. *Ticaret ve Turizm Eğitim Fakültesi Dergisi, 1*, 76–88.

Koçel, T. (2005). *İşletme Yöneticiliği, Yönetim ve Organizasyonlarda Davranış Klasik-Modern-Çağdaş ve Güncel Yaklaşımlar. Baskı*. İstanbul: Beta Yayınları.

Kohn, L. T., Corrigan, J. M., & Donaldson, M. S. (2000). Errors in healthcare: A leadingcause of dealthandinjury. In L. T. Kohn, J. M. Corrigan, & M. S. Donaldson (Eds.), *Toerr is human: building a safer health system* (pp. 26–48). Washington, DC: Institute of Medicine National Academy Press.

Kolade, O., & Ogunnaike, O. (2014). Organizational citizenship behaviour, hospital corporate image and performance. *Journal of competitiveness, 6*(1), 36-49.

Kolb, D., Lublin, S., Spoth, J., & Baker, R. (1986). Strategic management development: Using experiential learning theory to assess and develop managerial competencies. *Journal of Management Development, 5*(3), 13–24. doi:10.1108/eb051612

Kondo, N., Sembajwe, G., Kawachi, I., van Dam, R. M., Subramanian, S. V., & Yamagata, Z. (2009). Income inequality, mortality, and self rated health: Meta-analysis of multilevel studies. *BMJ (Clinical Research Ed.)*, ▪▪▪, 339.

Koray, K. (2011). Sağlık Hizmetlerinin Örgütlenmesinde Kamu-Özel Ortaklığı. *Ankara Üniversitesi Sağlık Bilimleri Fakültesi Dergisi, 66*(3), 217–262.

Koray, M. (2005). *Sosyal Politika, İmge Kitapevi, Güncellenmiş ve Gözden Geçirilmiş 3*. Ankara: Baskı.

Korkmaz, A. (2010). *Vahit Bademci'nin Paradigma Değişikliği Üzerine Bir Araştırma. Testler Değil, Ölçümler Güvenilirdir"". Yayımlanmamış Yüksek Lisans Tezi*. Zonguldak: Zonguldak Karaelmas Üniversitesi, Sosyal Bilimler Enstitüsü.

Kornai, J., & Eggleston, K. (2001). *Welfare, choice and solidarity in transition: Reforming the health sector in Eastern Europe*. Cambridge University Press. doi:10.1017/CBO9780511492464

Kosroshahi, N. H. (2018). *Sosyo-Ekonomik Değişkenlerin Sağlık Göstergeleri Üzerindeki Etkisi*. Atatürk Üniversitesi Sosyal Bilimler Enstitüsü, Doktora Tezi.

Kouzes, J. M., & Posner, B. Z. (2006). *The leadership challenge* (Vol. 3). John Wiley & Sons.

Kovacı, S., Belke, M. & Bolat, S. (2018). Ülke Gruplarına Göre Ekonomik Gelişme ve Sağlık Harcamaları İlişkisi. In *Uluslararası Sosyal Bilimler ve İnovasyon Kongresi* (pp. 165-179). Academic Press.

Krawiec, R. J., Housman, D., White, M., Filipova, M., Quarre, F., Barr, D., . . . Tsai, L. (2016, August). Blockchain: Opportunities for health care. In *Proc. NIST Workshop Blockchain Healthcare* (pp. 1-16). Academic Press.

Kronfol, N., Khalife, J., Romanos, J., Makouk, J., Noun, P., & Ammar, W. (2014). Observations on the Ministry of Public Health program of support to the hospitalization of patients in Lebanon. *Lebanese Medical Journal*, *103*(1006), 1–7. PMID:24684124

Kulyk, P., & Augustowski, L. (2017). Convergence of Health Expenditure in EU 12 and V4 States. *Copernican Journal of Finance & Accounting*, *6*(2), 33–43. doi:10.12775/CJFA.2017.009

Kumar, R. D. (2013). Leadership in healthcare. *Anaesthesia and Intensive Care Medicine*, *14*(1), 39–41. doi:10.1016/j.mpaic.2012.11.006

Kuo, T. T., Kim, H. E., & Ohno-Machado, L. (2017). Blockchain distributed ledger technologies for biomedical and health care applications. *Journal of the American Medical Informatics Association*, *24*(6), 1211–1220. doi:10.1093/jamia/ocx068 PMID:29016974

Kurt, S. (2015). Government health expenditures and economic growth: A Feder-Ram approach for the case of Turkey. *International Journal of Economics and Financial Issues*, *5*(2), 441–447.

Labilloy, B. (2003). *European Insurance Regulation: New Opportunities for Insurers and Consumers*. Brussels: CEA.

Lantz, P. M. (2008). Gender and leadership in healthcare administration: 21st century progress and challenges. *Journal of Healthcare Management*, *53*(5), 291–301. doi:10.1097/00115514-200809000-00004 PMID:18856135

Larson, J. S. (1991). *The measurement of health: Concepts and indicators* (Vol. 31). Greenwood Publishing Group.

Latapy, M., Magnien, C., & Del Vecchio, N. (2008). Basic notions for the analysis of large two-mode networks. *Social Networks*, *30*(1), 31–48. doi:10.1016/j.socnet.2007.04.006

Latham, G. P., & Pinder, C. C. (2005). Work motivation theory and research at the dawn of the twenty-first century. *Annual Review of Psychology*, *56*(1), 485–516. doi:10.1146/annurev.psych.55.090902.142105 PMID:15709944

Lau, M. C. K., & Fung, K. W. T. (2013). Convergence in Health Care Expenditure of 14 EU Countries: New Evidence from Non-Linear Panel Unit Root Test. *MPRA*.

Lau, A. Y. S., Gabarron, E., Fernandez-luque, L., & Armayones, M. (2012). Social media in health – what are the safety concerns for health consumers? *The HIM Journal*, *41*(2), 30–35. doi:10.1177/183335831204100204 PMID:23705132

Lau, M. C. K., Fung, K. W. T., & Pugalis, L. (2014). Is Health Care Expenditures Across Europe Converging? Findings from the Application of a Nonlinear Panel Unit Root Test. *Eurasian Business Review*, *4*(2), 137–156. doi:10.100740821-014-0014-9

Lawton, R. (1998). Not working to rule: Understanding procedural violations at work. *Safety Science*, *28*(2), 75–95. doi:10.1016/S0925-7535(97)00073-8

Leape, L. L., Brennan, T. A., Laird, N., Lawthers, A. G., Localio, A. R., Barnes, B. A., ... Hiatt, H. (1991). The nature of adverse events and negligence in hospitalized patients: Results of the Harvard Medical Practice Survey study II. [PubMed]. *The New England Journal of Medicine*, *324*(6), 377–384. doi:10.1056/NEJM199102073240605

Leatt, P., & Porter, J. (2003). Where are the healthcare leaders" the need for investment in leadership development. *Healthcare Papers*, *4*(1), 14–31. doi:10.12927/hcpap.2003.16891 PMID:14660891

Lee, R., & Miller, T. (2002). An Approach to Forecasting Health Expenditures with Application to the U.S. Medicare System, *Heatlh Servies Research.* 37(5), 1365-1386. Retrieved from http://onlinelibrary.wiley.com/wol1/doi/10.1111/1475-6773.01112/full

Leibfried, S., & Pierson, P. (1992). Prospects for social Europe. *Politics & Society*, *20*(3), 333–366. doi:10.1177/003232929202000305

Leonard, N. H., Beauvais, L. L., & Scholl, R. W. (1999). Work motivation: The incorporation of self-concept-based processes. *Human Relations*, *52*(8), 969–998. doi:10.1177/001872679905200801

Leppink, C. K. (2010). Pygmalion Training in a For-Profit Organization: The Nondeceptive Creation of the Pygmalion Effect [Doctoral Thesis]. Regent University, Virginia.

Lerner, D., Amick, B. C. III, Lee, J. C., Rooney, T., Rogers, W. H., Chang, H., & Berndt, E. R. (2003). Relationship of employee-reported work limitations to work productivity. *Medical Care*, *41*(5), 649–659. doi:10.1097/01.MLR.0000062551.76504.A9 PMID:12719689

Lerner, D., & Henke, R. M. (2008). What does research tell us about depression, job performance, and work productivity? *Journal of Occupational and Environmental Medicine*, *50*(4), 401–410. doi:10.1097/JOM.0b013e31816bae50 PMID:18404013

Letvak, S., & Buck, R. (2008). Factors influencing work productivity and intent to stay in nursing. *Nursing Economics*, *26*(3), 159. PMID:18616053

Leung, D., Law, R., van Hoof, H., & Buhalis, D. (2013). Social Media in Tourism and Hospitality: A Literature Review. *Journal of Travel & Tourism Marketing*, *30*(1–2), 3–22. doi:10.1080/10548408.2013.750919

Leung, R. C. (2013). Increasing Dynamic Capabilities of Health Organizations with Social Media. In *Social Media in Strategic Management* (Vol. 11, pp. 129–142). Emerald Group Publishing Limited; doi:10.1108/S1877-6361(2013)0000011011

Leung, X. Y., Sun, J., & Bai, B. (2017). Bibliometrics of social media research: A co-citation and co-word analysis. *International Journal of Hospitality Management*, *66*, 35–45. doi:10.1016/j.ijhm.2017.06.012

Levin, A., Lin, C. F., & Chu, C. S. J. (2002). Unit root tests in panel data: Asymptotic and finite-sample properties. *Journal of Econometrics*, *108*(1), 1–24. doi:10.1016/S0304-4076(01)00098-7

Liang, X., Zhao, J., Shetty, S., Liu, J., & Li, D. (2017, October). Integrating blockchain for data sharing and collaboration in mobile healthcare applications. In *Proceedings of the 2017 IEEE 28th Annual International Symposium on Personal, Indoor, and Mobile Radio Communications (PIMRC)* (pp. 1-5). IEEE. 10.1109/PIMRC.2017.8292361

Liang, L. L., & Tussing, A. D. (2019). The Cyclicality of Government Health Expenditure and Its Effects on Population Health. *Health Policy (Amsterdam)*, *123*, 96–103. doi:10.1016/j.healthpol.2018.11.004

Lichtenberg, F. R. (2000). Sources of U.S. Longevity Increase 1960-1997. *CESifo*. Retrieved from https://www.econstor.eu/bitstream/10419/75781/1/cesifo wp405.pdf

Liedtka, J. M. (1998). Strategic thinking: Can it be taught? *Long Range Planning*, *31*(1), 120–129. doi:10.1016/S0024-6301(97)00098-8

Li, H., & Huang, L. (2009). Health, education, and economic growth in China: Empirical findings and implications. *China Economic Review*, *20*(3), 374–387. doi:10.1016/j.chieco.2008.05.001

Linden, M., & Ray, D. (2017). Life expectancy effects of public and private health expenditures in OECD countries 1970–2012: Panel time series approach. *Economic Analysis and Policy*, *56*, 101–113. doi:10.1016/j.eap.2017.06.005

Linn, L., & Koo, M. (2016). Blockchain for health data and its potential use in health it and health care related research. In *Proceedings of the ONC/NIST Use of Blockchain for Healthcare and Research Workshop*. ONC/NIST.

Lin, W. Y., Zhang, X., Song, H., & Omori, K. (2016). Health information seeking in the Web 2.0 age: Trust in social media, uncertainty reduction, and self-disclosure. *Computers in Human Behavior*, *56*, 289–294. doi:10.1016/j.chb.2015.11.055

Liu, W., Zhu, S. S., Mundie, T., & Krieger, U. (2017, October). Advanced block-chain architecture for e-health systems. In *Proceedings of the 2017 IEEE 19th International Conference on e-Health Networking, Applications and Services (Healthcom)* (pp. 1-6). IEEE. Retrieved from https://www.iim.ftn.uns.ac.rs/is17/papers/28.pdf

Livingston, J. S. (1988). Pygmalion in Management. *Harvard Business Review*, 121–130. PMID:12545926

Li, X., Yao, R., Liu, M., Costanzo, V., Yu, W., Wang, W., ... Li, B. (2018). Developing urban residential reference buildings using clustering analysis of satellite images. *Energy and Building*, *169*, 417–429. doi:10.1016/j.enbuild.2018.03.064

Li, Y., Wang, X., Lin, X., & Hajli, M. (2018). Seeking and sharing health information on social media: A net valence model and cross-cultural comparison. *Technological Forecasting and Social Change*, *126*, 28–40. doi:10.1016/j.techfore.2016.07.021

Lonsdale, C. (2005). Post-contractual lock-in and the UK private finance initiative (PFI): The cases of National Savings and Investments and the Lord Chancellor's Department. *Public Administration*, *83*(1), 67–88. doi:10.1111/j.0033-3298.2005.00438.x

Lubitz, J., Cai, L., Kramarow, E., & Lentzner, H. (2003). Health, Life Expectancy, and Health Care Expenditure Among the Elderly. *The New England Journal of Medicine*, *349*(11), 1048–1055. doi:10.1056/NEJMsa020614 PMID:12968089

Luecke, R. (2010). *Strateji, Çev: Turan Parlak*. İstanbul: Türkiye İş Bankası Kültür Yayınları.

Lu, H., While, A. E., & Barriball, K. L. (2005). Job satisfaction among nurses: A literature review. *International Journal of Nursing Studies*, *42*(2), 211–227. doi:10.1016/j.ijnurstu.2004.09.003 PMID:15680619

Lum, L., Kervin, J., Clark, K., Reid, F., & Sirola, W. (1998). Explaining nursing turnover intent: job satisfaction, pay satisfaction, or organizational commitment? *Journal of Organizational Behavior: The International Journal of Industrial. Occupational and Organizational Psychology and Behavior*, *19*(3), 305–320. doi:10.1002/(SICI)1099-1379(199805)19:3<305::AID-JOB843>3.0.CO;2-N

Lund, C., Breen, A., Flisher, A., Kakuma, R., Corrigall, J., Joska, J., ... Patel, V. (2010, August). Poverty and common mental disorders in low and middle income countries: A systematic review. *Social Science & Medicine*, *71*(3), 517–528. doi:10.1016/j.socscimed.2010.04.027 PMID:20621748

Lund, D. B. (2003). Organizational culture and job satisfaction. *Journal of Business and Industrial Marketing*, *18*(3), 219–236. doi:10.1108/0885862031047313

Lundvall, B. Å. (Ed.). (2010). *National systems of innovation: Toward a theory of innovation and interactive learning* (Vol. 2). Anthem press.

Lustig, N. (2007). Investing in health for economic development: The case of Mexico. In*Advancing Development* (pp. 168–182). London: Palgrave Macmillan. doi:10.1057/9780230801462_10

Luthans, F. (1995). *Organizational Behavior, international edition*. İstanbul: Literatür Yayıncılık.

Mackey, T. K., Kuo, T. T., Gummadi, B., Clauson, K. A., Church, G., Grishin, D., ... Palombini, M. (2019). 'Fit-for-purpose?'–challenges and opportunities for applications of blockchain technology in the future of healthcare. *BMC Medicine*, *17*(1), 68. doi:10.118612916-019-1296-7 PMID:30914045

Mackey, T. K., & Nayyar, G. A. (2017). A review of existing and emerging digital technologiesto combat the global trade in fake medicines. *Expert Opinion on Drug Safety, 16*(5), 587–602. do i:10.1080/14740338.2017.1313227 PMID:28349715

Madathil, K. C., Rivera-Rodriguez, A. J., Greenstein, J. S., & Gramopadhye, A. K. (2015). Healthcare information on YouTube: A systematic review. *Health Informatics Journal, 21*(3), 173–194. doi:10.1177/1460458213512220 PMID:24670899

Maddala, G. S., & Wu, S. (1999). A Comparative Study of Unit Root Tests with Panel Data and A New Simple Test. *Oxford Bulletin of Economics and Statistics, 61*(s1), 631–652. doi:10.1111/1468-0084.61.s1.13

Mahoney, J. (2001). Leadership skills for the 21st century. *Journal of Nursing Management, 9*(5), 269–271. doi:10.1046/j.1365-2834.2001.00230.x PMID:11879469

Mahsud, R., Yukl, G., & Prussia, G. (2010). Leader empathy, ethical leadership, and relations-oriented behaviors as antecedents of leader-member exchange quality. *Journal of Managerial Psychology, 25*(6), 561–577. doi:10.1108/02683941011056932

Malafronte, I., Porzio, C., & Starita, M. G. (2016). The nature and determinants of disclosure practices in the insurance industry: Evidence from European insurers. *International Review of Financial Analysis, 45*, 367–382. doi:10.1016/j.irfa.2015.02.003

Mangi, A. A., Kanasro, H. A., & Burdi, M. B. (2015). Motivation tools and organizational success: A criticle analysis of motivational theories. *The Government-Annual Research Journal of Political Science, 4*(4).

Margarita, I. Å. (2013). Motivation tools though lenses of prospective employees. *Entrepreneurship and Sustainability Issues, 1*(2), 116–123. doi:10.9770/jesi.2013.1.2(6)

Martin, D., & Singer, P. (2003). A strategy to improve priority setting in health care institutions. *Health Care Analysis, 11*(1), 59–68. doi:10.1023/A:1025338013629 PMID:14510309

Martin, M. J., Gonzalez, M. P. L., & Garcia, M. D. G. (2011). Review of the literature on the determinants of healthcare expenditures. *Applied Economics, 43*(1), 19–46. doi:10.1080/00036841003689754

Marx, D. (2001). Patient safety and the 'just culture': a primer for health care executives. In *MERS: Medical event reporting system for transfusion medicine*. Washington, DC: AHRQ.

Maslach, C., & Leiter, M. P. (2016). Burnout. In Stress: Concepts, Cognition, Emotion, and Behavior (pp. 351-357). Academic Press.

Mathers, C. D., Sadana, R., Salomon, J. A., Murray, C. J., & Lopez, A. D. (2001). Healthy life expectancy in 191 countries, 1999. *Lancet, 357*(9269), 1685–1691. doi:10.1016/S0140-6736(00)04824-8 PMID:11425392

Mazgit, İ. (1998). *Ekonomik kalkınma sürecinde Türkiyede sağlık sektörünün yeniden yapılanması* [Doctoral dissertation]. DEÜ Sosyal Bilimleri Enstitüsü.

Mazzaschi, A. (2011). Surgeon and safari: Producing valuable bodies in Johannesburg. *Signs (Chicago, Ill.)*, *36*(2), 303–312. doi:10.1086/655941 PMID:21114075

Mbaku, J. M., & Kimenyi, M. S. (1997). Macroeconomic Determinants of Growth: Further Evidence on the Role of Political Freedom. *Journal of Economic Development*, *22*(2), 119–132.

McClelland, D. C. (1987). *Human motivation*. CUP Archive.

McFadden, K. L., Henagan, S. C., & Gowen, C. R. III. (2009). The Patient Safety Chain: Transformational Leadership's Effect on Patient Safety Culture, Initiatives, and Outcomes. *Journal of Operations Management*, *27*(5), 390–404. doi:10.1016/j.jom.2009.01.001

McFarlane, C., Beer, M., Brown, J., & Prendergast, N. (2017). Patientory: A Healthcare Peer-to-Peer EMR Storage Network v1. 0. Retrieved from https://patientory.com/patientory_whitepaper.pdf

McGough, S. F., Brownstein, J. S., Hawkins, J. B., & Santillana, M. (2017). Forecasting Zika Incidence in the 2016 Latin America Outbreak Combining Traditional Disease Surveillance with Search, Social Media, and News Report Data. *PLoS Neglected Tropical Diseases*, *11*(1), e0005295. doi:10.1371/journal.pntd.0005295 PMID:28085877

McNatt, B. (2001). *The Pygmalion Effect Managing The Power of Expectations: Leader's Guide*. CRM Learning.

Mediledger. (n.d.). Retrieved from https://www.mediledger.com/

Mehrara, M., Musai, M., & Amiri, H. (2010). The relationship between health expenditure and GDP in OECD countries using PSTR. European Journal of Economics. *Finance and Administrative Sciences*, *24*, 1450–2275.

Meryem, K., & Alper, T. (2000). *Sosyal Politika. Baskı*. Ekim.

Metcalfe, J. S. (1994). Evolutionary economics and technology policy. *Economic Journal (London)*, *104*(425), 931–944. doi:10.2307/2234988

Mettler, M. (2016). Blockchain technology in healthcare: The revolution starts here. In *Proceedings of the 2016 IEEE 18th International Conference on e-Health Networking, Applications and Services (Healthcom)*. IEEE.

Meydan, C. H., & Polat, M. (2010). Liderin Güç Kaynaklari Üzerine Kültürel Bağlamda Bir Araştirma. *Ankara Üniversitesi SBF Dergisi*, *65*(4), 123–140.

Milanovic, B. (2016). *Global Inequality: A New Approach for the Age of Globalization*. Harvard University Press. doi:10.4159/9780674969797

Miles, R. E., Snow, C. C., Meyer, A. D., & Coleman, H. J. Jr. (1978). Organizational strategy, structure, and process. *Academy of Management Review*, *3*(3), 546–562. doi:10.5465/amr.1978.4305755 PMID:10238389

Miner, J. B. (1978). Twenty years of research on role-motivation theory of managerial effectiveness. *Personnel Psychology*, *31*(4), 739–760. doi:10.1111/j.1744-6570.1978.tb02122.x

Ministry for Foreign Affairs Sweden. (2016). Regional Strategy for Sweden's Development Cooperation with the Middle East and North Africa (MENA) 2016-2020.

Mintzberg, H. (1987). The strategy concept I: Five Ps for strategy. *California Management Review, 30*(1), 11–24. doi:10.2307/41165263

Mısırlı, İ. (2007). *Genel ve Teknik İletişim Kavramlar,İlkeler ve Uygulamalar*. Ankara: Detay Yayıncılık.

Mitchinson, A. R., Kim, H. M., Geisser, M., Rosenberg, J. M., & Hinshaw, D. B. (2008). Social Connectedness and Patient Recovery after Major Operations. *Journal of the American College of Surgeons, 206*(2), 292–300. doi:10.1016/j.jamcollsurg.2007.08.017 PMID:18222382

Mongeon, P., & Paul-Hus, A. (2016). The journal coverage of web of science and scopus: A comparative analysis. *Scientometrics, 106*(1), 213–228. doi:2-015-1765-5. doi:10.10071119

Moorhead, S. A., Hazlett, D. E., Harrison, L., Carroll, J. K., Irwin, A., & Hoving, C. (2013). A new dimension of health care: Systematic review of the uses, benefits, and limitations of social media for health communication. *Journal of Medical Internet Research, 15*(4), 1–16. doi:10.2196/jmir.1933 PMID:23615206

Moran, M. (1999). Governing the health care state: a comparative study of the United Kingdom, the United States, and Germany. Manchester University Press.

Morden, T. (2016). *Principles of strategic management*. Routledge. doi:10.4324/9781315602172

Morrisey, M. A. (2001). Competition in hospital and health insurance markets: A review and research agenda. *Health Services Research, 36*(1 Pt 2), 191. PMID:11327174

Mosa, A. S. M., & Yoo, I. (2013). A Study on Pubmed Search Tag Usage Pattern. Pdf. *Medical Informatics and Decision Making, 13*(8), 1–14. PMID:23289362

Mossialos, E., Thomson, S., & World Health Organization. (2004). *Voluntary health insurance in the European Union*. Copenhagen: WHO Regional Office for Europe.

Muhsin, K. (2003). Kamu harcama çeşitlerinin ekonomik büyüme üzerine etkisi. *Ankara Üniversitesi SBF Dergisi, 58*(3).

Mumford, M. D., Medeiros, K. E., & Partlow, P. J. (2012). Creative thinking: Processes, strategies, and knowledge. *The Journal of Creative Behavior, 46*(1), 30–47. doi:10.1002/jocb.003

Muniz, A. M. J. Jr, & O'Guinn, T. C. (2001). Brand Community. *The Journal of Consumer Research, 27*(4), 412–432. doi:10.1086/319618

Murali, V., & Oyebode, F. (2004). Poverty, social inequality and mental health. *Advances in Psychiatric Treatment, 10*(3), 216–224. doi:10.1192/apt.10.3.216

Murat, S., & Eser, B. (2013). Türkiye'de Ekonomik Büyüme ve İstihdam İlişkisi: İstihdam Yaratmayan Büyüme Olgusunun Geçerliliği. *Emek ve toplum, 2*(3), 92-123.

Murphy, R. (2018). Local Consumer Review Survey. Bright Local. Retrieved from https://www.brightlocal.com/research/local-consumer-review-survey/

Murphy, L. (2005). Transformational leadership: A cascading chain reaction. *Journal of Nursing Management, 13*(2), 128–136. doi:10.1111/j.1365-2934.2005.00458.x PMID:15720482

Murray, W. B., & Foster, P. A. (2000). Crisis Resource Management Among Strangers: Principles of Organizing a Multidisciplinary Group for Crisis Resource Management. *Journal of Clinical Anesthesia, 12*(8), 633–638. doi:10.1016/S0952-8180(00)00223-3 PMID:11173002

Mushtaq, Y., & Khalidi, M. (2016). A Study on Pygmalion Effect: A Case of Academic Training in a Military Unit. *Market Forces, 11*(1), 35–48.

Mütercimler, E. (2006). *Yüksek Stratejiden Etki Odaklı Harekâta Geleceği Yönetmek*. İstanbul: İkinci Baskı, Alfa Basım.

Nalimov, V. V., & Mul'chenko, Z. M. (1969). *Naukometriya, The study of the development of science as an information process*. Moscow: Nauka.

Narayan, A., Van der Weide, R., Cojocaru, A., Lakner, C., Redaelli, S., Mahler, D. G., & Thewissen, S. (2018). *Fair Progress?: Economic Mobility Across Generations Around the World*. World Bank Publications.

Narayan, P. K. (2007). Do Health Expenditures 'Catch-Up'? Evidence from OECD Countries. *Health Economics, 16*(10), 993–1008. doi:10.1002/hec.1196 PMID:17238220

Narayan, S., Narayan, P. K., & Mishra, S. (2010). Investigating the relationship between health and economic growth: Empirical evidence from a panel of 5 Asian countries. *Journal of Asian Economics, 21*(4), 404–411. doi:10.1016/j.asieco.2010.03.006

Nelson, R. (1959). The simple economics of basic scientific research. *Journal of Political Economy, 67*, 297-306.

Newman, M. E. J. (2006). Modularity and community structure in networks. *Proceedings of the National Academy of Sciences of the United States of America, 103*(23), 8577–8582. doi:10.1073/pnas.0601602103 PMID:16723398

Newstrom, J. W., Davis, K., & Pierce, J. L. (1993). Organizational behavior: Human behavior at work.

Ng, K. Y., Van Dyne, L., Ang, S., & Ryan, A. M. (2012). Cultural intelligence: A review, reflections, and recommendations for future research. In *Conducting multinational research: Applying organizational psychology in the workplace* (pp. 29-58). APA.

Ng, R. (2013). Cultural intelligence. In The Encyclopedia of Cross-Cultural Psychology (pp. 310-313). Academic Press.

Nghiem, S. H., & Connelly, L. B. (2017). Convergence and Determinants of Health Expenditures in OECD Countries. *Health Economics Review*, *7*(1), 1–11. doi:10.118613561-017-0164-4 PMID:28819772

Nguyen, T., Larsen, M. E., O'Dea, B., Phung, D., Venkatesh, S., & Christensen, H. (2017). Estimation of the prevalence of adverse drug reactions from social media. *International Journal of Medical Informatics*, *102*, 130–137. doi:10.1016/j.ijmedinf.2017.03.013 PMID:28495341

Nielsen. (2015). Winning Strategies for an Evolving Media Landscaping. Retrieved from https://www.nielsen.com/sa/en/insights/report/2015/global-trust-in-advertising-2015/

Nixon, J. (2000). Convergence of Health Care Spending and Health Outcomes in the European Union, 1960-95. *The University of York Centre for Health Economics.*

Nixon, J., & Ulmann, P. (2006). The relationship between health care expenditure and health outcomes. *The European Journal of Health Economics*, *7*(1), 7–18. doi:10.100710198-005-0336-8 PMID:16429295

Nketiah-Amponsah, E. (2019). The Impact of Health Expenditures on Health Outcomes in Sub-Saharan Africa. *Journal of Developing Societies*, *35*(1), 134–152. doi:10.1177/0169796X19826759

Noree, T., Hanefeld, J., & Smith, R. (2014). UK medical tourists in Thailand: They are not who you think they are. *Globalization and Health*, *10*(1), 29. doi:10.1186/1744-8603-10-29 PMID:24885204

Noree, T., Hanefeld, J., & Smith, R. (2016). Medical tourism in Thailand: A cross-sectional study. *Bulletin of the World Health Organization*, *94*(1), 30–36. doi:10.2471/BLT.14.152165 PMID:26769994

Normore, A. H., & Collard, J. (Eds.). (2009). *Leadership and intercultural dynamics*. IAP.

Northouse, P. G. (2018). *Leadership: Theory and practice*. Sage publications.

Novignon, J., Olakojo, S. A., & Nonvignon, J. (2012). The effects of public and private health care expenditure on health status in sub-Saharan Africa: New evidence from panel data analysis. *Health Economics Review*, *2*(1), 22. doi:10.1186/2191-1991-2-22 PMID:23232089

Noy, S., & McManus, P. A. (2015). Modernization, Globalization, Trends and Convergence in Health Expenditure in Latin America and the Caribbean. *Social Development*, *1*(2), 321–346. doi:10.1525od.2015.1.2.321

Nugent, T., Upton, D., & Cimpoesu, M. (2016). Improving data transparency in clinical trials using blockchain smart contracts. *F1000 Research*, *5*, 2541. doi:10.12688/f1000research.9756.1 PMID:28357041

Nutt, P. C., & Backoff, R. W. (1987). A strategic management process for public and third-sector organizations. *Journal of the American Planning Association*, *53*(1), 44–57. doi:10.1080/01944368708976634

O'Neil, H. F. Jr, Drillings, M., & O'Neil, H. F. (2012). *Motivation: Theory and research*. Routledge.

Obrizan, M. & Wehby, G.L. (2018). Health Expenditures and Global Inequalities in Longevity, *World Development, 101*, 28-36. doi:.08.003 doi:10.1016/j.worlddev.2017

Öcal, N., & Yıldırım, J. (2010). Regional Effects of Terrorism on Economic Growth in Turkey: A Geographically Weighted Regression Approach. *Journal of Peace Research*, *47*(4), 477–489. doi:10.1177/0022343310364576

Odhiambo, S. A., Wambugu, A., & Kriti-Ng, T. (2015). Convergence of Health Expenditure in Sub-Saharan Africa: Evidence from a Dynamic Panel. *Journal of Economics and Sustainable Development*, *6*(6), 185–205.

Odubunmi, A. S., Saka, J. O., & Oke, D. M. (2012). Testing the cointegrating relationship between health care expenditure and economic growth in Nigeria. *International Journal of Economics and Finance*, *4*(11), 99–107. doi:10.5539/ijef.v4n11p99

OECD. (2001). *Strategies for Sustainable Development*. France.

OECD. (2010). *Dedicated Public-Private Partnership Units: A Survey of Institutional and Governance Structure*. Paris: OECD Publishing.

OECD. (n.d.). Health spending. Retrieved from https://data.oecd.org/healthres/health-spending.htm

OECD. (n.d.). Infant mortality rates. Retrieved from https://data.oecd.org/healthstat/infant-mortality-rates.htm

OECD/EU. (2018). *Health at a Glance: Europe 2018: State of Health in the EU Cycle*. Paris: OECD Publishing. doi:10.1787/health_glance_eur-2018-

Ogden, J., Morrison, K., & Hardee, K. (2013). Social capital to strengthen health policy and health systems. *Health Policy and Planning*, *29*(8), 1075–1085. doi:10.1093/heapol/czt087 PMID:24277736

Okay, A. (2009). *Sağlık İletişimi*. İstanbul: MediaCat Yayınları.

Okay, A. (2014). *Sağlık İletişimi*. İstanbul: Derin Yayınları.

Okunade, A. A., Karakuş, M. C., & Okeke, C. (2004). Determinants of Health Expenditure Growth of the OECD Countries: Jackknife Resampling Plan Estimates. *Health Care Management Science*, *7*(3), 173–183. doi:10.1023/B:HCMS.0000039380.42784.20 PMID:15648560

Olalı, H., & Timur, A. (1988). Turizmin Türk Ekonomisindeki Yeri, İzmir: Ofis Ticaret Matbaacılık San. Ltd. Şti.

Olenski, S. (2013). How Johnson & Johnson Is Using Social Media To Save Lives. Forbes. Retrieved from https://www.forbes.com/sites/steveolenski/2013/07/10/how-johnson-johnson-is-using-social-media-to-save-lives/#7f371b81d773

Öngel, V., Altındağ, E., & Öngel, Ö. (2014). Kişi Başına Sağlık Harcamalarının Sağlık Göstergeleri Üzerindeki Etkileri: MINT ve BRIC Ülkelerinin Karşılaştırmalı Analizi. In *Proceedings of the International Conference on Eurasian Economies* (pp. 1-5). Academic Press.

Oni, L. B. (2014). Analysis of the growth impact of health expenditure in Nigeria. *IOSR Journal of Economics and Finance, 3*(1), 77–84. doi:10.9790/5933-03117784

Or, Z. (2000). Determinants of health outcomes in industrialised countries: a pooled, cross-country, time-series analysis. *OECD Economic Studies.*

Örücü, E., Yumuşak, S., & Bozkır, Y. (2006). Kalite Yönetimi Çerçevesinde Bankalarda Çalışan Personelin İş Tatmini ve İs Tatminini Etkileyen Faktörlerin İncelenmesine Yönelik Bir Araştırma. *Celal Bayar Üniversitesi İİBF Yönetim ve Ekonomi Dergisi, 13*(1), 39–51.

Oskay, Ü. (1992). *İletişimin ABCsi.* İstanbul: Simavi Yayınları.

Osterloh, M., & Frey, B. S. (2000). Motivation, knowledge transfer, and organizational forms. *Organization Science, 11*(5), 538–550. doi:10.1287/orsc.11.5.538.15204

Oyedele, O., & Adebayo, A. (2015). Convergence of Health Expenditure and Health Outcomes in Ecowas Countries. *International Journal of Economics Financial Management, 4*(2), 46–53.

Oyman, S. (2009). *Stratejik yönetim sürecinde performans ölçümü ve dengeli sonuç kartı uygulaması: Türkiye Cumhuriyet Merkez Bankası için bir değerlendirme.* Ankara: Uzmanlık Yeterlilik Tezi, Türkiye Cumhuriyet Merkez Bankası.

Özdemir, F. (2006). *Örgütsel iklimin iş tatmin düzeyine etkisi: tekstil sektöründe bir araştırma. Yayımlanmamış doktora tezi.* Adana: Çukurova Üniversitesi, Sosyal Bilimler Enstitüsü.

Özel, H. A. (2012). Ekonomik Büyümenin Teorik Temelleri. *Çankırı Karatekin Üniversitesi İİBF Dergisi, 2*(1), 63-72.

Özer, A. R. I. K., İleri, Y. Y., & Buğra, K. A. Y. A. (2016). Sağlık Hizmetlerinde Tıbbi Cihaz Sektörü. *Hacettepe Sağlık İdaresi Dergisi, 19*(2).

Özkan, Z. (2011). *66 Soruda Sağlıkta İletişimin Gücü.* İstanbul: Optimist Yayınları.

Öztek, M. Y. (2005). Performans Ölçümünde Esas Alınan Ölçütler. *Öneri Dergisi, 6*(23), 19-22.

Pablo, A. L., & Javidan, M. (Eds.). (2009). *Mergers and acquisitions: Creating integrative knowledge.* John Wiley & Sons.

Paksoy, A. (2006). *Performansa Dayalı Ücretleme: Bir Alan Araştırması.* Kahramanmaraş: Yayınlanmamış Yüksek Lisans Tezi, Kahramanmaraş Sütçü İmam Üniversitesi Sosyal Bilimler Enstitüsü.

Paleari, S. (2019). Disaster risk insurance: A comparison of national schemes in the EU-28. *International Journal of Disaster Risk Reduction, 35*, 101059. doi:10.1016/j.ijdrr.2018.12.021

Palmer, A., & Koenig-Lewis, N. (2009). An experiential, social network-based approach to direct marketing. *Direct Marketing: An International Journal*, *3*(3), 162–176. doi:10.1108/17505930910985116

Palomo-Duarte, M., Berns, A., Yañez Escolano, A., & Dodero, J. M. (2019). Clustering analysis of game-based learning: Worth it for all students? *Journal of Gaming & Virtual Worlds*, *11*(1), 45–66. doi:10.1386/jgvw.11.1.45_1

Panopoulou, E., & Pantelidis, T. (2012). Convergence in Per Capita Health Expenditures and Health Outcomes in the OECD Countries. *Applied Economics*, *44*(30), 3909–3920. doi:10.1080/00036846.2011.583222

Panopoulou, E., & Pantelidis, T. (2013). Cross-State Disparities in US Health Care Expenditures. *Health Economics*, *22*(4), 451–465. doi:10.1002/hec.2816 PMID:22473657

Patel, V., Lund, C., Hatheril, S., Plagerson, S., Corrigall, J., & Funk, M. (2010). Mental disorders: equity and social determinants. In E. Blas & A. S. Kurup (Eds.), *Equity, social determinants and public health programmes* (pp. 115–134). Geneva: World Health Organization.

Patients Beyond Borders. (2019). *Medical Tourism Statistics and Facts.* Retrieved from https://patientsbeyondborders.com/medical-tourism-statistics-facts

Paul, S. (1982). *Strategic management of development programmes: guidelines for action (No. 19).* International Labour Organization.

Payne, J. E., Anderson, S., Lee, J., & Cho, M. H. (2015). Do Per-Capita Health Care Expenditures Converge Among OECD Countries? Evidence from Unit Root Tests with Level and Trend-Shifts. *Applied Economics*, *47*(52), 5600–5613. doi:10.1080/00036846.2015.1054070

Pearce, J. A., Robinson, R. B., & Subramanian, R. (2000). *Strategic management: Formulation, implementation, and control.* Columbus, OH: Irwin/McGraw-Hill.

Pedreira, M. L., & Marin, H. F. (2004). Patient Safety Initiatives in Brazil: A Nursing Perspective. *International Journal of Medical Informatics*, *73*(7-8), 563–567. doi:10.1016/j.ijmedinf.2004.05.001 PMID:15246036

Pedroni, P. (1999). Critical Values for Cointegration Tests in Heterogeneous Panels with Multiple Regressors. *Oxford Bulletin of Economics and Statistics*, *61*(s1), 653–670. doi:10.1111/1468-0084.61.s1.14

Pedroni, P. (2001). Fully modified OLS for heterogeneous cointegrated panels. In *Nonstationary panels, panel cointegration, and dynamic panels* (pp. 93–130). Emerald Group Publishing Limited.

Pedroni, P. (2004). Panel Cointegration: Asymptotic and Finite Sample Properties of Pooled Time Series Tests with an Application to the PPP Hypothesis. *Econometric Theory*, *20*(03), 597–625. doi:10.1017/S0266466604203073

Peker, Ö., & Aytürk, N. (2002). *Yönetim Becerileri (2. Baskı).* Ankara: Yargı Yayınevi.

Pekkurnaz, D. (2015). Convergence of Health Expenditure in OECD Countries: Evidence from a Nonlinear Asymmetric Heterogeneous Panel Unit Root Test. *Journal of Reviews on Global Economics*, *4*, 76–86. doi:10.6000/1929-7092.2015.04.07

Pelletier, B., Boles, M., & Lynch, W. (2004). Change in health risks and work productivity over time. *Journal of Occupational and Environmental Medicine*, *46*(7), 746–754. doi:10.1097/01.jom.0000131920.74668.e1 PMID:15247815

Pestieau, P. (2006). *The welfare state in the European Union: Economic and social perspectives*. Oxford University Press.

Peterson, M. F., & Hunt, J. G. J. (1997). International perspectives on international leadership. *The Leadership Quarterly*, *8*(3), 203–231. doi:10.1016/S1048-9843(97)90002-3

Peters, R. S. (2015). *The concept of motivation*. Routledge. doi:10.4324/9781315712833

Petre, A. (2017a). Leveraging Sustainable Innovation in Healthcare. Retrieved from http://www.ancapetre.com/leveraging-sustainable-innovation-healthcare

Petre, A. (2017b). Blockchain use cases in healthcare. Retrieved from https://www.linkedin.com/pulse/blockchain-use-cases-healthcare-anca-petre

Petri, H. L., & Govern, J. M. (2012). *Motivation: Theory, research, and application*. Cengage Learning.

Piabuo, S. M., & Tieguhong, J. C. (2017). Health expenditure and economic growth-a review of the literature and an analysis between the economic community for central African states (CEMAC) and selected African countries. *Health Economics Review*, *7*(1), 23. doi:10.118613561-017-0159-1 PMID:28593509

Pickering, J. F. & Matthews, D. (1997). The evolution of Rules for the Single European Market in Insurance. NIESR.

Pijoan-Mas, J., & Sánchez-Marcos, V. (2010). Spain is Different: Falling Trends of Inequality. *Review of Economic Dynamics*, *13*(1), 154–178. doi:10.1016/j.red.2009.10.002

Piketty, T. (2015). About Capital in the Twenty-First Century. *The American Economic Review*, *105*(5), 48–53. doi:10.1257/aer.p20151060

Pilkington, M. (2017). Can Blockchain Improve Healthcare Management? Consumer Medical Electronics and the IoMT. doi:10.2139srn.3025393

Plsek, P. E., & Wilson, T. (2001). Complexity, leadership, and management in healthcare organisations. *BMJ (Clinical Research Ed.)*, *323*(7315), 746–749. doi:10.1136/bmj.323.7315.746 PMID:11576986

Pollard, D., & Hotho, S. (2006). Crises, scenarios and the strategic management process. *Management Decision*, *44*(6), 721–736. doi:10.1108/00251740610673297

Porter, M. E. (1996). What is strategy.

Porter, M. E. (1998). Clusters and the new economics of competition. *Harvard Business Review*, *76*(6), 77–90.

Porter, M. E., & Locations, C. (2000). Company strategy. In *The Oxford handbook of economic geography* (pp. 253–274). Oxford press.

PPIAF. (2009). Toolkit for Public-Private Partnerships. In *Roads & Highways*. Public-Private Infrastructure Advisory Facility.

Prada, G. (2008). Exploring technological innovation in health systems: Is Canada measuring up? *Journal of Management & Marketing in Healthcare*, *1*(4), 362–374. doi:10.1179/mmh.2008.1.4.362

Prats, J., Demaestri, E., & Chiara, J. (2018). *Public–Private Partnership Databases*. Inter-American Development Bank.

Preble, J. F. (1997). Integrating the crisis management perspective into the strategic management process. *Journal of Management Studies*, *34*(5), 769–791. doi:10.1111/1467-6486.00071

Priyabhashini, A., & Krishnan, V. R. (2005). Transformational Leadership and Follower's Career Advancement: Role of Pygmalion Effect. *Indian Journal of Industrial Relations*, *40*(4), 482–499.

Pronovost, P., Weast, B., Rosenstein, B., Sexton, B., Holzmueller, C. G., Paine, L., ... Rubin, H. R. (2005). Implementing and Validating a Comprehensive Unit-Based Safety Program. *Journal of Patient Safety*, *1*(1), 33–40. doi:10.1097/01209203-200503000-00008

Psikoloji Sözlüğü. (2000). Rol karışıklığı. In *"Rol haritası", "Rol mesafesi", "Stereotip", "Pygmalion etkisi", "Pygmalionizm", "Toplum yanlısı saldırganlık", "Özdeşim teorisi". S. Budak (haz.)*. Ankara: Bilim ve Sanat Yayınları.

Purvanova, R. K., Bono, J. E., & Dzieweczynski, J. (2006). Transformational leadership, job characteristics, and organizational citizenship performance. *Human Performance*, *19*(1), 1–22. doi:10.120715327043hup1901_1

Rabah, K. (2017). Challenges & Opportunities for Blockchain Powered Healthcare Systems: A Review. *Mara Research Journal of Medicine & Health Sciences*, *1*(1), 45–52.

Rahman, M. M., Khanam, R., & Rahman, M. (2018). Health Care Expenditure and Health Outcome Nexus: New Evidence from the SAARC-ASEAN Region.

Randall, D., Goel, P., & Abujamra, R. (2017). Blockchain Applications and Use Cases in Health Information Technology. *J Health Med Informat*, *8*(276), 2.

Ravikumar, S., Agrahari, A., & Singh, S. N. (2015). Mapping the intellectual structure of scientometrics: A co-word analysis of the journal scientometrics (2005–2010). *Scientometrics*, *102*(1), 929–955. doi:10.100711192-014-1402-8

Reeves, A., Basu, S., McKee, M., Meissner, C., & Stuckler, D. (2013). Does investment in the health sector promote or inhibit economic growth? *Globalization and Health*, *9*(1), 43. doi:10.1186/1744-8603-9-43 PMID:24059873

Report, B. I. (2018) mHealth and Home Monitoring. Retrieved from http://www.berginsight.com

Reynolds, D. E. (2000). Pygmalion in Management: Understanding Supervisory Expectations As an Antecedent of Managerial Self-Efficacy [Doctoral Thesis]. Cornell University, NY.

Reynolds, M. M., & Avendano, M. (2018). Social Policy Expenditures and Life Expectancy in High-Income Countries. *American Journal of Preventive Medicine*, *54*(1), 72–79. doi:10.1016/j.amepre.2017.09.001

Ridic, G., Gleason, S., & Ridic, O. (2012). Comparisons of health care systems in the United States, Germany and Canada. *Materia Socio-Medica*, *24*(2), 112. doi:10.5455/msm.2012.24.112-120 PMID:23678317

Rigby, D., & Bilodeau, B. (2013). Management Tools & Trends 2013. Bain & Company. Retrieved from http://www.bain.com/consulting-services/strategy/fundamentals-of-growth.aspx

Riggio, R. E., & Cole, E. J. (1992). Agreement between subordinate and superior ratings of supervisory performance and effects on self and subordinate job satisfaction. *Journal of Occupational and Organizational Psychology*, *65*(2), 151–158. doi:10.1111/j.2044-8325.1992.tb00491.x

Riumallo-Herl, C., Canning, D. & Salomon, J.A. (2018). Measuring Health and Economic Wellbeing in the Sustainable Development Goals Era: Development of a Poverty-Free Life Expectancy Metric and Estimates for 90 Countries. *The Lancet Global Health*, *6*(8), e843-e858.

Rızvanoğlu, K. (2009). *Herkes İçin Web: Evrensel Kullanılabilirlik ve Tasarım*. İstanbul: Punto Yayınları.

Robbins, C. J., Bradley, E. H., Spicer, M., & Mecklenburg, G. A. (2001). Developing leadership in healthcare administration: A competency assessment tool/Practitioner application. *Journal of Healthcare Management*, *46*(3), 188–202. doi:10.1097/00115514-200105000-00010 PMID:11372221

Rodoplu, D. (2001). *Stratejik Yönetim Düzeyinde Zaman Yönetimi ve Yetki Devri". Yayımlanmamış Yüksek Lisans Tezi, TC Kocaeli Üniversitesi, Sosyal Bilimler Enstitüsü*. Kocaeli.

Rosenau, PV. (1999). *Introduction: The strengths and weaknesses of public-private policy partnerships.*

Rosenmöller, M., & Lluch, M. (2006). Meeting the needs of long-term residents in Spain. Patient Mobility in the European Union, 59.

Rosenthal, R. (1994). Interpersonal Expectancy Effects: A 30-year perspective. *Current Directions in Psychological Science*, *3*(6), 176–179. doi:10.1111/1467-8721.ep10770698

Rosenthal, R., & Jacobson, L. (1968). *Pygmalion in the classroom*. New York: Holt, Rinehart &Winston Inc. doi:10.1007/BF02322211

Rost, J. C. (1993). *Leadership for the twenty-first century*. Greenwood Publishing Group.

Rueda, D., & Stegmueller, D. (2015). *Preferences That Matter: Inequality, Redistribution and Voting*. Mimeo.

Russel, T. (2005). Special Address To The Midwest Surgical Association on Surgical Outcome Analysis and Patient Safety. *American Journal of Surgery, 189*(3), 264–267. doi:10.1016/j.amjsurg.2004.11.011 PMID:15792747

Rustichini, A., & Vostroknutov, A. (2014). Merit and Justice: An Experimental Analysis of Attitude to Inequality. *PLoS One, 9*(12), e114512–e114525. doi:10.1371/journal.pone.0114512 PMID:25490094

Saari, L. M., & Judge, T. A. (2004). Employee attitudes and job satisfaction. *Human Resource Management: Published in Cooperation with the School of Business Administration, The University of Michigan and in alliance with the Society of Human Resources Management, 43*(4), 395-407.

Sağlık Bakanlığı. 2019. Sağlık Turizmi Nedir? Retrieved from http://www.saturk.gov.tr/index.phphttps://saglikturizmi.saglik.gov.tr/TR,175/saglik-turizmi-hakkinda.html

Sahnoun, M. (2018). Does Health Expenditure Increase Economic Growth: Evidence from Tunisia? *Romanian Economic Journal, 20*(67).

Sala-i-Martin, X. X. (1996). The Classical Approach to Convergence Analysis. *Economic Journal (London), 106*(437), 1019–1036. doi:10.2307/2235375

Saltman, R. B. (2004). Social health insurance in perspective: the challenge of sustaining stability.

Şamkar, H., & Güner, D. (2018). OECD Ülkelerindeki Beş Yaş Altı Çocuk Ölüm Sayılarının Yanlı Tahmin Teknikleriyle Modellenmesi. *Ulikidince, 11*(21), 273–284. doi:10.18092/ulikidince.398068

Sampson, R. J., & Raudenbush, S. W. (1999). Systematic social observation of public spaces: A new look at disorder in urban neighborhoods. *American Journal of Sociology, 105*(3), 603–651. doi:10.1086/210356

Sarasohn-Kahn, J. (2008). The Wisdom of Patients: Health Care Meets Online Social Media. *Medical Benefits, 25*(13), 12. Retrieved from http://search.ebscohost.com/login.aspx?direct=true&db=bth&AN=32816528&site=ehost-live&scope=site

Sarpong, B., Nketiah-Amponsah, E., & Owoo, N. S. (2018). Health and Economic Growth Nexus: Evidence from Selected Sub-Saharan African (SSA) Countries. *Global Business Review*.

Sass, E. (2012). Social Health Site Sickweather Predicts Early Flu Season. Retrieved from https://www.mediapost.com/publications/article/190027/social-health-site-sickweather-predicts-early-flu.html

Saxena, S., Thornicroft, G., Knapp, M., & Whiteford, H. (2007). Resources for mental health: Scarcity, inequity, and inefficiency. *Lancet, 370*(9590), 878–889. doi:10.1016/S0140-6736(07)61239-2 PMID:17804062

Sayılı, U., Sayman, Ö. A., Vehid, S., Köksal, S. S., & Erginöz, E. (2017). Türkiye ve OECD Ülkelerinin Sağlık Göstergeleri ve Sağlık Harcamalarının Karşılaştırılması. *Online Türk Sağlık Bilimleri Dergisi, 2*(3), 1–12.

Sayım, F. (2011). Mena Ülkelerinde Sağlık Ekonomisi. In H. Genç & F. Sayım (Eds.), *Ortadoğu ve Afrika Ülkelerinin Ekonomik Yapısı MENA Ülkeleri Ekonomisi* (pp. 151–175). Bursa: MKM Yayınları.

Schein, E. H. (2010). *Organizational culture and leadership* (Vol. 2). John Wiley & Sons.

Schelling, T. C. (1980). *The strategy of conflict*. Harvard university press.

Schendel, D. E., & Hatten, K. J. (1972). Business policy or strategic management: A broader view for an emerging discipline. In Academy of management proceedings (No. 1, pp. 99-102). Briarcliff Manor, NY: Academy of Management. doi:10.5465/ambpp.1972.4981324

Schmitt, C., & Starke, P. (2011). Explaining Convergence of OECD Welfare States: A Conditional Approach. *Journal of European Social Policy, 21*(2), 120–135. doi:10.1177/0958928710395049

Schoemaker, P. J. (1995). Scenario planning: A tool for strategic thinking. *Sloan Management Review, 36*(2), 25–50.

Seeman, N., Ing, A., & Rizo, C. (2010). Assessing and Responding in Real Time to Online Anti-vaccine Sentiment during a Flu Pandemic. *Healthcare Quarterly, 13*(sp), 8–15. doi:10.12927/hcq.2010.21923

Seiler, S. (2007). *Determining factors of intercultural leadership: A theoretical framework. In Cultural challenges in military operations* (pp. 213–228). Rome: NDC.

Seitz, J., & Wickramasinghe, N. (2017). Blockchain technology in e-health: The case of electronic prescriptions in Germany. In *Proceedings of the XVII International Scientific Conference on Industrial Systems*. Academic Press.

Şencan, N. (2013). Sağlık çalışanları ve eczacılar üzerinde yapılan iş doyumu ve örgütsel bağlılık araştırmaları. MÜ. *Eczacılık Dergisi., 17*, 106.

Şenkal, A., & Sarıipek, D. B. (2007). Avrupa Birliği'nin Karşılaştırmalı Refah Modelleri ve Sosyal Politikada Devletin Değişen Rolü. *Kocaeli Üniversitesi Sosyal Bilimler Dergisi*, (14), 146-175.

Şenkal, A. (2007). *Küreselleşme sürecinde sosyal politika*. Alfa Basım Yayım Dağıtım.

Serinkan, C. (2008). *Liderlik ve Motivasyon Geleneksel ve Güncel Yaklaşımlar*. Ankara: Baskı, Nobel Yayın Dağıtım.

Shang, B., & Goldman, D. (2008). Does Age or Life Expectancy Better Predict Health Care Expenditures? *Health Economics, 17*(4), 487–501. doi:10.1002/hec.1295 PMID:17935199

Shaw, J. W., Horrace, W. C., & Vogel, R. J. (2005). The determinants of life expectancy: An analysis of the OECD health data. *Southern Economic Journal, 71*(4), 768–783. doi:10.2307/20062079

Sheridan, E. (2005). *Intercultural leadership competencies for United States business leaders in the new millennium* [Doctoral dissertation]. University of Phoenix.

Shi, L., & Starfield, B. (2000). *Primary Care, Income Inequality, and Self-Rated Health in the United States: A Mixed-Level Analysis. International Journal of Health Services, 30(3),* 541–555.

Shiokawa, H., Fujiwara, Y., & Onizuka, M. (2013). Introduction to strong mixing conditions. In Fast Algorithm for Modularity-Based Graph Clustering Hiroaki (pp. 1170–1176). Academic Press.

Shi, X., Li, J., Wang, F., Dinçer, H., & Yüksel, S. (2019). A Hybrid Decision-Making Approach for the Service and Financial-Based Measurement of Universal Health Coverage for the E7 Economies. *International Journal of Environmental Research and Public Health, 16*(18), 3295. doi:10.3390/ijerph16183295 PMID:31500288

Shneiderman, B. (1999). 7 31). Pushing Human-Computer Interaction Research to Empower Every Citizen: Universal Usability. *Communications of the ACM, 43*(5), 85–91.

Shoaf, C., Genaidy, A., Karwowski, W., & Huang, S. H. (2004). Improving performance and quality of working life: A model for organizational health assessment in emerging enterprises. *Human Factors and Ergonomics in Manufacturing & Service Industries, 14*(1), 81–95. doi:10.1002/hfm.10053

Shrivastava, P. (1986). Is strategic management ideological? *Journal of Management, 12*(3), 363–377. doi:10.1177/014920638601200305

Shrivastava, P. (1994). *Strategic management: Concepts & practices.* South-Western Publishing Company.

Signorini, A., Segre, A. M., & Polgreen, P. M. (2011). The Use of Twitter to Track Levels of Disease Activity and Public Concern in the U.S. during the Influenza A H1N1 Pandemic. *PLoS One, 6*(5), e19467. doi:10.1371/journal.pone.0019467 PMID:21573238

Simic, M., Sladic, G., & Milosaljevic, B. (2017). A Case Study IoT and Blockchain powered Healthcare. In *Proceedings of the 8th PSU-UNS International Conference on Engineering and Technology (ICET-2017).* Academic Press.

Simsek, M., & Nursoy, M. (2002). *Toplam Kalite Yönetiminde Performans Olçümü.* Istanbul: Hayat Yayınları.

Şirvan, N., & Alp, Ö. S. (2017). Türev Piyasa Araçlarının Türk Bankacılık Sektöründe Riske Olan Etkileri1. *Başkent Üniversitesi Ticari Bilimler Fakültesi Dergisi, 1*(1), 130–157.

Siyal, A., Junejo, A., Zawish, M., Ahmed, K., Khalil, A., & Soursou, G. (2019). Applications of Blockchain Technology in Medicine and Healthcare: Challenges and Future Perspectives. *Cryptography, 3*(1), 3. doi:10.3390/cryptography3010003

Smailhodzic, E., Hooijsma, W., Boonstra, A., & Langley, D. J. (2016). Social media use in healthcare: A systematic review of effects on patients and on their relationship with healthcare professionals. *BMC Health Services Research*, *16*(1), 1–14. doi:10.118612913-016-1691-0 PMID:27562728

Small, H. (1999). Visualizing science by citation mapping. *Journal of the American Society for Information Science*, *50*(9), 799–813. doi:10.1002/(SICI)1097-4571(1999)50:9<799::AID-ASI9>3.0.CO;2-G

Smith, K. (2000). Innovation as a systemic phenomenon: Rethinking the role of policy. *Enterprise and Innovation Management Studies*, *1*(1), 73–102. doi:10.1080/146324400363536

Snyder, J., & Crooks, V. A. (2010). Medical tourism and bariatric surgery: More moral challenges. *The American Journal of Bioethics*, *10*(12), 28–30. doi:10.1080/15265161.2010.528510 PMID:21161839

Socialbakers. (2018). Facebook statistics directory. Retrieved from https://www.socialbakers.com/statistics/facebook/

Solow, R. (1956). A Contribution to the Theory of Economic Growth. *The Quarterly Journal of Economics*, *70*(1), 65–94. doi:10.2307/1884513

Sözcü. (2019, April 30). *E Nabız nedir? Nasıl kayıt olunur?* Retrieved from https://www.sozcu.com.tr/2019/ekonomi/e-nabiz-nedir-nasil-kayit-olunur-szcu1-4612566/

Spector, P. E. (1997). *Job satisfaction: Application, assessment, causes, and consequences* (Vol. 3). Sage publications.

Spector, P. E., Chen, P. Y., & O'Connell, B. J. (2000). A longitudinal study of relations between job stressors and job strains while controlling for prior negative affectivity and strains. *The Journal of Applied Psychology*, *85*(2), 211–218. doi:10.1037/0021-9010.85.2.211 PMID:10783537

Spiteri, J., & von Brockdorff, P. (2019). Economic development and health outcomes: Evidence from cardiovascular disease mortality in Europe. *Social Science & Medicine*, *224*, 37–44. doi:10.1016/j.socscimed.2019.01.050 PMID:30738235

Spitzer, A., Camus, D., Desaulles, C., & Kuhne, N. (2006). The Changing Context of Western European Healthcare Systems: Convergence versus Divergence in Nursing Problematics. *Social Science & Medicine*, *63*(7), 1796–1810. doi:10.1016/j.socscimed.2006.03.023 PMID:16782252

Ssozi, J., & Amlani, S. (2015). The effectiveness of health expenditure on the proximate and ultimate goals of healthcare in Sub-Saharan Africa. *World Development*, *76*, 165–179. doi:10.1016/j.worlddev.2015.07.010

Stankūnas, M., Sauliūnė, S., Smith, T., Avery, M., Šumskas, L., & Czabanowska, K. (2012). Evaluation of leadership competencies of executives in Lithuanian public health institutions. *Medicina*, *48*(11), 85. doi:10.3390/medicina48110085 PMID:23455893

Starbucks. (2017). Share. Vote. Discuss. See. Retrieved from https://www.starbucks.com/coffeehouse/learn-more/my-starbucks-idea

Statista. (2019a). Most popular social networks worldwide as of July 2019, ranked by number of active users (in millions). Retrieved from https://www.statista.com/statistics/272014/global-social-networks-ranked-by-number-of-users/

Statista. (2019b). Number of monthly active Twitter users worldwide from 1st quarter 2010 to 1st quarter 2019 (in millions). Retrieved from https://www.statista.com/statistics/282087/number-of-monthly-active-twitter-users/

Steers, R. M., Mowday, R. T., & Shapiro, D. L. (2004). The future of work motivation theory. *Academy of Management Review*, *29*(3), 379–387.

Steiner, G. A. (1971). *Business and society.*

Steinfield, C., Ellison, N. B., & Lampe, C. (2008). Social capital, self-esteem, and use of online social network sites: A longitudinal analysis. *Journal of Applied Developmental Psychology*, *29*(6), 434–445. doi:10.1016/j.appdev.2008.07.002

Sternberg, R. J., & Detterman, D. K. (1986). *What is intelligence? Norwood.* New York: Ablex.

Stiglitz, J. E. (2012). *The Price of Inequality: How Today's Divided Society Endangers Our Future*. WW Norton & Company.

Stockport, G. J. (2010). Semco: Cultural transformation and strategic leadership. *International Journal of Technology Marketing*, *5*(1), 67–78. doi:10.1504/IJTMKT.2010.033297

Stogdill, R. M. (1974). *Handbook of leadership: A survey of theory and research*. Free Press.

Stokes, R. (2011). The Essential Guide to Digital Marketing (4th ed.). Quirk e-marketing Pty Ltd.

Strauss, J., & Frost, R. (2013). *E-Marketing: Pearson New* (International Edition). Essex, UK: Pearson Education Limited.

Strickland, A. J., & Thompson, A. A. (1984). *Strategic management: concepts and cases*. Plano, Tex.: Business Publications.

Suhrcke, M., Mckee, M., Arce, R. S., Tsolova, S., & Mortensen, J. (2005). The Contribution of Health to the Economy in the European Union. *Health & Consumer Protection Directorate-General*. Retrieved from **Error! Hyperlink reference not valid.**https://ec.europa.eu/health/archive/ph_overview/documents/health_economy_en.pdf

Sünter, A. T., Canbaz, S., Dabak, Ş., Öz, H., & Pekşen, Y. (2006). Pratisyen hekimlerde tükenmişlik, işe bağlı gerginlik ve iş doyumu düzeyleri. *Genel Tıp Dergisi*, *16*(1), 9–14.

Swan, M. (2015). *Blockchain Blueprint for a New Economy*. USA: O'Reilly Media.

Swayne, L. E., Duncan, W. J., & Ginter, P. M. (2006). *Strategic Management of Health Care Organizations (5. bs.)*. Cornwall: Blackwell Publishing.

Szewczyk, P. (2017). *Potential applications of the blockchain technology in helthcare*. Zeszyty Naukowe. Organizacja i Zarządzanie/Politechnika Śląska.

Tabak, R. (2006). *Sağlık İletişimi*. İstanbul: Literatürk Yayıncıık.

Tamkoç, M. N., & Torul, O. (2018). Cross Sectional Facts for Macroeconomists: Wage, Income and Consumption Inequality in Turkey. Bogaziçi University.

Tampoe, M., & Macmillan, H. (2000). *Strategic management, process, content and implementation*. Oxford University Press.

Tang, L., & Huang, H. (2016). A Study on the Influences of human capital investment in health on economics growth in Hunan Province. *International Journal of Simulation--Systems, Science & Technology*, *17*(49).

Tansüyer, T. (2010). *Hasta Güvenliği ve Tıbbi Hatalar Konusunda Sağlık Personelinin Görüşlerini Belirlemeye Yönelik Bir Alan Araştırması*. Ankara: Gazi Üniversitesi Sosyal Bilimleri Enstitüsü Yayınlanmamış Yüksek Lisans Tezi.

Taylor, P. (2016). Applying blockchain technology to medicine traceability. Retrieved from https://www.securingindustry.com/pharmaceuticals/applying-blockchain-technology-to-medicine-traceability/s40/a2766/#.XLt6tOgzY2y

Teece, D. J. (2010). Business models, business strategy and innovation. *Long Range Planning*, *43*(2-3), 172–194. doi:10.1016/j.lrp.2009.07.003

Teece, D. J., Pisano, G., & Shuen, A. (1997). Dynamic capabilities and strategic management. *Strategic Management Journal*, *18*(7), 509–533. doi:10.1002/(SICI)1097-0266(199708)18:7<509::AID-SMJ882>3.0.CO;2-Z

Teker, D.L. (2008). Sağlık Sektöründe Proje Finansman Modelleri: Türkiye İçin Bir Model Önerisi ve Bir Hastane Projesinin Fizibilite Analizi. *Muhasebe ve Finansman Dergisi*, (37), 1-18.

Teker, S. Teker, D., & Çimen M. (2013). Ulaştırma projeleri finansmanı için bir model önerisi: kamu-özel sektör ortaklığı ile yap-işlet-devret. *İşletme Araştırmaları Dergisi*, *5*(1), 116-129.

Teker, D., Teker, S., & Sönmez, M. (2012). *Ekonomik Değişkenlerin Kadın ve Erkeğin Yaşam Süresine Etkisi. İşletme Araştırmaları Dergisi*, *4*(3), 118–126.

Tekin, AG. (2007). Kamu-Özel Sektör İşbirlikleri-Kamu-Özel Ortaklıkları. *İdarecinin Sesi Dergisi*, *21*(122), 10-14.

Templer, K. J., Tay, C., & Chandrasekar, N. A. (2006). Motivational cultural intelligence, realistic job preview, realistic living conditions preview, and cross-cultural adjustment. *Group & Organization Management*, *31*(1), 154–173. doi:10.1177/1059601105275293

Tengilimoğlu, D., & Yiğit, A. (2005). Hastanelerde liderlik davranışlarının personel iş doyumuna etkisini belirlemeye yönelik bir alan çalışması. *Hacettepe Sağlık İdaresi Dergisi*, *8*(3), 374–400.

Tetik, S. (2003). İşletme performansını belirlemede veri zarflama analizi. *Yönetim ve Ekonomi: Celal Bayar Üniversitesi İktisadi ve İdari Bilimler Fakültesi Dergisi*, *10*(2), 221–230.

Thaiwebsites.com. 2019. *Cost of Medical Treatment in Bangkok*. Retrieved from http://www.thaiwebsites.com/cost-medical-treatment.asp

The Guardian. 2014. Baby Gammy may be given Australian citizenship, government suggests. Retrieved from http://www.theguardian.com/world/2014/aug/04/baby-gammy-australian-citizenship-government-suggests

The World Bank. (n.d.). World Development Indicators Database. Retrieved from https://databank.worldbank.org/source/world-development-indicators/preview/on.

The World Bank. (n.d.). World Health Organization's Global Health Workforce Statistics Database. Retrieved from https://data.worldbank.org/indicator/SH.MED.PHYS.ZS

Thevenot, G. (2007). Blogging as a social media. *Tourism and Hospitality Research*, *7*(3–4), 287–289. doi:10.1057/palgrave.thr.6050062

Thomas, H. (1984). Strategic decision analysis: Applied decision analysis and its role in the strategic management process. *Strategic Management Journal*, *5*(2), 139–156. doi:10.1002mj.4250050205

Thomas, R. K. (2003). *Society and health: sociology for health professionals*. Springer Science & Business Media.

Thune, T., & Mina, A. (2016). Hospitals as innovators in the health-care system: A literature review and research agenda. *Research Policy*, *45*(8), 1545–1557. doi:10.1016/j.respol.2016.03.010

Timuroğlu, M. K. (2010). *Stratejik Düşünce, Öğrenme Yönlülük Ve Yenilik. Yayınlanmamış Doktora Tezi*. Erzurum: Atatürk Üniversitesi, Sosyal Bilimler Enstitüsü, İşletme Anabilim Dalı.

Titrek, O., & Zafer, D. (2009). İlkögretim Okulu Yöneticilerinin Kullandıkları Örgütsel Güç Kaynaklarına İlişkin Öğretmen Görüşleri. *Kuram ve Uygulamada Eğitim Yönetimi*, *60*(60), 657–674.

Törenli, N. (2005). *Yeni Medya, Yeni İletişim Ortamı*. Ankara: Bilim ve Sanat Yayınları.

Torul, O., & Öztunalı, O. (2018). On Income and Wealth Inequality in Turkey. Central Bank Review, 18(3), 95-106. doi:10.1016/j.cbrev.2018.06.002

Tosunoğlu, H. (2014). *Liderlik Tarzı Algısının Örgütsel Bağlılık Üzerindeki Etkisinde Örgüte Güvenin Aracı Rolü: Bir Örnek Olay İncelemesi, Hacettepe Üniversitesi Sos*. Ankara: Bil.Ens. Yüksek Lisans Tezi.

Trastek, V. F., Hamilton, N. W., & Niles, E. E. (2014). Leadership models in health care—A case for servant leadership. *Mayo Clinic Proceedings*, *89*(3), 374–381. doi:10.1016/j.mayocp.2013.10.012 PMID:24486078

Triandis, H. C. (2006). Cultural intelligence in organizations. *Group & Organization Management*, *31*(1), 20–26. doi:10.1177/1059601105275253

Trist, E. (1990). *Culture as a psycho-social process. The Social Engagement of Social Science*. London: Free Association.

Tübitak, & Kalkınma Bakanlığı. (n.d.). *Kamu İnternet Siteleri Rehberi İnternet Sitelerinde Kullanılabilirlik*. Ankara: Tübitak. *Kalkınma Bakanlığı*.

Tüfekçioğlu, H. (1997). *İletişim Sosyolojisine Başlangıç*. İstanbul: Der Yayınları.

TUIK. (n.d.). Uluslararası Seçilmiş Göstergeler. Retrieved from https://biruni.tuik.gov.tr/secilmisgostergeler/tabloOlustur.do.

Tunceli, K., Bradley, C. J., Nerenz, D., Williams, L. K., Pladevall, M., & Lafata, J. E. (2005). The impact of diabetes on employment and work productivity. *Diabetes Care*, *28*(11), 2662–2667. doi:10.2337/diacare.28.11.2662 PMID:16249536

Türk, S., Aydoğan, E., & Kansu, N. (2003). İçsel Motivasyonun İş Tatmini Üzerindeki Etkisi, Türk Tarih Kurumu Matbaası ve Nurol Matbaası'nda Yapılan Bir Araştırma, 1. Matbaa Teknolojileri Sempozyumu, Eylül, Ankara. Matbaa Teknolojileri Sempozyumu, Eylül, Ankara. Retrieved from http://w3.gazi.edu.tr/web/msturk/yayinlar/pdf/motive.pdf

Turner, L. (2008). Cross-border dental care:'dental tourism' and patient mobility. *British Dental Journal*, *204*(10), 553–554. doi:10.1038j.bdj.2008.403 PMID:18500297

Turunç, Ö. (2006). Bilgi Teknolojileri Kullaniminin İşletmelerin Örgütsel Performansina Etkisi Hizmet Sektöründe Bir Araştirma. *Toros Üniversitesi İİSBF Sosyal Bilimler Dergisi*, *3*(5), 225–247.

Tüylüoğlu, Ş., & Tekin, M. (2009). Gelir Düzeyi ve Sağlık Harcamalarının Beklenen Yaşam Süresi ve Bebek Ölüm Oranı Üzerindeki Etkileri. *Çukurova Üniversitesi İktisadi ve İdari Bilimler Fakültesi Dergisi*, *13*(1), 1-31.

Tüylüoğlu, Ş., Tekin (2009). Gelir Düzeyi ve Sağlık Harcamalarının Beklenen Yaşam Süresi ve Bebek Ölüm Oranı Üzerindeki Etkileri, *Çukurova Üniversitesi İktisadi ve İdari Bilimler Fakültesi Dergisi*, 13(1), 1-31.

Twitter Inc. (2017). Twitter Usage & Company Facts. Retrieved from https://about.twitter.com/company

U.S. Dept. of Health and Human Services. (2019). MEDLINE: Description of the Database. Retrieved from https://www.nlm.nih.gov/bsd/medline.html

Udler, M. S., Kim, J., von Grotthuss, M., Bonàs-Guarch, S., Cole, J. B., Chiou, J., ... Mercader, J. M. (2018). Type 2 diabetes genetic loci informed by multi-trait associations point to disease mechanisms and subtypes: A soft clustering analysis. *PLoS Medicine*, *15*(9). doi:10.1371/journal.pmed.1002654 PMID:30240442

Uğurlu, M. (2018). *Sağlık Teknolojisi Değerlendirmesi Ülke Uygulamaları ve Türkiye İçin Model Önerisi*. Ankara: T.C Maliye Bakanlığı Strateji Geliştirme Başkanlığı Yayınları.

Ülgen, H., & Mirze, S. K. (2004). Isletmelerde stratejik yonetim. İstanbul: Literatür yayıncılık.

Ülgen, B. (2016). *Örgüt Yönetiminde Duygular, Nobel Dağıtım, 1.* Ankara: Baskı.

Ülgen, H., & Mirze, K. (2006). *İşletmelerde Stratejik Yönetim, Literatür Yayınları, 3.* İstanbul: Basım.

Ülgen, H., & Mirze, S. K. (2010). *İşletmelerde stratejik yönetim (5. Baskı).* İstanbul: Beta Basım Yayım Dağıtım.

Umer, M., Zofeen, S., Majeed, A., Hu, W., Qi, X., & Zhuang, G. (2018). Spatiotemporal Clustering Analysis of Malaria Infection in Pakistan. *International Journal of Environmental Research and Public Health, 15*(6), 1202. doi:10.3390/ijerph15061202 PMID:29880778

UNDP. (n.d.). İnsani Gelişme Endeksleri ve Göstergeleri: 2018 İstatistiksel Güncellemesi Türkiye. Retrieved from **Error! Hyperlink reference not valid.**http://www.tr.undp.org/content/dam/turkey/hdr2018/tr/Turkey%20Briefing%20NoteTurkey%20Briefing%20NoteTRv01.pdf

United Nations–Economic Commission for Europe. (2000). *Guidelines on Public-Private Partnerships for Infrastructure Development.*

Uno, H., & Zakariasen, K. (2010). Public health leadership education in North America. *Journal of Healthcare Leadership, 2*, 11–15. doi:10.2147/JHL.S9727

UNWTO. (n.d.). [Conference Note]. In *Proceedings of the 22nd Session of the UNWTO General Assembly.* Academic Press.

Urry, J. (2002). *The tourist gaze.* London: Sage Publications.

Usher, D. (1964). The welfare economics of invention. *Economica, 31*(123), 279–287. doi:10.2307/2550623

Üstünel, B. (1988). *Ekonominin Temelleri, 5.* Baskı.

Uygun, B. (2013). Yeni Bir İlişki Türü: Kamu Özel Ortaklığı. *Hukuk Gündemi*, 24-27.

Uysal, Ş. A., Keklik, B., Erdem, R., & Çelik, R. (2012). Hastane yöneticilerinin liderlik özellikleri ile çalışanların iş üretkenlik düzeyleri arasındaki ilişkilerin incelenmesi. *Hacettepe Sağlık İdaresi Dergisi, 15*(1), 25–57.

Üzün, C. (2000). *Stratejik yönetim ve halkla ilişkiler.* Dokuz Eylül Yayıncılık.

Vaitkuviene, L., Balvociute, R., & Stoskus, S. (2010). The comparative analysis of employee motivation tools: The case of Lithuanian and Swedish manufacturing companies. *Oranizciju Vadyba, 3*, 97–113.

Valdes, B. (1999). *Economic Growth: Theory, Empirics and Policy.* USA: Edward Elgar.

Valente, T. W. (2010). *Social Networks and Health: Models.* Methods and Applications. doi:10.1093/acprof:oso/9780195301014.001.0001

Van den Heuvel, W. J., & Olaroiu, M. (2017). How important are health care expenditures for life expectancy? A comparative, European analysis. *Journal of the American Medical Directors Association, 18*(3), 276–289. doi:10.1016/j.jamda.2016.11.027 PMID:28131720

Van Dyne, L., Ang, S., & Livermore, D. (2010). Cultural intelligence: A pathway for leading in a rapidly globalizing world. In *Leading across differences* (pp. 131-138). Academic Press.

Van Eck, N. J., & Waltman, L. (2007). Bibliometric mapping of the computational intelligence field. *International Journal of Uncertainty Fuzziness and Knowledge-Based Systems, 15*(5), 625–645. Available: 488507004911 doi:10.1142/S0218

VanYperen, N. W., Van Den Berg, A. E., & Willering, M. C. (1999). Towards a better understanding of the link between participation in decision-making and organizational citizenship behaviour: A multilevel analysis. *Journal of Occupational and Organizational Psychology, 72*(3), 377–392. doi:10.1348/096317999166734

Velasco, E., Agheneza, T., Denecke, K., Kirchner, G., & Eckmanns, T. (2014). Social media and internet-based data in global systems for public health surveillance: A systematic review. *The Milbank Quarterly, 92*(1), 7–33. doi:10.1111/1468-0009.12038 PMID:24597553

Venkatraman, N., & Camillus, J. C. (1984). Exploring the concept of "fit" in strategic management. *Academy of Management Review, 9*(3), 513–525.

Ventelou, B., & Abu-Zaineh, M. (2016). Medicine and democracy: The importance of institutional quality in the relationship between health expenditure and health outcomes in the MENA region. *Health Policy (Amsterdam), 120*(8), 928–935. doi:10.1016/j.healthpol.2016.06.005 PMID:27370915

Vroom, V. H., & Jago, A. G. (1988). *The new leadership: Managing participation in organizations*. Prentice-Hall, Inc.

Wang, L. (2002). Health Outcomes in Low-Income Countries: Empirical Findings from Demographic and Health Surveys. *World Bank.*

Wang, H., & Yazbeck, A. S. (2017). Benchmarking health Systems in Middle Eastern and North African Countries. *Health Systems & Reform, 3*(1), 7–13. doi:10.1080/23288604.2016.1272983 PMID:31514711

Wang, Z. (2009). The Convergence of Health Care Expenditures in the US States. *Health Economics, 18*(1), 55–70. doi:10.1002/hec.1343 PMID:18273915

Waring, J., Allen, D., Braithwaite, J., & Sandall, J. (2016). Healthcare quality and safety: A review of policy, practice and research. *Sociology of Health & Illness, 38*(2), 198–215. doi:10.1111/1467-9566.12391 PMID:26663206

Wasem, J., Greß, S., & Okma, K. G. (2004). The role of private health insurance in social health insurance countries.

Weaver, B., Lindsay, B., & Gitelman, B. (2012). Communication technology and social media: Opportunities and implications for healthcare systems. *Online Journal of Issues in Nursing*, *17*(3). doi:10.3912/OJIN.Vol17No03Man03 PMID:23036059

Weberg, D. (2012). Complexity leadership: A healthcare imperative. *Nursing Forum*, *47*(4), 268–277. doi:10.1111/j.1744-6198.2012.00276.x PMID:23127241

Webster, P. R. (1990). Creativity as creative thinking. *Music Educators Journal*, *76*(9), 22–28. doi:10.2307/3401073

Weiss, H. M. (2002). Deconstructing job satisfaction: Separating evaluations, beliefs and affective experiences. *Human Resource Management Review*, *12*(2), 173–194. doi:10.1016/S1053-4822(02)00045-1

Wheelen, T. L., Hunger, J. D., Hoffman, A. N., & Bamford, C. E. (2010). *Strategic management and business policy*. New Jersey: Prentice Hall.

Whittaker, A., & Speier, A. (2010). "Cycling overseas": Care, commodification, and stratification in cross-border reproductive travel. *Medical Anthropology*, *29*(4), 363–383. doi:10.1080/01459740.2010.501313 PMID:21082483

Wikström, E., & Dellve, L. (2009). Contemporary leadership in healthcare organizations: Fragmented or concurrent leadership. *Journal of Health Organization and Management*, *23*(4), 411–428. doi:10.1108/14777260910979308 PMID:19862865

Williams, M., Burden, R. L., & Al-Baharna, S. (2001). The role of the individual in motivation theory. In *Motivation and second language acquisition*. Second Language Teaching & Curriculum Center.

Wilson, J. Q., & Kelling, G. L. (1982). Broken windows: The police and neighborhood safety. *Atlantic Monthly*, *211*, 29–38.

Wisk, L. E., Nelson, E. B., Magane, K. M., & Weitzman, E. R. (2019). Clinical Trial Recruitment and Retention of College Students with Type 1 Diabetes via Social Media: An Implementation Case Study. *Journal of Diabetes Science and Technology*, *13*(3), 445–456. doi:10.1177/1932296819839503 PMID:31010315

Wissema, J. G., Brand, A. F., & Van Pol, H. D. (1981). The incorporation of management development in strategic management. *Strategic Management Journal*, *2*(4), 361–377. doi:10.1002mj.4250020405

Wong, A., Mazumder, B., & Halliday, T. (2019). *The Intergenerational Transmission of Health in the United States: A Latent Variables Analysis*. University of Hawaii.

Wooldridge, B., & Floyd, S. W. (1990). The strategy process, middle management involvement, and organizational performance. *Strategic Management Journal*, *11*(3), 231–241. doi:10.1002mj.4250110305

World Health Organization, (2017). Tracking universal health coverage: 2017 Global Monitoring Report.

World Health Organization. (2005). *World health development indicators*. Washington, D. C.

World Health Organization. (2006). Constitution of the World Health Organization, 45th Edition of Basic Documents.

World Health Organization. (2007), European Regional Patients for Patient Safety Workshop Report. Dublin.

World Health Organization. (2009) World Alliance for Patient Safety Forward Programme, France.

World Tourism Organization and European Travel Commission, UNWTO. (2018). *Exploring Health Tourism – Executive Summary*. Retrieved from https://www.e-unwto.org/doi/pdf/10.18111/9789284420308

Wortman Vaughan, J. (2018). Making Better Use of the Crowd: How Crowdsourcing Can Advance Machine Learning Research. *JMLR, 18*(193), 1–46. Retrieved from https://www.microsoft.com/en-us/research/publication/making-better-use-of-the-crowd-how-crowdsourcing-can-advance-machine-learning-research/

Xia, Q. I., Sifah, E. B., Asamoah, K. O., Gao, J., Du, X., & Guizani, M. (2017). MeDShare: Trust-less medical data sharing among cloud service providers via blockchain. *IEEE Access, 5*, 14757–14767. doi:10.1109/ACCESS.2017.2730843

Yakut, İ. (2008). *Sağlık İletişiminde Katılımın İşlevi Hasta ve Hasta Yakınları Açısından*. İzmit: Umuttepe Yayınları.

Yalçın, A. Z., & Çakmak, F. (2016). Türkiye'de Kamu Sağlık Harcamalarının İnsani Gelişim Üzerindeki Etkisi. *Atatürk Üniversitesi İktisadi ve İdari Bilimler Dergisi, 30*(4), 705–723.

Yammarino, F. (2013). Leadership: Past, present, and future. *Journal of Leadership & Organizational Studies, 20*(2), 149–155. doi:10.1177/1548051812471559

Yang, F. C., Lee, A. J. T., & Kuo, S. C. (2016). Mining Health Social Media with Sentiment Analysis. *Journal of Medical Systems, 40*(11), 236. doi:10.100710916-016-0604-4 PMID:27663246

Yang, M., Kiang, M., & Shang, W. (2015). Filtering big data from social media - Building an early warning system for adverse drug reactions. *Journal of Biomedical Informatics, 54*, 230–240. doi:10.1016/j.jbi.2015.01.011 PMID:25688695

Yardımcı, F., Başbakkal, Z., Beytut, D., & Muslu, G. & Ersun, A. (2014). Bir Devlet Hastanesinde Sağlık Çalışanlarının Hasta Güvenliği Kültürü Algısının İncelenmesi. *Anadolu Tıbbi Araştırmalar Dergisi, 8*(4), 173–179.

Yaşar, M. F. (2015). *Şehir Hastaneleri ve Kamu Özel İşbilirği (PPP).* Modeli.

Yaylalı, M., Yusuf, A. K. A. N., & Cem, I. Ş. I. K. (2010). Türkiye de Ar&Ge Yatırım Harcamaları Ve Ekonomik Büyüme Arasındaki Eş-Bütünleşme Ve Nedensellik İlişkisi: 1990–2009. *Bilgi Ekonomisi ve Yönetimi Dergisi*, *5*(2).

Yazbeck, A. S. (2017). *Tamer S. Rabie & Aaka Pande*. Health Sector Reform.

Yereli, A. B., Kobal, İ., & Köktaş, A. M. (2016). *Türkiye'de Sağlık Harcamalarını Arttıran Faktörler*. İstanbul: Uluslararası Bilgi, Ekonomi ve Yönetim Kongresi, İstanbul Üniversitesi İktisat Fakültesi.

Yıldırım, C. (2016a). Patent Başvurusu ve İhracat Arasındaki İlişki: Panel Veri Analizi. *Bartın Üniversitesi İİ BF Dergisi*, *7*(13), 226–249.

Yıldırım, C. (2016b). Tüketici Fiyat Endeksi ile Faiz Oranı İlişkisinin Ekonometrik Bir İncelemesi. *Kastamonu Üniversitesi İktisadi ve İdari Bilimler Fakültesi Dergisi*, *12*(2), 431–445. doi:10.21180/kuiibf.20161218337

Yıldız,, T., Eriten,, G., Erdem,, İ., Gökay,, N.S., & Kulaç,, M., & Alp, R. (2012). Mezuniyetin ve Profesyonel Sağlık Personeli Olarak Çalışmanın Hasta Güvenliği Bilinci Üzerine Etkileri. *Kafkas J MedSci*, *2*(3), 94–98. doi:10.5505/kjms.2012.03511

Yılmaz, V., & Yentürk, N. (2015). Türkiye'de sağlık harcamalarına tarihsel bir bakış. *İstanbul Bilgi Üniversitesi Sivil Toplum Çalışmaları Merkezi*, 1-17.

Yip, K. (2017). Blockchain & alternate payment models. In *Proceedings of the ONC/NIST Use of Blockchain for Healthcare and Research Workshop*. ONC/NIST.

Young, A. T., Higgins, M. J., & Levy, D. (2008). Sigma Convergence versus Beta Convergence: Evidence from U.S. County-Level Data. *Journal of Money, Credit and Banking*, *40*(5), 1083–1093. doi:10.1111/j.1538-4616.2008.00148.x

Yrle, A. C., Hartman, S., & Galle, W. P. (2002). An investigation of relationships between communication style and leader-member exchange. *Journal of Communication Management*, *6*(3), 257–268. doi:10.1108/13632540210807099

Yücel, D. (2013). Pygmalion Etkisi Kapsamında Yönetici Beklentilerinin Astlar Tarafından Algılanmasının Astların Performansı Üzerindeki Etkileri ve Bir Araştırma [Doktora Tezi]. Marmara Üniversitesi Sos.Bil.Ens., İstanbul. Retrieved from http://www.artfulliving.com.tr/kultur-ve-yasam/pygmalion-bir-kadin-yaratmak-ve-onunla-aska-dusmek-i-6059

Yue, X., Wang, H., Jin, D., Li, M., & Jiang, W. (2016). Healthcare data gateways: Found healthcare intelligence on blockchain with novel privacy risk control. *Journal of Medical Systems*, *40*(10), 218. doi:10.100710916-016-0574-6 PMID:27565509

Yukl, G. (2011). Contingency theories of effective leadership. In The SAGE handbook of leadership (pp. 286-298). Academic Press.

Yukl, G. (2008). How leaders influence organizational effectiveness. *The Leadership Quarterly*, *19*(6), 708–722. doi:10.1016/j.leaqua.2008.09.008

Yukl, G., & Mahsud, R. (2010). Why flexible and adaptive leadership is essential. *Consulting Psychology Journal: Practice and Research, 62*(2), 81–93. doi:10.1037/a0019835

Yukl, G., Mahsud, R., Hassan, S., & Prussia, G. E. (2013). An improved measure of ethical leadership. *Journal of Leadership & Organizational Studies, 20*(1), 38–48. doi:10.1177/1548051811429352

Yüksel, E. at el. (2014). Check Up Sağlık İletişimi Kaynak İleti ve Hedef Kitle Bağlamında Sağlık Konulu Yayınların Analizi. Konya: Literatürk.

Yüksel, S. (2017). The Impacts of Research and Development Expenses on Export and Economic Growth. *International Business and Accounting Research Journal, 1*(1), 1–8. doi:10.15294/ibarj.v1i1.1

Yüksel, S., & Oktar, S. (2017). Okun Yasasının Farklı Gelişme Düzeyindeki Ülkelere İlişkin Ekonometrik Analizi. *Marmara Üniversitesi İktisadi ve İdari Bilimler Dergisi, 39*(1), 323–332. doi:10.14780/muiibd.329945

Yürüşen, S. (2011). *Veri zarflama analizi ile bayi performansının hesaplanması: otomotiv sektöründe bir uygulama* [Doctoral dissertation]. Fen Bilimleri Enstitüsü.

Zeren, F., Özcan, B., & Menteşe, E. Y. (2016). Health Care Convergence Analysis in Turkey on the Province Level: Spatial Quantile Method. *Procedia Economics and Finance, 38*, 90–97. doi:10.1016/S2212-5671(16)30181-2

Zerenler, M. (2005). *Performans ölçüm sistemleri tasarımı ve üretim sistemlerinin performansının ölçümüne yönelik bir araştırma*. Ekonomik ve Sosyal Araştırmalar Dergisi.

Zhang, Y., & Xu, G. (2008). Using Web clustering for Web communities mining and analysis. In *Proceedings of the 2008 IEEE/WIC/ACM International Conference on Web Intelligence, WI 2008* (Vol. 1, pp. 20–31). IEEE. 10.1109/WIIAT.2008.415

Zhang, X. (2018). Pythagorean fuzzy clustering analysis: A hierarchical clustering algorithm with the ratio index-based ranking methods. *International Journal of Intelligent Systems, 33*(9), 1798–1822. doi:10.1002/int.21915

Zhang, Z., Zhu, G., & Shen, Y. (2018). Data clustering analysis of early reflections in small room. *The Journal of the Acoustical Society of America, 144*(4), EL328–EL332. doi:10.1121/1.5065073 PMID:30404478

Zhao, X., Wu, Y. P., Ren, G., Ji, K., & Qian, W. W. (2019). Clustering Analysis of Ridership Patterns at Subway Stations: A Case in Nanjing, China. *Journal of Urban Planning and Development, 145*(2), 04019005. doi:10.1061/(ASCE)UP.1943-5444.0000501

Zhou, L., Zhang, D., Yang, C. C., & Wang, Y. (2018). Harnessing social media for health information management. *Electronic Commerce Research and Applications, 27*, 139–151. doi:10.1016/j.elerap.2017.12.003 PMID:30147636

Zichermann, G., & Cunningham, C. (2011). *Gamification by Design: Implementing Game Mechanics in Web and Mobile Apps*. Sebastopol, CA: O'Reilly & Associates Inc. doi:10.1093/intimm/dxs132

Ziesemer, T. (2016). The Impact of Development Aid on Education and Health: Survey and New Evidence for Low-income Countries from Dynamic Models. *Journal of International Development*, *28*(8), 1358–1380. doi:10.1002/jid.3223

Zılhoğlu, M. (2003). *İletişim Nedir?* İstanbul: Cem Yayınevi.

Zupic, I., & Čater, T. (2015). Bibliometric Methods in Management and Organization. *Organizational Research Methods*, *18*(3), 429–472. doi:10.1177/1094428114562629

About the Contributors

Hasan Dinçer is an Associate Professor of finance at Istanbul Medipol University, Faculty of Economics and Administrative Sciences, Istanbul-Turkey. Dr. Dinçer has BAs in Financial Markets and Investment Management at Marmara University. He received PhD in Finance and Banking with his thesis entitled "The Effect of Changes on the Competitive Strategies of New Service Development in the Banking Sector". He has work experience in finance sector as portfolio specialist and his major academic studies focusing on financial instruments, performance evaluation, and economics. He is the executive editor of the International Journal of Finance and Banking Studies (IJFBS) and the founder member of the Society for the Study of Business and Finance (SSBF).

Serhat Yüksel is an Associate Professor of finance in İstanbul Medipol University. Before this position, he worked as a senior internal auditor for seven years in Finansbank, Istanbul-Turkey and 1 year in Konya Food and Agriculture University as an assistant professor. Dr. Yüksel has a BS in Business Administration (in English) from Yeditepe University (2006) with full scholarship. He got his master's degree from the economics in Boğaziçi University (2008). He also has a PhD in Banking from Marmara University (2015). His research interests lie in banking, finance and financial crisis. He has more than 130 publications (books, book chapters, scientific articles, etc.).

***

Zafer Adiguzel is an Assistant Professor in 2006, Kocaeli University, Faculty of Economics and Administrative Sciences. In 2010 he graduated from Cardiff Metropolitan University with an MBA in Finance. In 2016 he graduated from Gebze Technical University, Department of Management and Organization. Presently, he continues his academic career as a faculty member at Istanbul Medipol University, Medipol business school.

Gökhan Aydın received his Ph.D. in Management Engineering from Istanbul Technical University in 2009. He worked for 12 years in marketing, sales and retail management departments in leading companies in Turkey. He is currently employed as an Assoc. Professor at Istanbul Medipol University. He is lecturing on various marketing classes in graduate and undergraduate programmes and his areas of interest include brand equity & management and digital marketing (mobile, SNS, etc.).

Serhat Burmaoglu is a Professor of Quantitative Decision Making. His research interest is investigating the relationship between economic growth, productivity, competitiveness, innovation, and knowledge economy in macro-economic level by using multivariate statistical analysis and data mining applications for extracting usable patterns to direct technology policy. He performs bibliometric analysis and patent analysis on emerging technology subjects to prepare scenario-based foresight studies. He published many book chapters and articles in different national and international journals.

Işıl Çekçi is a specialist in Health Management. She continues her research in the fields of innovation, health systems and medical documentation. She is also in preparation for her doctoral education.

Amit Chatterjee is presently an Assistant Professor in Economics at MIT-WPU University, Pune. He is a registered PhD research scholar at the Department of Economics, The University of Burdwan, India. His areas of research lie in rural economy, information and technology, education, etc.

Ramesh Chandra Das is currently an Associate Professor of Economics at Vidyasagar University, West Bengal, India. Previously he was Associate Professor of Economics at Katwa College, India. He has obtained Masters, M. Phil and Ph. D Degree in Economics from the University of Calcutta. He has twenty years of teaching and research experience in different fields of economics including theoretical and empirical economics, financial economics, environmental economics and political economics. Dr. Das has contributed several research papers to national and international journals and completed three MRPs sponsored by UGC, India. He has written textbooks on Microeconomics and Macroeconomics (coauthor) for different fields of readers and academician. He is the editor-in-chief in Asian Journal of Research in Business Economics and Management, Associate Editor of International Journal of Research on Social and Natural Sciences. He has edited a number of handbooks on globalization, investment and growth, economic and political convergence, infrastructure, microfinance, military expenditure, terrorism, etc. and worked as a guest editor of IJSEM's Special Issue (2 parts) published by IGI Global, USA.

Ihsan Eken was born in 1986 in Istanbul. He studied Visual Communication Design at Istanbul Commerce University. Later on, he received his master's degree in Advertising and Brand Management at Bahcesehir University. He received his doctorate degree with his thesis on "Accessible Communication for Everyone, Mobile Accessibility of Visually Impaired Users: Analysis of Mobile Applications With Usability Approach" in Istanbul Commerce University Media and Communication Program. He is currently working as an assistant professor at Istanbul Medipol University Faculty of Communication. He is the Media and Visual Arts Program Vice Head of Department. He has won numerous awards in national and international festivals. Finally, he has national and international scientific publications

Serkan Eti is a mathematics graduate at Yildiz Technical University. He is a graduate of Quantitive Methods at Marmara University. He has his doctorate in Quantitive Methods. At the same time, he has been a lecturer at Medipol University since 2017.

Başak Gezmen was born in 1978 in Izmir. She received her master's degree in Journalism at Marmara University. She received her doctorate degree with her thesis on "Technological developments in Journalism in Turkey" in Marmara University Journalism Program. She is working as an assistant professor at Istanbul Medipol University Communication Faculty. She has published in national and international scientific publications.

Yurdagül Meral Chair is in the International Management and Finance Dept. Istanbul Medipol University School of Business and Management Science ymeral@medipol.edu.tr www.medipol.edu.tr +90 216 681 753 *CDCS–certificate of documentary credit specialist http://cdcs.ifslearning.ac.uk/ holder. *PhD in Business Management and Organization and *MBA from Istanbul University. 30 years (1986-2016) of 'International Trade' finance experience (including two years in Frankfurt) in banking. After having her associate Degree in Business Management, from Boğaziçi University, started to work in international trade finance departments of Interbank (has completed one year 'Management Trainee' program), Koç-American Bank (formerly American Express Bank) including Frankfurt Branch and Tekstil Bank and Şekerbank respectively. She taught International Trade Rules (ICC) and Practise in Banks and Bankers Association.

Eray Ekin Sezgin was born in Elazığ in 1989. She completed her primary, secondary and high school education there. In 2012, he graduated from Karadeniz Technical University, Faculty of Economics and Administrative Sciences, Department of Business Administration. In 2014, he completed his master's degree in Firat University, Institute of Social Sciences, Department of Business Administration. After completing his master's degree, he started his doctorate education in 2014 at Fırat University. In 2018, he completed his PhD at Fırat University, Institute of Social Sciences, Department of Health Management. His academic interests include Health Management and Management and Organization. He is working as an Assistant Professor in Health Management at Munzur University.

Orhan Torul is an Assistant Professor at the Department of Economics at Boğaziçi University, where he has been a faculty member since 2013. He graduated in 2013 with a Ph.D. degree in Economics from University of Maryland, College Park; and he completed his undergraduate and graduate studies at Middle East Technical University and Boğaziçi University, respectively. Dr. Torul worked as a visiting researcher at the Istanbul School of Central Banking in 2015 and University of Oslo in 2017. Dr. Torul's research interests lie in the area of macroeconomics, political economy, distributional economics, public economics, computational economics, and applied econometrics.

Index

H

I

L

M

N

O

P

R

S

T

U

V

W

Ensure Quality Research is Introduced to the Academic Community

Become an IGI Global Reviewer for Authored Book Projects

The overall success of an authored book project is dependent on quality and timely reviews.

In this competitive age of scholarly publishing, constructive and timely feedback significantly expedites the turnaround time of manuscripts from submission to acceptance, allowing the publication and discovery of forward-thinking research at a much more expeditious rate. Several IGI Global authored book projects are currently seeking highly-qualified experts in the field to fill vacancies on their respective editorial review boards:

Applications and Inquiries may be sent to:
development@igi-global.com

Applicants must have a doctorate (or an equivalent degree) as well as publishing and reviewing experience. Reviewers are asked to complete the open-ended evaluation questions with as much detail as possible in a timely, collegial, and constructive manner. All reviewers' tenures run for one-year terms on the editorial review boards and are expected to complete at least three reviews per term. Upon successful completion of this term, reviewers can be considered for an additional term.

If you have a colleague that may be interested in this opportunity, we encourage you to share this information with them.

www.ingramcontent.com/pod-product-compliance
Lightning Source LLC
LaVergne TN
LVHW061527290926
849162LV00004B/698